Torts – A Wider View

Torts – A Wider View

Stephen D. Sugarman

Roger J. Traynor Professor of Law
UC Berkeley Law School

Vandeplas Publishing, LLC

United States of America

Torts – a wider view

Sugarman, Stephen D.

Published by:

Vandeplas Publishing, LLC – August 2014

801 International Parkway, 5th Floor
Lake Mary, FL. 32746
USA

www.vandeplaspublishing.com

ISBN 978-1-60042-225-6

Why Read This Book?

The goal of this book is to provide 1L students (and their instructors) with a very different set of outside readings to accompany the study of Torts -- different from what is currently available in the *wider* view they take of the subject.

Students often are looking for something to read beyond what is contained within the covers of their casebook. At the start of the term, my usual advice to my students is that they should use the time to read the assignment again. But after a while I begin to refer them to supplemental material. There are, of course, the articles referred to in notes in the casebook from which I teach – but those tend to be much deeper examinations of the doctrine under review. For those who are seeking a sophisticated but pithy doctrinal presentation, I have tended to refer them, for example, to the mini-treatises by Professors Abraham or Geistfeld (among many other good ones that are on the market).

But what about those students who are looking for broader perspectives on Torts and its role in our society? At least two nice collections of selections from the work of a large number authors who have written about Torts in a serious way are available (edited by Professors Levmore and Sharkey on the one hand and by Professors Davies, Levine and Kionka on the other). Yet both of these volumes are centrally aimed at helping readers gain a deeper understanding of doctrine (as I see it), and are structured to march along with the presentation of tort law in most casebooks.

Far broader in its sweep is the collection of classic pieces gathered by Professor Rabin in his "**Perspectives**" book. This is well worth having students read (or at least read from). Yet there are virtually no even remotely contemporary pieces included (partly, but only partly, because Rabin's fourth and last edition appeared in 1995).

This volume offers a wider view of Torts. All seventeen of the pieces were written by me (which is perhaps a drawback). They are already plausibly available to any student who wants to track them down – although a number were published abroad. Moreover, in this volume each of the pieces comes with an introductory overview, and, where appropriate, updating. (Two of the chapters contain "postcripts" that discuss very recent in press work of mine and further supplement the relevant chapter.) These seventeen chapters don't track the study of tort doctrine. But they are meant to help the reader to adopt a whole range of broader perspective on Torts than the usual 1L course (and casebook) provides.

Part I collects five articles and book chapters that set Torts in its ideological, political, and historical context – in ways that are different from what others have written. I argue that Torts is essentially a "conservative" (rather than "liberal" or "libertarian" or "communitarian") way of dealing with the social problem of accidents. But then I explore how it has come to pass that in the U.S. it is Democrats who are today's tort defenders, and Republicans its critics. I explain that tort law in the 21st century is very different from tort law in the 19th century because of changes that I argue are bigger and more important than doctrinal change (albeit there has been a lot of that as well). I address whether tort law should be made (and reformed) by state court judges, by state legislatures, or by Congress; and I show how governors can sharply impact tort law through their judicial appointments. These topics should engage students, but they are little addressed by today's casebooks or the supplemental volumes noted above.

Part II provides four comparative law chapters. Most students studying Torts learn next to nothing about the way tort law and its alternatives function today in other countries. Largely unlike those other supplemental readers, this Part helps students realize that we might learn from others, and that we narrow our outlook by restricting our focus to variation among our 50 states. Part III contains three chapters that examine difficult contemporary problem areas for tort law – medical injuries, auto accidents, and disasters – and presents discussions of potential reforms that lie largely outside of tort. Most 1L students are little exposed to these sorts of ideas.

Part IV is about tort doctrine, but not in the usual way. Four chapters present arguments are about how and why tort law can and should be significantly simplified – playing off the American Law Institute's (ALI) current project to adopt an updated Restatement (Third) of Torts. Both specific doctrinal areas and, ultimately, the entire Restatement of Torts (Third) are shown to be unnecessarily complicated, and illustrations are offered showing that Torts would not only be easier to understand but also better and more consistent if various complexities were removed. The final chapter argues that while the Restatement (Third) of Torts is a move in the right direction, a better pathway to an imagined Restatement (Fourth) might well have been charted had the ALI kept alive its Enterprise Liability project – which itself took a much wider view of Torts and is, ultimately, the inspiration for this book.

Aware of this structure, some readers might find it attractive to push through the material as presented. Others might well want to pick and choose or at least move around among the chapters to engage topics as they become salient to them (or perhaps their instructors guide them, playing off what is provided here with their own views that may well different from what I offer).

Two personal notes: In 1989 I published "**Doing Away With Personal Injury Law**" that drew on a long article of approximately the same name as well as a number of shorter pieces that pushed in the same direction. At the time I wondered whether I would continue to publish on Torts. But it turns out that I have, and this book brings the core of that more recent work together in one place.

I exclude from this volume my attack on tort theory which I develop through an examination of my favorite torts case Vincent v. Lake Erie Transportation Co. *The "Necessity" Defense and The Failure Of Tort Theory: The Case Against Strict Liability For Damages Caused While Exercising Self-Help In An Emergency* is nearly book-length itself and is readily available via my website: http://www.law.berkeley.edu/sugarman.htm. My shorter and less trenchant exploration of the *Vincent* case appears as a chapter in Professor Rabin's and my co-edited book of "**Torts Stories**."

Table of Contents

Part I

The Bigger Picture - Ideology, History and Politics

Most law students begin the study of Torts by jumping directly into the reading of opinions of judges in cases involving what we today call tort law. This is understandable because one of the key skills that would-be lawyers must master is the careful reading and analysis of judicial opinions. Moreover, because Torts is the pre-eminent common law course, this skill is arguably best developed in that context.

Yet it is equally important not to lose sight of the forest for the trees. What are the wider contexts in which these cases are being decided? Since is it not inevitable that tort law is the way for a society to deal with the matters arising in the cases being studied, what are the alternatives? Moreover, where is tort law located in the wider world of politics and political ideology? And, why is it that the politics of tort law has largely solidified along partisan political lines in ways that would have been hard to predict fifty years ago?

Furthermore, while it quickly becomes clear to students in their study of Torts that tort doctrine changes over time, how much is doctrinal change – in contrast to other changes – really responsible for the fact that the real world of tort law in the 21st century is dramatically different from the world of tort law at the end of the 19th century?

So long as tort law plays a key role in the U.S. in dealing with personal injury and death, as well as damage to property, emotional harm, and financial loss, what branches of government do and should shape its development over time? State judges? State legislatures? Governors? Congress?

These are some of the primary themes addressed in the five chapters that comprise Part I of this book.

Chapter 1

Is Tort Law Liberal, Conservative, Libertarian, or Communitarian?

Although many Torts casebooks begin with an examination of at least a portion of what is usually termed the law of intentional torts, the heart of the first year study of Torts is focused on what is best described as the "accident" problem, and some books start right in with this aspect of the law of torts. Accidents happen and people are injured. These could be motor vehicle or other transportation accidents, medical accidents, accidents caused by the use of products, accidents occurring in recreational injuries or simply on someone else's premises, and so on. In the 1L Torts course, the main focus is on those accidents (whether carelessly caused or not) which lead to bodily injuries and death, and to a lesser extent to the damage or destruction of real property like buildings or personal property like motor vehicles. These sorts of accidents provide most of the business for a large share of the lawyers whose practice is centered on tort law, and for that reason many such lawyers are frequently termed "personal injury lawyers." To be sure, tort law involves lots of other injuries caused both accidentally and intentionally. And clearly there are, alas, a vast number of intentional torts that occur but never lead to tort claims because the attacker has no means of paying any damages award that tort law would impose. So far as the law is concerned, these wrongdoers are conventionally dealt with, if at all, via the criminal justice system.

Thinking about injuries caused by accident, a brief investigation demonstrates that tort law is clearly not the only way in which a society can deal with them. Indeed, as some Torts courses (eventually) reveal, accidents leading to personal injuries and death at the workplace are handled outside of tort law in the U.S., and in New Zealand tort law for personal injury and death has, as a practical matter, been eliminated (and replaced by social insurance arrangements). In other contexts, students learn, not only do American victims of careless behavior have no remedy in tort, they have no publicly provided remedy at all.

In this first chapter, four different models of how a society might deal with the accident problem are presented. More importantly, they are discussed as mechanisms that are associated with four quite different ideological positions about the role of government in general. Followers of these four political perspectives are termed here: Liberals, Conservatives, Libertarians, and Communitarians.

This chapter originally appeared as Chapter 15, "Personal Injury and Social Policy: Institutional and Ideological Alternatives" in **Torts Tomorrow -- A Tribute to John Fleming** (N.J. Mullany and A.M. Linden, eds., 290- 304, The Law Book Company 1998) and is reproduced with permission of Thompson Reuters (Professional) Australia Limited, www.thomsonreuters.com.au. This volume collected several essays honoring the scholarly career of Professor Fleming, the leading comparative law scholar of tort law in the 20th century and long time faculty member at the University of California's Berkeley Law School.

PERSONAL INJURY AND SOCIAL POLICY- INSTITUTIONAL AND IDEOLOGICAL ALTERNATIVES

In the four decades between the publication of the first[1] and ninth[2] editions of Professor John Fleming's *The Law of Torts* his field has undergone enormous change. Considering social policy toward personal injuries, tort law has come to play a more central role-with respect to product injuries, medical accidents, toxic spills and more. Yet, as John Fleming well appreciated, today's fault-and-lawsuit-based system suffers from many shortcomings -- shortcomings that have generated a wide range of proposals, some enacted, to replace personal injury law in part or entirely.[3] In this chapter, I compare the judicially-administered negligence regime with three competing institutional and ideological alternatives and speculate about the possible ousting of tort from its current prominence over the next four decades.

SOCIAL POLICY GOALS

Accidents happen. As a consequence, people are injured. Although society has an interest in reducing the frequency and severity of accidents, it would be foolish for society to attempt to eliminate all accidents. To try to achieve such a goal would be far too costly. Moreover, it would require restricting people's activities in a highly intrusive and undesirable way. Instead, society should be concerned about reducing accidents where the reduction can be achieved efficiently. As Guido Calabresi, the intellectual founder of "law and economics", put it years ago, there is an "optimal" level of accidents a society should aim for.[4]

Moreover, when accidents occur, society also has an interest in ensuring that the costs of those accidents are distributed fairly. Yet people may differ in their views as to what is fair. For some, the paramount concern is that economic losses are widely spread, so that no individual has to bear the full financial brunt of the harm he or she accidentally suffers. From this point of view, it is bad enough that he or she has to bear the physical consequences. For others, fairness in the allocation of costs is most importantly a matter of assigning responsibility for those costs to the party who caused the accident. From this perspective, an ex post assessment is necessary in order to determine who should pay.

INSTITUTIONAL ALTERNATIVES

In pursuit of both efficiency and fairness objectives, there are several institutionally distinct ways a society might deal with the management of the risk of accidents and the allocation of the costs of accidents that occur. I will describe four models:

(i) lawsuit-driven, fault-based compensation;
(ii) accident-cost-internalising, focused compensation plans;
(iii) social insurance paired with government regulation; and
(iv) the market.

In most societies the arrangements employed to address the risks and costs of accidents do not reflect purely one form. Rather, societies tend to combine elements from the different models in their own special ways. Nonetheless, the models described reflect distinctive strategies.[5]

Model one is conventional fault-based liability law, as it is generally understood throughout the common law and civil law worlds. In this model, people are threatened with financial penalties if they unreasonably fail to prevent accidental injuries to others-if they fail to exercise "due care". The financial penalties are meant to create a deterrent effect—enticing would-be injurers to take appropriate precautions. To the extent the strategy is successful reasonably avoidable accidents do not occur. Since the accidents that do occur are, therefore, not efficiently avoidable by someone else, society leaves the cost of those accidents on the victims. However, victims are permitted, ex ante, to make private insurance arrangements to cover those losses.

Of course, in practice, fault-based tort law is not fully effective at discouraging all reasonably avoidable accidents. So, when actors fail to take reasonable precautions and injure others, the victims are permitted to sue the negligent parties so as to shift the costs of those accidents to the unreasonable injurer.

This regime is considered fair because it allows innocent victims to shift costs to misbehaving injurers, and efficient because it encourages rational people to behave properly.[6] This approach puts its faith in the judicial process being able to determine, ex post, which risks of harm were unreasonably imposed and which were not.

Model two is reflected in both focused compensation schemes as well as "strict liability in tort." Workers' compensation is a good example. In this model, large organisations (often business enterprises) are asked to take responsibility both for managing the risks that fall within their domains and for paying for the accidental injuries that occur-regardless of fault. Rather than leaving the courts to decide which accidents should be reasonably avoided, the organisation has the obligation to compensate all its victims thrust upon it by government. Put differently, by imposing all accident costs on the responsible organisation, society gives it the incentive to take safety precautions when it is efficient to do so.[7]

This model is thought fair to the organisation because it has power over, and often makes profit in, the domain of its responsibility and fair to the victim who benefits from an assured loss-spreading regime and need not worry about arranging for private insurance. This regime is thought efficient because the organisation is encouraged to decrease accidents everywhere it can do so by spending less on precaution than it would have to spend compensating victims.

This model puts its faith in the idea that the compensation obligation will cause the organisation to take the socially desirable precautions and that the right organisation has been given the responsibility to do so. Notice how both workers' compensation and strict tort liability for extra-hazardous activities[8] reflect this model's key features, even though the compensation rules and the procedural settings of the two schemes differ.[9]

In model three, government takes direct responsibility for both the accident-optimising and the compensation objectives – but through independent institutions. Government safety agencies adopt regulations designed to promote the right level of precaution and governmental social insurance mechanisms provide victim compensation. The regulatory bodies have no responsibilities for compensation. They are meant to be neutral experts in safety and they may act by setting behavioural standards ex ante. It is in these respects that model three should be distinguished from model one in which the government acts ex post by enabling the judicial system to apply a generalised "fault" standard in awarding compensation where it is due.

In model three the funding of the social insurance system is independent of any accident prevention goal. So, for example, it is likely to be financed by broad-based revenue sources, like sales or income taxes, that are not linked to the level of accidents associated with firms or individuals. In model two, by contrast, the funding obligation is organisation-specific (based on the accidents that occur in its domain) and it is this cost internalisation that provides the financial incentive for safety.

Moreover, on the benefit side of model three, accident victims are not singled out for special treatment as they are in model two. Rather, they are treated in the same way as other citizens in need of health care, basic wage replacement and the like—by having access to the governmental safety net. Model three is thought fair because society collectively ensures compensation to all victims and those who carelessly cause accidents are collectively punished by a regulatory agency, and efficient because society discourages avoidable accidents through its regulatory regime.

Model three puts its faith in the effectiveness of the regulatory system in managing risk. Although this model may be conventionally associated with a "command and control" regulatory style, that is not necessarily required. Regulators might choose to deploy an incentive-based regulatory strategy. The key that distinguishes this model from the others is the separation of the compensation function from the safety function.

Model four relies upon individual responsibility and the market. As for safety, private parties have the obligation to take precautions to prevent injuries to themselves. If those precautions are better taken by others, then those precautions are worked out through the market. So, for example, buyers and sellers of goods and services manage risk together by agreeing on the precautions that are to be employed in connection with their voluntary transactions. This model permits individuals with different tastes for risk to trade off risk against other factors (for example, cost, aesthetics, performance and the like). It assumes that individuals rather than courts, agencies or large organisations should decide what risks are reasonable to run and what risks should be reduced in the name of accident prevention. Hence, if enterprises have risk management thrust upon them, it is through voluntary contract and not through the coercive arm of the state.

Model four also relies upon individuals to make compensation arrangements for themselves. This may involve arranging for private insurance or for compensation to be tied to the provision of a product or service. Indeed, it is up to the parties to decide whether individual compensation is to be paid in case the service or product provider fails to take a promised precaution. Would-be victims might prefer to have their own insurance and to rely upon reputational concerns to entice would-be injurers to take the agreed precautions. This is to be contrasted with the other models in which compensation is provided by some third party in all cases where an accident should have been avoided but was not.

Model four is thought fair and efficient because the parties decide for themselves what risks should be taken and how losses are to be allocated. This model puts its faith in the market. The governmental role is essentially reduced to enforcing the contracts that individual parties make.

It is easy to see, in principle, how the market might deal with those categories of accidents involving voluntary interactions-work injuries, public transportation injuries to passengers, product injuries to consumers, medical injuries, recreational injuries on commercial premises and the like. Yet it is difficult to even imagine how the market would regulate accidents that do not arise out of market transactions-like motor vehicle accidents and other injuries to "strangers". Hence, this model might apply to only certain domains. In this respect, model four is like model two, since in model two an appropriate organisation may not exist to take responsibility for all categories of accidents. Of course, inequalities in information and bargaining power make many people sceptical about the effectiveness of using the market to manage risk, even in the voluntary transaction setting.

ASSOCIATED POLITICAL IDEOLOGIES

Many people bring to politics, and the role of government generally, a commitment to a certain ideological way of looking at things. Many have a basic attitude toward individual and collective responsibility that orients the way they think about all policy issues, whether it is a matter of welfare policy, education policy, defence policy, environmental policy or accident policy. Moreover, these different mind-sets tend to predispose people to favour specific sorts of institutional solutions to policy issues. In this vein, the four models I have just described reflect four distinct ideological outlooks. I connect the models with (i) conservatives, (ii) social democrats, (iii) communitarians, and, (iv) libertarians, respectively.[10]

I associate model one with conservative values because it emphasises individual responsibility for wrong-doing. Model one focuses on providing deserving victims individual rights of redress. At the same time, it imposes on individual victims the costs that are incurred when others are not to blame for their injuries. These themes--individual rights and individual responsibility--reflect conservative outlooks on crime and welfare policy. By threatening punishment, it is hoped that people will take their social responsibilities seriously and that government will not be needed to intervene. Government's role is only activated when an individually aggrieved victim comes forward with a complaint against another private party, minimising the role of government bureaucracy.

Model two reflects the social ideology that led to the post-World War II welfare state. From this perspective, little weight is put on individual fault. Larger institutional forces are seen as the key actors in society. This is reflected in how the left looks at unemployment and crime. Moreover, in this view, it is more important that "rough justice" is achieved and people have basic needs met, than having a system of exquisite and costly individual justice with winners and losers. Capitalism is by no means rejected, but government properly forces large private organisations to carry out public purposes-here the management of the risk and cost of accidents.

Model three is connected to what I call communitarianism. The state is the larger collectivity through which we all act to serve the needs of our greater community. Those with this outlook care, for example, about the needs of disabled people generally. It does not matter whether people are disabled at birth, by disease, by aging, or by accidental injury. The risk of temporary or permanent disability can strike any person, and communitarians believe that society in general owes to those with temporary or permanent disabilities fair access to medical care and related services, as well as income replacement. The costs of accidents should be borne by and diffused across society. On the other side of the model three equation, communitarians also want the community, self-consciously, to set standards of conduct, at least where the risk of harm to others is at stake, to reduce the risk of accidents in the first instance. Under the communitarian ideology, individuals have a duty to participate in their collective self-government and through that participation government becomes neither feared nor ridiculed, but rather the voice of the people.

Model four represents libertarian values. Like the model four solution, libertarians believe in individual choice and are sceptical about government regulation. Just as libertarians believe that government should generally take a hands-off approach to controlling the behaviour of its citizens, this outlook extends to the management of risk. Individuals should be allowed to manage their own risks without government intervention. The dominant value is liberty and libertarians highly value the market as a mechanism to both preserve and promote liberty.

UNITED STATES CONSUMER AND VICTIM GROUPS EMBRACE A CONSERVATIVE INSTITUTION

Most societies have a complex set of institutional arrangements for dealing with the risk and costs of accidents that do not mirror, in pure form, any one of the four models set out earlier. One explanation for this layering is that, over time, the four ideological perspectives just described wax and wane and the political parties in charge of the government, each with their own mix of ideological guiding principles, come and go. Moreover, individual accident problems become politically salient in different eras, as technology advances and different modes of production are used to manufacture new products. For example, factory work injuries became prominent problems early on in the age of industrialisation, motor vehicle accidents rose to prominence in the 1950s and 1960s as more people drove larger and faster cars and mass injuries due to prescription drugs and aeroplane crashes have gained prominence more recently with increasing access to those products and services.

Another explanation for this complex institutional arrangement is that, within any democratically run country at any time, there is likely to be a diversity of ideological opinion. This diversity of opinion among public groups usually means that advocates of each ideological perspective will be successful, at one time or another, in capturing power or influence within the system and succeed in gaining passage of a law or program that reflects their preferred view of how to manage accident risks and costs. Moreover, it is often more difficult to repeal an existing governmental program or regulatory regime than it is to add a new one. This, too, contributes to the existence of multiple, and sometimes ideologically contradictory, approaches within the same society.

There is a further complication that I will now address. I have described conventional tort law as a conservative institution and in many countries it operates in a solidly conservative manner. Moreover, in such settings the politically conservative actors in the society (the heads of large enterprises, for example) are likely to be quite content with it.

But in the United States, starting in the 1960s, tort law became identified with the left. Why did that happen? One explanation is that at that time, it appeared to some that tort law was abandoning its commitment to the individualised determination of fault and instead embracing strict liability for injuries attributable to enterprise activities. In other words, many began to see that tort law would be transformed from a model one institution into a model two regime.[11]

The endorsement in 1964 of "strict products liability" by the American Law Institute in § 402(a) of the *Restatement of Torts, Second* was seen as an important early harbinger. And yet, as the past 25 years have played out in the United States, strict liability has really gone nowhere (at least nowhere important) as a *doctrinal* matter. Strict liability for product injuries now squarely applies only to manufacturing defects.[12] Moreover, these defects appear to account for a relatively small share of product accidents, and in any event, the application of strict liability to those accidents has brought about only a small change in the outcome of cases, given the availability of res ipsa loquitur under the fault regime. Put differently, complaints about a product's design or warnings, on the whole, must still be based in negligence.[13]

Additionally, United States courts have shown virtually no willingness to deem products "defective" on the basis of danger alone; that is, without requiring the plaintiff to demonstrate a feasible alternative design.[14] Even more sweeping strict liability--in which causation alone would suffice--has never been seriously entertained.[15] Moreover, true strict liability for service-providing enterprises has hardly been given a moment's thought.[16]

Nevertheless, some people believe that American negligence law in action has often become strict liability in fact. The argument may be made in at least two ways. One is that, as United States courts have been increasingly allowing juries to decide whether an individual defendant was at fault, those juries have been increasingly willing to find negligence where it does not exist. The claim is that these juries find non-existent negligence in order to provide compensation for victims, who have large medical bills and lost wages, at the expense of "deep pocket" defendants, who are not at fault but can still afford to compensate the injured plaintiffs. Yet, one should not make too much of this claim, even if juries have behaved in that way in some individual cases. Certainly, victim lawyers go to great lengths to prove the defendant's fault in most cases; and certainly defendants win a fair share of personal injury cases that actually go to trial.[17]

A second argument is that in the settlement process defendants pay out large sums whether they are at fault or not. To be sure, strict liability may be the law in action in certain small-value cases where the plaintiff's claim contains a certain nuisance value, that is, the defendant does not want to pay to litigate and finds it cheaper just to pay the victim off. But in more serious injury cases, it seems far more likely that defendants settle for large sums for other reasons. Often they know they have been at fault and want to avoid the negative publicity that might come from a trial. Moreover, in these settlements their fear is not that juries will find them negligent even though they exercised due care. Rather, defendants fear that juries will impose large punitive damage awards when their conduct was merely negligent, and not reprehensible, as the doctrine is supposed to require before an award of exemplary damages is made. To the extent juries are too quick to impose punitive damages, this may reveal a discontinuity between tort law on the books and tort law in action, but it is not a problem of turning conservative fault law into strict enterprise liability.

A more convincing explanation, I believe, for the embrace of tort law by victim and consumer groups--along with its fault requirement--is tort law's resonance with the David and Goliath story. Individual lawyers, acting, in effect, as private attorneys general, are able to expose corporate wrongdoing that government regulators have ignored (or have been pressured into overlooking). This is what Linden JA has called the "ombudsman" function of tort law.[18]

In other words, starting in the 1960s, those on the left in the United States saw that a conservative institution, in which government's role was merely to referee the resolution of private disputes, could be converted, at least in some important cases, into a forum for what is in effect "public interest litigation". Just as American lawyers turned to the courts to combat civil rights violations by government, so too lawyers aroused the judiciary in the campaign against corporate misconduct in the personal injury field.[19] It is also worth recalling that during the period between 1968 and 1992, the American presidency was in the hands of Republicans for all but the four Carter years. In those circumstances especially, it is not surprising that the left would conclude that their efforts to attack corporate wrongdoing would be better received by judges (many of whom had earlier been appointed by Democrats) than through the executive branch. The situation in many American States reflected--indeed continues to reflect--this same pattern.

Viewed as public interest litigation, tort law allows the previously powerless individual victim to take on the economic powerhouses of the country. With the fearless and charismatic personal injury lawyer at his or her side, the victim suddenly has his or her David to fight against Goliath. To be sure, many would argue that the victims' lawyers (that is, the Davids) are really in it to line their own purses rather than for the public good. But, even if this were true for many lawyers, it may not matter. With the United States system of compensating lawyers on a contingent fee basis, these two interests are basically aligned.

Of course, most torts cases are not public interest cases. Most claims involve ordinary automobile accidents and claims against other motorists.[20] Many involve routine "slip and fall" injuries and so on. To be sure, "money" (typically an insurance carrier) is usually on the other side (otherwise victims would not bother to sue), but rarely is some important general "principle" at stake in the individual case. Still, even in these routine cases, some victim advocates have adopted what I have here termed a conservative perspective, by rejoicing in United States tort law's recognition of the victim's dignity. Never mind that most plaintiffs do not seem to enjoy the litigation experience.[21] At least, a very generous award of pain and suffering damages can put lots of cash in the victims' pockets.[22]

The upshot of the embrace of the expanded United States tort system by the left has been that the conservatives are the ones who have primarily complained about the American negligence law system. Tellingly, however, conservatives generally do not want to eliminate tort law--certainly not if that risks model one being replaced by model three. Rather, conservatives seek to tame tort law--to bring it back to more of the model one institution it was in an earlier era. In practice, this has most importantly meant trying to limit the amount of damages victims can recover, to control the legal fees that victim attorneys may obtain, and to get judges (who nowadays are more likely to have been Republican appointees) to more carefully supervise the administration of the fault principle.[23] In more recent years, conservatives have somewhat successfully carried out their campaign in individual State legislatures.[24] Indeed, their general message about the "runaway" tort system has also arguably had an impact on judges and juries.[25]

PROPOSED REFORMS OF TRADITIONAL SOCIAL DEMOCRATS

Although America's most famous consumer advocate, Ralph Nader, is wildly and resolutely in favour of tort law,[26] not all of those who might call themselves social democrats are so enraptured. Indeed, from the mid-1960s onward, many have argued that the basic conservative underpinnings of tort law make it incapable of dealing properly with the contemporary accident problem. Some of their key points are: (i) tort law inevitably provides incomplete coverage of accident victims, thereby requiring an additional compensation mechanism; (ii) tort law is very expensive to administer and is beset with delays; (iii) akin to a "lottery", tort law is idiosyncratic in how much it pays, lavishing pain and suffering awards on some victims while denying recovery altogether to others who are identically or nearly identically situated; and (iv) tort law is not successful in shaping behaviour in socially desirable ways.[27]

In short, these critics attacked model one from all angles: as they view negligence law, not only is it inadequate in theory (because it fails to compensate victims of unavoidable accidents), but worse it is especially unfair and inefficient in action. This sort of argument hasn't moved Nader. His response, as I see it, is to favour a combination of models one and three: (i) let us have lots of governmental safety regulation; and (ii) let us have comprehensive social insurance (these are the model three features); but (iii) let us keep tort law (model one) especially because it allows wronged victims to strike back at corporate wrongdoers and teach them a lesson.

Unlike Nader, many critics of the United States version of model one in action have pushed for model two reforms. Some have concluded that the compensation arrangements envisioned by model three are politically implausible, but many simply prefer the model two approach. They believe that accident cost internalisation by enterprises (model two) is a more promising way to optimise safety than through regulation (model three).

Hence proposals have been floated for all sorts of focused compensation plans (variations on workers' compensation) that would internalise accident costs to an appropriate organisation or industry-giving that enterprise the twin duties of both managing risk and compensating victims regardless of fault. Proposals have covered injuries such as those caused by pharmaceutical drugs,[28] aeroplane crashes,[29] medical accidents,[30] and toxic chemicals.[31] Indeed, the call for a medical accident compensation scheme has been renewed by Justice Englard in this volume.[32]

Some more adventuresome scholars have envisioned even more sweeping reforms in the model two vein. These all owe their debt to Calabresi J's pioneering work. For example, Professors Franklin and Pierce advanced rather similar proposals that go beyond tailored compensation schemes to cover accidental injuries in general.[33] Although both Franklin and Pierce included some model three features in their schemes (that is, some victims would be compensated from money raised from general taxes), both rely on cost internalisation as the key strategy for enticing large enterprises to take safety precautions. Later, Professor Latin took a similar position, although his reforms would rely upon sweeping enterprise liability in tort, rather than imposing accident costs on organisations via a new compensation scheme.[34] Most recently Professors Nolan and Ursin, writing together, have renewed the Calabresi-Latin line on behalf of enterprise liability.[35]

However, in practice, in the United States, little has come of these efforts. A modest childhood vaccine injury scheme is in place.[36] Sweeping strict liability in tort stands ready in case there is a large-scale calamity at a nuclear power plant.[37] A few small arrangements exist at the State level, such as compensation schemes for badly injured newborns in Virginia and Florida.[38] But the more ambitious proposals have languished.

Indeed, even motor vehicle no-fault plans (which do not really fit model two very well because they do not impose strong responsibility on organisations) have made few inroads since they first burst onto the United States scene at the end of the 1960s.[39] By now only a couple of States have ambitious no-fault schemes (Michigan and New York), a few others have modest schemes and none has anything approaching, say, Quebec's comprehensive no-fault approach to auto accidents.[40]

A LIBERTARIAN COUNTER-ATTACK

Some American scholars have responded to what they saw as the highjack of tort law by the left by proposing libertarian solutions.[41] At least in settings in which the injurer and victim were in an economic relationship prior to the accident, libertarian scholars have advocated that the parties should be able to make their own "deal" as to who should take responsibility for managing the risk and what would be the financial consequences were there an accident. This regime could cover, for example, the highly contentious areas of product injuries and medical accidents.

Doctrinally, this libertarian approach has meant arguing that individuals ought to be able to waive their tort rights in advance of an accident. More precisely, for this approach to work would-be injurers need to know that courts would uphold "agreements not to sue" that goods and services providers would have their customers and patients enter into. Therefore, as a practical matter, this approach translates into the deployment of exculpatory clauses, regardless of libertarian philosophy's reliance on individual market-based solutions. This is not a judgment on whether it would be right or wrong to let would-be victims waive their right to sue. Rather, it is only a recognition that proponents of libertarian contractual agreements are unlikely to urge would-be injurers to agree to be strictly liable. The whole thrust of the libertarian argument is that individuals can count on market pressures to manage risks and that, in return for a lower price for a product or service, they might well prefer to take on the financial risk of loss themselves, especially if they were already well insured.

However, little has happened on this reform front either. Some may fear that to ask for an agreement not to sue will harm the enterprise's marketing efforts. But the most likely explanation for the lack of uptake of the libertarian program is that potential defendants fear that courts will not respect exculpatory clauses. Such attempts to limit liability were harshly treated early on,[42] and they seem to crop up these days primarily in the recreational activity setting. In the recreational setting, some risk of non-negligent injury is usually clear and the parties may rationally decide that it is, therefore, not worthwhile to ask the legal system to make what might be a very difficult ex post decision as to who was at fault. Moreover, these activities are clearly voluntary activities (that is, they are neither necessary medical interventions nor basic consumer products).

Yet, even these most logical agreements not to sue have not fared very well in State courts and legislatures.[43] Rather, courts are more likely to uphold a tort waiver only when a reasonable compensation substitute is offered.[44] However, this is not the libertarian way; it is rather the solution sometimes suggested by pragmatic reformers with model two in mind.[45]

A COMMUNITARIAN FUTURE?

Most writing on behalf of model three reforms has come from outside the United States. For example, Terrence Ison from Canada has promoted this point of view for decades.[46] A British group, headed by Donald Harris at Oxford University's Centre for Socio-Legal Studies, also pushed this way of thinking for a short while.[47] I have been something of a lonely voice for this approach in

America. [48] Most important, of course, has been the embrace by New Zealand of an accident compensation scheme that closely resembles model three.[49]

Understandably, at a time when capitalism is reigning and former socialist economies are in disarray and when the large social insurance schemes of many Western European welfare states, as well as the United States social security system, are under great financial pressure, it might seem odd to talk about a communitarian future in which other countries would follow and expand upon the New Zealand approach--especially when there is talk about that the New Zealand government may privatise at least part of the system.

Yet, tort law's shortcomings are obvious and they have yet to be eliminated or even substantially reduced by recent reforms. Tort law remains heavily laden with transactions costs. Tort law can never provide the compensation security that all accident victims need. The system continues to deliver uneven individual justice, and whatever its positive effects toward safety (if any), they are plainly insufficient.

Victims still rely on other compensation arrangements (including private insurance and social insurance) that tort law duplicates and society still needs more effective risk management mechanisms. Although the solutions could follow a model two approach, I think that approach is unlikely for the long run, if for no other reason than significant model three compensation arrangements are already in place that would be duplicated by a comprehensive model two strategy.

In short, if more is to be done about the problem of accidents and their costs, I foresee that the changes will have a communitarian cast. Here are two plausible examples. First, the government transforms workers' compensation into a more general model three social insurance scheme, by having it provide around-the-clock coverage for workers and their dependents. In the United States, this would not only broaden the availability of health insurance but it would also greatly strengthen workers' income disability protection. Secondly, the government creates a "whistle- blower" scheme that rewards individuals and their lawyers for exposing enterprise misconduct that creates or increases the risk of accidents. [50] This scheme would be designed to allow society to capture whatever whistle- blower benefits tort law now provides.

Were both of these (or similar) reforms enacted then tort law's compensation and behavioural control functions would have been primarily consigned to other institutional arrangements. As a result, tort law's continued application to personal injury cases (apart from instances of deliberate harm that merit punitive damages) would become a redundant and an excessive luxury that would mainly benefit lawyers. This thought experiment leads me to conclude that the prospect for a communitarian future depends upon convincing the public that: (i) tort law is not and cannot achieve society's accident policy goals; and (ii) that a model three substitute would serve society more efficiently and effectively than layering on one more partial supplement in an attempt to fill the substantial gap in coverage of tort law.

Although one way to reach a communitarian outcome is to adopt a substitute regime all at once, as New Zealand did, this is not the only possible scenario. Alternatively, tort law might be eroded from within.

Suppose, as an initial step, tort law were made secondary-and in two senses. One, as John Fleming wrote so thoughtfully,[51] the collateral sources rule could be reversed so that tort would, at most, serve a gap-filling role on the compensation side. Two, compliance with regulatory standards could increasingly count as a complete defence to a suit in negligence so that tort would be understood to play only a back-up role in terms of risk regulation. In this posture, as communitarian solutions expanded, tort law's role would be naturally undermined, until such point as it might become sufficiently marginal as to be abandoned.

I recognise that this is unlikely to happen very soon (at least in the United States) and my crystal ball gazing for the longer run may be way off the mark. Twenty-five years ago John Fleming attributed the replacement of personal injury law in New Zealand with what I have called a communitarian solution at least partly to the existence of "a strong sense of group identity, a feeling that one's neighbour's welfare is almost as important as one's own".[52] Yet, during the 1980s and 1990s, selfish individualism has triumphed around the globe. Even so, I still find it hard to imagine that tort law will become even more prominent in the future than it has become during its chronicled ascendancy through the many editions of Professor Fleming's great treatise. Rather, if we adopt a generous time horizon, I still think he was right to predict in 1984 that "the law of tort will yield more and more ground to accident compensation in the coming years".[53]

ENDNOTES

1. J G Fleming, *The Law of Torts* (1st ed, The Law Book Co Ltd, Sydney, 1957)

2. J G Fleming, *The Law of Torts* (9th ed, LBC Information Services, Sydney, 1998).

3. See generally J G Fleming, *The American Tort Process* (Clarendon Press, Oxford, 1988); J G Fleming, "Is There a Future for Tort?" (1984) 58 ALJ 131; J G Fleming, "The Pearson Report: Its 'Strategy' "(1979) 42 MLR 249; J G Fleming, "The Decline and Fall of the Law of Torts (or Law of Delict?)" (1973) 6 Comp and Int'l LJ of Southern Africa 259.

4. G Calabresi, "Optimal Deterrence and Accidents" (1975) 84 Yale LJ 656.

5. American Law Institute, *Enterprise Responsibility for Personal Injury: The Institutional Framework* (American Law Institute Publishers, Philadelphia, 1991), Vol 1, Ch B, pp 55-233, Ch D, pp 351-448.

6. For simplicity's sake, I ignore here the situation when both injurer and victim can efficiently avoid the accident. Contemporary tort law, of course, largely deals with this

7. Again, I put aside for simplicity's sake situations in which the victim could have readily avoided the accident but did not. In practice, focused compensation schemes tend to ignore all but the most egregious cases of victim fault.

8. American Law Institute, *Restatement of Torts, Second* (American Law Institute Publishers, St Paul, Minnesota, 1977), §§519-520 (Abnormally Dangerous Activities).

9. In this volume Professor Stanton examines the retreat from strict liability for ultra-hazardous activities in English and Australian law: see K M Stanton, "The Legacy of Rylands v Fletcher", Ch 6.

10. For earlier thinking of mine along these lines see generally S D Sugarman, "Proposals for Reform" (1993) 15 U Haw L Rev 659; S D Sugarman, "A Restatement of Torts" (1992) 44 Stan L Rev 1163.

11. See generally G Calabresi, *The Cost of Accidents* (Yale University Press, New Haven, I970). In this volume Professor Klar bemoans this expansion of enterprise liability and calls for a return of tort law to its traditional fault-based anchors: see L N Klar, "Downsizing Torts", Ch 16.

12. American Law Institute, *Restatement of Torts, Third* (American Law Institute Publishers, Philadelphia, 1997), § 2 (Products Liability) (Proposed Final Draft).

13. Ibid.

14. *O'Brien v Muskin Corp* 463 A 2d 298 (1983) is the exception to this general rule and it has been overturned by the New Jersey legislature: see NJSA §§ 2A:58c-3 (West Publishing Co, St Paul, Minnesota, 1998). The Supreme Court of California's passing mention in *Barker v Lull Engineering Co Inc* 573 P 2d 443 n 10 (1978) of allowing liability on the basis of danger alone has never gone anywhere.

15. This position has lately been revived in the literature by Professors Croley and Hanson, but with no indication yet that any courts are at all interested: see S P Croley and J D Hanson, "Rescuing the Revolution: The Revived Case for Enterprise Liability" (1993) 91 Mich L Rev 683.

1 6. California flirted slightly with this idea in *Becker v /RM Corp* 698 P 2d I I 6 (1985) (imposing strict liability on the purchaser of an apartment building when a tenant was injured by a shower door that was in defective condition at the time the defendant purchased the building). However, that case was overturned in *Peterson v Superior Court* 899 P 2d 905 (1995) (denying strict liability claim of guest against hotel owner where the guest slipped in a defective bath tub). For discussion of American and Canadian developments see S M Waddams, "New Directions in Products Liability", Ch 8.

17. See T Eisenberg et al, "Litigation Outcomes in State and Federal Courts: A Statistical Portrait" (1996) 19 Seattle U L Rev 433 at 436 (reporting that for 1991-1992, defendants won 51 per cent of cases in State court jury trials; 45 per cent of cases in federal court jury trials).

18. See A M Linden, *Canadian Tort Law* (6th ed. Butterworths, Toronto, 1997), pp 20-27. Justice Linden reviews and expands upon this argument in this volume: see Han AM Linden, "Torts Tomorrow-Empowering the Injured", Ch 17.

19. See R Nader and J A Page, "Automobile Design and the Judicial Process"(1967) *55* Cal L Rev 645.

20. See Eisenberg et al, op cit n 17, Table I.

21. See E A Lind and T Tyler, *The Social Psychology of Procedural Justice* (Plenum Press, New York, 1988).

22. Some scholars have estimated that pain and suffering damages account for 50 per cent of many personal injury damage awards: see S P Croley and J D Hanson, "The Nonpecuniary Costs of Accidents: Pain-and-Suffering Damages in Tort Law" (1995) 108 Harv L Rev 1785 at 1787; E J McCaffery et al, "Framing the Jury: Cognitive Perspectives on Pain and Suffering Awards" (1995) 81 Va L Rev 1341 at 1346. But compare D R Hensler et al, *Compensation for Accidental Injuries in the United States* (RAND Institute for Civil Justice, Santa Monica, 1991), pp 100-101 (estimating that out of a total of $15.7 billion a year in liability payments for accidental injuries, damages for pain and suffering amounted to $5.2 billion).

23. See G L Priest, "Economic Problems of Accidents and Compensation" (1993) 15 U Haw L Rev 544. See also P W Huber, *Liability: The Legal Revolution and its Consequences* (Basic Books Inc, NewYork, 1988).

24. See, for example, S J Carroll, *Assessing the Effects of Tort Reform* (RAND Institute for Civil Justice, Santa Monica, 1987) (discussing tort reforms enacted in 1986); R L Rabin, "Federalism and the Tort System" (1997) 50 Rutgers L Rev 1 at 3-4 (noting tort reform campaigns from the 1970s to the 1990s).

25. See T Eisenberg and J A Henderson, "Inside the Quiet Revolution in Products Liability" (1992) 39 UCLA L Rev 731 at 794 (discussing how judges may have been influenced by negative public opinion about the tort and product liability systems); M Galanter, "Real World Torts: An Antidote to Anecdote" (1996) *55* Md L Rev 1053 at 1110-1112 (noting contemporary juror research that shows juror scepticism towards personal injury plaintiffs).

26. See, for example, A Tobias, "Ralph Nader is a Big Fat Idiot" (1996) Worth 93.

27. See, for example, J O'Connell, *The Lawsuit Lottery: Only the Lawyers Win* (Free Press, New York, 1979).

28. See R A Merrill, "Compensation for Prescription Drug Injuries" (1973) *59* VaL Rev I.

29. See S D Sugarman, "Right and Wrong Ways of Doing Away with Commercial Air Crash Litigation: Professor Chalk's 'Market Insurance Plan' and Other No-Fault Follies" (1987) 52 J Air Law and Com 681.

30. S D Sugarman, "Doctor No" (1991) 58 U Chi L Rev 1499 (review of PC Weiler, *Medical Malpractice on Trial* (Harvard University Press, Cambridge, 1991)).

31. See R L Rabin, "Some Thoughts on the Efficacy of a Mass Toxics Administrative Compensation Scheme" (1993) 52 Md L Rev 951.

32. See Hon I Englard, "Informed Consent-The Double-faced Doctrine", Ch 10.

33. See M A Franklin, "Replacing the Negligence Lottery: Compensation and Selective Reimbursement" (1967) 53 VaL Rev 774; R Pierce, "Encouraging Safety: The Limits of Tort Law and Government Regulation" (1980) 33 Vand L Rev 1281.

34. See H A Latin, "Problem-solving Behavior and Theories of Tort Liability" (1985) 73 Cal L Rev 677. Whereas Calabresi seemed to envision imposing strict tort liability on the "cheapest cost avoider", Latin would impose it on enterprises that could be counted on to engage in "problem solving behavior". Both of them rejected the idea that juries should ordinarily determine fault on a case-by-case basis.

35. See V E Nolan and E Ursin, *Understanding Enterprise Liability: Rethinking Tort Reform for the Twenty-first Century* (Temple University Press, Philadelphia, 1995).

36. See Rabin, op cit n 31.

37. See *Price-Anderson Act* 42 USC § 2210, 1988 (creating strict liability in tort for nuclear power plants involved in an "extraordinary nuclear occurrence").

38. See *Birth Related Neurological Injury Compensation Act* (Injured Infant Act), Va Code Ann,§ 38.2-5000-5021, Supp 1987; *Birth Related Neurological Injury Compensation Plan,* Fla Stat Ann,§§ 766.301-766.316, 1998 (West Publishing Co, St Paul, Minnesota, 1998).

39. See R E Keeton and J O'Connell, *Basic Protection for the Traffic Victim* (Little, Brown & Co, Boston, 1965).

40. See S D Sugarman, "Quebec's Comprehensive Auto No-Fault Scheme and the Failure of Any of the United States to Follow" (1998) Cahiers de Droit, Universite Laval, Quebec (forthcoming).

41. See P H Rubin, *Tort Reform by Contract* (AEI Press, Washington, 1993); Huber, op cit n 23; PC Choharis, "A Comprehensive Market Strategy for Tort Reform" (1995) 12 Yale J on Reg 435; R A Epstein, "Medical Malpractice: The Case for Contract" [1976] Am B Found Res J 87.

42. See, for example, *Hennigsen v Bloomfield Motors Inc* 161 A 2d 69 (1960) (striking down express disclaimers limiting liability); *Vandermark v Ford Motor Co* 391 P 2d 168 (1964) (rejecting contractual disclaimers limiting tort liability); *Tunkl v Regents of University of California* 383 P 2d 441 (1963) (rejecting a release from liability for future negligence imposed as a condition for admission to a charitable research hospital).

43. *Dalury v S-K-1 Ltd 610* A 2d 795 (1995) (rejecting a broad release from liability required by a ski resort); *General Obligations Law* NY,§ 5-326, 1997 (declaring void against public policy efforts to contract out of liability by health clubs). Compare *Barnes v New Hampshire Karting Association Inc 509* A 2d 151 (1986) (upholding a release-from- negligence agreement signed as a condition of participating in karting races); *Okura v United States Cycling Federation* 186 Cal App 3d 1462 (1986) (upholding release covering negligence as a condition of participating in bicycle race).

44. See, for example, J O'Connell, "An Alternative to Abandoning Tort Liability: Elective No-fault Insurance for Many Kinds of Injuries" (1976) 60 Minn L Rev 501 at 519.

45. See, for example, J O'Connell, "Expanding No-fault Beyond Auto Insurance: Some Proposals" (1973) *59* VaL Rev 749. See also S D Sugarman, *Doing A way with Personal Injury Law* (Quorum Books, New York, 1989), Ch 9.

46. See T G Ison, *The Forensic Lottery: A Critique on Tort Liability as a System of Personal Injury Compensation* (Staples Press, London, 1967); T G Ison, "The Significance of Experience Rating" (1986) 24 Osgoode Hall LJ; T G Ison, *Compensation Systems for Injury and Disease: The Policy Choices* (Butterworths, Toronto, 1994).

47. See D Harris et al, *Compensation and Support for 1//ness and Injury* (Clarendon Press, Oxford, 1984).

48. See generally Sugarman, op cit n 45.

49. See G W R Palmer, *Compensation for Incapacity* (Oxford University Press, Wellington, 1979). For recent developments in New Zealand see Han G Palmer, "The Design of Compensation Systems: Tort Principles Rule, OK?" (1995) 29 Val U L Rev 1115.

50. See Sugarman, op cit n 45, Ch 7.

51. See J G Fleming, "The Collateral Source Rule and Loss Allocation in Tort Law" (1966) 54 Cal L Rev 1478.

52. See Fleming, ''The Decline and Fall of the Law of Torts (or Law of Delict?)", op cit n 3,at 271.

53. See Fleming, "Is There a Future for Tort?", op cit n 3, at 142.

Chapter 2

Ideological Flip-flop – Why Democrats and Republicans Switched Sides on Tort Law

Chapter 1 shows how the core features of tort law appear to mesh well with conservative political ideology, and that those with views to the left – liberals and communitarians – might be expected to favor other mechanisms for dealing with the accident problem. This chapter first argues that this is roughly how things stood in the U.S. in the early 1960s. At that time, critics of tort law were primarily liberals from academia who envisioned replacing tort law for personal injuries and death with some sort of government compensation scheme – as New Zealand eventually did in the 1970s. Conservatives were then largely content with tort law, and business leaders, who mostly had few financial concerns about the tort system, could embrace the idea that tort law helped weed out the "bad apples" from their midst (which they certainly were not, or so they claimed).

But as this chapter next argues, things are turned upside down today. We've had a dramatic "flip-flop" with conservatives and business leaders together crusading (for quite some time now) against tort law and liberals having become its main supporters. Moreover, the leading voices on the left now come primarily from practicing personal injury lawyers and no longer from academia. Why did this ideological flip-flop come about? This chapter explores that question. It also examines how tort law itself has become highly politicized in both the legislative process and the judicial selection process – enormously more so than it was fifty years ago.

This chapter originally appeared as a chapter in **Essays on Tort, Insurance, Law and Society in Honour of Bill W. Dufwa** (Volume 2, pages 1101-1122 , Jure Forlag AB 2006) and is reprinted with permission of the publisher . These essays (mostly from non-American contributors) were gathered as a Festschrift to honor Professor Dufwa of the University of Stockholm on the occasion of his retirement.

Ideological Flip-Flop: American Liberals Are Now the Primary Supporters of Tort Law

This essay explores in ideological terms the transformation in who supports American tort law.[1] Traditionally structured to function to favor defendants, tort law around 1960 was a regime that conservatives defended and liberals[2] sought to replace or reform. Today, many on the left embrace tort law, and it is the right that is pushing for "tort reform." Along with this ideological somersault, American tort law has become much more politically prominent.

I. Tort Law Resonates with Conservative Values (while Liberal Values have an Uneasy Relationship with Tort Law)

At its core, tort law (at least in theory) comfortably resonates with conservative ideology.[3] There are two basic points here. *First,* in the U.S., as throughout the industrialized world, civil liability for accidental or intentional harms almost always requires proof of fault by the defendant. This means that tort law embraces the principle of personal responsibility for wrong-doing, and this is normally a core conservative value. This value is reflected, for example, in widespread conservative support for the criminal law and in the frequent desire by conservatives to impose punishment in response to misconduct. Moreover, some conservatives have emphasized that tort law serves to help weed out the "bad apples" - firms and professionals that might otherwise stain the reputations of socially-responsible enterprises and professionals who work to promote everyone's well-being.

By contrast, the ideology of the left is conflicted on the. idea of fault. On the one hand, many on the 1eft are reluctant to blame individuals for bad social outcomes and instead to attribute social woes to structure factors in the society. In turn, the left tends to be much less enamored with punishment as a response to social deviance (e.g., as illustrated by proposals for the decriminalization of drug use and prostitution). Yet, this rejection of individual blame tends to focus on the "have-nots" in society. Others on the left - what might be termed the "populist" wing -- have long been eager to blame both business and political leaders for abusing their power at the expense of the ordinary citizen. Hence, tort law resonates well with this sort of liberal populist thinking. Note next that by saying that blameworthy conduct is to be punished, tort law simultaneously says that non-faulty conduct is (generally) not to be punished, even if it· causes harm to another. This means, for example, that technological development can escape paying for the harm that it does when that harm is not readily avoidable. This result is consistent with views of many political conservatives who believe that "progress" brought about by business (and the "market") is inherently desirable.

By contrast, many on the left (especially the "Greens") have become much more skeptical about whether technological progress really is "progress" -- as illustrated, for example, by the widespread opposition on the left to genetically modified crops. As a consequence, those on the left might be expected to much more quickly espouse a regime of tort liability without fault ("strict liability") as a social engineering mechanism deployed in pursuit of general social welfare values. One way to put this is that what is claimed to be "progress" should be forced to prove that it truly is progress by paying its way (i.e., by paying for the externalities it produces). Strict liability would achieve that objective more fully than does fault liability.

Second, as a system of behavior control, tort law relies upon privately-initiated litigation. Instead of public agencies or public prosecutors telling people how to behave. The threat of tort liability is meant to induce people to act reasonably without government intervention. To be sure, courts are there in reserve to deal with private disputes if a victim claims that an actor did not act properly and caused harm. But the principle underlying the system (as much elaborated by "law and economics" scholars)[4] is that deterrence generally achieves socially desirable levels of accident prevention (safety) without regulation. This approach is highly attractive to conservatives who prefer "market" solutions and whose ideology generally favors "small" government.

Again, the left is divided on this matter. Many on the left would much prefer a system of direct governmental regulation to the indirect mechanism of tort law. Yet, the populist Wing of the left is eager to play the David role in the fight with Goliath, and welcomes the spectacle of individual private heroes (lawyers in this case) battling, and sometimes defeating, the captains of industry.

II. The Structure of Tort Litigation Historically Has Favored Enterprise Defendants (and Insurers of Defendants)

In practice, the typical tort claim pits an ordinary citizen against either an enterprise (a corporation or a governmental body) or an insurer who financially stands behind the defendant. This pattern traditionally has disadvantaged claimants in a number of respects.

First, the claimant must carry the burden of proof by demonstrating 1) that the defendant is at fault, 2) that the defendant's fault is that cause of the victim's loss, and 3) the extent of the loss suffered. Imposing this burden on the claimant is generally justified on the ground that tort law should not hold someone responsible unless the judicial system is convinced this is the correct outcome (and the corollary principle that defendants should not be hauled into court and then ordered to demonstrate their innocence).

Indeed, when tort cases are brought to trial, the elaborate apparatus of the legal system is there for the purpose of trying to assure that "precise justice" is achieved.[5] Fault-finding is highly individualized to the facts of each case. In this way, the outcome of the tort mechanism becomes a public declaration of the "truth" as to who was wronged by whom (if at all).

While conservatives have traditionally been happy to embrace the twin ideas that tort law metes out "precise justice" and that defendants are deemed innocent until proved otherwise, the left is again somewhat divided on this matter. On the one hand, those on the left are quick to support the idea that the moving party must carry the burden of proof when litigation pits the government against an ordinary citizen (e.g., in criminal cases) or when powerful economic actors, like employers or landlords, seek to take away critical assets, such as someone's job or home. Nevertheless, many people on the left are rather less concerned about the niceties of proving individual fault when, as in the typical tort case, the structure of the litigation is reversed - ordinary citizens claiming compensation from either impersonal enterprises or insurance companies. Not only are these defendants economic powers rather than people, but also the financial harm arising from the mistaken attribution of fault is viewed as fur less serious than are the consequences of an erroneous determination against an individual.

In any event, a problem for victims with the way tort law assigns the burden of proof is that sometimes the judicial system simply cannot be certain whether the defendant was to blame. As a result, a lack of crucial evidence can create an insurmountable hurdle that may preclude deserving victims from recovery. This is especially unfair if, as sometimes happens, the relevant evidence actually exists and is in the possession of the defendant, but is not disclosed.

Second, rules concerning the payment of legal fees can raise the hurdle to recovery even further.6 In most nations, the loser of a torts case is responsible for both his legal fees and the fees of the other side. As a result, in cases of uncertain outcomes, the fear of losing the lawsuit and having to bear both sides' fees can preclude some injured parties from suing who actually would have won their case had they tried. In the U.S., by contrast, a victim who loses his case normally pays the fees of neither side. The defense side pays its own lawyer, since under the American rule each side bears his own legal fees; but a losing victim in a torts case also owes nothing to his own lawyer, since personal injury lawyers in the U.S. charge fees that are contingent on winning (i.e., the fee is a share of the recovery). Nonetheless, this fee arrangement presents would-be claimants with a different problem. Simply put, the better lawyers tend to screen out weaker cases, leaving deserving victims who have less certain claims with the risk of being stuck with inexperienced or less competent representation, if any.

Third, tort defendants are typically repeat players in the litigation process, and this may give them several advantages over claimants who tend to be bringing their once-in-a-lifetime lawsuit. Not only are defendants much more experienced with the pre-trial process, the settlement-negotiation process, and the trial process itself, but also they have usually developed a network of reliable lawyers and experts to handle their cases. By comparison, victims are often quite unsophisticated in these matters and have to seek out help only after they are in the midst of suffering from the injury upon which their claim rests.

Furthermore, as parties with financial strength and frequent claims experience, defendants (or their financial backers) generally do not face a "bet the company" sort of lawsuit. As a result, the defense side can typically be "risk neutral" as to many aspects of the tort litigation process - knowing that, over time, the odds will tend to balance out the consequences of various uncertainties. By contrast, the one- time claimant is typically risk averse and, comparatively speaking, a great deal more is likely to be at stake. This means that victims are likely to be more cautious. Among other things; this means that they are likely to compromise their claim by accepting a lower settlement than a risk neutral party would accept.

The upshot is that the regime of tort liability has traditionally been satisfactory both to those who accept the conservative ideology and the big business and insurance company interests with whom they are typically politically connected.

III. Traditionally It Has Been the Left that Has Wan to Reform the Tort System

By the 1960s, liberals in the U.S. were beginning to voice a chorus of complaints about tort law. These were of three very different sorts, however. *First,* the response of many on the left was to call for the replacement of tort with alternatives, an uprising that was especially vociferous in the late 1960s as automobile no-fault plans begin being presented to state legislatures.[7] The primary focus of this social-engineering oriented wing of tort reformers was on the failure of tort law to provide compensation to all of the accident victims who need it.

They pointed out that, by its own terms, tort law's fault system does not well serve the compensation needs of 1) those who cannot prove the other side to be at fault even if they actually are, 2) victims injured by those who are judgment proof, 3) people who are victims of no one's fault, as well as 4) those who the tort system deems to be at fault for their own injury. From a compassionate perspective, however, regardless of the explanation for the injury, a victim still needs health care services and sufficient income replacement to keep bread on the table, a roof over his and his family's head, and so on.

Once victim compensation became some critics' most important goal it seemed only natural that many on the left would favor the adoption of a separate mechanism-a compensation plan-to deal squarely with victim needs. The historic precedent for this was the successful push for industrial injury compensation plans (called workers' compensation in the U.S.) in the early years of the 20th century. In the U.S., these plans are generally a complete substitute for tort recovery - at least with respect to claims against the victim's employer. As such, they represent a clear commitment to deal with work injuries through collectively-provided social insurance instead of via the hit-and-miss process of individual litigation. And even though industrial injury victims in many other countries may still sue their employer under tort law, those victims also turn first and primarily to the social insurance mechanism to deal with their compensation needs. Today, this progressive strategy is well-reflected, for example, in Quebec's auto no-plan, adopted in 1977, which has since spread to other Canadian provinces.[8]

Under the Quebec scheme, auto accident victims no longer make tort claims. Instead they receive compensation from a specialized governmental agency, which collects auto insurance premiums from all motorists and promptly pays out benefits to victims regardless of fault. In the last third of 20th century, scholars in common law nations proposed additional compensation plans of this same general sort that would deal with more classes of accidents, like airplane crashes, medical accidents, and drug side-effects.[9] Within the U.S., Jeffrey O'Connell has been the most persistent and innovative advocate of no-fault substitutes for tort.[10]

Moreover, other scholars developed even broader schemes to replace much more of tort law with administrative compensation plans. In the U.S., for example, both Marc Franklin[11] and later Richard Pierce[12] developed sweeping accident compensation schemes of a sort also proposed by Canadian scholar Terrence Ison for British Commonwealth nations.[13] A group at England's Oxford University, headed by Donald Harris, called for an even wider plan that would, for example, cover those with disabilities caused, not only by accidents, but also by illness and birth defects.[14]

Twenty years ago, I proposed an even more· radical plan.[15] And, New Zealand actually moved in this more sweeping direction. In the early 1970s a broad accident compensation scheme was adopted there as a nearly complete substitute for tort. Much amended over the years (especially at times when more conservative governments have been in power), the core features of the plan remain in place.[16]

Second, during this same period, a different tort reform group on the left sought, not to replace tort law, but rather to substitute strict liability for fault liability. These reformers concluded that the compensation goal that so many on the left held dear could actually be attained (or at least much more fully realized) through tort law itself Simply put, for them, the objective was to dramatically widen tort law's reach, and "enterprise liability" became their rallying cry. Berkeley's Albert Ehrenzweig and Yale's duo of Fleming James and Guido Calabresi are now widely viewed as early exemplars of this perspective.[17]

Third, still other reformers were content with the basic idea of fault-based tort law. To them, the main problem was that the formal doctrine then in place provided too many instances of legal protection for defendants who were actually at fault. The most important academic scholar with this view was

Berkeley's Dean William Prosser, the author of the most important American torts· treatise of the twentieth century and the Reporter for the American Law Institute's Restatement of Torts (Second) during the 1950s and 1960s. Prosser was hardly a left winger. Yet, most of the important doctrinal changes he championed (and frequently achieved) were decidedly pro-victim.

Prosser and other similarly-minded tort law critics objected to decisions of courts, some rooted in the 19th century, that had used fears of crushing liability, or a flood of litigation, or the squelching of socially valuable activities as arguments for limiting the scope of tort law's reach. These critics made specific doctrinal objections, just to illustrate a few, to limited duties owed 1) to those on the premises of others, 2) by charities to their victims, and 3) to those who were emotionally harmed by the defendant's fault. An additional doctrinal target was the common law rule that the victim's fault, regardless of how modest in comparison to the defendant's, normally altogether barred recovery. Other objections emphasized procedural roadblocks to victim recovery. Examples in this category included 1) having to find a home town doctor to testify in a medical malpractice case, 2) having to sue defendants endlessly (i.e., one victim at a time) for what were essentially identical harms caused by the same product or activity, and 3) being unable to access damning evidence of fault that defendants hid and refused to divulge.

Note well that each of these three groups of tort reformers· was led by leaders from academia. By contrast, certainly in the early 1960s, most of the actual lawyers who represented plaintiffs in torts cases had little by way of an important voice in the call for tort reform. (If asked, they most likely would have sided with the Prosser view of things.) Indeed, many in academia looked down upon these lawyers as "ambulance chasers," and within the legal profession they generally were at or near the bottom in terms of prestige.

IV. Changes in Lawyering and the Law since 1960 Have Eroded Many of the Defense Side's Advantages in Tort Litigation

In trying to understand why many of those in the U.S. who are on the political left currently favor a robust tort law and are cool to alternatives, it should first be emphasized that a many changes have occurred over the past 40-50 years that have decidedly cut into the advantages the defense side historically has had in the operation of the tort system.[18]

First, plaintiff personal injury lawyers in America as a group appear to be more talented today than in the past, or, at least, there are more very effective lawyers doing this sort of work. Although it is difficult to trace the direction of causation here, several points can be made.

One, the status of the personal injury lawyer is now much higher than it was in days in which this part of the bar was routinely stigmatized as "ambulance chasers." Part of the status no doubt comes from the role of these lawyers in winning huge awards in high profile cases.[19] This, of course, has meant more earnings for this class of lawyers, and presumably that, in turn, attracts more able lawyers to this sort of work. Also, while there continues to be a great deal of complaining about the tactics and antics of personal injury lawyers, at the same time they are, at least on some important occasions, grouped with other "public interest" lawyers who are seen to help the ordinary citizen in exposing the wrongdoing of powerful interests in the society. Indeed, plaintiff personal injury lawyers often seek to portray themselves as analogous to civil rights lawyers who led the battle for the rights of racial minorities and women; and, of late, they have, at least in some places, re-labeled themselves as "consumer" attorneys instead of "trial lawyers." The enhanced reputation attached to the nature of their work probably serves to lure additional talent to this line of practice.

Two, along with greater numbers of plaintiff personal injury lawyers and the diversity of cases they bring (e.g., medical malpractice, product injuries, transportation injuries, injuries blamed on property owners and the like) has come increased specialization. Individual attorneys are able to focus their practice (at least for a while) in a fairly narrow way (e.g., airplane crash cases, machine tool injury cases, asbestos injury cases, auto design defect cases, pharmaceutical drug cases, serious birth injury cases, etc.). This specialization also brings with it both deeper experience and greater expertise.

Three, because (as already noted) plaintiff lawyers in the U.S. take a cases on a contingency fee basis, and because the successful lawyers in this field will typically have· a substantial portfolio of broadly similar cases going at once, the defense side advantages of both experience and risk neutrality are by now substantially undermined. Once the defense side realizes that the lawyer for the victim is quite prepared to see the case through trial and take a chance of receiving no fee, the bargaining power of the defense in settlement negotiations is reduced. Moreover, although plaintiff personal injury lawyers continue largely to practice as individuals or with small firms, in very large cases it is now not uncommon to affiliate on a case-by-case basis with lawyers in other firms who provide additional expertise, legwork, and perhaps the crucial financing necessary to keep the case going. This too makes for a more equal legal battle between victim and injurer.

Four, it is no longer so difficult for plaintiff side lawyers to gain access to expert witnesses who will testify on their side of the case. Gone are the days in which no physician could be found who would be willing to testify against a fellow doctor. This change is the result of many factors: more doctors and urbanization means that local doctors are less likely to be personal friends (golfing partners, for example); as malpractice litigation increases, more doctors realize that they can make a career of testifying in these sorts of cases; the nationalization of medical standards, combined with subtle changes in the legal rules governing malpractice cases, no longer require a plaintiff witness to come from the same town as the defendant doctor; and university-based doctors in particular seem increasingly willing to condemn very bad doctoring when that is what they believed occurred. Some of these points apply to other accident fields as well, where, for example, accident reconstruction experts, engineers, and the like are now eager to display their sophisticated knowledge (for a fee, of course) in furtherance of the plaintiff side of the case.

Five, class actions, although still atypical, are now possible in some torts cases. Alternatively, case aggregation (where many claims are simultaneously pursued before the same judge) is now often possible where a large number of victims are similarly situated. Both of these procedural developments allow some cases to be presented that simply would not have been brought before.

In addition, where there are huge numbers of victims of a single event or a single product or course of action, the presentation of a package of claims all at once sharply raises the stakes for the defense side. Nowadays defendants may indeed confront a "bet the company" problem if they choose to litigate to the end rather than settling, regardless of what the defense believes to be the genuine merits of the case. This too shifts the balance in the structure of the tort system away from the defense side.

Second, in addition, both courts and legislatures have helped tort plaintiffs over the years through common law and statutory developments on various fronts. These include changes in substantive rules of tort law, rules of evidence, and rules of procedure that, in one way or the other, reduce the litigation burden the plaintiff faces. For example, some rules concerning the proof of "causation" have been relaxed when it has struck the courts as highly unfair to force the victim to prove something when the relevant evidence is very likely to be in the hands of the defense side. As another example, old rules that sharply restricted duties of injurers have been eroded and replaced with softer principles that require an inquiry into the reasonableness of the defendant's conduct in the specific case. Further, the rules of "discovery" that now govern civil litigation make it fur more difficult for defendants to hide evidence they possess that is harmful to their case. In short, most of Prosser's agenda has been achieved and more.

Besides, and almost unique to the U.S., tort cases continue to be tried to juries. This wild card means that the defense side can never be sure that what it considers to be a clear winner of a case will, in the end, be so viewed by a group of local citizens who have been selected to serve on the jury, in significant respects, owing to their considerable ignorance of the issues at stake. And while it appears from research findings that juries usually decide cases the same way judges would have decided them had the judge tried the case without a jury, there is the off-chance of a very unexpected outcome, and especially of an exceptionally high monetary award. The latter seems to be especially true now that high level awards are frequently publicized in the media so that jurors are more likely to be aware of huge verdicts that other juries gave. This gives the talented plaintiff lawyer a weapon that can be effectively employed either to extract a more generous settlement or, in the end, to bring home a gigantic victory.

V. Enthusiasm on the Left for Alternative Compensation Plans has Largely Evaporated

Despite what many might see as the long-term success of the New Zealand approach to accident compensation, other developed countries have simply not followed this example. Early on, Australia came close, but since then no wealthy nation has even seriously considered the New Zealand solution. Why is that? After all, even though many industrialized nations have had some periods in which their governments have been in the hands of conservative parties, most have had years (often many years) of more progressive governments.

In trying to explain New Zealand's exceptional status, it is essential to recognize the social safety net that has been constructed in most of the developed world and that exists altogether apart from tort law. Throughout Western Europe for example, there are well-entrenched schemes of national health insurance and social security income replacement covering death and both long and short-term disability, to say nothing of a myriad of other social support mechanisms for those in need of assistance. In these countries, despite recent cutbacks of the social safety net in some of them, the core compensation goal that so strongly prompted advocates of industrial injury compensation plans a hundred years ago is largely being met - separate from either tort or any specific accident compensation scheme.

In the U.S. the picture is much more complex because there is no national health care plan and the thinner social safety net for income replacement has more holes in it. Nonetheless, even in the U.S., in practice, a vast share of citizens has reasonably good health insurance, assured death benefits, and at least some income protection for complete long-term disability. Moreover, a substantial share of the population has reasonable short-term disability income protection and more generous long-term disability coverage.[20]

Hence, in important respects, so far as the compensation goal is concerned, the adoption of a New Zealand-like scheme would be largely redundant for a significant share of victims—as it indeed is in New Zealand itself. The same can be said for the Quebec auto no-fault plan. And when this fact is put together with the reality that in recent years many industrialized countries have been trimming, rather than expanding their social welfare states, the failure of others to copy New Zealand may at first seem readily explained.

Yet, it remains the case that plans like those in New Zealand and Quebec fill in some important holes in the compensation web that otherwise would exist. Moreover, compensation plan advocates have pointed to additional benefits that such plans can bring.

One, it seems clear that auto insurance is markedly less expensive in Quebec under its no-fault plan than it would be under the tort system - even though more victims are covered, and in many cases their coverage is now superior to what it had been under tort law.[21] This is achieved by a combination of savings on legal and other litigation-related expenses, the elimination of commissions, advertising and other costs associated with a private insurance regime, and the elimination of pain and suffering awards for those with minor temporary injuries. In sum, a wholly different ground on which some of those on the left might favor alternatives to tort is that such plans leave ordinary consumers with more money in their pockets to spend on something else they need or want.

Two, some on the left have long argued that safety is better promoted through mechanisms other than tort. For certain compensation plan advocates, this is a matter of the funding of the compensation mechanisms themselves. If, rather than paying for victim compensation through general or broad-based taxes, the compensation plan funding is targeted to those enterprises that cause claims, then, it is argued, the desire to save money will prompt firms to make sensible investments in accident prevention. This, of course, is the same "law and economics" argument that supports the claim that tort law efficiency promotes safety. Yet, some compensation plan devotees have argued that because the operation of those plans is more predictable, the safety-promoting signal they give is clearer and more effective than the one sent by the threat of tort liability.

To be sure, compensation plan advocates on the left appear to be divided over whether a society's accident prevention strategy should importantly rest on financial incentives created by plan funding rules. Skeptics would rather place safety policy more squarely in the hands of government agencies whose prime mission is accident prevention.

In all events, the fact remains that the adoption of a compensation plan as an alternative to tort has remained a relatively rare phenomenon throughout the economically developed world. Indeed, it is important to notice that, in recent decades in the U.S., specialized plans of this sort that have actually come into effect are the result of pressure from business interests. For example, America's childhood vaccine compensation program[22] was enacted in order to assure that drug companies would continue to make vital vaccines. The Florida and Virginia plans to compensate severally neurologically injured newborns were created to prevent obstetricians from curtailing their medical practice in those states.[23] Even the national compensation plan adopted in response to the World Trade Center and related terrorism of September 11, 2001 was motivated in significant respects by a desire to limit the potential legal exposure of the U.S. airlines whose planes were used by the terrorists.[24] This is not to say that those on the left opposed these schemes, but rather to emphasize that their adoption was not part of the agenda of the left.

In the end, for the U.S., perhaps the most important explanation for the near evaporation of support for alternative compensation plans by those on the left, is that the loudest voices speaking out in favor of tort law now come, not from academia, but from victims' rights advocates—the plaintiffs' lawyers and their allies.

VI. The Previously Political Roles Have Been Reversed with Prominent American Liberals Now Tort Law's Biggest Boosters

As already explained, around 1960, liberals in the U.S. were not generally enthused about the state of tort law, and many reformers on the left began to promote compensation plan alternatives.

To be sure, as also noted above, others on the left toyed with the idea of expanding tort's doctrinal and operational reach so as to create an accident compensation scheme through tort the tort system itself. After all, great strides in this direction could be achieved through a combination of the substitution of 'strict liability for fault-based liability, the complete elimination of the defense of victim fault, and the assurance that those likely to cause injuries are adequately insured so as not to be judgment proof. Yet, none of those changes has been achieved.

Nevertheless, in the U.S. today those on left are the ones who are the main supporters of the fault-based tort system - calling it a crucial weapon in support of progressive causes.

In some respects, it is hardly surprising that victims (and their lawyers) today are more satisfied with tort law as compared with the past. As noted above, much of the structural advantage that the defense side previously had has been neutralized, and common law judges and legislatures have liberalized substantive tort doctrine itself. Moreover, widely publicized reports of jury verdicts have made it well known that personal injury lawyers increasingly win very large verdicts for their clients. For example, earlier on, it was a select few lawyers who had won $1 million or more in an individual case. Nowadays, such awards are common. In 1961, the largest reported award for pain and suffering in a California personal injury case was $134,000.[25] Even if that would come to more than $600,000 in today's money, these days individual awards of more than $1 million for pain and suffering are so frequent that they may well not even make the newspaper.

Perhaps most importantly, by defending fault-based tort law, today's leading voices from the left embrace the same values that seem naturally congenial to the right. Indeed, these liberal supporters today seem uninterested in converting tort law itself into an efficient victim compensation machine. They are not generally pushing to turn tort law from a fault system into a strict liability system. To the contrary, from the viewpoint of plaintiff-side personal injury lawyers, this is because, as a litigation strategy, they want to be able to allege and prove fault anyway as a way of achieving larger verdicts.

Basically, the business community is portrayed as all-too-often behaving badly - regularly cutting corners by sacrificing safety in order to increase profits. Rather than seeing the problem as one of a few "bad apples," this perspective views business misconduct as rampant. Tort law, then, is depicted as *the* key barricade that prevents enterprises from simply rolling over consumers and workers on behalf of their owners. While this critique of business as being socially irresponsible was also voiced in the 1960s, it has, in more recent decades, become a mantra of the left.

Moreover, the private litigation feature of tort law is now more widely embraced by liberals. Here the argument is that government regulators - once seen as the solution to business misconduct - are too overworked, too lazy, or too easily captured by those they are meant to regulate. This reflects a general disenchantment by many on the left with "big government." This does not mean that American liberals oppose government safety regulation, but rather that many are now unwilling to rely on government regulation to the exclusion of private litigation.

Joining with left wing populists, these liberals argue that it is crucial for independent outsider "private attorney general" sorts of public citizens (i.e., the plaintiff's lawyer) to be able to wield power against enterprises so as to expose, punish and, one hopes, deter unreasonably dangerous activities that government is failing to control. Liberal supporters of U.S. tort law also now praise it as providing the kind of moral satisfaction that ordinary people desperately need when victimized by powerful interests. The recapture of one's dignity is said to be achieved in the quintessentially American way of, not merely winning the litigation, but winning a lot of money.

It bears re-emphasizing that most of the important voices from the left that are raised in the U.S. today on behalf of tort law are not those of academics. Rather they are the voices of personal injury lawyers themselves, or of organizations they sponsor or run. These personal injury lawyers have a huge amount at stake, both economically and in terms of self-identity. Moreover, they are now well organized, and they now have lots more money to devote to their cause - money that, ironically, comes directly from the pockets of those they rail against. And they use their money strategically - seeking, among other things, to win the support of politicians (both legislators and judges) to whose election and re-election campaigns they make generous donations.

One special advantage that U.S. plaintiff personal injury lawyers have had for some time is the unreservedly whole-hearted endorsement of tort law by Ralph Nader—America's leading consumer advocate.[26] Although Nader's reputation in recent years is perhaps altered (and in some progressive quarters it is diminished) because of his two quixotic campaigns for the Presidency, nonetheless he continues to be viewed by many as an unselfish voice for consumers and for the public at large. And when he echoes what the personal injury lawyers are saying, this provides considerable weight for their claim that their position is not simply one of greed.

Especially because of Nader's voice, there seems lost in the U.S. today voices of consumer advocates on the left who continue to find tort 1) wasteful because of its enormous administrative costs (most importantly, legal fees), 2) lottery-like in its determination of who wins cases and the amount of their victory, 3) largely ineffectual in promoting safer conduct, 4) structurally inadequate to compensate needy victims, and so on.[27]

Yet, even those consumer groups not under the personal sway of Nader are generally defenders of tort law these days. Perhaps one explanation is that their support has tended to come in the context of efforts by the other side simply to do away with victim rights without providing clear benefits to anyone other than shareholders and insurers.

VII. In turn, Now it is Conservatives in the .U.S. Who Complain About Tort Law

For the past two decades, defendants and their ideologically conservative allies have mounted a well-funded attack on U.S. tort law. Much of their legislative reform effort has been cloaked in anecdotes. Real or imagined cases are portrayed as having preposterous outcomes. This strategy is at the heart of the campaign to convince both the public and policy-makers that U.S. tort law is wildly reeling out of control.

When it comes to statutory specifics, conservatives have difficulty mounting a wholesale attack on tort law because of its continued formal reflection of values that are normally congenial to conservatives. This has forced American conservatives to object to tactics, procedures, uncertainties, "bet the company" risks, inconsistencies in case outcomes, etc. that they say characterize the tort system. This is not an objection so much to tort law on the books, but rather to what they claim is tort law· in action (i.e., in practice). Put differently, they claim to have lost faith in the idea that tort law actually provides "precise" justice. Not surprisingly, then, they say they are for "tort reform" but not its replacement.

Put generally, conservative political entrepreneurs simultaneously seek both to reduce and stabilize the exposure faced by their business and insurer allies, while remaining committed to the basic idea of private law as society's core mechanism for accident regulation and victim compensation.

To be sure, one can point to a few examples of where political conservatives in the U.S. have sought to restrict the substantive reach of tort doctrine around the edges. Yet, their main efforts have been to reformulate the law of damages from that which common law courts have evolved over the years. A central target is the open-ended award by juries of pain and suffering damages (i.e., general damages for non-economic loss). Instead, defense interests have tried to win legislative limits on recovery (i.e., financial maxima such as $250,000 per victim). Instead of having the tort system ignore other sources of compensation a victim might have as "collateral" (e.g., social or private insurance), defendant interests have lobbied to reverse that rule. Instead of holding multiple tortfeasors each fully liable for the entire amount of the damages they together have caused - with the risk of absent or insolvent defendants falling on the defense side - conservatives have sought statutory change that imposes liability on a defendant enterprise only to the extent of its share of the fault in bringing about the loss. And so on.[28]

Over the past twenty years, punitive damages have also been seen to loom as a serious threat over the heads of defendant firms whose employees have misbehaved. In fact, punitive damages are awarded only in a small minority of cases, and, as a matter of legal doctrine, they are supposed to be imposed only for the worst sort of wrongdoing. Moreover, American jury verdicts granting punitive damages are often reduced or eliminated by the trial judge or by courts on appeal. Furthermore, the U.S. Supreme Court has now intervened into this controversy, concluding that it would normally be unconstitutional for punitive damages to be awarded in an amount that is ten or more times the amount of compensatory damages in the case.[29]

Nonetheless, the risk of suffering the economic and public relations pain of large punitive awards in torts cases has embittered many who would have been defenders of the tort system of the past. They allege that the actual award of punitive damages is lottery-like and irrational in amount, and that frequently the risk of punitive damages is large enough to force defendants to settle cases for far more than they otherwise would be worth. This concern has caused defense interests to seek statutory reform of the law of punitive damages, at a minimum by tightening the criteria for their award and reining in the amount that can be awarded and, where possible, by eliminating punitive damages entirely.

Broadly speaking, the business community and its political friends long for the tort law of circa 1960. But the actual legislative fight over tort reform is carried out over the subtle details, as defense interests seek to roll back victims' rights in very specific ways that are aimed at reducing both the frequency of claims and the level of awards, while holding on to the basic norm of fault-based liability.

VII. As a Result American Tort Law is Now a Highly Contentious and Politicized Issue

In the early 1960s, when Dean Prosser was completing the most important sections of the Restatement of Torts (Second), American tort law was the most traditional of common law subjects. Putting aside the academic social engineering visionaries, it seemed as if both claimants and defendants, as well as the actual lawyers for both sides, broadly shared the view that if tort law was going to change, it would do so largely through the opinions of common law judges. As if by implied agreement, neither side in actual litigation was to seek help from the legislative process.

During most of the 1960s, then, such "tort reform" as was achieved (as already discussed) meant pro-plaintiff doctrinal evolution brought about by common law judges. Often in response to Prosser's suggestions, many state courts did indeed liberalize many of tort law's traditionally restrictive rules, thereby significantly expanding victims' legal rights - albeit while retaining the fault principle for nearly all of tort law's coverage (defectively manufactured products being the main exception to which strict liability attached, starting in the mid-1960s).

But soon, most state legislatures stepped squarely into tort law's realm. At first, this seemed to be the result of coalition politics. For example, the most important initial wave of reform, starting in the late 1960s and spilling over into the 1970s, was the elimination of the old common law rule that victim fault (contributory negligence) was a complete bar to recovery. While this seemed to be a pro-victim change, it should be emphasized that the adoption of these statutory changes was often as much or more the product of defendant-side efforts as it was victim-side initiatives. Indeed, the comparative fault laws that were legislatively adopted often continued to bar recovery to victims who were half or more a fault. This is to be contrasted with the more pro-plaintiff rule adopted by common law judges who replaced the complete bar rule with a more pure form of comparative fault that provided victims with some compensation even if they were primarily at fault in causing their harm. Moreover, it seems that many auto insurers at the time saw relaxation of the contributory negligence complete bar rule as a strategy for preventing the adoption of auto no-fault laws that those insurers then opposed.

In the late 1960s and 1970s, and originally at the initiative of liberal academic reformers, a number of American state legislatures began adopting auto no-fault schemes - notwithstanding the opposition of some insurers, just noted, whose strategy of blocking auto no-fault with the embrace of comparative negligence thereby failed. As noted earlier, liberal advocates of auto no-fault tended to see themselves as inheritors of the workers' compensation tradition. Yet, on the ground, it took other insurers who favored auto no-fault joining with those academics to produce the political might necessary to achieve these changes. Furthermore, opponents of auto no-fault were not only other insurers, but also plaintiff lawyers. The latter did not want to lose business, especially the large cases. In the end, and reflecting the growing political muscle of lawyers who handled major injury cases, of the approximately twenty states that adopted auto no-fault plans, only two or three enacted schemes that substantially replaced tort with a compensation plan for auto injuries, and none acted as Quebec did to adopt a complete' substitution.

Before long, however, cross-party and ideologically mixed political coalitions appeared to fade. As the voices on the left became more and more the voices of the plaintiff lawyers, and the voices on the right became more and more embittered with how "their" system was functioning, the battles over tort law became more strident and politically more partisan.

For example, in California in 1986, conservative interests successfully campaigned to have the voters recall from office Chief Justice Rose Bird and two other left-leaning members of the California Supreme Court. Although the public campaign against these three was waged on the ground that they were "soft on crime" (especially with respect to the death penalty), it is widely believed that defense interests in torts cases provided much of the money for the recall effort, hoping to have these judges replaced with those who would not be so quick to move the common law in a pro-plaintiff manner. And, they were successful. In the nearly twenty years since the ouster of Chief Justice Bird and her two colleagues, the California Supreme Court has become much more favorable towards defendants in its decisions than it had been in the prior two decades.[30]

Furthermore in California, the defense side took to the legislative initiative route as well. Hiring specialized firms to solicit voter signatures, business and insurance interests were able to present a number of propositions directly to the voters, and they were twice successful. Both of these popularly adopted laws restrict the recovery of pain and suffering awards in certain special cases - where there are multiple defendants[31] and where the plaintiff is an uninsured motorist or a drunk driver.[32]

Waves of specialized defense interests also went directly to the California legislature for relief from tort law, and many were successful - including physicians, public utilities and other property owners, tobacco and gun and alcohol manufacturers, and so on. Many of these legal changes overturned specific pro-plaintiff decisions of the California Supreme Court, or else precluded the Court from moving in a direction that defendant interests feared the Court was going.

This partisan fight over tort law was by no means restricted to California. As already described above, throughout the U.S., the defense side has sought legislative protection especially with respect to the law of damages. And it has achieved at least some defense-oriented reform in most states.[33] "Tort reform" is now understood primarily to be legislative, not judicial, reform; and the direction of the reform is decidedly now pro-defendant, not pro-plaintiff. In short, trial lawyers on the victim side are now the ones who are most eager for tort law to remain as much a common law system as possible, with no further intrusion by the legislative process.

Where they are out gunned in the legislative process, plaintiff lawyers often turn to the forum they know best - the courts. In several states they have gone all the way to state supreme courts seeking to have many of the defense-oriented tort reform measured invalidated as incompatible with the state constitution. These lawsuits generally charge that the statutes improperly invade the authority of the jury and/or the judges.[34] And, in several states this legal attack has succeeded, especially, it seems, when former plaintiff lawyers have been in positions of prominence on the state high court.

That, in turn, has made the selection and election of state Supreme Court justices itself a much more politically contested matter. For example, in states where judges are routinely elected by the public (Alabama, for instance), huge sums are spent by both sides of the personal injury law divide trying to put their favored candidate on the bench.

The bottom line is that, in America, tort law is no longer something of a legal and political backwater that is shaped primarily by specialized experts from academia and both sides of the bar, whose disputes were almost always taken only to state court judges for resolution. Now, the last several U.S. Presidents have taken a stand on tort law, the U.S. Supreme Court has joined the fray, defense interests regularly pressure the U.S. Congress to adopt nation-wide changes (a few of which have so far been successful around the edges of the tort system), and at the state level charges and counter-charges about tort law are regularly in the news, and legislative reform proposals are regularly in play. All in all, American tort law has become a highly politically partisan matter.

Stepping back and comparing things today with the way they were around 1960, the most dramatic change is that the main warriors defending tort law now come from those on the left who support Democratic politicians; and it is the right and their Republican party allies who are squealing about the operation of a system whose formal principles continue to resonate with their conservative values.

ENDNOTES

1. To be clear at the outset, "tort law" means primarily the law governing personal injuries and property damage. In the U.S., this area of the law remains mostly judicially-created "common law," and although each of the 50 American states has its own tort law, their central features are the basically the same.

2 We in the U.S. label "liberals" those who in Europe are frequently termed "social democrats."

3 Stephen D. Sugarman, Personal Injury and Social Policy- Institutional and Ideological Alternatives, in Torts Tomorrow: A Tribute to John Fleming (N. Mullany and A. Linden, eds.) 290 (1998).

4 Starting perhaps most importantly with Richard A. Posner, A Theory of Negligence, 1 J. Legal Studies 29 1972).

5 See generally, Stephen D. Sugarman, Precise Justice and Rough Justice: Scientific Causation in Civil Litigation as Compared with Administrative Compensation Plans and Mass Tort Settlements, in Scienza e Diritto Nel Prisma del Diritto Comparato (G. Comande and G. Ponzanelli eds.) 139 (2004).)

6 John G. Fleming, The American Tort Process 187 (1988).

7 For a very early call, see Jeremiah Smith, Sequel to Workmen's Compensation, 27 Harv. L.Rev. 235 (1913).

8 See generally, Stephen D. Sugarman, Quebec's Comprehensive Auto No-Fault Scheme and the Failure of Any of the United States to Follow, (1998) Les Cahiers de Droit 109.

9 See, e.g., Stephen D. Sugarman, Right and Wrong Ways of Doing Away with Commercial Air Crash Litigation, 52. Air L. & Com. 681 (1987); John G. Fleming, Drug Injury Compensation Plans, 30 Am.J. Comp. L. 297 (1982); and Clark Havighurst, "Medical Adversity Insurance: -Has Its Time Come?, 1975 Duke L.J. 1233.·

10 See, e.g., Jeffrey O'Connell, The Injury Industry and the Remedy of No-Fault Insurance (1971); Jeffrey O'Connell, Ending Insult to Injury: No-Fault Insurance for Products and Services (1975); Jeffiey O'Connell, The Lawsuit Lottery: Only the Lawyers Win (1980); and Jeffrey 0'Connell, The Blame Game: Injuries, Insurance and Injustice (with Kelly) (1986).

11 Marc Franklin, Replacing the Negligence Lottery: Compensation and Selective Reimbursement, 53 Va. L. Rev. 774 (1967).

12 Richard Pierce, Encouraging Safety: The Limits of Tort Law and Government Regulation, 33 Vand. L. Rev. 1281 (1980).

13 Terrence Ison, The Forensic Lottery (1967).

14 Donald Harris, et al, Compensation and Support for Illness and Injury (1984).

15 Stephen D. Sugarman, Doing Away With Personal Injury Law (1989). See also, Patrick S. Atiyah, Accidents, Compensation· and the Law (3d ed. 1980) and Jane Stapleton, Disease and the Compensation Debate (1986).

16 For the proposal leading to the New Zealand plan, see Woodhouse Report, Royal Commision of Inquiry, Compensation for Personal Injury in New Zealand (1967). More generally, see Geoffrey Palmer,

Compensation for Incapacity (1979) and Geoffrey Palmer, The Design of Compensation Systems: Tort Principles Rule, OK, 29 Val. U. L. Rev. 1115 (1995).

17 See, e.g., Albert Ehrenzweig, Negligence Without Fault, 54 Cal. L. Rev. 1422 (1966); Fleming James, Jr., Some Reflections on the Bases of Strict Liability, 18 Louisiana L. Rev. 293 (1958) and Fleming James, Jr., Accident Liability Reconsidered: The Impact of Liability Insurance, 57 Yale L.J. 549 (1948); and Guido Calabresi, The Costs of Accidents (1970). See also, Virginia E. Nolan and Edmund Ursin, Understanding Enterprise Liability 1995).

18 See generally, Stephen D. Sugarman, A Century of Change in Personal Injury Law, 88 Cal. L. Rev. 2403 (2000).

19 John A. Jenkins, The Litigators: Inside the Powerful World of America's High-Stakes Trial Lawyers (1989).

20 Reporters' Study, Enterprise Responsibility for Personal Injury Volume 1 (American Law Institute 1991) and Stephen D. Sugarman, A Restatement of Torts, 44 Stan. L. Rev. 1163 (1992).

21 Daniel Gardner, Comparer L'Incomparable: Les Indemnities Pour Prejudice Corporel en Droit Commun et dans la Loi sur L'assurance Automobile, (1998) Les Cahiers de Droit 229.

22 The National Childhood Vaccine Injury Act o£1986.

23 Birth Related Neurological Injury Compensation Plan, Fla.. Stat. Ann. 766.301 (West1998); Birth Related Neurological Injury Compensation Act (Injured Infant Act) Va. Code Ann 38.2-5000 (Supp. 1987).

24 See generally, Robert L. Rabin, The Quest for Fairness in Compensating Victims of September 11, 49 Cleveland State L. Rev. 573 (2001) and Robert L. Rabin, the September 11th Victim Compensation Fund: A Circumscribed Response or an Auspicious Model?, 53 DePaul L. Rev. 769 (2003).

25 Seffert v. Los Angeles Transit Lines, 56 Cal.2d 498 (1961).

26 See generally, Stephen D. Sugarman, Nader's Failures? The Struggle for Auto Safety, 80 Cal. L. Rev. 289 (1992).

27 An exception is Professor Jeffrey O'Connell, who has relentlessly carried on as America's leading scholar-advocate for replacing various parts of tort law with no-fault compensation schemes.

28 See generally the web site of the American Tort Reform Association, at www.atra.org.

29 State Farm Mutual Automobile Insurance Co. v. Campbell, 123 S. Ct. 1513 (2003).

30 Stephen D. Sugarman, Judges as Tort Law Un-Makers: Recent California Experience with "New" Torts 49 DePaul L. Rev.455 (1999).

31 Proposition 51, adopted in 1986.

32 Proposition 213, adopted in 1996. Stephen D. Sugarman, Put a Limit on Uninsured Motorists' Right to Sue, Sacramento Bee, April 26, 1995; see generally Stephen D. Sugarman, The Uninsured Motorist Puzzle, (1998) Crossroads 1.

33 Stephen D. Sugarman, United States Tort Reform Wars, 25 UNSW L.J. 849 (2002).

34 See e.g., Sofie v. Fibreboard Corp. 771 P2d 711 (Wash. 1989), Brannigan v. Usitalo, 587 A2d 1232 (NH 1991), Best v. Taylor Machine Works, 689 NE2d 1057 (Ill. 1997), and State ex rel Ohio Academy of Trial Lawyers v. Sheward, 715 NE2d 1062 (Ohio 1999).

Chapter 3

Torts Then and Now – Across the 20th Century, the Legal Background Changed Faster than Tort Law Itself

Tort law in the 21st century is importantly different from what it was at the end of the 19th century. In the course of 100 years, tort doctrine has centrally coalesced around a robust law of negligence, anchored in contemporary concerns about fairness, loss spreading, and safety promotion. Students studying Torts learn this by reading judicial opinions from many different eras. Classic 19th century cases that stake out key common law principles are examined; 20th century decisions that elaborate, redirect, and in some cases overthrow prior decisions are discussed; and contemporary litigation is explored to understand where cutting edge tort law stands today. Along the way, students see how tort law contends with "new" problems as they arise. Yet, the central purpose of this engagement is to help the student master the art of "legal reasoning" through very careful attention to doctrinal development.

But, as this chapter argues, in comparing the state of tort law in the 19th century with that of the 21st century, far more important than doctrinal changes have been changes in American society, the professions, civil procedure and evidence law, as well as the introduction of liability insurance. Together, these other developments have made it far easier and more natural for accident victims to sue. In addition, work, home, and leisure activities have altered dramatically since the era of the Robber Barons, thereby significantly changing the nature of the accidents that we now suffer. Moreover, some injuries that were central to the operation of tort law in 1900 have been removed from personal injury law. The upshot is that the size and nature of the personal injury law system today differs enormously from the system in place in the year 1900. Nevertheless, many of the shortcomings of personal injury law that were apparent to reformers then still plague tort law's operation today.

In contrast with Chapters 1 and 2, this chapter is historically focused (rather than ideologically focused). Its sweep is much longer with an empirical emphasis on the non-doctrinal changes that are often ignored in the study of Torts by 1L students.

This chapter first appeared as an article in the California Law Review as part of a centennial symposium that broadly examined legal change over the course of the 20th century. Stephen D. Sugarman, "A Century of Change in Personal Injury Law," 88 Cal. L. Rev. 2403 (2000) and is reprinted with permission of the journal.

A Century of Change in Personal Injury Law

For well over 100 years, tort law has been a complex body of rules covering a wide range of civil injuries that, at times, have seemed rather unrelated to each other. Indeed, as late as 1900 it was by no means clear that "torts" was even a coherent field of the law or an identifiable subject of separate study.[1] Nevertheless, the law of personal injuries has been at the heart of American tort law throughout the twentieth century. In this Essay, I will focus primarily on changing personal injury law and the changing personal injuries it handles. More precisely, my Essay will concentrate on accidental injuries. Although much legal doctrine exists that covers intentional personal injuries, personal injury law throughout the twentieth century, in practice at least, has been fundamentally about accidents.[2]

The last 100 years have seen a significant change in the personal injuries with which tort law deals. Several forces have driven this change. First, tort law doctrine has been sharply altered. Second, the ability and willingness of accident victims to sue has markedly increased. Third, other forms of regulation have narrowed the role of tort law because of its perceived inadequacy. Fourth, the pattern of accidental bodily injuries is dramatically different today. I take these transformations up in Parts I-IV, respectively. After that, I address several other twentieth-century shifts in the background context of personal injury law: the creation of various social insurance arrangements, the development of the regulatory state and its attention to safety issues, and the enormous diversification in torts scholarship. Having reviewed these many changes, I then summarize how the business of personal injury law today differs from what it was in 1900. In the final sections of this Essay, I explore the questions of how well personal injury law serves our society as we begin the twenty-first century and what are the prospects for its future reform.

THE TRANSFORMATION OF PERSONAL INJURY LAW DOCTRINE

Personal injury law doctrine has changed significantly from the beginning to the end of the twentieth century. This transformation has not, however, resulted in the embrace of "strict liability" as many late twentieth-century advocates had hoped. Rather, defendant liability has consolidated around the "fault" principle.

A. *The Failure of "Strict Liability" to Take Hold*

Especially in the last third of the twentieth century, many tort scholars wrote on behalf of "enterprise liability." Guido Calabresi's work[3] played a key role, as did the legal opinions of Roger Traynor.[4] In terms of fairness, the basic vision behind "enterprise liability" is that those who choose to engage in business activities and gain the benefits from those activities ought to pay for the accident costs associated with them. Two key instrumental justifications for enterprise liability are that it prompts commercial actors to carry out their business more carefully (the deterrence objective), and that it spreads the financial loss from accidents among all those who buy from the enterprise, rather than concentrating the loss on unlucky victims (the risk-spreading objective).

As a doctrinal matter, "enterprise liability" in its strong form calls for the imposition of "strict liability" or "liability without fault" on commercial sellers of goods, providers of commercial services, owners of commercial property, and so on. Yet, there has been very little acceptance of strict liability in tort. Strict liability law today is largely restricted to product injury cases involving manufacturing defects.[5] And in that setting, strict liability usually makes little difference because victims typically could win anyway under negligence law, especially since the rule of *res ipsa loquitur* would commonly apply. Strict liability also applies to injuries caused by so-called abnormally dangerous activities, such as dynamite blasting, that occur despite the exercise of due care.[6] But, by definition, these extra-hazardous activities and the injuries they cause are uncommon.[7] So, while blasting injury and similar cases continue to provide fascination for the torts classroom, they matter little to the day-to-day life of tort law.

Scholars like Charles Gregory and Morton Horwitz[9] have argued that during much of the nineteenth century (and before) tort law was dominated by strict liability. Were that actually so, then the twentieth-century transformation in tort doctrine might be described as one in which that prior way of thinking was soundly overruled. But the better reading of the historical record, as shown primarily by the work of Gary Schwartz, is that strict liability was highly unusual before the twentieth century as well.[10]

B. *The Consolidation of the Principle of Defendant Liability Based on Fault*

The central change in personal injury law doctrine that has taken place since 1900 is the evolution of a robust law of negligence. Making defendants take legal responsibility for accidents that they have unreasonably failed to prevent, but only for those accidents, is the core principle of personal injury law today. Interestingly enough, "enterprise liability" thinking has played a role here. The fault principle itself is increasingly defended on deterrence and risk-spreading grounds, rather than simply on the basis of fairness as between the plaintiff and the defendant.

Personal injury law's coalescence around the fault principle has resulted in a simplification of the substantive law in this area, a trend Harry Kalven noted three decades ago.[12] The most important shift in doctrine since 1900 has been the elimination of many long-standing rules that previously immunized defendants from liability, a theme best explored in an article published twenty years ago by Robert Rabin. [13]

In the nineteenth century (and well into the twentieth), tort law contained many rules that limited a defendant's legal duty. Although juries might well have concluded that reasonable precautions were available to defendants that would have prevented harm to victims, judges applied legal doctrines that protected those defendants from liability. By the end of the twentieth century, however, this picture had been radically altered. In the first place, many old "no duty" rules have been abandoned. Perhaps most important is the overthrow of the rule that manufacturers owed no duty of care to consumers for harms done to them as a result of negligently made products, unless the consumer had bought the product directly from the manufacturer (the "privity" requirement)--an uncommon practice in a modem world dominated by independent retailers. Cardozo's justly famous opinion in the *MacPherson* case prompted this change in the law relatively early in the twentieth century.[14] Since then, many other "no duty" rules have also fallen. For example, emotional distress claims no longer require physical touching to be actionable,[15] land owners and occupiers are liable to trespassers and social guests in circumstances in which they previously owed those victims no duty of care, [16] and intra-family immunity (another "no duty" principle) has been widely abandoned.[17] The general acceptance of "enterprise liability" thinking (both the deterrence and risk- spreading objectives) helps explain why exempting these various defendants from liability would seem so odd to most lawyers and academics at the end of the twentieth century.

Second, the common law has expanded to find new duties where few people earlier would have dreamed they could exist. Auto makers now have a duty to exercise due care in making their vehicles reasonably safe in the event of crashes; [18] physicians have a duty to conform to national standards of medical practice[19] and to disclose to their patients the risks of proposed medical treatment (and non-treatment);[20] and commercial establishments must take affirmative steps to protect their customers from the foreseeable dangers of criminal assaults on their premises.[21] Again, "enterprise liability" thinking at least partially underlies these changes.

The emphasis of today's tort law in imposing financial responsibility on at-fault defendants is also reflected in the near universal rejection (typically by statute) of contributory negligence as a complete defense, a robust rule of tort law in 1900.[22] Now, negligent defendants (certainly those who are predominately at fault) no longer escape merely because their victims also failed to exercise due care. Instead the financial loss of the accident is shared according to the relative fault of the parties. In the same vein, the assumption of risk defense, which was also vigorously applied in 1900, has now been contained, albeit (alas) not eliminated.[23]

The upshot, therefore, is that, although the jury must be convinced that the defendant was at fault, many a victim's legal burden in personal injury cases is considerably lighter than it was a century ago.

II
THE INCREASE IN THE ABILITY AND WILLINGNESS OF PEOPLE TO SUE FOR PERSONAL INJURIES

In 1900, misfortune was a more accepted part of life. Today, people are more willing to blame others for their injuries and go to court to obtain redress. In this section I want discuss a variety of ways in which people's ability to pursue tort remedies has been enhanced over the past 100 years. Along the way I will comment on how these and other factors may have influenced tort victims' willingness to sue.

A. *Changed Cultural Meaning Attached to Suing for Personal Injury*

In the past in many communities, suing in tort would stigmatize the plaintiff. Suing was seen as a hostile and inappropriate act. Accident victims were told to just "lump it" or, perhaps, reach a quiet informal resolution of their concerns without litigation.

Now, in many communities the exact opposite norm prevails. People are expected to sue if they are injured. They may be made to feel the fool if they don't. Friends and family encourage accident victims to "get theirs" since "everybody else is doing it." Many victims are eager to see themselves as entitled to recovery from another, and are eager to transfer blame for their predicament away from themselves and to another if at all possible. Many quickly buy into the idea that by suing they are a modern day version of David on the attack against the evil Goliaths in our society (businesses, insurance companies, governments, and the like).

In some quarters, accident victims today are viewed as too aggressive, too selfish, too greedy and so on. But this point of view may well fail to constrain litigation, even if the victim perceives it. Perhaps the greater "individualism" of our society is relevant here. Perhaps the concentration of our population in larger, more anonymous urban areas is as well. The media may also have played a role: in recent years, newspapers, popular magazines, and TV have appeared to give much greater attention to personal injury cases and the large awards made in some of them.

B. A Better and More Specialized Plaintiff's Bar

For a large part of the twentieth century, personal injury lawyers were widely and disparagingly viewed as sleazy "ambulance chasers" who worked on the fringe of the profession, doing personal injury work because they were not talented enough to succeed at other kinds of law. Starting fairly early in the century, canons of legal ethics were widely adopted that were designed in large part to rein in practices of many who practiced personal injury law.[24] The social status of the personal injury bar is still controversial today, and some lawyers continue to make their living by running "mills" that process vast numbers of small (mostly auto accident or slip and fall) cases by negotiating settlements with insurance company adjustors. Little "law" is practiced by these attorneys, and some of them still obtain clients through what are generally thought to be unsavory practices, such as paying hospital orderlies and other "runners" to had out their business cards. However, as we enter the twenty-first century, the reputation of personal injury lawyers is much changed. Now, the elite members of the personal injury bar are among the wealthiest and most famous big shots in the profession, and in some quarters they are among the most admired.[25]

Although the stars of this sector of the profession still attract scorn, those who obtain tens of millions of dollars in fees from class actions, toxic spills, and the like, and those who are now obtaining hundreds of millions (or even billions) in fees from tobacco litigation, are clearly no longer fringe actors. They have become prominent players in the legal world. The changing status of personal injury legal work is also reflected by the fact that, on the defense side, many large, big-city, elite law firms that earlier on would not touch personal injury defense work are now lead counsel on behalf of defendants in many important cases.

The upshot is that today it is widely recognized that many financially successful "trial lawyers" (a phrase, oddly, that has been usurped by the plaintiffs' side) are extremely effective lawyers. Perhaps this is because this part of the profession is now so much more lucrative.[26] Whatever the reason, it means that victims are increasingly likely to find someone who is highly competent to represent them.

Moreover, many personal injury lawyers now specialize. If a family member is a plane crash victim, there are several experts in plane crash cases to whom one might tum. If medical malpractice is your complaint, you can find many lawyers who do only, or mostly, these sorts of cases. In the product injury field, victims can find lawyers who specialize in certain types of products. This sort of specialization also tends to raise the average quality of the representation victims obtain.

The plaintiff side has also been helped by organized cooperation among trial lawyers. Although most personal injury lawyers still work on their own or in relatively small firms, the creation of their national trade association, the Association of Trial Lawyers of America (ATLA), and its state counterparts has provided important forums that benefit plaintiffs. For one thing, these associations serve as vehicles for lawyers to exchange information on similar cases on which they are working. For another, they have become the groups through which effective state-level political lobbying and campaign contributing take place. This political activity, of course, is primarily pursued on behalf of the interests of the trial lawyers themselves. But what is good for them tends to be good for plaintiffs too (which is not the same as saying that it is necessarily good for all accident victims or for society as a whole, a topic I take up in Parts IX and X).

C. *Advertising and Promotion*

Access to personal injury lawyers, and hence access to the courthouse, has also been enhanced by the legalization of, and intensive investment in, forms of marketing that were considered both unethical and illegal in the past. With the help of the U.S. Supreme Court's "commercial free speech" doctrine,28 personal injury lawyers now openly advertise on TV, via the Internet, in the yellow pages, on public transport vehicles, and so on. This change is likely to generate not only more clients for the advertisers, but also more public awareness of the existence of these legal services, how to find them, what they cost, and so on, thereby eliminating inhibitions that previously might have prevented some victims from seeking legal relief.

D. Availability of Expert Witnesses

A bigger, more urban nation, more money flowing through the tort system, less collegiality among physicians and others, and changing rules of evidence have combined to make it much easier for today's plaintiffs' lawyers to find credible expert witnesses to testify on behalf of their clients. Earlier in the century, for example, when the malpractice standard was based on local practice, getting one of a town's doctors to testify against another in a malpractice case was almost impossible. This difficulty effectively preempted most malpractice litigation regardless of whether serious malpractice had occurred. Today, with a malpractice standard based on national norms, finding a plaintiff-side qualified medical expert today is easy (assuming one has a plausibly valid case, or perhaps even if not).

E. Growth in Liability Insurance

It has almost never paid to sue in tort if the person you are suing is effectively financially judgment proof. While tortfeasors today who are insolvent, or nearly so, remain unpromising targets of litigation, the flowering of the liability insurance industry in the twentieth century has improved the recovery prospects for personal injury victims.

Motorists in most states are required to be insured, and although perhaps one in six is not[29] the great majority are now able to provide at least some tort compensation to anyone they negligently injure. Without that insurance, many fewer auto claims would be brought. Insurers have also built liability insurance (for non-auto accidents) into standard homeowner (and renter) insurance policies. So, what was traditionally intended to provide insurance against fire and theft has expanded not only to protect the injurer's other assets, but also to provide a deep pocket from which tort victims may be paid. On the commercial side as well, small merchants, who previously would have gone bankrupt if subjected to a tort claim, now typically have general commercial liability insurance, thereby providing an opportunity for litigation to succeed that frequently would not have been attempted in the past.

F. An Increase in the Sums Obtainable for Pain and Suffering

Although tort law has formally awarded general damages for the pain and suffering that accompanies personal injuries throughout the twentieth century, the sums juries award today (and in tum the sums lawyers can win for their clients in settlement of claims) dwarf those of 100 years ago, even accounting for inflation.[30] It stands to reason that the prospect of a larger award increases the willingness of victims to sue. This is especially true in today's world in which many victims, as discussed below, already have their health care and wage replacement needs reasonably assured.

If a personal injury lawsuit promised victims little more than they could get without it, or if most of what more it promised would wind up in the lawyer's pocket, then the incentive to sue would be modest. But if, even after paying your lawyer, you can net out a great deal more than is necessary to pay for your out of pocket expenses, then the economics of litigation look very different.

Perhaps it is because our nation is so wealthy; perhaps it is because we use juries for torts cases when other countries do not; perhaps it is for other cultural reasons; but for whatever reason, the amount our legal system awards victims for pain and suffering is much, much greater than is obtainable elsewhere in the world.[31]

G. An Apparent Much-Increased Willingness to Engage in Fraud to Collect a Tort Award

One dark side to our generosity in the award of general damages is the incentive it creates to engage in fraud. And, alas, our personal injury system seems much more riddled with fraud than it was in the past (although data on this change is hard to come by)[32] In any event, these days some people stage accidents, pretend accidents have occurred that did not, pretend they are more injured than they actually are, receive (or pretend to receive) medical treatment they do not need, and so on, all in furtherance of winning larger settlements for pain and suffering. Sometimes these system abusers are victims acting on their own; sometimes they are in cahoots with lawyers, doctors and the like, perhaps even put up to their misconduct by the lawyers involved.

The bottom line is that, in addition to changes in tort law, changes in institutional and cultural facets of American life surrounding the personal injury law system have facilitated a greater tendency by accident victims to seek financial remuneration from their injurers (or alleged injurers).

III
THE NARROWING OF THE ROLE OF TORT LAW BECAUSE OF ITS PERCEIVED INADEQUACY

In contrast to the two themes already explored, several other factors cause tort law in the year 2000 to function somewhat more narrowly than it otherwise might. During the course of the twentieth century, new institutional regimes in the work injury and auto injury areas have taken bites out of the business of personal injury law. Moreover, for several other newly identified social/political problems, tort law has failed to provide a satisfying solution, and so its role has been eclipsed by other regimes.

A. Work Injuries Substantially Replaced with Workers' Compensation

In 1900, injured workers had to sue in tort to recover damages from their employer for occupational injuries. This regime was widely thought to be inadequate to provide coverage for the lost wages and medical care that victims needed. As a result, early in the twentieth century, tort law was supplanted by the system of workers' compensation that still dominates the treatment of workplace injuries as we begin the twenty-first century. [33] Moreover, unlike some other countries where victims can both file for an industrial injury benefit and sue, the United States adopted workers' compensation as a total replacement for tort claims against employers sounding in negligence.[34] Thus, twentieth century American personal injury law has lost a large area of business (although lawsuits by workers against third parties, such as product liability claims against machine tool makers, is a thriving mini-industry).[35]

Interestingly enough, tort law has now partly or fully jettisoned three important doctrinal barriers faced by workers at the end of the nineteenth century:

contributory negligence as a complete bar; assumption of risk when workers knowingly work in dangerous conditions; and the so-called fellow servant rule which restricted the principle of *respondeat superior* to cases in which the defendant company's tort was committed by a superior. Hence, many plaintiffs with workplace claims would actually fare far better today than they would have a century ago were tort law still available to them.

Nonetheless, at present there is little prospect that tort law will be widely reintroduced into the American law of workplace injuries. For one thing, employers today would strongly oppose such a change (even though they complain about workers' compensation costs being too high). In addition, while some successful claimants would do much better under tort law, a large share of workers still do better under workers' compensation than they would in tort. This is because so many worker injuries occur without fault or are the fault of the injured worker him or herself.

B. Auto Injuries Partially Replaced by No-Fault Schemes

In terms of number of suits, personal injury law's main business today concerns auto accidents, a point discussed at greater length below. My emphasis here is that in a few states (most importantly Michigan and New York) personal injury claims arising out of auto accidents have been substantially reduced by the adoption of auto no-fault laws, which extinguish legal rights of those suffering lesser injuries in return for assured compensation for out-of-pocket losses, regardless of who is to blame for the accident.[36] So, here too, though personal injury law doctrine is generally more liberal today than before, a bite (at least in some states) has been taken out of its reach.

The following comprise the main indictments of tort law on the auto injury front: (a) dispute resolution costs are too great, causing undesirably high auto premiums; (b) reaching a suitable settlement of an auto claim takes too long and is an unhappy experience for all too many victims; (c) seriously injured victims are vastly undercompensated by the system; (d) fraudulent claims are encouraged and widely occur; and, relatedly, (e) small claims are paid off at excessive levels by insurers who are eager to clear their dockets and afraid to take a chance that juries might award victims extravagantly high sums.[37]

Auto no-fault can make substantial headway against all these problems. However, in the United States to date, no state has embraced a no-fault scheme that effectively does so. Michigan has the most comprehensive auto no-fault plan in the United States, and while its no-fault plan does a fairly good job combating many of the problems just noted, that scheme does too little to compensate the most seriously injured victims (who are relegated back to tort).[38] Quebec has implemented a very promising model, in which generous and prompt payments are made to all auto accident victims on a no-fault basis, tort claims are abolished, and auto premiums are stunningly low. Nevertheless, the power of the plaintiffs' bar in the United States has blocked serious consideration of copying that solution here.[39]

C. The Eclipse of Tort as the Vehicle for Dealing with Other Policy Problems

Several important socio-political issues have come to the fore in the second half of the twentieth century that, in principle, are grist for the tort law mill. But often tort law has been eclipsed as the central mechanism by which our society deals with the problem. Here are a few examples.

Discrimination on the basis of race (and gender and so on) is one important instance. Despite some early decisions suggesting that such discrimination might be fought with tort suits sounding in "emotional distress,"[40] tort law has not become an important legal weapon of the civil rights movement. Instead, special statutory schemes, both federal and state, have done the heavy lifting, even as they sometimes provide tort-like remedies (including general damages which compensate for the pain and suffering of having been a victim of discrimination).

Police misconduct, another problem area, could also be battled by lawsuits for battery, invasion of privacy, and so on. Instead, the "exclusionary rule," police review boards, and the like have been the front- line weapons. Moreover, to the extent that police brutality lawsuits are brought against individual officers, they tend to be based on federal civil rights laws[41] that provide claimants advantages not available to them in regular tort claims.

Yet another example is the field of domestic violence. With tort law having swept aside the old immunity (or no duty) rules protecting one spouse from being sued by another and preventing children from suing their parents, one might have imagined that tort law would become an important tool in the fight against domestic violence, at least in non-poor households. Yet, although such claims are now sometimes brought, they remain quite rare.[42] Instead, restraining orders, divorce law, police assistance, criminal complaints (and sometimes prosecutions), child protective services and foster care, special domestic violence statutes (providing their own remedies), and so on are the prime legal avenues through which domestic violence victims respond.

A final example concerns harm to the environment. While tort law can and sometimes still does provide remedies (both damages and injunctions) for both public and private nuisances,[43] tort has not been the main way our society legally combats environmental dangers. Instead, we have turned to special environmental laws and agencies with their own administrative mechanisms and remedies.

The preceding examples in this Part show how, as the twentieth century progressed, targeted solutions to pressing social/political problems have lessened the impact of tort law in certain spheres where it used to play or could have played a more prominent role.

IV
THE CHANGING PATTERN OF ACCIDENTAL INJURIES AND DEATH FROM 1900 TO 2000

A fundamental change in personal injury law over the past century has been brought about because of change in the nature of the injuries themselves. Alterations in places of work, modes of transportation, and patterns of behavior have all contributed to differences in the types of injuries which occurred in the course of the century.

A. Then

In 1900, the population of the United States was approximately 75 million.[44] Although data on deaths, accidental deaths, causes of death, and industrial accidents are sketchy and inconsistent, a general picture emerges. Despite conflicting reports, I estimate that there were probably around 100,000 accidental deaths in 1900.[45] Allocating the total number of accidental deaths to specific causes is also tricky. What is clear, however, is that railway accidents, drowning, fractures, and burns were important causes of accidental fatalities, and that injuries from other vehicles and machinery were not.[46]

Perhaps something like a quarter or more of the accidental deaths in 1900 were from work injuries. A 1908 study puts the number of fatal industrial accidents in the United States among employed males in the range of 30,000-35,000.[47] British data from the same period suggest that men suffered around 98% of fatal work accidents.[48] Nonfatal accidents, of course, were far more common than fatal ones, although how much harm is required for something to qualify as an accidental injury for these purposes is unclear. For example, one 1899 data set suggests that for every worker killed in railway accidents, there were more than fifteen injured sufficiently to have been counted.[49] Another study reported some New York industrial accident data for the period 1901 to 1906 suggesting that there were perhaps forty times as many injuries as fatalities, and that, of the reported injuries, more than 80% were temporary.[50]

The role of recreational injury at this time is quite uncertain. For example, as already noted, drownings were common, but most of these could have been work-related deaths at sea.

B. Now

In 2000, things are very different. The U.S. population has more than trebled, to over 275 million.[51] The National Safety Council reports that there were about 92,000 accidental fatalities in the U.S. in 1998.[52] That is a very substantial drop in the accidental death rate since 1900. The Council also calculates that in 1998 there were more than 200 accidents leading to disabling injuries for every accidental death.[53] It is difficult to compare these figures with the 1900 data.

The Council further reports that motor vehicle accidents caused more than 40,000 deaths in 1998, which is about 45% of all the accidental in fatalities that year.[54] This was, of course, a largely unheard-of source of death in 1900. In 1996, "falls" accounted for nearly 15,000 fatalities, and "poisoning by solids and liquids" and "drugs, medicaments and biologicals" each accounted for nearly 9,000 fatal injuries (although many of the deaths in the latter two categories were probably by suicide.)[55] The three other most important categories of accidental fatalities that year, according to the Council, were "fires and flames" (around 4,000), "drowning, submersion" (around 3,500), and "complications, misadventures of surgical, medical care" (around 3000).[56]

Turning from deaths to accidental injuries, a 1989 study by the RAND Corporation (using a very different methodology from that used by the National Safety Council) found that nearly 20% of all accidents involved motor vehicles, about 40% involved slips and falls, and about 30% involved a varied set of products such as toys, sports equipment, household appliances, or industrial hand tools.[57]

The Consumer Product Safety Commission's National Electronic Injury Surveillance System (NEISS) provides more detailed information about the connection between consumer product injuries and treatment in hospital emergency rooms.[58] In the NEISS data, the "product" category that accounts for the largest number of estimated injuries is "stairs, ramps, landings and floors."[59] The categories of "beds, mattresses, pillows," "chairs, sofas, sofa beds," "bathroom structures & fixtures," "desks, cabinets, shelves, racks," "tables," and "doors" are also sources of a very substantial number of injuries.[60] Although the Commission does not specify the cause of injury, a great share of all of the injuries so far mentioned from the NEISS data must be from falling off of, or bumping into, the listed products. Sports and other recreational injuries represent other important contributions to the accident rate, with the categories "basketball" and "bicycles & accessories" leading the way, and "football," "baseball, softball," "playground equipment," and "exercise, exercise equipment" coming next.[61]

Reports on industrial injuries and fatalities also show substantial changes since 1900. A 1998 National Safety Council report states that the unintentional work death rate per 100,000 population was reduced by 90% between 1912 and 1998.[62] This report estimates that there were 18,000-21,000 occupational deaths in 1912, but that by 1998, the number was reduced to 5,100 at a time when the workforce had more than trebled.[63] Although transportation incidents were still the leading cause of work- related fatalities, the pattern was much changed from 1900. Motor vehicle injuries accounted for about 40% of occupational fatalities in 1998,[64] but there were only eighty-three work-related railway fatalities that year.[65]

The National Safety Council put disabling work injuries at about 20% of all accidental injuries in 1998,[66] a proportion in the same range as my estimate for 1900. Yet, the type of work accidents has changed substantially. For example, the Bureau of Labor Statistics reports that there were 5.5 million occupational injuries in 1998, plus another 400,000 occupational illnesses.[67] Of those, mining accounted for only 29,000 and railroading a mere 8,600.[68] There were, by contrast, more than 1.5 million injuries in manufacturing, nearly 1.5 million in wholesale and retail trades, and 1.3 million in service industries.[69]

These data I have presented reflect, of course, the changing nature of the non-natural dangers that Americans faced at the end of the century as compared to the beginning. Our work, leisure, and home lives have altered enormously. Many previously dangerous activities have been either made much safer or largely abandoned. Yet all sorts of new dangerous activities have been taken up. Our embrace of personal highway motor vehicles is plainly the most significant change. One further point to note is that the data presented here so far focus on accidents, by which the studies mean some acute event. But, we are now quite aware that many products "accidentally" cause not just acute trauma but disease as well. I will return to this theme in Part VIII where I compare the business handled by today's personal injury law with that of a century ago.

V
THE DRAMATIC CHANGE IN ALTERNATIVE COMPENSATION SCHEMES

In 1900, if someone suffered an accidental personal injury or death, the adverse financial consequences would probably have been met, if at all, from personal savings, family and friends, churches and charities, or perhaps fledgling benevolent societies and, in a small share of the incidents, through personal injury law. By 2000, for most Americans, this situation had dramatically changed due to the development of other compensation schemes.

A. Enormous Expansion of Medical Care Access and Use

In 1900 doctors certainly existed and they treated at least some of those in need, although medicine then was often far more an art than a science. Today, we have a system of sophisticated hospitals, a vast network of general physicians and specialists, and tremendous advances in the medical treatment of victims of both accidents and disease. And nearly all Americans today expect to be able to take advantage of these improvements.

They can do so primarily because of our health insurance system. Although America lags behind a large number of rich nations in failing to adopt a comprehensive national health insurance scheme, our patchwork quilt of arrangements nonetheless assures reasonable access to good quality health care to the vast majority of our citizens.[70] Private employment- based health insurance, Medicare for the elderly, and Medicaid for many of the poor or near poor provide most of the coverage. These are all twentieth-century developments.

B. Dramatic Expansion of Income Replacement Protection

Americans are also now much better protected against wage losses caused by personal injuries than they were in 1900.[71] For long term disability and death, our expanded Social Security system, first enacted in 1935, provides substantial income replacement benefits, in amounts that cover a reasonably high share of lost wages of those with relatively low earnings. Higher earners often have supplemental disability insurance and life insurance that is privately obtained or employment-based. For short-term non-occupational disability caused by accident, a large share of U.S. workers has job-based sick leave and many have short-term disability insurance (which is now mandatory in a handful of states).[72]

C. The Interplay of Insurance and Personal Injury Law

These vast compensation arrangements have important implications for both personal injury law and workers' compensation schemes. These arrangements exist because people realize that they need insurance against health care costs whether or not the event that occasions their accident (or illness) is caused by the fault of another or at the workplace; and those dependent on their own wages or the wages of another also realize that what they need is around the clock protection, not just protection of those wages against disruption caused by a tort or a work injury.

But the consequence for those with good health insurance is that the benefits provided by both tort and workers' compensation are often redundant in dealing with the accident victim's health care needs. On the tort side this typically means either that the victim obtains a windfall double recovery (obtaining a cash payment to cover medical expenses that have already been paid for by insurance) or else, more commonly, that a complicated process is set in motion by which the health insurer recoups its expenses from the tort award, a process that adds significant transaction costs. Workers' compensation plans are typically "primary," and hence either they pay for the victim's health care directly, or else they reimburse regular health insurers for medical expenses arising out of work-related injuries for which those plans paid. But from the worker's perspective, the point is that those expenses would generally have been paid for anyway even if workers' compensation were unavailable.

On the income side, tort awards are generally added on top of whatever sick leave, disability insurance, life insurance and the like that is available to the accident victim and/or the victim's survivors in cases of death. Hence, wage losses are often doubly compensated. However, most of those suffering non work-derived, permanent, partial disabilities do not have non-tort disability insurance and may well have to rely on tort (when available) to provide for the accompanying loss in wages. On the job injury side, workers' compensation does provide benefits for partial, permanent disability (as well as temporary and permanent total disability and death), although this category of benefit is the most contentious and probably the most unsatisfactory part of the scheme in many states.

The main point, then, is that personal injury law serves a very different compensation function in the year 2000 than it would have served had these alternate compensation schemes not been created. Indeed, as a practical matter, the main compensation for many tort victims provided by the legal system is not for out of pocket economic losses. That is, a great deal of money is provided both for "pain and suffering" and to duplicate other sources of recovery. To be sure, the victim's legal expenses often consume a substantial share of this money. But enough still often goes to the victim to cause many to seek this extra compensation via litigation.

VI
A GREAT EXPANSION OF THE REGULATORY REGIMES COVERING THE MAIN TYPES OF ACCIDENTS WHERE PERSONAL INJURY LAW OPERATES

In Part III, I noted certain social issues over which tort law could have exerted a greater influence had its role not been eclipsed by other institutional arrangements. In this Part, I want to focus on areas in which personal injury law is thriving despite the twentieth-century development of parallel schemes aimed at preventing the same types of personal injuries that tort law is meant to deter.

As the motor vehicle has come to dominate our lives in the twentieth century, we have by no means been content to rely upon personal injury law to reduce highway injuries. A vast criminal law regime has been created to discourage, capture and punish careless drivers. A complex administrative regime has been developed to train, license, and re-license individual drivers. And to the extent that auto makers are seen to be part of this picture, they are answerable not only to personal injury lawsuits but also to the rules and regulations of the National Highway Transportation Safety Administration (NHTSA).[73]

Something of the same story could be told about injuries caused by the health care industry. Although doctors long seemed free from regulation, this is now rapidly changing as hospitals, insurers, state licensing boards, and other agencies have moved in to try to impact the quality of care provided. And on the drug and medical device side, the Food and Drug Administration plays an active role in protecting heath care consumers from dangers.

Whether these regulatory schemes duplicate, reinforce, or contradict tort law, or do some of each of those things, is a controversial matter. Nor do I mean to suggest here that any of these regulatory mechanisms is especially effective. Rather, the main point to be emphasized here is this: looking back to 1900, personal injury law was arguably society's main line of defense against certain types of unsafe conduct (even if it was not a very strong defense); today, by contrast, tort functions in an environment in which other complex, safety promoting, regulatory schemes also operate.

VII
TRANSFORMATION IN LEGAL SCHOLARSHIP

Just as tort law has changed, so too has the legal academy's approach to tort law. During the early decades of the twentieth century, torts scholarship was dominated by work on legal doctrine. Even though Oliver Wendell Holmes had some soaring things to say about torts in his famous 1881 lectures on the common law,[74] the typical legal scholarship of that era focused on making sense of the rules. Indeed, many academics saw themselves as scientists out to discover the patterns in a mass of previously under-analyzed data in the form of legal opinions from around the nation. A good example of that approach is Francis Bohlen's influential analysis of "incomplete privileges" published in 1926 in the Harvard Law Review.[75]

Although certain exceptions can be identified, attention to doctrine remained central in tort law scholarship until the 1960s, and is epitomized by two monumental achievements. First is the Restatement of the Law of Torts, a project of the American Law Institute initially issued in 1934 and revised in its second edition starting in the early 1960s (with portions of the Restatement Second dribbling out over many years). Second is the 1941 publication of William Prosser's treatise on Torts, which not only compiled a stupendous number of cases and rules, but also presented Prosser's own critique of some of them and his now famous calls force retain doctrinal changes that were later embraced by the courts.

Starting in the late 1960s, the focus in tort scholarship has changed dramatically. Writing about new doctrinal developments in tort law is now largely (although not entirely) the work of law students and practitioners. Professors, at least those who see themselves as "scholars" and especially those from the "leading law schools," have (alas) generally shunned writing about the details of tort doctrine. This is, of course, an exaggeration. Some of the best writing in torts by leaders in our field, like John Fleming,[76] Robert Rabin[77] and Gary Schwartz[78] has been about doctrinal matters--all of whom also, I should add, incorporate "new" dimensions in their work as well.

One of these "new" dimensions is the empirical study of tort law in action. This is the contribution of the "law and society" (or "socio-legal studies") movement to tort. Through the work of scholars like Deborah Hensler[79] and Marc Galanter[80] we have a much better understanding of how the personal injury law system actually works than we ever did. Recently, the "case study" approach has further enhanced our understanding of tort law in action. In this approach, one case or a related series of cases is examined in depth, not so much in order to describe and critique the legal analysis of the judges in the published opinions, but more to understand what our personal injury law is about through the lens of a single problem. Peter Schuck's book on the Agent Orange controversy well illustrates this genre.[81]

Torts scholarship has also become highly interdisciplinary, or perhaps better put, personal injury law is increasingly being examined with the tools of, and from the vantage point of, other disciplines. "Law and economics" is perhaps most prominent, as illustrated first in the writings of Calabresi[82] and later, for example, in other pioneering work by Richard Posner,[83] Steven Shavell,[84] and many others. "Law and philosophy" has also had its say, as those with a moral philosophy bent, like Jules Coleman,[85] Ernest Weinrib,[86] and George Fletcher[87] have weighed in to help us better understand the many notions of justice that tort law might, or does, serve. Perhaps latest on this scene are those, led initially by Howard Latin,[88] who examine the contributions that cognitive psychology can bring to our understanding of tort law.

The main importance of all this scholarship, in my view, is that it provides insight into how we should appraise personal injury law as a whole, a matter to which I will tum in the final sections of this Essay.

VIII
THE BUSINESS OF PERSONAL INJURY LAW-THEN AND NOW

Having now surveyed changes in accident patterns and tort law's reach during the twentieth century, as well as other background factors relevant to tort law, let me sketch the main differences I see between the business of personal injury law in 1900 as compared with 2000.

In his study of tort law in Alameda County, California, at the end of the nineteenth century, Professor Lawrence Friedman reports that only about seventeen personal injury lawsuits per year were filed in the county between 1880 and 1900.[89] Tort cases were only 2% of the superior court filings between 1880 and 1900;[90] by contrast, they were more than a quarter of the cases in 1970, when the rate of filing had grown from 1 in 2,200 persons in the county to 1 in 333.[91] In the last two decades of the nineteenth century, about two-thirds of the cases were brought against railroads and street railways, and although injured passengers were the most common plaintiffs, other claimants included injured workers and those involved in grade crossing accidents.[92] Medical malpractice cases were filed less than once every two years on average.[93] As compared with today, a far higher proportion of the filed claims, just over 30%, went to trial. Although plaintiffs won 75% of the cases that finally went to jury verdicts, defendants obtained many nonsuits and had many cases overturned on appeal, so that, in the end, plaintiffs in only 10% of the claims initially filed won damages in court.[94] Of those who won and held on to their victory after appeal, no plaintiff obtained more than $14,000, and the average award was around $3,500.[95]

Today personal injury law cases are predominantly auto injury cases; data for 1996 from the nation's seventy-five largest counties shows that auto cases made up nearly half of all trials of torts cases.[96] Other important categories of personal injury cases today include injuries incurred on the property of another ("slip and fall" cases as well as many other types of harms), accounting for just over 20% of large county state court torts trials in 1996,[97] injuries incurred in the course of medical treatment, product injuries, non-auto transportation injuries, and injuries caused by the escape of powerful forces that ought to have been under human control (explosions, fires, electricity, and the like). Many of these categories of cases were unimportant or completely absent 100 years ago for a combination of the reasons explored earlier. Perhaps most pointedly, suits in significant numbers against motorists, doctors, and product manufacturers are all a result of twentieth-century changes.

Another great difference in personal injury law today as opposed to the past is the problem of the mass injury, and the field of "mass tort" law that has come of age to try to deal with it. The difference is not merely that negligent airline companies can and sometimes do easily kill more people all at once than just about any careless defendant could have killed at once in 1900. A few hundred airline deaths is actually small potatoes when compared with the number of injuries that some other modern products have caused. Nowadays, if certain dangerous products proliferate and cause havoc before their dangers are appreciated, enormous numbers of consumers and others can be put at risk. This has happened with asbestos, certain birth control devices, some pharmaceutical drugs and medical appliances, and other products. And sometimes products proliferate not via purchases by victims, but through "leaks" or "escapes" into the water, air and so on. Moreover, as indicated earlier, many dangerously toxic products today do not cause acute trauma, but instead induce debilitating or deadly diseases. Cigarettes, a product that was of little importance in America in 1900, are perhaps the most important example.

Yet, as is evident from the data presented earlier, personal injury law still only deals with a small share of accidental injuries, and by no means all accidental fatalities. RAND's 1989 study found that only about 10% of all accident victims even filed claims for compensation, including 44% of auto accident victims, 7% of work accident victims, and 3% of other accident victims.[98] About half of the claimants hired a lawyer and most of those had obtained some recovery; of those who pursued their claim without a lawyer, only around half obtained any compensation.[99]

IX
AN APPRAISAL OF How WELL TORT LAW SERVES OUR SOCIETY AT THE START OF THE NEW CENTURY

A. Failure on the Compensation Goal

Decades ago Fleming James and others imagined that, were enterprise liability to become the central principle of tort law, then tort might possibly become a reasonably comprehensive mechanism for compensating accident victims.[100] Yet, things have not turned out that way. First, as already noted, strict liability has so far failed as a doctrinal matter. Second, as also shown above, a substantial share of accidental injuries are not touched by personal injury law today. And they are likely to remain beyond the reach of any readily imaginable scheme of enterprise liability; to give but one example, who thinks that basketball makers (or basket makers, or basketball court makers) should really be liable for all basketball injuries? Hence if personal injury law is to be judged as a mechanism for accident compensation, it must be deemed a failure.

Its defenders instead need to focus the risk-spreading goal on the narrower question of how well our system serves to compensate those who are entitled to compensation under tort law's own rules.[101] Here, too, alas, the system fares quite poorly.

Most importantly, the vast majority of seriously injured auto accident victims are under-compensated because our society, as a practical matter, permits people to drive with little or no auto insurance.[102] We tolerate this situation because of the high cost of auto insurance and the burden it imposes on the poor; and yet the irony is that the cost of insurance is so high precisely because our tort law is so generous. The upshot is that our scheme dramatically favors auto accident victims with small injuries over those with large injuries. Indeed, in my view, we have things entirely up- side down. We undercompensate those most in need, and yet we overcompensate those with small injuries by awarding them excessive sums for transitory pain and suffering that is ordinarily long gone before the money is paid out.[103]

Personal injury law fails to compensate large numbers of deserving victims of many other types of wrongdoing as well. Medical malpractice is a good example. Based upon a well-known Harvard study, I estimated that of every 1000 medical malpractice victims, somewhat fewer than 50 obtain compensation from personal injury law. At the same time, nearly as many claimants who are not malpractice victims are also compensated either through settlements or erroneous jury decisions.[104]

B. Qualms about Whether Justice Is Being Served

I am skeptical about whether a large share of those who actually bring lawsuits obtain a satisfying sense of "justice" from the system. First, hardly any claimants obtain a jury verdict in their favor, because nearly all claims are either settled or dropped. Hence, it is a rare victim who is able to hold his or her injurer accountable in court. Research conducted by the RAND Corporation's Institute for Civil Justice suggests that the claims experience is not very satisfying to victims.[105] Often victims' lawyers pay little attention to them, their cases drag on seemingly forever, and suddenly they are presented with a dollar figure to accept or reject.

Those who are actively involved in litigation often have mixed experiences. There is probably a rush of excitement when the lawyer is hired and the lawsuit is filed. Enduring a deposition or cross examination in court is often harrowing. At trial, the case too often plays out to the victim in mysteriously stylized ways, and the tactics and witnesses for the defense side are frequently infuriating. To be sure, a seven figure or more jury award is probably exhilarating; yet even that is rarely the end of it, as the victim often has to endure years of post-verdict motions, appeals, and further settlement negotiations.

My judgment overall is that for some victims the system works fine, but for most it does not. The experience of victims is often quite different from that enjoyed by the personal injury lawyer. For many attorneys doing this work, the fight, the tension, the risk taking, and the like can be very satisfying. Moreover, many honestly believe that they represent a thin line of consumer protection against a rapacious business and insurance complex. Others, however, are cynical about their work, even if it provides them with a generous living standard.

C. Ineffective as Punishment

Personal injury law is sometimes defended as a means by which just punishment is visited on wrongdoers. I have always found this to be a mysterious claim as applied to the world of accidental injuries. Individual defendants are usually sued only if they have liability insurance. Enterprise defendants are not generally individuals. They are pieces of paper, and the individuals within their ranks who were at fault in causing the harm are rarely punished either by the legal system or by the enterprise itself. Personal injury law might punish (at least financially) if we, for example, required individual wrongdoers to pay at least some of the award or settlement arising out of their misconduct, but we do not.

Punitive damages are, by definition, a mechanism of punishment. They are infrequently available in personal injury cases,[106] as they are not supposed to be imposed where the harm was only accidentally caused, albeit carelessly. Rather, punitive damages are meant to be reserved for much more serious wrongdoing. Even so, punitive damages are problematic as a punishment device. In most claims against individuals, their possible award may enable the plaintiff's lawyer to obtain a larger settlement, but an actual jury award of punitive damages will result only rarely if for no other reason than most individual defendants would not be able to satisfy the judgment. And obtaining a larger settlement from an insurer hardly punishes the wrongdoer. Therefore, punitive damages are now primarily a device for punishing enterprises.

The concerns I have here are twofold. On the one hand, I doubt whether our system accurately punishes the worst corporate actors. I fear that a large number of enterprises are inappropriately subjected to punitive damages while others escape who should not, and that the sums actually awarded are highly inconsistent from case to case. On the other hand, I remain perplexed about who we think we are really punishing. Enterprises subjected to punitive damages are often publicly owned corporations. Is it the shareholders we are trying to punish? But they are not the ones who acted egregiously. Is it that we are trying to devalue the stock options of executives in the firm? But that would imply that we think that all of those with stock options have engaged in horrendous behavior, which is typically not the case. It seems rather that we want to think of the corporation as a person and to punish it as an institution. But this is a flight of fancy.

D. Deterrence--The Jury Is Still Out

In my view, we are left, then, with behavioral channeling, the promotion of safer conduct and safer products, as the key justification for our existing system of personal injury law. Perhaps the most important contribution of the law and economics movement is the notion that personal injury law ought to be able to promote "efficient" levels of accidents--though its devotees are still fighting over whether it is a regime of negligence (which we have) or a scheme of strict liability (which others prefer) that best serves that goal.107 The proof, in any event, is not in the theory (although that helps us think about where to look for evidence). Unfortunately, empirical studies of the influence of personal injury law on enterprise behavior are extremely difficult to carry out in a convincing manner. Still, many are making the effort, and their efforts are getting more sophisticated.

When I first wrote about this issue fifteen years ago, I was quite unpersuaded that personal injury law had important positive impacts on con- duct.108 I noted that for the threat of liability to matter it would have to achieve desirable improvements in safety beyond those which would have occurred anyway as a result of personal moral scruples, fear of harm to oneself, market pressures towards safe conduct, and regulatory regimes promoting safety. Moreover, I pointed out that several factors tend to undermine whatever good personal injury law might do in closing the gap between what those other forces achieved and the socially optimal level of safe conduct. These factors include the blunting impact of insurance, trumping interests that cause actors deliberately to risk danger to others despite the possibility of tort liability, and limits on the ability of enterprises to control those in their employ.

These considerations made me extremely dubious that the threat of personal injury law makes for safer drivers or better doctors, and yet, even in these areas, some authors have claimed positive results for tort law. [109] Other scholars have emphasized that personal injury law's main promise lies in directing corporate behavior in desirable directions, and some empirical evidence has been marshaled in support of that prediction (although others have pointed to socially undesirable impacts the threat of tort law seems to have on corporate innovation in certain industries). [110]

I suppose that a fair appraisal as we start the twenty-first century is that the jury is still out on this issue. What remains clear to me is that, as a society, despite the urging of some of the law and economics crowd, we are quite unwilling to rely on tort law alone to regulate the risk of accidents. That is, we are decidedly not ready to give up our regulatory and criminal regimes directed towards safety. Hence, the real policy issue is what sort of mixture of personal injury law and other regulatory mechanisms work best for the money, recognizing that personal injury law carries very high transaction costs to operate. [111]

Some scholars believe that personal injury law serves additional important social functions that are somehow different from the fairness and deterrence goals. One claim is that personal injury claims help to alert administrative agencies of dangerous products and activities that the agencies would otherwise be slower to regulate. Another claim is that through personal injury law we satisfy our collective need to identify and assign blame for wrongdoing when fellow members of society are hurt by that misconduct. Yet another claim is that through jury processing of individual cases we best develop a social consensus about what are the reasonable precautions that members of our society should take to protect others from harm. Recently, Peter Bell and Jeffrey O'Connell have thoughtfully written about these and related social benefits that may be achieved by tort law today. [112] I agree that what might be called "ombudsman," "educational," or "political" benefits, as well as other possible benefits of the personal injury law system, deserve further attention. But it must be remembered that the overwhelming majority of personal injury law claims that are filed, that is, routine cases that are almost always settled or abandoned, have almost nothing to do with these objectives.

X
LOOKING AHEAD

In thinking about the place personal injury law will have in the twenty-first century, I find myself dwelling on the billions of dollars in legal fees that trial lawyers are beginning to obtain from their role in tobacco litigation and the ability those trial lawyers may have to deploy even a small share of that money in politically effective ways. That is not to say that the plaintiffs' bar always wins. After all, one important recent experience in California is to the contrary.

In the late 1970s, when liberal, pro-plaintiff, Democratic appointees controlled the California Supreme Court, the judges decided that defendants' insurers committed a tort and were subject to both compensatory and punitive damages if they failed to act in good faith in their negotiations with the plaintiff and the plaintiff's lawyer. [113] Ten years later, when Republican appointees dominated the California Supreme Court, this tort was abolished, the Court noting that only California had recognized such a cause of action. [114] In 1999, as soon as the Democrats finally regained control of the state's governorship, senate, and assembly, a statute was passed to reinstate this bad faith cause of action. But then in early 2000 the voters rejected the law in a referendum election. [115] Put simply, that election was won by the insurance industry, whose TV commercials and mass mailings overcame the campaign waged by the trial lawyers on the other side.

But just as this experience suggests that the insurance industry can sometimes defeat legal changes sought by the plaintiffs' bar, so too the past fifteen years have shown that the trial lawyers can frequently defeat changes sought by insurers and other defense interests. Much legislative tort law reform during this period has been of the "roll back victims' rights" sort,[116] and although most states have passed some of these "reforms," few have adopted strong comprehensive reforms. Where that has happened, state courts have often stepped in at the behest of the trial lawyers and struck the reforms down. [117] At the ballot box, the insurance industry has been quite unsuccessful in selling auto no-fault to the public. [118]

Given the ability of the competing special interest groups to block changes sought by the other side, one should not expect a great deal of change in personal injury law itself. To be sure, during the 1990s, courts in some states have become somewhat more pro-defendant in terms of personal injury law doctrine, and this trend may continue.[119] So, too, juries in some places (but decidedly not in others) are becoming less extravagant in what they award. But these are changes of modest scope. [120]

The prospects for more dramatic change will probably require some outside factor to enter into play. Another crisis in auto insurance rates, for example, could trigger a new round of interest in auto no-fault plans. Auto no-fault advocates, led by Jeffrey O'Connell (personal injury law's most inventive reformer), this time have "auto choice" plans at the ready. [121] The idea behind these plans is that individual drivers should be able to elect to be in either the fault or the no-fault regime as they wish-an ingenious notion that could catch on in the right circumstances, especially if motorists could be made to understand how much of their auto insurance premium they could save by electing the no-fault option.[122]

Similarly, growing tensions in managed care and ongoing pressures for more comprehensive health insurance schemes could trigger reform in the medical malpractice field. Paul Weiler's nifty proposal to replace medical malpractice law with a no-fault scheme covering all serious medical accidents could finally get a full airing.[123]

Erosion of the role of personal injury law from within remains a possibility. Several states have already reversed the collateral sources rule, thereby awarding tort damages only for medical expenses and wage loss not covered by social insurance and health care plans.[124] More might be coaxed to do so if Americans obtain better compensation arrangements to cover those out-of-pocket expenses that tort is meant to compensate. The simple point here is that if tort were only to compensate for losses not otherwise covered, and if those collateral sources grow, then tort would recede.

Again, the adoption of comprehensive health insurance could play a role here. Moreover, although improving Social Security's reach was thought impossible during the past decade when the future bankruptcy of Social Security was most on people's mind, the picture is now beginning to change as the existing federal debt is possibly on its way to disappearing and the health of Social Security's future is being secured. At a minimum, before too long I predict that calls for turning workers' compensation into an around-the-clock scheme will resurface.125 Rather than broadening workers' compensation itself, however, a different solution is imaginable. It would involve parceling out workers' compensation's functions to other regimes: for example, the health care portion could go to comprehensive health insurance and the wage replacement function could go to a combination of Social Security plus a new employment-based scheme for short term disability. 126

Another potential source for the erosion of the role of personal injury law is the voluntary relinquishment of the right to sue. Already in the health care field we see a growing shift to people's willingness to commit in advance to arbitration of personal injury claims rather than litigation. This trend could expand. Even more dramatically, several writers have imagined other ways in which potential victims could parlay their potential personal injury law rights in advance into more attractive financial benefits.127 This could possibly turn personal injury law into a simpler, inter- insurance company administrative scheme.

Potentially important, too, are changes in our regulatory regimes. As I suggested earlier, many of those who laud personal injury law as an effective promoter of accident prevention also criticize most other public forms of regulation. Yet, as I stated above, I do not believe that our major regulatory systems are very much at risk of being dismantled. At the same time it remains unclear whether our society will ever have sufficient confidence in those other regimes to let go of personal injury law as a parallel deterrence mechanism. If the public really believes that the personal injury lawyer serves a socially valuable function both in exposing and preventing enterprise misconduct, then we should look for ways to de-couple this function from the function of providing accident victim compensation. Lawyers and victims who first identify and prove unreasonably dangerous corporate behavior would need to be amply rewarded for that work without using the apparatus of personal injury law as we know it.

One fairly moderate package that would move our society in that direction would include the reversal of the collateral sources rule, the imposition of a high threshold of harm before victims may recover pain and suffering damages, plus the creation of easier access to both moderate punitive damages and the payment of plaintiffs' legal fees from serious wrongdoers. But those punitive damages and legal fees would only be available to those who actually serve our society by ferreting out seriously at-fault behavior.

In the end, the role of personal injury law at the end of the twenty-first century is probably as unpredictable as its current role was at the end of the nineteenth. Not only might personal injury law doctrine and the back- ground institutions to tort law change significantly, but also technological advances may well change the pattern of accidental bodily injury that will exist 100 years from now in ways we cannot anticipate.

ENDNOTES

1. *See generally* G. EDWARD WHITE, TORT LAW IN AMERICA: AN INTELLECTUAL HISTORY 18-19, 38-39, 60-62 (1980).

2. By narrowing my Essay as I have, I do not mean to deny that business torts, for example, are an important area of the law-arguably one of rapidly growing importance today. So, too, tort law plainly deals with personal harms that involve other than physical injuries to the body-including harm to reputation which is protected by the law of defamation, the right to be left alone which is protected by privacy law, and so on. Furthermore, damage to tangible property is clearly a very important part of tort law's realm, and, of course, many bodily injuries are accompanied by damage to property as well-auto accidents being the exemplar. Nonetheless, because this is a brief essay with a 100 year sweep, I have decided to center my attention on accidental bodily injury. I also note that this portion of tort's work is what most contemporary law school courses on tort law feature.

3. GUIDO CALABRESI, THE COSTS OF ACCIDENTS (1970).

4. Most importantly, see Escola v. Coca Cola Bottling Co., 150 P.2d 436 (Cal. 1944).

5. *See* RESTATEMENT (THIRD) OF TORTS: PRODUCTS LIABILITY § 2 (1998).

6. *See* RESTATEMENT (SECOND) OF TORTS §§ 519-20 (1977).

7. *See id.*§ 520(d) (describing such activities as "not a matter of common usage").

8. *See* Charles 0. Gregory, *Trespass to Negligence to Absolute Liability,* 37 VA. L. REV. 359 (1951).

9. *See* MORTON J. HORWITZ, THE TRANSFORMATION OF AMERICAN LAW, 1780-1860, at 67-108 (1977).

10. *See* Gary T. Schwartz, *The Character of Early American Tort Law,* 36 UCLA L. REV. 641 (1989); Gary T. Schwartz, *Tort Law and the Economy in Nineteenth Century America: A Re-interpretation,* 90 YALE L.J. 1717, 1727-34 (1981).

11. *See* Robert L. Rabin, *Some Thoughts on the Ideology of Enterprise Liability, 55* MD. L. REV. 1190 (1996).

12. *See* Harry Kalven, Jr., *Tort Law: Tort Watch,* 34 ATL L.J. 1 (1972); Harry Kalven, Jr., *TortLaw: Negligence on the Move,* 33 ATL LJ. 1 (1970).

13. *See* Robert L. Rabin, *The Historical Development of the Fault Principle: A Reinterpretation,* 15 GA. L. REV. 925 (1981).

14. *See* MacPherson v. Buick Motor Co., 111 N.E. 1050 (N.Y. 1916).

15. *See, e.g.,* Dillon v. Legg, 441 P.2d 912 (Cal. 1968).

16. *See, e.g.,*Rowland v. Christian, 443 P.2d 561 (Cal. 1968).

17. *See, e.g.,* Waite v. Waite, 618 So.2d 1360 (Aa. 1993).

18. *See, e.g.,* Larsen v. General Motors Corp., 391 F.2d 495 (8th Cir. 1968).

19. *See, e.g.,*Jones v. O'Young, 607 N.E.2d 224 (111. 1992).

20. *See, e.g.,* Korman v. Mallin, 858 P.2d 1145 (Alaska 1993).

21. *See, e.g.,* Kline v. 1500 Mass. Ave. Apartment Corp., 439 F.2d 477 (D.C. Cir. 1970).

22. *See* Williams v. Delta Int'l Mach. Corp., 619 So.2d 1330 (Ala. 1993).

23. *See, e.g.,* Knight v. Jewett, 834 P.2d 696 (Cal. 1992). *See generally,* Stephen D. Sugarman, *The Monsanto Lecture: Assumption of Risk,* 31 VAL. U. L. REV. 833 (1997). The prominence of "fault" in personal injury law has further increased because the law now downplays rules of causation as ways for defendants to escape liability. Careless defendants, who earlier escaped liability because of narrow applications of the "but for" test of causation, now often must face the more liberal "substantial factor" test. *See, e.g.,* Mitchell v. Gonzales, 819 P.2d 872 (Cal. 1991). Careless defendants who previously were able to hide behind the plaintiff's inability to identify which specific defendant actually "did it" are now sometimes held responsible on the basis of "alternative liability," "concerted action,'' or "market share" theories. *See, e.g.,* Hymowitz v. Eli Lily & Co., 539 N.E.2d 1069 (N.Y. 1989).

24. *See* HENRY S. DRINKER, LEGAL ETHICS 63-65, 210-73, 309-25 (1953) (discussing "ambulance chasing," and advertising and solicitation, as well as the 1908 canons adopted by the American Bar Association and the First Code of Professional Ethics adopted in the United States by the Alabama State Bar Association in 1887); *see also* Max Radin, *The Achievements of the American Bar Association: A Sixty Year Record,* 26 A.B.A. J. 135 (1940).

25. *See, e.g.,* JOHN A. JENKINS, THE LITIGATORS: INSIDE THE POWERFUL WORLD OF AMERICA'S HIGH-STAKES TRIAL LAWYERS (1989).

26. For recent empirical evidence on the personal injury bar, see Herbert M. Kritzer, *The Wages of Risk: The Returns of Contingency Fee Legal Practice,*47 DEPAUL L. REv.267 (1998).

27. *See* Association of Trial Lawyers of America (visited June 27, 2000) <http://www.atla.org>.

28. For the development of legal doctrine as applied to marketing by lawyers, see *Florida Bar v. Went For It, Inc.,*515 U.S. 618 (1995).

29. *See 1.* DANIEL KHAZZOOM, WHAT WE KNOW ABOUT UNINSURED MOTORISTS AND HOW WELL WE KNOW WHAT WE KNOW, RESOURCES FOR THE FUTURE DISCUSSION PAPER 98-09; David W. Sommer eta!., *Financing Uninsured Motorists,* 13 J. of Ins. Reg. 359 (1995).

30. See the discussion in *Seifert v. Los Angeles Transit Lines,* 364 P.2d 337 (Cal. 1961).

31. For a discussion of pain and suffering award levels in Europe, *See* PAUL SZOLLOSY, COMPENSATION FOR PERSONAL INJURY IN WESTERN EUROPE (1992).

32. *See, e.g., Fraud Facts* (visited June 27, 2000) <http://www.InsuranceFraud.org>.

33. *See generally* Lawrence M. Friedman & Jack Ladinsky, *Social Change and the Law of Industrial Accidents,* 67 CoLUM. L. REv. 50 (1967).

34. *See* ARTHUR LARSON, WORKMAN'S COMPENSATION LAW§ 114.10 (2000).

35. *See generally* 2 A.L.I, REPORTERS' STUDY: ENTERPRISE RESPONSIBILITY FOR PERSONAL INJURY 183-98 (1991).

36. *See* James K. Hammitt & John E. Rolph, *Limiting Liability for Automobile Accidents: Are No Fault Thresholds Effective?,* 7 LAW & POL'Y 4 (1985).

37. *See generally* STEPHEN D. SUGARMAN, "PAY AT THE PUMP" AUTO INSURANCE (1993).

38. As of 2000, wage loss protection in Michigan is limited to $ 3,760 per month. *See* MICH. COMP. LAWS. ANN. § 500.3107(b) note (West 2000) (Informational Statement re: Procedural Guidelines Issued Pursuant to Act 306 of the Public Acts of 1969 as Amended).

39. *See* Stephen D. Sugarman, *Quebec's Comprehensive Auto No-fault Scheme and the Failure of Any of the United States to Follow,* LES CAHIERS DE DROIT, *numero special,* 109 (1998).

40. *See, e.g.,* Alcorn v. Anbro Eng'g Inc., 468 P.2d 216 (Cal. 1970).

41. Under 42 U.S.C. § 1983 most importantly.

42. *See generally* Ira Mark Ellman & Stephen D. Sugarman, *Spousal Emotional Abuse as a Tort?, 55* Mo. L. REv. 1268 (1996).

43. *See* RESTATEMENT (SECOND) OF TORTS § 822 (1977).

44. *See* U.S. CENSUS BUREAU, STATISTICAL ABSTRACT OF THE UNITED STATES 39 tbl. 25 (1922).

45. Although detailed data from that period is available from only a limited number of states, one "vital statistics" report of the death rate between 1900 and 1909 shows it to be in the range of 15-20 per 1,000 (or 1,500-2,000 per 100,000) for a total of between 1.2-1.5 million deaths in 1900. *See* FORREST E. LINDER & ROBERT D. GROVE, FEDERAL SECURITY AGENCY, VITAL STATISTICS RATES IN THE UNITED STATES 1900-1940, at 122 (1976). A 1908 study, however, put the total number of deaths of males over age 15 in 1900 at just under 1.4 million. *See* Frederick L. Hoffman, *Industrial Accidents,* 17 BULL .OF THE BUREAU OF LAB. 417,422 (1908). The "vital statistics" report shows that the death rate from "external causes" was Jess than 100 per 100,000, and that included suicide, acute poisoning, and homicide. *See* LINDER & GROVE, *supra,* at 214-15. This would amount to somewhat less than 75,000 total deaths from "external causes"-or approximately *5%* of all deaths reported in the relevant table. The 1908 study noted above, however, put the number of accidental deaths of males over 15 at just over 125,000 in 1900. *See* Hoffman, *supra.* In that study, accidents to males over 15 accounted for about 9% of all deaths to men in that age group.

46. According to the "vital statistics" report, the death rate from "accidental drowning" was 12.1 per 100,000, from "railroad accidents and injuries" 9.7 per 100,000, from "fractures" 9.2 per 100,000, and from "burns and scalds" 7.5 per 100,000. These were the largest subcategories. By contrast, death rates per 100,000 were 1.4 from horse and vehicle injuries, 0.4 from injuries by machinery, 0.4 from injuries in mines and quarries, and 0.4 from electric shock. Death rates from streetcar and auto accidents in 1900 were too small to warrant separate categories (although streetcar death rates reached 3.8 per 100,000 in 1907 at a time when the auto accident death rate reached 0.7 per 100,000). *See* LINDER & GROVE, *supra* note 45, at 214-15. The 1908 report, however, puts railroad deaths in 1900 at nearly twice that of drowning, and nearly three times that of burns and scalds (which, by the way, killed females at twice the rate of males); as with the "vital statistics" report, however, railroad deaths dwarfed machinery deaths. *See* Hoffman, *supra* note 45, at 423. If the "vital statistics" figures are to be believed, then approximately 7,300 persons died in 1900 from "railroad accidents and injuries." LINDER & GROVE, *supra,* at 214-15. Other tum-of-the-century data about industrial accidents suggests that 2,200 railway employees were killed by railway accidents in 1899. *See* W. F. Willoughby, *Accidents to Labor as Regulated by Law in the United States,* 32 BULL. OF THE DEP'T OF LAB. 1, 8 (1901). This implies (if the two data sets may be combined) that around 5,000 of those killed in railway accidents in 1900 were people other than employees, presumably passengers and those struck by trains at crossings, among others. The 1908 report at one point puts the total number of deaths from

railroad accidents at around 6,000 in 1900. *See* Hoffman, *supra* note 45 (which is at least in the same ballpark as the "vital statistics" estimate of 7,300). On the other hand, this may just be a coincidence. As noted, the "vital statistics" data indicate a national death rate from mine and quarry accidents of 0.4 per 100,000 which implies a total of300 such deaths, most of which probably were workers killed in mines and quarries. Yet, different industrial accident data suggest that there were nearly 1200 coal mining deaths in the U.S. in 1899. *See* Willoughby, *supra* at 18.

47. *See* Hoffman, *supra* note 45, at 418.

48. *See id.* at 421.

49. *See* Willoughby, *supra* note 46, at 8. This amounted to a total of around 35,000 injuries or approximately 37 injuries for every 1,000 railway workers. *See id.*To get a feel for the dangerousness of other industries, I note that another part of that same study showed that the estimated injury rate in New York in 1899 was slightly more than 37 per 1,000 employees in the chemical, oil, explosives, pulp, paper and cardboard industries, and in public utilities; it was around 25 per 1,000 in the building industry and in metals and machinery industries; under 20 per 1,000 in stone and clay products, wood, food, tobacco, and liquors; under 10 per 1,000 in printing and textiles; only 3 per 1,000 in leather and just over 1 per 1,000 in clothing, millinery, and laundering. *See id.*at 25.

50. *See* Hoffman, *supra* note 45, at 420.

51. *See* U.S. CENSUS BUREAU, STATISTICAL ABSTRACT OF THE UNITED STATES 834 (1999).

52. *See* National Safety Council, *Injury Facts* (visited April 28, 2000) <http://www.nsc.org/lrs/statinfo/ 99002.htm>.

53. *See id.* Somewhat different findings are presented in a Report to Congress published in 1989, based largely on 1985 data, which distinguished among nonfatal accidents; that Report found that there were 15 times as many hospitalized injured persons as fatalities, and more than 300 times as many non- hospitalized injured persons as fatalities. DOROTHY P. RICE ET AL., COST OF INJURY IN THE UNITED STATES: A REPORT TO CONGRESS 1989, at xxi (1989).

54. *See* National Safety Council, *supra* note 52.

55. *Id.*

56. *Id.*

57. DEBORAH R. HENSLER ET AL., COMPENSATION FOR ACCIDENTAL INJURJES IN THE UNITED STATE 31 (1991). According to the National Safety Council, motor vehicles were responsible for about 11% of all disabling injuries in 1998 (over 2 million in total).*See* National Safety Council, *supra* note 52. Some other highlights of the RAND study are that about 30% of accidents occurred while people were relaxing. *See* HENSLER, *supra* at 27. About a third reported suffering their accidents while in their own homes (or those of friends). *See id.* at 28. Seven percent were rated by RAND as "very serious" and an additional21% were rated "moderately serious." *Id.* at 41. The Report to Congress did not identify products as a cause of injury, as the RAND study did, but it estimated that, as among unintentional injuries, falls accounted for nearly half of hospitalizations and 13% of fatalities. *See* RICE, *supra* note 53, at xxi. In the Report to Congress, drowning remained a fatality category worth separate attention, accounting for about 6% of unintentional fatalities according to the Report to Congress, as did bums and fires which accounted for about 6% of the fatalities and 3% of the hospitalizations. *See id.* The Report to Congress found that while the male injury rate was almost 40% higher than the female rate, the male death rate was nearly three times the female rate. *See id.* at 13. For motor vehicles, females actually had a higher injury rate than males, but the male death rate was two and a half times as great *See id.*

58. In considering these data, note that the Commission's jurisdiction and the NEISS reports exclude certain products which are important causes of accidental injuries, including motor vehicles, drugs, guns, and tobacco products. *See* Consumer Product Safety Commission, *National Injury Information Clearinghouse* (visited June 27, 2000) <http://www.cpsc.gov/about/clrnghse.html> (explaining NEISS); Consumer Product Safety Commission, *Who We Are-What We Do For You* (visited June 27, 2000) <http://www.cpsc.gov/cpscpub/pubs/103.html> (explaining jurisdiction).

59. *NEISS Data Highlights,* CONSUMER PRODUCT SAFETY REv.{U.S. Consumer Product Safety Comm., D.C.), Fal11999, at 3.

60. *Id.* at 6-7.

61. *Id.* at 3-4.

62. *See* NATIONAL SAFETY COUNCIL, INJURY FACTS 48 (1999).

63. *See id.* This number should be compared with the estimate of 30,000-35,000 occupational fatalities for 1900 noted earlier. *See supra* text accompanying note 47.

64. *See* National Safety Council, *supra* note 52.

65. *See* Bureau of Labor Statistics, United States Department of Labor, News (USDL 99-208) August 4, 1999 Table 1.

66. *See* National Safety Council, *supra* note 52. The RAND study found that about 21% of accidents were work related (plus about 5% more which were incurred while commuting to work). *See* HENSLER, *supra* note 57, at 28.

67. *See* Bureau of Labor Statistics, *supra* note 65, at 4.

68. *See id.*

69. *See id.* Note that according to the National Safety Council, disabling occupational injuries numbered 3.8 million in 1998 (not *5.5* million as quoted in the Bureau of Labor Statistics report cited above), which amounted to more than 700 times the number of work-related deaths. *See* National Safety Council, *supra* note 52. In any event, it is difficult to compare these ratios with the 1900 data because the definition of a nonfatal injury has no doubt changed, and changes from report to report.

70. *See generally* 1 A.L.J, REPORTERS' STUDY: ENTERPRISE RESPONSIBILITY FOR PERSONAL INJURY 129-56 (1991) (discussing public access to health insurance in a tort context).

71. *See id.* at 157-202 (discussing disability and life insurance as alternatives to tort law).

72. *See* Wilmer L. Kerns, *Protection Against Income Loss During the First 6 Months of Illness or Injury,* 57 Soc. SEC. BULL. 88 (1994).

73. Concerning the effectiveness of NHSTA over auto safety, see generally, Stephen D. Sugarman, *Nader's Failures?,* 80 CALIF.L. REv. 289 (1992).

74. OLIVER WENDELL HOLMES, THE COMMON LAW (1881).

75. Francis H. Bohlen, *Incomplete Privilege to Inflict Intentional Invasions of Interests of Property and*

Personality, 39 HARV. L. REV 307 (1926).

76. *See, e.g.,* John G. Fleming, *Comparative Negligence at Last-By Judicial Choice,* 64 CALIF. L. REV. 239 (1976).

77.*See, e.g.,* Robert L. Rabin, *Enabling Torts,* 49 DEPAUL L. REv.435 (1999).

78. *See, e.g.,* Gary T. Schwartz, *Foreword: Understanding Products Liability,* 67 CALIF. L. REV. 435 (1979).

79. *See, e.g.,* HENSLER, *supra* note 57.

80. *See, e.g.,* Marc Galanter, *Real World Torts: An Antidote to Anecdote, 55* MD. L. REV. 1093 (1996).

81. PETER H. SCHUCK, AGENT ORANGE ON TRIAL: MASS TOXIC DISASTERS IN THE COURTS (1986).

82. *See* CALABRESI, *supra* note 3.

83. *See, e.g.,* RICHARD A. POSNER, ECONOMIC ANALYSIS OF LAW (1972).

84. *See, e.g.,* STEVEN SHAVELL, ECONOMIC ANALYSIS OF ACCIDENT LAW (1987).

85. *See, e.g.,* JULES L. COLEMAN, RISKS AND WRONGS (1992).

86. *See, e.g.,* ERNEST J. WEINRIB, THE IDEA OF PRIVATE LAW (1995).

87. *See, e.g.,* George Fletcher, *Fairness and Utility in Tort Theory,* 85 HARV. L. REV. 537 (1972).

88. *See* Howard Latin, *"Good" Warnings, Bad Products, and Cognitive Limitations,* 41 UCLA L. REV. 1193 (1994).

89. *See* Lawrence M. Friedman, *Civil Wrongs: Personal Injury Law in the Late Nineteenth Century,* 1987 AM. B. FOUND. J. 351, 359 [hereinafter Friedman, *Civil Wrongs].*

90. *See* Lawrence M. Friedman and Thomas D. Russell, *More Civil Wrongs: Personal Injury Litigation,* 1901-1910, 34 AM. J. LEGAL H!ST. 295,296 (1990).

91. *See* Friedman, *Civil Wrongs, supra* note 89, at 360.

92. *See id.* at 361.

93. *See id.*

94. *See id.* at 364-65.

95. *See id.* at 365; *see a/so* RANDOLPH E. BERGSTROM, COURTING DANGER 11-30 (1992) (describing tort litigation in New York in the period 1870-1910).

96. *See* BRIAN J. OSTROM & NEAL B. KAUDER, EXAMINING THE WORK OF STATE COURTS, 1998: A NATIONAL PERSPECTIVE FROM THE COURT STATISTICS PROJECT 96 (1999).

97. *See id.*

98. *See* HENSLER, *supra* note 57, at 121.

99. *See id.* at 124, 137.

100. *See* George L. Priest, *The Invention of Enterprise Liability: A Critical History of the Intellectual Foundations of Modem Tort Law,* 14 J. LEGAL STUD. 461, 470-83 (1985).

101. *See generally* PETER A. BELL AND JEFFERY O'CONNELL, ACCIDENTAL JUSTICE: THE DILEMMAS OF TORT LAW 46-67 (1997).

102. See Jeffrey O'Connell, *A Draft Bill to Allow Choice Between No-Fault and Fault-Based AutoInsurance, 21* HARV. J. ON LEGIS. 143, 152 n. 32 (1990).

103. *See generally SUGARMAN,*"PAY AT THE PUMP" AUTO INSURANCE, *supra* note 37.

104. *See* Stephen D. Sugarman, *Doctor No, 58* U.CHI.L. REV. 1499 (1991).

105. *See* HENSLER, *supra* note 57, at 139-40 (noting that more than 66% of those who filed a lawsuit considered the process unfair); E. Alan Lind et al., *In the Eye of the Beholder: Tort Litigants' Evaluations of their Experiences in the Civil Justice System,*24 L. & Soc'Y. REv. 953 (1990).

1 06. *See* 1 A.L.I., *supra* note 70, at 231-65.

107. *See, e.g.,* Steven P. Croley & Jon D. Hanson, *Rescuing the Revolution: The Revival Case for Enterprise Liability,* 91 MICH. L. REV. 683 (1993); Jon D. Hanson & Kyle D. Logue, *The First-Party Insurance Externality: An Economic Justification for Enterprise Liability,* 76 CORNELL L. REv. 129 (1990).

108. *See* STEPHEN D. SUGARMAN, DOING AWAY WITH PERSONAL INJURY LAW 3-34 (1989); Stephen D. Sugarman, *Doing Away with Tort Law,*73 CALIF.L. REV. *555,*559-90 (1985).

109. *See, e.g.,* Gary T. Schwartz, *Reality in the Economic Analysis of Tort Law: Does Tort Law Really Deter?,* 42 UCLA L. REV. 377 (1994); BELL & O'CONNELL, *supra* note 101, at 68-100.

110. *See* DON DEWEES ET AL., EXPLORING THE DOMAIN OF ACCIDENT LAW: TAKING THE FACTS SERIOUSLY (1996); THE LIABILITY MAZE: THE IMPACT OF LIABILITY LAW ON SAFETY AND INNOVATION (Peter W. Huber & Robert A. Litan, eds., 1991).

111. *See* JAMES S. KAKALIK & NICHOLAS M. PACE, COSTS AND COMPENSATION PAIN IN TORT LITIGATION (1986).

112. *See* BELL & O'CONNELL, *supra* note 101, at 138-69.

113. *See* Royal Globe Ins. Co. v. Superior Court, 592 P.2d 329, 333-35 (Cal. 1979).

114. *See* Moradi-Shalal v. Fireman's Fund Ins. Cos., 758 P.2d 58, 63-64, 68 (Cal. 1988).

115.*See Vote 2000-CaliforniaPrimary Election* (visited June 27, 2000) <http://www.vote2000.ss.ca.gov/retums/prop/OO.htm>.

116. *See* SUGARMAN, DOING AWAY WITH PERSONAL INJURY LAW, *supra* note 108, at 75-99.

117. *See, e.g.,* Knowles v. United States, 544 N.W.2d 183 (S.D. 1996) (rejecting malpractice damages as unconstitutional).

118. For example, in 1988 and in 1996, California voters defeated insurance industry-supported auto no-

fault plans, propositions 104 and 200. *See California Ballot Proposition Database, Hastings College of the Law Library* (visited July 10, 2000) <http://www.holmes.hastings.edu>.

119. *See* Gary T. Schwartz, *The Beginning and the Possible End of the Rise of Modem American Tort Law,* 26 GA. L REv.601 (1992); Stephen D. Sugarman, *Judges as Tort Law Un-Makers: Recent California Experience with "New" Torts,* 49 DEPAUL L. REV. 455 (1999).

120. *See* James A. Henderson, Jr., & Theodore Eisenberg, *The Quiet Revolution in Products Liability,* 37 UCLA L. REV. 479 (1990).

121. *See* Jeffrey O'Connell et al., *The Costs of Consumer Choice for Auto Insurance in States Without No-Fault Insurance,* 54 MD. L. Rev. 281 (1995); Stephen D. Sugarman, *Choosing Among Systems of Auto Insurance for Persona/Injury,* 26 SAN DIEGO L. REV. 977 (1989).

122. *See* Stephen Carroll, *Effects of an Auto-Choice Automobile Insurance Plan on Costs and Premiums* (visited July 13, 2000) <http://www.rand.org/publications/CT/CT141/>.

123. *See* PAUL C. WEILER, MEDICAL MALPRACTICE ON TRIAL (1991).

124. *See* MARC A. FRANKLIN & ROBERT L. RABIN, TORT LAW AND ALTERNATIVES 692 (6th ed.1996).

125. *See* Stephen D.Sugannan, *Serious Tort Law Reform,* 24 SAN DIEGO L. Rev. 795 (1987).

126. *See* Stephen D. Sugarman, *Short Tenn Paid Leave: A New Approach to Social Insurance and Employee Benefits, 15* Calif. L. Rev. 465 (1987).

127. *See* Robert Cooter & Stephen D. Sugarman, *A Regulated Market in Unmatured Tort Claims: Tort Reform by Contract, in* NEW DIRECTIONS IN LIABILITY LAW 174 (Walter Olson ed.,1988).

Chapter 4

Who Should Reform Tort Law?
Congress, State Legislatures, or Judges?

Tort law in the U.S. is traditionally a matter of state law. It is one of those many legal realms that, pursuant to principles of "federalism," Congress has largely left untouched. Tort law is also largely a matter of "common law" (in contrast to, say, family law which, while also left centrally to the states to determine, is largely statutory). Hence, in practice, our U.S. tort law is better described as comprised of 50 different common laws (or perhaps 49 common laws plus the civil law of torts in Louisiana). It need not have turned out that way.

Many nations survive, perhaps even thrive, on a single national tort law – typically adopted by statute (a "code") enacted, and over time amended, by the national legislature (e.g., parliament). Indeed, even in other common law countries, it seems fair to say, there is but a single common law of torts. Consider Canada and Australia, for example. In both of those nations a uniform binding countrywide common law of torts is developed by the Canadian Supreme Court and the High Court of Australia and imposed on the various provinces and states (Quebec's special civil law status aside). But in the U.S., in light of *Erie v. Tompkins* (as 1L students of Civil Procedure learn), we have no single federal common law of torts.

To be sure, in many respects tort law is very similar from state to state across the U.S. This tendency is affirmatively promoted by the American Law Institute's (ALI) "Restatement" project, which seeks to articulate what might be termed the dominant (or wisest) solutions to most of the issues that come before state common law judges. Given the fairly high status that the ALI has attained – through a combination of the qualifications required for membership and the very careful deliberative process the ALI members engage in before adopting a "Restatement" – its announcements have carried considerable weight in convincing state court judges how to resolve matters before them. Indeed, the Restatement of Torts, now in the middle of its Third revision, has probably been the ALI's most influential project. Nonetheless, states are not at all bound to follow the Restatement, and here and there many do not. Moreover, sometimes states are out in front of the Restatement as new problems come before them, and they may well decide to resolve those issues differently. So, while it is probably something of an exaggeration to term the U.S. as having a "crazy quilt" of tort law, still tort law varies around the nation. Indeed, one of the key things that takes place in the typical 1L Torts class is that the professor and the students try to figure out how courts have justified coming to different results on similar facts (and perhaps they try to determine which is the "better reasoned" result).

State legislatures sometimes modify the law of torts for their state, something that seems to have become considerably more frequent since, say, 1970. Most of the "tort reform" effort, discussed in Chapters 2 and 3, has been carried out through state legislatures (although the heart of the common law of torts remains primarily intact across the country).

Should this continue to be so? Or should Congress step in and make substantial, even revolutionary, changes to the law of torts? This chapter explores that question. The first part examines claims by business and other defense interests that they are being unfairly treated by state tort law and need Congress to rescue them. The second part raises the possibility that Congress could supplant state tort law, not with a new national tort law, by with a much broader non-tort scheme for compensating accident victims (a theme signaled in Chapter 1 and which will be explored again in more detail in later chapters). Finally, attention is paid to the possibility that Congress could change the jurisdiction of federal courts hearing tort cases.

This chapter was written in the mid-1990s and contributed to a conference held at the University of Michigan Law School on the question of whether tort reform, especially proposed Congressional tort reform which was then on the political front-burner, was primarily a matter of true substantive change or mere political rhetoric. It was published as Stephen D. Sugarman, "Should Congress Engage in Tort Reform?" 1 Michigan Law & Policy Review 121 (1996).

Although "tort reform" was a key plank in the Republican party's "Contract with America" that swept a Republican majority into the House of Representatives in the 1994 elections, that Congress was not successful in turning its provisions into law. Indeed, although Congress has tinkered around the edges of tort law in the two decades that followed, tort law today remains very much a state law matter. Perhaps the most important Congressional change has been to make it easier for defendants to remove cases from state courts and obtain federal court jurisdiction over some important tort disputes, especially in the product liability arena (a topic raised at the end of this chapter). But it remains true that federal judges apply substantive state law in deciding these cases.

Was Congress too timid? Should tort law (or its replacement) be uniform throughout the U.S? This chapter explores this topic.

SHOULD CONGRESS ENGAGE IN TORT REFORM?

Should Congress engage in tort reform? I first appraise, and find rather unpersuasive, arguments that defense interests might offer in favor of Congressional action on personal injury law. Then I explore reasons why consumer and victim advocates might seek Congressional action with respect to personal injuries. Although some good arguments can be made on this side, their political prospects are currently slim. Turning to the tort reform proposals now pending in Washington, I criticize them as asking Congress to take on an inappropriate role. Finally, I raise some issues about what clearly is a proper Congressional role -determining the place of federal courts in personal injury cases.

I. ARGUMENTS DEFENSE INTERESTS MIGHT OFFER IN FAVOR OF CONGRESSIONAL ACTION ON PERSONAL INJURY LAW

For more than two decades defense interests have captured the "tort reform" label They have broadly argued that liberal judges have allowed or encouraged personal injury law to get out of control, and they have appealed to legislatures at both the state and federal level for relief. In this section, I address a variety of justifications that defense interests assert (or could assert) in support of tort reform by Congress. The issue in each case is whether a convincing argument has been made for national legislation with respect to personal injuries, a field which has long been dominated by state law, primarily common law. My conclusion is that none of the claims canvassed in this section is convincing.

A. Adopting a National Fault-Based Theory of Tort Law

Defense interests have argued that the United States should embrace fault-based liability as our national legal theory of tort law. Reflected in conventional "negligence" doctrine, I associate this perspective with traditionally conservative values. Its core principle is that when someone acts badly and causes harm to another, the government should make its courts available as a forum for redress if the victim seeks to hold the wrongdoer accountable. In this model of tort law, individuals pursue justice and serve the collective good in the process. This happens because potential injurers, fearing liability if they misbehave, will have an incentive to exercise due care in the way they act. This outlook arguably dovetails with the ideology behind the Republican Party's "Contract With America" -- in welfare, for example, the Contract also emphasizes the tenet of personal responsibility.

Of course, Congressional endorsement of a single ideological view of tort law is not the only way to achieve national consistency. For example, the National Conference of Commissioners on Uniform State Laws, an organization with representatives from every state, regularly tries to accomplish that same result by promulgating so called "uniform laws" that states are urged to adopt. The aspiration is that the country will converge on a single vision legislature-by-legislature. This has been attained, perhaps most spectacularly, with the Uniform Commercial Code. The Restatement project of the American Law Institute is another, perhaps more subtle, approach to the same end. By lending the prestige of its members to what they conclude is the better reasoned doctrine in important, traditionally common law areas, the Institute hopes to convince state court judges to fall in line.

Nevertheless, Congressional action in significant legal fields previously left to the states is certainly not unheard of even in the area of tort law. Consider, for example, the Sherman antitrust law and the federal securities laws. They created dominant national visions of how to deal with the financial problems they address, thereby importantly supplanting, if not actually preempting, state tort doctrine in the areas of conspiracy and fraud.

On this basis, I can understand the business community pressing, starting around 1970, for a sweeping federal products liability law grounded firmly in the fault principle. At that time, the new and competing ideology of "enterprise liability" was very much in the air -- backed by a few venturesome judges and several prominent torts scholars and given at least some backing by the Restatement (Second) of Torts. Rather than being individual fault-based, enterprise liability reflects a liberal perspective on the role of tort law. It imposes strict liability on organizations whose products cause harm, whether or not it can be shown in specific cases that injury could have been avoided by the product manufacturer through the exercise of reasonable precaution. Many believed that enterprise liability would become the new tort law paradigm at least in the products area, and fear of that outcome provided defense interests a reason for seeking Congressional re-affirmation of the traditional fault principle. This was indeed the thrust of the Model Product Liability Act, developed in the mid1970s by the Department of Commerce. Although drafted as though it would be adopted by individual states, it was quickly understood that Congress itself might impose its provisions nationwide. Even though bills of this sort were introduced, they did not pass in the face of Democratic opposition.

With Republicans finally taking control of Congress in 1995 is it time to revive such bills? I do not think so. The reason is that as the past 25 years have unfolded, enterprise liability has failed to take hold as legal doctrine. On the whole, state courts just have not been won over to the idea of using tort law as an accident compensation scheme in the tradition of Workers' Compensation -- apart from the arena of manufacturing defects where tort law simply adopted contract warranty notions, in place for decades, that present no real threat to the business world. Simply put, through vigorous litigation efforts and state-level political efforts, the threat of enterprise liability has been largely beaten back.

Instead, conservative ideology and the fault principle have continued to carry the day. Even in New Jersey, a change of heart by the supreme court plus state legislative reform have pulled what was perhaps the doctrinally most liberal state squarely back into the fault camp. This is why I simply see no need today for Congress to embrace fault-based tort law for product injuries—a point that has been made painfully clear to defeated advocates of strict liability in preliminary drafts of a new Restatement of Torts covering product injuries that is now in the adoption process.

To be sure, some of those on the defense side argue that, despite the formal legal doctrine, enterprise liability is the law in action as applied by juries. Business executives can often relate a favorite anecdote about how their firm or another they know about was held liable for an injury that, in their view, could not plausibly have been avoided by actions taken at the time of manufacture. As they see it, either jurors are disregarding the judge's instructions or plaintiffs' lawyers are capitalizing on knowledge gained from the benefit of hindsight and fooling juries into believing that warnings should have been given or that products should have been made in different ways.

It is not easy, however, for conservatives to offer a principled remedy to this complaint. After all, the fault idea to which they claim such attachment depends upon having confidence that juries can do well exactly what some claim juries often do poorly -- determine whether or not due care was taken. Indeed, opponents of the current regime often mistakenly attack what they call "strict products liability" law when juries find that a product should have been designed differently, apparently not realizing that this is exactly the sort of issue that conventional fault law requires juries to address.

Of course, it could be argued that judges should replace juries as the decision-makers in torts cases. Yet, juries themselves, as a matter of political philosophy, are something of a conservative institution in the sense that they have been understood to stand in the way of the abuse of power by government. To be sure, one could favor maintaining juries in criminal cases but not in civil cases, as is largely the situation in England today. Yet, the traditionalism of the American civil jury is so ingrained as to make a conservative attack on its very existence sound radical -- especially if the proposal put on the table is that Congress should tell states that they may no longer use juries in torts cases. Besides, in the end, it is by no means clear as a practical matter that defense interests would routinely fare better if there were no civil jury. After all, it is not infrequent that the defense, not the plaintiff, asks for a jury trial.

Perhaps certain procedural changes to the current system could be adopted that would make the fault principle more accurately implemented in the eyes of the defense. But, once more, it seems an exceedingly odd step to ask Congress to take so long as tort cases continue to be heard in state courts -- a matter to which I will return below.

B. Protecting Vital International Interests of the United States

An entirely different defense-oriented justification for Congressional tort law reform is that it is necessary to protect vital international interests of the United States. After all, national legislation on matters of international trade is commonplace, and the international competitiveness of American firms and products is surely a legitimate matter of Congressional concern.

Turning specifically to products liability law, the claim is often voiced that pro-plaintiff state law verdicts harm U.S. firms which are out there battling in today's global market. I find this argument unpersuasive.

The first point to notice is that, despite all the attention it gets, in the end tort law is not a very important financial drag on U.S. business typically costing firms well under 2% (often under 1%) of gross sales. As a result, even if the "tort liability" tax in the U.S. is relatively much larger than, for example, in Europe and Asia, to the great majority of firms these differentials are nonetheless far less important than international wage, tax and regulatory differentials. German firms, for example, typically face much higher payroll taxes than do American firms; Korean firms typically face much lower wage costs -- differences that dwarf tort cost differentials.

Moreover, foreign manufacturers who do business in the U.S., and thus compete here with American firms, are also subject to American law. Hence, when foreign made products injure U.S. consumers, their manufacturers or importers are typically burdened in the same way as American manufacturers selling in the U.S. market. For example, Toyota is on the same footing as Ford (whether Toyota's cars are made here or abroad) for vehicles sold and used in Illinois. It is possible that, in some instances, there is a problem with thin capitalization of firms that make or import foreign products, but the absence of evidence demonstrating this suggests it is not a serious problem.

As for sales of U.S. products abroad, the "level playing field" result would be that injuries to non-Americans in their home nation would lead to claims filed there under foreign law. Increasingly, this appears to be the result. American courts today (both state and federal) seem routinely willing to dismiss such claims—typically on the grounds that the forum is inappropriate even if jurisdiction technically is available.

The upshot is that we just do not seem to be differentially hobbling our own firms to any significant extent in their fight for market share either at home or abroad.

C. Protecting Out-of-State Business Defendants

A rather different claim is that Congressional action is needed to protect out-of-state defendants (e.g., national corporations headquartered elsewhere) from in-state judges and juries. The argument is that state law functions in a way that is systematically biased against outsiders. This claim formed the heart of a book published some years ago by Richard Neely, a former justice of the West Virginia Supreme Court, who portrayed West Virginia judges and juries as deliberately socking it to out-of- state defendants.

The first doubt I have about this assertion stems from an absence of systematic empirical evidence. Suppose that certain states would choose to adopt this strategy through legal doctrine. By adopting strong rules of liability, states with few in-state manufacturers could attempt to impose the burdens created by those rules mainly on out-of-staters. Yet, so far as I have been able to determine, there is no factual support for this supposition. That is, the law on the books does not seem especially pro-plaintiff in states with little in-state manufacturing. Indeed, some of the least industrial states often appear to be the most pro-defendant in terms of tort doctrine.

Second, I question whether the law in action, regardless of the law on the books, particularly disfavors out-of-state businesses. As I look across America it seems to me that complaints about tort law have not been coming especially from out-of-state defendants. Rather, we have been hearing just as loudly from doctors and municipal governments, two very local categories of defendants.

Third, it appears to me that what research we have on this topic shows that if there is any bias in the law in action, it is against all corporate defendants and not just out-of-state businesses. For example, work by the RAND Institute of Civil Justice suggests that an otherwise similar case yields a higher judgment if the defendant is a corporation instead of an individual (and even larger, it should be noted, if the defendant is an organ of government). Besides, if out-of-state defendants are mistreated by the law in action rather than the law on the books, it is by no means clear that they would fare any better under a Congressionally adopted national tort law (putting the issue of federal damages rules aside until later).

Finally, even if there were something to this concern about bias, it seems to me that it is already addressed by the principle of "diversity" jurisdiction, which gives out-of-state defendants the right to remove such cases to federal court. To be sure, since the Erie decision it is clear that federal courts will apply state law to tort claims brought to them on the basis of diversity jurisdiction. Still, there is reason to believe that federal courts will be rather less provincial than state courts, and hence less likely than outlier, local courts and juries to engage in or tolerate rank discrimination against out-of-state defendants.

I realize that there is arguably a defect in this reliance on the current rules for diversity jurisdiction in the sense that a plaintiff can typically defeat a manufacturer's effort to remove a case to federal court in a product injury case by suing a local retailer as well. On the other hand, since state tort law in product injury cases typically holds the retailer liable to the same extent as the manufacturer, in order to impose extravagant liability on the outsider, the jury will usually also have to do the same thing to the local retailer. If this is still considered insufficient protection, then perhaps Congress could think about changing the grounds on which cases may be removed to federal courts, an issue to which I will return at the end.

D. Preventing Inappropriate Forum Shopping

In a somewhat different vein, it is sometimes claimed that victims inappropriately forum shop their cases, seeking out places where the law is more favorable to them. A uniform national law would curtail this inappropriate behavior. But it is by no means clear what defense interests think plaintiffs gain from such behavior.

All states have "choice of law" rules, and while they are not exactly the same, ordinarily in tort cases the same law is applied whether the claim is litigated in California where the plaintiff bought the product and was injured, in Texas where the defendant manufactured it, or in New York where the defendant's national headquarters is located. Usually, that is, all states will conclude that California tort law should apply to this case.

This is not to say that nothing turns on the location of the suit. There are procedural differences from place to place that might be thought to favor one side or the other. But it is easy to over-emphasize such differences; besides, these differences are likely to remain even with a uniform national substantive tort law. Again, if the law in action as opposed to the law on the books, favors plaintiffs more in one state than in another, that is not easily altered with a new law on the books. To be sure, some plaintiffs may be able to have more favorable damages laws applied to their case as a result of forum shopping; I explore the idea of a national tort damages law below.

Finally, as I see it, most of the complaints about forum shopping actually are based on variation within a state—such as urban juries being far more generous than are suburban ones, or that juries in certain blue collar communities are especially anti-business. But this problem exists where there already is a uniform law applicable from forum to forum, and hence is unlikely to be solved with a different uniform substantive tort law.

E. Eliminating Conflicting Legal Requirements

A still different complaint by defense interests is that it is intolerable for national companies to be subject to so many different state tort laws. Again I fail to see what is really so serious about this variety.

First of all, it bears re-emphasizing that, in fact, state tort laws today are broadly the same in product injury cases. Basically, all states impose strict liability for injuries caused by products that were defectively manufactured, but require plaintiffs to plead and, as a practical matter, prove negligence when an entire product line is challenged for its design or warning features. Hence, most of the time, a firm will be liable or not for the same sort of injury wherever it occurs and whatever defendant is sued.

To be sure, around the edges there are genuine state-to-state differences both in terms of damages law and as to certain arguably important doctrinal details including the formal burden of proof. Yet, pointing to these details hardly suffices to demonstrate that there is a serious problem. After all, firms doing business in many states always have to contend with different state laws on all sorts of matters and they seem to manage without undue difficulty. Besides, assume that state A has more generous damages laws than does state B, or suppose state A has a more plaintiff-oriented contributory negligence law than does state B. It is difficult to see how this would really mean anything more than that the cost of doing business in state A is higher than in state B. This, of course, is something enterprises know going in and can deal with in advance—just as they do when one state's tax or regulatory regime imposes higher costs of doing business in that state than another.

Ordinarily, this would simply mean charging slightly higher prices in state A. Since we are typically talking about cost differences that would amount to only a fraction of one percent of the sales price, imposing this differential certainly seems feasible (if it were even thought necessary). For such differences, manufacturers will not generally have to deal with complaints by their retailers that customers are going across state lines to make their purchases. Of course, this cost accounting will be somewhat upset because some accidents will be the result of products that were bought in state Y injuring people in state Z because the product has been brought into state Z when, say, its user moved there. But surely this phenomenon accounts for a fairly small share of accidents. Furthermore, perhaps just as often the product will have been purchased in a place where a higher cost would have been imposed in anticipation of a possible injury in that state, but then the product was taken to a place with more pro-defendant tort rules and lower prices. And finally, where there is a more regional market for goods and activities, there is reason to expect that surrounding state law is likely to be fairly homogeneous.

It is sometimes argued in response that considerably more is involved than mere differences in the cost of doing business from one place to another. Suppose California courts condemn certain auto designs that New York courts do not. For example, suppose gasoline tanks mounted outside the vehicle's frame are found to be defective in the former jurisdiction, but not in the latter. What, then, is General Motors supposed to do? Making a special California version might be possible, as we have seen with the creation of special California cars with tighter emission controls. But while California is a huge market, making a special Oregon version, for example, is perhaps far less feasible. And it probably becomes increasingly less feasible as either the state-to-state variety increases beyond two and/or the product is less expensive than an automobile. While this does put General Motors (and other product makers) in something of difficult position, let us consider the alternatives more carefully.

In the first place, if we asked General Motors whether it would prefer to face a uniform national law which was the same as California's in this example of the gas tank location, or else legal variety among the states with most adopting the hypothetical New York position, I would be very surprised if General Motors did not opt for the diverse law result. In short, defendants are far more attracted to the idea of uniformity when it is uniformly pro defendant.

One ground for my prediction about General Motors' preferences is my instinct that a significant share of cases where states treat product designs or warnings differently occur after an older design has been attacked, and go only to whether or not money will have to be paid to the plaintiff. By the time of litigation, that is, the product's current national design standard is already very different.

Finally, suppose that, in my example, the more restrictive California tort law makes General Motors feel that it has to make all of its models contain the design solution that the California courts decided was safer—even though, let us assume, General Motors engineers are convinced that the cost of the design change simply is not worth the (alleged) safety benefit thereby attained. In that event, it seems to me, it ought to be the consumers in other states who should be complaining because, I trust, they will now have to pay for the new design in the vehicles they buy. But I note that we certainly don't hear such complaints. Indeed, I bet that national consumer groups are far more likely to complain if General Motors were to take the position that it would simply pay the damages claims when people are injured by the design in California and stick to its preferred design everywhere.

II. ARGUMENTS CONSUMER AND VICTIM ADVOCATES MIGHT OFFER IN FAVOR OF CONGRESSIONAL ACTION WITH RESPECT TO PERSONAL INJURIES

Although the general tort reform bills that have been introduced into Congress in the course of the past two decades have come almost entirely from the defense side (and largely from Republicans), this need not have been, nor need it continue to be, the case. Consumer and victim advocates might also try to make an argument for federal legislation. Indeed, I believe there are better arguments for Congress undertaking these reforms than those urged by the defense side. As a political matter, however, I concede at the start that such changes are quite unlikely right now.

A. Adopting a Uniform National Enterprise Liability-Based Tort Law

One approach is exactly the opposite of that with which I began. Instead of opponents trying to block enterprise liability its advocates might have gone to

Congress seeking to have it adopted for the nation. Indeed, the unwillingness of the states to break with the fault principle may make federal enactment of enterprise liability now all the more urgent in the eyes of its supporters. One justification for a federal statute would be that a perverse incentive problem prevents action by individual states and requires instead what is in effect concerted action among them through the mechanism of Congress. According to this argument economic threats by business make it especially difficult for any single state to get out in front of others by imposing extra burdens on enterprises, even if a majority of citizens in most, or even every, state actually favored that result.

The simple version of this argument is not terribly persuasive, however, under current law the direct threat an individual firm could make against a state trying to adopt enterprise liability would only be not to sell its goods in the state and that sort of threat would probably be viewed as rather empty. What states might more seriously fear is a threat not to locate business operations in the state, since this means jobs. As we have seen, however, place of manufacture is now usually unimportant in determining whether a state's strict liability rules will apply to any specific product injury.

Therefore, the more effective pressure from the business community is less likely to be in the form of an individual enterprise threatening to retaliate against tort reform specifically and more likely to come from the business community as a whole. Groups like the Chamber of Commerce argue that adoption of enterprise liability would reflect hostility by the state to business generally, thereby discouraging firms from locating there. This pressure is more likely to be effective against state legislatures than against state courts, because business is a well-organized interest group in the direct political arena. Nonetheless, business organizations also file amicus briefs in key tort law litigation.

In light of this analysis, it seems to me that had prestigious national bodies strongly supported enterprise liability as a desirable reform for the country, it might have prompted a serious political fight in Congress over the idea. But despite early support from some scholars and courts, in the end groups like the American Bar Association and the American Law Institute that have explored tort reform since the 1970s have not generally endorsed this approach. Hence, no real case has been made that leaving tort reform to the states yields a "race to the bottom" so far as victim and consumer interests are concerned.

B. Enacting a Nationwide Accident Compensation Plan

A quite different comprehensive solution to the problem of accident victim compensation could come through congressional enactment of a new social insurance scheme (or an expansion of existing national programs).

This approach could be modelled after the accident compensation plan adopted by New Zealand in 1974. Although certain features of the New Zealand system have been modified in the 1990s with the election of a conservative, more market-oriented government, it remains basically true that if you suffer injury by accident in that nation, you qualify for wage replacement and health care benefits that are provided by the central government and funded nationally. Proposals later offered (but not enacted) in Australia and Great Britain were even more sweeping in their reach, designed to provide benefits through the same program to the full range of disabled people, whether the disability was caused by accident, illness, congenital disability, etc.

I have previously broached what I consider to be an even more wide ranging idea, in which a single scheme would be aimed at all needs for income support, health care and rehabilitation. Such a program might actually pay somewhat different benefits to, say, the retired, the unemployed, and the disabled. But tradeoffs among these groups and judgments about relative need and dessert would be made within a single program with a single administration.

Thus, those who favor the "compensation plan" approach for the U.S. have several models from which to choose. If Congress were to start from, our existing social insurance base, any of these proposals would probably involve an expansion of the Social Security and Medicare programs. For example, Social Security could be enlarged to provide income security for those workers who are only partially disabled as well as for those people who become disabled but were not in the work force at the time. This is hardly unprecedented. Social Security has already managed the transition from a scheme of benefits for retired workers to a broader program that includes benefits for totally and permanently disabled former workers and the survivors of former workers.

Although this is not the place to explore these ideas in any detail, a few matters bear mention. I acknowledge that the precise nature of the income and health care benefits any such plan would provide, as well as the mechanism(s) employed to finance and administer such benefits, would be difficult to work out and controversial in many respects. For example, to what extent should funding be tied to activities that generate claims on the plan? Nevertheless, with reasonable technical solutions to these matters in the design, victim and consumer groups could strongly favor such legislation, at least if there were any hope of its adoption as a political matter. I concede that almost no one these days seems to be advocating such a program apart from me. But they might do so, and perhaps will do so in the future. I also admit that it is imaginable that states on their own could move in this direction, although coordination with existing Social Security benefits for the disabled could be awkward. Nonetheless, a state's workers' compensation plan, for example, could be expanded to cover both non-work injuries and a worker's dependents. But the feasibility of certain state level solutions does not invalidate the legitimacy of a nationwide program any more than does the existence of private pension plans make Social Security illegitimate. If our society concludes that all Americans should have income security and health care protection against disabilities caused by accidents (or arising from other causes), I consider this to be a sound basis for congressional action.

Returning then to the possibility of a national accident compensation scheme (or even a broader plan), two more points need emphasizing. First, such a reform should be seen as part of tort reform, whether or not tort law itself is in any way altered, simply because this reform would directly address a central function of tort law. That is, it would pay compensation to qualified plaintiffs who suffer wage loss and medical expenses, even though, of course, the class of those provided benefits would be much wider than that comprised of those who today could be successful tort plaintiffs.

Second, were a social insurance scheme of this sort adopted by Congress it would in any event become essential then at least to decide what the implications, if any, should be for tort law itself. Several approaches are possible. Congress could simply provide the new social insurance benefit and leave it to states to determine how to blend their own tort law with the new program. States could, for example, allow double recovery or, more likely, could reduce the benefits that victims could obtain by the amount to which they are entitled under the new federal plan.

Congress might also take a more active stance. For example, it might order states to abandon the common law rule on collateral sources and preclude tort plaintiffs from collecting damages already covered by the federal plan. Or, on the contrary, Congress might provide that the new federal plan stands in the shoes of plaintiffs and is entitled to reimbursement from tortfeasors as a matter of law, precluding states from abandoning the collateral sources rule. This approach would presumably minimize direct federal costs and would arguably internalize costs of certain accidents into the activities that cause them. This is basically what Germany does today. It is a country with a strong first party social insurance scheme in which the social insurance providers retain a right of reimbursement from tort defendants and their liability insurers.

Of course, in order to engage in what some consider to be good social cost accounting, this approach would generate considerable transaction costs by shifting funds from the pocket of one insurer to another, and on that ground I have grave doubts about the wisdom of such a solution.

In any event, in contrast to the German approach, I want to put on the table an even bolder proposal on the other side. Along with the new national social insurance scheme, Congress might decide to abolish state tort actions for ordinary accident victims—perhaps retaining the right to sue for punitive damages for those who are victims of intentional misconduct.

This result would be justified first from a pragmatic perspective. With a comprehensive national plan in place of the sort I have discussed, there is simply no need to provide victims with tort damages. To be sure, this solution would deny victims recovery for pain and suffering damages as well. But that too might be justified. On the one hand it can be argued that these damages today go primarily to pay for legal fees and expenses which would be largely eliminated under the new plan. Moreover, it might also be argued that: (a) awards for pain and suffering are inappropriately given today by tort law to those victims with modest injuries who don't really have lasting pain and suffering; (b) the availability of such awards too often promotes fraudulent and exaggerated claims; and (c) because of practical realities, such awards are rarely provided to seriously injured people (since most tortfeasors who cause grave harm with their cars or weapons are either completely judgment proof or effectively so above modest automobile insurance liability policy limits of, for example, $50,000). Moreover, the new national social insurance scheme itself might provide some extra compensation to those who are seriously impaired or disfigured, as New Zealand has done.

Clearly, those who believe that tort law today effectively serves other important social functions besides victim compensation would be alarmed by this proposal. I have primarily in mind those who view tort law as predominantly serving either to deter careless conduct or to provide precise individual justice. To placate those with these outlooks, perhaps tort law has to remain in place as in Germany, even after the new national compensation plan is adopted. Indeed, some deterrence devotees might object to the compensation plan altogether. First, they might fear that some victims who, in their view, should sue to help keep up the deterrence pressure would choose not to do so. Second, they might worry that some victims would be more careless in their own conduct or slower to recover from an injury because of the availability of the plan's benefits.

Yet, maintaining the tort law remedy is not the only way to respond to these concerns. On the one hand, new behavior control mechanisms might be enacted along with the new social insurance plan. I have, for example, proposed a scheme of paying bounties to whistle-blowers who identify dangerous products before manufacturers themselves come forward and disclose those dangers. Others might favor promoting safer products through the compensation plan's funding mechanism, in the tradition of workers' compensation, as was long ago advocated by Professors Marc Franklin and Richard Pierce.

On the other hand, there are also routes to achieving victim satisfaction apart from maintaining tort remedies. These deserve consideration especially given the relatively low level of satisfaction that victims in fact seem to attach to today's tort liability regime. Ours is a system, after all, in which few plaintiffs ever actually win at trial. Instead, most obtain a compromised settlement award in a process typically marked by a lack of regular communication between the plaintiff's lawyer and the plaintiff and by minimal participation by the claimant in the settlement process. Moreover, individual wrongdoers are rarely directly punished by tort awards, as they are almost always paid, if at all, by insurance companies, enterprises, or governmental agencies. By contrast, in Japan, for example, where victims sue much less often, it has been worked out culturally that injurers (or top executives of firms that have caused injuries) come around and make what appear to be sincere apologies.

The main thing to see is that a new national accident compensation plan, perhaps coordinated with other national legislation, may well be viewed as simply incompatible with the maintenance of individual lawsuits for personal injuries.

Or, perhaps more pragmatically, Congress might decide that it was only fair to give defendants, especially business defendants, relief from state tort law in return for imposing on them the new costs of the expanded social insurance regime (assuming that at least some of the funding would come from expanded payroll taxes, for example). In other words, it might be concluded that a compensation plan minus tort is a better package on balance than tort with no compensation plan, putting aside the option of having both systems.

By this same way of thinking Congress might restrict state medical malpractice laws (or even state tort law generally) as part of the adoption of a national health insurance scheme. This is an issue that Congress would have had to resolve if President Clinton's health care reform proposals had been adopted.

A still different approach was embraced in the National Childhood Vaccine Injury Act of 1986 -- the only significant federal statute adopted in the past twenty-five years concerning personal injury law. There, for public health reasons, Congress stepped into a very narrow and special area of state tort law in order to assure a continued supply of children's vaccines after lawsuits at the state level drove some manufacturers from the field and the one or two that remained threatened to quit. A national compensation plan was created for children who, shortly following vaccination, can be shown to have certain listed health problems. It is not required to show an actual causal connection between the two. If found eligible for the program, the liberal benefits include medical care, future wage loss reimbursement if appropriate, and even up to $250,000 for pain and suffering. If a claimant doesn't like the fund's compensation offer, however, it may be rejected and the victim is then free to sue in tort in court. However, Congress insisted that in such cases, manufacturer fault has to be demonstrated (or that a defective batch of the vaccine was the source of the injury). In short, the state tort option is maintained, albeit somewhat modified in certain states by Congressional direction, but the victim must select between the two remedies. It is readily imaginable that this solution could be expanded by Congress to cover, for example, all cases of serious adverse reactions to pharmaceutical products, perhaps to medical treatment generally, or even to all accidental injuries.

C. Permitting or Encouraging State Level Experimentation

This analysis so far has assumed that if Congress is to act it would do so either by adopting some substantive tort law regime or by creating a compensation plan substitute for tort. But Congressional action need not necessarily come in the form of uniform national schemes. Instead Congress could aggressively encourage state-level experimentation, or at least pave the way for state experimentation by getting other existing federal rules out of the way. A few examples will illustrate the point.

I have been trying to get states to experiment with an employee benefit scheme that I call "short term paid leave." It would, among other things, replace tort law recovery for short term disabilities with a kind of mandated individual savings account. Employees would "earn" from their employer one paid leave day for, say, every five days worked. This paid leave bank could be drawn on to provide income during periods of temporary disability arising from accident or illness.

The account would also be used to fund vacation pay, paid public holidays, short term unemployment, etc. and would eliminate the payment of short term wage replacement benefits in workers' compensation. For our general purposes here, however, the most important thing about the proposal is that, if also combined with a state-wide health insurance scheme, it could provide the basis for eliminating a very large proportion of existing tort claims. But in order to enact the short term paid leave plan states would need waivers from federal unemployment compensation rules. And in order to adopt employer-based state health insurance programs, states would need Congress to waive the requirements of ERISA, the federal pension law, that preclude such legislation. In short, what I see as consumer-oriented state level changes, which would probably include tort law reform in the package, are being thwarted by existing federal controls.

A rather different example involves my idea for substituting what I call "pay at the pump no-fault auto insurance" for our traditional tort and liability insurance scheme. In this proposal auto accident victims would no longer make tort claims. Instead they would file first party (no-fault) claims with their own insurer. Funding of the insurance premium would come primarily from charges imposed at the time fuel is purchased (like gasoline taxes). Experimentation with this plan would be much more likely to occur were Congress to make certain modifications in the existing federal gasoline tax laws.

If state level programs like these were to gain widespread support among both business and consumer interests, then perhaps Congressional action enabling and promoting those experiments would indeed be forthcoming.

III. TORT REFORM PROPOSALS CURRENTLY BEFORE CONGRESS

The Republican "Contract with America" calls for tort reform at the national level, and as of this writing the House of Representatives has actually passed tort reform legislation. These proposed changes seem to me to be relatively marginal adjustments around the fringes of traditional tort law. The House bill would restrict tort damages in certain respects. Punitive damages would be limited in amount in all cases to the greater of $250,000 or three times economic loss, and pain and suffering awards would be limited to $250,000 in medical malpractice cases (but not in product liability cases). If one side rejected a settlement offer from the other side and later went on to do worse in court, that side would have to pay the legal fees and costs of the other side that had accrued since the offer was rejected. To protect "deep pocket" defendants, joint and several liability would be abolished for pain and suffering damages, although states could maintain it for economic loss if they wished. Finally, in quite a different vein, a 15 year statute of repose would apply to most product liability cases, thereby cutting off claims against old products.

Whatever else it is, this package of reforms is neither a comprehensive national product liability law nor a comprehensive national law of tort damages. Several bills now before the Senate are decidedly in this same spirit, although they differ in details. I do not mean to argue that the specific proposals are misguided; on the contrary I believe that at least some of them are on the right track, even though I would prefer a rather different package.

What is troubling, however, is that Congress is now acting like a state legislature in an area that has conventionally been left to actual state legislatures. In short, what is the point of this ad hoc central government activism, given that the overall ideology of the Contract with America appears to be much more oriented toward reviving state's rights?

Some explanations lie in basic politics, I suppose. Defense interests have been trying to get some sort of product liability reform through Congress for 20 years. They tend to be supporters of the Republicans. So, with their party now in power, the Republicans may feel a certain obligation to respond to the pressure of these constituents and set aside ideological consistency about federalism. In short, this legislative activity may be understood simply as repayment to important financial contributors to the new Republican controlled Congress. More broadly, like other provisions in the Contract With America, the most important thing may be the Republicans' ability to say to the voters "we said we would make change and we have," regardless of the actual content of the individual provisions. Under this analysis, the crucial thing is to explain why tort law reform got on the Contract in the first place, and the probable answer is that it was something that polls say Republicans generally like.

There is also a more cynical way to look at this Congressional activity. With the Republicans having a weaker position in the Senate and facing the threat of a Presidential veto, perhaps the congressional supporters of tort reform never really expected to pass reform legislation. Instead, these bills serve to allow Republicans to raise even more campaign contributions from a business community that hopes eventually to get its way. In the same vein, these bills may provide a good issue for Republican candidates to run on in the 1996 elections. This is reminiscent of President Reagan's continued talk in favor of "family values" along with the failure of his administration to do much to achieve federal policy changes in support of that talk.

It could be argued that these bills should be seen as a threat primarily designed to force states to act. This is perhaps a good way to understand the tort reform activities of the Reagan Administration which supported far more sweeping changes than those now before Congress. And whether or not the Reagan officials can fairly take credit for it, the fact is that most states did indeed soon thereafter adopt their own tort reform provisions. (Something similar occurred in the 1970s in the field of workers' compensation when threatened federal action was followed by considerable state level reform.)

But the very fact that most states have already engaged in tort reform in recent years makes it much less convincing to think about current Congressional activity as designed to push states to take tort reform seriously and do something about it. Indeed, a large number states have already restricted recovery for pain and suffering, tightened the rules covering punitive damages, cut back on joint and several liability, altered their rules on the payment of legal fees, and so on -- the very subjects of the proposed federal legislation.

To be sure, not every state has curtailed plaintiff rights, certainly not in all these areas. Maybe federal tort reform should be seen as achieving a mop-up of what the states started, spreading the "right" solutions everywhere. But this analysis is also highly problematic because the specific solutions contained in the House and Senate bills certainly do not reflect anything like a consensus among those who favor tort reform as to what exactly should be done in the areas covered. There is a great variety of opinion as to precisely how punitive damages and pain and suffering damages should be reduced, and there are widely differing views about just what protection to give to "deep pocket" defendants now subject to joint and several liability. These differences show up vividly in the tort reform provisions that states have already adopted. Hence, were Congress to adopt some version of the House and Senate bills it would be second guessing many states that have already acted from the same general outlook but have called the issue somewhat differently, perhaps disturbing the careful political alliance in individual states that allowed tort reform to be adopted on the terms it was.

In other words, it seems to me insulting for Congress, for example, to tell a state that: punitive damages must be proved by "clear and convincing" evidence; pain and suffering awards must be limited to $250,000 but only for medical malpractice cases; and there may be no joint and several liability at all when that state already has, for example, restricted punitive damages to "despicable" conduct, limited pain and suffering awards across the board to $500,000, and eliminated joint and several liability for any defendant that was less than 25% at fault. To re-emphasize the point, it would be one thing for a new state legislature to modify the old set of reforms to embrace those in the House bill, but there does not seem to be a principled justification for Congress to do this. So, although I am not saying that it would violate the Constitution for Congress to so act, it does seem inappropriate to do so.

Additional undesirable consequences would result if Congress engages in tort reform of the sort now being considered. Legislative action by Congress would emphatically undermine tort as a common law subject, thereby blunting certain opportunities for common law change. This is a situation, it seems to me, in which the symbolism of federal intrusion is great even if the actual statutory impact is not.

The evolution of tort law over the years has enjoyed a certain elegance that stems from the fact that change has not been so clearly a matter of raw political power, but rather the more subtle transformation of doctrinal rules to reflect changing social mores. Hence, I consider it no trivial loss to have that tradition cast aside cavalierly. Indeed, this sort of federal pre-emption seems especially off the mark because, at this very moment, recently appointed state court judges are using common law techniques to move tort law in a more pro-defendant direction. Furthermore, this is hardly a case in which Congress must act in order to provide relief for an interest group that is structurally blocked from the political process at the state level. In recent years, defense interests have enjoyed widespread success convincing state legislators to engage in tort reform, regardless of what sometimes appears to be the political might of the plaintiffs' bar.

Finally, it remains unclear what theory of tort law underlies the provisions of these bills. To be sure, restricting tort damages law by formula can have a pro-defendant impact. But the sharp reduction this brings in jury discretion seems fundamentally at odds with the administration of the fault theory of tort law favored by defense interests which relies upon the wisdom of the jury to come to the fair result on a case by case basis.

IV. CHANGING THE ROLE OF THE FEDERAL COURTS

As I explained earlier, "diversity" jurisdiction in federal courts exists in part to permit out-of-state defendants to escape local courts when they are sued by a local citizen. The right of removal to federal court is frequently used by defendants for the purpose of obtaining what they consider to be a somewhat less parochial forum, even if the substantive law applied to the case remains the same. However, as I noted already, because of today's "complete diversity" requirement, plaintiffs can often prevent removal to federal court by joining a second defendant in the case, such as a retailer, who is a citizen of the same state as is the plaintiff. Perhaps, then, out-of-state product-maker defendants might wish to redirect their efforts at reform by urging Congress to alter the rules governing diversity jurisdiction in order to provide them more assured access to the federal courthouse.

This line of thinking suggests that defense interests might want a broader role for federal courts than exists today. Yet, many defendants may have the opposite view. I have in mind now the apparently increasing involvement of federal courts in product liability cases brought as class actions. Although in some of these cases the defense forces the case into the federal forum, in others the plaintiffs initially file in federal court. The aspiration of the attorneys for the class is to bring about a nationwide solution to the problem—typically by engaging in sufficient pre-trial litigation to convince the defense that some sort of mass settlement is the best way to resolve the conflict. Then, payment arrangements for claimants are devised under the guidance of an active federal judge. This has occurred in several celebrated mass tort cases, such as the Agent Orange litigation, and seems to be what the plaintiffs' class action lawyers are counting on in the large scale breast implant and cigarette litigation currently pending.

To be sure, in some of these situations both sides may see mutual advantages in federal court litigation and a nationwide resolution. Yet, sometimes the defense might well have wanted to force plaintiffs to litigate piecemeal in state courts, perhaps hoping to discourage claims they consider to be without merit. In such cases, the development of the entrepreneurial federal judge who aggressively manages the matter is not really what the defense prefers.

Some federal judges must feel a great sense of satisfaction in presiding over settlements of immense and enormously complicated litigation that might otherwise have dragged on for years. Yet, these cases can also drain the very limited resources of the federal judiciary, taking up so much time and attention of a judge who would otherwise be moving forward with the local caseload. Furthermore, while these activist federal judges may be seen to be making the best of a terrible mess, the fact remains that a portion of the federal judiciary is being turned into a social welfare benefits distribution agency, a function for which other federal bodies, such as the Social Security Administration, seem better suited.

There is finally a certain irony about these mass tort cases that is worth noting. The managing judges seem to be applying what turns out to be a uniform national legal standard. That is, when they certify a national class and arrive at a nationwide settlement agreement, no attention appears to be paid to the vagaries of local law; claimants get the same settlement offer regardless of where they reside. The courts appear to justify this uniformity by giving unsatisfied claimants the opportunity to opt out of the settlement and sue locally. (Defendants, however, are not permitted to single out claimants for exclusion from the class based on their state of residence.) As a result, defendants in some of these mass injury cases are not altogether happy facing something of a uniform national tort law after all, and might favor Congressional action to decrease the role of federal judges in tort litigation.

For now I merely raise these matters without trying to resolve them. My point here is simply that, instead of seeking federal tort reform directly, defense interests might be better advised to press Congress to rethink the jurisdiction of federal courts—a plainly proper subject for national legislation.

Chapter 5

Governors Can Change the Direction of Tort Law with their Judicial Appointments

At one time it was conventionally thought that the common law should be seen as akin to the law of physics in the sense that, through the application of logic and the scientific method, one could discover what the correct answer was to a newly presented legal issue. Common law judges, in this vision, were to be understood as more like scientists than political actors who imposed their values and policy choices through the exercise of the power that comes with their office. This outlook was rejected by "realist" thinking in the early part of the 20th century. Today, it is widely agreed that common law courts "make" law, rather than "find" the law.

But if the application of logic and the careful analysis of prior opinions are not by themselves sufficient to determine the outcome of torts cases brought before courts, how are those cases to be decided? The answer, oversimplifying considerably, lies in politics. What are the political and ideological views of the judges? This does not mean that judges are simplistically pro-victim or pro-defendant and so will always predictably decide torts cases in favor of plaintiffs or injurers. For one thing, so long as there is tort law, then, as explained in Chapters 1 and 2, even conservatives, who might be thought to be pro-business and pro-defendant in their leaning, will want certain clear wrongdoers to take responsibility for the harm they cause to others by being held liable in tort. So, too, even liberals who might be thought to be pro-victim will sometimes concede that, under tort law, this victim is not deserving of compensation from this defendant.

Moreover, while judges are political actors, they come from the ranks of lawyers and they have been taught to "think like lawyers," which, in this context means they have formed a view of what the purpose of tort law is and how it should be implemented. Trial judges and intermediate courts of appeal judges have some discretion to put their own views of the purpose tort law into play in the cases before them. State Supreme Court justices have far more discretion. To be sure, even the latter are understandably concerned about the legitimacy of the institution they represent, and so they do not want to appear reckless or ridiculous in the eyes of either the lawyers who come before them or the public at large. This, together with a concern about either creating judicial chaos or bringing upon themselves an overwhelming amount of work, means that most justices are faithful to the common law ideal of *stare decisis* – the at least somewhat binding nature of the Court's prior decisions. But it is widely understood that a state's highest court may properly overthrow (or neatly distinguish) a prior common law decision if following that earlier case or the path it laid down would yield a result that the justices believe is ill suited to contemporary circumstances. The upshot is that tort doctrine, as noted in Chapter 3, has changed considerably over the past 100 years.

In recent times, there has been a sharp division in the academy, spilling over to some in the judiciary, as to just what work tort law is supposed to do. As noted in Chapters 1 and 2, some liberals have seized upon the fundamentally conservative nature of tort law and embraced its broad features as a mechanism for a much greater shifting of losses from personal injury victims to those enterprises that have injured them or failed to protect them from harm (as well as to defendants in general, who are seen as readily able to deal with victim's losses through liability insurance).

This "modern" thinking is well reflected in the writings of Professor (later Dean and Judge) Guido Calabresi. In his book "The Cost of Accidents" (1970) and later writings, Calabresi (following a line of earlier scholarship by Yale Law School colleague Fleming James) promoted what, as a practical matter, meant the far wider application of "enterprise liability." Writing from what we would today call a "law and economics" perspective, Calabresi invited readers (scholars, students and judges) to impose liability on the party that sensibly appeared to be the "cheapest cost avoider." This would be the party, as between the relevant classes of injurers and victims, who is most likely best positioned to have avoided the accident in the first place, or if that was not practical, then who is most likely best positioned to widely spread the loss so that it is not crushingly felt by a single party. Most of the time, the application of the "cheapest cost avoider" way of thinking pointed in the direction of defendant liability.

Notice carefully the instrumental nature of this way of thinking about the accident problem. The social goal here is not to reach some highly individualized determination of who should fairly bear the cost of the accident. Rather, it is to put in place a mechanism that, while trying to minimize the costs of administration, will promote both greater safety (or as Calabresi put it, an "optimal" level of safety) and a more widespread distribution of the loss. To be sure, in some cases that meant victims themselves should take responsibility for preventing the injury (and arranging in advance for insurance if the harm were to occur anyway). But most of the time the Calabresian way of thinking pointed to what many have termed "enterprise liability."

But Calabresi's way of thinking by no means swept the field. First, other law and economics scholars, while agreeing with the social goals that Calabresi advanced, saw them best realized in the careful application of traditional negligence law principles (rather than Calabresi's more rule-of-thumb approach that as a practical matter was much more analogous to strict liability). Second, other scholars and many judges concluded that Calabresi's way of thinking would lead to the imposition of liability on defendants who in the particular case had not done anything wrong and would be unfairly be treated if held liable in tort. And unfairness to defendants was a value that weighed heavily with them – at least with respect to those sorts of defendants who were otherwise viewed as importantly contributing to America's economic success (i.e. enterprises).

This clash of views has clearly played out in the torts decisions of the California Supreme Court, which are the focus of this chapter. During the period between, say, 1963 and 1986, the California Supreme Court was widely viewed as the leading court in the nation with regard to tort law, and it was clearly seen as the leading court in shifting tort law in the pro-plaintiff direction (a role subsequently taken over by the New Jersey Supreme Court). Countless earlier California decisions that had favored defendants were slowly and sometimes abruptly cast aside. New issues that had never been presented to courts before were routinely resolved in ways that favored victims. Many in the academy lauded these decisions as finally getting tort law right, freeing the law from many of its unduly harsh doctrinal constraints. Berkeley Law's Dean William Prosser, the leading doctrinal torts scholar of the second half of the twentieth century, not only praised many of these decisions, in many cases these decisions actually adopted positions Prosser had earlier taken in his scholarship (and to some extent in his role as the chief Reporter for the Second Restatement of Torts on behalf of the ALI).

While Calabresi's "least cost avoider" approach was not explicitly embraced by the California Supreme Court, his general outlook was clearly influential in guiding the justices in their openly policy-oriented reasoning that was grounded in a pro-victim and enterprise liability way of thinking. This point is demonstrated in the first part of this chapter by a review of the personal injury decisions decided by the California Supreme Court during the last three years in which Rose Bird served as Chief Justice (1984-1986).

In fall 1986, however, in a highly contested election California voters refused to retain the Chief and two of her very liberal colleagues. This, plus retirements, created a dramatic change in the composition of the Court. Before the retention election, six of the seven justices had been appointed by Democratic governors (five by Jerry Brown and one by his father and prior governor Pat Brown). By March, 1987, five of the seven justices sitting on the Court had been appointed by Republican Governor George Duekmejian, and in the period up until 1998 covered by this chapter the Court's composition was almost entirely made up of appointees of Duekmejian or his successor Republican governor Pete Wilson.

Since then the California Supreme Court has continued to be dominated by Republican appointees, including those appointed by Governor Arnold Schwartzenegger. Democrat Governor Gray Davis who served from 1999-2003 and was then "recalled" by the voters appointed but one justice. Current California Governor Jerry Brown, who is back after a long time away for second stint, has so far made one appointment (Berkeley Law Professor Goodwin Liu) and that was to replace Davis' appointment. Hence, between 1987 and 2014, at least five and often six of the seven justices have been Republican appointees.

This shift in 1987 in who appointed the justices was accompanied by a dramatic shift in California tort law. The Republican-appointed judges quickly established and maintained a strong pro-defendant outlook. This was manifested in two ways – the outright overturning of a number of high points of the Bird era and the refusal to continue on the Bird path when new issues presented themselves. It is clear from the new court that Calbresian and enterprise-liability thinking has been put aside.

This chapter was originally presented in 1999 at the Fifth Annual Clifford Symposium held at DePaul Law School in Chicago, and published as Stephen D. Sugarman, "Judges as Tort Law Un-Makers: Recent California Experience With 'New' Torts", 49 DePaul Law Review 455-488 (1999) and is reprinted with permission of the journal.

The theme of that year's Clifford Symposium was Judges as Tort Lawmakers. In this chapter, two overall themes are presented. First, as already described, the dramatic shift from Democratic-appointed to Republican-appointed justices on the California Supreme Court was accompanied by a sharp move in tort law from pro-plaintiff to pro-defendant outcomes. Second, it was not only doctrinal shifts that occurred. The Bird court not only made new law, it also struck down old legal rules under which judges had decided cases in favor of defendants as a matter of law (without cases ever getting to juries). The Bird Court shifted many of these decisions away from judges and turned them over to juries – to be decided by having juries apply general "reasonableness" standards to the facts before them. This move was, in a sense, the "unmaking" of the law of torts.

The post-Bird Court did the opposite. It "unmade" the law by overturning prior decisions. But at the same time it also "made" law by re-establishing many "rules" that returned decision-making to trial judges in ways that once again allowed them to decide cases as a matter of law before allowing juries to consider them.

JUDGES AS TORT LAW UN-MAKERS: RECENT CALIFORNIA EXPERIENCE WITH "NEW" TORTS

A straightforward reading of the title captures my central point: in the past dozen years the California Supreme Court has repealed many provisions of tort law that had been adopted by the court in earlier years. The fundamental reason for this turnabout is a change in court personnel with liberal Democrats, led by Chief Justice Rose Bird, generally replaced with moderate or conservative Republicans. I do not dwell on this readily understandable political explanation for the change in the law.

My goals are first, simply to document the extent of the retreat from the court's previously pro-plaintiff inclination. Those who have not been following the court may no longer recognize the California Supreme Court they thought they once knew.[1] Second, in the process of describing this u-turn, I emphasize the extent to which the new court has rejected some basic outlooks held by the old court on what tort law of the late twentieth-century was supposed to be about.[2]

Finally, I demonstrate an ironic sense in which the new court is creating some "new" torts.[3] The old court tended to eliminate law, in the sense of overturning defense oriented "rules" and separate legal "doctrines." The new court, at least in several areas, is doing the opposite by embracing "new" (or older) rules. Hence, in some important respects, it is re-establishing a tort "law" that removes power from juries and returns it to judges (and also tilts in favor of defendants). In light of this shift, one may read my title quite differently: it was the old court that un-made law and the new one that is making it.

For this study, I examined the California Supreme Court's *personal injury law* decisions for the past fifteen years (1984-1998), and uncovered approximately fifty cases of at least moderate importance -- an average of about three per year. I excluded from the study cases involving only property damage, economic loss, defamation and privacy, insurance policy interpretation, as well as others not squarely concerned with physical injuries. No doubt other scholars would add or exclude some cases from my category (or wish I had bounded the category differently), but I am confident that most torts professors would basically agree that I have captured the court's important personal injury law decisions of the past fifteen years. To make one thing clear at the outset, I do not mean generally to endorse or oppose the stance of either the old or the new court.

I. 1984-1986 THE END OF THE BIRD ERA

At the start of my study period, the court's membership included five appointees of Democratic Governor Jerry Brown and one appointee of his father, Democratic Governor Pat Brown.4 Soon the seventh position was filled by the new Republican Governor George Deukmejian.5 Only these justices (apart from an occasional temporarily appointed justice) heard and decided the cases handed down in the first three years of my study period. I think it fair to characterize a majority of the justices during this initial period as broadly pro-plaintiff in their approach to tort law; this is especially true of then Chief Justice Bird.

Nine of the approximately fifty cases in my study come from the last three years of the Bird era 1984-1986. Taken as a whole, these decisions reveal a court very willing to expand tort liability for modern policy reasons-primarily that defendants are well-positioned both to protect the public from harm and, when harm does occur, to bear the burden of compensation by spreading losses through liability insurance and/or via the prices they charge for what they sell.

A. Background

This pro-plaintiff outlook was not new to the court in 1984. It is more accurate to say that, by 1984, it was well entrenched. The California Supreme Court's embrace of modern policy reasons in support of defendant tort liability is perhaps best traced to two famous opinions from prior eras. The first is Justice Traynor's 1944 concurring opinion in *Escola v. Coca Cola Bottling Co. of Fresno,*[6] in which the former Berkeley law professor argued that a manufacturer should incur "an absolute liability when an article that he has placed on the market, knowing that it is to be used without inspection, proves to have a defect that causes injury to human beings."[7] Traynor openly rested his call for what we have come to term "strict product liability" on a variety of policy considerations, including safety promotion and loss spreading.[8] Traynor was still on the court nearly twenty years later when his views about the proper legal treatment of defective products were unanimously embraced in *Greenman v. Yuba Power Products, Inc*.[9]

The second famous opinion I have in mind is that of Justice Peters on behalf of the court in 1968 in *Rowland v. Christian.*[10] There, the California Supreme Court overthrew the ancient common law regime that based liability for injuries incurred by those on one's property upon the status of the victim-trespasser, licensee, or invitee.[11] Not only did the court usher in a new era in which these cases would be decided under basic negligence principles, but also it based the change in the law upon its balancing of a series of considerations (which I call here the *"Rowland* factors") that plainly included modern policy reasons:

> the foreseeability of harm to the plaintiff, the degree of certainty that the plaintiff suffered injury, the closeness of the connection be- tween the defendant's conduct and the injury suffered, the moral blame attached to the defendant's conduct, the policy of preventing future harm, the extent of the burden to the defendant and consequences to the community of imposing a duty to exercise care with resulting liability for breach, and the availability, cost, and prevalence of insurance for the risk involved.[12]

As a doctrinal matter, the *Rowland* decision still grounds occupier liability in the fault system and not strict liability; yet, the final three considerations on its list of factors to be addressed clearly reflected the thinking of those scholars in the era who were arguing for what has generally been termed "enterprise liability."

Perhaps the most important contribution to that scholarly literature is Guido Calabresi's now famous 1970 book called *The Costs of Accidents.* In this and other writings, Calabresi argued against conventional tort law-which he identified with the practice of making a careful inquiry in every case as to whether this particular defendant could reasonably have prevented this particular victim's injury-what one might call "retail" decisionmaking.[14] Calabresi favored, instead, what I call "wholesale" decision making. One should rather ask whether, in general, for the type of injury involved, defendants or plaintiffs are more likely to be best positioned to know about the risks and to take precautions designed to avoid the accident -- a search for what Calabresi called the "cheapest cost avoider."[15] Although the costs of some accidents might fall on victims under this approach, it was clear that commercial and governmental actors (i.e., defendants) would far more often be deemed cheaper cost avoiders than individual victims would be.[16] Moreover, in deciding on whom to place the costs of accidents, Calabresi further argued that one should consider whether defendants or plaintiffs were more likely to be best able to spread the loss, and in particular, to spread the loss in a way that connected the cost to the type of accident involved.[17] This latter inquiry almost always would point towards injurer liability.

In the thirty years since Calabresi presented his ideas, no state supreme court has fully and openly embraced them, even though some courts occasionally use the phrase "cheapest cost avoider."[18]

Nonetheless, I believe that the safety promotion and loss spreading considerations he so well-articulated, factors that would lead to "enterprise liability" in most circumstances, substantially influenced the California Supreme Court throughout the 1970s and for so much of the 1980s as Justice Bird sat on the court.

This influence is well reflected, I believe, in the nine cases I examined from the last three years of the Bird era. Seven of those nine decisions were won by plaintiffs in decisions that expanded tort law in the plaintiffs' direction. Plaintiffs lost two cases and in both of them Chief Justice Bird objected to the majority's opinion on the ground that the court failed to broaden the application of the principle of strict products liability to cover the facts at issue. The seven plaintiff victories all involved efforts to hold defendants responsible for injuries suffered either on the defendants' properties or from use of the defendants' properties. And the reasoning throughout has a decidedly Calabresian bent.

In the next sections, I will briefly describe these three years of decisions, both to provide some doctrinal details and to give the gist of the court's thinking. I have grouped the cases under three headings.

B. Responsibility for the Wrongdoing of Others

Five of the cases, taken together, may be seen to have consolidated California law around what some might call a "new" tort: you must take reasonable precautions with respect to your property to protect victims from foreseeable wrongdoing by third parties. One way to understand this group of cases is that the court concluded that it would lend its hand to the crime-fighting effort of the day by enlisting property owners in the battle through the threat of tort liability.

The first case involved a "key in the ignition," a problem the court first addressed in 1954 in *Richards v. Stanley.*[19] Back then, the court was unsympathetic to the victim's claim against the vehicle owner when an unauthorized third party took the vehicle and injured the plaintiff. In addition to the fact that the owner in *Richards* had not left his vehicle in a particularly dangerous area, the court seemed to focus on the victim's need to look to the driver, not the car's owner, for recompense.[20]

As a practical matter, however, owners, who usually carry vehicle insurance, are much more likely to be able to provide victim compensation than an unauthorized driver, who might well be a teenage joy-rider. Moreover, through the simple precaution of taking the keys away, the driver/owner might easily forestall the injury in the first place. Ten years later, the court began carving out exceptions to *Richards,* starting with *Hergenrether v. East.*[21] There, the court allowed the jury to impose liability where the "special circumstances" of the case made the defendant's conduct foreseeably quite dangerous.[22]

The court returned to the "key in the ignition" problem in 1984 in *Palma v. U.S. Industrial Fasteners, Inc.*[23] The plaintiff claimed that the owner left a commercial truck overnight in a high crime industrial area, unlocked, with the key in the ignition, and that the truck was then stolen and carelessly driven by a third party who ran over the plaintiff. The court pointed to several specific allegations, including the type of people who frequented the area where the truck had been left and the difficulty of safely operating the vehicle, in finding that the defendant should not have been granted a summary judgment and that the plaintiff had a right to have the case heard by the jury.[24]

Although the court did not overrule *Richards* outright and continued to talk in terms of the "special circumstances" noted in *Hergenrether,* the opinion makes clear that, as a practical matter, legal analysis of this type of accident was to be brought inside the core of basic negligence law. As the court put it, the factual issue for the jury was simply "whether the circumstance in which [the defendant's] truck was left created a foreseeable risk of harm that was unreasonable and thus imposed on [the defendant] a duty of care to prevent harm to third persons by refraining from creating that risk."[25]

This application of general negligence principles to cases where a third party uses the defendant's vehicle to harm the victim was made even more explicit in a second "key in the ignition" case decided at nearly the end of the Bird era. In *Ballard v. Uribe,* [26] the plaintiff offered proof that the defendant knew that his vehicle, an aerial lift, was in need of repair and quite dangerous to use in its existing condition. Yet, according to the victim's witnesses, the defendant left his lift with the keys in the ignition in a place where others could readily gain access to it. Sure enough, the lift was operated by an unknowing co- worker of the plaintiff, and when the basket flipped backwards because of the broken condition of the lift, the plaintiff, who had been in the basket, was thrown out and hurt.[27] The court held that the defendant had a duty to protect others from the operation of its vehicle by third parties.28 It argued that, given the dangers involved, holding an owner liable for negligently failing to control the unauthorized use of his vehicle benefitted public safety without imposing an undue burden on the owner.[29]

In a separate opinion, Chief Justice Bird called for the outright overruling of *Richards.*[30] Although the court concluded that this was not the "occasion to consider the continued vitality of *Richards," 31* I believe that, by the time the court is through with *Ballard,* owners have a general duty, because the vehicles belong to them, to exercise due care to protect victims from injury caused by unauthorized third party use of those vehicles. The jury is to bring to bear, in the specific case, considerations of the size of the risk and the burden of precautions.[32] The court also made clear that in its deliberations a jury can readily find that, since the burden is so small, an owner may be held liable for leaving his or her keys in the ignition-provided that the circumstances in which the vehicle was left portend significant danger.[33]

Turning now to three other cases involving injuries caused by third party wrongdoers (this time on the defendant's property), we again see the Bird Court brushing aside specific legal requirements of earlier case law. Instead, as with the "key in the ignition" cases, the court embraces the general idea that with the ownership of property comes the duty to protect persons on the property, even from the danger of third party criminals. A breach of that duty depends, in turn, on an individualized determination by the jury in each case of whether a reasonable owner would have taken the specific precaution that the victim identifies as lacking.

First came *Peterson v. San Francisco Community College District,*[34] which involved an attempted daytime rape in the parking lot area of the defendant's campus. The student plaintiff alleged that there had been similar attacks in that region of campus that the defendant should have warned her about and that the defendant should have trimmed foliage growing near the stairway where the attack occurred. The court overturned the trial court and held these allegations sufficient to support a claim for "maintaining a dangerous condition of public property" under section 835 of the California Tort Claims Act.[35]

In *Peterson,* the court put aside earlier cases like *Hayes v. State of California*[36] which generally held that third party conduct does not constitute a "dangerous condition" for which a public entity may be held liable.[37] In *Hayes,* where two young men were attacked on a university beach at night, the court applied modern policy analysis in reaching its pro-defendant result. It worried that imposing tort liability could lead to the closure of public facilities, and it belittled the benefits of warnings about crime when the public was already well aware of the risk of violent crime "particularly in unlit and little used places."[38]

But in *Peterson,* the court openly applied the earlier-quoted *Rowland* factors in the other direction, now finding it wholly appropriate for the defendant to have a duty to protect its students from the criminal wrongdoing of third parties.39 Emphasizing that the plaintiff had been attacked in a much-used place in broad daylight, the court now argued that warnings would be very beneficial. Adopting what I would call Calabresian analysis, the court said that, "as a community college district responsible for overseeing the campus, the defendant and its agents are in a superior position to know about the incidences of crime and to protect against any recurrences."[40]

Next in this line came *Isaacs v. Huntington Memorial Hospital,*[41] in which a doctor sustained injuries when shot by an unknown assailant in the defendant hospital's parking lot. The case focused on the plaintiff's claim that the defendant hospital should have provided increased security measures in that parking lot. Precisely at issue was whether, in deciding the question of the defendant's duty of care, the court should apply the "prior similar incidents" test that had been required by several previous lower court decisions.[42]

Once again the court applied the *Rowland* factors and concluded that the jury should decide whether or not to impose liability based upon the "totality of the circumstances."43 As the court put it, limiting liability to instances of "prior similar incidents" on the defendant's property violated public policy by discouraging landowners from taking precautions and denying recovery to the first victim.[44] By contrast, because the danger in this case was clearly foreseeable (the hospital was in a high crime area and thefts and threatened assaults had occurred nearby) and the burden on the hospital of providing adequate security was comparatively low (two lights in the lot where the assault occurred were not working and a security guard and TV camera were used to monitor another of the hospital's lots), the court concluded that the "value to the community of imposing such a duty is manifest."[45]

Finally, in *Lopez v. Southern California Rapid Transit District,*[46] the court held that, under California Civil Code Section 2100, a publicly- owned, common carrier could be liable for injuries sustained when a fight broke out on one of its buses.[47] Based on the accepted general duty of common carriers to their passengers, the court determined that the carrier could meet its duty with respect to wrongdoing by others by, for example, stopping the bus, requesting the disruptive passengers to desist or leave, or alerting police.[48] Such precautions would provide considerable public safety while imposing a minimal burden on the carrier. Again, using what I would call Calabresian analysis, the court emphasized the crowded and confining nature of buses and that "passengers have no control over who is admitted on the bus and, if trouble arises, are wholly dependent upon the bus driver to summon help or provide a means of escape."[49] The court went on to say that "[t]hese characteristics of buses are, at the very least, conducive to outbreaks of violence between passengers and at the same time significantly limit the means by which passengers can protect themselves from assaults by fellow passengers."[50]

To be sure, the California Supreme Court had earlier broken new ground in holding defendants responsible for the wrongdoing of third parties because of their relationship to either the victim or the third party. For example, that is the general principle underlying cases like *Tarasoff v. Regents of the University of California,*[51] holding therapists potentially responsible for harms caused by their patients, and *Johnson v. State of California,*[52] holding state officials potentially liable for harms caused by foster children to their foster parents. The five newer cases I have described from 1984-1986 may be seen to have extended the prior doctrine by seeing the legal duty as arising from the defendant's relationship, not to a person, but to his property.

Another way to see these newer cases is as an extension of *Rowland* itself. The five cases from 1984-1986 expanded the *Rowland* rule so that it applies, not only to dangers emanating from the property itself, but also to dangers connected to the property that are created by third parties. One may argue the results in these cases from 1984-1986 were readily predictable from yet two other earlier California Supreme Court *cases-Coulter v. Superior Court*[53] and *Weirum v. RKO General, Inc.*[54]

Coulter imposed tort duties on social hosts who serve alcoholic beverages to guests who then become drunk and carelessly injure others. Hence, the court there arguably based one's legal responsibility on the connection between your property (your booze) and the wrongdoing of third parties.[55] *Coulter* was subsequently overturned by legislation.[56] *Weirum,* following *Rowland,* suggested that an individualized jury determination about risk-taking and prevention might apply to all tort cases cast in negligence, with specific legal rules largely dropping out of the picture. There, the court said that the defendant radio station could be held liable for the misconduct of others who were enticed into their misconduct by the unreasonably dangerous advertising the station ran (awarding prizes to those who were first to physically find an on-the-move disc jockey).[57]

Given these various earlier decisions, I do not want to make too much of the idea that the five cases I have just discussed from 1984-1986 really do establish a "new" tort. I am confident, however, that they show the court at work as "lawmaker" candidly examining and relying upon policy reasons for expanding the reach of tort doctrine in various circumstances.

C. *Strict Liability for Product Injuries*

As I mentioned at the start, the California Supreme Court in *Greenman* had already imposed strict liability on their manufacturers for defective products. Indeed, it had subsequently extended the principle to cover others involved in the marketing chain, such as retailers[58] and lessors.[59] One case from the 1984-1986 period took a giant step in further expanding strict product liability by applying it to landlords. In two other cases, both involving pharmaceutical drugs, the court declined to further expand products liability. Chief Justice Bird dissented in both cases, emphasizing the same policy reasons that drove the court's other decisions from this era.

By imposing strict liability for defects in the condition of rental units, *Becker v. IRM Corp.*[60] was perhaps the most venturesome of any of the court's decisions during the 1984-1986 period. The case involved a tenant falling against a glass shower door which shattered, severely lacerating his arm.[61] The court held the landlord strictly liable for the injury-treating the door, in effect, as a defective product because it was made of a type of glass prone to shattering.[62] The court characterized this as a sensible and reasonably logical extension of its earlier applications of strict liability for products. Just as parties involved in the distribution of products are in a better position than consumers to prevent and carry the burden of harm, landlords were seen to be in a better position than tenants to carry the burden of inspection and the cost of injuries. In an openly Calabresian way, the court opined "[t]he cost of protecting tenants is an appropriate cost of the enterprise" and "the landlord ... may be able to adjust rents to reflect such costs."[63]

Two other cases from this era also concerned product liability, both involving pharmaceutical drugs. In its earlier decisions, the California Supreme Court seemed determined to expand the principle of strict liability to cover more than manufacturing defects. Even for products manufactured as intended, the court consistently emphasized that California had left negligence principles behind.[64]

Nonetheless, as scholars and other courts soon discovered, it was not obvious what a design or warning defect could be if there were no negligence with respect to the product's design or warning. Put differently, if a court truly rejected negligence in those settings, would it require anything more than the fact that someone was injured? If not, that would seem to equate "defect" with "cause." One set of cases concerns dangers that are revealed only after the time of manufacture. Imposing strict liability would mean judging knowledge about the danger at the time of trial rather than at the time of manufacture. This same approach could be applied to newly dis- covered technological developments, which, if judged as of the time of trial instead of the time of manufacture, would also impose strict liability. Earlier, the California Supreme Court seemed to head down this "hindsight" route in *Barker v. Lull Engineering Co., Inc.* [65]

It was not clear, however, just why liability should fall on these manufacturers and not on others whose products caused harm but did not experience technological advancements or newly revealed knowledge between the time of manufacture and the time of trial. Moreover, some commentators began to express concern that this hindsight approach would impose inappropriate, uncertain, and potentially crippling liability on manufacturers of products of great social value, such as pharmaceutical drugs.[66] They pointed out that Dean Prosser himself had sought, in comment k to Section 402A of the *Restatement (Second) of Torts,* to preclude liability for socially valuable, but unavoidably unsafe, products like prescription drugs.[67]In *Finn v. G.D. Searle & Co.,*[68] the first of two prescription drug cases from the end of the Bird era, the victim suffered visual damage from a drug which was later determined to be harmful. Following a jury verdict for the defendants, the plaintiff appealed.[69] The court, however, was able to duck the question of whether to apply hindsight- based strict liability to the case because it was clear to the majority that the plaintiff's trial theory was based upon the claim that the defendant knew, or should have known, of the drug's danger at the time the plaintiff took it -- a negligence-based notion. On that theory, the court concluded that the plaintiff had a fair hearing by the jury.[70]

Chief Justice Bird disagreed with the court, arguing for the application of strict liability. She emphasized that the policies underlying strict liability in general-deterring poor manufacturing, design, testing, and compensating victims by imposing the cost of injury on the party best positioned to pay-apply equally well to prescription drugs as to other products to which the court had extended strict liability.[71] Bird cited the serious injuries caused by defective drugs, as well as the large numbers of consumers who take them with minimal awareness of possible risks, arguing that a drug manufacturer is in a better position to absorb the costs of injury. According to Bird, a drug manufacturer should be strictly liable whenever a drug fails to meet ordinary consumer safety expectations, or to provide a benefit that greatly out- weighs its risk.[72] Explicitly embracing the hindsight test, Bird advocated basing the manufacturer's knowledge on the information available at the time of trial, not at the time of manufacture.[73]

The second pharmaceutical drug case, *Murphy v. E.R. Squibb & Sons, Inc.,*[74] went against a plaintiff (4-3) who sought to hold her pharmacist strictly liable for providing her with a harmful drug. Although some commentators had earlier proposed extending strict liability from products to services, and although some courts began crossing the line into what appeared to be hybrid product-service cases, the California Supreme Court, having just taken one large step in imposing strict liability on landlords in *Becker,* refused to take the next giant step in *Murphy.*[75] Instead, the court analogized a pharmacist's role of dispensing drugs to a service like manufacturing blood plasma which was protected against strict liability by Section 1606 of the California Health and Safety Code.[76] The court also relied on policy grounds, stating that "if pharmacies were held strictly liable for the drugs they dispense, some of them, to avoid liability, might restrict availability by refusing to dispense drugs which pose even a potentially remote risk of harm, although such medications may be essential to the health or even the survival of patients" or by selecting "the more expensive product made by an established manufacturer when he has a choice of several brands of the same drug."[77]

Chief Justice Bird, joined by Justices Broussard and Kaus, dissented, finding that the pharmacist's role as salesman predominates his or her role as service provider.[78] Moreover, she argued, in Calabresian style, that applying strict liability to pharmacists would serve all the policies served by strict liability in general-by encouraging the pharmacist to take precautions, as well as preventing the individual unlucky patient from having to bear the financial burden of his or her own injuries.[79]

Summing up these product liability decisions, many would say that *Becker* established a "new" tort. In any event, what I see is a court carefully considering new policy proposals put before it in the products liability area, and deciding, much like a legislature, whether it would, on balance, be wise to sharply expand defendant responsibility. One large step in that direction was taken and two other steps were put off, at least for the time being.

D. Responsibility for the Negligent Infliction of Emotional Distress

The remaining case from the end of the Bird era that I will discuss involved the negligent infliction of emotional distress ("NIED") upon a family member based on harm occurring to a child. The California Supreme Court broke ground on NIED claims nearly twenty years earlier in *Dillon v. Legg,*[80] which allowed recovery in certain circumstances by those who witness a close relative's harm. *Ochoa v. Superior Court*[81] was one of several cases that had come before the California courts since then, asking the court to determine the boundaries of an NIED cause of action. In *Ochoa,* the Bird Court liberalized the boundary by allowing a mother to recover for the emotional distress she suffered when watching her son deteriorate from the lack of proper medical attention while he was held in a juvenile hall infirmary.[82]

Before *Ochoa,* however, an NIED claim seemed to require a "sudden occurrence" of harm; the court now concluded that such a requirement "arbitrarily limits liability when there is a high degree of foreseeability of shock to the plaintiff and the shock flows from an abnormal event, and, as such, unduly frustrates the goal of compensation -- the very purpose which the cause of action was meant to further."[83] Hence, *Ochoa* portended the possibility that, a la *Rowland,* injuries might soon decide all NIED cases on a case-by-case basis in terms of the foreseeability of harm under the specific circumstances.

E. Overall

As noted already, the seven plaintiff victories in the 1984-1996 period generally reflect Calabresi's ideas. *Becker,* which extended strict liability to landlords for defective shower doors, surely does. Landlords, more than new tenants, are plainly better positioned to know and do something about replacing dangerous shower doors and other dangerous conditions in the apartment. In any event, through rent, landlords can spread across all tenants the cost of inevitable accidents from shower door injuries to unlucky victims.

Although couched in the language of negligence law, I think cases like *Lopez, Isaacs,* and *Peterson* also reflect this Calabresian outlook. These commercial or governmental property owners and operators are much better positioned than individual victims to take precautions to prevent injury by third-party wrongdoers. These property owners can also spread the cost of accidents over the prices they charge for their activities, whether it is for bus fares, parking lot fees, or college tuition.

To be sure, victims in these sorts of cases were supposed to prove that the proposed safety precautions were not only feasible, but would really have made a difference -- the sort of retail decision making that Calabresi opposed. This evaluation, of course, was to be made by jurors -- participants who, at the time, many observers suspected were all too willing to impose costs on corporate and governmental defendants without being too picky about the subtleties of tort law's fault requirement.

This point leads me to another over-arching theme. Writing in the early 1970s, Harry Kalven, in many respects an ideological opponent to Calabresi, observed that tort law was becoming simplified and stream-lined.[84] Courts were tossing aside many of the old specific "rules" of tort law. *Rowland* was perhaps the most prominent example scuttling complex rules about the law of occupier liability to invitees, licensees, and trespassers.85 From all around the nation there were many other cases in this same vein-especially those that cast aside old "no duty" rules, including, for example, cases that eliminated so-called spousal immunity,[86] brushed aside automobile "guest statutes,"[87] and recognized rights of consortium in both spouses.[88] Kalven seemed to applaud this development, although he noted it was ironic that, just as minor irregularities and inconsistencies of tort law were being eliminated, there was developing an enormous inconsistency in tort law—with some domains governed by the fault principle and others by the principle of strict liability.[89]

The practical result of the elimination of many of these old rules (seen most clearly in the occupier liability area) was to transfer much power from judges to juries. To be sure, judges, at least in theory, could still grant summary judgments and directed verdicts in appropriate individual cases. But these hurdles were usually easy to jump, perhaps in part as a result of the increased sophistication of the plaintiff's bar and the growing availability of expert witnesses who would say just about anything. In short, the purification of the negligence regime increasingly meant that the law was what an individual group of jurors said it was. In its favor, this trend had, among other things, a kind of egalitarian spirit to it that well fit the thinking of many 1960s liberals.

Whether or not surreptitiously intended as a way of creating strict liability, many of the Bird Court's decisions I have discussed pushed California tort law in this "lawless" direction as well. This substitution of jury decision making for judge-applied legal rules is clearly seen in cases like *Ochoa,*[90] *Isaacs,*[91] and the "key in the ignition cases."[92]

Again, each generally moved those sorts of cases out of the hands of judges into the hands of juries.[93]

As an aside, there is one final case from this era that I cannot resist mentioning, even though it is outside my category. *Seaman's Direct Buying Service, Inc. v. Standard Oil of California*[94] capped an important series of earlier decisions by the California Supreme Court that viewed defendants as having abused their positions under contract law. These included employers who wrongfully discharged employees, insurers who wrongfully refused to pay valid claims, landlords who wrongfully evicted tenants, and so on.[95] *Seaman's* involved the wrongful refusal to acknowledge the existence of a contract.[96] Not wanting to limit victims to their conventional contract rights, the court adopted the "bad faith" concept that, when violated, constituted a tort, thereby providing victims with access to both compensatory pain and suffering damages and punitive damages.[97] Many would say this "bad faith" area of the law amounts to a "new" tort.

In sum, though perhaps not amounting to gigantic expansions of tort law, the California Supreme Court cases I have reviewed from the 1984-1986 period surely constitute definite extensions of the law. Even if not "new" torts, the pro-plaintiff decisions certainly represent the embracing of new legal duties, particularly for landlords, vehicle owners, and other property owners.

II. THE PAST TWELVE YEARS - THE POST-BIRD ERA

A. *The Voters Refuse to Retain*

Under California Law, the governor appoints supreme court justices, but the voters must later approve them for new terms in periodic "retention" elections.[98] Three pro-plaintiff judges, Chief Justice Bird and Associate Justices Reynoso and Grodin, came up for retention simultaneously in 1986. In a bitter election, fought in public primarily over "death penalty" issues, the voters rejected these justices and thereby removed them from the court. Other justices promptly replaced them, and with that came an abrupt change in the ideological stance of the court as a whole.

By March of 1987 the only Democratic-appointed justices left on the court were Justices Mosk and Broussard, and the latter retired in 1991. Today, Justice Mosk soldiers on having now served for thirty-five years since his appointment by Governor Pat Brown in 1964. By now, all but two of Governor Deukmejian's eight appointees have also left the bench, having been replaced by four appointees of Republican Governor Pete Wilson.

B. *Reversing Gears*

I have identified about forty personal injury decisions of the California Supreme Court from the past twelve years that I consider to be at least moderately important. Taken as a whole, they present a dramatically different picture from the one painted so far. Plaintiffs did not lose every one of these cases, but they lost most of them. Some decisions involved the court's refusal to expand tort law further.

Many involved retrenchment from earlier positions. Several cases openly overruled highly visible decisions of the Bird era.

Taken as a whole, the cases decided by the California Supreme Court in the past twelve years, in my judgment, reflect a very different outlook on tort law than we saw under Chief Justice Bird's leadership. First, although the court still faithfully rehearses the *Rowland* factors, it now frequently draws very different conclusions about the direction they point. Simply put, the court now broadly opposes the imposition of liability on a defendant on the grounds that he either is well positioned to spread the cost of the accident or, as a general matter, is probably better positioned to avoid the accident. In short, Calabresian "enterprise liability" thinking is out of favor with the court. Second, the court is now strongly inclined to reintroduce more detailed rules into tort law -- to take power back for judges and away from juries (and thereby to give defendants clearer ideas about just what their precise legal obligations are).

In this latter respect, we are confronted with the nice linguistic irony that I noted at the outset: as the court has been cutting back on the reach of tort law, it has made much new law in the sense of substituting "rules" for "jury discretion."[99] These are the main themes I will illustrate as I skate over approximately forty personal injury law decisions of the California Supreme Court since 1986. As in Part I, my analysis groups these more recent cases under several headings.

C. Taking Responsibility for the Mis-Conduct of Others

As before, I will start with the issue of taking responsibility for the wrongdoing of third parties. Here, in two important decisions, the California Supreme Court has sharply shifted gears by taking a strong pro-defendant stance.

In *Ann M. v. Pacific Plaza Shopping Center,*[100] an employee in the defendant's shopping center, who had been raped by a stranger, charged that the defendant was negligent in not providing security guards. As Justice Mosk emphasized in his dissent, the court essentially scuttles the "totality of the circumstances" test of *Isaacs* and resurrects the "prior similar acts" test.[101] The court stated that because there were no prior similar incidents on the defendant's property, this limited the foreseeability of the danger, and so the precaution requested by the victim was too burdensome.[102] While the court tries to cast its evaluation as a matter of the defendant's legal "duty" (an issue for judges), this, of course, is exactly the sort of determination that the Bird Court sought to give to juries in *Isaacs. Ann M.* is additionally notable for the court's open assertion that "random, violent crime is endemic in today's society. It is difficult, if not impossible, to envision any locale open to the public where the occurrence of violent crime seems improbable."[103] This reflects a very different attitude than that of the Bird Court about what is realistic to expect landowners to do to prevent crime.

In *Kentucky Fried Chicken of California, Inc. v. Superior Court,* [104] the plaintiff alleged that she was a customer in the defendant's restaurant when an unidentified criminal seized her and held her at gun point, threatening to harm her if the employee at the cash register did not give him money. When the employee failed promptly to comply, the criminal threatened to shoot the plaintiff, who screamed out in fear for her life. Only then did the clerk open the cash register drawer, after which the criminal took the money and ran. Although the plaintiff was not shot, she claimed serious injury. The court held that the defendant had no legal duty to comply with the robber's unlawful demands, emphasizing the defendant's legal right to defend his own property.[105] Once more, the court takes for itself the question of whether it should impose certain safety precautions (to protect customers from crime) on corporate defendants, and once again concludes it should not.[106] Again, this is quite inconsistent with the Bird Court's approach in *Isaacs* and *Peterson* which turned these matters of reasonably required safety measures over to the jury.

Not all of the court's post-Bird decisions involving responsibility for the wrongdoing of third parties were decided for defendants, however. A pair of decisions imposes a duty based upon "negligent misrepresentation."

First came *Garcia v. Superior Court,*[107] where a convicted murderer on parole kidnaped and killed the plaintiffs' mother. They claimed that the defendant parole officer knew that the murderer had threatened to kill their mother but nevertheless told her that he would "not come looking" for her.[108] The court concluded that an action would lie if the jury was convinced that the defendant had "negligently misrepresented" the risk to the mother.[109] Next came *Randi W. v. Maroc Joint Unified School District,*[110] where the plaintiff, a student, alleged that she was sexually assaulted by someone who had been the subject of prior charges of sexual misconduct. According to the plaintiff, her school district had hired her assailant because his prior school districts employers gave him unqualified positive references even though they knew about the sexual impropriety complaints against him.[111] Consequently, she sued those former employers, and the court held this stated a cause of action for negligent misrepresentation, relying upon *Garcia.*[112]

Hence plaintiffs in both *Garcia* and *Randi W.* were permitted to hold their defendants liable for the criminal wrongdoing of third parties-provided, of course, that they could prove at trial the allegations of their complaints. Two points are worth noting about the limited nature of the duties imposed in these cases. First, if the defendant parole officer and school districts had just kept quiet, there would apparently have been no basis for imposing liability upon them for not disclosing what they knew about the dangerousness of the third party in question. It was their affirmative misrepresentation of the danger that created potential liability. Second, plaintiffs in both cases were also required to show that the misrepresentation was actually relied upon-by the victim herself in *Garcia* and by the hiring school district in *Randi W.* The more pro-plaintiff dissenters in both cases offered analyses that would not have required that reliance.

Next, I want to turn to quite different tort law settings in which doctrine can serve the purpose of making one party responsible for the fault of another. For example, in *Privette v. Superior Court,*[113] a worker, who sustained injuries when instructed by an independent contractor to carry hot tar up a ladder, sued the property owner. The court stated that "under the peculiar risk doctrine, a person who hires an independent contractor to perform work that is inherently dangerous can be held liable for tort damages when the contractor's negligent performance of the work causes injuries to others."[114] In effect, this doctrine treats the independent contractor as though he were an employee by imposing vicarious liability on the defendant. Another way to put this rule is to call it a "non-delegable duty." Ever since *Woolen v. Aerojet General Corp.,*[115] California law had permitted *employees* of the independent contractor to invoke the "peculiar risk" doctrine.

In *Privette,* however, the court overruled that longstanding precedent, essentially on the grounds that the victim's access to workers compensation benefits should be his exclusive remedy.[116] Put differently, it saw the old rule as providing access to a deep pocket, one that the court concluded was not really necessary when workers compensation was already available. The court also thought it unfair that the defendant who was not at fault would have greater responsibility to the victim than the careless independent contractor, against whom no tort claim by the victim, or claim for indemnity from the defendant, would lie.[117] Of course, a parallel situation sometimes applies in other workplace settings in which the employer is at fault and the employee sues a third party, such as a manufacturer who is held strictly liable for a defective product.[118]

Cutting off access to a second deep pocket through tort law when workers compensation is available has been a recurring theme for the new court. For example, in *Cole v. Fair Oaks Fire Protection District ,*[119] the court decided that when a worker suffers a physical injury, workers compensation provides the exclusive remedy.[120] Thus the worker may not sue the employer in tort for emotional distress, even if tort law would compensate damages when workers compensation does not.[121]

Conventional vicarious liability of employers for the torts of their employees is, of course, another setting in which the doctrine of strict liability applies and serves, among other things, to give the victim access to a presumptively deeper pocket. It also arguably gives additional safety incentives to those who are "cheaper cost avoiders" than the victims. The court in recent years has confronted several difficult vicarious liability cases involving intentional sexual misconduct by employees.

In *John R. v. Oakland Unified School District,*[122] the court held vicarious liability was inapplicable when a junior high school pupil was allegedly sexually molested by his math teacher, in the teacher's apartment, while participating in an officially sanctioned extracurricular program. The doctrinal issue in these sorts of cases has traditionally been cast as whether the tort was committed "within the scope of employment."[123] At the time of *John R.* there was a division of opinion as to how to treat sexual assaults by employees both in courts around the nation and in the lower California courts.

The new court decided in favor of the defendant in *John R.* after exploring the policy goals underlying vicarious liability. A Calabresian analysis would probably impose vicarious liability on both loss spreading and safety promoting grounds. But the California Supreme Court asserted that loss spreading was inappropriate here both because it would make insurance more difficult for already-strapped school districts to obtain and because this injury was not fairly part of the risk allocable to the district.[124] The court was equally skeptical about the accident prevention rationale, claiming that "strict liability in this context would be far too likely to deter districts from encouraging, or even authorizing, extracurricular and/or one-on-one contacts between teachers and students or to induce districts to impose such rigorous controls on activities of this nature that the educational process would be negatively affected."[125]

In *Farmers Insurance Group v. County of Santa Clara,*[126] the court put forward essentially the same policy analysis, holding that the county was not responsible for the acts of a deputy sheriff who lewdly propositioned and offensively touched other deputy sheriffs.[127] Finally, in *Lisa M. v. Henry Mayo Newhall Memorial Hospital*[128] the court, focusing more this time on issues of basic fairness, held that a hospital was not vicariously liable for the conduct of a hospital technician who sexually molested a patient under the pretense of conducting an ultrasound examination.[129]

Oddly enough, despite these three pro-defendant rulings, the court, in *Mary M. v. City of Los Angeles* [130] (decided after *John R.* but before *Farmers* and *Lisa M.)* concluded that a city could be held vicariously liable for the conduct of its police officer who raped a woman he had detained and taken to her home.[131] The court held that when a police officer detains a person and then misuses his authority while she is in his custody, it is the jury's decision to find whether he was acting within the scope of his employment.[132] In contrast to *John R.,* the court in *Mary M.* rejected the claim that liability would generate a perverse behavioral response by the defendant; to the contrary, it asserted that vicarious liability might actually lead to socially desirable prevention measures by the police department.[133] I will not try to reconcile these four vicarious liability decisions, which were all decided by a divided court with a changing membership. Rather, I will simply note that, if nothing else, the difficulties the court had with these cases at least shows that sweeping "cheapest cost avoider" and "cheapest loss spreader" considerations are clearly insufficient to create liability.

This trend appears in other cases as well, including two in which the court refused to impose a duty on the defendant to take responsibility for harms to victims that were more directly caused by a party other than the defendant. In *Nally v. Grace Community Church of the Valley,*[134] the parents of a young suicide victim sued a large, wealthy church when one of its clergymen failed to prevent the suicide through religious counseling. The church could easily be viewed as the "cheapest cost avoider" and surely the "cheapest loss spreader" in this situation, and yet the court declined (for arguably very good reasons) to impose liability on the basis of an alleged negligent performance of spiritual counseling.[135] In *Artiglio v. Corning, Inc.,*[136] plaintiffs sought to hold Dow Chemical liable for injuries alleged to have been caused by silicone breast implants manufactured by its partially owned, and now bankrupt, subsidiary Dow Corning. Their case was based upon the theory that when Dow Chemical had "undertaken" certain research and testing activities, this created an ongoing obligation for it to take responsibility for the safety of the product in question.[137] Dow Chemical was certainly a "cheaper loss spreader" than the plaintiff and because of its expertise in product testing, an apparently far superior source of accident prevention. Yet, the court showed no interest whatsoever in deciding this case at the wholesale level, finding instead that, as a matter of law, the risk of harm to these plaintiffs was unforeseeable when Dow Chemical had undertaken those specific instances of silicone research and testing in the past, and hence the grant of defendant's summary judgment motion was proper.

D. *Strict Product Liability*

I turn next to the core of products liability, where the retreat from prior law is stark. Perhaps most strikingly, in *Peterson v. Superior Court,*[138] the new California Supreme Court simply overruled *Becker.* There, a hotel guest was injured by slipping on the surface of an allegedly defective bathtub. Portions of the opinion read very much like the report of a legislative committee that has decided a previous law has not worked out very well, or perhaps even more like the report of a legislative committee whose minority has recently become its majority. Noting that California had stood virtually alone in imposing strict liability on landlords, the new court membership claimed that "only in rare cases would the imposition of strict liability upon the landlord or hotel owner create an impetus to manufacture safer products."[139] As for the question of which party was more likely to discover the defect, the court focused in on the issue at the retail level, asserting "a tenant cannot reasonably expect that the landlord will have eliminated defects in a rented dwelling of which the landlord was unaware and which would not have been disclosed by a reasonable inspection."[140]

Moreover, the new court sounded very wary of simply providing another deep pocket (a good loss spreader) for the innocent victim of a product defect to sue a theme we saw already in the third party wrongdoer cases just discussed and will encounter again and again below. In short, the victim was relegated back to negligence law so far as the landlord is concerned although the victim could still pursue the bathtub maker in strict liability.

This *Peterson* decision is but one example of the court's retrenchment on products liability. In several other cases, with import both large and small, the court (despite some rhetoric to the contrary) is slowly, but steadily, pushing California products liability law away from any remaining pretense of strict liability into a decidedly fault-based framework (apart from routine manufacturing defect cases).

In *Brown v. Superior Court,*[141] the court rejected the application of its then basic products liability doctrine as articulated in *Barker. Brown* was a DES case which clearly involved a product that surprised the plaintiff by turning out to be dangerous.[142] The court first decided that *Barker's* "consumer expectations" test was inapplicable because, with pharmaceutical drugs, the consumer's expectations are based on the doctor's warnings, not the drug itself, and a manufacturer should not be liable for a doctor's failure to warn.[143] The court also cited public policy reasons for not imposing strict liability on the manufacturer based on the "consumer expectations" test, asserting that, in the case of drugs, it would result in marketing delays or reluctance on the part of manufacturers to develop new drugs.[144] Second, the court rejected the applicability of strict liability via the "hindsight" test to the defective warning aspect of the case-saying that the defendant could not be held liable for "risks inherent in a drug ... it neither knew nor could have known by the application of the scientific knowledge avail- able at the time of distribution."[145] In short, drug makers would be held to something that sounds to me very much like the fault principle thereby, laying aside the uncertainty that remained after *Finn.*

After *Brown,* the court decided *Anderson v. Owens-Corning Fiberglass Corp.,*[146] an asbestos case. I find this opinion something of an indecipherable mish-mash. The court claims that it is continuing to apply strict liability to non-drug warning cases because the defendant is to be precluded from arguing that it was reasonable to fail to disclose dangers known to it at the time of manufacture.[147] Of course, it would almost always be negligent to fail to disclose any substantial known danger; the more important issue was what to do about unknowable dangers. As to that, the court clearly rejected the "cheapest loss spreader" ideology that seemed to underlie decisions of the Bird era.[148] It admitted that although "an important goal of strict liability is to spread the risks and costs of injury to those most able to bear them . . . it was never the intention of the drafters of the doctrine to make the manufacturer or distributor the insurer of the safety of their products."149 By emphasizing "How can one warn of something that is unknowable?"150 the court clearly rejects Calabresi's wholesale approach which would surely view chemical manufacturers as generally far more likely than chemical users to find out in advance about the dangers of their products and take actions to prevent injuries. As for loss spreading, the court makes the point in *Anderson* that, when the risk is unforeseeable, even large corporations might well be unable to spread losses widely.151 Moreover, although the court argues that its embrace of fault-based responsibility for warning defects is to be distinguished from how California law treats design defects, as we will see next, the court has now largely imposed a negligence-like approach there as well.

In *Soule v. General Motors Corp.,*[152] the plaintiff's ankles were badly injured when her car collided with another vehicle. She claimed that her GM car was defective because its left front wheel broke free, collapsed rearward, and smashed the floorboard into her feet.[153] The plaintiff made two main legal claims that her car had been improperly welded (manufacturing defect) and that Ford had a better safety design that GM should have adopted (design defect).[154] GM disputed both of these points. Over GM's opposition, the trial court charged the jurors that they could find for the plaintiff on the "consumer expectations" test -- a test that, if applied to GM in this setting, could clearly be used to impose liability without fault on the carmaker.[155]

Expanding the reach of *Brown* beyond pharmaceutical drugs, the California Supreme Court decided that "the consumer expectations test is reserved for cases in which the *everyday experience* of the product's users permits a conclusion that the product's design violated *minimum* safety assumptions"[156] a condition absent from this case. Instead, the court said that these sorts of cases, where there realistically are no consumer expectations about wheel collapses in crashes, must be evaluated under the risk/benefit test.[157]

To be sure, the court in *Soule* explicitly refused to overrule the consumer expectations test for all cases, as GM had pressed and some other states have done.[158] Indeed, the court made clear that doing so would mean, in effect, relegating all design defect cases to negligence law -- something it was unwilling to do, at least at the time. Furthermore, the court also rejected GM's effort to reverse California's law that imposed the burden of proof with respect to design defects on the defendant.[159] Nevertheless, it seems to me that for a great number of complex products, *Soule,* as a practical matter, turns the trial of design defect cases in California into proceedings virtually indistinguishable from what they would be were the plaintiff required to prove design negligence.[160]

The new dominance of a fault orientation in the product liability arena may also be seen in *Mexicali Rose v. Superior Court,*[161] where the court refused to follow the lead of more plaintiff-orientated jurisdictions when dealing with "natural" substances found in restaurant food. There, a patron claimed to suffer throat injuries when he swallowed a one inch chicken bone that unexpectedly appeared in his chicken enchilada. Application of strict liability via the consumer expectations test, so much touted in *Barker,* might well have been justified by the court on the grounds that, since the victim had no warning, the defendant was best situated to avoid these sorts of injuries or spread the risk when they inevitably occurred. However, the court concluded that when the substance is "natural" to the food, as a bone is natural to chicken, the victim is not entitled to expect complete safety and hence may only proceed against the defendant in negligence.[162]

One final fact-specific product injury case is also worth noting. In *Ramirez v. Plough, Inc.,*[163] the court decided that a children's aspirin was not a defective product when the manufacturer provided the warnings only in English even though it widely advertised and sold the product in parts of the state where large numbers of monolingual Spanish speakers lived. The court rejected the pro-plaintiff result of an earlier New Jersey decision on similar facts and instead decided that drug manufacturer compliance with federal and state warning regimes should, as a matter of law, dictate that the product was not defective.[164] This decision was not a matter of federal pre-emption, but rather the court's own, very self-conscious, choice to opt for a clear uniform rule, rather than allow the jury to decide the issue of adequacy of the warning from the facts on a case-by-case basis.

Although the new court in *Ramirez* does in the products liability area what I earlier emphasized it has been doing in negligence cases -- i.e., adopting rules of law that take cases from the jury—I should acknowledge here that several of the other product liability cases I have discussed go the other way. That is, in rejecting strict liability for negligence, in for example, *Mexicali Rose* and *Peterson* (the hotel bathtub case), as well as in the cases discussed above that reject the "consumer expectations" test, the court, all the while making the law more pro-defendant, nonetheless creates a role for the jury.

E. The Boundaries of NIED Claims

A sharp change of direction also marked the new court's treatment of NIED cases. In *Thing v. La Chusa,*[165] the court effectively over-ruled the *Ochoa* approach established at the end of the Bird era. In *Thing,* a mother heard about an accident involving her child and arrived at the scene moments later to find her badly injured child lying in the road. The mother sued the driver who ran over her child for NIED, but the court rejected the claim.[166] Rebuffing the way *Ochoa* had treated the problem, the court resurrected the *Dillon* factors as absolute legal requirements in NIED cases.[167] No longer were those factors merely guidelines to indicate the sorts of factors that would help assure the genuineness and seriousness of the plaintiff's emotional distress. In this way, returning to one of my main themes here, power was removed from the jury and given to the trial judge who is enabled to rule for defendants in appropriate cases as a matter of law.

Even before *Thing,* the new court expressed its desire to restrict the availability of NIED claims. In *Elden v. Sheldon,*[168] the court rejected a lawsuit by an unmarried heterosexual domestic partner who witnessed the negligent killing of her cohabitant when in a car together. Once more adopting a clear legal rule rather than allowing the jury to make an individualized judgment about the closeness of the relationship, the court announced that NIED suits were restricted to those who are legally married to the direct victim of the defendant's fault.[169]

Later, in *Christensen v. Superior Court,*[170] the new court adopted a restricted rule to govern who might sue for emotional distress arising from the negligent (or even intentional) mishandling of a decedent's remains, thereby narrowing the class of valid claimants who had been recognized by the court of appeals.

This is not to say that no plaintiffs won their NIED cases before the new court. In *Marlene F.v. Affiliated Psychiatric Medical Clinic, Inc.,*[171] the court concluded that a mother had a cause of action for NIED against a therapist who was counseling both her and her sons (after the therapist allegedly sexually molested the sons). It appears that the mother's own professional relationship with the therapist gave her the "direct victim" status required by prior case law.[172] Furthermore, in *Burgess v. Superior Court,*[173] the same approach allowed a mother to state an NIED claim against a doctor who negligently injured her child in the course of delivering the baby. Since the doctor was hired by her, she was a "direct victim."[174]

However, the court called a halt to this development in *Huggins v. Longs Drug Stores California, Inc.*[175] Parents in that case unwittingly injured their son by giving him a prescription overdose because the defendant pharmacy had mis-instructed them as to the proper dosage. They sued for NIED but the court refused to treat them as "direct victims."[176] As the majority saw it, the parents were customers on behalf of their child, but they were not patients of the pharmacy in the conventional sense.[177]

The court also denied NIED recovery in *Potter v. Firestone Tire and Rubber Co.,*[178] where a group of landowners brought suit against a tire manufacturer for fear of acquiring cancer from the hazardous wastes the manufacturer dumped in a nearby landfill. The court held that, barring physical injury or illness, a plaintiff must prove a fear based on reliable medical and scientific opinion that he or she is more likely than not to develop cancer in the future due to exposure.[179] My point here is that we yet again see the court taking upon itself the decision as to where to draw the boundary around NIED claims, in contrast to the direction the Bird Court seemed to be moving in *Ochoa.*

F. *Other Areas of Tort Law: Win Some, Lose Some*

1. *Assumption of Risk*

In *Knight v. Jewett,*[180] the court recognized that some so-called "assumption of risk" cases are really better understood as "comparative fault" cases (in which the careless victim should receive a partial recovery from the also careless injurer), whereas other cases are better understood as "no duty" cases (in which the victim should recover nothing).[181] It would have been better, in my view, had the court just abolished the use of the "assumption of risk" label and allocated the cases to the other appropriate doctrinal categories.[182] The court did not do that. More importantly for my purposes here, it chose to attach the "no duty/assumption of risk" label in a sweeping way to recreational injury cases.[183]

In *Knight,* the plaintiff and defendant were playing a casual game of "touch" football. According to the victim, she had already told the defendant to stop playing so roughly and he promised to be more careful when, on the next play, he knocked her down, stepped on her hand, and injured her. In what I view as a dubious empirical judgment, the court claimed "vigorous participation in such sporting events likely would be chilled if legal liability were to be imposed on a participant on the basis of his or her ordinary careless conduct. . . . [I]mposition of legal liability for such conduct might well alter fundamentally the nature of the sport."[184] In short, no duty was to lie apart from "conduct that is so reckless as to be totally outside the range of the ordinary activity involved in the sport."[185] Once more, the court here adopts a rule pursuant to which, as a matter of law, certain victims will not recover, thereby denying the plaintiff the opportunity to convince a jury that, under all the circumstances, the defendant's conduct was socially unacceptable. I do not mean to suggest that this is the wrong function for a "no duty" rule to serve, but rather to indicate my disagreement with the policy judgment that recreational injuries are an appropriate place for such a "no duty" rule.

Apparently, to make sure that the lower courts get the point, the court revisited the same basic issue three more times to emphasize the idea that in the typical recreational injury case, juries are not to decide whether, in the specific setting, this defendant had actually been unreasonably careless. The first was

Ford v. Gouin[186] the companion case to *Knight,* which involved a water skier who was injured and sued the driver of the boat that was pulling him -- on the grounds the driver carelessly drove too close to the riverbank.[187] The second was *Parsons v. Crown Disposal* Co.,[188] where the plaintiff was thrown from his horse after loud noises from a nearby garbage truck frightened the horse,[189] The third was *Cheong v. Antablin,*[190] where friends skiing together crashed into each other, injuring the plaintiff, who sued his fellow skier claiming negligence on the part of the defendant.[191]

2. Other

As indicated already, not all plaintiffs lost their cases before the new court. For example, in *Neighbarger v. Irwin Industries, Inc.,*[192] the court refused to apply the so-called "firefighter's rule" (which bars recovery as a matter of law) to private employees who were injured while battling a negligently set fire (restricting the rule's reach to public firefighters).[193] In *Alcaraz v. Vece,*[194] the court ruled in favor of a tenant plaintiff who sued his landlord after stepping into a water meter box with a missing or broken cover. The box was located in the front lawn of the property, but technically on the property owned by the city, not the defendant. The court concluded (4-3) that if the defendant exercised control over that adjacent property that was not noticeably separate from his, he would have a duty to warn his tenants of dangers on that property.[195] These decisions (and others already noted above) make clear that the new court is not single-mindedly pro-defendant; rather, these two cases at least show the judges at work trying to work out in a sensible way the details of negligence law as it applies to newly presented situations.[196]

The potentially most pro-plaintiff decision from the past twelve years, in my judgment, is *Mitchell v. Gonzales*[197] in which the court decided that trial courts should no longer give the "but for" jury instruction on causation, but should instead give a "substantial factor" instruction.[198] This particular case involved the drowning of one of three young children who had been playing together on a paddle board in water deeper than they were tall. It appears that there may have been some misunderstanding by the jury about the idea that more than one cause can be a proximate cause of an injury.[199] But this decision could be enormously beneficial to plaintiffs in other cases (and highly disruptive of traditional tort doctrine) if the shift in jury instructions here ordered also undermines (as it would appear to) traditional notions about "cause in fact." The court, in passing, tries to make light of this possibility, saying that "[i]f the conduct ... had nothing at all to do with the injuries," it could not be a substantial factor in causing them.[200] Yet this misses some far more difficult problems than the court seems to acknowledge. However, this is not the occasion to go into these matters.[201]

G. *Bad Faith Retreat*

Finally, again as an aside, let me simply note that the new court has largely gutted the "bad faith" law that was so steadfastly erected during the Bird era and earlier. In *Freeman & Mills v. Belcher Oil,*[202] the court overruled the Bird Court's 1984 decision in *Seamans.* In *Moradi-Shalal v. Fireman's Fund Insurance Cos.,*[203] the court over-ruled *Royal Globe v. Superior Court,*[204] an earlier California Supreme Court decision which had allowed tort victims to bring bad faith claims against their defendant's insurers when the latter refused to settle. In *Foley v. Interactive Data Corp.,*[205] the court sharply curtailed the tort rights of employees claiming "wrongful discharge."[206] Moreover, on a related front, the court in *Cedars-Sinai Medical Center v. Superior Court*[207] rejected the claimant's plea to create a "new" tort for the "spoilage of evidence" in the context of a plaintiff asserting the defendant had destroyed records that were crucial to his case.[208]

III. CONCLUSION

I have not tried to count up the numbers in any precise way, but my recitation should make clear that the rate of success by tort plaintiffs in the California Supreme Court is dramatically different over the past dozen years than it was at the end of the Bird era. Calabresian thinking about enterprise liability as a way of dealing with the cost of accidents is currently dead in the Golden State. At the same time, we have lots of new rules and judicial decision making in cases that, in prior years, would have gone to juries with vague instructions about fault attached. And so, I hope I have shown that, in their very different ways, both the old and new courts have made and un-made a new law of torts.

ENDNOTES

1. For a somewhat different appraisal of the work of the new court in the post-Bird era, see Ellis Horvitz, An Analysis of Recent Supreme Court Developments in Torts and Insurance Law: The Common-Law Tradition, 26 LOY. L.A. L. REV. 1145, 1153-62 (1993).

2. I do not mean to suggest that the California Supreme Court is alone in its shift to a more pro-defendant tort law. See, e.g., James A. Henderson, Jr. & Theodore Eisenberg, The Quiet Revolution in Products Liability, 37 UCLA L. REV. 479 (1990) (arguing that the current trend in judicial decisions favors defendants); Gary T. Schwartz, The Beginning and the Possible End of the Rise of American Tort Law, 26 GA. L. REV. 601 (1992) (arguing that the movement to expand tort liability has ended). California is perhaps an especially important case, however, because its supreme court was clearly one of the nation's most pro-plaintiff as of the end of 1986. Timothy D. Howell, So Long "Sweetheart": State Farm Fire & Casualty Co. v. Gandy Swings the Pendulum Further to the Right as the Latest in a Line of Setbacks for Texas Plaintiffs, 29 ST. MARY'S L.J. 47, 93 (1997).

3. For other writings about "new" torts, see, for example, Anita Bernstein, How to Make a New Tort: Three Paradoxes, 75 TEX. L. REV. 1539 (1997) (examining "new tort" causes of action and cases); Robert F. Blomquist, "New Torts": A Critical History, Taxonomy, and Appraisal, 95 DUKE L. REV. 23 (1990) (explaining the creation and use of the "new tort" concept).

4. Governor Jerry Brown's appointees were Rose E. Bird, Otto M. Kaus, Allen E. Broussard, Cruz Reynoso and Joseph R. Grodin. Stanley Mosk was appointed by Governor Pat Brown.

5. The seventh position was filled by Malcolm M. Lucas in 1984.

6. 150 P.2d 436 (Cal. 1944) (Traynor, J., concurring).

7. *Id.* at 440.

8. *See* id. at 441.

9. 377 P.2d 897 (Cal. 1962).

10. 443 P.2d 561 (Cal. 1968).

11. *See* id. at 568.

12. *Id.* at 564.

13. Guido CALABRESI, THE COSTS OF ACCIDENTS: A LEGAL AND ECONOMIC ANALYSIS (1970).

14. *See* id. at 251.

15. *See* id. at 136.

16. *See* id. at 262.

17. *See* id. at 284-85.

18. *See*, e.g., Rankin v. City of Wichita Falls, 762 F.2d 444 (5th Cir. 1985); Union Oil Co. v. Open, 501 F.2d 558 (9th Cir. 1974); Schneider Nat'l, Inc. v. Holland Hitch Co., 843 P.2d 561 (Wyo. 1992).

19. 271 P.2d 23 (Cal. 1954).

20. *See* id. at 29.

21. 393 P.2d 164 (Cal. 1964).

22. *See* id. at 167.

23. 681 P.2d 893 (Cal. 1984).

24. *See* id. at 902.

25. *Id.* at 901.

26. 715 P.2d 624 (Cal. 1986).

27. *See* id. at 626.

28. *See* id. at 629.

29. *See* id.

30. *Id.* at 640 (Bird, C.J., concurring and dissenting).

31. *Id.* at 628 n.5.

32. *See* Ballard, 715 P.2d at 629.

33. *See* id.

34. 685 P.2d 1193 (Cal. 1984).

35. *Id.* at 1203.

36. 521 P.2d 855 (Cal. 1974).

37. *Id.* at 858.

38. *Id.*

39. *See* 685 P.2d at 1200-01.

40. *Id.* at 1202.

41. 695 P.2d 653 (Cal. 1985).

42. *See* id. at 657.

43. *Id.* at 661.

44. *See* id. at 655.

45. *Id.* at 662.

46. 710 P.2d 907 (Cal. 1985).

47. *See* id. at 914.

48. *See* id. at 911.

49. *Id.* at 912.

50. *Id.*

51. 551 P.2d 334 (Cal. 1976).

52. 447 P.2d 352 (Cal. 1968).

53. 577 P.2d 669 (Cal. 1978).

54. 539 P.2d 36 (Cal. 1975).

55. Coulter, 577 P.2d at 675.

56. CAL. Bus. & PROF. CODE § 25602(c) (West 1977).

57. Weirum, 539 P.2d at 41.

58. *See* Vandermark v. Ford Motor Co., 391 P.2d 168 (Cal. 1964).

59. *See* Price v. Shell Oil Co., 466 P.2d 722 (Cal. 1970).

60. 698 P.2d 116 (Cal. 1985).

61. *See* id. at 117.

62. *See* id. at 122.

63. *Id.* at 124.

64. *See* Cronin v. J.B.E. Olson Corp., 501 P.2d 1153 (Cal. 1972).

65. 573 P.2d 443 (Cal. 1978).

66. *See* James A. Henderson, Jr., Coping with the Time Dimension in Products Liability, 69 CAL. L. REV. 919, 921 (1981).

67. *See* RESTATEMENT (SECOND) OF TORTS§ 402A cmt. k (1965).

68. 677 P.2d 1147 (Cal. 1984).

69. *See* id. at 1151.

70. *See* id. at 1154.

71. *Id.* at 1164

72. *Id.* at 1168.

73. *Id.*

74. 710 P.2d 247 (Cal. 1985).

75. *See* id.

76. *See* id. at 252.

77. *Id.*

78. *Id.* at 258 (Bird, C.J., dissenting).

79. *Id.*

80. 441 P.2d 912 (Cal. 1968).

81. 703 P.2d 1 (Cal. 1985).

82. *Id.* at 9.

83. *Id.* at 7.

84. *See*, e.g., Harry Kalven, Jr., Tort Watch, 34 ATLA L.J. 1 (1972) (commenting on the growth of strict liability) [hereinafter Kalven, Tort Watch]; Harry Kalven, Jr., Negligence on the Move, 33 ATLA L.J. 1 (1971) (commenting on the growth in the law within the negligence principle).

85. Rowland v. Christian, 377 P.2d 897 (Cal. 1968).

86. *See* Waite v. Waite, 618 So. 2d 1360 (Fla. 1993).

87. *See* Brown v. Merlo, 506 P.2d 212 (1973).

88. *See* Diaz v. Eli Lilly & Co., 302 N.E.2d 555 (1973).

89. Kalven, Tort Watch, supra note 84, at 2.

90. As discussed in supra Section D. Ochoa rejected Dillon's rules for individualized inquiries in NIED cases.

91. *See* supra Section B for Isaacs rejection of "prior similar incidents" for a "totality of the circumstances" test.

92. Ballard v. Uribe, 715 P.2d 624 (Cal. 1986); Palma v. U.S. Indus. Fasteners, 681 P.2d 893 (Cal. 1984).

93. I do not mean to argue that all of the Bird-era cases I reviewed are of this sort. Becker v. IRM, for example, took the issue of individualized fault determination away from the jury by imposing strict liability on the landlord. See Becker v. IRM Corp., 698 P.2d 116, 122 (Cal. 1985).

94. 686 P.2d 1158 (Cal. 1984).

95. *See* id. at 1166.

96. *See* id.

97. *See* id. at 1167.

98. *See* CAL. CONST. art. 6(a), § 16 (1966).

99. Again, I do not want to be understood as arguing that the court is doing this in every case-as I will point out below.

100. 863 P.2d 207 (Cal. 1993).

101. *See* id. at 216.

102. *See* id. at 215-16.

103. *Id.* at 215.

104. 927 P.2d 1260 (Cal. 1997).

105. *See* id. at 1269.

106. *See* id. at 1262.

107. 789 P.2d 960 (Cal. 1990).

108. *See* id. at 962.

109. *See* id. at 965.

110. 929 P.2d 582 (Cal. 1997).

111. *See* id. at 584.

112. *See* id. at 587.

113. 854 P.2d 721 (Cal. 1993).

114. *Id.* at 723.

115. 369 P.2d 697 (Cal. 1962).

116. 854 P.2d at 731.

117. *See* id. at 728.

118. In Toland v. Sunland Housing Group, 955 P.2d 504 (Cal. 1998), the court reaffirmed and slightly expanded the reach of Privette.

119. 729 P.2d 743 (Cal. 1987).

120. *Id.* at 744.

121. See also Livitsanos v. Superior Court, 828 P.2d 1195, 1197 (Cal. 1992). In Livitsanos, the court expanded Cole to cover situations in which emotional distress damages were sought in tort and no physical injury was alleged. /d. Still, workers compensation was to be the victim's only remedy even if it provided no compensation. Later, the court eased up a bit on the "exclusive remedy" rule both in Snyder v. Michael's Stores, Inc., 945 P.2d 781, 782 (Cal. 1997) (holding that the exclusive remedy principle did not bar a claim by a child who was in utero when allegedly injured from her mother breathing carbon monoxide while at work) and Fermino v. Fedco, Inc.,872 P.2d 559, 560 (Cal. 1994) (concluding that a claim for false imprisonment was not barred by workers' compensation law). For another example of the new court restricting access to a deep pocket, see Evangelatos v. Superior Court 753 P.2d 585 (Cal. 1988). There, in passing, the court (albeit in dicta) seems to have abandoned the position taken earlier in American Motor Cycle v. Superior Court, 578 P.2d 899 (Cal. 1978), as to how the risk of insolvency is to be born in cases with multiple tortfeasors. Evangelatos, supra at 590. In American Motor Cycle, the court seems to say that the California rule was that the solvent defendants would be responsible for any share of the loss otherwise assigned to an insolvent defendant-and that no part of the insolvency would be borne by the victim, even at-fault victims. But with no discussion, Evangelatos embraces the view (supported by some subsequent lower California decisions) that the risk of insolvency would also be proportionately shared by any plaintiff who was also at fault. Evangelatos, supra at 595.

122. 769 P.2d 948 (Cal. 1989).

123. *Id.* at 953.

124. *See* id. at 956.

125. *Id.*

126. 906 P.2d 440 (Cal. 1995).

127. *See* id. at 444.

128. 907 P.2d 358 (Cal. 1995).

129. *Id.* at 359.

130. 814 P.2d 1341 (Cal. 1991).

131. *See* id. at 1342.

132. *See* id. at 1352.

133. *See* id. at 1348.

134. 763 P.2d 948 (Cal. 1988).

135. *See* id. at 952.

136. 957 P.2d 1313 (Cal. 1998).

137. *See* id. at 1318.

138. 899 P.2d 905 (Cal. 1995).

139. *Id.* at 915.

140. *Id.* at 918.

141. 751 P.2d 470 (Cal. 1988).

142. *See* id. at 473.

143. *See* id. at 476-77.

144. *See* id. at 478.

145. *Id.* at 480.

146. 810 P.2d 549 (Cal. 1991).

147. *See* id. at 559.

148. The Bird era, led by Chief Justice Rose Bird, repealed many provisions of tort law previously adopted by the court.

149. Anderson, 810 P.2d at 559.

150. *Id.*

151. *Id.* at 559 n.14. I do not believe that my position as to the state of "warning" law in California after Anderson is undermined by Carlin v. Superior Court, 920 P.2d 1347 (Cal. 1996), a subsequent pharmaceutical drug case about warnings decided by a panel including three temporarily-assigned lower court judges. Although Justice Mosk's opinion for the court again tried to make a big deal of the difference between failure to warn in the strict liability context and the negligence context, this still seems of little moment to me. Basically, the court concluded that a drug maker could be liable for the "failure to warn about the known or reasonably scientifically knowable dangerous propensities of its product." !d. at 1348. This is a restatement of the holding in Anderson, and still basically sounds like negligence to me.

152. 882 P.2d 298 (Cal. 1994).

153. *See* id. at 301.

154. *See* id. at 302.

155. *Id.* at 303.

156. *Id.* at 308.

157. *Id.* at 309.

158. Soule, 882 P.2d at 310 and n.7.

159. An advantage, by the way, that I understand experienced plaintiffs' lawyers will never rely upon unless they are completely unable to come forward in their part of the case with alternative design proposals.

160. Note that the court in Soule ultimately decided that giving the consumer expectations test instruction was harmless error since the plaintiff so clearly emphasized fault-based theories-bad welding and bad design-in the presentation of her case. 882 P.2d at 310-12.

161. 822 P.2d 1292 (Cal. 1992).

162. *See* id. at 1294.

163. 863 P.2d 167 (Cal. 1993).

164. *See* id. at 178.

165. 771 P.2d 814 (Cal. 1989).

166. *See* id. at 829-30.

167. *Id.* at 820. See also Dillon v. Legg, 441 P.2d 912 (Cal. 1968) (allowing recovery in certain circumstances by those who witness a close relative's harms).

168. 758 P.2d 582 (Cal. 1988).

169. *See* id. at 585-86.

170. 820 P.2d 181 (Cal. 1991).

171. 770 P.2d 278 (Cal. 1989).

172. *See* id. at 281.

173. 831 P.2d 1197 (Cal. 1992}.

174. *See* id. at 1203.

175. 862 P.2d 148 (Cal. 1993).

176. *See* id. at 150.

177. *See* id. at 154.

178. 863 P.2d 795 (Cal. 1993).

179. *See* id. at 800.

180. 834 P.2d 696 (Cal. 1992).

181. Although the court did not acknowledge it, still other "assumption of risk" cases are better understood as "no breach" cases and perhaps "no proximate cause" cases.

182. *See* generally Stephen D. Sugarman, Assumption of Risk, 31 VAL. U. L. REV. 833 (1997) (discussing alternatives to the "assumption of risk" label such as informed consent, no duty rules, and comparative negligence).

183. *See* Knight, 834 P.2d at 708-09.

184. *See* id. at 710.

185. *Id.* at 711.

186. 834 P.2d 724 (Cal. 1992).

187. *See* id. at 726.

188. 936 P.2d 70 (Cal. 1997).

189. *See* id. at 71.

190. 946 P.2d 817 (Cal. 1997).

191. *See* id. at 819.

192. 882 P.2d 347 (Cal. 1994).

193. *See* id. at 355-56.

194. 929 P.2d 1239 (Cal. 1997).

195. *See* id. at 1253.

196. Two more exotic cases were faced by the new court. First, San Diego Gas and Electric v. Superior Court, where plaintiffs sued a public utility alleging injuries from exposure to electromagnetic fields created by power lines adjoining their property 920 P.2d 669 (Cal. 1996). The court barred the action under Public Utility Code Section 1759 as an impermissible interference with the Public Utility Commission's broad regulatory authority, *id.* at 704-05. Second, Moore v. Regents of the University of California, was a very special "informed consent" case in which the plaintiff successfully claimed that the defendants improperly used his cells for potentially lucrative medical research without obtaining his prior permission 793 P.2d 479, 480 (Cal. 1990).

197. 819 P.2d 872 (Cal. 1991).

198. *See* id. at 877-82.

199. *See* id. at 875-76.

200. *Id.* at 878.

201. For another more defense-oriented foray by the court into the world of "causation," see Rutherford v. Owens-Illinois, Inc., 941 P.2d 1203, 1214-22 (1997).

202. 900 P.2d 669 (Cal. 1995).

203. 758 P.2d 58 (Cal. 1988).

204. 592 P.2d 329 (Cal. 1979).

205. 765 P.2d 373 (Cal. 1988).

206. *Id.* at 384-86.

207. 954 P.2d 511 (Cal. 1998).

208. *Id.* at 515-17.

Part II

Learning from Other Countries

In most 1L Torts classes, no serious attention is paid to the tort law of other countries, apart perhaps from the reading of mostly older English common law cases that are seen to lay the groundwork for later U.S. developments. Contemporary U.K. decisions are usually ignored, as are the robust recent common law tort decisions of courts like the Supreme Court of Canada and the High Court of Australia. Civil law treatment of accidental and intentional injuries is almost always completely ignored, with these examples left to be covered in courses on Comparative Law. To most casebook editors and U.S. authors it seems daunting enough to try to keep track of and make sense of divergent U.S. decisions across the country.

Nonetheless, Americans can learn from the judicial decisions of other nations, especially from places where judges publish written decisions justifying their results. Those comparisons are mainly about tort doctrine and the questions that need be answered in deciding whether the defendant is to be held liable or not. But this is not the only realm in which the U.S. might learn from developments elsewhere. This Part II is primarily about those other realms.

Some 1L Torts students learn, fleetingly or possibly in some detail, about how New Zealand has replaced tort law for personal injury and death with a national accident compensation scheme. Personal injury victims in New Zealand obtain financial recovery for a large share of their lost income and reasonable medical and related expenses that are not already be covered by that country's national health insurance scheme. Their own fault or the fault of others is irrelevant to their recovery. In certain cases modest payments are made as well in compensation for what in the U.S. we would call pain and suffering. To emphasize the point, tort suits for personal injury damages have been eliminated. The New Zealand plan is well written up by others and is not the focus of this part, which primarily explores other differences between the U.S. and elsewhere – e.g. the auto accident problem, tort reform of damage awards, and pain and suffering awards. Each of the chapters argues that other places have dealt with important aspects of the accident problem in ways that are arguably better than the comparable treatment here.

Chapter 6

Why Can't We Be More Like Quebec?

In the early 1900s, it became clear that tort law in the U.S. was not well serving victims of workplace accidents. Reformers looked to both Germany and Great Britain and learned that both nations had introduced a scheme of industrial accident compensation outside of the tort system. Adapting those approaches to their own needs, American states soon began to put what were then called "workmen's compensation" plans in place, and today in all U.S. jurisdictions workers' compensation, not tort law, is where victims of work injuries turn.

The introduction of the automobile soon created somewhat similar explosion of injuries and deaths, and before long tort law critics began to complain that motor vehicle accident victims were also not being well served by the common law. By the mid-1960s several advocates were urging the adoption of something that from the victim's perspective would function similarly to workers' compensation.

Of course, for auto accidents there is no one occupying the position of the employer to whom the legislature could turn to require putting in place insurance arrangements that would provide benefits to motorists. Instead, the focus turned to car owners and drivers themselves. What if, instead of requiring motorists to purchase liability insurance, which paid their tort liability if they carelessly injured another, motorists were required to buy coverage for their own injuries that would cover their losses regardless of how those injuries came about (that is, regardless of whether they or anyone else was at fault in causing their harm). And so the concept of "auto no-fault" was born.

Critics of the tort system complained that: (1) it wasted way too much money on administrative costs, including legal fees, so that less than half the money motorists paid for liability insurance actually went to victims (and most of that was not for hard out-of-pocket economic losses, but rather to duplicate other benefits like those provide by health insurance or for so-called "pain and suffering"); (2) it took too long for victims to be paid (with trials of auto accident cases often occurring many years after the event); (3) a substantial share of auto accident victims recovered nothing from the system because either they were at fault (at the time contributory negligence was a complete defense) or no one was at fault, or because the negligent party who injured them had failed to buy insurance (this was true for perhaps 20% or more of the cars on the road) and was personally judgment proof; (4) even when careless motorists had insurance, it was typically far too little to cover the full loss of any seriously injured victim, whereas by contrast savvy automobile claims "mills" had figured out ways of quickly obtaining lump sum recoveries for dubious "whiplash" and other such harms that critics felt were undeserved, but which auto insurance companies paid out to get these nuisance cases off their books; and (5) drivers were upset that their auto insurance bills were "too high" (and some feared that the ranks of uninsured motorists would grow even larger).

Forcing motorists to insure themselves on a no-fault basis promised to take lawyers largely out of the system and dramatically reduce overhead costs, thereby freeing up more than enough money to provide coverage for all auto accident victims who would receive compensation in a prompt and non-adversarial manner analogous to what happens if your car is stolen or destroyed in a fire. Benefits could also be shifted to emphasize the needs of the seriously injured rather than the trivially injured. And in the process, auto no-fault advocates promised, insurance premiums would fall. It seemed almost too good to be true – apart from what it would do the legal practice of many attorneys who specialized in auto injury cases.

Yet, true auto no-fault has never been adopted in any U.S. state. But it has been put in place in many other jurisdictions. Quebec, Canada is one important example, and this chapter discusses the Quebec solution, adopted in the 1970s and still thriving. A key focus is on why the Quebec solution has spread to some other Canadian provinces but not to the U.S. Issues covered include the political power of plaintiffs' lawyers and the political preferences of automobile insurers in the two countries, the differing structure of government and public attitudes towards government running insurance programs here and there, differences in Canadian and U.S. ideology concerning individual and collective responsibility, the potential impact of auto no-fault plans on auto accident rates, and differences between U.S. and Canadian tort law that present reformers with different trade-offs in U.S. states as compared with Quebec.

This chapter was presented initially at an international symposium on 20 Years of No-Fault Insurance hosted by Laval University in Quebec in 1998 and was published as Stephen D. Sugarman, "Quebec's Comprehensive Auto No-Fault Insurance Scheme and the Failure of Any of the United States to Follow," 39 Cahiers de Droit, numeros 2-3, 303-333 (1998) and is reprinted with permission of the journal.

Quebec's Comprehensive Auto No-Fault Scheme and the Failure of Any of the United States to Follow

Quebec adopted a comprehensive auto no-fault plan more than twenty years ago.[1] As will be detailed below, it has apparently served Quebec very well. This approach has been pointed to with envy by no-fault devotees in other jurisdictions on both sides of the Canadian-U.S. border[2]. Yet, during this period, not one of the United States has embraced the Quebec example. In this article, I will discuss some reasons for this failure to act. At the end, I will explore ways in which some U.S. jurisdictions might begin to move in Quebec's direction. Although I will give special attention to the situation in California where I am based, my analysis is meant to apply generally across the U.S.

1. A Brief History of Auto No-Fault in North America

1.1 Beginnings

In North America, auto no-fault insurance began in Canada with the adoption of a scheme by Saskatchewan in 1946.[3] This was one of the models pointed to by Professors Robert Keeton and Jeffrey O'Connell when they published their famous blueprint for U.S.-style, auto no-fault in 1965.[4] In the U.S., a somewhat more modest version of the Keeton-O'Connell plan was adopted in 1970 by Massachusetts (where Keeton then taught and where auto insurance rates were annoyingly high).[5] In the next few years, many other states and provinces followed suit.[6]

1.2 Partial Plans in the U.S.

Yet, in the U.S. neither the Keeton-O'Connell proposal nor the enacted plans were comprehensive. Basically, the approach that won political acceptance in the 1970s was rooted in the goal of trying to rid the legal system of the huge mass of auto accident cases involving small injuries. These little cases were swamping the system. They took what seemed like ages to resolve. Some victims were obtaining substantial awards for pain and suffering for minor injuries, injuries that were long healed, and in some senses forgotten, well before the matter was put to rest legally. Other victims were getting nothing. Enormous legal fees and other expenses were incurred on both sides. Therefore, he thinking that won the day in nearly two dozen legislatures was that everyone would be better off if these little cases could be taken care of quickly, with all auto victims being assured that their medical expenses in minor injury cases were paid for and that at least a moderate amount of their wage loss was replaced. Put differently, why not dispense with often fruitless and costly inquiries into "fault" when the money spent on transactions costs could be put to use instead either to compensate victims who failed to recover under tort law or else to reduce auto insurance premiums.[7]

In some states, no-fault plans have successfully removed at least a substantial share of the smaller claims from the tort system. This goal was generally best achieved in jurisdictions that imposed a formal legal hurdle to the recovery of damages in tort for pain and suffering. In those states, minor injury victims effectively had no-fault benefits as their only remedy. These are generally termed the "modified" jurisdictions-because the right to tort recovery is modified.[8]

Other states, however, imposed no restriction on tort recovery for pain and suffering and their no-fault schemes are generally termed the "add on" plans[9]. There, the only limit in tort is that claimants can't recover damages for items already compensated by no-fault benefits. The hope for fewer tort claims in these states depends on the willingness of the victim voluntarily to settle for prompt coverage of out of pocket losses and to forego the litigation route. While this seemed to have occurred in Saskatchewan under its original "add on" scheme[10], in the U.S. no-fault benefits in "add-on" states all too often have served instead to encourage claimants to file tort claims and then to refuse to settle early because the no-fault benefits took care of their basic needs[11]. It should be no surprise that the U.S. "add-on" schemes have tended to increase auto insurance premiums overall[12].

Fewer than a handful of the states removed even a modest share of the more serious injuries out of the tort system. To do so basically requires a combination of a) generous no-fault benefits for economic loss and b) a high "serious injury" threshold on suits for pain and suffering damages. Indeed, in the U.S. it is probably fair to say that really only Michigan and New York (two states bordering Canada) have adopted anything like a widespread auto no-fault plan. Even in those two jurisdictions, however, the most serious injuries have continued to be handled by tort law and not by no-fault. In Michigan, for example, about half of a motorist's insurance premium for bodily injury continues to fall on the liability insurance side (and about half on the no-fault side) [13].

As auto no-fault became a hot issue in the U.S. in the 1960s and 1970s, some insurers proposed a "comprehensive" solution[14]. There would be no more tort remedy at all against other motorists (apart perhaps from intentional injury and drunk driving cases). But all (or virtually all) auto accident victims would be reimbursed for their full economic losses, usually from their own insurer, regardless of who might have been at fault in causing the accident. The argument on behalf of the comprehensive solution was that the most important benefits of the no-fault approach were just as applicable to serious auto injuries as they were to minor ones. In short, under this sweeping approach, auto insurance for bodily injury would become like insurance for the loss of one's vehicle owing to fire or theft.

Yet, rather than expanding on the initial, more-modest auto no-fault legislation, states went off in the other direction. Not only did the U.S. no-fault movement come to a halt, but a few states even repealed their no-fault plans[15]. Moreover, in Michigan the most recent political response designed to reduce premiums (so far unsuccessful) has been to try to reduce no-fault coverage rather than to widen tort law's repeal[16]. And in New York, there seems to be no visible support to expand its plan to be as generous as Michigan's.

1.3 Bolder Plans in Canada

In Canada the story has been very different. Following the early Saskatchewan initiative, many provinces adopted no-fault plans and later expanded them[17]. Quebec, as noted at the outset, made the most dramatic reform by adopting a comprehensive scheme in 1977. In more recent years, Manitoba enacted a comprehensive scheme[18] and Saskatchewan expanded its plan to make it fully comprehensive[l9].

2. Why Has No State Followed the Quebec Example?

By now, the Quebec model is hardly new. To the contrary, it has for two decades been there to be seen, studied and followed (or to be modified and then followed). Yet, not one of the American states has chosen to do so. Is this because the Quebec solution is a bad idea, or at least would be in the U.S.? If not, then why has it been rejected? Let me tum to a series of reasons that, I believe, explain our inaction south-of-the-border.

2.1 Politics

2.1.1 The Power of the Plaintiffs' Lawyers

Due to the "checks and balances" system of state politics in the U.S., the election of a candidate from a particular party, favorable to your interests, to the top job *(i.e.,* governor) hardly suffices to ensure favorable legislative outcomes as it may in Canadian provinces. This is because the other major political party may still control one or the other (or both) houses of the state legislature, hence controlling the committees through which legislation must pass. Moreover, sometimes a member of the governor's or dominant party will maintain control over a key legislative committee and yet have a different agenda from that of the governor or the party generally. These key committee chairs have enormous power to block legislative reform.

Given this system, in the U.S., so-called "special interests" are often able to influence the outcome of political issues of particular concern to them. One of the best ways is to have built up the support of legislators who chair or serve on committees with jurisdiction over the matters most salient to the special interest group. And one way to win *that* support is through campaign contributions. In most states in the U.S., lawyers who represent accident victims have organized themselves to take advantage of the political and campaign contributions systems, and have, as a result, obtained considerable leverage with key state legislators. In general, the plaintiffs' bar has allied itself with and funded Democrats, and like the Democratic party, the lawyers portray themselves as the defenders of ordinary people (consumers and victims). They characterize their opponents, the Republicans, as representatives of the powerful corporate interests in the society.

So, for example, when the business community seeks to limit the amount of money that accident victims can recover under tort law for pain and suffering, the Democratic legislators and the plaintiffs' lawyers form a natural alliance in opposition. The self-interest of the lawyers in this and similar settings is clear, especially because of the near universal practice in the U.S. of lawyers handling personal injury cases on a contingent percentage basis. That is, legal fees typically are approximately one third of the total recovery, and so any change that reduces what victims may be awarded directly reduces the lawyers' incomes as well.

Yet sometimes the interests of consumers and victims may not coincide with those of the trial lawyers. Quebec-style auto no-fault is a good example. The Quebec plan's supporters claim that it benefits consumers enormously by providing quick and generous compensation to more victims at a lower overall cost to motorists. But since one of the main effects of implementing Quebec's comprehensive no-fault plan in the U.S. would be to reduce plaintiff personal injury lawyers' fees dramatically, it should not be surprising that these lawyers have tried to discredit its attractiveness as a consumer/victim measure.

In California, for example, comprehensive automobile no-fault plans appear to have no chance legislatively so long as Democratic friends of the trial lawyers' lobby control one of the key committees (Insurance or Judiciary) in either the state Senate or Assembly (something they have done for many years now despite the election of Republican governors). This has prompted proponents of auto no-fault to seek reform through the "initiative" process. A frequently employed mechanism in California and a few other states, initiatives are a way that citizens may force a popular vote on matter, in effect bypassing the ordinary legislative process.

For example, in 1988, key players in the auto insurance industry sponsored Proposition 104. By this I mean that industry leaders drafted the initiative, paid people to gather the required number of voter signatures needed to get the measure put on the ballot, and then carried the lion's share of the cost of advertising and other measures carried out on its behalf[20].

Proposition 104 was by no means a comprehensive auto no-fault scheme. It was, rather, a modest "modified" plan providing moderate no-fault benefits and curtailing tort law recovery for pain and suffering in less serious injury cases. This measure was badly defeated by the voters 21.

In the 1990s a new effort was launched. This time a comprehensive auto no-fault plan was put on the ballot in the spring of 1996 in the form of Proposition 200. This measure would have provided victim compensation broadly comparable to what Quebec provides, and it would have eliminated nearly as much of the tort law as Quebec has eliminated. But, unlike Quebec, this proposal assumed that private insurers would continue to sell and administer the no-fault-bodily-injury insurance mandated by the plan. Proposition 200 was the brainchild of a gadfly U.S. reformer named Andrew Tobias who lives in Florida, writes national columns for prominent publications, and had been promoting versions of auto no-fault for years. The insurance industry lent some support to the effort. Tobias also obtained considerable financial backing from parts of the business community (especially high tech companies located in California's Silicon Valley) by yoking his measure politically to two other ballot initiatives that were also advertised as litigation-reducers[22]. Proposition 200 was also strongly rejected by the voters (65% to 35 %)[23].

The plaintiffs' lawyers' lobby in California was the main source of the funds that were used to advertise against both Propositions 104 and 200[24]. They were also the main opponents in Hawaii where the legislature in 1995 passed a comprehensive no-fault scheme that would have expanded that state's existing, more-limited plan. But that measure was vetoed by the Democratic governor, himself a trial lawyer before entering politics[25]. The trial lawyers are greatly assisted in their fight against auto no-fault by having, from time to time, the support of certain important consumer groups, and, most importantly, the steadfast support of Ralph Nader.

2.1.2 Ralph Nader's Devotion to the Civil Justice System

Ralph Nader won his reputation in the U.S. as "Mr. Consumer" in the 1960s when he campaigned against unsafe automobiles[26]. At that time, General Motors helped make him especially famous by engaging in tactics against him that resulted in a lawsuit by Nader against GM for invasion of privacy in which Nader won a great deal of money and GM emerged with a very black eye[27]. It seems from the outside at least, that Nader's own experience in successfully using the civil justice system to combat wrong-doing by a large corporation has made him a stalwart defender of tort law and the trial lawyers' most important ally.

Whereas the trial lawyers might be dismissed as merely mouthing consumer protection arguments as cover for what is their own self-interest, this hardly applies to Nader, who has a reputation for exceptional selflessness and asceticism in his personal life. Some have tried to tar Nader by saying that his support for the trial lawyers is based upon the financial support they, in turn, supply to some of the organizations he has founded[28]. But I think that most close observers have rejected this claim, concluding instead that Nader truly believes in tort law in all of its reach.

It is fairly easy to see why Nader would, for example, oppose eliminating product liability suits against major manufacturers, even if they were replaced with a generous compensation scheme: this would deprive consumers of the role that some people (including Nader) think that tort law plays in preventing and/or exposing corporate misconduct. And while others might believe that a better solution would be a combination of a product injury compensation fund and a scheme that rewards whistle-blowers who disclose wrong-doing by product makers[29], this is an issue on which neutrals can conclude that there are reasonable arguments on both sides. Accordingly, Quebec has not broadly replaced tort law for product injuries with a compensation plan.

When it comes to routine auto injuries, however, the story is very different. Tort defendants here aren't generally corporations, but rather other drivers. It is clear that under U.S. tort law approximately half of the bodily-injury, liability-insurance premium paid for auto insurance goes for transactions costs, primarily to pay the legal fees of one side or the other[30]. Moreover, of the remainder that is paid out to victims, far more goes as compensation for pain and suffering or to duplicate benefits that victims already have from health insurance and other sources than is paid to compensate for true out-of-pocket economic losses[31].

Still, Nader is adamantly against auto no-fault schemes of all sorts, apparently on the ground that Americans have an absolute right to access to the civil justice system that cannot be denied to them, and the belief that it is important for victims to win as much in pain and suffering as juries or settlement will provide[32]. Nader's opposition has made it very difficult for no-fault advocates to convince people in the U.S. that the right sort of plan could actually be a great benefit to consumers overall.

2.1.3 Opposition of the Insurance Industry

Although most major U.S. auto insurers have supported the so-called “modified” auto no-fault strategy, and many would support a comprehensive auto no-fault plan as well, they are, obviously, opposed to certain aspects of the Quebec solution. The insurers want to stay in the business of providing coverage for bodily injury from auto accidents, and Quebec's plan gives that business to a government monopoly. Understandably, the U.S. companies would not be content merely writing the property damage coverage that private insurers are limited to providing in Quebec. Tobias' Proposition 200, on the other hand, allowed private insurers to continue to sell and administer the bodily injury coverage mandated by the plan. Hence, some insurers supported it. Yet this support was not terribly enthusiastic, in part because these companies thought that the initiative probably wouldn't pass anyway and in part because of concerns that open support by insurers would make Proposition 200 even less popular. Moreover, some insurers didn't like Proposition 200 because they oppose any scheme that will lower the amount of premiums they collect, even if the scheme is more predictable and easier for them to administer[33].

In contrast to the insurers' limited support for Proposition 200, when Tobias and I earlier circulated auto no-fault proposals that would be funded primarily "at the pump" (i.e., with fuel surcharges) the industry totally opposed us[34]. Even though we included the private insurers in our proposals as claims administrators (and even though some versions would have allowed them to continue to serve as risk spreaders), the insurers took the position that "pay at the pump" involved too much government control for their taste; it was, in effect, too much in the direction of the Quebec solution.

This stance, in a broad sense, mirrors the industry's position on workers' compensation. The insurers strongly support workers' compensation as a nearly complete substitute for tort claims against the employer (which is the rule in all of the United States), but they strongly oppose its implementation in those few states where the state government has created a single, government-run and publicly-owned insurer to handle the business. And the insurers have generally been successful in this opposition, since, in the great majority of states, either private workers' compensation insurers are the exclusive providers, or else the private firms share the market with a competitive state insurer that usually garners only a small portion of the employers as customers[35].

In short, with the trial lawyers, Nader, and the insurance companies all against the Quebec auto no-fault solution, political realities alone may fully explain why no U.S. state has enacted a similar scheme.

2.2 Public Perceptions

Yet, beyond mere politics, opponents of importing the Quebec approach to the U.S. are able to trade on certain public perceptions that are noticeably different in the states as compared with Canada.

2.2.1 Public Distrust of Government

For one thing, in the U.S. there is a fairly strong block of voters who take a dim view of any proposal that calls for a government agency to run the scheme at issue. This does not mean that it is absolutely implausible for the Quebec arrangement to be transplanted to the U.S. After all, the California legislature recently created the California Earthquake Authority which is charged with the role of making earthquake insurance available to property owners[36]. But this scheme was adopted only because very few private insurers were willing to sell earthquake insurance. Additionally, because California law required those selling homeowner's insurance *(i.e.,* broad "fire and theft" insurance) to offer their clients earthquake coverage as well, this was creating a crisis in the availability of the basic homeowner's insurance. Nonetheless, a plan to replace the now functioning auto insurance market (there are literally hundreds of companies selling auto insurance in California) with a monopoly public-provider is sure to run into widespread skepticism about how efficiently, effectively, or fairly the government insurer would operate.

2.2.2 Public Distrust of Insurance Companies

While distrust of government may help explain why the precise Quebec solution would face a very high hurdle to its enactment in the U.S., that does not explain why a state might not embrace Quebec's treatment of tort and no-fault benefits in a way that is administered by the private insurance industry (as California's Proposition 200 envisioned). But, here too, we run into a public perception problem: the equally widespread distrust of the insurance industry.

California's Proposition 103, barely passed in 1988 with Nader's support in the election that saw Proposition 104's no-fault scheme go down to defeat, was promoted on the basis that the auto insurers had, in effect, conspired to gouge consumers with unreasonably high premiums and then to mistreat them when claims were filed[37]. Furthermore, reflecting distrust of insurers, California most particularly, but now more and more states, have allowed insurance consumers to file tort actions (entitling winners to both open ended awards for pain and suffering and largely unconstrained sums for punitive damages) when their insurers in "bad faith" resist paying claims[38].

While, of course, the current auto injury compensation scheme also relies on the private insurance industry to provide the benefits, at least most victims with any sizable claim are able to enlist a lawyer to fight for them a lawyer who can be paid a contingent fee out of the generous pain and suffering benefits the lawyer can obtain in the settlement (or trial). But comprehensive, auto no-fault is meant to be administered largely without lawyers, and there is typically no generous "cushion" in its benefit structure to pay for legal representation if that is desired. Some people in the U.S. fear this will leave claimants, especially low income claimants, at the mercy of the insurance companies.

What all this means to me is that if a comprehensive auto no-fault plan to be run by private insurers is proposed and the plan is endorsed by the insurers, it will start out facing widespread opposition from the public at large.

2.2.3 Public Skepticism about the Financial Benefits

Those public misgivings might well be ameliorated if people could be convinced that motorists would save a great deal of money under a comprehensive auto no-fault scheme like Quebec's. Looking at the Quebec experience, one ought to be able to conclude that adopting a similar plan, say, in California would save motorists billions of dollars. Astoundingly, in Quebec the annual premiums motorists pay for no-fault bodily injury protection today are not substantially more than they were when the plan was enacted 20 years ago -- $142 (Canadian) for a good driver in 1998, as compared to about $100 in 1978[39]. Yet in that same period the benefits paid out under the plan have more than tripled, as wages and other costs have increased sharply (if nothing else because of inflation)[40]. Moreover, a study by the RAND Corporation's Institute for Civil Justice found that significant savings would occur were California's Proposition 200 adopted[41]savings that could be translated into sharply lower auto insurance premiums. Yet it is by no means clear that the public believed this about Proposition 200.

First, and perhaps most importantly, auto no-fault in the U.S. simply does not have a reputation as a money-saver for motorists. Of course, those in-the-know realize that experience with "add-on" plans is a very poor indicator of what would happen under a Quebec-style plan. But for the U.S. public, no-fault is an idea that has been around for quite some time now and its supporters are hard put to point to places where car owners have come out way ahead. Of course, supporters could point to Quebec, but the political reality in the U.S. (alas) is that experience from other nations is typically not terribly persuasive, especially in this context when there seems to be some U.S. experience that is contrary (even if not really analogous) to Quebec's.

This perception about no-fault might be overcome if other "government" insurance programs had good track records in terms of saving money that could be pointed to by way of analogy. But here too the U.S. track record is not attractive. For example, workers' compensation insurance rates (another no-fault scheme, after all) have risen sharply over the past two decades (in terms of percent of payroll); and the U.S. scheme for providing public health insurance to the elderly (Medicare) has become dramatically more costly in the three decades since its adoption and has regularly far out-paced cost projections.

Altogether, then, it is a very difficult uphill battle to convince the U.S. public generally that a no-fault idea imported from Quebec is going to save motorists a great deal of cash -- even if it will.

2.3 Cultural Traditions

Even if the public was convincingly shown that legal costs would be reduced and motorist premiums would be sharply lowered, Quebec-style auto no-fault runs counter to important U.S. cultural traditions.

2.3.1 Ideological Commitment to Individual Responsibility

For one thing, there is in the U.S. strong ideological support for the notion of individual responsibility, an idea which lies behind tort law and is rejected by comprehensive no-fault. Conservatives typically embrace this value on many issues, most notably the "crime problem" which liberals have tended to blame, at least in part, on the economy, the education system and the like. Recently, the U.S. has addressed "welfare reform" and in this round the Democrats, with President Clinton leading the way, joined with Republicans in emphasizing the personal responsibility theme. Given this bi-partisan support at least in the welfare area, there would surely be ideological disinclination to abandon it for motorists.

Of course, in practice, it is rather misleading to say that the tort system holds careless drivers personally responsible for their misconduct. If they are uninsured, they are not sued. If they are insured, then it is their insurance company that pays. Although this might be translated into higher individual premiums the next year, this is a private, not a public, penalty. Moreover, since few auto accident cases go to trial, tort law rarely serves the function of publicly denouncing the defendant's conduct as improper. Hence, it is more the symbolism of personal responsibility that people in the U.S. must be reluctant to overthrow for no-fault.

To be sure, workers' compensation is a no-fault plan that is well entrenched in the U.S., and there is no serious move to return workplace injuries to the tort system. But there the employer is formally obligated to provide benefits for injured workers, an outcome that trades on the idea that the employer has control over the workplace and so should take responsibility for what happens there. In auto no-fault, by contrast, rather than imposing strict liability on those who crash into other vehicles, drivers must look to their own insurers for coverage of accidents that occur in settings where the other car's driver could well have been at fault.

2.3.2 Lack of Support for Collective Responsibility

The other side of the "personal responsibility" coin is the relative lack of ideological commitment in the U.S. to the principle of collective responsibility, at least as compared with Canada. To be sure, there are wonderful stories of people in the U.S. coming to each other's aid in times of emergency, all sorts of disaster relief assistance is provided through government programs, and, of course, there is a strong commitment to collective responsibility for things like education. But as just noted above, there has recently been a retreat from that norm in the public benefits area, and there has never been a strong endorsement of it in the health care area, making the U.S. in this respect quite unlike most industrially-developed nations. In short, in a country where there is, in general, a rather patchy safety net, it is not surprising that no special effort has been made to assure compensation to victims of auto accidents despite the very prominent role that they play in the universe of serious and fatal accidents[42]. Indeed, as noted already, to the extent that states have embraced auto no-fault at all, all but two of them have excluded from its reach those very victims most in need of a thicker safety-net that is, the most seriously injured.

2.4 Trade-offs

When Quebec in 1977 embraced comprehensive auto no-fault and abandoned tort law for auto accidents, some people were worse off as a result. But, on balance, the trade-offs then made seemed quite fair, at least to the Quebec government that made the decision. In the U.S., however, the trade-offs would be somewhat different and, as explained below, would generate stronger objections from the losers (or those who claim to speak on their behalf).

2.4.1 A More Generous Tort Law

Speaking generally, Quebec's pre-1977 tort law was less generous than U.S. tort law. Of course, each state has its own tort law, and so eliminating tort recovery as part of a comprehensive no-fault plan would mean something different from place to place. Moreover, state tort law has changed since 1977 so that as it changes the tradeoff also changes.

For example, at the time Keeton and O'Connell put forward their auto no-fault proposal in 1965, the formal law in nearly all states treated the contributory negligence of the victim as a complete bar to recovery. Although it was then widely believed that juries commonly ignored this rule, it surely played an important role in discouraging some potential claimants from filing at all and gave insurers in certain cases extremely strong bargaining positions. By now, nearly every state has adopted a comparative fault regime that, at least when the victim is less at fault than the injurer, merely reduces compensation rather than barring it completely[43]. Indeed, many believe that comparative negligence was enacted in many places in the 1970s, at least in part, in order to blunt the demand for no-fault.

Also in 1965 several states still had "guest statutes" on their books, which generally denied passengers recovery against negligent drivers. Now these have all but disappeared[44]. For these two examples, then, as compared to today there would have been many fewer "losers" back in the 1960s had comprehensive auto no-fault then been adopted and tort law for auto accidents eliminated. That is, comparatively speaking on those two dimensions, even more would have to be given up were the tort regime overthrown today instead of in the 1960s. Overall, however, that conclusion must be tempered because more recently many states have cutback the amount of damages that may be awarded in tort cases. This has had the opposite effect reducing the amount of recovery that would be given up were comprehensive auto no-fault adopted today.

2.4.2 Especially Generous Awards for Pain and Suffering

Nevertheless, what is (and was) the most important difference between U.S. tort law and Canadian tort law is the much greater generosity in the U.S. in the amount of money paid out for pain and suffering, also called "general damages." This difference, which certainly existed in the 1960s, is probably even more pronounced today. Moreover, this is the head of damages that Nader and the trial lawyers emphasize in their fight against no-fault.

Several points bear attention here. Perhaps most interesting for the U.S. audience is the fact that Quebec's auto no-fault plan actually pays out sums for pain and suffering. In 1994, for example, about 12 % of the costs of the scheme went to fund such awards[45]. This is probably quite surprising to most people in the U.S. who know anything about auto no-fault, because discussions of auto no-fault in the U.S. have almost all been premised on the assumption that pain and suffering benefits will not be provided. (Of course, if only "modified" plans are being considered, then pain and suffering awards are curtailed in only the non-serious injury cases.)

In any event, the level of the awards for pain and suffering made under the Quebec plan is quite modest as compared with U.S. tort law. Although the most seriously injured claimant will be able to obtain as much as $175,000 Canadian starting in 1999[46], large amounts are rarely awarded, and in any case this is more than an order of magnitude less than what can be awarded in U.S. cases now. By contrast, in Quebec in 1977 the cutback in the amount awarded for this purpose was substantially less. So, to emphasize the point directly, some U.S. auto accident victims would receive enormously less money than they do today (even after paying their legal fees) were the Quebec scheme simply transferred to the U.S.

At least two qualifications to this point are in order, however. The first is that a state could always adopt the Quebec plan in general and yet make the pain and suffering awards substantially larger. This would, of course, make the plan substantially more expensive. But since the U.S. tort system is currently so generous in what it awards, this means that insurance rates are much higher than they would be in Quebec were Quebec to go back to its old tort law, and hence, even with a more generous no-fault benefit package, there is still considerable room for premium reduction.

Second, the problem of "uninsured" and "under-insured" motorists in the U.S. also reduces the amount that would be given up were comprehensive auto no-fault adopted. That is, while some U.S. victims win millions for pain and suffering, most victims are unable to recover anything like that amount not because of tort law, but because of the limited ability of their victims to pay. Nationwide it is estimated that about 17% of U.S. drivers are uninsured[47], and another 50% have liability insurance in the amount of $50,000 (U.S.) or less[48]. Together these facts mean that, despite tort law's superficial generosity, most seriously-injured victims are vastly under-compensated, often recovering only a small share of their economic losses and nothing for pain and suffering[49].For these victims, a Quebec-style approach would actually deliver much better benefits. Still, there is no doubt that a small minority of the gravely injured who are able to sue a defendant with very deep pockets would trade off quite a bit of money were a comprehensive no-fault scheme adopted.

Also, the modestly injured with an insured at-fault defendant to claim against would also probably be worse off (and relatively more so than in Quebec) under plausible U.S. comprehensive plans. Is this bad? Many of us believe that, in return for a good no-fault scheme, pain and suffering awards should be readily abandoned for such victims (most of whose pain and suffering is in the past before they see the money paid in compensation). Yet, the political support for these very victims appears to be precisely what has lead to so many states enacting "add on" plans rather than "modified" plans.

Thus, the general point remains that, in the U.S. setting, the inevitable pain and suffering "take away" will loom as a larger trade-off than it did in Quebec. This is something which tort defenders make good rhetorical use of especially so long as they don't have to disclose how many U.S. claimants (especially the seriously injured) fail to tap into this bonanza.

For some tort critics, the idiosyncratic pattern of recovery we observe in the U.S. whether because of insurance availability and amount or because of inconsistent jury results or uneven lawyer bargaining ability provides a strong argument for replacing the common law system with a reliable and routinely more uniform compensation plan. Yet, it is by no means clear that this view would be broadly embraced by the U.S. public.

That is, it sometimes seems that many people enjoy the lottery-like aspect of U.S. tort law that makes some people rich by the luck of the draw. This is perhaps consistent with the interest many people in the U.S. have in playing lotteries in general. In order to deal with this phenomenon, Tobias reported making a wickedly clever proposal to Nader as a way to try to win his support. Tobias suggested that a special lottery would be held every so often that would be open only to those who had made successful claims under the comprehensive auto no-fault plan. Tickets would simply be given out to the claimants along with their recovery under the no-fault scheme (perhaps with more tickets going to those who had been more seriously injured). The lucky winners would get lump sum prizes of various sizes. Tobias asserted that results of this lottery would not differ dramatically from how tort law in action now works, and yet this lottery would be enormously cheaper to administer and fund. We may assume that Nader was not amused.

2.4.3 The Uninsured Motorist Problem

As noted above, it is estimated that perhaps one in six car owners in the U.S.

goes without automobile liability insurance-even though having this insurance is compulsory in more than 40 states[50]. In some places the uninsured rate is strikingly higher; in California, for example, nearly 30% of motorists are thought to be uninsured[51].

It is typically claimed that many of the uninsured are poor people. The picture painted by some is that the poor desperately need their old car to get to work (given the poor public transportation system throughout most of the U.S.), but would have to deprive themselves and their children of food if they bought car insurance. While this portrait is surely true of some of the uninsured, some suggest that many could afford to buy insurance and don't[52]. It seems that they don't buy partly because they don't expect to be in an accident at which they are at fault and don't expect to get caught without having the required insurance (since enforcement of the compulsory insurance laws has been notoriously lax in most states). But, in addition, it seems that many of the uninsured just figure that they will be essentially judgment-proof if they do happen to cause an accident, and that without insurance they just won't be sued. Surely many talk themselves into adopting this morally dubious posture because automobile insurance rates are so high in the U.S. in large part due to our Rolls Royce-like tort law.

The prevalence of uninsured motorists has been one of the strong arguments in favor of adopting a comprehensive auto no-fault scheme in the U.S. Because premiums would come down, more would buy coverage, and, more importantly, those who still failed to do so would now be depriving themselves of protection instead of their victims.

But there is another, somewhat bizarre, side of this coin. If a plan like Quebec's were adopted, not only would it be compulsory, but also we could expect that vigorous efforts would be made to enforce participation. In Quebec, for example, uninsured motorists risk having their cars impounded, among other penalties. A compulsory, well-policed no-fault scheme would help achieve the near universal coverage of accident victims that is intended by its designers. Yet, returning to the California data, this would mean an extra financial burden for the 30% of drivers who don't buy insurance now. Even if the burden were far less than what auto insurance would cost them today, it still would be an increase in the out-of-pocket costs of car ownership. Although some would welcome the ability to obtain coverage and comply with the law at a modest price, many others would prefer to continue to “go bare” (especially if the cost in the U.S. were around $300 U.S. a year as was envisioned under Proposition 200, rather than the less than $150 Canadian charged by the Quebec scheme)[53].

As a result, I imagine that many of today's uninsured drivers would oppose an effectively-enforced, no-fault scheme. While their position is a difficult one to present in public debate, it nonetheless lurks in the background and can be acted on individually at the ballot box when initiatives are proposed (although it is probably true that the uninsured are very disproportionately non-voters). In short, the greater ease with which one can be an auto insurance scofflaw is yet another "benefit" of the existing U.S. scheme that would have to be traded away were the Quebec solution to replace it.

2.5 Some Policy Concerns About the Quebec Model

My discussion so far has focused on obstacles to enactment in the U.S. of a Quebec-style auto no-fault plan on the assumption that, from a certain frame of reference, the Quebec approach is a desirable one. Now, however, I want to discuss to some concerns that may be raised about it by objective policy analysis.

2.5.1 Safety Fears

Perhaps the most important worry is that comprehensive auto no-fault generates more auto accidents. Although one might even be willing to accept this outcome as part of the price for an otherwise very desirable scheme, surely this would be a strong argument against its adoption. Moreover, this is exactly the reputation that the Quebec solution has garnered among scholars south of the border. This reputation is the result of a variety of studies conducted both inside and outside Canada. The two Canadian studies generally discussed are those of Gaudry[54] and Devlin[55]. Both found there were more auto accidents with the Quebec plan than there would have been without it. These findings are also consistent with a widely publicized study of U.S. no-fault by Landes[56] as well as research on no-fault in Australia[57].

However, carrying out a convincing study of the impact of no-fault is extremely difficult. For one thing, since auto accident rates have been dropping generally, the researcher has to try to figure out whether the drop would have been greater had tort remained and no-fault not been adopted. Two research strategies are: 1) to explore whether the trend-line under tort law was shifted under no-fault and 2) to compare accident rates in matched tort and no-fault jurisdictions. But, as with all research of either a time series or cross-sectional nature, there are always extremely difficult data problems. For example, something else might have happened in the no-fault period that accounts for a trend change that should not be attributed to no-fault; and in cross-sectional studies there is always the risk that the jurisdictions being compared are different in unmeasured ways, thereby again leading to the attribution to no-fault of accident outcomes that were actually caused by something else. To overcome these conundrums, very complicated research strategies have been employed, frequently using highly sophisticated, multiple-regression-analysis techniques that are too complex for the ordinary reader to evaluate.

At the theoretical level at least three models, containing quite different predictions about safety under the Quebec plan, could be constructed. One would rest on the idea that fears about harming one's own body, fears of getting a traffic citation or facing other criminal charges, and general moral feelings about not risking harm to others provide all the deterrence that can be achieved. Under this model, tort law has no additional impact on making people drive more safely. Therefore, eliminating tort law would not lead to a deterioration in driving conduct.

The second model predicts that, not withstanding those other pressures to drive safely, tort law does promote better driving, perhaps due to fears, even exaggerated fears, of incurring higher auto insurance premiums. Hence this second model would predict worse driving under no-fault.

Moreover, two other features of the Quebec approach that might yield more accidents could be incorporated into this model. For one thing, lowered insurance costs make driving more affordable, thereby permitting more people to become motorists. That, in turn, would be expected to yield more accidents, and especially so if the new drivers are disproportionately young people who had been most effectively priced off the highway by a tort liability regime that charged them (particularly young men) well more than average (assuming, as in Quebec for many years, the state-run, no-fault plan charged all drivers the same premium)[58].

Yet, in other areas of life, we don't normally consider the lowered costs of a product or service to be undesirable, even if it causes more people to use it, thereby bringing about more accidents. For example, if someone invents a new type of ski equipment that is no more dangerous than existing equipment, but is so much cheaper as to make skiing much more affordable, the number of skiers lured onto the slopes would probably increase. Yet, we would not object to the introduction of this equipment even if it also meant more ski accidents due to the increased number of skiers.

The second factor is that by providing comprehensive compensation to victims, Quebec's plan could have the effect of causing people either to be less cautious about injury to themselves or less quick to recover once injured. This is often termed the "moral hazard" problem. While "moral hazard" could potentially lead to undesirable results, many would be reluctant to forego the Quebec approach on this ground alone. After all, that analysis would equally apply to workers' compensation plans, health insurance schemes, private disability schemes and the like. But surely most will conclude that the benefit of providing people needed insurance well outweighs the moral hazard risk. Further, the risk is typically dealt with by providing victims less than full compensation through the plan[59].

In contrast to this second model that predicts higher accident rates associated with the Quebec no-fault plan, a third model predicts lower accident rates. The theory here is that when a government agency is charged with responsibility for running the scheme that has to charge premiums to the public, it will be under great political and public pressure to keep those premiums low. As a result, it will also be under pressure to find ways to lower accident rates so as to reduce claims on the scheme, through public education and specific safety-promotion measures.

Interestingly enough, despite the early negative empirical findings about the Quebec plan on safety grounds, there is now reason to reject those results. For one thing, officials running the Quebec plan claim they have been highly effective in reducing accident rates and can point to specific safety-promoting measures they have generated[60]. To be sure, without the application of sophisticated research methodologies, one should not rely too heavily on these officials claims. Yet Gaudry himself has released a much more recent study that comes to the opposite conclusion from his earlier work suggesting now that the Quebec plan lowered the accident rate more than would have occurred without it[61]. Furthermore, recent critiques have cast doubt on the persuasiveness of Devlin's work[62]. Finally, there are U.S. studies contradicting Landes[63].

For me, the bottom line is that we should not fear that importing the Quebec regime to the U.S. would yield an undesirable increase in accidents. Moreover, it is not necessary to embrace the flat fee rules that prevailed in the early years in Quebec. Motorists with bad driving records could easily be charged more;

indeed, since 1992 Quebec has done exactly that by making bad drivers pay extra to renew their driving licenses[64]. Furthermore, unlike Quebec, young drivers, or novice drivers generally, might be charged an additional surcharge for their first three years on the road (with a refund of some or all of that surcharge if they were accident free for those three years)[65].

2.5.2 Cost Fears

The Quebec experience ought to allay cost fears. Although overall program costs certainly have increased, for example from just under $500 million Canadian in 1990 to over $700 million Canadian in 1994, nevertheless, as noted earlier, the insurance cost to motorists if adjusted for inflation is decidedly less than what it was 20 years ago. It is important to appreciate, however, a major contributor to today's low cost is that the government agency in charge wound up in the early years with far more premium income than was necessary to pay claims and wisely invested this surplus. As a result, about 40 percent of the cost of the system is now paid for by investment income[66]. U.S. insurers, of course, also enjoy investment income on premiums (since they collect in advance) which in turn holds premiums down somewhat. But the relative amount of investment income available to the Quebec authorities is larger than would typically occur in a competitive market. Hence, if Quebec's system today enjoyed only the average amount of investment income obtained by a U.S. insurer of comparable size, the Quebec premiums would have to increase (although they would have been still lower in the earlier years). Nevertheless, it seems reasonably clear that even if Quebec had to pay for the full cost of its plan out of current premiums (and earnings on those premiums), although the rates would go up, they still would be less in 1998 than they were in 1978 in real terms that is, if discounted for inflation.

However, as previously pointed out, the U.S. experience with workers' compensation has been far worse. Because of that experience, some people in the U.S. will want to hold down the cost of a comprehensive auto no-fault plan by making its benefits secondary to payments by health insurance plans and other sources like Social Security. Moreover, this approach has certain administrative attractions-most importantly avoiding the transactions costs of one insurer recouping from another. Nevertheless, hypersensitivity to health care costs in the U.S. today may make this a particularly bad time for that sort of cost-shifting. The upshot is that a state importing the Quebec scheme to the U.S. might simply have to take it on faith that it could approximate Quebec's ability to control costs as compared with U.S. experience in workers' compensation.

A quite different cost concern arises from the size of the benefit package under the no-fault plan as compared with the typical liability insurance benefit package. Today, as noted already, most U.S. motorists carry either the minimum allowable auto insurance (often only $10,000-$25,000 U.S. per person injured) or else modest amounts above the minimum ($50,000 U.S. or less). If the auto no-fault plan is to be truly comprehensive it will have to provide a far higher dollar level of coverage than $50,000 U.S. This, of course, will make the program commensurately more expensive.

Proposition 200 in California sought to deal with this issue by making the default insurance policy have a benefit maximum of $1 million (with certain internal limits, for example, on wage replacement), while at the same time permitting buyers to opt, if they wish, for a cheaper plan with only $50,000 of coverage. This has the advantage of allowing the plan's promoters to emphasize how little one would pay for a $50,000 policy. Yet if most people were actually to buy that coverage, this would leave many seriously injured victims substantially under-compensated. Of course, as noted, $50,000 is all that many seriously injured victims now obtain, and here it would be a matter of consumer choice. Still, there is some reason to fear that too many people would buy less coverage now and later be very regretful. On the other hand, again, forcing everyone to buy the $1 million coverage makes the plan relatively less attractive as a money-saving proposal compared with the current regime, and understandably makes the initiative more difficult to sell to the voters in 30 or 60 second sound bites that dominate most election campaigns. After all, these reforms come at a time when motorists are far more likely to respond favorably to insurance premium reductions than to distant promises of better benefits in case they are badly injured. Still, although I recognize the difficulty of the judgment that was involved, I am not convinced that the promoters of Proposition 200 dealt with these competing considerations in the wisest manner.

I do agree that the cost problem is most importantly confronted in the details of the program's design. That is, the real cost and cost escalation worries, I believe, depend upon the precise nature of the benefits provided. But before tolerating a ceiling of $50,000 for those with no other sources of compensation, other avenues should be pursued. For example, one would want the medical benefits to be offered in ways that take advantage of the sorts of sensible and fair cost containment strategies now beginning to be used in the U.S. in workers' compensation and health insurance plans; one would want to be careful that rehabilitation benefits are provided in reasonably proper amounts where they can be effective and not lavishly wasted; and one would want to avoid over-generosity in the level of replacement services benefits provided. Indeed, the drafters of Proposition 200 were very mindful of at least some of these very points. Nonetheless, I believe that with these sorts of internal controls and limits in place, sufficient financial savings could be promised to today's drivers even in a plan with $1 million benefit maximum.

I have not yet mentioned legitimate concerns about fraudulent claims. Workers' compensation and health care schemes in the U.S. face this problem, and surely a comprehensive auto no-fault plan would as well. Indeed, fraud in the non-fault aspects of auto and homeowners' insurance is an ongoing problem. But the concern here ought to be a comparative one since, alas, the automobile liability system in the U.S. is allegedly rife with fraud. There are ongoing reports of staged accidents, deliberate accidents, deliberate malingering after accidents, claims to reimburse the cost of medical services that were never rendered, and the like. Some argue that U.S. auto liability insurance premiums are 10-20% higher than they would be without this sort of fraud[67].

No doubt, the present system especially encourages fraud because of the availability of open-ended pain and suffering damages. This is the grease that draws together, for example, the crooked lawyer and doctor with the willingly fraudulent claimant. By pretending to have medical needs, the economic losses claimed are increased, thereby also increasing the amount of pain and suffering obtainable in settlement, and generating extra funds for the lawyer and for the cheating patient.

I am convinced that this sort of fraud would be less popular in a plan that didn't pay pain and suffering benefits, or at least didn't pay the amounts now paid in the U.S. Yet, on the other hand, since fault would no longer be an issue, other types of smaller-scale fraud would be encouraged. Still, on balance, especially since fraud does not seem to a matter of serious concern in Quebec, there is reason to hope that the fraud problem would become smaller were Quebec's auto no-fault plan adopted in the states.

2.5.3 Slippery-Slope Fears

Some no-fault critics, probably Nader, worry that comprehensive auto no-fault would be just a foot in the door to the adoption of other no-fault arrangements, arrangements they far more strongly oppose. Others hope for exactly that auto no-fault leading to, for example, no-fault coverage of medical accidents, pharmaceutical drug injuries, recreational injuries, and the like[68]. If the Quebec experience is to be any guide, auto no-fault might at first be seen as a step in the direction of other no-fault plans. That is, Quebec's auto no-fault plan was followed by a liberalizing reform of the province's workers' compensation scheme, a similar revision of the scheme to compensate victims of violent crime (now not in force), and the adoption of a scheme to compensate those who suffer side-effects from vaccinations against disease[69]. Moreover, there is now some discussion in Quebec about how accidental victims of medical treatment might be covered on a no-fault basis.

On the other hand, in the years since Keeton and O'Connell proposed auto no-fault in the U.S., we too have witnessed a substantial liberalization of workers' compensation, the widespread adoption of (fairly ineffective) programs for compensating victims of violent crime, and the enactment of a national childhood vaccine injury scheme. In addition, there has been much talk in the U.S., although not any action yet, about handling the medical injury problem on a no-fault basis. Put differently, to the extent that Quebec has slid down the "slippery slope," so has the U.S. but without a Quebec-style auto no-fault plan to lead the way.

This suggests to me that "slippery slope" fearing opponents of comprehensive auto no-fault should not be so fearful, and "foot-in-the-door" proponents should not feel so hopeful.

3. Creeping Toward the Quebec Solution?

Although no U.S. state has yet followed the Quebec auto insurance precedent, perhaps in future years that will occur, or at least we will see moves in that direction. Just because California's Proposition 200 was defeated and Hawaii's comprehensive no-fault plan was vetoed does not mean that those ideas are dead, especially as other changes are afoot that could facilitate their rejuvenation.

3.1 Auto No-fault "Choice" Plans

Realizing that "add-on" plans were probably making things worse, and that trial lawyer political power continues to block state legislative enactment of comprehensive no-fault, O'Connell and others have proposed a "choice" scheme under which individual motorists can elect to be in either the fault system or the no-fault system. O'Connell's argument is that it should be harder for the lawyers to defeat something that is a matter of consumer choice as compared with conventional no-fault which is forced on everyone. His assumption, however, is that once given the choice, the vast majority of motorists would elect no-fault because of its lower cost and in some circumstances far better benefits.

But so far the trial lawyers, who can read the tea leaves too, have been able to block choice plans. And at least one time it was put to the voters of a state (in Arizona) advocates found they were outmatched by the lawyers' campaign and the proposal was badly defeated[70]. Hence, O'Connell and others have now taken their campaign to Congress where, at least for the moment, Republicans, who aren't so beholden to the plaintiffs' bar, wield considerable political power. Yet, it is by no means clear that this approach is going to get anywhere any time soon.

3.2 Pay at the Pump

While this is not the place to discuss pay at the pump schemes in detail, suffice it to say that policy analysts have proposed several auto compensation plans that would be funded primarily with surcharges on the purchase of gasoline (or other vehicle fuels). These proposals are usually tied to no-fault benefit schemes although that does not necessarily follow. They have certain politically desirable attributes. First, they would largely eliminate the uninsured motorist problem in the sense that all drivers would have to pay into the plan since everyone would have to buy gasoline and relatively little fraud is likely. Second, pay at the pump is attractive to environmental groups, public transportation advocates, and those concerned about energy efficiency because they appear to promise a combination of less driving and the purchase of more fuel efficient vehicles.

To be sure, pay at the pump plans currently seem politically remote, if nothing else because they bring out the opposition of the "highway lobby" that a) favors more driving rather than less *(e.g.,* motel owners, fast food restaurateurs, freeway builders, the oil companies, etc.) and; b) jealously guards the principle that "gas taxes" should be used only for the building and maintenance of roads. Nevertheless, pay at the pump could possibly become the stalking horse for a Quebec-style plan a lesser of evils that insurers and others could get behind to forestall pay at the pump.

3.3 Crackdowns on the Uninsured Motorist

Throughout the U.S., the public seems up in arms about the uninsured motorist problem. This has prompted the adoption of increasingly tougher sanctions against the uninsured including high fines, driving license suspension, vehicle confiscation and so on. Many thoughtful observers find these growing penalties draconian, especially when levied against poor people with few options.

Most recently, an approach called "no pay, no play" has been promoted[71] and has so far been adopted in a few states, including California. It comes in two versions. In both, anyone who is uninsured and hurt in an auto accident has his right to recover in tort limited. The idea is that since he belongs to a class of drivers who aren't paying their fair share of money into the plan, then members of that class should be restricted in what they draw from the plan when they sue. In California such motorists are denied pain and suffering damages; in Louisiana they are forced to bear some of their own out of pocket losses[72]. One version of "no pay, no play" limits tort recovery *in addition* to any other penalties already imposed on uninsured motorists; in the second version, tort limits are imposed *instead of* other penalties in effect, one is permitted to go without liability insurance so long as he agrees that he won't recover fully in tort if he is injured.

My goal here is not to discuss the merits of the various approaches to the uninsured motorist problem. I want only to emphasize what was noted earlier. Under comprehensive no-fault, the uninsured motorist problem has an entirely different meaning. Instead of cheating someone you negligently injure out of recovery, your failure to insure only hurts you (and perhaps your own family). Hence, if these escalated attacks on the uninsured motorist do not achieve satisfactory results, this might be another pressure for moving to Quebec-style no-fault as a different way to combat the uninsured.

Conclusion

I believe that adoption in California of a Quebec-style comprehensive automobile no-fault plan (perhaps administered by the private sector), would be a great benefit to most consumers and to most victims (especially those who are most seriously injured). Possibly, a few years of good experience with the Quebec model in Manitoba and Saskatchewan will demonstrate its export potential. Or, perhaps we just need to get Nader to spend a lot of time in Quebec.

ENDNOTES

1. *Automobile Insurance Act,* R.S.Q. 1977, c. A-25.

2. See *e.g.,* J. O'CONNELL and C. TENSER, "North America's Most Ambitious No-Fault Law: Quebec's Auto Insurance Act", (1987) 24 *San Diego L Rev.* 917; J. DAW, "Does Quebec Have the Answer?", *The [Toronto] Star* (16 May 1995) Dl. See also the text of N. Weatherston published in this issue.

3. M.A. FRANKLIN, *Tort Law and Alternatives,* 2nd ed., Mineola, The Foundation Press, 1979, pp. 797-798; R. KEETON and J. O'CONNELL, *Basic Protection for the Traffic Victim: A Blueprint for Reforming Auto Insurance,* Toronto, Little, Brown and Co., 1965.

4. R. KEETON and J. O'CONNELL, *op. cit.,* note 3.

5. M.A. FRANKLIN and R.L. RABIN, *Tort Law and Alternatives,* 6th ed., Westbury, The Foundation Press, 1996.

6. See U.S. DEPARTMENT OF TRANSPORTATION, *State No-Fault Automobile Insurance Experience 1971-1977,* Washington, Department of Transportation, June 1977, pp. 6-12; U.S. DEPARTMENT OF TRANSPORTATION, *Compensating Auto Accident Victims: A Follow Up Report on No-Fault Insurance Experiences,* Washington, Govt. Print. Off., May 1985, pp. 23-24.

7. M.A. FRANKLIN and R.L. RABIN, *op. cit.,* note 5, pp. 756-757 (reprinting, *Automobile Insurance... For Whose Benefit?,* A Report to Governor Nelson A. Rockefeller by the INSURANCE DEPARTMENT OF THE STATE OF NEW YORK, Albany, Insurance Department, 1970, pp. 17-44).

8. See, *e.g.,* J. O'CONNELL and J. BARKER, Compensation for Injury & Illness : An Update of the Conrad-Morgan Study", (1986)47 *Ohio St. L. J.* 913, 930; see also M.A. FRANKLIN and R.L. RABIN, *op. cit.,* note 5, pp. 756-757 (referring to "mixed" plans).

9. R.H. JOOST, *Automobile Insurance and No-Fault Law, 2*nd ed., Deerfield, Clark, Boardman & Callaghan, 1992, section 1:1, 3; J. O'CONNELL and J. BARKER, loc. *cit.,* note 8, 930.

10. M.A. FRANKLIN, *op. cit.,* note 3, p. 798.

11. J. O'CONNELL and R.H. JOOST, "A Model Bill Allowing Choice Between Auto Insurance Payable With and Without Regard to Fault", (1990) 51 *Ohio St. L. J.* 947, 947-948.

12. See, *e.g.,* U.S. DEPARTMENT OF TRANSPORTATION, *op. cit.,* note 6 (May 1985); J. O'CON- NELL and R.H. JOOST, "Giving Motorists a Choice Between Fault and No-Fault Insurance", (1986) 72 *Va. L. Rev.* 61.

13. U.S. DEPARTMENT OF TRANSPORTATION, *op. cit.,* note 6, p. 34 (May 1985).

14. M.A. FRANKLIN, *op. cit.,* note 3, pp. 801-803 (citing plan by American Insurance Association recommending comprehensive no-fault system and abolition of all tort law for automobile accidents).

15. R.H. JOOST, *op. cit.,* note 9, p. 8, section 1:2.

16. R.H. JOOST, *Automobile Insurance and No-Fault Law,* 2nd ed., Deerfield, Clark, Board- man & Callaghan, Supp. 1997, p. 29, section 1:20.

17. R.H. JOOST, *op. cit.,* note 9, p. 6, section 1:2.

18. R.H. JOOST, *op. cit.,* note 16, p. 118, section 7:6.

19. *Id.,* p. 53.

20. It is now common that ballot initiatives in California are actually promoted by well- organized interest groups rather than loose collections of grass roots voters who have arisen to support a cause-defeating the original vision behind the initiative process. So, too, it is common for sponsors to pay people to collect the signatures necessary to put initiatives on the ballot. See A. TOBIAS, "Ralph Nader is a Big Fat Idiot", *Worth* (Oct. 1996) 92, at 100.

21. Proposition 104 was defeated 74 to 26%. See *The [San Diego] Union Tribune* (9 November 1988) A4.

22. See A. TOBIAS, *loc. cit.,* note 20, 105. Proposition 201 would have limited people's right to sue when the value of stock they bought dropped, and would have helped high tech enterprises especially. Proposition 202 was designed to reduce legal fees in cases taken on a contingent fee basis. *Id.,* at 172-173.

23. *The [San Francisco] Examiner* (27 March 1996) A6.

24. *Ibid.* See also, A. TOBIAS, *loc. cit.,* note 20, 175-176.

25. See A. TOBIAS, *loc. cit.,* note 20, 174-175.

26. See, *e.g.,* R. NADER and J.A. PAGE, "Automobile Design and the Judicial Process", (1967) 55 *Cal. L Rev.* 645.

27. See *Nader* v. *General Motors Corp,* 25 N.Y.2d 560, 255 N.E.2d 765 (1970); see also, M.A. FRANKLIN and R.L. RABIN, *op. cit.,* note 5, p. 1069 (discussing *Nader* v. *General Motors Corp..)*

28. See P. BRIMELOW and L. SPENCER, "Ralph Nader, Inc.", *Forbes* (17 Sept. 1990) 117; A. TOBIAS, *[oc. cit.,* note 20, 176.

29. See generally, S.D. SUGARMAN, *Doing Away With Personal Injury Law,* Westport, Quorum Books, Greenwood Publishing, 1989.

30. M.A. FRANKLIN and R.L. RABIN, *op. cit.,* note 5, pp. 756-757 (reprinting, *Automobile Insurance... For Whose Benefit?, op. cit.,* note 7, pp. 17-44); see also U.S. DEPARTMENT OF TRANSPORTATION, *op. cit.,* note 6, p. 43 (June 1977).

31. M.A. FRANKLIN and R.L. RABIN, *op. cit.,* note 5, pp. 756-757 (reprinting, *Automobile Insurance... For Whose Benefit?, op. cit.,* note 7, pp. 17-44).

32. See, *e.g.,* R. NADER, The Corporate Drive to Restrict Their Victims' Rights", (1986-87) 22 *Gonz. L. Rev.* 15; see also, R. NADER and J.A. PAGE, "Automobile-Design Liability and Compliance with Federal Standards", (1996) 64 *Geo. Wash. L. Rev.* 415 (noting that tort law is an essential supplement to federal regulation and the proper role of auto-design product liability suits is to help reduce the number of traffic accidents and the severity of injuries).

33. See A. TOBIAS, *loc. cit.,* note 20, 173, 175.

34 *Id.,* at 96-97.

35. In the U.S. approximately 60% of employers obtain worker's compensation coverage through private carriers, approximately 20% obtain coverage through state funds, and approximately I % of employers "self-insure" against their employees' injuries. See THE AMERICAN LAW INSTITUTE, *Reports' Study, Enterprise*

Responsibility for Personal Injury 121, Vol. I, Philadelphia, American Law Institute, 1991.

36. See generally, *West Cal. Ins. Code,* Section 10089.5 et seq.; D. ADAMSON and D. McNARY, "Quest for Quake Insurance Some Californians Finding Fault with State-Operated Coverage Plan", *The [Los Angeles] Daily News* (5 January 1997) Bl.

37. See generally, S.D. SUGARMAN, "California's Insurance Regulation Revolution: The First Two Years of Proposition", (1990) 103 *San Diego L Rev.* 683.

38. See, *e.g.,* R.C. HENDERSON, "The Tort of Bad Faith in First-Party Insurance Transactions After Two Decades", (1995) 37 *Ariz. L. Rev.* 1153.

39. In 1997 Quebec motorists paid $112 (Canadian) for their bodily injury protection, paying for it in two parts, $87 at the time of vehicle registration and $25 at the time of driver's license renewal. In 1998, the amount paid at the time of vehicle registration increased to $117, returning to the 1996 level. See interview with Andre Viel, Chef de Service des Etudes et des Strategies en Assurance Automobile, *Societé de l'assurance automobile du Quebec,* email, January 29, 1998.

40. See SOCIETÉ DE L 'ASSURANCE AUTOMOBILE DU QUEBEC, *Annual Report,* Quebec, S.A.A.Q., 1994. Because of inflation, the Canadian consumer price index is 275% of what it was in 1978 : interview with Daniel Gardner, Professor of Law, Université Laval, email on February 2, 1998.

41. S. CARROLL and A. ABRAHAMSE, *The Effects of a Proposed No-Fault Plan on the Costs of Auto Insurance in California,* Issue Paper, Santa Monica, RAND Institute for Civil Justice, March 1995.

42. In 1996 there were 43,300 unintentional motor-vehicle deaths, out of a total of 93,400 unintentional deaths. Also, in 1996 there were 2,600,000 motor-vehicle related disabling injuries, out of a total of 20,700,000 disabling injuries. *National Safety Council Accident Facts (Injury Statistics),* http://www.nsc.org (visited on March 9, 1998).

43.V.E. SCHWARTZ, *Comparative Negligence,* 3rd ed., Indianapolis, A. Smith Co., 1994, pp. 2-4; R.H. JOOST, *op. cit.,* note 9, pp. 14-15, section I :3.

44. R.H. JOOST, *op. cit.,* note 9, p. 16, section I :5.

45. SOCIETÉ DE L'ASSURANCE AUTOMOBILE DU QUEBEC, *op. Cit.,* note 40.

46. As soon as the proposed modification to the actual s. 73 of the *Automobile Insurance Act* will be adopted: *Loi modifiant la Loi sur l'assurance automobile,* Projet de loi 429, 2e session, 35e legislature (Quebec), s. 21.

47. J.D. KHAZZOOM, *What We Know About Uninsured Motorists and How Well We Know What We Know,* Discussion Paper 98-09, Washington, Resources for the Future, December 1997, Table III.3.

48. See J. O'CONNELL," No-Fault Auto Insurance: Back by Popular (Market) Demand?", (1989) *26San Diego L. Rev.* 993, 1000, note 18; S.J. CARROLL and J.S. KAKALIK, *No-Fault Automobile Insurance: A Policy Perspective,* Santa Monica, RAND Institute for Civil Justice, R-4019/1-ICJ, 1991.

49. See S.J. CARROLL and J.S. KAKALIK, *No-Fault Approaches to Compensating Auto Accident Victims,* Santa Monica, RAND Institute for Civil Justice, RP-229, 1993, pp. 278-281; see also S.J. CARROLL *et al., No-Fault Approaches to Compensating People Injured in Automobile Accidents,* Santa Monica, RAND Institute for Civil Justice, R-4019-ICJ, 1991.

50. See INSURANCE INFORMATION INSTITUTE, *Insurance Issues Update,* New York, Insurance Information

Institute, October 1997 (noting 43 states and the District of Columbia require liability insurance); see also R.H. JOOST, *op. cit.,* note 9, p. 21, section 1:8.

51. J.D. KHAZZOOM, *op. cit.,* note 47, Table III:1.

52. T.E. TROXEL, Ph.D., Remarks at the "No-Pay-No-Play: Addressing The Uninsured Motorist Issue" Conference, San Diego, CA (15 December 1997).

53. Actually, the compulsory Quebec charge is more because one condition of car ownership in Quebec is that you carry $50,000 in tort liability insurance for property damages (to vehicles and other property). This is privately sold and varies in cost, but $179 (Canadian) is what a good driver in Quebec City might expect to pay annually. See interview with Andre Vie!, Chef de Service des Etudes et des Strategies en Assurance Automobile, *Societé de l'assurance automobile du Quebec,* email, January 29, 1998.

54. See M. GAUDRY, "Measuring the Effects of the No-fault 1978 Quebec Automobile Insurance Act with the DRAG Model", in G. DIONNE (ed.), *Contributions to Insurance Economics,* Boston, Kluwer Academic Publisher, 1992; M. GAUDRY, *The Effects on Road Safety of the Compulsory Insurance, Flat Premium Rating and No-Fault Features of the 1978 Quebec Automobile Act,* Prepared for the inquiry into motor vehicle accident compensation in Ontario, 1987.

55. See R.A. DEVLIN, "Liability Versus No-Fault Automobile Insurance Regimes: an Analysis of the Experience in Quebec", in G. DIONNE (ed.), *op. cit.,* note 54; R.A. DEVLIN, "Some Welfare Implications of No-Fault Automobile Insurance", (1990) 10 *Int'l Rev. L. & Econ.* 193-205; R.A. DEVLIN, *Liability Versus No-Fault Automobile Insurance Regimes: an Analysis of Quebec's Experience,* Presented to Canadian Economic Association meeting, Windsor, Canada, 1988.

56. E.M. LANDES, "Insurance, Liability, and Accidents: A Theoretical and Empirical Investigation of the Effect of No-Fault Accidents", (1982) 25 *J. L & Econ.* 49.

57. See R.I. McEWIN, "No-Fault and Road Accidents: Some Australasian Evidence", (1989) 9 *Int'l Rev. L & Econ.* 13-24.

58. This was the initial Quebec solution.

59. Moreover, there is skepticism about whether people really do take increased risks to their lives when insurance is available. But it seems that, in the right setting, some do so. Of course, if one were to incorporate this moral hazard idea into a model of how an auto no-fault plan might work, then one would also address the moral hazard aspects of tort law.

60. See SOCIETÉ. DE L'ASSURANCE AUTOMOBILE DU QUEBEC, *op. cit.,* note 40.

61. See M. GAUDRY *et al., DRAG-2, un modele econometrique applique au kilometrage, aux accidents et a leur gravite au Quebec-Partie 4-Application du modele aux accidents, a leur gravite et aux victimes de la route,* Direction des etudes et des analyses, Societe de l'assurance automobile du Quebec, May 1995; M. GAUDRY *et al., DRAG-2, un modele economerrique applique au kilometrage, aux accidents et a leur gravite au Quebec-Partie l-Estimation et analyse du kilometrage et des victimes d'accidents de la route au Quebec entre 1957 et 1989,* Direction des etudes et des analyses, Societe de l'assurance automobile du Quebec, October 1993; M. GAUDRY *et al., Application of econometric model DRAG-2 to the frequency of accidents in Quebec according to different levels of severity,* Proceedings of the 8th Canadian Multidisciplinary Road Safety Conference, Saskatoon, Saskatchewan, June 1993.

62. See, *e.g.,* N. GLICK and J. BERKOWITZ, *Statistical Evidence of fatality increases in response to "no-fault" insurance ?,* Paper prepared for the Insurance Corporation of British Columbia (unpublished).

63. See P. EXETER and A. LUND, "Re-analysis of the effects of no-fault auto insurance on fatal crashes", (1986) 53 *J. Risk & Ins.* 226-241 (critiquing Landes statistical regressions and conclusions); see also P.S. KOCHANOWSKI and M.V. YOUNG," Deterrent Aspects of No-Fault Automobile Insurance: Some Empirical Findings", (1985) 52 *J. Risk & Ins* 269-288.

64. *See* SOCIETÉ DE L'ASSURANCE AUTOMOBILE DU QUEBEC, *op. cit.,* note 40; R.H. JOOST, *op. cit.,* note 9, p. 21, section 7:5.

65. *See, e.g.,* S.D. SUGARMAN," *Pay at the Pump" Auto Insurance: The California Vehicle Injury Plan (VIP) for Better Compensation, Fairer Funding, and Greater Safety,* Berkeley, Institute of Governmental Studies Press, 1993, p. 18.
66. SOCIETÉ DE L'ASSURANCE AUTOMOBILE DU QUEBEC, *op. cit.,* note 40.

67. The Coalition Against Insurance Fraud estimates that there was $13.4 billion in auto- mobile insurance claims fraud in 1994 based upon the National Insurance Crime Bureau estimate of a 16.44% fraud rate. http://www.InsuranceFraud.org/press (visited on March 9, 1998).

68. See, *e.g.,* P.C. WEILER, *Medical Malpractice on Trial,* Cambridge, Harvard University Press, 1991 (advocating for no-fault for medical accidents); R. MERRILL," Compensation for Prescription Drug Injuries", (1973) 59 *Va. L. Rev. 1* (advocating no-fault for prescription drug injuries); J. O'CONNELL, "No Fault Liability by Contract for Doctors, Manufacturers, Retailers, and Others", (1975) *Ins. L. J.* 531 (advocating no-fault regimes for a variety of injuries).

69. *Act Respecting Industrial Accidents and Occupational Diseases,* L.Q. 1985, c. 6 (French version at L.R.Q., c. A-3.001); *Act Respecting Assistance and Compensation for Victims of Crime,* L.Q. 1993, c. 54 (not yet in force; will replace the 1971 *Act Respecting Compensation for Victims of Crime* and copy the automobile scheme in respect of compensation levels); *Act to Amend Various Legislation Respecting Social Affairs,* L.Q. 1985, c. 23, s. 18, adding ss. 16.1 to 16.11 to the *Public Health Protection Act,* L.R.Q., c. P-38, expressly referring to the *Automobile Insurance Act* in respect of compensation levels (s. 16.3).

70. See R.H. JOOST, *op. cit.,* note 16, p. 26, section 1:2C.

71. See, *e.g.,* J. O'CONNELL, "Allowing Motorists a Choice to Be Legally Uninsured by Surrendering Tort Claims for Noneconomic Loss {With Some Further Thoughts on Choices Between PIP and Tort Coverage)", {1995) I *Conn. Ins. L J.* 33.

72. In California, the" no pay, no play" law was passed by, as Proposition 213, by 76 percent of Californian voters in November 1996. The constitutionality of Prop 213 is currently on appeal to the California Supreme Court; however, two lower courts of appeal have sustained Prop 213's constitutionality. In Louisiana, the no pay, no play law-formally called the *Omnibus Premium Reduction Act of 1997,* or *Act of 1476*-is also under constitutional attack. The law is currently on appeal to the Supreme Court of Louisiana. See also, INSURANCE INFORMATION INSTITUTE, *Insurance Issues Update,* R. GASTEL (ed.), New York, Insurance Information Institute, October 1997.

Chapter 7

Pain and Suffering -- Nations Differ but We are Off the Chart

In the U.S., tort victims who suffer personal injuries are entitled to money damages in compensation for a range of losses. Two major types of recovery are readily understood in dollar terms even if the precise amounts that should be awarded can be highly contested. These are recovery for medical (and similar) expenses and lost income (or earning power) that were incurred as a result of the injury. Because tort awards are made in a lump sum, for someone with an ongoing, say, permanent injury, the amount that should be provided (whether by a jury or a judge or through a settlement) will necessarily be somewhat speculative as to how much the victim's losses will be going forward into the future. Still, experts are typically brought into estimate these numbers and the system resolves disputes among them in a logically coherent (if not necessarily consistent) manner. These types of damages are variously termed "economic" or "pecuniary" or "financial" or "hard" or "special" and the like.

Things are very different for the third major type of damages to which victims are entitled and which are the subject of this chapter. These are quite frequently called damages for "pain and suffering," although other labels like "non-economic" or "non-pecuniary" or "soft" or "general" damages are also often used. If the defendant's conduct has burned your face or cost you your arm or leg or deprived you of your hearing or sight or made you a wheelchair-bound paraplegic or quadriplegic, it is widely understood that you have suffered a loss beyond the medical expenses and lost income connected with your injury. You have incurred a permanent invasion (or even a temporary one) to your bodily integrity and that invasion is not only perhaps an assault on your dignity and identity but also it frequently is physically painful and/or prevents you from doing things you used to enjoy, thereby denying you pleasure you otherwise would have experienced.

These losses are not readily translated into money terms, but since awarding money is what tort law does, the legal system has determined that money will be the way that these non-economic losses are compensated. The longtime common law rule is that the appropriate amount to be awarded for pain and suffering is a question for the trier of fact, usually the jury, subject to review by the trial court. This serves to limit jury discretion when the amount awarded smells of caprice, malice, discrimination and the like. An additional important feature of our system is that U.S. juries are not told about what prior juries awarded in arguably similar cases and instead come to what they believe is the proper award afresh each time. Of course, most tort claims are settled, but the settlement is influenced by predictions on both sides about the range of what a jury might award were the case to go to trial.

Most other nations around the globe these days also permit private lawsuits for personal injury, and they also award money damages for what we call pain and suffering even if they use different phrases to describe the nature of the award. In almost all other nations, however, these awards are made by judges and not juries.

This chapter compares awards for pain and suffering across nations, drawing in particular from data gathered on 19 European countries. The first part of the chapter compares these European nations with each other. Two major findings are 1) with some exceptions there is a reasonably common rank ordering among countries of classic injury types in terms of their seriousness and in turn the relative amounts awarded for these harms, and yet 2) in terms of the actual amount of Euros awarded, European nations vary wildly from one to another. Simplifying, this means that across the continent the loss of a leg or an arm is frequently awarded in the range of, say, 30-35% of what is awarded to someone who has been rendered quadriplegic. But in, say, Ireland and England one suffering the same injury might well be awarded more than ten times as much money as is awarded in, say, Denmark and Greece.

The chapter next turns to U.S. data which first demonstrates that, while we too tend to rank injuries in terms of their relative seriousness much as the Europeans do, there are two stark differences. First, the amount awarded for any specific type of injury tends to vary even more widely within the U.S. than do the extremes across Europe. Second, a central point of the chapter is that the actual amount awarded in the U.S. for a specific injury averages many times that which is awarded in even the most generous European country. This latter finding is the basis for this chapter's title that U.S. is off the chart.

Two very important caveats are then introduced to limit this last finding. First, the norm in Europe is that the successful victim's legal fees are paid for by the defendant on top of the rest of the damages provided. (Although in some places the sum provided for attorneys is sufficiently modest that the victim must use some of his or her recovery to supplement what the defendant pays, even then the amount plaintiffs' lawyers are paid in these cases is relatively much less than in the U.S.) Second, some U.S. states have legislatively adopted caps on pain and suffering awards and in some states these caps are not very high. Awards in those states that are made to very seriously injured victims may not be more than is provided in generous European nation. Even more importantly, once legal fees are taken into account the picture becomes radically different. In those circumstances with low caps on pain and suffering awards, the victim may well have to pay more than 100% of his or her award for pain and suffering to his or her lawyer. The result is that victims in those U.S. cases are now off the chart in the opposite direction with net pain and suffering awards effectively in the negative and sharply less than even the least generous European nation – hence a different basis for this chapter's title.

This chapter was first presented to the Eleventh Annual Clifford Symposium held at DePaul Law School, published as Stephen D. Sugarman, "A Comparative Law Look at Pain and Suffering Awards," 55 DePaul Law Review 399-434 (2006), and is reprinted with permission of the journal. Subsequent to this presentation, I have extended the comparison of the U.S. approach to that of a wider number of nations around the world. Those findings, which are consistent with those discussed above, are summarized in a postscript to this chapter.

A COMPARATIVE LAW LOOK AT PAIN AND SUFFERING AWARDS

INTRODUCTION

Most discussions of "pain and suffering" awards in American tort law look inward, at most comparing one state with others. This Article looks outward, exploring what other "Western" nations award in pain and suffering damages, and comparing those outcomes with the American practice.

As a starting point, there is a fundamental commonality. The legal systems of Western Europe, Canada, and Australia all provide financial compensation to personal injury victims for what we in the United States interchangeably call "pain and suffering," "noneconomic losses," and "general damages." However labeled, this is money meant to compensate for things like the physical pain and suffering that goes along with a physical trauma, the emotional harm that can come from an injury to one's self or a loved one, the disappointment or embarrassment arising from one's changed appearance or altered abilities to engage in pleasurable activities and favorite pastimes as a result of an injury, the harm to one's dignity or one's health from being wrongly injured by another, and so on. These injuries are widely acknowledged by Western democracies by ordering legally liable defendants to pay money to their victims in recognition of these harms.

Despite this basic similarity among nations, the U.S. regime in most states is enormously more generous than other legal systems in the amounts it awards for pain and suffering. In some American states, gravely injured plaintiffs can win millions of dollars of such damages from their defendants. These sums are unheard of elsewhere. Indeed, as shown below, for the same injuries, typical American awards are often more than ten times as much as those awarded in even the most generous of the other nations.

Some critics of the American common law of personal injury damages have long objected that the sums we award for pain and suffering are inappropriately large.[1] In recent years, several American states have bluntly responded by putting a cap on the amount of pain and suffering damages that a single plaintiff obtains (e.g., $250,000).[2] Usually, these caps require trial judges to wipe out any amounts that juries award above the allowable maximum. As a result of these statutory changes, U.S. law on pain and suffering awards now varies considerably from jurisdiction to jurisdiction -- at least for those with more serious injuries who are affected by these caps. Several other wealthy nations have also put a limit on awards for pain and suffering, although their solution, as explained below, is actually quite different from ours.

Some critics of the American regime object to the uneven nature of our awards.[3] As they see it, different juries award those with similar injuries very different sums for reasons other than the inherent justice of their claims. Critics point out that our juries ordinarily learn nothing of what other juries previously awarded in similar cases, and so they are probably importantly influenced by their own experience, the talents of the lawyers in the case before them, their empathy for the victim or dislike of the defendant, and so on. To be sure, most American tort claims are settled without a trial, and lawyers on both sides are generally familiar with outcomes of prior trials and settlements. Hence, all things equal, we would expect U.S. settlements to have less variability than trial outcomes. Even so, practitioners with experience bargaining in the "shadow of the law" are well aware that the amount claimants can obtain in settlement may depend on variables such as whether the case would be tried in an urban or rural area of the same state, or how the plaintiff is likely to be viewed by the jury.

I briefly explore here how several nations have been able to assure greater consistency in their pain and suffering awards. When contrasting the United States with other nations on this dimension, it should be remembered that these days we are largely alone in relying heavily on jury trials in personal injury cases. Yet, American states could adapt other nations' consistency-promoting strategies to our jury-based scheme if they wished.

Notwithstanding the success of many other countries in achieving less internal variability in awards than we have, it should not be assumed that other Western legal systems generally have similar award levels. To the contrary, I will also show that other nations vary enormously in the amounts they generally award for pain and suffering for similar injuries. This nation-to-nation variation has nothing to do with juries, however, and presumably arises from different national values.

In comparing the United States with other nations, it is also important not to forget the different ways in which lawyers are compensated. Outside the United States, a "loser pays" rule generally applies.[4] This means that a liable defendant pays the plaintiff's legal expenses. American victims, by contrast, have to cover their legal expenses out of their awards. Attorney fees are generally set by contract as a percentage of the recovery, frequently thirty-three percent. Although this means that the legal fee is assessed against the entire award, I believe it is fair to assume that, as a psychological matter, U.S. claimants understand that the burden of attorneys' fees and related costs comes first from their pain and suffering awards. And the question for claimants is how much money, if any, is actually going to be left for them for pain and suffering. That is, how much will they net beyond what they are receiving for out-of-pocket losses like medical expenses and lost income?

My findings, shown below, demonstrate that, because of this difference in the payment of lawyers, those victims with relatively high awards for out-of-pocket losses may well find themselves no longer advantaged by the American regime of large payments nominally in- tended for pain and suffering. Instead, American lawyers are often the main beneficiaries.

My findings also show that the obligation in the United States to pay one's own lawyer additionally means that the caps on pain and suffering awards that are typically proposed and enacted in the United States will often leave seriously injured American tort victims worse off than their counterparts in many other wealthy nations.

II. THE EUROPEAN PICTURE

In this part, after explaining where I obtained the data upon which I base my analysis, two broad themes are explored. The first, which I call "vertical equity," considers the extent to which European countries similarly view the relative seriousness of various injuries. For example, do they consistently treat losing an arm with the same gravity ratio (for example, fifty percent as grave) relative to becoming blind? I term the second theme a matter of "horizontal equity." There I examine the degree to which awards differ from one European nation to another for the same sort of injury, such as losing a leg.

A. Data Sources

I have not gathered primary data about European awards for pain and suffering. Instead, I rely upon the work of others who have explored this issue, and most importantly on *Personal Injury Awards in EU and EFTA Countries,* which contains reports from experts from twenty nations.[5] This compilation, edited by David Mcintosh and Marjorie Holmes, is the third edition of the same project, the other two having been published in 1991 and 1994. This volume generally reports data from 2000 (although there is modest variation from nation to nation).

In the Mcintosh and Holmes study, expert lawyers were told to imagine two different tort victims who were not at all at fault in causing their own injuries -- a married male doctor, age forty, with two children, and an unmarried female legal secretary, age twenty, with no dependents. The experts were to then assume that the victims suffered fifteen alternative injuries, ranging from instant death to repetitive strain. They were then instructed to report how much money these victims would likely recover in tort for each of the injuries. In predicting the overall amount of recovery, the reporters were also told to indicate separately how much of that amount would likely be awarded for pain and suffering, and those are the numbers that I concentrate on here.[6]

I put aside the experts' reports on total compensation and its component parts other than pain and suffering. I concede that it is possible that cross-nation comparisons of pain and suffering are flawed because in some nations the amount awarded for pain and suffering could depend on what is included or excluded in the other categories of compensation. But, based upon advice I have received from European law scholars, I do not believe this is important for purposes of this Article.

I also recognize (as do the study directors) that the experts' numbers used in the Mcintosh and Holmes project might be in error. A few of the national reports rely on a team of experts in order to arrive at the numbers they submitted, and that may help improve the reliability of the reporting. Yet, in most of the reporting nations, one person alone provided the sum. As shown in Table 8, below, for most nations, a precise figure was reported, whereas a modest range (usually less than a thirty percent range) was reported for a few of the nations (primarily for Ireland, Germany, and the Netherlands). As a general matter, it is difficult to know whether to take more comfort in precision. A range might reflect sensible uncertainty, or perhaps a keen awareness of variation among similar cases (perhaps from place to place around the country or perhaps in other ways). A single number might convey a false precision.

In any event, the reliability of the national reports is likely to depend on other differences among the countries. In Germany, for example, there are very good compilations of primary data on personal injury awards for all sorts of different harms.[7] Hence, to the extent that the hypothetical injuries in the study parallel injury types contained in these compilations, the German reporters would be expected to be quite confident about their replies. In nations without such compilations, the task of the expert in providing a reliable report would be harder.

Indeed, in connection with the first version of this project, the experts from Italy pressed the study directors to provide a number reflecting the percent disabled they should assign to each of the injuries that they were to convert into predicted damage awards, and the directors complied. The directors based the percentages on how they believed the English Department of Social Services would rate each disability in connection with the award of workers' compensation benefits (although the directors also instructed reporters to base their estimates on different percentages if other numbers were used in their own nation).[8]

And finally, because of the way the Spanish data is reported, clearly separate sums for noneconomic loss are not readily identifiable, and hence in this Article I have ignored the Spanish data and include results from only nineteen of the twenty nations in the Mcintosh and Holmes project.

As I have explained, the Mcintosh and Holmes study on which I primarily rely is based on expert predictions about hypothetical cases. As a check on their reliability, I have compared these predictions against some results in actual cases, relying for that purpose, among other things, on two other helpful volumes.[9] Based on those comparisons, I have concluded that the Mcintosh and Holmes expert valuations are reasonably reliable. Mcintosh and Holmes have also done some cross-checking and, while they realize that individual results in real cases are likely to vary from the numbers they provide, they too are reasonably confident that their study reports broadly accurate estimates.[10] I should also add that it appears that the Mcintosh and Holmes experts saw it as their job to report how much the hypothetical victims would obtain in court, rather than in settlement, although, based on informal conversations with European lawyers, I have a sense that the settlement discount is much less there than in the United States.

Moreover, for my purposes, even fairly large errors in the numbers reported by Mcintosh and Holmes are not terribly important because my attention is primarily on, gross differences, both among the reporting nations and as between them and the United States. Before discussing the results of the Mcintosh and Holmes project, I should make clear that this effort says nothing about the frequency of litigation for similar accidents and similar harms from nation to nation.[11] Nor do I directly concern myself with the availability of alternative compensation schemes in the countries, the existence of which could be an important factor in litigation rates.

A. *Results*

My analysis focuses on six of the fifteen hypothetical injuries covered in the Mcintosh and Holmes survey: quadriplegia, total blindness, deafness, amputation of an arm above the elbow, amputation of a leg above the knee, and facial burns. Intuitively, these seemed to reflect a diverse range of reasonably distinct harms. To be sure, the actual pain and suffering of any individual could easily vary because of the imprecision of the descriptions used in the study. For example, was the amputated arm the person's writing arm? Precisely how bad were the facial burns? Had the person who lost a leg been an avid skier? Nonetheless, as already noted, for the most part, the expert reporters had little trouble specifying a single sum as the amount likely to be awarded in their country for pain and suffering for each of the hypothetical injuries.

1. *Basic Data*

TABLE 1
PREDICTED AWARDS FOR PAIN AND SUFFERING IN THE MEDIAN NATION BY TYPE OF INJURY AMONG NINETEEN EUROPEAN NATIONS (€1000s)

Quadriplegia	92
Blindness	65
Leg Amputation	41
Arm Amputation	38
Deafness	31
Facial Burns	14

Table 1 shows the predicted median award (in euros) for pain and suffering for the hypothetical doctor suffering each of the six injuries I explore (i.e., the nation whose predicted award for that injury ranked tenth among the nineteen examined here). For example, what might be termed the "typical" European pain and suffering award is €38,000 for the loss of an arm, €65,000 for blindness, and so on. Shortly, I will present the range of these awards for the nineteen nations and then compare them with U.S. data. This section presents some data relevant to the question of whether there is general agreement among European nations (as reflected by the expert reports) as to the relative seriousness of these six injuries.

2. *Relative Seriousness of the Various Injuries ("Vertical Equity" Within Europe)*

Do the nineteen reporting nations broadly agree on which injuries deserve more money for pain and suffering and which deserve less? And, if so, do they broadly agree as to what should be the relative size of the awards for each of these harms? .This inquiry can be viewed as a matter of "vertical equity."
I calculated a "relative-seriousness" rating for the six injuries for each nation by determining what percentage each predicted award amount is of the largest predicted award for that nation. (Where a range of predicted recovery was supplied, I used the middle of the range.) Table 2 displays the results for the nineteen countries for the injured doctor case. This table allows the viewer to see not only the ordering of the injuries for each nation, but also the range between the injuries in each nation.

TABLE 2
NATIONAL AWARD PROPORTION FOR EACH INJUR
A PERCENTAGE OF HIGHEST PREDICTED FOR EACH NATION

	Facial Burn	Deaf	Arm Loss	Leg Loss	Blindness	Quadriplegia
Austria	11	30	34	44	46	100
Belgium	23	58	54	56	73	100
Denmark	21	59	59	59	100	72
England	37	32	37	37	70	100
finland	18	52	58	41	100	100
France	8	31	58	41	100	100
Germany	13	13	13	15	25	100
Greece	29	35	47	47	100	100
Iceland	21	42	53	44	100	100
Ireland	32	39	67	67	94	100
Italy	8	52	20	20	90	100
Liechtenstein	14	30	34	45	46	100
Luxembourg	26	100	41	51	96	85
Netherlands	12	29	32	37	58	100
Norway	11	40	28	28	100	100
Portugal	10	70	60	60	90	100
Scotland	19	14	42	42	77	100
Sweden	7	44	44	32	88	100
Switzerland	10	65	50	50	99	100

Table 2 indicates that in most countries, quadriplegia and blindness are considered most serious and facial burns as least serious. Reporters for twelve countries predicted the highest pain and suffering award for quadriplegia, one predicted the highest pain and suffering award for blindness, and five predicted essentially equal awards for both. (One reporter ranked deafness ahead of both blindness and quadriplegia.) At the other end, seventeen of the nineteen national reports predicted the lowest pain and suffering award for facial burns. Among the other three injuries-deafness, loss of an arm, and loss of a leg—there was no clear rank ordering. Overall, it seems fair to say that all three of those injuries were treated as likely to attract roughly the same awards by most reporters, although the data provided by the reporters is least consistent with respect to deafness.

In comparing the predicted awards of the secretary with those predicted for the doctor, I found that in six of the countries there was little or no difference in the sums, regardless of the injury.[12] In eight of the countries, the awards predicted for the secretary were modestly higher for most or all injuries. I will assume that, in these nations, age is taken into account in determining the amount of pain and suffering and the extra sum for the secretary basically reflects that she is fifteen years younger in the hypothetical and so has more years ahead of her to live with her disability.

The differences between the predicted awards for the doctor and the secretary are harder to understand for the remaining countries. In Belgium, for example, the secretary was predicted to receive more than the doctor only for facial burns. Perhaps this discrepancy reflects an assumption that, as a young, unmarried woman, this disfigurement was seen as more painful to her than to him, even when blindness would not be. More difficult to understand is the report from Switzerland, for example, where both deafness and facial burns were predicted to yield higher pain and suffering awards to the secretary, even though loss of limbs, blindness, and quadriplegia were not. Given what are relatively modest differences in predicted outcomes for both victims, the data I present here is drawn only from the numbers predicted for the doctor case.

TABLE 3
EUROPEAN "VERTICAL EQUITY": MEDIAN NATION AWARD PROPORTIONS (%) (FROM TABLE 2)

Quadriplegia	100	Arm	44
Blindness	90	Deafness	40
Leg	44	Facial Burns	14

Drawing on the data from Table 2, Table 3 presents the median nation's percentage for each of the six injuries. To be clear, Table 3 shows that the median nation—the one with the tenth highest proportion of the nineteen reporting-was expected to award forty-four per- cent as much in pain and suffering for a leg amputation as compared with what the median was expected to award for whatever it viewed as the most serious injury of the six. Hence, Table 3 presents a rough, comparative measure of the European-wide average seriousness of the six injuries.

TABLE 4
EUROPEAN "VERTICAL EQUITY": PRESUMPTIVE DISABILITY PERCENTAGES PROVIDED BY THE STUDY DIRECTORS

Quadriplegia	100
Blindness	100
Deafness	50
Leg Amputation	35
Arm Amputation	30
Facial Burns	Up to 20

Recall, at the request of the Italian team, the study directors previously provided percent—disabled figures for each of the hypothetical injuries. Table 4 presents those numbers. Comparing them with the numbers calculated and presented in Table 3, one sees a reasonably close fit between the median nation data and the study director's estimates of percent-disabled. (To be sure, for some reporters, the study directors' percent-disabled message may have been too influential, thereby contributing to a similarity between the rankings on the two tables.)

TABLE 5
EUROPEAN "VERTICAL EQUITY": RANGE OF AWARD PROPORTIONS (%)
FOR FIFTEEN (OF NINETEEN) MIDDLE-RANKING NATIONS

Quadriplegia	85-100
Blindness	46-100
Deafness	29-65
Leg	28-60
Arm	28-59
Burns	10-26

Averages can be deceiving. Table 5 draws together data from Table 2 by showing a restricted range of the percentages calculated for each injury. For this illustration, I have eliminated the two nations at both extremes. But even for the middle fifteen nations, Table 5 shows a range of percentages of at least a two-to-one ratio for the five injuries generally rated less serious than quadriplegia.

To illustrate this point with a few examples (drawn from Table 2), the Netherlands reporter predicts an award for deafness at twenty- nine percent of the award in the Netherlands for quadriplegia, whereas in Switzerland the deafness award is sixty-five percent of quadriplegia. In the same vein, the predicted arm loss award in Norway is twenty-eight percent of the quadriplegia award, whereas in Denmark it is fifty-nine percent. Moving to blindness, the pain and suffering award in Austria is predicted to be only forty-six percent of the quadriplegia award, whereas in several nations it is equal to the quadriplegia award.

In short, looked at in this latter way, I see considerable variation from country to country in its assessment of the relative seriousness of the six injuries.

3. *Awards From Country to Country ("Horizontal Equity" Within Europe)*

"Horizontal equity" refers to the extent to which victims with the same injuries are awarded the same sums for pain and suffering. The nineteen-nation survey provides little useful information on this question with respect to intra-national differences. As noted, most reporters offer a single sum for each injury, and only a few provide a range. Moreover, as earlier suggested, those providing a range of recovery may well be saying only that there are different sorts of cases captured by these broad injury titles. Greater attention will be given below to intra-national consistency.[13]

But these nineteen-nation reports do permit the examination of horizontal equity by making inter-national comparisons *across nations* for the same injury. Of course, there may be quite understandable reasons why different nations would award different sums for the exact same injury, reflecting different values that different legal systems seek to advance with pain and suffering awards. Nonetheless, in preparing to make a comparison with the United States, this inquiry allows us to consider how uniformly Europeans approach the issue.

TABLE 6
NATIONAL RANKINGS (ONE TO NINETEEN) BY AMOUNT OF AWARD
BY INJURY AND OVERALL AVERAGE

	Burns	Deaf	Arm	Leg	Blind	Quad	Average
Ireland	1	4	1	1	1	1	1.5
England	2	5	3	3	3	3	3
Belgium	3	3	2	2	5	6	3.5
Italy	7	2	7	10	2	4	5
Luxembourg	6	1	5	5	6	9	5
Scotland	4	17	3	3	4	5	6
Germany	5	9	12	11	10	2	8
Netherlands	10	7	9	8	9	7	8
Liechtenstein	8	8	8	7	13	8	9
Iceland	9	12	10	12	8	13	11
Austria	12	15	11	9	15	10	12
Finland	11	10	13	14	11	14	12
France	15	14	6	6	18	11	13
Switzerland	17	6	14	13	12	16	13
Norway	13	13	18	16	7	12	13
Portugal	18	11	15	17	16	17	16
Denmark	14	18	17	15	17	18	17
Sweden	19	16	16	18	14	15	17
Greece	16	19	19	19	19	19	19

Before turning to the detailed monetary figures that the reporters predicted would be awarded for various injuries under their nation's legal system, Table 6 presents the relative rank of each nation in terms of how much money its reporter predicts would be provided in pain and suffering damages to the hypothetical doctor for each of the six injuries. For example, a "six" under burns means that the amount of this nation's pain and suffering award for burns was the sixth highest of the nineteen, whereas a "thirteen" under burns means that this nation's award for burns was thirteenth highest.

Not surprisingly, no nation shows exactly the same rank for all injuries. Nonetheless, some patterns emerge. Looking at both their average rank and their individual scores, it appears that all but one of the nineteen nations falls reasonably easily into one of four subgroups.

Six "Group One" nations—Ireland, England, Scotland, Belgium, Luxembourg, and Italy—represent the most generous countries in terms of pain and suffering awards. Nearly all of their comparative numbers are seven or less. At the other end, four "Group Four" nations—Greece, Portugal, Sweden, and Denmark—represent the least generous countries. Nearly all of their comparative numbers are fourteen or more.

Five "Group Three" nations—Finland, Iceland, Switzerland, Austria, and Norway—have reasonably similar numbers that put this group somewhat above the least generous group. Three "Group Two" nations—Germany, Netherlands, and Liechtenstein—appear clustered somewhat below Group One in terms of generosity. France, with such varied numbers shown in Table 6, resists categorization.

Although I will not make too much of it here, there are national characteristics (or some might say, stereotypes) that one might associate with these groups. At the least generous end (Groups Three and Four) we find that:

- two relatively poor nations among the nineteen (Greece and Portugal) perhaps simply cannot afford the more generous awards paid elsewhere in Europe;[14]
- five Scandinavian nations (Sweden, Denmark, Norway, Iceland, and Finland) are well known for having strong social welfare programs, and that may cause these countries to favor putting national resources into their more collective schemes instead of individualized tort law recoveries; and [15]
- two Germanic nations (Switzerland and Austria), whose citizens I think of as being relatively "tough," might translate that characteristic into relatively lower monetary awards.

At the more generous end (Groups One and Two) we find that:

- three common-law nations (England, Scotland, and Ireland) not only have a historic tradition of jury-based awards that may influence today's award levels, but also the common-law experience might translate into a more individualized sense of corrective justice; and
- four highly Catholic states (Belgium, Luxembourg, and Italy-plus Ireland, as well) are relatively more generous for reasons that are not at all clear to me—although one European colleague suggested to me that it is possible that Catholics may pity victims more than Protestants who may be more stoic.

TABLE 7

EUROPEAN "HORIZONTAL EOUITY" AMONG THE NINETEEN NATIONS, MEDIAN NATION AND RANGE OF NATIONAL AWARDS FOR PAIN AND SUFFERING BY TYPE OF INJURY (IN €1000s)

	Median	Range
Quadriplegia	92	15-250
Blindness	65	22-235
Leg Amputation	41	10-166
Arm Amputation	38	10-166
Deafness	31	7-124
Facial Burns	14	4 -80

Turning now to actual monetary figures, Table 7 shows the full range of predicted pain and suffering awards for each of the six injuries for the nineteen reporting nations. The extremes of the range are very substantial. Notice that for each of the six harms, the most generous system is predicted to award *more than ten times* what is paid by the least generous system. Table 7 also repeats the data from Table 1, showing the award for each injury for the median nation. Those data reveal that the extremes vary substantially in both directions from what I am terming the typical award.

For those wishing to see the fuller data set, I present in Table 8 detailed monetary figures for each nation for each assumed injury in the doctor's case.

TABLE 8
NINETEEN-NATION DATA: PAIN AND SUFFERING AWARDS
BY TYPE OF INJURY (IN EUROS)

	Burns (face)	Deafness	Amputation arm (above Elbow)	Amputation leg (above knee)	Total Blindness	Quadriplegia
Austria	6980-12692	27286	31729	41247	41882	92013
Belgium	41206	101400	94827	98839	128128	175217
Denmark	7971	22037	22037	22037	37100	18521-34932
England/ Wales	79750	68875	79750	79750	152250	217500
Finland	10689	31004	29400	24586	59881	59881
France	7324	27296	50596	59917	29958	86548
Germany	22308-44615	31230-33462	26770-35692	33462-40153	58000-71385	178462-312308
Greece	5124-7688	7688	10250	10250	21780	15374
Iceland	14992	29983	37978	31983	71961	71961
Ireland	66483-94083	83085-110687	199031	166031	221374-249046	221374-276718
Italy	15785-15883	104877	40899	40899	178805	199671
Liechtenstein	15699	33751	39246	51018	51804	113812
Luxembourg	32437	124986	50894	63403	120749	106233
Netherland	13866	29713-39617	29713-47541	39617-49522	59427-79235	19235-158471
Norway	8135	29022	20897	20897	73126	73126
Portugal	4356	30489	26132	26132	39199	43555
Scotland	36250	26100	79750	79750	130500	188500
Sweden	1241-6634	26536	25967	19144	51366	58758
Switzerland	5732	37252	28656	28656	57313	57313

C. *European Conclusion*

Based on the data reported here, these nineteen European nations tend to rank fairly similarly the "relative-seriousness" of the six injuries. Nonetheless, there are some noticeable differences in national perceptions of relative-seriousness of the six injuries. But this modest amount of vertical inequity is dwarfed by a much higher level of horizontal inequity. Simply put, European nations are predicted to award vastly different amounts for pain and suffering damages to victims with the same injury. While the cause of these differences exceeds the scope of this article, it is at least clear that the legal awards for pain and suffering across Europe are enormously varied from country to country.

III. THE U.S. PICTURE

This section presents American data on pain and suffering awards to victims who suffered broadly similar injuries to the six injuries discussed in Section II.

A. Data Sources

The American data is from the results of both actual trials and settlements {although, so far as we could tell, none of the reported results was reduced in amount because of a statutory cap on pain and suffering awards). These data come primarily from James P. Munger, *What's It Worth: A Guide to Current Personal Injury Awards and Settlements,* and Jacob A. Stein, *Stein on Personal Injury Damages.*[16]

There are good reasons not to treat these data as precisely capturing typical American awards. On the other hand, there are good reasons to view them as being roughly in the ballpark in terms of what American tort victims with these sorts of injuries might expect to recover.

It is important to remember that a victim will often suffer multiple injuries, and we have sought to exclude those cases. Thus, as best we can determine, the U.S. outcomes here reflect awards for victims with a single basic harm. Most of the American data we draw on here includes information on both the amount of pain and suffering damages awarded and the total amount awarded, although there are some incomplete reports.

Nonetheless, I appreciate that the cases we found are neither a complete nor random sample of all the cases in which victims recovered at trial for the harms we examined. Hence, there is reason to be concerned that the data sources we relied upon exaggerate recovery levels because they may not include a representative share of the cases in which a lower recovery was obtained. It is also fair to assume that settled cases (which are most cases, after all) on average result in lower recovery than tried cases, and I would be willing to assume a discount of one-third.

Still, as will become clear in the analysis, it would appear that all of my basic points would follow even were the numbers reported here twice as much as (or even more than) the typical results in the real world.

B. Pain and Suffering Awards for Broadly Similar Injuries to Those in the European Study

1. Quadriplegia

Research revealed seventeen reported awards in quadriplegia cases from a wide range of U.S. jurisdictions from the years 1986-2003, with most of the cases coming from years fairly close to 2000. Of these, the pain and suffering portion has been separately identified in twelve of them.

TABLE 9
U.S. "HORIZONTAL EQUITY": PAIN AND SUFFERING AWARDS IN TWELVE QUADRIPLEGIA CASES (IN $ MILLIONS)

1.0
1.5
2.0
2.5
3.0
3.4
Median
3.5
4.0
4.6
4.9
6.0
6.0

As shown on Table 9, the median pain and suffering award was just under $3.5 million. As the awards ranged from one million to six million dollars, the highest award was six times that of the lowest award.[17]

2. *Leg Amputation*

We identified twenty-six U.S. leg amputation cases from 1983 through 2003 (again with most of the cases coming from years fairly close to 2000), and we have separate amounts for the pain and suffering awards in seventeen of them. Of these, only four involved amputation of one leg above the knee—the facts of the European hypothetical discussed earlier.

TABLE 10
U.S. "HORIZONTAL EQUITY": PAIN AND SUFFERING AWARDS IN SEVENTEEN LEG AMPUTATION CASES (IN$ MILLIONS)

• Above the Knee:	0.400, 4.000, 5.600, 7.500
• Both Legs:	0.1500, 6.000
• One Leg Below the Knee:	0.150, 0.200, 0.400, 0.490, 0.500, 0.615, 1.000, 1.550, 1.750, 5.580, 9.750

The results for all seventeen cases are shown in Table 10. For the four above-the-knee amputation cases, the range of the pain and suffering awards was huge. Two cases involved loss of both legs and the pain and suffering awards in those cases were also radically different. Most of the cases we uncovered involved an amputation at or below the knee of one leg. These awards also varied enormously, with the largest recovery more than sixty times that of the smallest. The median of all seventeen of the awards for pain and suffering was one million dollars.[18]

3. *Blindness*

TABLE 11
U.S. "HORIZONTAL EQUITY": PAIN AND SUFFERING AWARDS IN ELEVEN BLINDNESS CASES (IN $ MILLIONS)

• Both eyes:	4.400, 4.500, 5.000
• One eye:	0.245, 0.300, 0.500, 0.500, 0.800, 1.500, 5.600

We identified only six reasonably recent U.S. cases of total blind ness, and the awards separated pain and suffering for only three of them. Table 11 shows that in those cases, amounts of $4.4 million, $4.5 million, and $5.0 million were awarded for pain and suffering.

Thirteen fairly recent U.S. cases were identified in which one eye was blinded and, of these, pain and suffering awards were separated out in eight. For those eight cases, as shown in Table 11, pain and suffering awards ranged from $245,000 to $5,600,000, a ratio of more than twenty to one.

4. *Arm and Finger Loss*

TABLE 12
U.S. "HORIZONTAL EOUITY": PAIN AND SUFFERING AWARDS
(IN $1000s)

Seven Finger-Loss Cases (P&S in $1000s)	20, 50, 100, 137, 400, 569, 850
Five Arm-Loss Cases (P&S in $1000s)	700, 1470, 1500, 2454 (various types)

To provide something of a contrast with lost arm cases, we identified eight recent U.S. cases of a lost finger, with pain and suffering awards separated out for seven of them. As shown in Table 12, those seven awards ranged from $20,000 to $850,000 with a median of $137,000.

We also identified five arm amputation cases (see Table 12), two below the elbow and one involving the loss of both arms. Because of the low numbers of cases and their variety, perhaps not much should be made of these awards, although the median pain and suffering award for them was $1,500,000.

5. *Vertical Equity in the United States*

Because of the limited data, I am reluctant to draw too strong conclusions about comparing the relative ranking of the injuries examined in the United States with the European picture. Let me simply report that (as shown in the prior tables) the median awards for quadriplegia, loss of an arm (all types), loss of a leg (all types), and loss of a finger, were $3.5 million, $1.5 million, $1 million, and $137,000, respectively. The very few total blindness cases averaged $4.5 million (with $500,000 as the median award for the loss of one eye). Generally speaking, then, the median awards for quadriplegia, leg loss, and arm loss in the United States suggest a congruence with European awards, as described above, in terms of their relative seriousness. With respect to total blindness, just as a few European nations treated it as or more serious than quadriplegia, the limited U.S. data suggests something of the same thing here.

6. Ratio of High Versus Low American Awards for Types of Loss

TABLE 13
U.S. "HORIZONTAL EOUITY": U.S. RATIOS OF FULL RANGE OF
PAIN AND SUFFERING AWARDS BY TYPE OF INJURY

Finger	42/1
Arm	3.5/1
One Eye	23/1
Leg	65/1
Quadriplegia	6/1

Table 13 presents the ratio of the high and low awards identified for the various injuries on which we are focusing in the U.S. data. What these numbers show is that, like variations in awards from European nation to nation, American awards can vary enormously from case to case. I want particularly to emphasize that we found ratios of more than twenty to one for several of the injuries.

Because state law caps do not appear to have been involved in these cases, it is not likely the case that the formal common law of damages varied importantly from state to state for these cases. Therefore, judges probably give roughly similar jury instructions on pain and suffering awards in most places. Still, variations in results from case to case could be the product of evidentiary and other rules that differ from place to place as to what lawyers are permitted to argue (for example in their closing arguments) and introduce as evidence (such as to what the daily life of the victim is now like). I believe it is more likely, however, that these widely varying results are more importantly a reflection of what I noted at the start-the American regime of pain and suffering awards makes no use of precedent, and so the amount awarded in each case typically reflects what a single jury concluded would be fair from everything it learned and considered on this occasion.

IV. AMERICAN-EUROPEAN COMPARISONS

TABLE 14 CROSS-NATIONAL AWARD SIZE COMPARISON COMPARING U.S. MEDIAN PAIN AND SUFFERING AWARDS WITH EUROPEAN AWARDS

	U.S. Medians in $1000s	U.S. Medians in €1000s (approx.)	European Medians €1000s	European Range €1000s
Finger	137	100		
Arm			38	10-166
Leg	1000	750	41	10-166
One Eye	500	375		
Blindness	4500	3375	65	22-235
Quadriplegia	3400	2550	92	15-250
(€1 = $1.333)				

Having provided separate data as to award levels for the different legal systems, this section turns to American-European comparisons. Drawing on the prior tables, Table 14 first displays median U.S. pain and suffering awards in both dollars and euros for the type of injuries examined.[19] Then, Table 14 displays what I earlier termed the typical European nation award, plus the full range of predicted European nation awards.

The most important point these numbers show is that the amounts awarded for pain and suffering in the American cases we examined are vastly greater than the predicted awards in Europe. This is true when looking at averages as well as the full range of European awards. Indeed, these data show that the U.S. median awards are enormously larger than the highest predicted awards for similar injuries in Europe, notwithstanding the great diversity of award levels throughout Europe.

More specifically, the median pain and suffering award in the United States for quadriplegia was more than twenty-five times greater than the predicted award for quadriplegia in the median European nation and more than ten times the highest predicted European award.

For loss of a leg, the; median American award, even taking into ac- count a wider range of leg injuries including the perhaps lesser injury of a loss below the knee, was nearly twenty times the predicted award in the median European nation, and more than four times the highest predicted award. Indeed, the loss of a finger in the United States tends to generate almost three times the median European nation pain and suffering award for loss of an arm.

Loss of one eye in the United States tends to attract more for pain and suffering than does total blindness in Europe.

V. TAKING LEGAL EXPENSES INTO ACCOUNT

From the data presented so far, it appears as though the United States is far more lavish than Europe when awarding pain and suffering damages. As noted at the outset, however, one must remember that, in Europe, losers in torts cases pay the legal fees and costs of winners. Therefore, the European pain and suffering awards represent what the victims (approximately) keep.

In the United States, by contrast, each side pays its own expenses. For purposes of this exercise, I am going to reduce the American plaintiff's total award by thirty-three percent to account for attorneys' fees and expenses. I view this as a conservative estimate. This is because, apart from special cases (e.g., those involving minors), it would be rare for the lawyer's fee itself to be less than thirty-three percent in a case that actually goes to trial (and often it would be forty percent). Moreover, litigation costs are typically increased by the ordinarily substantial out-of-pocket expenses of litigation for expert witnesses, depositions, investigations, and the like. On the other hand, I concede that cases that are settled relatively quickly typically require considerably fewer expenses and generally involve a lower fee for the successful lawyer (say, twenty-five percent).

As I explained earlier, fees and costs in the United States are not assessed against any specific portion of the recovery, but against the total recovery. Nonetheless, it seems sensible to assume that the fees and costs are best understood by the victim as coming (first) out of the pain and suffering award. After all, if the victim pays the fees and costs out of the portion of the recovery that is based on lost income or medical expenses, then those economic losses will not be fully compensated (although admittedly, in the United States, a substantial share of the economic loss awarded in cases of serious harm is likely to be based on often uncertain projections as to future medical expenses and wage losses).

Once the matter of legal expenses is taken into account, American-European comparisons become more complicated to make. This is because the net position of American victims is strongly influenced by the relative share of the total award that is meant for pain and suffering. This is made especially vivid when comparing leg amputations with quadriplegia.

TABLE 15
WHAT IS LEFT FOR VICTIM PAIN AND SUFFERING AFTER TAKING LEGAL FEES INTO ACCOUNT: U.S. LEG AMPUTATION AWARDS

P&S Amount ($1000s)	Total Award ($1000s)	P&S%of Total	P&S left (minus 33%for legal expenses) ($1000s)	P&S left (€1000s)
150	500	30	(20)	(15)
200	1442	14	(280)	(210)
150	400	38	20	15
400	435	92	250	190
452	633	71	240	180
490	573	86	300	225
500	734	68	260	195
615	716	86	380	285
1000	1500	67	500	375
1550	2420	64	740	555
1750	4493	39	250	190
4000	7568	53	1480	1110
5580	6343	88	1890	1420
5600	7670	73	3040	2280
6000	7497	80	3500	2625
7500	7510	100	5000	3750
9750	11426	85	5940	4460

For the seventeen leg amputation cases (of all types) presented earlier, there is data available on both the total amount of the award and the share of that awarded for pain and suffering. These data (in dollars) are shown in the first two columns of Table 15. The third column shows what share (percentage) of the total award was for pain and suffering, and one can see that it was more than sixty percent of the award in thirteen of the seventeen cases, and more than thirty-three percent in all but two cases. The upshot is that, in all but those two cases, the U.S. victim winds up with some money left for pain and suffering after paying assumed legal expenses of thirty-three percent out of the pain and suffering award. Indeed, as the fourth column of Table 15 shows, fourteen of the seventeen victims are assumed to wind up with fairly substantial amounts for pain and suffering, ranging from $240,000 to nearly six million dollars.

Column five then converts these net numbers to euros. Notice how much larger many of these numbers are than is the median European award (€41,000) or even the European maximum (€166,000) predicted for leg amputations above the knee.

On the other hand, looking more carefully at the data, note that three of the seventeen are actually worse off than they would be in the most generous European nation, seven are near or modestly above the European high end, and only seven are well beyond the European maximum, six of which are dramatically so. In sum, even taking legal expenses into account as done here, American leg amputation victims typically net at least as much for pain and suffering and often enormously more than everywhere in Europe.

Although not fully discussed in this Article, the cases found for blindness (whether in one or both eyes) and for amputation of a finger or an arm generally suggest a similar pattern.[20] That is, even after reducing awards for legal expenses, U.S. victims in these types of cases tend to have more—often enormously more—money left for pain and suffering than those who lose their sight or their arm in Europe.

By contrast, however, the pattern in the quadriplegia cases is very different as shown by Table 16.

TABLE 16
WHAT IS LEFT FOR VICTIM PAIN AND SUFFERING AFTER TAKING LEGAL FEES INTO ACCOUNT: U.S. QUADRIPLEGIA AWARDS

P&S Amount ($1000s)	Total Award ($1000s)	P&S % of Total	(legal expenses) ($1000s)	P&S left (€1000s
1,000	3,950	25	(320)	(240)
1,500	19,100	8	(5370)	(4025)
2,000	7,345	27	(450)	(340)
2,500	7,872	32	(125)	(95)
3,000	8,972	33	10	10
3,400	6,670	51	1180	885
3,500	8,187	43	770	580
4,000	17,770	22	(1920)	(1440)
4,600	21,360	22	(2520)	(1890)
4,900	9,500	52	1730	1300
6,000	9,000	67	3000	2250
6,000	16,530	36	490	370

Patterned after the prior table on leg loss, Table 16 demonstrates that because the share of the award intended for pain and suffering is often smaller than thirty-three percent, many of the victims face legal expenses in excess (and often substantially in excess) of the amount awarded for pain and suffering. As revealed in column five, after paying their presumed legal expenses, seven of the twelve victims would be worse off in the United States than in the typical European nation, where €92,000 was the predicted pain and suffering award.

Most strikingly, three American victims have more than a million euros deficit in pain and suffering and would have to surrender a significant share of their award for out-of-pocket losses to their lawyer. On the other hand, because of the variability in the U.S. data, two victims still wind up with more than a million euros for pain and suffering even after paying legal expenses, and therefore would still be financially far better off than in even the most generous European nation (€250,000).

The data shows that in the quadriplegia cases, although the total awards tend to be higher than in the leg loss cases, the typical share of the total award for pain and suffering is relatively much smaller. I assume that the reason for this is that the quadriplegia cases tend to involve high levels of both ongoing care and lost income. Notice that this analysis assumes that on the out-of-pocket loss side, both American and European law, one way or another, basically provide full compensation; I am not confident that this is a very reliable assumption, but I could not see what else to do given the data I have.

Despite the initial appearances that come from looking at the gross amount of the awards for pain and suffering, American victims need to have pain and suffering awards of, perhaps, at least half or more of their total award in order to meet or exceed the more generous European nations in terms of pain and suffering compensation. And while we see that this frequently occurs for grave injuries like the loss of leg that may carry with them relatively moderate medical costs and in- come loss, that pattern may not follow for severe disabilities with very large, ongoing medical and related expenses.[21] Simply put, even generous American juries seem unwilling to consistently award the necessary seven or eight-figure amount for pain and suffering.

VI. LESSONS FROM ENGLAND AND COMMONWEALTH NATIONS

Although England (and Wales), Canada, and Australia remain largely common-law nations as to the substance of tort law (Quebec aside), they treat pain and suffering damages quite differently than does the United States.[22] Most interesting, in my view, is the statutory scheme recently adopted in New South Wales, Australia.[23]

Under the new law, injuries are to be ranked, percentage-wise, in terms of their severity in comparison with the most extreme case.[24]

Hence one injury, say a leg amputation, might be rated as thirty-five percent as severe as the most severe. In that case, a victim with this injury would receive in pain and suffering thirty-five percent of the sum that would be awarded to someone with the most severe injury. Moreover, the new law sets the maximum award at 350,000 Australian dollars (which is about $265,000 at current exchange rates), with that sum to be indexed by inflation.[25] Hence, an injury with a thirty-five percent rating would, for now, qualify for an award of about $120,000 Australian (or $90,000).

It is additionally critical to note that, as shown in Table 17, under the New South Wales scheme, for injuries that are thirty-three percent less severe than the most extreme, the awards for pain and suffering are not to be proportional to their severity. Instead, injuries rated as less than fifteen percent as severe as the most severe are to receive nothing for pain and suffering. And for injuries between fifteen percent as severe and thirty-three percent as severe as the most severe, the awards are increased to bridge the gap-two percent for an injury that is seventeen percent as severe as the most severe, five percent for one that is twenty-three percent, ten percent for one that is twenty- seven percent, twenty-three percent for one that is thirty percent.

TABLE 17
NEW SOUTH WALES DISABILITY SEVERITY AND CORRESPONDING PARN AND SUFFERING AWARD

Severity	Damages
15%	1%
16%	1.5%
17%	2%
18%	2.5%
19%	3%
20%	3.5%
21%	4%
22%	4.5%
23%	5%
24%	5.5%
25%	6.5%
26%	8%
27%	10%
28%	14%
29%	18%
30%	23%
31%	26%
32%	30%
33%	33%
34-100%	34%-100%
respectively	

Put differently, New South Wales has imposed a threshold on awards for pain and suffering, requiring that an injury be at least fifteen percent as severe as the most severe for any award to be made, and then it has graduated the amount of the award in a way so that once the injury becomes thirty-three percent or more as severe as the most severe injury, the percentages are in lock step with the award linked to that made in the most serious case.

TABLE 18
"VERTICAL EQUITY": EUROPEAN-STUDY HYPOTHETICAL INJURIES
UNDER NEW SOUTH WALES LAW

	Percentage Disability of the Most Severe	Percentage of Maximum Award for P&S in New South Wales
Quadriplegia	100	100
Blindness	100	100
Deafness	50	50
Leg	35	35
Arm	30	23
Burns	20	3.5

Table 18 illustrates how this new Australian law works by applying the New South Wales approach to the six injuries discussed in the European study, using the percentages of disability provided by Mcintosh and Holmes to their expert reporters, and assuming for these purposes that quadriplegia is treated as the most severe injury. (In some sense, this is clearly not the case, because one can imagine someone suffering a combination of quadriplegia and blindness, for example; but this simplification is necessary for purposes of illustration.)

Looking at Table 18, note how the New South Wales scheme has an especially sharp impact on the loss of a leg as compared with the loss of an arm because those two disability percentages are stipulated as falling slightly on either side of thirty-three percent. Looking back to Table 2, no European nation's vertical equity percentages seem to precisely fit the assumed New South Wales pattern for loss of leg and loss of arm. Nonetheless, it is perhaps worth noting that Austria, Liechtenstein, and Luxembourg all award pain and suffering for a loss of a leg at least ten percentage points higher than loss of an arm. (Yet, note also that Finland, Iceland, and Sweden rank arm loss at least nine percentage points higher than leg loss.)

Table 18 makes vivid how the New South Wales scheme sharply reduces the award for harms that are only twenty percent as severe as the most severe. Hence, under this assumed application of the New South Wales law to the six injuries, the pain and suffering award for facial burns would be only 3.5% of that sum awarded for the most severe injury. No European reporter predicted an award for burns that is as low as 3.5% of the highest award for the reporter's nation. Nonetheless, several did report awards for burns that were quite low-seven percent of the highest in Sweden, eight percent in Italy and France, and ten percent in Switzerland and Portugal. Hence, one might well be seeing the rough equivalent of the New South Wales approach in these places. If nothing else, there appears to be a sharp discounting in these four nations for relatively lesser injuries.

It is also useful here to compare the Canadian approach. Some years ago the Canadian Supreme Court set a ceiling on awards for pain and suffering of 100,000 Canadian dollars, a sum that has grown with inflation to about 300,000 dollars today (or about US $250,000).[26]

But this limit is not generally thought to work like caps do in the United States. Although there is some disagreement among Canadian courts, the dominant view appears to be that the maximum award is to be made only for the most serious injuries and that the awards for other injuries should be scaled back from the maximum based on their relative seriousness.[27]

As noted earlier, caps in the United States seem intended only to influence the actual judgments awarded to those who receive jury verdicts above the maximum. Hence, one expects those victims with a wide variety of injuries to wind up clustered at the maximum.[28] By contrast, if the Canadian and New South Wales approaches were embraced in the United States, the ceiling would as well be intended to affect all of those plaintiffs whose jury verdicts are currently at or below the cap.

Comparing the Canadian practice with the New South Wales law, what appears quite special about the latter approach is the explicit threshold of a seriousness requirement before any pain and suffering award is to be made. With very little experience so far under the new law, however, it is not altogether clear what sorts of harms are going to be reliably excluded from pain and suffering recovery. To be sure, neither Canada nor Australia makes much use of juries in personal injury cases,[29] but as discussed later, this alone need not preclude American states from seeking to adapt the regimes of the sort just described.

Something very much like this "percentage of the most serious harm" approach recently adopted in New South Wales is already reasonably well developed in nations like Italy and France. There, injuries are, in effect, assigned a percentage of disability based upon expert medical determinations.[30] Once a victim's harm is assigned its percentage point, this number is then put into a formula (or a table) that determines the approximately appropriate sum to be awarded to that victim for noneconomic loss.

As for the details, for Italy at least, as reported and endorsed by Professor Giovanni Comande in an unpublished article on pain and suffering, the formula (like the New South Wales table) is not simply linear.[31] Rather, Comande argued that courts both do and should in- crease pain and suffering awards in more than a linear way as injury severity increases.[32] This, broadly speaking, is what the New South Wales law does for injuries with severity rankings between fifteen per- cent and thirty-three percent, but not for those with rankings above thirty-three percent-as is done in Italy.

Courts in England and Germany have adopted what at first blush appears to be a different practice. In these legal systems very careful records about past awards for specific types of injuries are kept and publicly reported.[33] This reporting is done by private firms in Germany and by a quasi-public body in England. Courts then are quite faithful in following these past award sums from case to case (again, increasing the awards over time for inflation).

But so long as the pattern of past awards reflects a sense of relative seriousness of injuries, and so long as new types of injuries are thoughtfully compensated with amounts for other injuries in mind, this approach, in the end, seems little different than the "percent of the most serious harm" approach used elsewhere. Put differently, in England and Germany, the courts do not go through the intermediate step of assigning a specific harm a percentage of disability and then translating that percentage to a specific award. Yet, the British and German approach implicitly has that same strategy in mind.

One advantage of the "percent of the most serious harm" approach is that it is not necessary to keep track of inflationary adjustments for every injury. Instead, it suffices simply to keep the percent disabled ratings for each injury constant over time and then to increase the highest award with inflation. Moreover, if a nation concludes that its award schedule, in general, is lower than seems just, it can easily upwardly adjust all awards again simply by raising the ceiling. If such a decision were made in England or Germany, it would require that all the specific-injury reports to be upwardly adjusted accordingly (which, in the end, is not all that difficult to do).

VII. POLICY DISCUSSION

A. *Caps Without Change in the Payment of Legal Expenses?*

Some U.S. advocates have called for a legislative cap of $250,000 on pain and suffering awards, and some states have already adopted a limit of this sort (often somewhat higher and often applicable only to medical malpractice cases).[34] As already explained, it is important to appreciate that, in the American context, a cap is generally intended only to affect awards that otherwise would be above the cap. That is, juries are not told of the limit, but if they make awards above the cap, their awards are simply reduced. Put differently, the financial burden of caps in the United States is meant to be borne only by those with the most serious injuries. The point of a ceiling elsewhere, however, is to create a framework within which all injuries are scaled and victims with similar injuries are awarded reasonably consistent sums from case to case.

The materials presented here demonstrate that, so long as winners in U.S. personal injury cases have to pay their own legal expenses, a cap of $250,000 in pain and suffering will typically leave a large share of U.S. victims with serious injuries considerably worse off than their European counterparts.

TABLE 19
U.S. LEG AMPUTATION AWARDS ADJUSTING FOR
LEGAL FEES AND A CAP ON PAIN & SUFFERING OF $250,000 ($1000s)

Unadjusted		With $250K P&S Cap		P & S left	
P&S	Total	P&S	Total	(minus 33%) ($)	P&S left (€)
150	500	150	500	(20)	(15)
200	1,442	200	1442	(280)	(210)
150	400	150	400	20	15
400	435	250	285	155	120
452	633	250	431	110	80
490	573	250	333	139	105
500	734	250	484	90	70
615	716	250	351	130	100
1,000	1,500	250	750	0	0

1,550	2,420	250	1120	(125)	(95)
1,750	4,493	250	2993	(750)	(560)
4,000	7,568	250	3818	(1020)	(765)
5,580	6,343	250	1013	(90)	(70)
5,600	7,670	250	2320	(525)	(395)
6,000	7,497	250	1747	(330)	(250)
7,500	7,510	250	260	165	125
9,750	11,426	250	1926	(392)	(295)

Table 19 shows what are assumed would be the awards for U.S. leg loss victims (drawn from Table 15) were pain and suffering amounts simply capped at $250,000. First, note that, as a result of the cap, fourteen of the seventeen victims would have their awards reduced, and in most cases by a dramatic amount.

Second, note that nine of the seventeen victims would find themselves with pain and suffering awards of less than thirty-three percent of their total award, thereby requiring them to pay legal expenses partially from their recovery for out-of-pocket losses.[35] All of these victims would, on my assumptions, clearly be worse off in terms of pain and suffering recovery as compared with similar victims in all of the European nations. Moreover, of those eight with some money left over for pain and suffering after covering legal expenses, none would net more than $160,000 or €120,000, and two of those eight would wind up with nearly nothing for pain and suffering. This compares with the median predicted European nation award of €41,000 for the loss of a leg and the highest predicted European award of €166,000 for the loss of a leg (see Table 14). Hence, on balance, on my assumptions, a $250,000 cap on pain and suffering would leave the typical American leg loss victim worse off than his or her European counterpart in terms of net recovery for pain and suffering (after legal expenses).

For the American quadriplegia victims we identified, were a $250,000 cap on pain and suffering in place, then every one of them would wind up having to use all of that award plus substantially more to cover his or her legal expenses. Indeed, as shown in Table 20 (drawn from Table 16), every one of the twelve victims with quadriplegia would have to use up all of the pain and suffering money and then dip into economic loss recovery by a minimum of $800,000 to pay the assumed legal expenses.

TABLE 20
U.S. QUADRIPLEGIA AWARDS ADJUSTING FOR LEGAL FEES AND A CAP ON PAIN & SUFFERING OF $250,000 ($1000s)

Unadjusted			
P&S Share	Total Award	Total Award w/$250K Cap	P&S left (minus 33% for legal fees)
1,000	3,950	3,200	(820)
1,500	19,100	17,850	(5700)
2,000	7,345	5,595	(1615)
2,500	7,872	5,622	(1624)
3,000	8,972	6,222	(1824)
3,400	6,670	3,520	(924)
3,500	8,187	4,937	(1395)
4,000	17,770	14,020	(4423)
4,600	21,360	17,010	(5420)
4,900	9,500	4,850	(1367)
6,000	9,000	3,250	(833)
6,000	16,530	10,780	(3343)

In short, U.S.-type caps of $250,000, when added to U.S. rules on legal expenses, are extremely harsh on seriously injured victims. Many American victims would find themselves far outside the range of European awards on the low side. This is in dramatic contrast to the way American victims are nominally treated by uncapped jury awards for pain and suffering.

Suppose U.S. jurisdictions adopted a scale of awards for pain and suffering like that of New South Wales, and set the highest award in 2005 at $500,000. Then, at today's currency conversion rates, nominal U.S. pain and suffering awards would be moderately above the high end of the awards made in Europe, Australia, and Canada, but they would not be way off the charts -- as our awards are today.

Nevertheless, under such a scheme, unless victim legal expenses were also paid by defendants, many seriously impaired American victims would still likely wind up worse off than their counterparts in at least many of the comparison nations.

A New Regime for Both Pain and Suffering and Legal Fees?

To bring the American law broadly into line with the high end (or moderately above the high end) of the European and Commonwealth nations discussed here, a two-pronged change would be needed. That is, first, American states could adopt a ceiling approach of the sort used elsewhere—perhaps that recently enacted in New South Wales. As above, imagine for these purposes a ceiling of $500,000 (to be adjusted for inflation). Second, liable defendants would also be required to pay the victim's reasonable attorneys' fees and costs of litigation.

Under such a regime, a critical issue would be the method for determining what constitutes reasonable fees. One could adopt European-type approaches that envision payment based on the specific efforts performed (sometimes also taking into account the time put into the unpopular with plaintiffs' lawyers in the United States, many of whom detest the idea of keeping time sheets to record the specifics of their effort on the case. They would prefer to maintain a contingent fee percentage. If that mechanism were employed, however, it is not evident that so-called "market" rates now charged by lawyers would have to be embraced by statute.

For example, I have elsewhere proposed legal fees (paid by defendants) equal to ten percent of what defendants offer within, say, ninety days of the injury, and then forty percent of any amount eventually won beyond the amount of the initial offer.[37] This strategy is designed to stimulate a reasonable early offer and, in turn, a quick settlement. A different approach would be to adopt the fee schedule (or something like it) now contained in California's law governing medical mal- practice cases.[38] Plaintiffs' lawyers may charge no more than:

> (1) Forty percent of the first fifty thousand dollars ($50,000) recovered.
>
> (2) Thirty-three and one-third percent of the next fifty thousand dollars ($50,000) recovered.
>
> (3) Twenty-five percent of the next five hundred thousand dollars ($500,000) recovered.
>
> (4) Fifteen percent of any amount on which the recovery exceeds six hundred thousand dollars ($600,000).[39]

While I have not been able to gain any hard data on the level of legal fees in Europe as compared with tort recoveries, contacts of mine have informally reported that, in the end, lawyers in many countries wind up with legal fees of approximately ten percent of the tort award, regardless of the formal mechanism used to determine those fees. Compared with that, the California medical malpractice schedule is generous.

Just to illustrate how a new regime of the sort proposed here might work, Table 21 provides some examples drawn from the leg-loss and quadriplegia numbers used here (with a bit of rounding to make the presentation easier to follow).

For simplicity, the table assumes that the maximum pain and suffering award would be paid to the quadriplegia victim ($500,000) and forty percent of that sum to the leg loss victim ($200,000). The table also assumes that defendants would pay victim legal fees according to the schedule of maximum legal fees applicable to California malpractice cases, as noted above.

TABLE 21
EXAMPLES COMPARING THE EXISTING REGIME
WITH A PROPOSED NEW REGIME ($1000s)

Existing Regime						Proposed New Regime			
	(1)	(2)	(3)	(4)	(5)	(6)	(7)	(8)	(9)
	P&S	Total Paid by Defendant	Legal Fees	Net P&S to Victim	Net Total to Victim	P&S	Total To Victim	Legal Fees	Total Paid by Defendant
Leg	500	750	(250)	250	500	200	450	125	575
Leg	1000	1500	(500)	500	1000	200	700	177	877
Quad	1000	4500	(1500)	(500)	3000	500	4000	672	4672
Quad	3000	9000	(3000)	0	6000	500	6500	1047	7547
Quad	6000	9000	(3000)	3000	6000	500	3500	597	4097
Quad	4000	15000	(5000)	(1000)	10000	500	11500	1797	13297

The examples set out in Table 21 show that under the proposed regime as compared with the common-law regime: (1) some victims would net more and others less (compare columns five and seven); (2) plaintiff lawyers would earn less (compare columns three and eight); (3) and defendants would generally pay less overall (compare columns two and nine). Put differently, from the victim's viewpoint, the reduction in the pain and suffering award (column one minus column six) is sometimes greater than and sometimes less than the saved legal fees (column three). And from the defendant's viewpoint, the reduction in pain and suffering obligation (column one minus column six) is usually greater than the new obligation to pay legal fees (column eight).

Not illustrated by this table is the envisioned impact on those with smaller injuries. In those cases, the predicted recovery for pain and suffering would generally be both less in amount (indeed zero in the least severe cases) and more consistent from case to case. Net recovery to victims and total cost to injurers would vary from the current regime based on the same factors already noted.

C. *Values and Politics*

In the end, I personally favor a reform of the American law of tort damages of the sort discussed here: (1) liable defendants would be obligated to pay the victims' reasonable legal expenses, just as they are obligated to pay victims' reasonable medical expenses; and (2) pain and suffering awards would be modeled after the New South Wales approach, but with an initial ceiling of, say, $500,000 (instead of $350,000 Australian).[40]

The New South Wales approach could be implemented in our jury-based system by (1) instructing juries to determine the percent this victim's harm is as compared with the most serious harm, (2) allowing both sides to introduce evidence as to how past juries have rated roughly similar harm, and (3) instructing juries to award the amount of pain and suffering damages as the legislative-administrative table calls for when the percent of the most serious harm is as they have found it to be in the case.

Yet, perhaps people in the United States would not want the reform favored here, or perhaps this reform could not be politically achieved even if favored by the majority. First, Americans may actually prefer nominally to award huge sums for pain and suffering, a substantial share of which goes to plaintiffs' lawyers. Americans may like the current practice because, being a very wealthy nation, we may believe that victims of wrongdoing are entitled to enormous awards by world-wide standards -- awards that we, as consumers, may be quite willing to pay for in the cost of our goods and services. Or perhaps because we are so rich, and so value money in our culture, we wish to assign extremely large money values to diminished life experiences when we think those worsened experiences are undeserved. Or maybe it is that we so value what personal injury lawyers do for us as consumers that we are more than happy to have them take a large bite from what are gigantic awards by worldwide standards.

Moreover, although many Americans might in some respects disapprove of unequal treatment of similar victims, we as a society may be unwilling to do anything to reduce our disparities because of our cultural commitment to individual juries doing what they see as individual justice to individual victims personally before them in the courtroom.

Furthermore, even if most Americans agreed that our pain and suffering awards are nominally too large, too unevenly awarded, and wrongly used to pay legal fees assessed against a victim's total recovery, legislatively enacting the sorts of reforms suggested here will be extremely difficult.

Not only is the personal injury bar politically very strong, but also it may well take some doing to convince ordinary people that reforms that lower the overall cost of tort liability to defendants are actually translated into reduced costs of goods, services, insurance, and the like for society in general. In sum, as strange as what we now have seems to me, it may well be what most of my fellow Americans (on balance) want.

After all, pain and suffering damages are what drive our tort "lottery," and a large share of Americans seems to enjoy playing "lottery" games, notwithstanding their bad odds. Perhaps, therefore, a first step in selling my proposed reforms to the public would be to include a promise that, along with their monetary awards for pain and suffering in a U.S. version of the New South Wales plan, successful tort victims would also be given a number of actual lottery tickets in their state's lottery (or the equivalent).

ENDNOTES

1. *See* 2 AM. LAW INST., REPORTERS' STUDY: ENTERPRISE RESPONSIBILITY FOR PERSONAL INJURY 199 (1991). *See generally* Mark Geistfeld, *Placing a Price on Pain and Suffering: A Method for Helping Juries Determine Tort Damages for Nonmonetary Injuries,* 83 CAL L. REV. 773 (1995); Louis L. Jaffe, *Damages for Personal Injury: The Impact of Insurance,* 18 LAW & CONTEMP. PROBS. 219 (1953); David W. Leebron, *Final Moments: Damages for Pain and Suffering Prior to Death,* 64 N.Y.U. L. REV. 256 (1989); Jeffrey O'Connell & Rita James Simon, *Payment for Pain & Suffering: Who Wants What, When & Why?,* 1972 U. ILL L.F. 1.

2. A reasonably up to date list of state reforms may be found on the website of the American Tort Reform Association (ATRA), http://www.atra.org/show/7340 (last visited Sept. 15, 2005)[hereinafter ATRA site].

3. *See generally* Randall R. Bovbjerg et al., *Valuing Life and Limb in Tort: Scheduling "Pain and Suffering,"* 83 NW. U. L. REV. 908, 924-27 (1989); Oscar G. Chase, *Helping Jurors Determine Pain and Suffering Awards,* 23 HOFSTRA L. REV. 763, 768-69 (1995); Shari Seidman Diamond et al., *Juror Judgments About Liability and Damages: Sources of Variability and Ways to Increase Consistency.* 48 DEPAUL L. REV. 301, 313-17 (1998); Frederick S. Levin, *Pain and Suffering Guidelines: A Cure for Damages Measurement "Anomie,"* 22 U. MICH. J.L. REFORM 303, 307-11 (1989); Frank A. Sloan & Chee Ruey Hsieh, *Variability in Medical Malpractice Payments: Is the Compensation Fair?,* 24 LAW & SOC'Y REV. 997, 997-99 (1990); W. Kip Viscusi, *Pain and Suffering in Product Liability Cases: Systematic Compensation or Capricious Awards?,* 8 INT'L REV. L. & ECON. 203 (1988).

4. For a comparison between the U.S. rule and the rules elsewhere, see JOHN G. FLEMING, THE AMERICAN TORT PROCESS 187-234 (1988).

5. PERSONAL INJURY AWARDS IN EU AND EFFA COUNTRIES (David McIntosh & Marjorie Holmes eds., 2003) [hereinafter PERSONAL INJURY AWARDS].

6. A somewhat similar strategy of the hypothetical case was employed in a different comparison of European tort law. *See* COMPENSATION FOR PERSONAL INJURY IN A COMPARATIVE PERSPECTIVE (Bernhard A. Koch & Helmut Koziol eds., 2003). This project did, however, generate the sort of detailed information by which comparisons can be made of the sort presented here. For an earlier effort to compare European awards using several hypothetical cases, *see* PAUL SZOLLOSY, COMPENSATION FOR PERSONAL INJURY IN EUROPE (1992); Paul Szollosy, *Recent Trends in the Standard of Compensation for Personal Injury in a European Context,* 3 NORDISK FORSIKRINGSTIDSSKRIFT 191 (1991).

7. *See, e.g.,* ALLGEMEINER DEUTSCHER AUTOMOBIL-CLUB (ADAC), SCHMERZENSGELD·BE-TRAGE (Susanne Hacks et al. eds., 17th ed. 2001)[hereinafter ADAC).

8. PERSONAL INJURY AWARDS, *supra* note 5, at 2.

9. *See* DAMAGES FOR NON-PECUNIARY LOSS IN A COMPARATIVE PERSPECTIVE (W.V. Horton Rogers ed., 2001); THE JUDICIAL STUDIES BOARD, GUIDELINES FOR THE ASSESSMENT OF GENERAL DAMAGES IN PERSONAL INJURY CASES (6th ed. 2002 & 7th ed. 2004) (reporting detailed results for specific injuries from England and Wales).

10. *See* PERSONAL INJURY AWARDS, *supra* note 5, at 3.

11. For a general discussion of lawsuit frequency from country to country, see Erhard Blankenburg, *Civil Litigation Rates as Indicators for Legal Cultures, in* COMPARING LEGAL CULTURES 41 (David Nelken ed., 1997). For more general information comparing the personal injury law schemes throughout Europe (and elsewhere), see INTERNATIONAL PERSONAL INJURY COMPENSATION (Dennis Campbell ed., 1996); PERSONAL INJURY COMPENSATION IN EUROPE (Marco Bona & Philip Mead eds., 2003).

12. The data for the secretary is not shown here, but is available from the author.

13. Professor Giovanni Comandé elsewhere reports that, within Italy, different jurisdictions assign different multipliers to what are in effect the same tables, thereby awarding different sums for pain and suffering for the same injury based on the location of the trial. Giovanni Comandé, Non-Pecuniary Damages for Personal

Injury in Europe and the U.S.A.: A Proposal for Judicial Scheduling Models (unpublished article, on file with author).

14. *See* World Bank Group, http://www.worldbank.org/depweb/english/modules/economic/gnp/dataeuro.html (last visited Nov. 10, 2005) (revealing that Greece and Portugal have a fairly low gross national product (GNP) per capita ($11,740 and $10,670 respectively), while other countries such as Germany, Switzerland, and Austria each have a GNP of $26,570, $39,980 and $26,830 respectively).

15. *See* COLUMBIA ENCYCLOPEDIA (6th ed. 2005), *available at* www.bartleby.com/65/so/socwelf/html (indicating that "[n]ot all governments have equally extensive social welfare systems. Great Britain and the Scandinavian countries, often termed 'welfare states,' have wide ranging social welfare legislation").

16. *See* JAMES P. MUNGER, WHAT'S IT WORTH: A GUIDE TO CURRENT PERSONAL INJURY AWARDS AND SETTLEMENTS (2004); JACOB A. STEIN, STEIN ON PERSONAL INJURY DAMAGES (3d ed. 2003).

17. The level of these U.S. quadriplegia awards does not generally decrease with age (data on file with the author). Indeed, the average award for those ages twenty to thirty is slightly higher than the average award for those under age twenty. In general, there is little variation on average by decade of life.

18. Unlike the case of quadriplegia, for the leg amputation cases there is a reasonably strong connection with age (data on file with the author). The highest of the five awards made to those over fifty was $615,000, whereas all seven of the awards over one million dollars, where we know the age, were made to those under age fifty.

19. I converted dollars to euros at the rate of $1.333 per euro. This is admittedly somewhat arbitrary, since the euro's value against the dollar has been quite volatile in the past few years, amounting to $1.22 per euro at the time this is written. The U.S. case reports are possibly, on average, somewhat newer than the European data, suggesting that taking account of a year or two of European inflation might be warranted. On balance, the figure appears to be sensible.

20. Data on file with author.

21. Overall, recovery for pain and suffering in the United States is generally thought to amount to about fifty percent of total compensatory awards. *See* Steven P. Croley & Jon D. Hanson, *The Nonpecuniary Costs of Accidents: Pain-and-Suffering Damages in Tort Law,* 108 HARV. L. REV. 1785, 1789 (1995); Geistfeld, *supra* note 1, at 777 (stating that "[a]t present, pain- and-suffering damages account for about half of the total tort damages paid in products liability and medical malpractice cases").

22. *See generally* P.S. ATIYAH, ACCIDENTS, COMPENSATION AND THE LAW (1970); JOHN G. FLEMING, AN INTRODUCTION TO THE LAW OF TORTS (1967); ALLEN M. LINDEN, STUDIES IN CANADIAN TORT LAW (1972).

23. *See generally* Stephen D. Sugarman, *Tort Reform Through Damages Law Reform: An American Perspective,* 27 SYDNEY L. REV. 507 (2005); Prue Vines, *Faith, Hope, and Personal Injury: The Ipp Report and the Civil Liability Acts,* AUSTRALIAN CIV. LIABILITY 1 (2004). On Australian damages law generally, see HAROLD LUNTZ, ASSESSMENT OF DAMAGES FOR PERSONAL INJURY AND DEATH (4th ed. 2002).

24. Civil Liability Act, 2002, c. 16 (N.S.W.).

25. *Id.*

26. Andrews v. Grand & Toy Alberta Ltd., [1978] 2 S.C.R. 229, 65. *See generally* D. GARDNER, L'EVALUATION DU PREJUDICE CORPOREL (2d ed. 2002).

27. *See, e.g.,* White v. Gait, [2004] 224 D.L.R.4th 347; Hodgson v. Walsh, [1999]121 O.A.C. 255.

28. For some empirical evidence of the role of caps in slicing off recoveries for those with the most serious injuries, see David M. Studdert et al., *Are Damages Caps Regressive? A Study of Malpractice Jury Verdicts in California,* 23 HEALTH AFF. 54 (2004).

29. *See generally* FLEMING, *supra* note 4.

30. Comandé, *supra* note 13.

31. *Id.*

32. *Id.*

33. *See, e.g.,* ADAC, *supra* note 7.

34. *See* ATRA site, *supra* note 2. *See also* Stephen D. Sugarman, Op-Ed, *The Legal Sting of Pain and Suffering,* L.A. TIMES, June 5, 2005, at M5 (stating that both President Bush and Senate Majority Leader Bill Frist advocate a $250,000 cap on pain and suffering awards in medical malpractice claims).

35. I put aside here the possibility that the jury would become aware of the cap and end run its limit by increasing its award for out-of-pocket losses by the amount of pain and suffering money it wishes to award above the cap. *See generally* Catherine M. Sharkey, *Unintended Consequences of Medical Malpractice Damages Caps,* 80 N.Y.U. L. REV. 391 (2005).

36. For a discussion of legal fees in a variety of nations, see William B. Fisch, *Professional Services, in* 8 INTERNATIONAL ENCYCLOPEDIA OF COMPARATIVE LAW 78-86 (1999). *See also* FLEMING, *supra* note 4.

37. Sugarman, *supra* note 23.

38. CAL. BUS. & PROF. CODE § 6146 (a) (West 2003).

39. *Id.*

40. I would most prefer to join these with other reforms in the law of damages that I do not address here. *See* Sugarman, *supra* note 23. *See also* STEPHEN D. SUGARMAN, DOING AWAY WITH PERSONAL INJURY LAW: NEW COMPENSATION MECHANISM FOR VICTIMS, CONSUMERS, AND BUSINESS (1989).

Postscript

Recent research has updated some of the data for some European nations described in Chapter 7 and has provided some comparative information for a number of additional countries around the world. (See Stephen D. Sugarman, "Tort Damages for Non-economic Losses (in cases of physical injury to the person)" *Comparative Tort Law Research Handbooks in Comparative Law* (M. Bussani and A. Sebok eds. Edward Elgar 2014). http://www.law.berkeley.edu/files/journals/Sugarman_Non_economic_loss_ReformattedFinal.pdf .

Table I shows the approximate amount likely to be awarded for pain and suffering (in Euros) for a tort victim who has been made quadriplegic by the accident, comparing six European nations in the years 2000 and 2012.

Table I Estimated Awards for Pain and Suffering (in Euros) for Quadriplegia (2000 and 2012)

	2000	2012
Denmark	27,000	88,500
Sweden	59,000	122,000
Netherlands	125,000	192,000
England	218,000	330,000

Germany	240,000	614,000
Italy	200,000	1024,000

This table reveals a number of things. First, in both time periods the amounts awarded for the same injury varied enormously from country. Second, award levels are sharply up in recent time (and in a number of places by well more than can be accounted for by inflation). Third, countries more or less (Italy aside) kept their relative generosity ranking over the period.

Now consider Table II that provides roughly comparable data for seven other nations.

Table II Estimated Awards for Pain and Suffering (in Euros) for Quadriplegia (2012)

China	9,000
Poland	75,000
Israel	102,000
South Africa	108,000
Canada	255,000
Japan	267,000
Australia	433,000

It is important not to be misled by the seeming precision of these numbers. They are not only estimates, but also for most of the countries they are averages of ranges that have been identified for each nation (with the width of the range varying considerably from place to place).

Nonetheless, again a number of basic points may be made. First, and foremost, once again we see that nations vary enormously in how much they are likely to award in pain and suffering damages to tort victims with similar injuries. Second, while the wealth of a nation partially predicts where a country will relatively rank, that alone cannot account for the differences. Third, by looking at Tables I and II, and even putting aside the top and bottom outliers (Italy and China) one still sees great variation. Fourth, comparing Tables I and II with U.S. data through 2003 shown earlier in this reveals that the U.S. awards are still well outside the range of other places. The average award for quadriplegia then in the U.S. was 2,700,000 Euros (based on current exchange rates).

And yet, it continually must not be forgotten that in the U.S. victims must pay their legal fees, whereas in the other nations listed here those expenses are supposed to be paid by the loser (i.e., the defendant in these cases). So, even if sometimes in other nations, despite the loser-pays rule, victims in practice still have to partially pay out of their tort recovery for legal fees, it remains true that the first blush difference between the U.S. and elsewhere can be a mirage. Indeed, for injuries as serious as quadriplegia, as explained above, U.S. victims might well wind up turning over all of their pain and suffering award (and then some) to their lawyer, and of course in such settings, the net amount retained by the victim for pain and suffering could well be less than even in the lowest-ranking nations identified here. (This puts aside as well, of course, the matter of how nations might differently award damages for actual economic loss – lost wages/earning power and expenses, like medical expenses, arising from the injury.)

Chapter 8

Changing the Law of Damages – Australia Uses a Scalpel Where We Use a Sledgehammer

"Tort reform" has been the agenda of U.S. defendants for several years now, and as discussed in Chapter 2, the focus of that reform has been far more on the law of tort damages than on the substantive basis for imposing tort liability. Not only is there rather little that could plausibly be changed in the way of tort doctrine that would still leave the core negligence system in place, defense side interests quickly realized that there was far more money to be saved by going after tort damages law.

For several decades now, business, municipal government, insurance, and health care professional lobbyists (in various combinations) have pressed in state after state for a large scale statutory "roll back" of victims' rights to recover. And they have been successful in a hit and miss way with legislatures in most jurisdictions.

This chapter looks at tort damages from a comparative law perspective. It proposes a package of reforms starting from the basic common law regime – a package that is not so nearly one-sided as what has been pitched to U.S. lawmakers in recent years by defense-side interests. This proposal draws on a number of changes that have been made elsewhere in the world in recent years, especially in New South Wales, Australia as part of that state's tort reform efforts.

This article was written for a special 2005 issue of the Sydney Law Review honoring University of Melbourne Professor Harold Luntz on the occasion of his retirement. It was published as Stephen D. Sugarman, "Tort Reform through Damages Law Reform: An American Perspective," 27 Sydney Law Review 507-524 (2005) and is reprinted with permission of the journal. Professor Luntz, one of Australia's most outstanding torts scholars, is the author of the leading book on tort damages in Australia.

Tort Reform Through Damages Law Reform: An American Perspective

Substantive tort liability depends on whether the defendant breached a duty of care and thereby caused an injury that is fairly part of the risk the defendant took. Yet, whether the defendant is liable or not is only part of the story. The way we determine the amount of money awarded to successful plaintiffs also critically impacts upon tort law's social function. Indeed, sweeping changes in the law of damages can dramatically transform tort law.[1] Perhaps this explains why Professor Harold Luntz has made damages a central focus of his scholarship.[2]

At common law, tort damages were meant to provide complete compensation for the tort victim's loss. When a wrongdoer caused harm, the goal of tort damages was to force the defendant to pay for everything necessary to make the specific plaintiff whole. Awards were meant to be highly individualized as to their amount, so as to reflect the unique circumstances of every individual case. Precise justice was understood to be as important in the award of monetary recovery as it was in the determination of liability itself.

Many people continue to embrace this view, and it clearly reflects the perspective of many judges and legislators in a large number of United States jurisdictions. American tort lawyers who represent plaintiffs in court typically make their reputations by convincing juries that an enormous sum is required to put a particular victim equivalently back in the position he or she would have been in but for the tortious conduct of the defendant.

Yet, in some American states, and in other nations around the world, different values have been brought to bear on the law of tort damages. These other perspectives can be importantly traced to experience in the design and implementation of social insurance schemes that compensate people suffering from disabilities (such as industrial injury compensation plans). Those social insurance schemes generally rest on the notion that it suffices to provide victims with rough justice when attempts at achieving precise justice cost too much. Costs here include both the financial costs of more individualized administration and the moral cost of inconsistent treatment of equals. Furthermore, whereas tort law conventionally has been understood to be exclusively about corrective justice, social insurance schemes almost always contain a distributional justice perspective. Put simply, those plans worry more about the actual monetary needs of ordinary people than the needs of those who are financially well off or otherwise well provided for.

Once it is appreciated that some or all of the typical features of social insurance schemes might be substituted for common law principles, the possibilities of large- scale changes in the tort damages law become evident.

In this essay, I explore several core issues with respect to tort damages in personal injury cases. In the process I propose ways in which the common law and traditional US rules might be changed so as to make recovery in tort considerably more like recovery under social insurance schemes. Along the way, I point out that Australia in general, and New South Wales in particular, have already moved in the direction I suggest. Although a few American states have also begun a similar shift, the process is slower, in part because the underlying politics has been so easily characterized as no more than 'taking away victims' rights.'

My proposals are not meant merely as a package of pro-defendant changes, even if, on balance, they would considerably reduce the cost of tort liability. My central motivation is not simply to enable enterprises and individuals to purchase cheaper tort liability insurance, even if this consequence should also yield general social benefits in the form of lower priced goods and services. Rather, my goal is a reformed law of tort damages in personal injury cases that better meets what I see as genuine victim need.

1. Primary v. Secondary

Conceptually, the most crucial initial issue that must be resolved in constructing the law of damages for personal injury is whether tort should be the primary or a secondary source of compensation for victims with valid tort claims. Put differently, should victims turn to tort initially, or only as a matter of last resort to fill in where compensation is otherwise not available?

More than a century ago, the answer to this question mattered little, because then most accident victims had no other source of compensation. But today that is all changed. Every developed nation has some institutional structure in place, altogether apart from tort law, to deal with its citizens' medical and related expenses and their loss of income.

In many countries, all residents have access to free or low cost health care, and the social insurance scheme replaces a considerable share of lost earnings arising from disability, retirement, unemployment and death. In robust systems, disability benefits attend to both short and long term needs, as well as to both partial and total disabilities.

Despite its wealth, the United States has a less comprehensive scheme, and we rely on both private insurance and the labor market to a far greater extent than countries with a broader political consensus on the social welfare role of the state.[3]

For example, although most of our elderly and many of our poor have government-funded free or low cost health care, most Americans access health care through private health insurance provided in connection with the employment of one or more household members. As a consequence, perhaps 15 to 20 per cent of Americans are without health insurance.[4] They must go without health care, pay out-of-pocket for care, or else seek care as charity patients. So, too, the US lags behind most wealthy nations with respect to income protection. Our national Social Security scheme provides moderate wage replacement benefits to survivors of deceased former workers and to workers and their families if the worker is totally and permanently disabled. Beyond that, those injured on the job have some wage replacement protection through workers' compensation schemes; those schemes are mandated by the fifty individual states, not the national government, and a substantial majority of employees are protected through insurance their employers purchase from private carriers. To provide income replacement in case of total disability beyond that made available through social insurance, many workers are provided, or permitted to purchase, group-based private disability insurance through their employment, and there is an individual market in long-term disability insurance policies that caters especially to high earners. Only a handful of states mandate income replacement for non-occupational short-term disabilities, and sick leave benefits are nowhere required by law. On the other hand, larger employers commonly provide such benefits to their regular employees.

Notwithstanding this 'crazy quilt,' even in the US, there is a good chance that anyone who happens to be an accident victim with a valid tort claim will today have at least some substantial alternative source of compensation.

Historically in the US, and at common law generally, these so-called 'collateral sources' have been formally ignored in tort litigation.[5] Defendants are not permitted to lower the amount of damages they owe merely because advance provision has otherwise been made for victim need. Nor, traditionally, are American juries meant to learn about such other sources of compensation any particular victim might have had. This approach has been variously justified: the wrongdoer should not get off easy; safety incentives would be undermined; proper social cost accounting would be disrupted; victims and/or society pay for the collateral sources and that advance planning was not done to benefit wrongdoers.

Nonetheless, the rule has been much criticized, even by those who concede that 'precise justice' might be better served, for example, by a careless driver's auto insurer paying full tort damages to the victim, and that victim, in turn, reimbursing his own health and disability insurers. The central objection to this arrangement is practical, not theoretical. Put simply, the transaction costs of shifting losses from one insurer to another are so large that, it is claimed, society as a whole would be better off forgoing the luxury of whatever exquisite justice is achieved by the common law solution. Moreover, if there is no reimbursement by the victim of the collateral sources, then, critics believe the victim winds up with a socially undesirable windfall of double recovery. Furthermore, in America, because legal fees are paid by victims and are generally calculated as a proportion of gross tort recovery, the common law rule is also seen by American critics as unjustly benefiting plaintiffs' lawyers at the expense of their clients. Finally, many American opponents of the common law collateral sources rule argue that by driving up the cost of tort liability it makes goods and services more expensive and for some crucial matters, like health care services, this can have the result of denying some members of the public adequate access to such things.

In response to these arguments, several American states have recently taken steps to overturn the conventional rule.[6] Some simply reverse the rule for specified sources. Others, somewhat opaquely, provide that juries may be told about certain collateral sources, presumably with the implied understanding that juries will appropriately reduce awards accordingly, but without specific instruction to that effect.

Although plaintiffs' lawyers and many consumer groups in the US view these reforms as part of a broader effort to 'take away victims' rights', I nonetheless conclude that a substantial reversal of the collateral source rule should be the centerpiece of what I envision (and will more fully describe later in this essay) as a balanced reform of the law of damages that would dramatically alter tort law's social role. As the first piece of the overall package, this reform would reserve tort for when it is most needed, that is, to deal with compensation needs that are not already met by the society's core social insurance arrangements. Put differently, if society is already assuring some income support and health care for all accident victims, then 'making them whole' does not require duplication (and complex follow on arrangements) through tort law itself.

Political leaders in many countries appear to have resisted this change on the ground that the reversal of the collateral source rule shifts costs away from liability insurance (and the causes of accidents) and onto social insurance schemes whose funding is especially politically sensitive. But since it should be clear to even those with modest sophistication that citizens generally pay for both social insurance and liability insurance (the latter via the costs of goods and services), it seems to me to be politically irresponsible to waste money in transaction costs merely on the basis of the public's misperceptions as to how costs are borne (i.e., allowing the public somehow to imagine that when the payment of tort claims comes from private insurance companies, then these costs really are not being borne by consumers).

Those especially concerned about social cost accounting (and the impact the assignment of accident costs may have on the level at which accident-causing activities are engaged in) might be placated if a reversal of the collateral source rule were joined with a tax (or some suitable substitute) on activities whose costs would otherwise be shifted onto basic safety net benefit schemes. As to auto injuries, for example, along with reversing the collateral source rule, petrol taxes could be increased and/or auto registration fees could be increased. While outside of tort law, the Quebec auto no-fault scheme has, in effect, adopted this approach.[7]

So far, however, US states that have somewhat reversed the collateral source rule have not taken this extra step of imposing new fees on activities that are relieved of costs because of the modification of damages law.[8]

Assuming there were to be a substantial reversal of the collateral source rule, this does not mean that it would be appropriate to reverse the rule for all collateral sources, however. Privately purchased life insurance is a good example. Indeed, American jurisdictions that have already altered the collateral source rule have made this distinction. They have not reversed the rule for private life insurance, but they have for US Social Security benefits, even though an important type of those benefits is the payment of pensions to deceased workers' survivors — in short, a life insurance policy whose benefits are paid out over time.

I agree with this distinction because the cultural understanding of these two collateral sources is very different. Private life insurance is viewed as providing a voluntarily-arranged supplemental source of income, aimed at improving the material well-being of policy beneficiaries on top of whatever else they might receive at the time of the insured's death — including stocks, bonds, real estate, personal property, and tort claims that might come to the survivors. Consistent with this perspective, it is unheard of for the standard life insurance policy to insist upon reimbursement if the policy beneficiary is successful in a wrongful death action in tort. By contrast, basic Social Security income replacement benefits and basic health insurance (as well as workers' compensation insurance) are widely understood as core safety net protections and not supplements.

The wisdom of continuing to ignore private life insurance when other benefits are being calculated is, in my view, re-enforced by our experience with the way life insurance was treated in the US by the compensation scheme set up in response to the airplane hijack terrorism events of September 11, 2001.[9] Contrary to past practice, in this case Congress provided that benefits payable to survivors of those killed on 9/11 would be reduced by life insurance payments obtained by those survivors. This was seemingly justified on the simple basis that, when survivors had life insurance proceeds, their need was correspondingly less. Moreover, the plan's designers probably thought this solution would be politically attractive with the public since its effect would be to lower what otherwise could be enormous payments to families of high earners killed in the terrorist attacks (since the 9/11 plan benefits were generally designed to reflect the lost earnings of those who died).

But in fact, as surely could have been anticipated, life insurance protection varied enormously among the victims. Hence, the 9/11 plan wound up 'valuing the life' of victims very differently — and most objectionably, devaluing the advance planning and thrift of the victim. As a result, it was commonly and powerfully argued that the family of a person who had paid US $12 000 a year for life insurance would get far less from the 9/11 plan than the family whose now-deceased breadwinner instead had more frivolously spent the same money to lease an expensive sports car.

Assume, then, that tort damages law is altered so that recoveries in personal injury and death cases are reduced from what they would otherwise be by subtracting benefits provided by basic social safety net schemes, but not subtracting private life insurance proceeds or other sources that are culturally understood to belong to the recipient beyond any tort recovery that is awarded. (As for how tort law should deal with private disability insurance that provides income replacement to high earners, see section 3 below.) Even reversing the collateral source rule to this limited extent would reduce sharply the role tort law in the US and in many other nations now plays in accident compensation. In addition, it would provide a mechanism for further diminishing the role for tort, were the basic social safety net to expand (as well as the mechanism for a renewed larger role for tort if a changing political climate or a decreased public fiscal capacity results in a reduced basic social safety net).

2. Compensation for Non-Economic Loss

The second most important issue in the law of damages for personal injury is its role in the compensation for what we in the US call pain and suffering, or general damages, or non-economic loss.[10] However labelled, this refers to losses based neither on lost income nor on out-of-pocket financial payments made (or owed) by victims. Rather, this is money to compensate for the physical pain and suffering that goes along with a physical trauma, the emotional harm that can come from an injury to one's self or a loved one, the disappointment or embarrassment coming from one's changed appearance or altered abilities to engage in pleasurable activities and favorite pastimes as a result of an injury, the harm to one's dignity from being wrongly injured by another, and so on.[11]

US tort law compensates these losses quite generously. The formal US rule is that the jury determines an appropriate pain and suffering award in the specific case. Hence, in principle, one's recovery is supposed to turn on a highly individualized appraisal of the victim's precise harm. In practice, the amount is also understood to turn on the talent of the victim's lawyer, the appeal of the victim to the jury, jury composition, the nature of the defendant's faulty conduct, and more. In reality, of course, the overwhelming share of tort claims is settled without a trial. In principle, settlement occurs in the shadow of a likely jury verdict in the individual case. In practice, lawyers for victims and lawyers and insurance adjustors for defendants negotiate in more rough and ready ways.

It is not true, as sometimes rumored, that in the US pain and suffering awards (general damages) are simply figured as three times the special (or hard, or economic) damages. Nonetheless, participants in the process report that there is more than a kernel of truth to the idea that the parties start their negotiations with that multiple well in mind, adjusting their demands and offers based upon all sorts of particulars in the case.

In any event, other things being equal, one ordinarily can anticipate a larger pain and suffering settlement if one has larger medical bills (or more lost income). While there is undeniably some common sense appeal to the idea that the greater your medical needs, the larger your pain and suffering, in the US this sort of thinking can all too often have the undesirable effect of victims running up larger health care costs in order to have a multiplier effect on their tort awards for pain and suffering. This is especially objectionable when victims are encouraged by their own lawyers to obtain what amount to fraudulent health care services. Some unscrupulous lawyers have a special arrangement with, say, a physical therapist, chiropractor, or other health care provider, who is happy to earn the extra income for services which may well not be needed (and in extreme cases are not actually provided, even though paper records are created). Under the US percentage-of- recovery-based system for the payment of victim legal fees, this inflation of health care costs not only means more money for the client and the friendly health care provider, but also more money for the lawyer. To be sure, defense interests know about these shenanigans and have good reason to make efforts to uncover them and expose the participants to punishment, which for the unethical lawyers involved could mean disbarment from future practice. Nonetheless, it is widely believed that undetected fraud of this sort is substantial.

In contrast to tort law, pain and suffering type harms are largely ignored in the US by a wide range of other compensation mechanisms. For example, basic social insurance plans and typical private disability insurance policies do not compensate for pain and suffering.

To be sure, there is a small private market in the US for so-called 'accident insurance'. These policies provide a specified (and usually relatively small) payment for the loss of an eye or an arm or a leg (but they typically do not cover many other common and painful injuries caused by accidents, like an injured back or neck, or nerve pain down the leg). It is also true that American workers' compensation plans typically provide modest payments for certain serious harms like major disfigurements or dismemberments.

Moreover, it is noteworthy that in the US at least two important non-tort national victim compensation schemes have provided for non-economic loss. The Childhood Vaccine Injury program awards up to US $250 000 for non-economic loss to seriously disabled young children who are accepted under the terms of the plan as having suffered their harm as a side-effect of a childhood vaccine. So too, the 9/1l compensation plan provided lump sum benefits to survivors of those killed as a consequence of the terrorist acts that were completely unrelated to any income or other out-of-pocket loss of the survivors. The amount set by the special master who managed the 9/11 plan was also US $250 000 per decedent, plus an additional US $100 000 for each surviving spouse and child. But while these may seem like large sums when compared with other nations' tort awards for non-economic loss, in the US 'deep pocket' careless defendants may well find themselves owing more than a million dollars (and occasionally more than ten million dollars) for pain and suffering to victims they have gravely disabled.

Many American scholars and business leaders have called for reform in the way that tort law deals with pain and suffering awards[12] — although earlier calls simply to eliminate this category of tort damages are not common today. Rather, the typical effort by defense-minded reformers in recent times has been to impose a ceiling (or cap) on the amount of such awards.[13] In California more than thirty years ago, for example, a cap of US $250 000 (that same amount again) was imposed on pain and suffering recovery in medical malpractice cases. Later, other states adopted ceilings that were often applicable to pain and suffering awards in all personal injury cases. These caps tended to range rather widely from, say, US $300 000 to US $850 000. But the major direct effect of any cap is the same. It is to cut back on what the most seriously injured victims can be awarded.

In the US a monetary cap also tends, in its effect, to harm the young more than the old, other things being equal. That is, under the American system, permanent pain and suffering is conventionally determined by taking into account the future life expectancy of the victim — i.e., the number of years of suffering that lie ahead. So, other things being equal, a 25 year old would be expected to obtain more money for the same huge injury than a 55 year old would. For this reason, some have envisioned that caps could be set in terms of annual limits (or, what is much the same, individuals would face shrinking caps the older they are). The legislature in the state of Washington tried a more flexible cap of this sort, taking victim age into account. However, the Washington Supreme Court found the law unconstitutional on other grounds and so the opportunity to assess the suitability of this age-related approach was lost.[14]

Indirectly, caps could also have an important additional effect. If the ceiling is understood to reflect what the legislature has determined should be paid to the most seriously harmed victim, then one might feel it appropriate to reconsider what are the proper sums payable to those who, prior to the cap, would have received an amount, say, nearly equal to the cap, but for a far less serious harm than one can suffer and yet now be restricted by the cap. Were that to occur, a cap could, in the end, have the effect of forcing a downward adjustment of pain and suffering awards not only on those above the cap, but also throughout the full range of harms.

Yet, it does not appear that caps in the US are intended to or importantly have such effects. Juries, for example, are generally not told about caps; rather, they are instructed to award damages as always, with the judge then later simply knocking off anything that turns out to be above the cap.

But, one could surely imagine a regime in which a cap amount was set to reflect what is thought appropriate for the most severe injury, with instructions to those managing the system to adjust accordingly. Indeed, perhaps the easiest way to envision such a scheme is to think about adopting a schedule that lists a wide range of harms, with presumptive benchmark sums for pain and suffering set from zero up to the highest figure, depending on the nature of the injury (with the largest amount becoming the cap). This approach appears to have taken hold somewhat informally in Great Britain.[15]

In Australia, a restrictive statutory approach to non-economic loss has been enacted in several jurisdictions.[16] Caps have been placed on recovery for general damages (typically ranging AU$250 000-$350 000).[17] Losses are then scheduled up to the cap, so that only the gravest injuries yield the maximum recovery. The New South Wales law provides that the severity of the loss in the individual case is to be compared with the most extreme case, and appropriate awards as a percentage of the maximum are set out by statute. For example, a non-economic loss which is 20 per cent of the most extreme case is to receive but 3.5 per cent of the maximum award; a non-economic loss which is 30 per cent of the most extreme case is to receive 23 per cent of the maximum award; and a non-economic loss which is 60 per cent of the most extreme case is to receive a full 60 per cent of the maximum award.[18] As for what per cent of severity is to be attached to specific sorts of injuries, courts are supposed to pay attention to what percentages have been assigned by other courts in similar cases.[19]

In my view, the most essential policy choice with respect to pain and suffering awards has not even yet been mentioned. It is deciding whether some harms should attract zero recovery. Put differently, the issue is whether there should be a threshold (or floor) on recovery for pain and suffering.

I favor that solution for a variety of reasons. First, these awards are today often paid out for small pains and emotional upsets that are long gone before the money is received. That is, there is no ongoing pain and suffering, and indeed that which the victim felt might well have been very temporary. Second, because of the nuisance value of these cases, victims are often able to exploit defendants' needs to get the claims off their books. Worse, because less is at stake, these are also cases in which devious victims are readily able to get away with running up unneeded care costs, to manufacture ailments, and the like.

Third, and this is perhaps most important, if combined with the reversal of the collateral source rule proposed above, a threshold on pain and suffering recovery provides the potential for simply eliminating entirely from the tort system an enormous share of current claims. After all, if you have your medical bills and lost income reasonably well replaced already, and if you are not injured enough to meet the threshold for recovering for pain and suffering, what is there to sue for? Indeed, as a practical matter, you might well be willing even to absorb modest shortfalls in recovery of economic losses if that is all you could recover in tort in any event. And while the latter means a modest burden for victims, the potential social gains of ridding the system of a giant share of current claims are very large. Obviously, there is the prospect of large savings in legal costs and payouts, as well as the reduced burden on the administration of the judicial system. Less evident, but perhaps equally important, there is the prospect of overturning the widespread American social norm that suing somebody else when you are hurt in an accident is what everyone does and what you are culturally expected to do.

Finally, combining a threshold on pain and suffering awards with a reversal of the collateral source rule means that the tort system would shift its focus towards the more seriously injured.

Based upon experience with auto no-fault plans in the US and Canada, there is good reason to believe that the imposition of a fairly high verbally phrased floor on recovery for pain and suffering for example, requiring serious disfigurement or dismemberment or at least three months of full disability — could achieve a very significant reduction in personal injury claims.

Such a threshold could be combined with a presumptive schedule of recovery for a range of increasingly serious injuries. With both a schedule and a threshold, presumably even those at the bottom of the schedule would be entitled to not insignificant sums. For example, under this approach, which I favour, pain and suffering awards might range from US $15 000–25 000 at the base to perhaps US $500 000 at the top. A US $500 000 maximum in the US would still target American awards considerably beyond those of other nations, but it would more like putting the US schedule at the edge of the chart instead of way off the chart.

Australia is again out in front in moving in this direction, as a few jurisdictions have already enacted thresholds on the recovery for pain and suffering. In New South Wales, for example, a non-economic loss which is less than 15 per cent as severe as the most extreme case does not entitle the victim to recover any damages for pain and suffering.[20]

3. Income Replacement: Progressive v Regressive

As already noted, tort law is conventionally understood to be a system in the service of corrective justice, not distributive justice. Put differently, the traditional role of damages law is to restore the victim to the position he would have been in absent the tort — at least to the extent that money can achieve that. To be sure, the fact that you get money rather than having your body instantly repaired and restored casts some doubt on how seriously tort law can pretend to achieve corrective justice after all.

Nonetheless, when it comes to replacing lost income, the long-standing commitment of tort law is to replace all lost income.[21] This means that higher earners will receive more from the system than will low earners, other things being equal. Of course, other things are not equal, and it is complicated to determine, for example, the relative likelihood of high and low earners becoming tort victims and whether the same sort of physical injury is likely to have a larger (or smaller) impact on the future earning potential of one, who, before the accident, was a higher (or lower) earner. But what is clear is that if two people of the same age are disabled for a month, or for five years, the amount to which they are entitled in tort will be greater for the one who was earning more at the time of the accident.[22]

The upshot is that tort law in action is understandably viewed as regressive — and especially when its funding arrangements are taken into account. After all, motorists, generally speaking, do not pay different sums for liability insurance simply because they earn different salaries. So, too, enterprise defendants do not pass the cost of tort liability on to consumers on the basis of consumer income levels. In short, for the same injury, higher earner victims as a class draw more from the tort system than do lower earner victims, but without paying more into it.

This need not be the law of damages. Indeed, social insurance schemes — even if wage-related — tend to resolve this issue very differently. In the US, benefits are wage-related in both our national Social Security scheme and our state workers' compensation plans. But these plans impose a limit on the level of wages that are replaced (and Social Security also replaces a smaller share of income the higher the income of the claimant). The basic social understanding of these plans, as already noted, is that they are aimed at core household needs. And as a corollary, these plans assume that those with much higher earning can choose, and except for deliberately high risk takers, will responsibly choose to purchase what they conclude is an appropriate level of supplemental protection (or will take jobs with employers who provide supplemental income protection as part of the employment package).

Given that social understanding, tort damages law could also adopt such an attitude, and I favor that sort of reform. Indeed, the case for this approach grows stronger in my view once it has been decided to reverse the collateral source rule with respect to basic social safety net benefits.

As just noted, high earners are the very ones best positioned to obtain extra insurance to protect wages that are not covered by social insurance. For those who buy this extra disability insurance, to then provide tort recovery as well would amount to unneeded double recovery in my view. To be sure, reversing the collateral source rule might suffice to deal with this problem if the reversal were applied, not merely to basic income replacement plans (as proposed above), but also to this sort of additional income protection as well. Yet, that would be an incomplete solution, in my opinion, when we next consider the victim who has not obtained supplemental income protection. Simply reversing the collateral source rule in an even more expansive way will have no effect on that high earning plaintiff, who would still draw generously from tort, thereby rewarding what strikes me as cavalier risk taking. Put differently, the point here is not that private disability insurance and private life insurance should be treated differently for purposes of the collateral source rule. It is rather that, from the perspective of distributive justice, tort law itself should be understood to compensate only for moderate levels of income loss to the extent that they are not already replaced by basic social insurance schemes. The result of this way of thinking would be to have tort law deny everyone recovery for the loss of high levels of income, once more bringing tort damages law closer to the policies governing social insurance.

If this policy were pursued, a difficult issue is just where the cut-off line should be. Again, experience in the US with the 9/11 compensation plan may offer some preliminary guidance. There, the plan administrator provided tables showing what benefits would be paid to survivors of those who had earned up to US $231 000 a year, which was said to be the cut off for approximately 98 per cent of American earners. Of course, the 9/11 plan was not understood to involve wrongdoers paying their tort victims. Moreover, there were complaints by families of high earners, especially when this seeming restriction on income replacement was combined with the set off of life insurance proceeds discussed earlier.[23] Yet, overall, there seemed little public opposition to a cap on benefits at the ninety-eighth percentile in income.[24] But this may well be inappropriately generous. Indeed, it seems to me that it might be quite sufficient for tort law to limit income replacement to, say, the seventy-fifth percentile, or perhaps at two or three times the average weekly wage. The latter in the US today would put the cap, not at US $231 000, but perhaps somewhere in the US $70 000–$100 000 range.

While some might favor completely eliminating the role of tort in replacing lost income, the modest level of income replacement provided by most US social insurance schemes would make this abrupt change in the US too harsh in my view. Put differently, the goal here is to exclude the really high earners from having all of their income replaced by tort law, and not to exclude the middle class from full wage replacement.

Once more, Australia has taken the lead on this issue, as several jurisdictions have restricted recovery for income loss to a multiple of the average annual earnings of full time adult workers — typically three times that amount, as in New South Wales.[25]

4. Sharing

The common law rule was that an at-fault victim, whose negligence contributed to his own injury in a causally relevant manner, could recover nothing from someone whose fault was also a cause of the injury. The law, in effect, conveyed the message that we do not open our courts to wrongdoers, especially those who could have avoided harm had they only been careful.

Nowadays all this has changed, and nearly everywhere a regime of comparative fault has taken over.[26] In what we in the US call the 'pure' form, even a victim who is 75 per cent at fault will recover 25 per cent of his loss from a defendant who is 25 per cent at fault. A majority of US states, however, have adopted the so-called 'modified' form, in which victims whose fault is greater than (or in some cases equal to) that of the injurer remain fully barred from recovering. These harsher rules continue to let off some wrongdoing defendants.

I propose a much more dramatic change in the effect of victim fault on damages recovery. In its strongest form, victim fault would be ignored, regardless of what share of the fault is attributable to the victim. An example of a more moderate reform would provide that, if the victim is no more at fault than the injurer, then the victim's fault would be ignored, but when the victim's fault is more than the defendant's, the defendant would be liable for damages equal to his share of the fault. Notice that, as compared to the 'pure form' of comparative negligence, this moderate reform provides greater compensation to victims who are less than half at fault. Regardless of the precise rule adopted, the sentiment behind reform of this sort rests on several considerations.

First, victims are the ones who suffer the physical harm. Hence, they already incur a substantial negative consequence of their fault. Second, from the viewpoint of punishing injurers, horizontal equity among injurers counsels against reducing a defendant's liability simply because that defendant's victim coincidentally also was to blame for the accident. Think of two drivers who carelessly speed through an intersection. One hits an innocent pedestrian and the other hits a carelessly inattentive second motorist. Both speeding drivers are equally at fault, but reducing the damages paid by the second (as comparative fault now does), imposes a lesser penalty on the second driver, who was no less careless than the first. Third, counterpart solutions in compensation plan alternatives to tort point in the same direction. In US workers' compensation schemes, for example, ordinary fault by victims is ignored.[27] That the employer is 'strictly liable' in workers' compensation is not itself the reason why employee fault is generally ignored. After all, defective product makers in the US are also strictly liable in tort. But the latter currently have available to them the partial defense of comparative fault (say, against a careless user of the product), when the employer does not. The reason that the employer does not goes to a wider understanding about the social need to provide medical care and income replacement to industrial accident victims whether or not they were injured through their own carelessness. My proposal for tort damages reform would ordinarily take away this defense from the defective product seller too, and hence, as with reform in the law covering income replacement discussed above, this reform would also bring tort damages law more in line with social insurance generally.

A different matter is the sharing of losses among defendants. Assume that the fault of more than one defendant was a cause of the victim's harm, and that the award is initially apportioned among them on the basis of defendant fault. The practical issue, then, is who should bear the risk that one or more of those who carelessly caused the victim's loss is either unable to be brought before the court (the absence problem) or financially unable to pay for his share of the damage award (the insolvency problem). The solution that best reflects a desire to use tort damages in order to provide backup compensation to tort victims is one that thrusts the risks of insolvency and absence on defendants. In the context of the other provisions here proposed, this is the solution I generally favor. In the US we call this a rule of joint and several liability.

The rule at the opposite extreme adopts the principle of what we call several liability. There, a defendant is liable for damages only up to its share of the fault (unless otherwise independently liable for the fault of another defendant, say, in co-conspirator cases). Hence under this rule, the risks of insolvency and absence are borne by victims.

In-between rules are also possible. In California today, for example, defendants bear those risks as to economic losses, but victims bear them as to non-economic losses. Or, under the rule proposed by the Uniform Comparative Fault Act (1979), those risks are shared by both defendants and plaintiffs.[28] Hence, if the victim is not at all at fault, insolvency and absence are problems for the deep pocket defendant before the court. But if the plaintiff is also at fault, then he shares those risks with the available defendant(s) — based on the relative fault of both plaintiff and defendant(s). While this latter solution has considerable appeal in the current US state of the law, it seems to me to be out of place if the proposal described earlier is embraced — that victim fault generally is to be ignored.

All things considered, then, a sensible victim-oriented compromise solution on the question of sharing might resemble something like this. Ordinarily, victim fault is ignored. If, however, the victim's fault is more than that of a single defendant, then, as between them, the victim bears his share of the available pain and suffering award based on his relative fault (but the defendant still bears all of the economic loss). In the same vein, if there are multiple defendants and one or more is absent and/or insolvent, then, only if the plaintiff is more at fault than the defendants as a group, would he bear any of those risks, and the risk would be restricted to pain and suffering damages, which the more at fault plaintiff would bear in proportion to his fault.[29]

5. Legal Fees

The typical rule outside the US is that the loser pays the winner's legal fees. In the US, however, the formal rule is that each side pays its own fees. But in practice, the American rule functions rather differently. On the defense side, although defendants officially have responsibility for their own fees, win or lose, those fees are almost always paid for by liability insurance (assuming defendants carry that insurance). Indeed, liability insurers not only pay for the legal defense, they normally control the defense (including selecting the lawyer and determining whether to settle, and if so for how much). After all, it is their money that is at risk. On the victim side, plaintiffs too have a kind of insurance. Even though claimants formally bear their own fees, win or lose, the contingent fee system that applies in virtually all personal injury cases means that there is no fee if there is no recovery. The plaintiff's lawyer, by taking on the case, in effect, provides the insurance that covers the fee (i.e., not charging) if the case is lost.

The major shortcoming of the American system is that when victims win, they have to pay their own legal fees out of their awards, and typically those fees now range between 20 and 50 per cent of the recovery depending on the nature of the case, who the victim is (e.g., minors are often charged less because courts may not approve higher fees in such cases) and at what stage of the litigation the case ends (e.g., after an early offer of settlement versus after a protracted appeal of a trial court verdict). In a world of high pain and suffering awards and where the collateral source rule remains, victims may well be able to pay for their legal fees out of what is understood as an extra bundle of recovery. Yet, this outcome happens idiosyncratically, depending on differences among cases that have little to do with the fairness of leaving the victim under-compensated as to real economic losses.

Hence, along with a partial repeal the collateral source rule and a restriction on the right of recovery for pain and suffering, I favor changing the law of damages in the US in a way that (unlike most other nations) continues to impose defense side legal costs on defendants win or lose, but (like most other nations) requires defendants to pay victim legal costs if the victim wins (and presumably settlements would be made that provide for coverage of the victim's legal fees). Put differently, under my proposal legal fees would be treated like other recoverable expenses that are incurred as a result of the accident.

Under such an approach one must decide what constitute reasonable fees. Although they might be set as a percentage of the recovery, which is how victim lawyers in the US now typically charge, there are many other options. Some say that, while it is true that tort recovery usually increases when the victim is harmed more, the plaintiff lawyer typically does not do proportionately more work to obtain such a recovery. On that view, the rule might be that, as recovery goes up, the fee owed by the defendant to the claimant's lawyer would decline as a proportion of damages won. For example, the fee might be 50 per cent of the first US $50 000 recovered, 25 per cent of the next US $100 000 and 10 to 15 per cent of the rest. Alternatively, some argue that the fee proportion should be higher (i.e., rather than lower) the more the victim wins. The theory here is that higher awards reflect greater effort or talent shown by the victim's lawyer.

There are other options as well. For example, victim legal fees could be based on an hourly rate tied to how much time the plaintiff's lawyer put into the case (which is how defense lawyers charge) or they could be set as a lump sum tied to the nature of the case (e.g., so much for an auto crash, so much for a slip and fall injury and so on).

A quite different solution would be to base the fee that the defense owes the victim's lawyer on a comparison of the amount of any early offer of settlement by the defense to the amount ultimately won at trial or achieved in settlement. For example, the plaintiff's lawyer might be awarded a fee equal to, say, ten per cent of whatever the defendant offers within, say, 90 days of the harm. But to the extent that the ultimate payout is more than the initial offer, the defense would owe the plaintiff's lawyer an amount equal to, say, 40 or 50 per cent of the difference. Moreover, if the final payout was less than the early offer, this might result in a reduced or even zero legal fee. This sort of formula arguably not only nicely approximates the value added to the case by the lawyer, but also provides strong incentives for the defense to make reasonable early offers and for victim lawyers to recommend to their clients to take such offers, if made. This would be an attractive way to establish claimant legal fees in my view.[30]

6. Punitive Damages

In US tort cases in most states, juries may award punitive damages for truly outrageous conduct. Defense interests in the US have been bitterly complaining about the award of punitive damages for several years, and they have been heard.

Even though such damages are actually awarded infrequently, and their amounts have long been reduced by trial judges, by appellate judges, and in post-verdict settlement agreements, the rare enormous award is terrifying to many company executives. Moreover, these executives and their lawyers complain that even a small risk of a potentially huge punitive award forces them to offer unduly generous settlements. Further, some argue that many punitive damages awards have been imposed for conduct that falls far short of the level of misconduct formally required by the law.

As a result of these complaints, some American states have responded by eliminating this sort of recovery altogether, leaving extra punishment to the criminal and administrative law systems. Other US states have limited recovery in a variety of ways, such as trying to assure that punitive damages are not awarded merely for negligence. This approach has also been taken by some Australian jurisdictions.[31] In some American states, punitive awards (or a portion of them) go, not to the victim, but to the state treasury, or some special fund set up by the state for this purpose. Furthermore, the US Supreme Court has recently weighed in, holding that certain punitive damages awards violate the US Constitution.[32]

The upshot is that those with substantial compensatory awards are now not normally supposed to receive punitive damages that are larger in amount than their compensatory awards, rarely more than four times the amount of their compensatory damages, and almost never more than 10 times as much. However, if the defendant fault is huge and the individual victim's harm rather minor, then higher multiples might be appropriate after all.

At an earlier time I recommended for the US that the determination of whether punitive damages should be awarded and, if so, the amount should be made by judges not juries. Although I still favor that solution, at this point in America perhaps it would be wisest to wait some years to see how the various recent reforms turn out in practice before making further changes. I mention punitive damages here primarily to acknowledge that their availability for victims of the worst sort of wrongdoing is not inconsistent with otherwise moving the law of tort damages towards the social insurance model. This is, after all, the solution reached in New Zealand, which has largely abolished tort law for accidental personal injuries and yet has maintained the right to sue for exemplary damages in egregious cases.[33]

7. Conclusion

To review, suppose tort damages in personal injury cases cover:

- otherwise un-reimbursed medical and related expenses caused by the tort;

- lost income up to no more than, say, three times the state average wage, to the extent that income is not otherwise replaced by core social insurance plans;
- pain and suffering, with amounts payable tied to a schedule that requires well more than a minor injury before any award is allowed and that tops out at, say, US $500 000 (or its cultural equivalent in other nations);
- victim losses, in most cases, regardless of whether the victim too was at fault;
- victim legal fees, based importantly upon how much recovery the plaintiff's lawyer obtains beyond what is promptly offered by the defendant; and
- punitive damages, for now, to the extent currently permitted.

As a result of these changes, damages law for personal injury in tort would much more reflect the values underlying the payment of benefits by non-tort compensation plans. A much greater share of the damages awarded in tort would go to fill genuine need, and more of the total payout would go to the more seriously injured. Were these changes put in place in the US, tort law for personal injuries would play a very different social role from the one it plays today. Put more informally, damages law in San Francisco would move somewhat closer to damages law in Sydney.[34]

Finally, I should emphasize that, along with Harold Luntz, I continue to believe that it would be even more desirable if both of our countries would emulate the law in Auckland.[35] Yet, I recognize that in today's political and economic climate in both the US and Australia, the prospects of adopting a New Zealand-style accident compensation scheme seem even further away than they were 20 years ago. Nevertheless, political currents, like ocean waves, come and go, and it seems to me that a country would be much better positioned to shift to a sweeping no-fault approach to accident compensation if its basic tort damages law were broadly in tune with social insurance thinking generally. Hence, the reforms recommended here, in my view, are desirable, not only in their own right as applied to our existing, largely fault-based tort law, but also as a future stepping stone to something even better.

ENDNOTES

1. For earlier American writing in this vein, see for example, Jeffrey O'Connell, 'A Proposal to Abolish Contributory and Comparative Fault, with Compensatory Savings by also Abolishing the Collateral Source Rule' [1979] University of Illinois LR 591; Jeffrey O'Connell, 'A Proposal to Abolish Defendants Payment for Pain and Suffering in Return for Payment of Claimants' Attorneys' Fees' [1981] University of Illinois LR 333; and Stephen Sugarman, Doing Away With Personal Injury Law (1989) at 174–191. Although the analysis presented here draws primarily on law in the United States, the concepts are relevant to all developed nations. This discussion applies only to personal injuries, however, so other actionable injuries are set-aside for now.

2. Harold Luntz, Assessment of Damages for Personal Injury and Death (4th ed., 2002).

3. See generally, American Law Institute, Enterprise Responsibility for Personal Injury, Vol. 1, The Institutional Framework (1991).

4. See at <http://www.census.gov/hhes/www/hlthins/hlthin03.html>.

5. See generally Harold Luntz, 'The Collateral Source Rule Thirty Years On' in Peter Cane & Jane Stapleton (eds.), The Law of Obligations: Essays in Celebration of John Fleming (1998) 377, and John Fleming, 'The Collateral Source Rule and Loss Allocation in Tort Law' (1966) 54 California LR 1478.

6. See generally Stephen Sugarman, 'United States Tort Reform Wars' (2002) 25 UNSWLJ 849.

7. Auto accident victims do not directly receive compensation from the Quebec auto no-fault plan for their motoring-related health care, since that is already provided by the Canadian national health scheme. But, each year, the auto scheme pays a lump sum to the health scheme, reflecting the approximate cost of health care provided to all auto accident victims. This cost, in turn, is passed on to Quebec motorists in the fees they pay into the auto plan. See generally Stephen Sugarman, 'Quebec's Comprehensive Auto No-Fault Scheme and the Failure of Any of the United States to Follow' (1998) Les Cahiers de Droit Numéro Spécial 109.

8. In countries like Australia, the pressures for and against the reversal of the collateral source rule appear to have resulted in an inconsistent resolution of the issue, both over time and as to different types of accidents. For the very complicated state of Australian law on this issue, see Luntz, above n2 at 423–478. See generally, Luntz above n5.

9. See generally Robert Rabin, 'The Quest for Fairness in Compensating Victims of September 11' (2001) 49 Cleveland State LR 573.

10. See Luntz, above n2 at 211–246, for the Australian position.

11. This is altogether apart from either medical care that might be sought to deal with those sorts of losses, or lost income that might result from these losses.

12. For a classic article, see Louis Jaffe, 'Damages for Personal Injury: The Impact of Insurance' (1953) 18 Law & Contemporary Problems 219.

13. See generally Sugarman, above n6.

14. Sofie v Fibreboard Corp 771 P2d 711 (1989).

15. See The Judicial Studies Board, Guidelines for the Assessment of General Damages in Personal Injury Cases (7th ed., 2004). Canada has also moved in this direction. See generally, Stephen Waddams, 'The Price of Excessive Damage Awards' (this issue).

16. See generally, Prue Vines, 'Faith, Hope and Personal Injury: the Ipp Report and the Civil Liability Acts' (2004) 1 Australian Civil Liability 1. See also Luntz, above n2 at 585–596 for a discussion of statutory limits in a variety of accident contexts. For a discussion of a wide range of recent Australian changes in damages law as applied to the field of medical accidents, see Harold Luntz, 'Damages in Medical Litigation in New South Wales' (2005) 12 JLM 280.

17. See for example, Civil Liability Act 2002 (NSW) §16 ($350 000 to be indexed over time as per §17).

18. Civil Liability Act 2002 (NSW) §16.

19. Civil Liability Act 2002 (NSW) §17A.

20. Civil Liability Act 2002 (NSW) §16.

21. For the Australian situation generally, see Luntz, above n2 at 301–354.

22. As with pain and suffering, completely destroying the future income potential of a younger person, other things being equal, yields a larger award than would be made to one near the end of his career.

23. Indeed, some have speculated that of the perhaps eighty or so claimants whose family members died in the 9/11 attacks and who have sued in tort, rather than accept the 9/11 plan benefits, a large share is comprised of those whose decedents were high earners with large life insurance policies.

24. The plan administrator denied that there was a hard cap on income replacement at the 98 per cent level, and information is not yet forthcoming about precisely how survivors of those in the top two per cent of earners were actually treated with respect lost income beyond the tables. But it is generally understood that, even if families of higher earners might have received something more, the principle of full income replacement was not applied to such stratospheric earning levels.

25. Civil Liability Act 2002 (NSW) s12. See generally, Harold Luntz, 'Damages for Personal Injury: Rhetoric, Reality and Reform from an Australian Perspective' (1985) 38 Current Legal Problems 29 and Harold Luntz, 'Keeping Professors in the Comfort to Which They Have Grown Accustomed' (1995) 3 Torts Law Journal 1.

26. For the Australian situation, see Luntz, above n2 at 133–148. See generally American Law Institute, Restatement of Torts (Third): Apportionment of Liability (2000).

27. To be sure, certain especially blameworthy worker misconduct can preclude any recovery from workers' compensation, and so too, extreme wrongdoing by victims might also appropriately serve as a continued bar under the general rule proposed here. Indeed, in comparative fault jurisdictions today, in instances of especially wrongful behavior, victims may be fully denied tort recovery just as they were under the common law rule.

28. 12 Uniform Laws Annotated 33 (1981 Supp).

29. In the Restatement of Torts (Third): Apportionment of Liability, ss28–31, the American Law Institute has recognized a large number of alternative solutions to this issue, but not the one I propose here. A related issue is what to do with the risk of under-settlement. Suppose the plaintiff has reached an agreement with one defendant, but that turns out to be for less money than what the judge or jury later determines to be that defendant's fair share of the liability. In such a setting, where the settlement was truly based on an estimate of the defendant's liability, and not, for example, on what was in fact the defendant's limited solvency, I would not oppose leaving the risk of under-settlement with the plaintiff, as the Uniform Comparative Fault Act (1979) generally recommends.

30. In Australia today, somewhat analogous rules now govern the award of legal fees to successful plaintiffs.

31. For example, Civil Liability Act 2002 (NSW) §21. For the Australian situation generally, see Luntz, above n2 at 71–90.

32. State Farm Mutual Automobile Insurance Co v Campbell 123 SC 1513 (2003).

33. For further support of this position, see generally, Harold Luntz, 'A Personal Journey Through the Law of Torts' (this issue) at notes 95–100.

34. To comply with these criteria, the law in New South Wales would also have to be somewhat altered. Although tort damages law in Sydney already contains several of the elements I favor, it would especially need revising as to both the collateral source rule and the consequences of victim fault. Indeed, as for the latter, unlike many other areas of tort damages reform discussed here, New South Wales currently seems to be moving in the opposite direction by becoming harsher to at-fault victims. See for example, Civil Liability Act 2002 (NSW) §5S.

35. See, for example, Harold Luntz, 'Proposals for a National Compensation Scheme' (1981) 55 Law Institute Journal 745 and Harold Luntz, 'The Case for No-Fault Accident Compensation' (1985) 15 Queensland Law Society Journal 167.

Chapter 9

American Tort Law – Better to Import than to Export?

As explored in Chapter 1, one might expect that people (or nations) with different political ideologies would favor different ways of dealing with the accident problem – that is, deterring unsafe acts and compensating victims in a just and administratively sensible manner. In practice, the U.S. and most other wealthy nations have embraced some combination of schemes to which accident victims of different sorts might turn. In the U.S. this means tort law for some injuries, social security and health insurance for others, and special compensation schemes like workers' compensation plans for still others. Moreover, some victims are able to obtain recovery from two or even three different sources.

This chapter provides a comparative law perspective on these three types of compensation arrangements – tort law, social insurance, and tailored compensation plans. Consideration is given to ways in which these schemes differ from each other and the key design issues that policy makers must resolve in setting their parameters, why different countries might favor one approach over the other or opt for different combinations of the three, and what nations might learn from each other in determining the role to be played by tailored compensation plans, in the way that monetary awards are determined under these various schemes, and in the way that lawyers are compensated for their roles, if any, in dealing with claims made under the full range of compensation arrangements.

Overall, the chapter argues that the U.S. might gain more wisdom about these compensation and safety promoting mechanisms by looking abroad than other nations are likely to gain from studying the U.S., and recommendations are made for American changes that draw on experience elsewhere. The chapter was presented at a conference held at Pepperdine Law School honoring Canada's Allen M. Linden, that nation's leading torts scholar and a justice on the Canadian Federal Court of Appeal, and later published as Stephen D. Sugarman, "Compensation for Personal Injury: What Nations Might Learn from Each Other,"

38 Pepperdine Law Review (2) 597-621 (2011). It is reprinted with permission of the journal.

Compensation for Accidental Personal Injury: What Nations Might Learn From Each Other

I. THREE TYPES OF COMPENSATION SCHEMES FOR ACCIDENTAL INJURY VICTIMS

I start by emphasizing three roles that government can play in providing compensation to people who suffer bodily injury by accident.

1. Government can provide accident victims with legal rights to sue those who have injured them (and make forums available where victims can enforce those rights). Tort law epitomizes this role.

2. Government can create general social insurance arrangements that provide compensation for lost income and pay for the medical (and perhaps related) expenses that accident victims incur. In the United States, Medicare pays for health care for the elderly and the totally disabled, Medicaid (and related plans) pays for the health care needs of the poor, and tax subsidies support our vast network of employer-provided health insurance. In Canada and most other rich nations, a comprehensive national health care system deals with this need. With regard to income replacement, in the United States as elsewhere, Social Security provides compensation to totally disabled former workers and their families.[1] Some other countries provide income support as well to workers who become partially disabled.

Although these schemes are available to accident victims, they do not focus on any particular type of accident, and indeed, they are not at all limited to accident victims.[2] Those suffering from diseases and congenital problems are also covered. Moreover, unlike compensation provided by tort law that is paid for by injurers (albeit often spread to others engaged in similar activities via liability insurance), social insurance is paid for by broad funding bases, like payroll taxes and income taxes, that are not connected to the cause of the accident that generates a claim for benefits.

3. In between these two extremes is a continuum of what has been called

tailored or focused compensation plans. Each of these provides compensation to victims of a specific type of injury, compensation that is made available other than through court-based litigation. [3] Moreover, in contrast to the anchoring norm of tort law, these tailored compensation plans do not seek to blame those who cause the covered injuries.[4] Yet, in many (but not all) instances, those whose conduct contributes to the need for compensation are asked to take responsibility for funding the relevant compensation plan.[5]

America's workers' compensation system is a good example of such a plan, providing medical and income replacement benefits (as well as vocational rehabilitation benefits) to those injured by accidents and diseases arising out of their employment.[6] Claims are made against employers (but not through lawsuits) who generally arrange in advance for the payment of valid claims via the purchase of workers' compensation insurance.[7] Another U.S. example is the National Vaccine Injury Compensation Program.[8] Children who receive vaccinations and then suffer harms that are caused by, or legally presumed to be caused by, the vaccine are entitled to receive money benefits from a fund that is financed by a charge imposed on all vaccinations.[9] In Canada, Quebec's pioneering automobile no-fault insurance scheme is yet another good example. [10] All drivers/car-owners are required to purchase insurance from a special governmental agency that in turns pays compensation to all of those injured in motor vehicle accidents. [11] New Zealand has for nearly four decades run a unique plan that provides compensation to all accident victims of whatever sort-work injuries, automobile injuries, home injuries, recreational injuries, and so on.[12]

II. THREE *KEY* ISSUES IN THE DESIGN OF THESE SCHEMES

I turn next to three key parameters on which designers of these various compensation arrangements must focus. The first concerns the nature of the benefits each scheme will provide. The second concerns the way in which the different compensation schemes interrelate to each other. The third concerns whether claimants will be represented by lawyers and, if so, how the lawyers are to be compensated.

1. With respect to benefit parameters, although I will not cover all of the issues

that arise in the design of a plan's benefits, the discussion will raise many of the key points. Turning first to income replacement (or compensation for lost earning capacity), it must first be decided whether the benefit will be standardized or whether it will vary based on the past earnings history and what is thought would have otherwise been the future earnings of the individual victim. If the latter, are victims' lost earnings to be fully replaced or partially so? If they are to be partially replaced, which, if any, of the following sorts of limits should apply: (1) the victim bears the first period (e.g., a week) of lost income; (2) the victim's earnings are replaced, not fully but at a reduced rate (e.g., 70%); or (3) a maximum limit is placed on the amount of earning covered (e.g., twice the average weekly wage in the jurisdiction)?

With respect to medical benefits, how broadly are they defined (e.g., including renovations to the homes of victims who are wheelchair bound and/or including the cost of attendant care for the seriously disabled), what controls are put on the decision as to whether claimed treatments are needed (e.g., physical therapy sessions), what limits are placed on the specific health care providers that victims may utilize, and so on?

Beyond these benefits, which are often termed "pecuniary," are benefits also to be provided with respect to "non-pecuniary" losses, and if so, how much and how are they determined? For example, should money be paid to compensate for the pain and suffering endured by the victim? What about the victim's lost ability to enjoy life in ways he or she previously did? What if the victim's body has been seriously disfigured or impaired? And what about the psychological upset of being harmed, especially if the injurer carelessly caused it to happen? As with lost income, if there is to be compensation provided for these harms, is it to be highly individualized or (relatively) uniform, and are there to be limits on recovery (like thresholds and ceilings)? [13]

Finally, if the victim suffers a long-term injury, should the benefits provided be paid once in a single lump sum, or should they be paid out over time? If the former, then it is likely that speculative projections into the future will be required. [14] If the latter, will adjustments in the benefits being paid be made over time as events unfold, or is the periodic payment of benefits mainly intended to protect the victim paternalistically from squandering a lump sum award?[15]

The discussion so far has assumed that the accident victim is the claimant, but what about situations in which the accident causes the death of the victim? If death is not instantaneous, are benefits provided to cover the period between the accident and the death, and if so, which benefits (e.g., non-pecuniary benefits)? [16] Once the direct victim is dead, are benefits provided to survivors? If so, which survivors receive those benefits and how much do they receive (e.g., lump sums, sums relating to the deceased's lost earnings, sums for grief, etc.)? [17]

2. Turning now to the way that the compensation schemes interrelate, the essential point is to appreciate that there are many possible answers. At one extreme, all of the schemes could ignore each other, and victims would be able to obtain and keep all the benefits to which they are entitled, even if this meant triple recovery. At the other, victims would never gain more than "full" recovery, although this principle alone says nothing about which scheme (or schemes) winds up bearing the loss. Nor does it say whether victims could temporarily obtain benefits from one scheme while awaiting them from another with the obligation to return funds to the prior out of those obtained from the latter. In between, a variety of solutions could permit victims to receive different sorts of double, but not triple, recovery. [18]

So far as tort law is concerned, this issue typically is addressed under the heading "collateral sources."[19] The common law rule is that collateral sources are ignored in a tort claim, thereby making tort law always "primary" in the sense that tort defendants always bear the loss.[20] The collateral source rule does not address whether victims can double-recover, however.[21] By statute, moreover, in some jurisdictions, the collateral source rule can be (and has been) revised in two major ways. [22] First, tort recovery may be deemed "secondary" and, hence, only available to the extent that collateral sources (or at least some of them) do not already cover the victim's losses.[23] Second, tort recovery simply may be repealed with respect to certain accidents and replaced with recovery via one or more collateral sources. To the extent that tort law is primary, the other schemes have to decide whether they will provide double recovery and, if not, whether they will at least advance benefits pending tort recovery.

As between general social insurance and tailored compensation plans, similar issues must be resolved, and if there is to be no double recovery, then it must be decided (a) which source is primary and (b) whether the primary source is to be a complete substitute or whether the secondary source remains available to compensate losses not covered by the primary source. [24]

Note further that there is more than one way to make, for instance, a tailored compensation plan that is primary to general social insurance. For example, with respect to an automobile no-fault plan, the plan might cover the victim's medical care, but if that care had already been provided by the country's national health scheme, then either the victim would be required to reimburse the health plan out of his automobile no-fault recovery or the automobile no-fault plan itself would directly repay the health plan.[25] But these are not the only options. For example, the health plan might provide the care, and the automobile plan could provide no health benefits to individual victims, but the automobile plan could make regular lump-sum contributions to the health plan that are designed to cover the cost (or estimated cost) of health care provided to large numbers of automobile accident victims. Indeed, in what amounts to much of the same thing, motoring could be taxed (e.g., via gasoline taxes) with proceeds used to an appropriate degree to fund the health plan.[26]

Finally, note that the determination of which plan will pay (when it is assumed that only one will) need not be determined by law but instead by the choice of the victim. For example, a victim might be entitled to choose between claiming compensation plan benefits and suing in tort, but he may not pursue both.

3. Turning now to the role and compensation of lawyers, the pattern is mixed, not only from country to country but also among the three types of compensation schemes. In general, lawyers play substantial roles in helping victims pursue tort claims, and they play only a small or rare role in helping victims pursue general social insurance benefits. Claims against tailored compensation plans fall in between, and indeed the participation rate of lawyers varies among the plans, although it is probably fair to say that the more serious the injury, the more likely a lawyer will be brought in to represent the claimant. There are many ways to compensate lawyers for both sides, which is a matter discussed further below.

IV.THREE REASONS WHY NATIONS' COMPENSATION SCHEMES MIGHT DIFFER

Although most rich nations have all three of the compensation schemes described above, each has its own special package of plans. Moreover, in their details, the schemes vary from place to place in terms of benefit parameters, the interrelationship of the schemes, and the role and compensation of lawyers. In this part, I will briefly offer three sorts of considerations that might help explain these differences.

1. Societies may view the purposes of their compensation schemes differently—especially tort law. Some may see tort law's central role as deterring socially objectionable (unreasonably dangerous) conduct; others may see it as helping to put victims back in the position they were before the accident (focusing on a victim's need); still others may see it as doing justice between injurer and victim. Of course, societies may value all of these objectives, though in differing proportions. With respect to both tort law and tailored compensation schemes, nations may differ in the importance they give (if any) to internalizing the costs of accidents into the causes of those accidents.

These different social outlooks might reflect underlying differences in culture and in political ideology. Does the society think of itself as highly individualistic or more as a community? Does it believe strongly in personal responsibility, or do its members more strongly believe that "accidents happen" and that society holds a collective responsibility for repairing the consequences of those accidents?

2. Nations have their own histories and experience their own special pattern of accidents, and perhaps because of path-dependence they find that their packages of compensation schemes differ as a result. [27] For example, countries experienced industrialization at different times and in different ways, thereby making workplace injuries a larger social problem in some societies than in others. Automobile travel too developed differently from place to place, and likewise, automobile accidents are not equally problematic in all places. Societies experience different types and frequencies of catastrophes (whether caused by nature or man), and they face different future catastrophic risks. These differences can yield different victim-compensation paths. Further,

because nations have differing governing arrangements, both adding new compensation arrangements and eliminating or limiting existing ones can be much more difficult in some places than others.

3. Lawyers are a much more powerful social force in some jurisdictions than in others. Their own interests, when combined with the political and social power they can exercise, may yield differing sorts of compensation schemes. I think it is generally recognized that practicing lawyers play especially prominent political roles in the United States as compared with elsewhere.

V. THREE AREAS IN WHICH NATIONS CAN LEARN (OR HAVE LEARNED) FROM EACH OTHER REGARDING TORT DAMAGES LAW[28]

I will not here systematically examine all the features of compensation plans to which I referred in Part II, but rather I will look at some selected matters on which U.S. law is (or has been) quite different, in search for insights that might help improve the law in one place or another. Given the points I have made in Part III, I acknowledge that what I call an improvement may well be just my opinion arising from personal values. I also recognize that achieving change is not always easy, especially when one opens the argument by pointing to how things are done in foreign places. Still, my hope is that this comparative exploration can at least help prompt informed conversations -- including among those who never realized that there are other ways in which things are done.

1. Consider tort compensation for non-pecuniary loss ("pain and suffering"). The United States is very different from other nations on this dimension.[29] We make juries available to the parties to decide civil disputes, and they are routinely used in tort cases, whereas most other legal systems have either never used juries for such cases or have fully or largely abandoned them.[30] What this means in the U.S. context is that (1) jurors have little or no past personal experience to go on in awarding to accident victims damages for non-pecuniary loss, and (2) juries are not given any instructions by judges as to past awards in similar cases.[31] As a result, in the United States, each successful claimant may be said to receive a personally tailored damages award determined by his or her peers.[32] On the other hand, it is widely believed, with respect to non-pecuniary loss, that

similar claims are treated much more variably in the United States than elsewhere.[33]

Moreover, for reasons that may or may not stem centrally from the use of juries, U.S. awards for non-pecuniary loss, on average, are far greater than in other nations (putting aside for the moment cases brought in U.S. states that have imposed a statutory cap on such awards). [34]

While it may seem like other countries might look to the United States and find our approach to this issue attractive, largely the opposite has actually occurred. Most nations have sought both to keep their non- pecuniary loss awards smaller than ours and to make their awards more consistent from case to case.[35]

This is not to say that all other nations make similar awards for non-pecuniary loss or that the U.S. record of very high awards has gone unnoticed and is decidedly without impact. For example, in recent years in both England and Italy there has been a substantial upward adjustment in the amount paid for non-pecuniary loss—change that, while not obviously embraced because of U.S. practice, moves those legal systems in the direction of American patterns.[36] Still, payments in these countries and the other more generous European (e.g., Ireland) and common law nations (e.g., Canada and Australia) still remain well below U.S. levels.[37]

It is also important to appreciate that non-pecuniary loss awards for various serious harms vary widely among other European nations -- with poorer countries, like Greece and Portugal, and countries with stronger social welfare systems, like Sweden and Denmark, providing perhaps only ten percent as much as is provided in higher paying European jurisdictions.[38]

What is more common among other rich nations, however, is the existence of a strategy designed to create case-to-case consistency, however generous or un-generous the nation's legal system is overall. In England and Germany, for example, careful records are kept as to how much money is awarded for certain types of harms, such as broken legs, lost eyes, paraplegia, lost arms, and so on.[39] These past award levels are then carefully followed by judges deciding new cases (with minor adjustments made where thought appropriate in individual cases).[40] In Italy and New South Wales, Australia, for example, a slightly different approach is used, yielding essentially the same result.[41] There, injuries are assigned a percentage based on severity. [42] In a case before the court, then, once the victim's disability percentage is determined, the presumptive award for non- pecuniary loss may be found on a table. [43]

Together these approaches create what might be termed "scheduled" awards, a solution that has been recommended by several scholars to U.S. courts, and which I also favor.[44] Notice that this strategy need not require the elimination of American juries.[45] Rather, juries could be given this sort of data and told that they should either approximately replicate what appears to be the past pattern of awards for this victim's type of harm, or if they wish to make a different award (higher or lower), they must give specific reasons justifying a deviation. [46] Based on the reasons given, trial judges could then decide whether to affirm such deviations or to reject them (in which case the losing party would perhaps have to either agree to a more typical award or go through a new trial).

Beyond seeking consistency from case to case, the Canadian Supreme Court, for example, explicitly acted to rein in awards of non-pecuniary damages in a way that might also be appropriate for U.S. jurisdictions to follow.[47] The court initially set a maximum on the award that may be given to the most seriously harmed victim at $100,000[48] with the understanding that this ceiling would grow over time with inflation.[49] At present, the maximum is about $300,000, which is similar to maxima recently set by legislation in Australian states.[50] What should be emphasized here is that this sort of maximum not only limits what may be awarded to the most seriously harmed, but also the courts and statutes have made clear that other injuries are to be scaled down from that maximum. So, for example, if a victim in New South Wales with a 100% disability rating were to receive $350,000 in non-pecuniary damages, then a victim with a 50% disability rating would receive only half as much.

This approach is to be contrasted with the way that U.S. jurisdictions impose monetary caps on awards for pain and suffering. The U.S. approach allows juries to make awards as usual, and then, if their award is above the cap, the judge cuts it off at the cap.[51] This means that harms of a wide range of seriousness might wind up being compensated at the cap, and nothing is done in U.S.

jurisdictions to scale down the award for less serious harms. [52]

Moreover, U.S. caps are generally not adjusted for inflation which seems, frankly, rather odd. [53] Hence, even if individual states wanted to be more generous than other nations, they might consider embracing the Canadian/Australian approach[54] by setting, say, $500,000 (adjusted for inflation) as the amount to be paid to the most gravely injured, with the understanding that those with lesser harms are to receive awards that are appropriately scaled down from that ceiling.

Other countries have also adopted strategies that U.S. jurisdictions might find attractive in dealing with non-pecuniary loss awards for minor injury cases. One approach, adopted not too long ago in New South Wales, is to impose a threshold on all personal injury tort claims.[55] There, unless the injury results in at least a 15% disability, no award is made for what we in the United States would call pain and suffering.[56] The idea is that these sorts of harms are either fairly modest or whatever pain and suffering the victim endured is gone by the time the case is resolved.

One attraction of this solution for U.S. jurisdictions is that it takes away the leverage that plaintiffs' lawyers now have in settling small cases. Both sides know that defendants are eager to get these cases off their books at a small cost, and because of that they wind up willing to settle for what many would think are extravagant pain and suffering sums, given the small scale of the injury, just because the defense side would incur even higher legal and other costs in actually defending such claims in court. If one agrees that U.S. victims now get windfalls in such cases, this threshold strategy is one way to address the problem.

Indeed, notice that this is roughly the way that Michigan and New York deal with small injury automobile injury claims under their automobile no- fault plans.[57] Both of these states provide substantial, but not at all comprehensive, no-fault benefits to cover income loss and medical and related expenses.[58] Seriously harmed victims may sue in tort as well both for pain and suffering and for pecuniary loss not compensated by the plans.[59]

But those who do not have serious injuries are precluded from seeking recovery for pain and suffering damages via tort law. [60] Neither Michigan nor New York uses the 15% disabled threshold used in New South Wales. Instead, they use language, regulations, and past practice to determine whether the threshold is met or not.[61] Nevertheless, evidence shows that the pain and suffering thresholds in those two states—when combined with no-fault benefits for pecuniary losses—take a very substantial share of automobile cases out of the tort system.[62]

Some Canadian provinces have adopted yet a different approach to minor injuries. They still allow pain and suffering awards in such cases, but they have put a fairly low statutory dollar cap ($4000 or less) on such claims.[63] This approach allows for at least some recovery for those who may have suffered intense, but transient pain, as well as those with lingering low-level suffering. But it makes clear to both sides in their settlement negotiations what a modest ceiling on such damages would face the victims if they went to court. My personal preference is for the New South Wales approach because it helps concentrate money paid out by the tort system on the more seriously injured, but I view the Canadian strategy as a creative compromise.

One other solution worth mentioning is the German practice of giving some victims (e.g., those injured by certain public utilities) the choice of suing in tort under a regime of strict liability (i.e., not having to prove defendant's fault) if they are willing, in exchange, to give up their claim for pain and suffering damages.[64]

In sum, there is a great deal that American jurisdictions might learn from the treatment elsewhere of damages for non-pecuniary loss.[65] Yet, I concede that this discussion of non-pecuniary loss recovery is incomplete without giving attention to the compensation of lawyers, a matter to which I will tum at the end.

2. More U.S. jurisdictions might consider changing the common law collateral source rule. Most states still follow the principle that tort recovery is always primary, although, during the past three decades of "tort reform," through efforts pressed on legislatures by defense interests, several American states

have already reversed the collateral source rule with respect to some other sorts of compensation.[66]

Perhaps most significantly, many legal systems do not allow tort recovery for medical expenses because the victim pays nothing for those services and instead merely receives medical treatment from the nation's health care system. As the United States has just now moved further in that direction, it seems a good time to consider whether more states should reverse the collateral source rule with respect to government -- or employer -- provided health insurance, as well as with respect to Social Security benefits, workers' compensation benefits, and other routine employer-based wage-continuation benefits like sick leave.

A big advantage of such a change, in my view, is to reduce the complexity of the common law system in which these other sources of compensation must either seek reimbursement from individual victims or allow double recovery.

Making tort recovery secondary to other basic social welfare compensation schemes is generally not popular with those who see tort's main function as promoting safety by threatening to impose accident costs on careless injurers and by actually internalizing those accident costs into the injurers' product or service when harm results because the defendant has failed to take the proper precautions. But notice that this goal might be substantially served in other ways. For example, along with altering the collateral source rule, the state could surcharge liability insurance policies (or equivalent corporate self-insurance arrangements) and direct the proceeds to health insurers and other relevant social insurance plans.

3. In light of our growing income inequality and the popular resentment of the stratospheric earnings of Wall Street plutocrats, it might also be time for American jurisdictions to reconsider the current practice of having tort law fully replace lost income (or lost earning capacity). Defenders of the current regime will argue that individual justice demands full compensation of victims, and perhaps that this is necessary to achieve tort law's deterrence goals.[67] Yet, from other viewpoints, the common law rule seems unfair and unnecessary.[68]

Generally speaking, we all pay the same price for a product that might injure people with a wide range of income levels. The same goes for those injured on the premises of others, those injured in transportation accidents, from medical injuries, and so on. Yet, the full recovery principle means that a rich victim gets more out of the tort system for the same injury than does a poor victim.[69] This seems undesirably regressive. Moreover, those with high incomes typically do not, and should not, need full recovery from tort law to make them whole with respect to their lost earnings. That is because higher earners tend to have, and if prudent should have, private disability insurance that already protects their income from a variety of risks including accidents that might lead to tort claims.

One way to alter tort law to deal with this issue is to restrict damages for income replacement in some way. Indeed, this has happened recently in Australia. In a change that I find quite attractive, New South Wales tort law now replaces lost earnings up to a maximum of three times the annual average earnings of full-time adult workers.[70] This would not be as revolutionary a change for the United States as it might appear at first blush once one considers that all of our workers' compensation plans, as well as our Social Security system, already place a limit on the amount of past wages that are considered in making benefit awards.[71]

An additional (and I believe sensible) reform would be to impose a modest deductible on income replacement by, say, having the first week of lost earnings fall to the victim. This is an amount that can be absorbed by most workers, especially those with paid sick leave (an employee benefit that the United States should make mandatory, but alas so far has not).[72]

This sort of provision would also mimic a common feature of workers' compensation laws and the laws of the five U.S. states that provide short- term income replacement for non-occupational disabilities.[73] When combined with the earlier-discussed changes in compensation for non-pecuniary losses and the collateral source rule, this would rid tort law of a huge number of small claims-leaving the tort system to focus on, and better focus its benefits on, the more seriously injured, which is a shift that I favor.

VI. THREE AREAS IN WHICH NATIONS CAN LEARN (OR HAVE LEARNED) FROM EACH OTHER REGARDING SOCIAL INSURANCE AND TAILORED COMPENSATION PLANS

Trying to get government to do more for victims is an uphill battle in a time of high unemployment and resistance to larger deficits. Moreover, in the United States especially, given the power of the plaintiffs' bar, it is never easy to make political headway with changes that would threaten lawyers' business, even if victims and consumers would, overall, be better off. Still, there are some win-win possibilities out there.

1. It is important to appreciate that nations differ in the ways they have made important tailored compensation plans either full, or only partial substitutes for tort law.[74] For example, in the United States, workers' compensation plans are, broadly speaking, complete substitutes for tort law. To be sure, in the rare instances in which employers intentionally harm victims, a tort remedy is likely to be available, and one who suffers a work injury may also sue a third party tortfeasor, such as the maker of a defective product that injured the plaintiff on the job. But, in the overwhelming share of work injuries, the victim's claim is exclusively against the employer and only under the workers' compensation scheme and not in tort.[75]

The American solution may seem obvious or natural here, but in most other places with workers' compensation plans, victims may sue in tort as well.[76] Normally they may only sue for losses not already covered by the workers' compensation scheme, but still, in serious injury cases, those losses-both with respect to income and pain and suffering—should be very substantial. In my view, a better solution is to liberalize workers' compensation benefits and keep the American complete substitute solution.

By contrast to U.S. workers' compensation rules, as already noted, America's two most generous automobile no-fault states (Michigan and New York) have put in place plans that are only partial substitutes for tort law.[77]

Yet, in places like Quebec and Israel, automobile no-fault plans, like our workers' compensation plans, are complete substitutes for tort claims.[78] It is also important to understand that in both Quebec and Israel, seriously injured automobile victims obtain some recovery from the no-fault scheme for pain and suffering.[79] This too is shatply at odds with American workers' compensation schemes, which do not provide such benefits.[80]

Overall, I believe that American victims and consumers would substantially benefit if (1) we adopted a Quebec/Israeli type, automobile no- fault scheme that fully replaces tort law,[81] and (2) we added moderate levels of pain and suffering benefits for seriously injured workers to our existing exclusive-remedy workers' compensation plans. This package, I believe, would be cheaper for consumers and would provide improved benefits for a large share of the seriously injured.

2. Many nations might be well served by adopting more tailored compensation schemes than they have at present. Northern Ireland and Israel, for example, have plans that cover terrorism victims that might be explored elsewhere.[82] Sweden has a plan for medical injuries that is worth studying. Many creative compensation plans for other recurrent or potentially catastrophic accidents have been proposed over the years in the United States (e.g., for side effects of pharmaceutical drugs) and are worth reconsidering.

All countries might profit from reconsidering their compensation approach to airplane accident victims—especially those killed in commercial air crashes.[83] Rather than having heirs sue the airlines in tort, where they are required to prove negligence on the part of the defendant's employees (and then recover losses based on the victim's past earnings), perhaps it would be more fair and administratively much more efficient to provide a uniform life insurance policy (of, say, $500,000) as part of the ticket price for all passengers, the proceeds of which would be paid out to the passenger's heirs in exchange for precluding a wrongful death tort claim.[84] This approach, which I find attractive, would treat with equal dignity the death of each passenger. [85]

This solution would allow those with substantial earning power the option to buy what they believe to be an appropriate amount of personal life insurance as a supplement to the policy provided by the airlines-policies that most people would (wisely) buy that would cover death in general and would not be restricted to airplane-crash death.[86] In fact, financially better- off passengers with dependent family members already typically have general life insurance policies (or other mechanisms providing financial security to their families) with the result that the benefit paid by those policies now duplicates recovery that is currently available to survivors who succeed in a tort claim. Also, in the same vein as suggested earlier of those who are keen to have carefully calibrated financial incentives intended to stimulate airline safety, fines might be imposed on a carrier when government inspectors (who examine all commercial crashes anyway) determine that a plane crashed due to carrier negligence.[87] The proceeds of such penalties could, for example, be put toward the construction of newer and safer airports or to support the national air control system.

In the spirit of treating all victims the same, it is worth noting how the U.S. 9/11 Victim Compensation Fund treated the families of those killed by the terrorists who crashed the four airplanes in the September 11, 2001 attacks.[88] The scheme's special administrator, Kenneth Feinberg, first decided that the fund would award $250,000 in non-pecuniary benefits for each life lost,[89] wisely and fairly refusing to treat families differently based on claims about how much the deceased suffered in the final moments before death.[90] To that flat sum, he also added flat sums if the deceased left a surviving spouse and/or children.[91]

Feinberg was additionally required by statute to pay benefits that reflected the lost earning power of the deceased to survivors.[92] This, all other things being equal, meant paying much larger sums to the families of high-wage earners as compared with low-wage earners-which, of course, is the tort law tradition, as well as the way Social Security works and the way workers' compensation generally works. [93] But after the program was wound up, Feinberg wrote that he felt it would have been fairer, as a special one-time benefit that acknowledged that these nearly 3000 people had altogether involuntarily lost their lives to terrorism, if the entire award to each surviving family would have been the same amount.[94] Some, both in the United States and abroad, might find this to be an attractive way to deal with death caused in a wide range of ways.

3. Nations might learn from each other about how tailored compensation plans are meshed with other forms of recovery. For example, if a society has a true

national health insurance scheme, what is the point of having medical care connected to work-related injuries be separately covered by workers' compensation plans as it is today in the United States? So, as America moves toward finally catching up with the rest of the world in having a comprehensive health care scheme,[95] I believe that our states should consider stripping those benefits from workers' compensation. Those benefits made much more sense a century ago when there was no other source of health insurance for workers. For those who are eager to have these work-related costs internalized into the cost of the relevant employer's goods or services, note that this already happens if the employer provides health insurance to its employees. Indeed, at present, the vast share of workers has duplicate sources to cover health care benefits for work- related injuries. As a result, workers and the two relevant insurers have to go through administrative busywork to sort out regarding which earner should ultimately bear the cost.

The 9/11 Compensation Plan ("9/11 Plan") contained one highly controversial feature for a tailored compensation plan: the benefits otherwise payable to survivors of those killed on 9/11 were fully reduced by the amount of life insurance the victim had.[96] This is a very rare feature, as normally workers' compensation, automobile no-fault plans, and other tailored compensation schemes ignore life insurance, which is treated as intended-to serve as a voluntary supplement to other benefits.[97] Indeed, even the jurisdictions that have reversed somewhat the collateral source rule for torts cases have not included life insurance proceeds as money to be deducted from the otherwise appropriate tort damages award.

Nonetheless, this feature of the 9/11 Plan had the twin virtues of making the plan benefits more carefully tailored to the actual need of the survivors and helping to keep the plan benefits from being even more heavily concentrated on the families of high earners. On the other side, however, survivors understandably howled when they received less from the plan than did otherwise identically situated families whose now deceased breadwinner voluntarily and irresponsibly chose not to purchase life insurance for his or her family but instead, for example, spent those would-be premium dollars on an expensive automobile.[98] Moreover, it is rumored that a large share of the relatively few families (perhaps 100 of 3000) that refused to seek funds from the 9/11 Plan and instead sued the airlines (and others) in tort did so because their now-dead loved ones had large life insurance policies, and as a result their 9/11 Plan benefits would have been very small. This experience suggests that Congress may have gotten the social balance wrong in the way it meshed 9/11 Plan benefits with other compensation sources.

Lastly, in meshing compensation plans and tort, several U.S. plans, both existing and proposed, include creative and somewhat varying options. Under the National Vaccine Injury Compensation Program ("Vaccine Plan"), for example, those who say that they or their children have been injured as a side effect of having been vaccinated must first file a claim for benefits under the program. [99] The plan administrators then determine whether the claimant is eligible [100] and, if so, how much money is appropriate to distribute. At that point the claimant has a choice—either accept the plan's offer or reject it forever and, if he or she wishes, then sue in tort. In this way the two compensation arrangements are exclusive from one another, but it is up to claimants to choose a scheme.

The 9/11Compensation Plan had a somewhat similar feature. If one filed a claim against the Fund, one could not sue in tort. [101] Unlike the Vaccine Plan, survivors were not required to first file with the fund to see what it would offer. To the contrary, if they did that, they were bound by what the fund decided to provide to them and forfeited their right to opt out and to sue the fund. [102] To help potential claimants figure out for themselves which route to take, the 9/11 Plan's administrator published extensive documentation setting out how benefits would be determined so that potential claimants and their advisors could be reasonably sure of what their benefit under the plan would be were they to file. [103]

Professor Jeffrey O'Connell has proposed a wide range of cleverly constructed choice schemes. To give but one example here, O'Connell designed a scheme in which motorists would, in advance of any accident, decide whether they wanted to be in the tort system or the no-fault system by buying one or the other type of insurance. [104] If two no-fault electing drivers crashed into each other, each of them could claim only no-fault benefits and only from his or her own insurer. [105] If two tort-electing drivers crashed into each other, they could claim from each other in tort, provided, of course, they could prove the other was at fault. [106] In one-car crashes, the no-fault electing driver could claim no-fault benefits from his or her insurer, and the tort-electing driver presumably would get no automobile insurance-related recovery, as he or she would have no one to sue in tort (putting aside situations in which the crash came about through a defective car or unreasonably maintained roads, etc.). [107] If a no-fault plan driver and a tort-system driver were involved in a crash, O'Connell proposed that the no-fault driver would claim from his or her no-fault plan. [108] The tort system driver could not sue the no-fault plan driver because the latter was immune from tort claims by having elected the no-fault regime. [109] But the tort system victim could claim from the "uninsured motorist" portion of his own automobile insurance-provided he could prove that the no-fault system driver had been at fault in causing the accident. [110] While it might at first seem unfair that the tort system driver had to pay for "uninsured motorist" insurance in this setting, notice how, as an offset, the tort system driver's liability insurance premium would be reduced under O'Connell's scheme as other drivers opted for no-fault and thereby gave up their right to sue tort system drivers. [111]

In fact, O'Connell believed that this ingenious scheme would function only in rare cases because he was confident that in short order most drivers would opt for the no-fault alternative, finding it not only substantially cheaper but also to provide no- (or lower-) hassle benefits regardless of who was at fault. [112] But so far, we have had no opportunity to test this prediction, as no state has embraced his proposal. Indeed, when Arizona voters were presented with the opportunity to put it into play, they rejected the idea. [113] For now, it is important at least to note that, in contrast with the choice features of the 9/11 Plan and the Vaccine Plan, O'Connell's automobile no-fault choice plan calls for people to make a choice before any injuries take place.

VII. THREE WAYS IN WHICH LAWYER COMPENSATION MIGHT BE ARRANGED

1. Defense lawyers under the American tort system are paid by defendants or by defendant insurance companies as part of the insurance contract [114] (a routine feature of motor vehicle liability insurance policies, for example). These lawyers

are normally paid on an hourly basis.[115] Claimant lawyers under the American system are almost always paid on a so-called contingent fee basis.[116] This arrangement has two important features. First, it means that the lawyers are only paid if they win, so that to some degree, winning claimants help fund the work done for losing claimants. The other feature is that when they win, the lawyers are paid a percentage of the award. This need not be the only form of payment. They could simply receive, for example, an extravagant hourly rate if they win. Nonetheless, the percentage-fee system is solidly in place, and a typical fee in torts cases is 33%, at least if the case settles. Sometimes, however, claimants can negotiate a lower percentage, and sometimes the agreed percentage can go up to, for example, 50% if the lawyer has to try the case and further defend a verdict on appeal.[117]

California has restricted attorneys' fees in medical malpractice cases by statute, allowing lawyers to charge no more than 40% of awards up to $50,000; 33.33% of the next $50,000 of recovery; 25% of the next $500,000; and 15% on all recovery beyond that.[118] This schedule appears to be based on the theory that relatively little extra work is required to obtain higher sums for victims. Because most medical malpractice cases that are brought involve substantial injuries, the upshot of the schedule is to reduce considerably the fees that successful lawyers would otherwise earn.[119]

While this has the effect of allowing victims to keep a greater share of their recovery, it has reportedly also meant that many experienced trial lawyers have left the practice of medical malpractice cases, leaving claimants potentially without representation or representation by less competent counsel.[120] Sometimes, then, victims might be financially worse off under the restricted fee regime than they would be under the conventional U.S. fee arrangement.[121]

2. This American practice of each side paying its own fees is atypical worldwide.[122] Many legal systems use a "loser pays" scheme.[123] This means that if the case goes to trial and the defendant wins, the plaintiff not only must pay his or her own lawyer (note the contrast with the U.S. system, where 33% of 0 is 0), but the plaintiff must also pay the defendant's legal fees (as approved by the court).[124] As this could be a considerable sum, this rule is said to discourage many claimants who do not feel confident that they have a winning case.[125]

From the societal perspective, this contrast means that in the United States the lawyers who represent victims play the role of screening out weak cases because they will earn nothing if no recovery is obtained. [126] In other systems, victims themselves (to be sure after obtaining initial legal advice) must serve the function of holding back on bringing weak cases. [127] Of course, victims with no real assets and little income would be in no position actually to pay either side's legal fees if their cases were lost.[128] In the United States, they can still find representation for decent claims.[129] Elsewhere, usually some legal assistance scheme is required to ensure representation in what might be viewed as somewhat borderline cases.[130]

Note also that in most places under the "loser pays" scheme, the lawyers are paid for the work they do---either so much for each task or so much per hour-although England recently has begun to introduce percentage fees on the claimant side. It is widely believed that lawyers on both sides of cases earn considerably less outside the United States than they do here for the handling of similar cases. [131]

Of course, if the claimant wins in court or obtains a settlement, then -- at least in principle -- in most other countries the claimant is able to retain the full amount of his or her recovery because the other side must cover his or her legal fees. [132] This principle is sometimes breached in countries where the loser is required to pay a sum that is understood to be well less than the fair legal cost of representing the victim and where the claimant's lawyer is permitted to charge the client the difference. In those instances some of the recovery goes to the lawyer, but as a general rule that amount is far less than it would be in the United States.

This difference in the compensation of lawyers is one very important reason why comparisons of gross awards in tort cases between the United States and elsewhere are misleading. If one assumes, as I do, that as a psychological matter, the American claimant thinks of his or her legal fees as coming out of the portion of the recovery allocated to pain and suffering, then one must take that into account when discussing the enormously higher awards for non-pecuniary loss made in the United States. [133] I have shown elsewhere that unless U.S. pain and suffering awards are several times the amount awarded for pecuniary loss, then the U.S. situation is no longer the outlier that it initially appears to be in comparison with the higher-paying European and common law nations.[134] To be sure, in many individual cases American claimants do win pain and suffering awards that are a very large share of the total award, but in cases where plaintiffs are gravely injured, this may not be so because the pecuniary award is so enormous.[135]

To me, this means that in the United States, any statutory reform of rules governing pain and suffering should take into account -- and perhaps also reform -- the rules on legal fees.[136] This has not happened, with the result that where pain and suffering awards are now limited in some U.S. jurisdictions to $250,000 or less, the actual sum retained by victims is much less than in comparable cases in other nations.[137] Indeed, often the victim's legal fee will be more than the full amount of his or her pain and suffering award so that some of the fee will have to come out of the rest of his or her damages.[138] In such cases, claimants are probably financially worse off in those states than are their counterparts in even those European nations that pay very little for non-pecuniary loss (like Denmark).[139]

3. These considerations lead me to favor a reform in the United States that would simultaneously change both the rules for recovery for pain and suffering and the rules for compensating lawyers. As for the former, I will add nothing here to the idea advanced in an earlier section about limiting pain and suffering recovery to, say, $500,000 (adjusted for inflation) for the most seriously injured, with recovery scaled down from there for lesser injuries (perhaps with juries being informed of the pattern of past awards in the hope of gaining greater consistency).[140]

As for legal fees in this new regime, I suggest a third way. Victims would never pay. If they lose, their own lawyer remains uncompensated (as they do now), but defendants would still have to pay their own lawyers (as they do now). But if claimants win, instead of their legal fees coming out of their award, defendants would pay those costs. While this is, of course, a new cost to defendants, it is offset by the reduced cost of pain and suffering awards that is part of the package.

Moreover, I also propose altering the way in which the victim's legal fees would be determined. I recommend keeping a percentage-fee basis but altering the percentage amount from the somewhat typical 33% now used. Instead, I would favor a regime something like the following. [141] If the defendant offers a settlement within, say, ninety days of the time the case is filed and the settlement is accepted, the lawyer for the claimant is paid an amount equal to I 0% of the settlement amount as the fee. If no settlement offer is made or if there is no settlement, and the case goes ahead, then the claimant's lawyer's fee is 10% of the amount of the initial settlement offer (if any) plus 40% of any amount obtained above the initial settlement offer.

This approach is based on the idea that at the start of the case, the claimant's lawyer has made only a modest effort, and hence a 10% fee is fair enough. Moreover, this arrangement strongly encourages the defendant to make a fair offer early on so as to keep her cost of the claimant's lawyer to a minimum. If the defendant is not forthcoming, then the claimant's lawyer's work typically becomes substantial and would be generously rewarded under my proposal.

This same sort of solution might be employed to compensate lawyers who represent claimants seeking benefits from tailored compensation plans and social insurance. Today, most people who file for Social Security do not use lawyers, but most of those claims are for retirement and survivor benefits that are usually not controversial as to eligibility or amount. On the other hand, many claimants seeking total disability benefits, especially those initially rejected, do turn to legal help in proving their disability. The same pattern applies to workers' compensation claims. The vast majority of claims are handled without lawyers, but when it comes to claims for permanent partial disability or total disability, lawyers often appear. For the 9/11 Plan, plaintiff tort lawyers around the nation volunteered to help people with claims against the plan on a pro bono basis, although a small number of families eventually hired attorneys to represent them. [142] Many—perhaps most—claimants under the Vaccine Plan have lawyers representing them.

Most of the lawyers who get involved with these cases today generally take them on a contingency fee basis with the fee paid out of the claimant's award. But the percentage of the award the lawyers take as a fee is generally considerably lower than in tort cases. For example, the traditional workers' compensation fee has been 10%, and often in these cases the client and the defendant insurer agree to a lump-sum payment insisted of ongoing monthly benefits. Among other things, this allows the lawyer to get the fee all at once, and the amount on which it is based is clear. Lawyers handling Social Security disability claims tend to get 25% of the back benefits they win for their clients (which generally is far less than 25% of the discounted present value of the entire award that has been won).

The Vaccine Plan, however, provides something of a precedent for my proposal. There, provided some minimal requirements are met, the plan will pay reasonable legal fees to lawyers who help people file claims. Indeed, reasonable legal fees are paid by the plan even in cases where benefits are denied. It might have been wise to have a similar arrangement for the 9/11 Plan. But as already noted, that turned out to be unnecessary. Wanting to appear patriotic and not wanting to appear to be profiting off the terrorist events of 9/11, the personal injury plaintiffs' bar generously agreed to pitch in for free on behalf of those who lost a loved one.[143]

The general principle I support, then, is that instead of having the claimant pay for his or her lawyer, the compensation plan should pay a reasonable fee to the claimant's lawyer in situations where we can have some confidence that the lawyer made a difference. For some plans, perhaps this means the plan should only have to pay after the claimant made an initial claim that was rejected (or only a low sum was offered) and now a lawyer participates so that the claim is recognized (or a much larger sum is offered). As with tort claims, the fee should be structured both to reward the effective lawyer without having to take the fee out of the victim's recovery and to entice the plan to make a reasonable offer before the lawyer must make a substantial effort on behalf of the client. Schemes like the Vaccine Plan seem to be different because the mounting of the initial claim can be quite difficult and waiting for a claim to be denied before offering to pay the claimant's lawyer does not make sense.

VIII. CONCLUSION

When it comes to the money paid to those who suffer personal injury by accident, U.S. law has not had a major impact on the laws of other rich nations, and perhaps that is just as well. To the contrary, the United States could benefit substantially by embracing aspects of the laws of other nations with respect to social insurance, tailored compensation plans, and tort law. These changes would still leave the United States with a robust (albeit reduced) tort law and a much stronger set of other compensation arrangements. These together, I believe, would constitute a package that would be more attractive to Justice Linden than our current package. If so, I urge advocacy on behalf of these reforms as a tribute to him.

ENDNOTES

1. BARBARA SAMUELS, SOCIAL SECURITY DISABILITY CLAIMS: PRACTICE AND PROCEDURE § 5:5 (2d ed. 2010); 42 U.S.C. § 402 (2010).

2. See, e.g., CANADIAN TORT LAW, *supra* note 1, at 602 (providing an example of a court considering whether artificial insemination that led patient to contract HIV could be held as a tort).

3. ORIN KRAMER & RICHARD BRIFFAULT, WORKERS' COMPENSATION: STRENGTHENING THE SOCIAL COMPACT 7 (1991).

4. See id. at 2.

5. *See* Stephen D. Sugarman, *A Restatement of Torts,* 44 STAN. L. REV. 1163, 1171 (1992).

6. *See generally* KRAMER & BRIFFAULT, *supra* note 5.

7. *See supra* note 7.

8. *National Vaccine Injury Compensation Program (VICP)* HEALTH RESOURCES AND SERVICES ADMINISTRATION, http://www.hrsa.gov/vaccinecompensation/ (last visited Oct. 16, 20 I 0).

9. Stephen D. Sugarman, *Cases in Vaccine Court-Legal Battles Over Vaccines and Autism,* 357:13 NEW ENG. J. MED. 1275, 1276 (2007).

10. Stephen D. Sugarman, *Quebec's Comprehensive Auto No-Fault Scheme and the Failure of Any of the United States to Follow,* 39 LES CAHIERS DE DROIT, *numero special,* 303 (1998).

11. *See generally,* Automobile Insurance Act, R.S.Q. 1977, c. A-25 (Can.).

12. GEOFFREY PALMER, COMPENSATION FOR INCAPACITY: A *STUDY* OF LAW AND SOCIAL CHANGE IN NEW ZEALAND AND AUSTRALIA 115-30 (1979).

13. Although outside the scope of my inquiry, which looks only at accidental injuries, plan designers must also think about instances in which the victim has been harmed by intentional wrongdoing (or perhaps the reckless disregard of the victim's interest in bodily integrity). Should additional sums be paid to victims that are designed to punish injurers, and if so, how much should the penalty be (or should this function be left to the criminal law)?

14. *See* P.S. ATIYAH, THE DAMAGES LOTTERY 13 (1997).

15. For a brief discussion of structured settlements and periodic payments, see VICTOR E. SCHWARTZ ET AL., PROSSER, WADE AND SCHWARTZ'S TORTS: CASES AND MATERIALS 560--61 (12thed. 2010).

16. *See id.* at 603-05.

17. *See id.*

18. *See, e.g.,* M.G. WOODROOF ET AL., AUTOMOBILE INSURANCE AND NO-FAULT LAW § 5:11 (1974).

19. *See generally,* John G. Fleming, *The Collateral Source Rule and Loss Allocation in Tort Law,* 54 CALIF. L. REV. 1478 (1966).

20. *Id.* at 1478.

21. *Id.* at 1496-97.

22. *See* SCHWARTZ, *supra* note 17, at 559.

23. *See* Fleming, *supra* note 21, at 548.

24. *See* Stephen D. Sugarman, *Tort Reform Through Damages Law Reform: An American Perspective,* 27 SYDNEY L. REV. 507, 508 (2005) [hereinafter *Tort Reform];* Stephen D. Sugarman, *A Century of Change in Personal Injury Law,* 88 CALIF. L. REv. 2403, 2422-23 (2000) (discussing the interplay of insurance and personal injury law).

25. *See* WOODROOF, *supra* note 20, § 5.2.

26. *See, e.g., Tort Reform, supra* note 26, at 516 ("Those especially concerned about social cost accounting ... might be placated if a reversal of the collateral source rule were joined with a tax (or some suitable substitute) on activities whose costs would otherwise be shifted onto basic safety net benefit schemes.").

27. *See* Anthony J. Sebok, *What's Law Got To Do with It? Designing Compensation Schemes in the Shadow of the Tort System,* 53 DEPAUL L. REV. 501, 501 (2003) ("It is a banal truism of life that where one starts off in a journey determines, to a great extent, where one ends up. This banal observation can be formalized under the rubric of 'path-dependency.'").

28. I do not address in this article the matter of substantive tort doctrine, except to note here that perhaps the most important lead role for American tort law has been to expand the sorts of accidents and injuries for which legal recovery is allowed. Starting in the 1960s, especially in California and then in New Jersey, substantive tort doctrine became more and more pro-victim. *See, e.g.,* O'Brien v. Muskin Corp., 463 A.2d 298, 303 (N.J. 1983) (establishing a pro-victim standard of analysis in products liability cases); Greenman v. Yuba Power Prods., Inc., 377 P.2d 897, 900 (Cal. 1963) (holding manufacturers strictly liable for all products placed on the market). I have in mind, for example, strict product liability rules, claims for emotional distress and wrongful birth, crimes committed by third parties on the defendant's premises, informed consent and lost chance claims in medical injury cases, and market-share awards in certain mass injury settings. Whether or not courts in other nations explicitly chose to follow American tort law when also moving to embrace these sorts of claims (or at least some of them), surely the lawyers who brought these novel claims in other nations were, in most instances, aware of U.S. developments.

29. Stephen D. Sugarman, *A Comparative Law Look at Pain and Suffering Awards, 55* DEPAUL L. REv. 399, 399 (2006).

30. *Id.* at 401.

31. *Id.* at 400, 417.

32. *Id.*

33. *Id.*

34. *Id.* at 418.

35. *Id.* at 432.

36. *Id.* at 410.

37. *See id.* at 422-23, 430.

38. *See* PERSONAL INJURY AWARDS IN EU AND EFTA COUNTRIES (David Mcintosh & Mrujorie Holmes eds., 2003); Sugarman, *supra* note 31, at 411; PERSONAL INJURY AND WRONGFUL DEATH DAMAGES CALCULATIONS: TRANSATLANTIC DIALOGUE (John 0. Ward & Robert J. Thornton eds., 2009).

39. For England, see generally, JUDICIAL STUDIES BOARD, GUIDELINES FOR THE ASSESSMENT OF GENERAL DAMAGES IN PERSONAL INJURY CASES (lOth ed. 2010). *See also* Sugarman, *supra* note 31, at 427.

40. Sugarman, *supra* note 31, at 427.

41. *Id.* at 426.

42. *Id.*

43. For Italy, see Giovanni Comande, *Towards a Global Model for Adjudicating Personal Injury Damages: Bridging Europe and the United Stales,* 19 TEMP. INT'L & COMP. L.J. 241 (2005); Sugarman, *supra* note 31, at 426.

44. *See, e.g.,* Randall Bovbjerg et al., *Valuing Life and Limb in Tort: Scheduling "Pain andSuffering,"* 83 NW. U. L. REV. 908 (1989).

45. *Id.* at 959.

46. *See* id.

47. Andrews v. Grand & Toy Alberta Ltd., [1978] 2 S.C.R. 229,233 (Can.).

48. *Id.* at 233.

49. *Id.* at 258.

50. For New South Wales, see Civil *Liability Act 2002* (NSW) pt. 2, div 3, §16 (Austl.) (setting maximum award for non-economic loss damages awards at $350,000).

51. *See* David M. Studdert et al., *Are Damages Caps Regressive? A Study of Malpractice Jury Verdicts* in *California,* 23 HEALTH AFF. 54, 54 (2004).

52. *Id.* at 55, 63.

53. *Id.* at 56.

54. *See, e.g.,* Bruce A. Thomas, *A Canadian View of the Product Liability Aspects of Innovation,*15 CAN.-U.S. L.J. 93,96 (1989).

55. *See Civil Liability Act 2002* (NSW) pt 2 (Austl.).

56. *Id.* pt 2, div 3, §16.

57. *See* N.Y. INS. LAW§§ 5101-09 (McKinney 2005); MICH. COMP. LAWS § 500.3135(1) (West 2006).

58. *See* N.Y. INS. LAW
§§5101-09; MICH. COMP. LAWS § 500.3135(1).

59. *See* N.Y. INS. LAW§ 5104(a); MICH. COMP.LAWS §500.3135(1).

60. *See* N.Y. INS. LAW§ 5104(a); MICH. COMP. LAWS §500.3135(1).

61. *See, e.g.,* N.Y. INS. LAW§§ 5102(d) (defining "serious injury").

62. *See* U.S. DEP'T OF TRANSP., COMPENSATING AUTO ACCIDENT VICTIMS: A FOLLOW-UP REPORT ON NO-FAULT AUTO INSURANCE EXPERIENCES 114-15 (May 1985) (reporting on declines in lawsuits filed in Michigan and New York); Thomas C. Jones, *The Michigan Study, in* No-FAULT AUTOMOBILE INSURANCE IN ACTION: THE EXPERIENCES IN MASSACHUSETTS, FLORIDA, DELAWARE AND MICHIGAN 379,383 (1977) (showing a huge decline in minor tort liability claims in Michigan).

63. *E.g.,* New Brunswick Injury Regulation (Insurance Act), N.B. Reg. 2003-20 § 4 (Can.) (capping non-pecuniary loss for all minor personal injuries at $2500).

64. *See* B.S. MARKESINIS, A COMPARATIVE INTRODUCTION TO THE GERMAN LAW OF TORTS 516 (1990).

65. *See Tort Reform, supra* note 26, at 512-16 (2005) (discussing U.S. and Australian methods of compensation for non-economic loss).

66. Joseph Sanders & Craig Joyce, *"Off to the Races": The 1980s Tort Crisis and the Law Reform Process,* 27 Hous. L.REV. 207, 223 n. 60 (1990).

67. *Tort Reform, supra* note 26, at 509.

68. *Id.* at 509-10.

69. *Id.* at 509.

70. *Civil Liability Act 2002* (NSW) s 12 (Austl.).

71. Stephen D. Sugarman, *Short Term Paid Leave: A New Approach to Social Insurance and Employee Benefits,* 75 CALIF. L. REV. 465,467 (1987).

72. *Id.*

73. *Id.*

74. *Id.*

75. *See id.*

76. *Tort Reform, supra* note 26, at 510.

77. *See supra* note 59 and accompanying text.

78. *Tort Reform, supra* note 26, at 511.

79. *Tort Reform, supra* note 26, at 511.

80. Awards that some states make that are based upon specific impairments, like loss of an arm or loss of an eye, are usually intended more as proxies for presumed income loss than for pain and suffering.

81. STEPHEN D. SUGARMAN, "PAY AT THE PUMP" AUTO INSURANCE: THE CALIFORNIA INJURY PLAN (VIP) FOR BETTER COMPENSATION, FAIRER FUNDING, AND GREATER SAFETY *5* (1993).

82. *But see* Robert L. Rabin & Stephen D. Sugarman, *The Case for Specially Compensating the Victims a/Terrorist Acts: An Assessment,* 35 HOFSTRA L. REV. 901 (2007).

83. *See* Stephen D. Sugarman, *Right and Wrong Ways of Doing Away with Commercial Air Crash Litigation: Professor Chalk's "Market Insurance Plan" and Other No-Fault Follies,* 52 J. AIRL.&COM. 681 (1987).

84. *See id.* at 686 (proposing an ideal plan in a "typical" no-fault system).

85. *See id.* at 687.

86. *See id.* at 686-88 (comparing two different no-fault systems using insurance).

87. *Cf* 49 U.S.C.A. §§ 40113-14 (West 2006) (describing the Federal Aviation Administration's responsibility to investigate and report).

88. *See generally* Robert L. Rabin, *The Quest for Fairness* in *Compensating Victims of September 11,* 49 CLEV. ST. L. REV. 573 (2001).

89. *See id* at 582.

90. *See id* at 585.

91. *See id.*

92. KENNETH R. FEINBERG, WHAT IS LIFE WORTH?: THE UNPRECEDENTED EFFORT TO COMPENSATE THE VICTIMS OF 9/II 34-35 (2005).

93. *See, e.g.,* Sugarman, *supra* note 85, at 685 (workers' compensation is based on lost earning power); *see also* Rabin, *supra* note 90, at 584 n.60 (benefits in workers' compensation cases are usually calculated by a percentage of decedent's weekly wage).

94. FEINBERG, *supra* note 94, at 182-83.

95. *See Health Care Reform,* N.Y. TIMES, http://topics.nytimes.com/top/news/health/diseasesconditionsandhealthtopics/health_insurance_and_managed_care/health_care_reform/index.html (last updated Dec. 13, 2010).

96. FEINBERG, *supra* note 94,at 35-36; *see* Rabin, *supra* note 90,at 578.

97. *See* Rabin, *supra* note 90, at 579-80.

98. *See id* at 583.

99. *Filing a Claim with the VICP,* HEALTH RESOURCES AND SERVICES ADMINISTRATION, http://www.hrsa.gov/vaccinecompensation/filing_claim.htm (last visited Dec. 20, 2010).

100. *Persons Eligible to File a Claim,* HEALTH RESOURCES AND SERVICES ADMINISTRATION, http://www.hrsa.gov/vaccinecompensation /persons_eligible.htm (last visited Dec. 20, 2010,) (outlining the parameters for eligibility).

101. *See* Rabin, *supra* note 90, at 586; Rabin & Sugarman, *supra* note 84, at 908.

102. *See* Rabin, *supra* note 90, at 586.

103. *See id.*

104. *See* Jeffrey O'Connell, *No-Fault Auto Insurance: Back by Popular (Market) Demand?,* 26 SAN DIEGO L. REV. 993 (1989).

105. *Id.* at 996.

106. *Id.*

107. *See id.*

108. *See id.*

109. *Id.*

110. *Id.*

111. *See id.*

112. *See id.* at 994; *see also* Gary T. Schwartz, *Auto No-Fault and First Party Insurance: Advantages and Problems,* 73 S. CAL. L. REV. 611,621 (2000).

113. *See* ROBERT H. JOOST, AUTOMOBILE INSURANCE AND NO-FAULT LAW § I :2C, at 26 (2d ed. 2002).

114. Robert H. Mnookin, *Negotiation, Settlement and the Contingent Fee,* 47 DEPAUL L. REV. 363, 365 (1998).

115. *Id.*

116. *Id.*

117. *See* Miss. State Bar v. Blackmon, 600 So. 2d 166, 176 (Miss. 1992) (Banks, J., dissenting); Hayseeds, Inc. v. State Farm Fire & Cas., 352 S.E.2d 73,80 (W.Va. 1986).

118. *See* CAL. Bus. & PROF. CODE§ 6146(a) (West 2003).

119. *See* Jane E. Reames, *Contingency Fees: Victim or Contributing Cause of Medical Malpractice Reform Acts?,* 62 CHI.-KENT L. REV. 271, 283 (1985).

120. *See id.* at284.

121. *See id.* at 288.

122. *See* W. Kent Davis, *The International View of Attorney Fees in Civil Suits: Why Is the United States the "Odd Man Out" in How It Pays Its Lawyers?,* 16 ARIZ. J. INT'L & COMP. L. 361, 400 (1999); *see also* Walter Olson, *Loser Pays,* POINTOFLAW.COM (May 21, 2004), http://www.pointoflaw.com/loserpays/overview.php.

123. *See Davis, supra* note 124, at 400.

124. *See id* at 403.

125. *See id* at 408.

126. *See id* at 377-78.

127. *See id* at408.

128. *See id* at 410.

129. *See* id at 377-78.

130. *See id* at 410; *see, e.g.,* MINISTRY OF JUSTICE, LEGAL AID: REFOCUSING ON PRIORITY CASES, 2009, C.P. 12/09, at 8 (U.K.) (demonstrating that "borderline" cases may be considered for legal assistance schemes where public interest considerations outweigh benefits to the individual litigants alone).

131. *See* Sugarman, *supra* note 31, at 401.

132. *See id* at 419.

133. *See id* at 40l.

134. *See id* at 421-22.

135. *Id.* at 422.

136. *See id* at 430-33.

137. *Id.* at 427-28.

138. *See id* at 428.

139. *See id.;* Stephen D. Sugarman, *The Legal Sting of Pain and Suffering,* L.A. TIMES, June5, 2005, http://articles.latimes.com /2005/jun/05/opinion/oe-sugarmans. To be sure, this analysis is further complicated to the extent that nations also differ in the amounts they award for pecuniary loss in comparable cases, a matter I put aside here.

140. *See supra* text accompanying note 56; *see also* Sugarman, *supra* note 31, at 430.

141. *Cf Tort Reform, supra* note 26, at 522 (offering an earlier version of this proposed regime).

142. *See* Kenneth R. Feinberg, *Speech: Negotiating the September II Victim Compensation Fund of200/: Mass Tort Resolution Without Litigation,* 19 WASH. U. J.L. & POL'Y 21, 29, (2005).

143. *See id* at 29.

Part III

Policy Reform

In recent years critics have been especially concerned about how the U.S. deals with three types of injuries that are the subject of this Part: 1) medical injuries, 2) auto injuries, and 3) injuries that arise from what are typically called disasters or catastrophes involving the harm to a large number of people from a single event. Each of these is a big deal in its own way. Auto accidents still kill more than 30,000 people each year in the U.S., and medical accidents probably kill more than three times that many. Catastrophes capture even more front-page news because of the concentration of loss surrounding a specifically identified event.

Tort law has come in for serious criticism in the way it functions in all three of these settings. Hoping to reduce harms arising from motoring, medical care, and disasters governments have adopted (and policy analysts have proposed) other safety-promoting regimes designed to complement or replace tort law. The same goes for schemes aimed at victim compensation for these sorts of injuries and deaths. Yet, disapproving judgments have also been made about these other regimes.

Part III deals with these important policy issues. Each chapter discusses ways that government might better deal with the relevant injuries through reforms that are primarily outside of tort law.

Chapter 10

Medical Malpractice: Doctor No

This chapter is about medical injuries, and its subtitle (perhaps too subtly taken from a James Bond movie of that name) draws from the now widely accepted estimate that more than 100,000 people die in the U.S. each year because of bad things that happen to them while in the hospital. Many or most of those deaths, experts believe, could and should have been avoided (although probably doctors themselves are directly responsible for only a moderate share of these deaths, the rest being more directly caused by other hospital personnel and conditions).

The law of medical malpractice, together with tort law's general negligence principle, is supposed to deter unsafe behavior by doctors and other hospital employees and then provide compensation when undeterred negligence causes patients harm. Although some scholars believe tort law in this setting serves to reduce the number of bad outcomes that occur during the course of medical treatment, it clearly is not doing enough.

Hard evidence of this large number of avoidable hospital-related deaths (and lesser harms) has spawned a "patient safety" movement, and a variety of strategies are now being tried out in hopes of reducing those negative outcomes. Reformers are concentrating on things like advanced technology to keep better track of patient records (say, as to drugs prescribed and taken), better training of and routinizing the conduct of surgical teams, more effective control of infection-causing agents inside hospitals, increased transparency in the reporting of avoidable harmful events and so on.

This chapter presents an essay written about Professor Paul Weiler's book "**Medical Malpractice on Trial**" and was published as Stephen D. Sugarman, "Doctor No," 58 University of Chicago Law Review 1499-1525 (1991). It is reprinted with the permission of the journal. Weiler's book draws on a key early empirical study that Weiler and his team carried out that demonstrated the substantial risk of iatrogenic injuries that hospital patients run. Weiler further showed that hardly any of those victims found their way into the medical malpractice system and that the legal regime was even more error-prone than the medical system (i.e., all too many malpractice victims who filed claims failed to recover and a substantial share of those who did recover were probably not malpractice victims even though they were injured). Weiler then proposed a number of creative legal reforms which are assessed in the essay, which also presents some other possible solutions. At the end of the chapter a postscript is provided that updates the picture from how it looked when the essay was written. In the larger picture, however, things are broadly the same today as they were then.

Doctor No

Paul Weiler's *Medical Malpractice on Trial*[1] is a splendid little book. In 161 very readable pages (plus sixty–eight pages of endnotes), he describes and critiques the current regime of medical malpractice law, surveys and evaluates a range of reforms previously proposed (and sometimes enacted), and offers a bold improvement package of his own. His most inventive and promising ideas are to substitute organizational liability (such as hospital liability) for individual physician liability (pp. 122–32) and to replace fault-based compensation with a no-fault scheme covering all medical accidents that lead to serious disability or death (pp. 132–58). Weiler tempers the boldness of his vision with a sensitive appreciation of both the political and practical problems of promptly achieving it. This appreciation leads him to advocate the immediate adoption of more modest steps in the direction he favors, including substantial changes in the measure of damages in malpractice cases and experiments with elective no-fault compensation in lieu of litigation.

Although I am persuaded that Weiler's recommendations would lead to a vast improvement over the current regime, he has not yet shown, as I will later explain, that his focused no-fault plan is the best long-range solution. Even so, I think this slim volume is a "must" for anyone who wants to understand contemporary issues surrounding medical malpractice. *Medical Malpractice on Trial* contains countless nuggets of information and analysis concerning a dazzling array of issues and contentions that have been featured in the debate over medical malpractice reform during the past twenty years. In the course of his presentation, Weiler pulls together nearly all of the best work by others who have written in this field.

Moreover, this book integrates the findings and analyses of two large and important projects for which Weiler has been centrally responsible. This information is otherwise only accessible in more awkward forms. While there is much to be gained from reading the more than 1,000-page final *Reporters' Study of Enterprise Liability for Personal Injury* (1991) for the American Law Institute[2] (*"Reporters' Study"*) (which covers many other topics besides malpractice) and *Patients, Doctors, and Lawyers: Medical Injury, Malpractice Litigation, and Patient Compensation in New York* (1990)[3] (*"Harvard Study"*) (the massive first report of the Harvard Medical Malpractice Study Group), Weiler's book is the place to start for a well-organized and compact examination of the medical malpractice field.

I. Medical Malpractice, Malpractice Law, and Malpractice Insurance Today

A. Patterns of Claiming and Collecting

Weiler paints a startling picture of current patterns of claiming and collecting which reveals the minor and idiosyncratic role malpractice law plays in the compensation of malpractice victims. Based on the Harvard Study, Weiler explains that of every 100,000 patients discharged from hospitals, nearly 4,000 suffered an "adverse event"[4] from their medical treatment. About one-fourth of these are the result of medical malpractice (p. 12). In short, hospital patients on average run about a four percent risk of an adverse event and about a one percent risk of medical malpractice.

These 100,000 patient discharges and 1,000 malpractice-caused injuries generate about 125 legal claims. About sixty of the 125 claimants actually receive compensation (p. 13). The rest of the claims lose at trial or are dropped. Of those sixty successful claimants, about twenty receive payment before they have filed a lawsuit, about thirty-five after a suit is filed but before (or during) trial, and only about five win at trial (pp. 53, 193 n 30).

According to neutral physicians reviewing the records, however, of every 125 claims that plaintiffs make, no malpractice occurred in about eighty-five cases. Based on Weiler's account and the Harvard study, I have calculated that most of the cases where malpractice occurred and a patient filed a claim lead to some award (thirty to thirty-five of forty); but some thirty percent of the claims where malpractice apparently did not occur also result in some payment (twenty-five to thirty of eighty-five), albeit a payment that is often substantially discounted from the amount of the claimant's likely recovery had liability been clear.

To put it in a somewhat different way, about thirty to thirty-five of every 1,000 malpractice victims use the legal system to obtain compensation for their losses, although only perhaps four out of every 1,000 obtain an award of individualized justice through a jury of their peers. At the same time, twenty-five to thirty people who were probably not victims of malpractice nevertheless receive payment from the system. In some cases these people probably have not even suffered any harm or a net detriment to health as a result of the medical treatment they complained about.

I've so far used the illustrative numbers of 1,000 tort victims out of every 100,000 hospital discharges in order to provide a ready feel for the data. In fact, we are talking about some forty million annual hospitalizations across America (p. 71). These numbers translate into about a million and a half adverse events and 400,000 torts (one percent of 40 million) every year. Yet, the system's compensation shortfall is enormous: only 25,000 medical malpractice claimants, out of 50,000 who claim and 400,000 who are injured, are likely to receive some compensation, of whom only 12,500 to 15,000 were actually malpractice victims.[5] Of course, many of those patients injured through medical malpractice suffer only minor injuries, about half incurring only minimal impairment and recovering completely within a month, and another substantial group fully recovering in less than six months (p. 136). Still, in as many as twenty-five percent of the cases of medical negligence the patient dies—at least in part as a result of malpractice.[6] In addition, about ten percent of the victims of medical malpractice suffer long-lasting disabilities.[7] Projecting the findings nationally, the Harvard Study suggests that every year the approximately 1.5 million adverse events from medical treatment in hospitals seriously and permanently disable approximately 150,000 people and kill more than 150,000 people (many of whom, admittedly, are elderly and perhaps frail at the outset).[8] Medical negligence accounts for greater than a quarter of those more than 300,000 substantial harms, only a small portion of which are actually compensated through the current tort system.

B. Administrative Costs, Insurance, and Other Burdens

Weiler also rightly emphasizes the enormous waste of the existing regime. In order to deliver $1 in net compensation into the hands of those medical malpractice claimants who receive something from the system, more than $1.35 is spent on claims processing costs. The legal expenses of both sides are the most significant costs.[9] And these figures don't even count the substantial additional transactions costs not directly attributable to claims processing, including commissions, marketing expenses, and taxes paid and profits earned by insurers, all of which probably amount to more than twenty percent of the cost of medical liability insurance (pp. 192–93 n. 28).

In states still following the common law rules as to tort damages, forty to fifty percent of the compensation paid is for pain and suffering (pp. 51, 55), the lion's share of which is concentrated on the five percent of successful claimants with the most serious injuries (who represent perhaps two or three of every 1,000 victims of malpractice) (p. 48). Moreover, of the remaining compensation paid through the legal system, perhaps as much as sixty percent is already covered by public and private insurance programs like Blue Cross and other forms of private health insurance, Medicare, Medicaid, Social Security, disability insurance, sick leave, and so on (p. 51).

A little arithmetic, then, shows that for every one dollar that is collected in malpractice insurance premiums, ten to fifteen cents has traditionally gone to reimburse claimants' actual out-of-pocket economic losses. Furthermore, delays of several years between the time of claim filing and receipt of compensation are not at all uncommon (p. 52).

Physicians, hospitals, and others paid a total of about $7 billion in medical liability insurance premiums in 1988. Weiler's data illustrates that around $1 billion of that amount will finally go to reimburse otherwise uncompensated economic losses. Claimants will actually probably receive a net cash total of between $2 and $3 billion (p. 99), depending upon how successful "collateral" sources (private and social insurance funds) are in recouping what otherwise would amount to double recovery by claimants.

The financial impact of the system on certain classes of physicians is enormous.

For example, high-risk specialists like neurosurgeons and obstetricians in high-risk states like New York and Florida pay annual medical malpractice insurance premiums of between $100,000 and $200,000 (p. 4). Still, as Weiler makes clear, the insurance burdens should not be over-dramatized since the national average malpractice insurance cost per doctor was only about $16,000 in 1988; the $7 billion in malpractice premiums paid in 1988 represented not much more than one percent of total annual expenditures for health care nationwide that year (p. 4).

To this cost, however, one must add at least some of the $9 or $10 billion spent annually by physicians on "defensive" medicine, in the form of extra record-keeping, extra tests given to patients, extra time with patients and the like (p. 85). Of course, some of those dollars might actually have benefitted patients and are cost-justified in an economic sense. But it is widely believed that many of these defensive measures do not help patients (and sometimes are even risky to patients); they serve primarily to help the doctor ward off malpractice claims (and, frequently, to increase the doctor's income as well) (p. 87).

Additional social costs of the existing legal system include (1) the psychological burden on those doctors who feel they are caught up in a Kafkaesque legal system (p. 81), (2) the refusal of competent physicians to enter or continue practice in certain high-risk specialties or to perform certain desirable but higher risk treatments (p. 85), and (3) the lost services of and earnings by doctors who must devote up to an average of five uncompensated days to defend against a typical malpractice claim (p. 81). So, while the "costs" generated by legal liability for medical malpractice do not loom large in the overall national health care budget, they are plainly not chicken feed.

In sum, from the viewpoint of compensating victims, whether we focus only on victims of malpractice or on all victims of adverse events from medical treatment, Weiler's analysis demonstrates that the current system is a disaster and a disgrace. The few are lucky lottery winners, so to speak, only about half of whom should even have been given lottery tickets. The many are ignored. Although it may not be fair to say that "*only* the lawyers win," it can hardly be said that, from the compensation perspective, patients as a class win.

C. Individualized Justice?

The system, overall, also fails to serve well the ideal of individual justice. As Weiler demonstrates, on the patient side, most "deserving" victims, those who have been wronged, get nothing, and only a trivial proportion of wronged victims have the satisfaction (if it turns out to be that) of winning in court. At the same time, many successful claimants are not "deserving" in the sense of having been wronged.

On the defendant side, physicians generally do not pay higher malpractice insurance premiums because of successful malpractice claims against them. Rather, rates turn far more importantly on the number and size of claims against other doctors practicing the same specialty and in the same region (p. 76).

Because nearly all the claims are either settled or dropped, "blame" as assigned by the current system is both highly selective and often misapplied. Insurance companies settle many undeserving claims for their nuisance value, often irritating the physicians involved (p. 15). And while doctors are actually vindicated about half of the time in court (p. 168 n. 8), victory in litigation is hardly the sort of justice they crave. (At the same time, some of those doctors who win at trial probably did commit malpractice, but win because of a lack of evidence, or a jury that is overly sympathetic to or awed by them.)

Meanwhile, most "malpractice" in the legal system turns out to be the sort of momentary slip of the hand that most people frequently display (p. 14). Unfortunately, in risky medical treatment settings those momentary errors can be extremely harmful. While we might agree that people victimized by these sorts of errors are in some sense "entitled" to better care, an error of this sort hardly makes someone a bad person, let alone a bad doctor. Contrary to widespread belief, repeat offenders are actually responsible for a small share of the malpractice that occurs (p. 79). A truer picture is that a large number of doctors regularly commit errors that are in theory avoidable, and only some of these doctors are unlucky enough to have those errors lead to significant patient harm.

D. Prevention

Weiler concludes, and I agree, that if the current legal system covering medical malpractice can be justified at all, it must be because of its role in preventing medical accidents by deterring acts of malpractice that would otherwise occur (p. 71). Of course, even if the present scheme had some positive impact on physician conduct, that would hardly end the inquiry. Alternative deterrence strategies would also have to be considered.

Weiler addresses the prevention issue in his marvelously helpful Chapter 4. Weiler believes that the existing malpractice regime does aid patient safety (p. 91). But he concludes that certain reforms would do better not only on this dimension, but also on other dimensions (such as better victim compensation, lower administrative costs, and less harm to physicians and medical practice) (p. 132). However, the goal of accident prevention remains central to Weiler's victim compensation reforms.

By contrast, I believe that the right strategy is to move toward the separation of the behavioral control and compensation functions—which, as I will explain, would take us away from both the current malpractice scheme and Weiler's favored alternative.

II. Track One Reforms: Substantial Changes In The Traditional Legal Regime

Weiler calls for reform along two tracks. Track two involves moving to what he calls "no-fault liability" for medical accidents. I will discuss this approach in the next section. Track one, my focus here, involves what he terms "serious reform" of the traditional system.

Weiler generally eschews doctrinal reform concerning the standard of care that physicians owe their patients. He quickly dismisses alternative dispute resolution procedures, like screening panels (p. 42). Instead, he concentrates on damages law. In Weiler's prescription, successful medical malpractice plaintiffs should not receive compensation for losses covered by "collateral sources" (pp. 47–54) and should have reduced recovery for pain and suffering (pp. 54–61). In return, they should receive compensation for their attorney's fees (pp. 61–69).

In favoring such a trade, Weiler basically endorses the solution that Professor Jeffrey O'Connell and I have recommended previously for personal injury cases generally—although, in the details, there are perhaps some important differences among us.[10]

A. Reversing the "Collateral Sources" Rule

Weiler, O'Connell, and I all favor a general reversal of the common law rule that ignores other "collateral" sources of compensation for the same loss when determining the amount of a victim's award in a tort case (pp. 50–52). Weiler does not pay much attention, however, to the details of just which collateral sources should count in reducing what otherwise would be the victim's malpractice award.

I assume Weiler would agree with me that a plaintiff should not recover in a lawsuit for losses already covered by social insurance or public assistance benefits or by basic work-related employee benefits, like health insurance. I also assume that Weiler would agree that malpractice law should continue to ignore the victim's savings and personally-purchased, permanent life insurance, even though they too are available to replace the losses incurred. After all, reversing the collateral sources rule isn't really meant to turn tort law into a means-tested compensation scheme.

Rather, the justification for the proposal is to channel the responsibility for the compensation into broadly applicable and far more cheaply administered first party loss insurance schemes and away from third party liability insurance which is so costly to administer. Yet, even given this general rationale, it is rather difficult to decide what to do about things such as disability insurance, especially when individually purchased by the victim outside the job context; and term life insurance, especially when automatically provided to all employees by the victim's employer. These are close questions that several state legislatures have already recognized in their attempts to turn the general pronouncements of law professors (and others) about the collateral sources rule into specific statutory provisions.[11]

Weiler contrasts the reversal of the collateral sources rule with the imposition of an overall ceiling on malpractice awards (p. 51), an approach, he notes, that has been followed in a few states (p. 49). He opposes the latter, and I agree, because it bites most in the relatively few cases with the greatest loss (p. 50). Reversing the collateral sources rule, by contrast, concentrates malpractice payments on cases of greater need.

B. Limiting and Standardizing Recovery for Pain and Suffering

Weiler, O'Connell, and I have somewhat divergent views with respect to tort compensation for pain and suffering. O'Connell's favored solution is to eliminate it altogether.[12] I do not favor that solution, at least for now, partly because it may be thought to represent too sharp a break with tradition, partly because of my empathy with the outrage that may be felt by those very seriously harmed through the fault of another, and partly because even workers' compensation law tends to pay some arbitrarily selected amounts to those who suffer serious permanent impairments.

Therefore, I propose retaining tort recovery for pain and suffering, also called "general damages," but in a quite restricted form. First, no one could recover general damages who had not suffered a serious injury, defined as involving either a disability that prevents one from returning to one's normal activities for more than six months, or a significant and permanent impairment or disfigurement. The idea is to eliminate payments to those claimants who now milk the defendant for the nuisance value of their claim, those claimants who feign or exaggerate soft tissue injuries, and, candidly, those who may well have suffered immediately following their injury, but who, by the time of trial, no longer have significant residual suffering from the accident.

This threshold is broadly based on the threshold employed by the Michigan auto no-fault scheme. It is intended, if applied to all torts cases, to bar the general damages claims of more than three-quarters of those now receiving some compensation for pain and suffering. In the medical malpractice context, however, one would expect proportionately fewer pain and suffering claims to be barred. This result is expected because the difficulties and expense of medical malpractice litigation already serve to exclude from the system a fairly large proportion of small injury cases.

Second, I propose a ceiling on pain and suffering recovery. It would be set at $150,000 (in 1988 dollars) and would grow with inflation.[13] Weiler rejects a ceiling of the sort I've proposed on the ground that it arbitrarily imposes reduced recovery only on those who have been most seriously injured (pp. 55–56). Yet, in practice, as I will shortly explain, I would hope that my proposal could work very much like the considerably more sophisticated regime that Weiler offers.

Weiler favors the creation of a "scale" (pp. 58–61). A scale is not the same as a schedule which would attempt to establish in advance a certain dollar sum for every sort of injury. Instead, the scale would assign so many dollars for each of a selected array of injuries. The top of the scale would be reserved for the most serious non-fatal injuries—such as an infant blinded or made quadriplegic at birth (p. 59). Other representative and less serious injuries would also appear on the scale, to which lesser dollar amounts of recovery would attach. In addition, the scale would take into account the age of the victim and hence the number of years of suffering ahead (id). The parties (in settlement negotiations) and juries and judges (in cases that go to trial) would be told about the scale and would seek to locate their claims at an appropriate place along it (pp. 59–60).

As Weiler well recognizes, a scale (as well as a schedule) would in fact contain its own ceiling. But Weiler says that the way existing ceilings work is that juries, unaware of the ceiling, decide on the amount of common law damages to which the victim is entitled. Afterwards, the judge simply applies the cap (p. 59). This process results in a range of injuries of quite different degrees of severity being treated alike at the top (p. 59).

Caps need not work that way, however. Suppose instead, judges, juries and litigators were told that the purpose of the cap is to serve as the highest point on Weiler's scale—as a sum reserved for the most serious and long-lasting harms only—with lesser injuries to receive appropriately lower amounts. With that understanding, the two schemes might well function much alike, although I concede that Weiler's proposal holds the promise of greater consistency among cases falling along the scale. The real dispute between us here is the comparative advantage, if any, of rule-making over individual adjudication. In this context, the English common law judges seem to have developed a *de facto* scale, without formally adopting one through the rule-making process Weiler proposes.[14] In any event, Weiler and I seem close here in principle, if not in administrative detail.

Another key point of agreement is that in order to reach even the bottom of Weiler's scale, the plaintiff would have to suffer at least the sort of serious injury I described in discussing my proposed threshold (pp. 59–60).

A possibly important difference between us is the current dollar value to be awarded for pain and suffering in the most serious injury cases and, in turn, the amount to be awarded along the scale to all seriously injured victims with valid claims. That is, Weiler might find my inflation-adjusted $150,000 rather too low as the top of his scale, although he is a bit coy on this question.

My idea is to provide enough money so that the most seriously injured victims could invest the award and comfortably earn the arbitrary sum of $1,000 a month in 1988 dollars—an amount that would significantly benefit most Americans, but would not make anyone rich. Given modest inflation and lowered interest rates since 1988, the $150,000 figure might be raised to $200,000 today.

Weiler first argues that the point of the pain and suffering award should be to allow the person to adjust socially and psychologically to his or her condition, just as the other damages awarded address medical and vocational adjustment (p. 58). He emphasizes the importance of inquiring whether the award really can be used to pay for things that would further those social and psychological goals (id). Yet, it is not clear that he favors individualized inquiries along these lines. He gives an example of a hobbyist piano player and a hobbyist chess player each losing a hand, suggesting that, other things being equal, the piano player should get a larger payment (pp. 60-61). But this illustration seems primarily to emphasize differences in lost enjoyment from similar injuries, not so much a difference in what each person needs to adjust, unless he has in mind the pianist taking lessons to learn how to play pieces written for one hand. So, too, when he suggests that a blind or quadriplegic child should be at the top of his scale (p. 59), he really doesn't justify this suggestion in terms of appropriate spending for social and psychological adjustment, but rather, it seems, in terms of the enormity of these injuries.

As a result, Weiler's analysis, like mine, provides no real basis for determining the range of the scale, and, like mine, his solution would involve a certain arbitrariness. At one point Weiler says that under his plan the amount paid at the ceiling "would likely fall well within the range of the statutory damage caps recently adopted by the state legislatures" (p. 58). I find this statement ambiguous. Does he have in mind as the range Maryland's $350,000 limit and New Hampshire's $875,000?[15] Is California's $250,000 cap in medical malpractice cases, adopted in the 1970s,[16] "recent" enough? While Weiler's discussion leaves me thinking that the top of his scale might approach $500,000, I note that he also favorably cites the Canadian approach in which the scale tops out at about $200,000 Canadian (close to my recommendation) (pp. 58, 195–96 n. 45).

C. Paying Successful Plaintiffs' Legal Fees

Weiler, O'Connell, and I all agree that successful claimants should be entitled to reasonable legal fees as part of their damage award, and that losing claimants should not be obligated to pay the legal fees of defendants (pp. 66–67). Frivolous claims aside, bringing a lawsuit is not a tort, and, given the current tort system, the cost of defending against non-frivolous claims seems fairly a part of the cost of the practice of medicine. By contrast, requiring the defendant to pay for those real costs incurred by winning plaintiffs seems just. This sense of justice is especially clear because the proposed changes would reduce recovery for pain and suffering and collateral sources—damages that are well understood, as a practical matter, to provide the money to pay for the plaintiff's lawyer.

I propose that plaintiffs who win at trial normally be awarded legal fees calculated as a declining percentage of the rest of their award, starting with forty percent of the first $50,000 awarded and decreasing to a sum equal to fifteen percent of the award above $600,000.[17] In a small proportion of cases involving special difficulty or ease, trial judges would be permitted to award higher or lower sums for the lawyers. For cases that settle reasonably early in the litigation process, I propose that a lower proportion of the award should be added on for legal fees. Although O'Connell's proposed statute provides for the payment of "reasonable attorney's fees" by defendants to successful plaintiffs, it does not address how to determine that sum.[18]

Weiler falls somewhere between O'Connell and me in terms of specificity. Although he does not take a firm stand, his tentatively favored solution seems to be one in which, like mine, the legal fees would be set as a percentage of the overall award (pp. 68–69). The specific percentage would not vary based on the amount of the award; instead, it would vary based on the point in the process at which the case is resolved (for example, fifteen percent if settled early and thirty-five percent if tried) (p. 64). Weiler appears to endorse part, but not all, of my proposal.[19]

We disagree over whether the attorney's percentage should be lower the higher the total amount of the award. The disagreement turns in large part on our different views of the current market for plaintiffs' legal services, which I believe is quite imperfect and Weiler does not. As I see it, most claimants do not shop for lawyers; they see only one, by referral or otherwise, and do not bargain over price. Of course, even if a small proportion of claimants shopped well, they might effectively police the market for everyone else. But I don't think that happens either.

Even when claimants shop among lawyers, frequently through referrals, I believe that malpractice attorneys try to convince claimants to employ them through non-price-cutting strategies. If nothing else, offering a lower price might inadvertently signal to the would-be client that the lawyer is less qualified. That danger is especially great in those cases where the plaintiff is highly risk-averse and unable to evaluate either how good the lawyer is or just what sort of lawyer is needed. Rather, the claimant generally wants the best lawyer possible, fearing that otherwise the case might be lost entirely. If I am right that claimants typically select their lawyer on the basis of reputation,[20] the result, in a socially perverse way, is that the lawyers with the best reputations will tend to get the easiest and most lucrative cases. Conversely, those with lesser reputations will handle the harder cases. The best strategy for ambitious and talented lawyers lower down in the pecking order, then, seems to be to work exceptionally hard in an effort to build a reputation in the legal community, not to charge a lower fee.

Were there to be negotiations among sophisticated parties for legal services in malpractice cases, I believe that contracts would provide for a lower percentage the more recovered, as is apparently true for real estate agent commissions on sales of homes. This result, I believe, is especially likely in the Weiler-reformed world in which far more of what the claimant receives would be readily predictable than is true today. Once the attorney makes a strong enough case for liability, the negotiations over the amount of damages should be less complicated and less difficult than now. Obtaining a large award would much more likely be a function of the plaintiff's actual loss than the attorney's skill.[21]

D. Summary and Likely Impact

In sum, Weiler's first track reform is thoughtful and well argued, even though it is neither as detailed as I would have liked, nor terribly original. The areas Weiler addresses are exactly the ones that legislatures, scholars, and commissions have been working to reform.

The most important quality of Weiler's proposal, in my judgment, is that it is balanced. This balance is in sharp contrast to the one-sided proposals from the Reagan and Bush Administrations[22] and, as Weiler points out, to the generally one-sided legislation that states have so far enacted. And Weiler's particular balance, it must be re-emphasized, would mesh the damages awarded in malpractice cases with malpractice claimants' actual losses far more sensibly than does the current system.

Given the wide array of legislation enacted by different states during the past twenty years, Weiler's package would have quite different meanings from state to state. For example, in those states that have already reversed the collateral sources rule and capped pain and suffering awards, or capped total awards (pp. 31–32), the total cost of the system to defendants might actually go up under Weiler's plan. By contrast, in a regime still embodying the basic common law rules, Weiler's package should reduce overall costs to defendants, as well as significantly altering who gets what.

Creating more predictability in awards by imposing a threshold on, and precluding extravagant awards for, pain and suffering is likely to lead to somewhat reduced administrative costs and to the elimination of a fair number of weak, modest-injury liability cases. On the other hand, there is little reason to think that this sort of package will either end the payment of invalid claims where there are serious injuries but no malpractice, or increase legitimate serious injury malpractice claims. And, of course, this package does not broaden coverage to seriously injured victims of adverse events in the absence of malpractice.

In sum, Weiler's package deserves support because, although it would not likely have a dramatic impact on malpractice insurance premiums, it would distribute money among plaintiffs in what I consider to be a far more socially desirable way than does the current system and is not easily labeled pro-plaintiff or pro-defendant.[23]

E. A Further Idea—Organizational Liability

Although it appears elsewhere in his book, Weiler recommends yet another change that I think should be included as part of his track one reform. He calls it "organizational liability" (pp. 122–32). Breathtakingly simple, and exceedingly inventive, organizational liability means that, for injuries incurred inside health care institutions, mainly hospitals, the institution—not the physician—would be liable for the physician's malpractice. Victims could not sue their surgeons or anesthesiologists, for example, but could sue the hospital instead. The proposal would treat doctors as employees of hospitals, even when they are, for other legal purposes, only independent contractors.

The direct consequences of organizational liability would be that doctors could no longer be named as individual defendants, except in cases concerning malpractice they might commit in their offices, and they would no longer purchase individual malpractice insurance to cover torts they commit in hospitals. As Weiler explains, this reform would largely conform medical practice to the prevailing situation in health maintenance organizations, some university and public hospitals, and other settings where the doctors are in fact employees of the institution and do not buy their own malpractice insurance (pp. 124–25).

While doctors in those other settings today may actually be named as defendants, everyone involved soon appreciates that any damage or settlement awards will be paid by the employer or its insurer.

Thus, although the formal common law rule is that employers who are held vicariously liable for the torts of their employees have a right of indemnity from their employees, this right simply is not asserted against negligent employees who impose costs on the organization. The upshot, as Weiler notes, is that doctors would basically be treated the way airline pilots are in cases arising out of plane crashes (p. 125). Pilots are not expected to carry individual insurance and, whatever the technical legal rights of their employer airlines, airlines simply do not seek indemnity from negligent pilots.

I agree with Weiler that two strong advantages of organizational liability would be that: (1) hospitals could better build medical malpractice costs into the overall cost of patient care than could doctors (p. 127), and (2) physicians would no longer labor under the fear of an individual judgment against them that they perceive to be unjust (p. 131).[24] For those reasons, I applaud and support this recommendation.

Weiler's own main reservation about his proposal concerns whether it might lead to more careless conduct by doctors (p. 129). But he concludes that, to the contrary, organizational liability should actually lead to fewer patient injuries as compared with the current rule (pp. 129–31). Weiler is keenly aware that, although airline pilots don't individually pay tort damages when their carelessness brings about passenger harm, airline liability, at least in theory, translates into the retraining, discipline, or even firing of negligent employees. Likewise, he envisions that hospitals would respond to the threatened imposition of organizational liability with new and more effective behavioral controls over their physicians. As a result, in Weiler's view, organizational liability would also prove beneficial in preventing accidents.

I am skeptical about these projected safety gains; at the same time, I am not worried that organizational liability would lead to more patient injuries. But I want to reserve my discussion of the question until I take up Weiler's track two no-fault reform proposal, which also contains organizational liability as a component and depends importantly for its intellectual justification upon the same alleged safety-promoting features.

III. Track Two Reforms: Toward a No-Fault System for Medical Accidents

A. The Plan

Most exciting of Weiler's recommendations is his call for a no- fault compensation scheme covering all seriously injured victims of medical treatment. Although he admits that he has not yet worked out the full details of his proposal, its main features are clear. Any hospital patient injured by medical treatment who is disabled for six months or more would be entitled to compensation from the hospital, regardless of fault (p. 136). That compensation would cover economic losses (such as lost income, lost household production, and medical and rehabilitation expenses) not otherwise covered through broad-based social and first party insurance schemes (id). It would also include modest payments for non-economic loss to the severely and permanently disabled, based upon a schedule that takes into account the victim's age at the time of injury and the nature of the impairment (p. 135).

Weiler is not the first to recommend a no-fault approach to medical accidents. O'Connell proposed an "elective" no-fault remedy for malpractice problems nearly twenty years ago.[25] Professors Clark Havighurst and Laurence Tancredi, separately and together, have been promoting various medical no-fault plans for just as long.[26] Weiler's analysis, however, is the first to claim that it is both affordable and administratively feasible for no-fault to cover the full range of patient harms from medical treatment, provided that coverage is restricted to the most seriously injured.

Previously, it was generally believed (or feared) that it would too often be too hard or too expensive to tell whether medical treatment caused the injury. After all, many people leave the hospital worse off than when they entered, not because of something done to them by their doctor or by hospital employees, but because their ailment has simply taken a turn for the worse. None of the advocates of medical no-fault plans believes that a no-fault program should cover those situations. People who die or decline from the disease or condition from which they suffer on entry are not the responsibility of the medical establishment. No-fault is meant to pay only for those patients the system accidentally harms, whether through malpractice or not. In addition to the causation problem, it has been feared that it would be much more expensive than in the current system to compensate all patients who are accidentally injured in the course of medical treatment.

Faced with these causal and fiscal conundrums, medical no-fault advocates have tended to favor creating a list of typical injuries that are generally caused by medical accidents and have reasonably well understood financial consequences. The no-fault plan would then cover only those things on the list (often called the "designated compensatory events"). This list might be generated legislatively to cover all hospitals, or it might be the product of decentralized market transactions in which individual hospitals and patients contractually agree that the no-fault plan and not malpractice law would cover specified injuries.

Weiler argues, however, that the Harvard study reveals two startling facts that go against the conventional wisdom. First, determining whether a patient is suffering from a medical accident or not was, in the Harvard study, not so difficult after all. Based upon expert reviews of medical files, only five percent of the cases were "close calls" (p. 144). So, while there will be hard cases, those situations evidently do not arise very often. Second, even though nearly fifty times as many patients suffer from medical accidents as recover on malpractice claims (p. 134), restricting the no-fault plan to the less than one-fourth of those victims who are seriously injured and then compensating them only for their net losses appears to make the scheme affordable (pp. 135–36).

Notice that this "same-cost" assertion assumes that the no-fault plan would substitute completely for the tort system, at least for injuries suffered in a hospital. The implication, then, is that Weiler's track one proposals are best seen as first step reforms of the traditional system.

It remains to be seen whether the ease of administration and affordable cost conclusions would stand up in practice, and the Harvard study has already run into criticism along these lines.[27] But I believe that Weiler has made a strong enough showing of his proposal's potential practicality that the proposal plainly deserves the more careful study and evaluation that Weiler seeks.

B. The Likely Impact of Weiler's No-Fault Plan

In order to decide what difference Weiler's no-fault plan would make, we must compare it to something. The most important comparison, I believe, is to the malpractice system altered by Weiler's track one reforms discussed above.

Consider, first, the seriously injured who would otherwise have valid malpractice claims. Because track one reforms would already restrict them to net economic losses and curtail payments for pain and suffering, in most cases their benefit package would not be terribly different under the no-fault plan. First, hospitals would be liable for pretty much the same net out-of-pocket losses under both schemes. To be sure, Weiler's no-fault plan would restrict lost wages to no more than 150 percent of the state average wage (p. 137), so that the relatively few no-fault claimants who earn more would be denied full recovery if they had failed to arrange for disability or life insurance on their own. But, of course, those higher earners are exactly the people who are most likely to have such private first party protection anyway.

In addition, the no-fault plan would probably cut back pain and suffering awards even further. Weiler doesn't acknowledge this directly, but the language he uses in describing those benefits (p. 135) and the workers' compensation analogy he draws upon (p. 132) suggest that would be the case. Whether this result would lower claimant recoveries to the range I have proposed for tort law, or even lower, remains to be seen.

In return for these reductions, claimants would be spared the burden of having to prove malpractice. Assuming the Harvard Study's findings about the eligibility determination under no-fault hold up, recovery would become enormously easier for those who now eventually show enough evidence of malpractice to win a settlement or verdict.

And, of course, no-fault would bring in a large new group of previously uncompensated claimants who suffer from adverse events not caused by malpractice. Unfortunately, Weiler does not make clear just how many new beneficiaries we are talking about, but it has to be many times the number who are currently compensated for serious injury caused by malpractice.

Most seriously disabled, elderly victims of medical accidents, now covered by Medicare and Social Security, would likely be eligible for little more than the no-fault plan's pain and suffering payment, because their uncovered economic losses are likely to be small. Some, however, would exhaust their Medicare coverage, or have special needs that no-fault, but not Medicare, would cover, and would substantially benefit from the plan. Most middle and professional class people with steady jobs would be largely restricted to recovering the pain and suffering component, because other insurance would already cover most of their economic losses. However, some people in those groups do not have adequate health insurance, rehabilitation coverage, or disability income protection, and could benefit considerably. If a member of one of these groups were killed in a medical accident, her heirs might qualify for substantial income replacement benefits under the plan, depending on the extent to which the plan allows duplication of the victim's own pension and life insurance benefits.

The plan would be of the most help to those people currently without much first party insurance protection. These individuals typically include homemakers, children and older students, the temporarily unemployed, and modest earners employed in the secondary labor force or by small employers without good employee benefit plans. As Weiler notes, income replacement is especially important, since, as the Harvard study found, insurance typically protects only a small portion of lost earnings (pp. 136–37).

By paying only after other basic compensation sources have been expended, Weiler's no-fault medical accident plan would be far better aimed at real need than are existing auto no-fault and workers' compensation schemes. Simplifying somewhat, those schemes, like the traditional tort system, are primary in the sense that if they and some type of first party insurance both cover the same loss, the loss falls on the compensation plan and not the insurance. By contrast, just as Weiler wants reformed malpractice law (in his track one reform) to pay only after "collateral sources" do, he also wants the medical no-fault plan to pay last.

C. How the Money Is Redirected

How are all those extra no-fault claims to be funded? There are three major sources of money. One portion would come from money saved as a result of lowered recoveries by those who are covered-lowered both from what Weiler's reformed malpractice system would pay and from what the current tort system pays.

The second major source of funds would be reduced costs of claims processing. Weiler believes that, instead of society spending more than fifty percent of the malpractice premium dollar on administration as is done today, the no-fault plan would reduce spending to fifteen to twenty percent on claims administration, more like what is spent in workers' compensation (pp. 139, 229 n. 38). This savings is to be achieved by employing an administrative compensation mechanism something like that which Social Security now uses in determining eligibility for disability benefits. Here Weiler writes somewhat approvingly of a recent proposal of the American Medical Association to shift medical malpractice claims to an expert administrative model and away from the current judicial model (pp. 114–22).[28] But for Weiler the AMA proposal is much too timid, as it would retain the basic fault criteria as the entry point into the system (pp. 117–18). Still, Weiler likes the AMA's idea of using specially trained hearing officers to decide doubtful cases (pp. 115–16). In any event, the aspiration is that the administrative model would drastically reduce the use and cost of lawyers on both sides. Weiler is quite aware that workers' compensation in America has not eliminated claimants' lawyers; on the other hand, their compensation is typically a far lower share of the recovery than that paid in tort suits. So, whether compared with legal fees paid for by both sides (as today) or by defendants (as under Weiler's track one reforms), the legal fees under the no-fault plan are meant to be considerably less.

The third main source of funds to cover new claimants under the no-fault plan would come from ·the elimination of malpractice claims by those without serious injuries (p. 136). Of course, many of those victims are *de facto* closed out of the current system because the costs of pursuing their cases, given the prospective recovery, make lawyers unwilling to take them. Even the payment of plaintiffs' legal fees by defendants under Weiler's reformed tort law is not likely to cause many more claims to be filed. The AMA's plan, by contrast, seeks to bring these lesser-injured victims into the system, by providing a lawyer for any claimant with a bona fide claim. Weiler's no-fault plan, however, not only excludes all the smaller-injury victims from coverage in the no-fault scheme, but also seemingly would deny them their tort rights. Weiler first disavows a position on the "exclusivity" issue (p. 134), but then proceeds on a "same cost" assumption (p. 135) which requires exclusivity if all the costs are to be used up by no-fault.

Weiler's approach to medical no-fault sharply departs from the American automobile no-fault practice. There, a few states like Michigan and New York aside, the plan is aimed almost entirely at small-injury cases, not the seriously injured. Automobile no-fault benefits are available with little or no deductible and no requirement of serious harm, and they have very low caps, such as $10,000. The seriously hurt are left to try their luck with tort law.[29] Weiler's medical no-fault is concentrated on the seriously injured. To keep costs under control, the plan would deny a tort remedy to anyone injured by a medical accident in a hospital.

I would be far more content to exclude those not seriously injured by medical accidents from both the tort and the medical no-fault plan were we to have a stronger social safety net for all Americans who are disabled for six months or less. That means reasonably assured first party health care benefits for lesser disabilities and well-designed, short term income replacement benefits. Having such programs in place, I believe, would also make Weiler's plan politically far more plausible.[30]

IV. Track Three Reforms: Broadening the Social Insurance Net and De-Coupling Prevention and Compensation

A. The Comprehensive Compensation Alternative

As are his track one reforms, Weiler's no-fault plan is hospital based—doctors would not be individually responsible for compensating hospital patients who suffer an accidental injury while under their care. As before, Weiler's justification is that imposing the costs on sophisticated organizations like hospitals will promote safer and more cost-effective medical practice.

Otherwise, Weiler would surely agree that there is no principled basis for advantageously singling out victims of medical accidents for compensation. After all, once fault is abandoned as the criterion, one cannot very forcefully argue that someone who is injured through the course of medical treatment has a greater entitlement to receiving compensation for his or her losses than does one who suffers losses directly from illness or birth defect, or by an accident occurring outside of the hospital.

Indeed, because I believe that all Americans suffering from disabilities of virtually every cause should have access to a program that takes reasonable care of their medical and related expenses and reasonably replaces their lost wages, I much prefer a comprehensive compensation solution that does not distinguish among medical accidents, auto accidents, product injuries, work accidents and the like. For me, such a solution would rely upon a broadened Social Security system and increased mandatory employee benefits.[31]

B. Do We Need Medical No-fault for Accident Prevention?

But what of the claim that we need focused plans, such as Weiler's medical no-fault scheme, in order to force those who are in a position to reduce accidents to internalize costs so that the accident rate will decline? There are two responses to this claim.

The first retort was given by Professor Marc Franklin more than twenty years ago and reiterated by Professor Richard Pierce more than ten years ago.[32] As they pointed out, it is quite possible to imagine a comprehensive compensation scheme that makes no distinctions among causes of harm on the benefits side, but which is funded by contributions that vary with the number and severity of accidents caused by the scheme's funding sources, which, of course, could include hospitals.

The second retort frontally challenges the prevention claim. A reduction of medical accidents is better promoted through behavioral control mechanisms that do not depend upon the hospital having a financial interest in paying out lower no-fault benefits or making lesser contributions to the compensation fund.[33]

For one thing, organizational no-fault liability also gives hospitals socially perverse incentives. For example, as is the case of employers under the existing workers' compensation scheme, hospitals will have a strong financial reason to fight claims by arguing that the claimant's injury was really caused by the condition that brought the patient to the hospital, and there will be pressure to organize the information collected at the hospital to lead to this conclusion. Hospitals are also likely to find it financially attractive to turn away patients whose health profiles make them most at risk of medical accidents, and to discourage or forbid the performance of medical treatment that most risks medical accidents—even when serving the patient and performing the riskier treatment are the socially desirable behaviors.

On the other hand, hospitals already have considerable incentives to police the conduct of independent contractor physicians, quite apart from any fear that courts might manipulate existing tort doctrine to hold them legally liable for the malpractice of doctors working there. First, a hospital does not want to gain the reputation that its patients are more commonly victims of malpractice than patients elsewhere. Second, hospital administrators and boards are concerned about the care received by patients they tend; although hospital managers may increasingly think of themselves as running businesses, surely there is still a strong self-imposed moral commitment to good medical care. Anyway, to the extent that business considerations do dominate, I believe that the changes brought about by recent health care cost containment pressures also give hospitals an incentive to get their doctors to do it right the first time. Now if the doctor fouls up and the patient has to stay longer for more treatment, this longer stay may well not be paid for by the private or public insurer standing behind the patient.

This does not mean that all or even most hospitals today adequately supervise doctors practicing there, require retraining for doctors who need it, or deny privileges to incompetent physicians when that drastic solution is warranted. But many of the barriers to such actions would remain under Weiler's no-fault plan, or, alternatively, might be removed quite apart from his plan. For example,

Weiler explains that the fear in the health care profession that a disciplined health professional will invoke antitrust laws may help explain some of the reluctance by hospitals to act more aggressively in policing those professionals (pp. 111–12).

The Harvard Study sought to develop and analyze new evidence on the impact of tort law on physician behavior through an econometric study that relied on the fact that the likelihood of being sued for malpractice varies considerably from place to place within New York state. For reasons not worth trying to detail here, I am skeptical about this aspect of the Harvard study. Perhaps more importantly, Weiler himself expresses grave misgivings about whether the study really proves that malpractice law actually causes better medical care. Still, he does assert that it is his "judgment" that malpractice law has a "modest . . . preventive effect" (p. 90).

Yet, if Weiler were right, we should expect to see lower malpractice rates in hospitals that are part of health maintenance organizations, other things being equal, as compared with hospitals in which independent physicians practice. After all, for the current malpractice system, HMOs face organizational liability of the sort Weiler is advocating. But I have seen nothing from the Harvard study or other research that demonstrates that HMOs or other hospitals with employee-physicians in fact do respond with the greater accident prevention efforts that Weiler's simple economic model predicts. An important part of the explanation for this lack of response, I believe, is the very point that Weiler himself emphasizes: a large amount of malpractice actually involves slips of the hand or momentary inattention that are extremely difficult to avoid (p. 129).[34]

Moreover, Weiler himself points to new developments on the regulatory front that hold considerable promise in terms of medical accident reduction quite apart from any cost internalizing strategy. Simply put, state medical boards are probably better advised to spend more of their resources on requiring hospital risk management and physician peer review rather than directly investigating and prosecuting doctors themselves (pp. 110–11).

To be sure, these boards may not currently have sufficient resources available to them to carry out their regulatory functions as effectively as we might like. But it would surely seem right to redirect toward regulatory enforcement some of the money that could be saved by eliminating the administrative costs of determining causation, as would occur were a comprehensive accident or disability compensation plan substituted for medical no-fault and other focused plans.

C. Medical No-fault as a Step

Nevertheless, I can support Weiler's medical no-fault plan, not as the best long-range solution, but instead as a step toward a more comprehensive system for compensating the seriously disabled. Taking political reality into account, we would expect to achieve Weiler's track one reforms sooner than his medical no-fault reform. Indeed, medical no-fault might be preliminarily tried on an elective basis or in a few experimental states, as Weiler suggests, before being applied universally (p. 151).

If, however, concurrent with the track one reforms an expanded temporary disability insurance scheme were adopted and combined with a strong national health insurance system, then people would realize that neither tort law, nor workers' compensation, nor auto no-fault or other no-fault plans such as Weiler's would need concern themselves with other than the most seriously injured.

Perhaps in the next stage, then, we might enact a series of such schemes focusing on the seriously injured—say, for victims of medical accidents, airplane accidents, prescription drug and vaccine side-effects, organized recreational sporting accidents and the like, as well as auto and workplace accidents. At that point, however, rather than continuing to add plans covering more and more specified groups, many might conclude that it would be wiser to consolidate this proliferation of schemes into a single compensation plan.

Whether we should define that overall plan in terms of accidents as New Zealand has,[35] or even more broadly in terms of the seriously disabled generally, as I have proposed, could then be debated. By then we should also know more about whether organizational no-fault liability for medical accidents had indeed contributed to patient safety (as Weiler predicts), in which case the funding of the comprehensive plan might well wish to target those hospitals experiencing relatively more accidents for larger contributions toward the funding of the comprehensive plan. Or, if, as I anticipate, we conclude (as New Zealand has so far) that fine tuning on the pay-in side is not really worthwhile, then the comprehensive plan would likely be funded by much broader-based revenue sources.

In sum, viewing both Weiler's track one and track two proposals as steps rather than ends, I find them highly attractive, and, as such, I very much hope that the prescriptions offered in *Medical Malpractice on Trial* gain the support they deserve.

ENDNOTES

1. Paul C. Weiler, Medical Malpractice on Trial (1991). All parenthetical page numbers in the text and footnotes refer to this text.

2. Reporters' Study of Enterprise Liability for Personal Injury (1991) (*"Reporters' Study"*).

3. Harvard Medical Practice Study Group, Patients, Doctors, and Lawyers: Medical Injury, Malpractice Litigation, and Patient Compensation in New York (1990) (*"Harvard Study"*).

4. In the Harvard Study, a hospital occurrence counted as an adverse event if it prolonged the patient's stay in the hospital by at least one day or caused the patient's death (p. 13).

5. Torts are also committed in doctors' offices—13% of malpractice claims arise out of conduct in doctors' offices as compared with 81% from hospitalizations and the rest from other locations such as nursing homes (pp. 225–26 n. 18). We know a lot less, however, about how often torts occur outside of hospitals and hence less about the proportion of those so injured who actually claim and recover.

6. Harvard Study at 6-21, table 6.5 (*supra* note 3).

7. *Id.* at 6-25, table 6.5.

8. I define the seriously disabled category more broadly than Weiler does. Weiler mentions 30,000 seriously disabled people (p. 12), but based on the report of the Harvard Study Group this figure must refer to people in the most severe disability category. The Harvard Study found that 9% of those suffering adverse events were disabled for more than six months and 14% died. Harvard Study at 6-1 (*supra* note 3). Between 2% and 3% were permanently disabled with a disability rating of more than 50%. *Id.* at 6-21, table 6.5. This puts the number killed in excess of 150,000, the number disabled for more than six months in the range of 150,000, and those in the most seriously disabled category at about 40,000 annually. Weiler notes that those not able to return to work within six months approached a quarter, numbering around 375,000, of the total annual number of adverse events (p. 136).

9. See James S. Kakalik and Nicholas M. Pace, Costs and Compensation Paid in Tort Litigation (1986).

10. O'Connell's proposed trades came in two sequential proposals that I have combined into a single recommendation for the purposes of this review. See Jeffrey O'Connell, *A Proposal to Abolish Contributory and Comparative Fault, with Compensatory Savings by Also Abolishing the Collateral Source Rule,* U. Ill. L. F. 591 (1979); Jeffrey O'Connell, *A Proposal to Abolish Defendants' Payment for Pain and Suffering in Return for Payment of Claimants' Attorneys' Fees,* U. Ill. L. Rev. 333 (1981); Stephen D. Sugarman, Doing Away With Personal Injury Law 167 (1989); and Stephen D. Sugarman, *Serious Tort Law Reform,* 24 San Diego L. Rev. 795 (1987).

Apart from issues discussed in the text, O'Connell and I both proposed that, as part of the trade, plaintiffs should gain an additional advantage through the elimination of the defense of plaintiff fault. Victim fault would constitute neither a complete bar to recovery, as in the common law regime, nor grounds for a reduced recovery, as is the case under modern comparative fault systems now in place in most states. Weiler does not include this change in his package. Of course, in medical malpractice cases, plaintiff fault is rarely an issue anyway, so this difference among us has little consequence in the malpractice context.

I would also have plaintiffs give up some access to punitive damages by making their availability and amount a matter for the judge, rather than the jury, to decide. This rule would bring punitive damages law in personal injury cases closer to the practice in civil rights law where a judge will often award large attorneys' fees in class action cases which expose and bring to justice especially bad conduct by the defendants. Weiler does not address the issue of punitive damages in his book, perhaps for the sensible reason that it has played relatively little role in the medical malpractice field. The Reporters' Study calls for restraints on the award of punitive damages. Reporters' Study at 231–65 (*supra* note 2).

11. More attention is given to the details of reversing the collateral sources rule in 2 Reporters' Study at 161–82 (*supra* note 2).

12. O'Connell, U. Ill. L. Rev. at 341 (1981) (*supra* note 10).

13. O'Connell's fallback position is less restrictive than mine. Were the legislature not to abolish pain and suffering awards altogether, his alternative statutory language would impose a threshold similar to mine, but no ceiling. *Id.* at 350.

14. But, of course, English personal injury cases generally do not use juries.

15. MD Cts. & Jud. Pro. Code Ann. § 11-108 (1989); NH Rev. Stat. Ann. § 508:4-d (Equity, Supp. 1990).

16. Cal. Civil Code § 3333.2 (West, Supp. 1991).

17. This percentage schedule is based on the California rule now in place that limits how much the plaintiff's lawyer may take out of the plaintiff's award. Cal. Bus. & Prof .Code. § 6146 (West, Supp. 1990).

18. O'Connell, U. Del. L. Rev. (1981) at 352 (*supra* note 10).

19. He also proposes several nice additional wrinkles to deal with both baseless suits and frivolous defenses, as well as unreasonable unwillingness by either side to settle during the process once an offer is made (p. 68).

20. For some insight into the process, see the story of Chicago's Philip Corboy, one of America's best-known malpractice lawyers, in John A. Jenkins, The Litigators, 315–70 (1989).

21. By contrast, in the present situation, one could argue that since what the claimant will get is such a crap shoot, the lawyer might justifiably claim an even larger share the more he or she is able to obtain through negotiation and/or jury skills. Of course, to admit this reality is largely to abandon the claim that the current system delivers individual justice and therefore may make it difficult for plaintiffs' attorneys as a class (staunch defenders of the system on "justice" grounds) to ask for more the more they win.

22. For the general views of the Reagan Administration on tort law reform, see US Attorney General, Tort Policy Working Group, Report on the Causes, Extent and Implications of the Current Crisis in Insurance Availability and Affordability (1986) (criticized in Sugarman, Doing Away at 78–82 (*supra* note 10)). For Reagan Administration proposals aimed specifically at medical malpractice, see Department of Health and Human Services, Report of the Task Force on Medical Liability and Malpractice (Aug. 1987). The views of the Bush

Administration are contained in S 1123, 102d Cong., 1st Sess. (Apr 25, 1991), in 137 *Cong. Rec.* S 6357 (May 22, 1991). A competing malpractice reform bill now before Congress is S 1232, 102d Cong., 1st Sess. (Jun 3, 1991), in 137 *Cong. Rec.* S 7307 (Jun 6, 1991) which emphasizes binding arbitration of malpractice claims. This bill is discussed in Clark C. Havighurst and Thomas B. Metzloff, *S.1232—A Late Entry in the Race for Malpractice Reform,* 54 L. & CONTEMP. PROBS. 179 (1991). For yet another approach, see The Health Care Injury Compensation and Quality Improvement Act of 1991, introduced by Senator Durenberger in October, 1991.

23. Subject to the reservations I have already noted as to some of the details.

24. Of course, malpractice litigation would still focus on whether the doctor acted carelessly.

25. Jeffrey O'Connell, *Expanding No-Fault Beyond Auto Insurance: Some Proposals,* 59 VA. L. REV. 749 (1973).

26. Clark C. Havighurst and Laurence R. Tancredi, *"Medical Adversity Insurance"—A No-Fault Approach to Medical Malpractice and Quality Assurance,* 51 MILBANK MEM. FUND Q. 125 (1973).

27. *See* MAXWELL J. MEHLMAN, THE HARVARD NO-FAULT PROJECT: A CRITIQUE (1989); Daniel Kramer, *The Harvard Study, An Analysis,* N.Y. L. J. 1 (Mar 9, 1990).

28. REPORT OF THE AMERICAN MEDICAL ASSOCIATION/SPECIALTY SOCIETY MEDICAL LIABILITY PROJECT, A PROPOSED ALTERNATIVE TO THE CIVIL JUSTICE SYSTEM FOR RESOLVING MEDICAL LIABILITY DISPUTES: A FAULT-BASED, ADMINISTRATIVE SYSTEM (1988). For wide-ranging analysis of the AMA proposal, see *Symposium: Taking Medical Malpractice Out of the Courts,* 1 CTS., HEALTH SCI. & L. 3 (1990).

29. DEPARTMENT OF TRANSPORTATION, COMPENSATING AUTO VICTIMS (May 1985).

30. For discussions of solutions to the short-term income replacement need, *see* SUGARMAN, DOING AWAY at 135–36 and 169–72 (*supra* note 10); Sugarman, 24 SAN DIEGO L. REV. at 808–15 (*supra* note 10); and Stephen D. Sugarman, *Short-Term Paid Leave: A New Approach to Social Insurance and Employee Benefits,* 75 CAL. L. REV. 465 (1987).

31. SUGARMAN, DOING AWAY at 127–52 (*supra* note 10).

32. *See* Marc A. Franklin, *Replacing the Negligence Lottery: Compensation and Selective Reimbursement,* 53 VA. L. REV. 774 (1967); Richard J. Pierce, Jr., *Encouraging Safety: The Limits of Tort Law and Government Regulation,* 33 VAND. L. REV. 1281 (1980).

33. For my general arguments against tort law as an effective deterrent, *see* SUGARMAN, DOING AWAY at 3–34 (*supra* note 10).

34. For very recent analyses of the impact of medical malpractice law on the promotion of safety and the slowing of innovation, see the following essays in THE LIABILITY MAZE (Peter W. Huber and Robert E. Litan, eds., 1991): Gary T. Schwartz, *Product Liability and Medical Malpractice in Comparative Context* 28; Stanley Joel Reiser, *Malpractice, Patient Safety, and the Ethical and Scientific Foundations of Medicine* 227; and Laurence Tancredi and Dorothy Nelkin, *Medical Malpractice and Its Effect on Innovation* 251.

35. For discussions and evaluations of the New Zealand plan, *see* TERENCE G. ISON, ACCIDENT COMPENSATION

(1980), and GEOFFREY PALMER, COMPENSATION FOR INCAPACITY (1979).

Postscript

In 2005 Professor Tom Baker published "**The Medical Malpractice Myth**" (University of Chicago Press), a response to those like Professor Weiler who have been long-complaining about the way tort law deals with medical accidents. As Professor Baker points out, defendant doctors win a super-majority of medical malpractice trials – as if to rebuke physicians for complaining about how they are treated by the legal system. But doctors may well read this data differently: to them, it might well feel as though they are constantly being victimized by unjustified lawsuits with their reputation as physicians put at risk by lawyers pursuing groundless claims on behalf of clients who face no legal expenses if they lose.

Professor Baker believes that the malpractice system makes fewer errors than suggested by Professor Weiler's study, a conclusion that is supported by later analysis. Yet, it still seems the case that the share of medical malpractice claims that are mistakenly handled (i.e., true victims of negligence who are not compensated plus those who are compensated but were not malpractice victims) remains higher than the rate at which the medical system errors in its treatment of patients (as argued in this chapter).

To be sure, the error rate in the medical system itself is at a socially unacceptably high level. A series of recent studies show that at least 100,000 people die each year because of errors that happen in U.S. hospitals. A large share of these errors are not committed by doctors but by other hospital employees (e.g. nurses and other staff), and one should not assume that everything that is counted as an "error" is also an example of "malpractice." Nonetheless, there is widespread agreement in the "patient safety" movement that hospitals and their medical staffs can and must do a much better job. For a fuller discussion of this matter, see Stephen D. Sugarman, "Outcome-Based Regulatory Strategies for Promoting Greater Patient Safety" 15 Theoretical Inquiries in Law 573 (2014). http://www.law.berkeley.edu/sugarman.

This high hospital-based error rate helps Professor Baker to drive home the point that it continues to be true that only a very small share of victims of medical malpractice actually sue – a finding emphasized earlier in this chapter as well. To him, this suggests that what society needs is more malpractice litigation, rather than less. Regardless of how one thinks about that claim, a different take-away is that our existing medical malpractice system utterly fails as a device for broadly compensating victims of physician error.

The legal system's primary justification lies here in its claimed deterrence effect. While others are skeptical about that, Professor Baker believes that patent safety would be in an even worse state absent tort law.

One possible tort reform strategy would be to alter the rules governing "informed consent" cases. Today, doctors have an affirmative obligation to disclose to patients not only the risks associated with the treatment proposed but also the alternative treatments (and their risks) available to the patient. But, despite a few exceptional cases to the contrary, doctors are not required to disclose their own success rate and bad side effect rate as compared with others in their field. While obtaining reliable information on these issues could be quite difficult, sometimes it is fairly readily available, and surely, if provided, it could help patients make more informed choices as to who to seek as their treating doctor. And the competitive effect of such a required disclosure could put considerable pressure on doctors to achieve better results (as well, perhaps, as some perverse conduct on their part). This possible reform strategy is further discussed in Sugarman, "Outcome-Based Regulatory Strategies for Promoting Greater Patient Safety" noted above.

Chapter 11

Auto Accidents – Nader's Failures?

Travel by motor vehicle is getting safer. Part of the recent decline in highway fatalities appears to have been caused by a combination of the economic recession and the increase in price of fuel both of which contributed to less driving. But more importantly, cars are safer, roads are safer, and perhaps people are driving more safely. Nonetheless, although things are moving in the right direction, we have a long way to go. More than 30,000 Americans die on the roads each year from motor vehicle accidents, many of which involve drunk drivers.

Tort law clearly aims to promote highway safety by threatening to impose liability on careless drivers for harms they cause and on motor vehicle manufacturers for product defects that lead to accidents that should not have happened. But tort law clearly is not fully up to the task, and for a long time our society has employed other means as well. These include the threat of criminal penalties for careless driving and the creation of the National Highway Traffic Safety Administration (NHTSA), a federal agency focused centrally on getting vehicle makers to produce safer cars.

This chapter presents an essay about a book written by Professor Jerry Mashaw and David Harfst titled **The Struggle for Auto Safety**. The essay was published as Stephen D. Sugarman, "Nader's Failures?," 80 California Law Review 289-305 (1992) and is reprinted with the permission of the journal.

Mashaw and Harfst show that NHTSA had been far less effective than had been hoped in improving auto safety – as compared with the ambition that Ralph Nader (American's most prominent consumer advocate) had for the agency when he successfully pushed for its creation. Mashaw and Harfst argue that a well-designed auto no-fault plan might better promote the introduction of safer vehicles and hence improved highway safety.

This chapter presents an even more ambitious auto no-fault plan that would be primarily funded "at the pump." (This is a much fuller presentation of the pay-at-the-pump idea briefly mentioned at the end of Chapter 6 on the Quebec approach to auto no-fault compensation plans.) The disappointing record of NHTSA together with Nader's stalwart opposition to auto no-fault plans of any sort are the "failures" referred to in this chapter's title.

Nader's Failures?

Jerry L. Mashaw and David L. Harfst's The Struggle for Auto Safety is a fascinating case study that seeks to demonstrate that the National Highway Traffic Safety Administration (NHTSA) has failed in its effort to promote motor vehicle safety, to explain why, and to offer reforms. Created out of the National Traffic and Motor Vehicle Safety Act of 1966 (pp. 4-6), the NHTSA was, many would say, Ralph Nader's "baby." Although the causal antecedents to the 1966 Act were many, Nader's book, Unsafe at Any Speed,[1] and his celebrated foul treatment by General Motors[2] played a prominent role in making auto safety a national issue. Moreover, Nader's sidekick, Joan Claybrook, a colleague since the early days of his battles with the auto industry, served in the late seventies as NHTSA's chief administrator.

The Struggle for Auto Safety, however, is hardly homage to America's most celebrated consumer advocate. I do not mean that Mashaw and Harfst blame Nader and Claybrook for NHTSA's failures. Nor would this be particularly noteworthy, as Nader well documented his own dismay with NHTSA's early efforts in his 1972 edition of Unsafe at Any Speed.[3] Nevertheless, according to Mashaw and Harfst, NHTSA is a dud when judged by the goals that Nader and its other architects initially set.[4]

The Vision

The Struggle for Auto Safety is one of several substantial recent studies covering traffic safety.[5] None dissent from this simple vision behind the Motor Vehicle Safety Act: that auto makers, who concentrate more on styling and performance, have the capacity to design and manufacture safer cars, and that the new NHTSA would force them to do so. The "technology forcing" strategy was meant to achieve much more than merely compelling all new vehicles to contain the best safety features currently available. Rather, under the spur of NHTSA, the Big Three auto manufacturers and their foreign competitors would work to bring to the showroom floor new technologies that would slash the highway death toll (p. 5).

As vividly portrayed by Mashaw and Harfst, auto accidents were seen as a public health sore thumb. While so many other public health problems were being licked, American motorists were continuing to maim and kill each other at alarming rates (p. 50). And, as with many other earlier and successful public health campaigns, the solution lay not in changing the behavior of ordinary people (p. 65). Driver education and efforts to discourage (and punish) reckless driving and driving under the influence had their place but were not solving the problem (pp. 1-2). From an epidemiological perspective, to concentrate on "the nut behind the wheel"[6] was to overlook far more promising environmental design changes. These included highway design and, more importantly, vehicle design. If vehicles could be made more forgiving, then (1) crashes might be avoided in the first place and (2) the consequences of auto crashes might be far less lethal (pp. 63-64).

In the mid-sixties the greatest hope seemed to lie along the latter route. Scientists like William Haddon (who became NHTSA's first administrator) had emphasized that enormous safety gains were potentially realizable if more attention were given to the "second collision" (p. 4).[7] If the tremendous force of the initial impact could be distributed away from, instead of into, the vehicle occupants, then the car could become considerably more "crashworthy." Padded dashboards, head rests, stronger windshields and side doors, and energy-absorbing steering columns are all part of the story. Undoubtedly, 1992 cars are improved on these fronts as compared with 1965 models.

Yet, from the outset Haddon and others believed that even more striking gains could be achieved through effective occupant restraints (pp. 65, 84). By 1964, auto lap belts were already standard equipment on all American cars. However, lap belts alone were not as useful as one would have liked (preventing user ejection more effectively than they did impact with the vehicle's interior) and, far more momentous, usage rates were exceedingly low-under 20% (p. 85). An alternative was needed. Consonant with the public health perspective, the focus turned to "passive" restraints in autos that could curtail the safety advocate's dependence upon millions of individual decisions to buckle up. From the beginning, Haddon's preferred solution was the air bag.

Requiring auto manufacturers to install effective passive restraints would appear, it was felt, as the perfect example of an agency's ability to force technological innovations that ultimately benefitted society. Preliminary development of the air bag was already underway by the early sixties. Setting safety performance standards for occupant restraints would accelerate both that development and the incorporation of safety features into vehicle design far more than would have market pressures alone (pp. 84-85). Moreover, by setting performance standards rather than imposing detailed design requirements, NHTSA could unleash constructive competitiveness among the auto makers and their suppliers. The competitors would battle to produce the best air bag or perhaps a better alternative passive-restraint device such as an effective, automatic seat belt that occupants would not disengage (p. 84).

The Record

In various ways NHTSA tried to pursue this agenda. Two decades after Haddon took over as administrator, however, there was virtually nothing positive to show for the passive-restraint effort. This is the central failure on which Mashaw and Harfst rest their case.

In the early seventies NHTSA temporarily opted for a different solution-mandating that auto manufacturers install an interlock device by which a car supposedly could not be started if the seat belts were not fastened. This encountered enormous consumer resistance (and bypass strategies), however, and the NHTSA requirement was overturned by Congress.

As Mashaw and Harfst further explain, frustrated by a lack of support by the courts, Congress, and the public, NHTSA's focus in the seventies began to shift away from technology forcing and towards the recall of defective vehicles (pp.

147-71). During Claybrook's tenure (1977-1980) NHTSA was especially active on this front. Yet, according to Mashaw and Harfst, recalling defective cars has little or no impact on safety. This is not only because so many owners of recalled vehicles fail to bring them in for refitting but more pivotally because such a small proportion of accidents are caused by vehicles with defects of the sort that the recall scheme reaches and corrects.[8]

In very recent years a growing proportion of new cars has been equipped with motorized shoulder belts that occupants generally do not or cannot detach. Moreover, starting with 1992 auto models, air bags are increasingly becoming standard equipment (and a selling point in ad campaigns). No one can really say whether we would have reached the same results by now (or sooner) without NHTSA. Unfortunately, we do know that what we have in 1992 is less than NHTSA had initially hoped for in 1972.

The Explanation

Other reviewers already have described and critiqued Mashaw and Harfst's theoretical explanation of NHTSA's performance.[9] I will offer but a few comments along those lines. The authors assert that American "legal culture" accounts for both NHTSA's retreat from technology forcing and performance standards and its shift to the recall strategy (p. 19). To simplify, the courts were hostile to the former but supportive of the latter.

To be sure, several key judicial decisions in the early seventies were antagonistic to NHTSA's mandatory performance standards when the agency lacked data showing sensible targets that auto manufacturers could actually meet (pp. 87-104). Given its premises, it should not have been surprising that the technology-forcing approach failed to generate in advance the information the courts were demanding. Mashaw and Harfst are right that this created a mismatch between what the courts would permit and what Congress' attempt to delegate the implementation of this strategy for auto safety to NHTSA required.

The "legal culture" explanation is a highly complex one to prove, however. As one reviewer explained, the courts in recent years appear as deferential to agency decisions as NHTSA could now reasonably ask.[10] Another pointed out that during the same period reviewed by Mashaw and Harfst, the courts were increasingly supportive of product-liability suits that attacked the automobile and its crashworthiness.[11] Finally, as Professor Michael Trebilcock suggested, perhaps NHTSA's record is better understood as the result of its creators having expected too much from the public health orientation they embraced.[12] Put a bit differently, maybe America's general social and political culture provides a better explanation for NHTSA's record than does its legal culture. In the next few paragraphs I will explore this theme further.

Another Explanation

By 1968, perhaps somewhat influenced by early NHTSA requirements, new cars contained lap belts and shoulder belts. The latter were uncomfortable, and to put both in place motorists were required to buckle twice. Nevertheless, if everyone had used these devices, occupants would have been protected almost as well as they are by a combination of air bags and lap belts in 1992 models. The question is: Why did so many American drivers refuse to buckle up?

One answer is that even though nearly everyone knows someone who has been seriously harmed or killed in an auto accident, many people are just unwilling to believe that it will happen to them. Devaluing their own risk of injury or death to almost nothing (far below the true risk), they are loath to impose on themselves even very minor burdens in terms of comfort and convenience. This is the attitude that the passive- restraint solution sought to defeat (p. 3).

A quite different answer to why people do not voluntarily buckle up is that they are aware of the risk of not wearing seat belts and they like it. This perspective has prompted a substantial and controversial literature about risk-taking that is sharply at odds with the public health approach to auto safety.[13] The idea is that while antilock brakes (the current rage) are much safer in principle, in predicting the overall impact on safety you must also take human reactions into account. With better brakes, the theory runs, people will drive faster, take turns more sharply, follow more closely, and so on. As a result, it may tum out that apparently safer vehicles do not translate into increased road safety after all. Some empirical studies claim to have found just this result.[14]

The concept that because of offsetting risk-taking, safer cars do not reduce auto accidents has not gone unchallenged. In a very sophisticated study, Robert Crandall and his colleagues at the Brookings Institution found that auto safety improvements since 1966 have had a substantial positive impact on reducing the occupant death rate.[15] Although the study found that non-occupant deaths were higher than predicted, owing perhaps to somewhat increased risk-taking by drivers of safer cars, the net effect was decidedly favorable. In view of earlier studies with less positive outcomes, Crandall's group was rather surprised to find that death rates were 30% lower in 1981 than would have been estimated had there been no auto safety improvements after 1965.[16] Even using conservative estimates for the value of a life saved, they determined that auto safety improvements ordered during the period under review were well worth their costs.[17]

One intuitively appealing explanation for the Brookings findings is that while drivers might substantially reduce the effects of brake and steering improvements by driving more dangerously, they are less likely to minimize the effects of vehicle improvements with respect to second- collision risks.[18] Drivers probably respond to the risk of an accident rather than the harm they might suffer in an accident (the second collision). Possibly drivers do not realize the degree of risk reduction achieved by measures aimed at the second collision.[19] Whatever the underlying explanation, I endorse the view supported by the Brookings study that safer vehicles are indeed responsible for a share of reduced highway fatalities and serious injuries

Mashaw and Harfst are not necessarily wrong about NHTSA's accomplishments despite its failures in court and before Congress. The Brookings study did not prove either that safer cars are attributable to NHTSA's actions or that NHTSA is really capable (the legal culture aside) of imposing costly passive restraints on American society before it is otherwise ready to accept them.

Consider first how many of the safety improvements ordered by NHTSA the market would have achieved anyway. This is very difficult to determine. Crandall and his colleagues estimated that all the safety improvements mandated from 1966 through 1984 increased the cost of a 1984 car about $500 in terms of equipment and about $100 more in higher fuel costs over the lifetime of the car.[20] But the analysis does not address whether these changes (or any single one of them) would have been made absent NHTSA regulation because of, say, increased safety- consciousness in the public at large.

Auto makers in the mid-sixties apparently thought that safety did not sell. Still, by 1984 they might well have put $100 per car into head rests, padded dashboards, stronger windshields and side doors, and safer steering columns, the approximate cost of NHTSA-ordered improvements in those areas.[21] Who is to say?

Air bags, however, are another matter, and, by contrast, I find it not surprising that they did not quickly come into the market during NHTSA's early years. Air bags were talked about as costing perhaps $200 in 1972,[22] a very substantial expense as compared with all of the other safety features NHTSA has ordered.[23] But if the primary reason people have not voluntarily buckled up has been their refusal to believe they are at risk, it would have been difficult to get them voluntarily to spend a significant extra sum for protection they have not believed is needed (even though it is). As for those who are well aware of the second collision risk and who routinely buckle up, why should they have wanted to purchase air bags that probably would not have given them a great deal of additional protection?

The key point is that given this double-barreled market resistance to air bags, it is unclear that NHTSA could have imposed air bags on the public early on even absent the judicial hurdles that Mashaw and Harfst emphasize. Would most safety-oriented motorists really have supported a requirement that would have forced them to pay considerably more in order, primarily, to assure the protection of others who are foolhardy? The public might well have forced Congress to overturn the paternalism of mandatory air bags, as it did in the case of the interlock solution.

As noted above, by the mid-nineties a substantial portion of newer cars on the road will have air bags. More than a result of NHTSA's recent efforts, however, this development might be the product of a changed public outlook, a different social culture. These days Americans appear to be more risk averse than in the past. Indeed, many seem eager that enterprises be forced to take precautions that are not cost justified even when large values are assigned to a life saved.[24] Maybe this caution comes with the aging of the baby-boom generation. Possibly it arises out of broad concerns about runaway health-care costs that "we" have to pay when "they" foolishly injure themselves, or, more narrowly, from an increased vulnerability that people might feel in today's smaller and lighter cars. Perhaps cautious people now overestimate how much additional protection air bags will provide those using seat belts; and maybe they do not realize how much reduced protection occupants have by relying on air bags instead of seat belts.[25]

American states have never achieved the level of seat-belt usage attained in several other countries (reportedly as high as 90% in some places in Australia as compared with an overall average of something over 40% in the U.S.).[26] Nevertheless, after a slow start as compared with the rest of the world, most states have, since 1984, formally mandated seat-belt use and many seriously enforce the law. Roughly speaking, adopting a law mandating seat-belt use appears to increase usage about 20% and effective enforcement of the law another approximately 20%.[27] Increased usage clearly seems to have a significant positive safety effect.[28]

That more than 80% of Americans live in jurisdictions with mandatory use laws suggests a change in the political culture.[29] In the sixties when seat belts were first generally available, no states adopted laws requiring their use. Given the lessened urgency for air bags as seat- belt use escalates, the irony may just be that the way was finally cleared for air bags, both politically and in the market, only after more and more people were already using seat belts.[30]

The Reform(s)

Mashaw and Harfst nearly advocate NHTSA's abolition. Instead, they withdraw that proposal and suggest, without real enthusiasm, that auto makers be required to wait until later in the standard-setting and enforcement process before being allowed to attack NHTSA requirements in court (pp. 245-47).[31] Mashaw and Harfst then consider the role that product-liability lawsuits play or might play and, wisely I believe, reject that avenue as the panacea (pp. 235-41).[32]

Amid this general gloom about effective governmental promotion of auto safety, Mashaw and Harfst more enthusiastically suggest auto no-fault insurance as an alluring, alternate solution. They point out that under the conventional tort/liability insurance system, gains in occupant safety would be primarily captured in reduced third-party liability insurance because tortfeasors would do less harm and hence be liable for lower damages awards (pp. 241-45). But it is not logical to expect insurers to lower the costs of an individual motorist's liability insurance if he or she drives a car with air bags, for example, because the premium charged is based upon the risk of injuring others, not yourself.[33] In other words, auto insurance generally fails to work as an institutional mechanism that can demonstrate effective passive restraints pay for themselves in losses avoided.

It is true that in states with the traditional fault system, insurers routinely offer motorists the opportunity to buy, in addition to third- party liability coverage, first-party protection against the risk of incurring medical expenses as a result of an auto accident. Moreover, major insurance carriers today commonly offer premium discounts on the medical-payments coverage if the car is equipped with air bags or automatic seat belts. But medical-payments coverage is typically a trivial portion of the total auto-policy cost, so the discount in turn is exceedingly small.[34]

By contrast, in no-fault states the financial benefit of having effective passive restraints can be significant. Currently, the major insurers in such states appear to offer 10-30% discounts on first-party personal- injury-protection (PIP) coverage for cars with air bags or automatic seat belts.[35] The more comprehensive the no-fault plan, the more the PIP premium and, hence, the greater the dollar value of the discount. A nationwide comprehensive substitute of auto no-fault for the current fault system, Mashaw and Harfst argue, could maximize this advantage (p. 253). Car buyers would be able to see, in a vivid way, how much better-off financially they are with such self-protection devices. Indeed, the present value of the insurance discounts they will eventually receive could well more than pay for the cost of their air bags.[36]

Under the no-fault solution Mashaw and Harfst envision, not only would a much larger proportion of motorists voluntarily buy air bags and other occupant safety features as they are introduced but also economic justice would result. Those who choose to put themselves at risk and later, as a result, need medical care, income replacement, and the like would pay for those benefits in higher auto insurance premiums. Today, by contrast, people who have employment-based health insurance and temporary disability insurance, as well as Social Security and other broad public and private insurance protection, plainly do not pay for the greater likelihood that they will need to use those benefits if they drive cars that are less safe for occupants. Although Mashaw and Harfst see certain technical problems with the no-fault solution, the biggest obstacle they anticipate is political (pp. 244-45).

Politics aside, not all will agree with Mashaw and Harfst's analysis and proposal. For example, although Professor Trebilcock decidedly favors public policies that employ charges to promote socially efficient conduct,[37] he objects to the switch to auto no-fault. Acknowledging that this might helpfully promote investment in self-protection, he fears that it risks undercutting the existing stimulus to exercise care toward others.[38] A common belief is that once motorists have acted upon self-preservation instincts, felt moral obligations to others, and feared criminal prosecution, there is little room left for tort law to further promote careful driving.[39] Others, however, believe that the fear of higher liability-insurance rates is still effective at the margin.[40] Empirical studies on the question are terribly difficult to carry out, and those that have been published are contradictory in their findings.[41] Nonetheless, at least one study of Quebec's no-fault plan (charging all drivers a fiat premium regardless of their age or driving record) found that, holding other factors constant, the shift away from the fault system was actually correlated with worse driving.[42] It is this outcome that accounts for Trebilcock's qualms about Mashaw and Harfst's proposal. I believe that both Trebilcock's and Mashaw and Harfst's objectives can be served through the adoption of a plan I have previously described elsewhere.[43]

A Better Reform

I favor the creation at the state level of an Auto Accident Compensation Corporation (AACC). The AACC would pay generous no-fault benefits to all auto-accident victims. I have preliminarily estimated that in California the AACC would be able to fund the following package: (1) 85% of otherwise unreimbursed lost earnings up to $50,000 a year (twice California's average wage); (2) otherwise unreimbursed medical expenses up to $500,000; (3) other reasonably incurred expenses up to $75 a day in the short term, $35 a day later on; and (4) moderate amounts for pain and suffering for those who either are fully disabled for longer than six months or suffer a permanent and serious impairment or disfigurement. In return, auto-accident victims could not sue their injurers in court.

I will not concentrate now on the benefit side of the program because funding of the AACC is the primary concern here. There would be three sources of funding. The most important in terms of money raised would be a surcharge on fuel consumption in the range of $0.30 a gallon. This, incidentally, should have a socially desirable impact in reducing the amount of driving people do.[44]

The next funding source for the AACC would be a charge imposed on drivers based upon (a) their driving record and (b) their experience. As for the driving-record charges, three categories of drivers would be established. Those with the best records -- no more than one moving violation in the past three years -- would pay a modest surcharge when renewing their driving license after three years. This might be $60, or $20 per year. In California this would probably cover 80% of drivers.[45] Drivers without such good records would fall in the second category, paying approximately $120 a year along with being required to renew their license annually. This might cover another 15-18% of drivers. Finally, in the third category would be drivers with the worst records, fewer than 5% of motorists, who might have to pay into the AACC $500 annually. These charges would respond to Trebilcock's concern that eliminating the need to purchase experience-rated liability insurance might tempt some people to drive carelessly.[46]

To respond to Trebilcock's additional concern that elimination of the fault system (and its higher insurance premiums for teenagers) would bring too many novices onto the roads,[47] drivers would also face surcharges based upon their experience. The surcharge might be $600 for sixteen- and seventeen-year-olds and $300 for both eighteen- and nineteen-year-olds and other new adult drivers.

The AACC's third source of funds would be a charge connected to the ownership of a vehicle. On the annual registration of an auto the owner would pay a sum based upon the model's safety record. Given currently available data and competing methods of analysis, there is sure to be controversy over how to measure a car's safety, so that some politically acceptable compromise over the calculation of these charges will be required.

One approach is to create a rating system blending the results of federal-government crash tests and data gathered by the AACC from actual on-road experience. One shortcoming of the crash-test data is that they are based upon experiments and not real-world situations. Another is that they only attempt to measure the danger of a head-on collision for vehicles in the same weight class.[48] Crash-test results are based upon crashing the car into a fixed barrier, which is equivalent to crashing it into an identical vehicle at the same speed. But, of course, a large proportion of real crashes occur through rollovers, through a single vehicle crashing into an object that at least partially gives way, and through the crash of two vehicles other than head-on and/or of sharply differing weights.[49]

Other things being equal, lighter cars are more dangerous to their occupants in a crash than are heavier cars. It makes good sense to appreciate that you are more at risk in a well-rated light car than in an equally well-rated heavy one. On the other hand, from the overall societal safety viewpoint, other things being equal, heavier cars are more dangerous to non-occupants than are lighter ones. Work by Leonard Evans showed that the danger to others caused by vehicles being heavier is more than offset by safety gains to the driver and occupants of heavier vehicles and that this holds true even taking into account that drivers of heavier cars are more likely to be involved in crashes than are drivers of lighter cars.[50] Perhaps this is because high-performance vehicles tend to be heavier and are driven more carelessly. In any case, from this perspective it would not be fair to ask owners of heavier cars to pay as much as owners of lighter cars with the same crash-test rating. Indeed, my conversation with Evans suggests that he would probably object to safety charges that are not solely, or at least largely, based upon the vehicle's mass. [51]

Unlike crash tests, on-road experience tells us about the actual performance of vehicles. Currently, widely disseminated data of this sort are compiled and analyzed by the Highway Loss Data Institute (HLDI), an affiliate of the Insurance Institute for Highway Safety.[52] But as just noted, those results are typically confounded by the fact that drivers of different types of cars might drive more carelessly. As an example, not long ago GM was advertising to a "new generation of Olds" drivers, emphasizing the sportiness of the new cars in this line. Assuming that Oldsmobile's have been traditionally driven by older and statistically safer drivers, and if the ad campaign were successful in attracting younger and statistically careless drivers, quite possibly Oldsmobile will show up as a more dangerous car on the HLDI statistics than it has in the past. The changes in the data would arise not because of any change in the car but because of its owners.[53]

At this point let me simply assume that the AACC would use the available data in a sensible manner and create, probably, three categories of vehicles. The first, or safest, category would include 15-20% of cars. Their owners might pay a charge of $40 a year. The second band would contain 60-70% of cars, and their owners would pay $80 a year. The remaining 10-20% of cars-the most dangerous ones-would be in the third band, and their owners would pay $120 (or possibly up to $200) a year.

New-car and commercial used-car sellers would have to post on the car's "sticker" the band in which the car falls. So long as insufficient data are available, a new model that is largely a continuation of a prior model would be placed in the same band as the prior year's model. If the new model were really a new design for which there is no experience or data, the model would simply be placed in the middle category.

In addition, a one-time safety fee, payable to the AACC, would be imposed on the purchase of a new car, against which credits would be allowed if the car has certain safety features. This information also would be posted on the "sticker." For example, the safety fee might start at $200, with a credit of $100 for air bags or automatic, motorized seat belts, and $50 for antilock brakes. These credits would be adjusted by the AACC for technology changes as new safety features come into the marketplace (side air bags, for example) and older features become more widespread.

This third AACC revenue source is intended to accomplish what Mashaw and Harfst seek through their advocacy of the no-fault solution. In addition to the actual financial incentives, putting the information on the "sticker" should help make safety more of a "talking point" in car sales.

I have made a preliminary estimate for California of the aggregate revenue that the AACC could expect to collect. It amounts to approximately $7.5 billion a year as shown below. This is roughly comparable to the amount of revenue now collected by California insurers on personal and commercial auto-insurance policies for liability insurance for bodily injury, medical payments, and uninsured-motorist protection for bodily injury.

ESTIMATED AACC REVENUES IN CALIFORNIA (1991 DATA AND DOLLARS)

Fuel surcharge:

$0.30 a gallon on 15 billion gallons $4.500 billion

Driving-license surcharge on just over 19 million drivers:

$ 20 on 15 million drivers	.300 billion
$120 on 4 million drivers	.480 billion
$500 on 200,000 drivers	.100 billion
	.880 billion

Annual vehicle registration surcharge on about 25 million vehicles:

$ 40 on 5 million vehicles	.200 billion
$ 80 on 15 million vehicles	1.200 billion
$120 on 5 million vehicles	.600 billion
	2.000 billion

New-car safety fees plus special surcharge on teen and other novice drivers:

Preliminary estimate	.120 billion
Grand total	$7.500 billion

A "typical" California motorist with a good driving record and a car of average safety who drives 13,000 miles a year and uses a gallon of gas for every twenty miles driven would pay just under $300 a year to the AACC from the three funding sources. This is certainly less than the typical California driver now pays for the insurance protection that would no longer be needed under the new plan.

I appreciate that there will be some objections to the idea of a government-run plan, even an independent AACC, on the ground that a public insurance monopoly is a recipe for trouble. Critics will point to possible administrative inefficiencies in implementing the program and the potential political inability of the AACC to differentiate among drivers and vehicles in the way that insurers do. But I believe that there are more than offsetting efficiency gains to justify these risks. The fee-collection process should assure that nearly all motorists contribute (as compared with current uninsured motorist rates of about 25% in California), and the considerable marketing and commission expenses that accompany the selling of auto insurance would be eliminated.[54]

I have several responses to those who ask about the impact of my proposal on the poor. Considering first those motorists who currently purchase auto insurance, I should emphasize that my plan promises many poor people sharply lower costs than they face under existing arrangements. A poor person with a good driving record could commute twenty-four miles a day even in an older, reasonably safe "gas guzzler" getting but twelve miles to the gallon and would have to pay about $250 annually to the AACC from all sources. By comparison, in Los Angeles today, for example, because of "redlining" and other reasons, many poor people are forced into the state's assigned-risk plan regardless of their past driving records and face annual liability-insurance premiums in the range of $1000 for the minimum required protection. Even poor motorists living in less urban counties, buying in the standard insurance market and eligible for good-driver discounts, are now likely to pay at least $300 a year for minimum liability and uninsured-motorist protection. Moreover, poor people will be gaining more useful protection under my plan. Today, if they are truly judgment proof, buying liability insurance amounts to morally proper, but financially wasteful, behavior.

Poor people who do not insure today will face increased costs (and will gain new benefits). Although a disproportionate share of our society's uninsured motorists is poor, it is by no means clear that their scoff- law behavior is widely approved. In California, for example, advocates for the poor have been searching for ways to provide them with affordable auto insurance that they could be expected to buy. I believe that my plan meets that standard.

If, in the end, the poor were thought too burdened by my plan, surely their plight should not block its adoption altogether. If necessary they could be provided with increased cash transfer payments or, if politically expedient, with transportation vouchers good for either public transportation or gasoline.

As for political resistance, the plan could well run into the opposition of the insurance and oil industries, trial lawyers, the "highway lobby,"[55] independent insurance agents and brokers, and truckers and travelling salespeople (who would perhaps pay more to the AACC than they now pay in insurance). But because of the plan's likely behavioral effects it should win the support of environmentalists, public-transport supporters, and fans of energy efficiency and independence. Most importantly, it should have the support of individual motorists and both consumer and traffic-safety groups.[56]

The figures provided earlier would produce for most California motorists a substantial reduction in their overall cost of driving. This is because their total contribution to the AACC would be less than currently incurred auto-insurance expenses that would no longer be necessary. Beyond overall public savings, the AACC system of charges is better designed than our current system to influence drivers, car buyers, and carmakers to act in more socially desirable ways or at least to reward them for doing so.

It is an open question, however, whether Nader would support the AACC proposal. Despite the attractiveness of the basic auto no-fault idea on many grounds -- including the auto-safety ground to which Mashaw and Harfst appeal -- Nader has long opposed auto no-fault.

Many insurers and consumer groups that back no-fault find this opposition bizarre. Some are inclined to credit recently published attacks on Nader that portray him as in bed with the plaintiff's bar.[57] I am more willing to accept his assertion that he simply opposes the idea of victims losing their right to sue.[58] After all, Nader himself has made successful use of the tort system, and shortly after he published Unsafe at Any Speed he teamed up with Professor Joseph Page to advocate product- liability litigation as a route to safer cars.[59] Whether he was right or wrong, I can well understand Nader's hostility to doing away with individual tort rights against large corporations.

But when the American tort law/liability insurance system is so obviously failing the public, his dogged objection to a sensible substitution for the right to sue other motorists mystifies me. I appreciate that American courts acknowledge the dignity of the individual by awarding pain and suffering damages that are in excess of what other nations do, and the AACC would, award and that Nader might find this quite attractive. But the reality is that a huge proportion of those seriously injured in auto accidents have no chance of benefitting from that generosity. Perhaps two-thirds of auto accidents are caused by drivers who are either altogether uninsured or have coverage of $50,000 or less.[60] Those with small injuries might be able to extract a fair amount from the system, particularly given the nuisance value of their claims; but even they wind up turning much or all of their compensation for pain and suffering over to pay their lawyers. The AACC would change all that, far better compensating victims, especially the seriously injured-and at a lower overall cost.

Assume I am right that the AACC represents either a better public approach to car safety than NHTSA has provided or at least a desirable supplement to NHTSA. If so, it would be ironic indeed if its adoption were blocked because of the quixotic opposition of the one public citizen most identified with auto safety in the first place.

ENDNOTES

1. Ralph Nader, Unsafe at Any Speed: The Designed-In Dangers of The American Automobile (updated ed. 1972).

2. *See* Nader V. General Motors Corp., 255 N.E.2d 765 (1970) (detailing Nader's charges against General Motors of invasion of privacy and intentional infliction of severe emotional distress).

3. Nader, *Supra* note 1, at xvii-lxxxvii.

4. Claybrook has a different view regarding NHTSA's success in regulating the auto industry. *See* Joan Claybrook & David Bollier, *The Hidden Benefits Of Regulation: Disclosing The Auto Safety Payoff,* 3 Yale J. On Reg. 87 (1985). *See Generally* Joan Claybrook et al., Retreat From Safety (1984).

5. *See, e.g.*, Robert W. Crandall et al., Regulating The Automobile (1986); Leonard Evans, Traffic Safety And The Driver (1991); Martin Friedland et al., Regulating Traffic Safety (1990); John D. Graham, Auto Safety: Assessing America's Performance (1989) [hereinafter Auto Safety]; John D. Graham, *Product Liability And Motor Vehicle Safety*, in The Liability Maze: The Impact Of Liability Law On Safety And Innovation 120 (Peter W. Huber & Robert E. Litan eds., 1991) [Hereinafter *Product Liability And Motor Vehicle Safety*].

6. Nader, *supra* note I, at xvi.

7. The "second collision" occurs in the instant after the vehicle crashes into an object-when passengers are flung from their seats into the dashboard, steering column, windows, etc., or out of the automobile altogether. See Caiazzo v. Volkswagenwerk A.G., 647 F.2d 241, 243 n.2 (1981).

8. Indeed, given that a large portion of the cars recalled do not actually have a defective part but must be worked on anyway, that some repair efforts made in response to recalls are faulty, and that motorists face accident risks when bringing their cars in for the recall, it is "not implausible to believe that the recall program is decreasing motor vehicle safety" (p. 168).

9. *See* Joseph A. Page, *The Struggle for Auto Safety*, Trial, May 1991, at 88; Michael J. Trebilcock, *Requiem for Regulators: The Passing of a Counter-Culture?*, 8 YALE J. ON REG. 497 (1991) (book review); Jorge L. Contreras, Book Note, *The Struggle for Auto Safety*, 4 HARV. J.L. & TECH. 307 (1991); Alexandra A. Shapiro, Book Note, *The Struggle for Auto Safety*, 91 COLUM. L. REV. 710 (1991). Trebilcock's is by far the most elegant review.

10. Shapiro, *supra* note 9, at 716.

11. Page, *supra* note 9, at 90. It should be underscored, however, that courts handling torts cases have resisted liability claims premised on the lack of air bags. For more on the role of product-liability law in promoting the installation of air bags, see *Product Liability and Motor Vehicle Safety*, *supra* note 5, at 156-60.

12. Trebilcock, *supra* note 9, at 504-06.

13. At its extreme, the argument is that if motoring were made unavoidably safe, then young men, for example, would find some other activity in which to indulge their taste for danger. See et al., *supra* note 5, at 123.

14. Among the most prominent work is that by University of Chicago economist Sam Peltzman, who vigorously promoted this type of analysis. *See* Sam Peltzman, *The Effects of Automobile Safety Regulation,* 83 J. POL. ECON. 677 (1975).

15. Crandall et al., *supra* note 5, at 66, 68.

16. *Id.* at 69.

17. *Id.* at 74-79.

18. Friedland et al., *supra* note 5, at 122.

19. Evans makes an extremely convincing case against the so-called "risk homeostasis" theory, showing that although drivers do respond to changes in vehicle and road conditions, it is implausible to conclude that they always seek a constant level of risk that inevitably wipes out any advances in safety. Rather, different interventions lead to differing sorts of responses, some of which achieve the safety effects intended, some more than expected, some less than expected, and some increased risk. *See* EVANS, *supra* note 5, at 282-309.

20. Crandall et al., *supra* note 5, at 37 (fable 3-4). Crandall's analysis assumes that over time manufacturers learn bow to meet earlier mandated changes at lower cost.

21. *Id.* at 34 (Table 3-2).

22. Auto Safety, *supra* note 5, at 42.

23. This is especially so when the large cost of required bumper improvements is taken out; they reduce vehicular damage in a crash but do little for occupants.

24. *See*, e.g., W. Kip Viscusi, Reforming Produci's Liability 120 (Table 6.1) (1991).

25. Evans estimated that the fatality-reducing effectiveness of lap/shoulder belts for drivers and right-front passengers is about 41% and that the addition of front-seat air bags raises the effectiveness percentage to about 46%. Reliance on air bags alone (that is, not using a lap belt ns well), according to Evans, should have a fatality-reducing effectiveness of about 17%. These percentages are as compared with no occupant-protection devices. Evans, *supra* note 5, at 244 (Table 9-6). Other estimates show a somewhat greater effectiveness for air bags alone (for example, 20% or more). *Id.* at 245 (Table 9-7).

26. *Id.* at 252.

27. *Id.* at 252-55.

28. *Id.* at 254-69.

29. *Id.* at 252.

30. The role of NHTSA, starting in the 1980s, in prompting states to adopt laws mandating seat-belt use is a complex one. For a discussion of this issue, see *Auto Safety*, *supra* note 5, at 120-23.

31. For a criticism of this solution, *see* Trebilcock, *supra* note 9, at 502.

32. *See also Product Liability and Motor Vehicle Safety, supra* note 5 (analyzing the role of product-liability law in promoting safer cars).

33. Some carriers are now offering small reductions in liability-insurance premiums for those motorists who have cars with antilock brakes, presumably on the theory that such motorists will cause fewer accidents. Telephone Interview with Stephen Oesch, General Counsel to the Insurance Institute for Highway Safety (Oct. 30, 1991). These discounts can also apply to collision coverage but apparently not to other first-party coverages.

34. In principle an insured with air bags might be thought entitled to a reduced premium for uninsured-motorist coverage because that covers the motorist's own tort loss when injured by someone else with either no insurance or too little insurance. But, according to Oesch, this does not appear to be the practice. *Id.*

35. *Id.* The discounts vary both by insurer and by the type of protective device (for example, air bags for the driver only or for the front passenger as well).

36. One cannot, however, assume this will be the case even if air bags really do pay their way from the social-cost perspective. This is because the transaction costs of insurance always make the actual premium larger than the pure premium calculated solely on the basis of risk.

37. *See, e.g.,* Michael J. Trebilcock, *The Social Insurance-Deterrence Dilemma of Modern North American Tort Law: A Canadian Perspective on the Liability Insurance Crisis*, 24 SAN DIEGO L. REV. 929 (1987).

38. Trebilcock, *supra* note 9, at 502.

39. Stephen D. Sugarman, Doing Away With Personal Injury Law 4-6 (1989).

40. *Id.* at 13-15, 21-23.

41. These studies are discussed in Friedland et al, *supra* note 5, at 68-74.

42. Friedland et al., *supra* note 5, at 70 (citing R.A. Devlin, Liability versus No-Fault Automobile Insurance Regimes: An Analysis of Quebec's Experience (paper presented at the Canadian Economics Association Meeting, Windsor, Ontario, Canada, June 3, 1988)).

43. Stephen D. Sugarman, *California's Insurance Regulation Revolution: The First Two Years of Proposition* 103, 21 SAN DIEGO L. REV. 683, 711-14 (1990) [hereinafter Sugarman, California's Insurance Regulation Revolution]; Stephen D. Sugarman, *Foreword: Choosing Among Systems of Auto Insurance for Personal Injury*, 26 SAN DIEGO L. REV. 977, 988-92 (1989); Stephen D. Sugarman, *The Case for Pay-at-the-*

Pump Car Insurance, SACRAMENTO BEE, June 9, 1991, Forum, at 1; Stephen D. Sugarman, *How to Slash Car Insurance Costs*, SACRAMENTO BEE, Apr. 1, 1990, Forum, at 1.

44. In the short run, given the current price of gasoline, the results of other studies seem to predict a reduction in driving of about 5%. Over time, fuel consumption would be expected to drop by up to 15% as people made more permanent adjustments. Those would include, on the one hand, a shift to more fuel-efficient cars and, on the other, a shift to public transportation and living closer to work. Mohamed M. El-Gasseir, State of California Energy Resources Conservation and Development Commission, The Potential Benefits and Workability of Pay-As-You-Drive Automobile Insurance (June 8, 1990) (unpublished report) (on file with author).

45. *See* Sugarman, *California's Insurance Regulation Revolution, supra* note 43, at 703.

46. Trebilcock, *supra* note 9, at 502.

47. *Id.* at 508-10.

48. *See, e.g.*, Jack Gillis, The Car Book 18 (1990).

49. *See* Evans, *supra* note 5, at 47 (Figure 3-3), 66-71.

50. *Id.* at 291.

51. Telephone Interview with Leonard Evans, Principal Research Scientist, General Motors Research Laboratories (Jan. 3, 1992).

52. *See, e.g.,* Highway Loss Data Institute, Injury and Collision Loss Experience by Make and Model (Sept. 1990) (pamphlet).

53. HLDI statistics are adjusted to take into account the age of the driver but not other characteristics. *See id*.

54. Moreover, I think it would be wise for the AACC to employ the claims-processing expertise of the existing insurance industry by contracting out that function in the way, for example, that Medicare contracts out its claim processing to the private sector.

55. The "highway lobby" includes concrete manufacturers, road builders, and owners of motels, fast-food outlets, and gasoline stations.

56. Whether auto makers back or oppose the plan will turn on whether the introduction of the AACC and especially the charge on new cars are seen as a proper quid pro quo for the elimination of auto-manufacturer product liability, manufacturing, and design and warning defects.

57. *See, e.g.,* Peter Brimelow & Leslie Spencer, *Ralph Nader. Inc.,* Forbes, Sept. 17, 1990, at 117; L. Gordon Crovitz, *Ralph Nader Is a Bargain for Trial Lawyers at $1,000 a Table*, WALL ST.J., Nov. 14, 1990, at 15.

58. *See, e.g.,* Ralph Nader, *The Assault on Injured Victims' Rights*, 64 DENV. U. L. REV. 625 (1988).

59. *See* Ralph Nader & Joseph A. Page, *Automobile Design and the Judicial Process*. 55 CALIF. L. REV. 645 (1967).

60. *See* Jeffrey O'Connell, *No-Fault Auto Insurance: Back By Popular (Market) Demand?,* 26 SAN DIEGO L. REV. 993, 1000 n.18 (1989).

Chapter 12

Roles of Government in Dealing with Disasters

Some "disasters" are commonly described as "natural" such as hurricanes (like Sandy that badly damaged New York and New Jersey and Katrina that badly damaged Louisiana and other Gulf states), earthquakes (like those in San Francisco and Los Angeles), floods (in Colorado), mudslides (in Washington), and so on, even if in retrospect claims are made that people were at fault for not preventing or minimizing the damage from the event, or at least that humans were in some sense the cause of the resulting harm. Other disasters (or catastrophes as they are sometimes termed) are immediately seen to be man-made (like the 911 terrorist attack, the BP oil spill in the Gulf, and the Oakland hills fire set by careless workers that destroyed 3000 homes and took some lives). Sometimes a mixture of forces is immediately seen to be involved (like the tsunami and resulting nuclear power plant failure in Japan).

Government plays a variety of roles in dealing with these disasters including prevention (or loss minimizing) efforts, rescue and stabilization efforts in the immediate aftermath of a disaster (as well as planning in advance for such efforts), and dealing with long term recovery. One potential government role of considerable interest concerns the compensation of individual disaster victims for a range of their losses -- death, personal injury/disease, property damage and destruction, and economic loss (like lost business profits).

In thinking about government's roles with respect to disasters, the place of tort law is important to consider. After all, one thing government can do is to have tort duties on the books and then enforce those legal obligations against liable parties after the disaster occurs. Moreover, the threat of future tort liability could play a role in preventing some disasters from occurring (or reducing the harm they do). At the same time, the prospect of tort liability in an amount that might well be crushing burden on a defendant might ex ante discourage enterprises from engaging in what are thought to be socially desirable economic activity and/or ex post destroy important economic institutions. These concerns raise the question of whether tort liability should be suspended (or constrained) with respect to certain disasters, and if so, whether it should be replaced by other arrangements.

From quite a different perspective, awareness of ordinary tort law's limited reach in compensating disaster victims might argue in favor of having government involved either in advance or after-the-fact in arranging for victim compensation outside of tort law.

Finally, are there some occasions in which government actors themselves are in some respect responsible for the bad consequences of the disaster (or even of the disaster itself occurring)? And if so, should tort liability or some alternative compensation arrangement be there to serve victims?

These are some of the main the questions addressed in this chapter. This chapter grew out of work carried out in connection with an American Bar Association task force on the role of law in disasters. It was presented as part of a UC Berkeley Law Symposium on Catastrophic Risks: Prevention, and Recovery, and published as Stephen D. Sugarman, "Roles of Government in Compensating Disaster Victims," Issues in Legal Scholarship (Article 1, 2007). It is reprinted with the permission of the journal.

Roles of Government in Compensating Disaster Victims

Disasters are going to occur, even if we don't know which ones they will be, when or where they will happen, or how devastating they will be. Beyond roles it might play in disaster prevention (or harm reduction), what is the responsibility of government with respect to victim compensation – compensation for personal injury and death, property losses, and financial losses? After setting out some preliminary considerations as to the nature of disasters and the place of both private insurance and tort law in providing disaster compensation, I suggest there are at least five potential roles for government:

- Facilitating the Receipt of Private Compensation for the Consequences of a Disaster
- Assuring Insurance Availability for Disaster Victims When the Market Fails

to Do So

- Providing Victim Compensation Either When Government Should Have Prevented the Disaster or When It Is the Sort of Disaster We Aspire to Have Government Prevent
- Providing Victim Compensation as an Alternative to Tort Recovery
- Providing Victim Assistance to Overwhelmed Communities For Reasons of Altruism and National Solidarity

Finally, I briefly explain that the decision to aid disaster victims is only the first step, and that an equally difficult next step is deciding in what form that aid should take.

I. Preliminary Considerations Concerning the Nature of Disasters

A. What Makes Something a Disaster? Individuals v. Society

At the individual level, even if no one else is directly impacted, a loss may be disastrous (or catastrophic, words I use interchangeably here). For example, if an otherwise healthy young person with no dependents falls down the stairs and becomes a quadriplegic, that person will be widely understood to have suffered a catastrophic loss. The victim will almost surely incur enormous harm – a dramatic change in personal lifestyle, huge medical and related expenses, and, very likely, a sharp reduction in earnings potential. Yet, regardless of how catastrophic to the individual, this is not the sort of event that is considered to be a societal disaster. The same might be said about a couple losing their precious home to a fire started in their kitchen or a gas stove explosion that leads to the deaths, say, of one of two parents and one of their two children. Even if crushingly disastrous for the victims (and the survivors), these events are not what we mean by societal disasters.

At the society level, a disaster is generally understood as an event that causes large losses to a substantial number of people. Such an event might also cause smaller losses to very many people, but even very widespread minor losses by themselves are not likely to be viewed cumulatively as amounting to disaster. Moreover, while events like hurricanes often cause disasters, many do not, thereby making clear that it is the consequences of an event that make it a disaster (or not).

Under the federal disaster relief program, which is largely run by the Federal Emergency Management Agency (FEMA), a "major disaster" is said to have occurred when the President, in response to a request from a state governor, declares it so (the President also has the authority on his own to declare an "emergency.")[1] Generally speaking, the President restricts these declarations to events with widespread and very grave consequences that are seen to overwhelm the capacities of state and local governments.[2] Under the governing law, a "major disaster" is supposed to be the result either of a "natural catastrophe" or of a fire, explosion, or flood, regardless of the cause.[3]

Events need not be declared disasters by the President to be considered societal disasters, however. For example, a mining accident in a small mining town, in which twenty miners are trapped and then die, may well be termed a disaster in that community. This implies that, even when confined to specific geographic locations, societal disasters can range from the smaller scale (the mining example) to the enormous (e.g., the consequences of hurricane Katrina).

The "event" that counts in determining whether there has been a societal disaster is sometimes ambiguous. Things like dynamite explosions, airplane crashes, and earthquakes are vivid occurrences, and when they do enough harm the boundaries of the resulting disaster are likely to be reasonably clear, even if the identities of those individuals who were seriously hurt or killed as a direct result of such events may not be entirely certain (to say nothing of those who were indirectly harmed).

But in other situations, the beginning and ending of an event may be quite fuzzy, and, in turn, just who is a victim of the disaster may be especially uncertain. Consider, for example, a terrible heat wave. We might be confident that more than 500 people in a certain city died from the disastrous heat, but determining on which days the heat wave began and ended, what geographic area to count as impacted by the heat, and just who died as a result of the heat may be quite difficult. Catastrophic famines and droughts have similarly uncertain temporal and geographic boundaries, and so the absence of a vivid triggering occasion may make it hard to appreciate just what are the disastrous consequences of such an "event." Other sorts of calamities lacking and a vivid triggering event can also unfold over time and space, like the enormously destructive consequences of the widespread use of asbestos decades before its latent dangers were appreciated.

Nor it is clear what are the minimum number of people who must be harmed, or the minimum amount of property that must be damaged, in order for something to qualify as a societal disaster. Besides, the way events are framed may determine whether what might otherwise be understood to be several separate incidents are to be lumped together and thereby understood to be sufficiently harmful to be characterized as a societal disaster. Suppose, first, a crazed student kills a dozen or more suburban classmates within seconds by firing off hundreds of rounds from a semi-automatic weapon. The consequence of that rampage will surely be termed a disaster for the community in which the school is located. Now suppose a serial killer murders a dozen people over a week's time in one community. That community is also likely to be said to have suffered a disaster. On the other hand, a long-past, out-of-town victim of the serial killer may well not be seen to be included in the disaster. Indeed, if the serial killer acts in a number of cities, the consequences of those acts may not be grouped together as a single societal disaster, and none of the individual communities may be understood to have suffered a societal disaster. The media probably plays a role in framing the way that the public views these sorts of events, and the media has an incentive to gather together separate occurrences in order to label something larger a disaster so as to get the public's attention.

Part of the problem of trying to reach an understanding of what we mean by a societal disaster is that the word "disaster" itself is now routinely tossed around in ways that wildly exaggerate the momentous nature of what is being described – such as, "my room is a disaster area" or "last night's date was a disaster" or "the basketball team's record so far this year is a disaster."

At the other extreme one can imagine catastrophic events on a scale that could destroy our civilization as we know it.[4] These include full scale war using weapons of mass destruction, endless global winters possibly caused by the earth being struck by an object from space, pervasive pandemics that wipe out a large share of the population, and so on. Such events could be so overwhelming to the American people and our national government as to make anything discussed here largely irrelevant, and for that reason I put aside potential occurrences of this enormity.

In the end, it is perhaps helpful to focus here on the idea of "major disasters" (as does FEMA) implying relatively large aggregate losses that a) are comprised, at least in part, of harms that are catastrophic to many individuals and b) are often sufficiently grave to overtax the capacity of even moderate size or larger communities to deal with the consequences.

B. Types of Disasters: Natural v. Manmade

Some major disasters are well understood to be naturally caused – like the consequences of some tornadoes and volcanic eruptions. And natural disasters are what typically come first to mind when one thinks about major disasters in general. Yet, a moment's reflection makes clear that many major disasters are the result of human acts – like the terrorist attacks on 9/11/01, wars, and riots, as well as the chemical leak in Bhopal and the nuclear reactor meltdown in Chernobyl.

This distinction is often blurred, however. Hurricane Katrina is a good example. The hurricane itself was obviously a force of nature (I put aside claims that hurricanes are becoming more frequent and more violent because of manmade global warming). But many are convinced that humans were importantly responsible for the catastrophic consequence of Katrina because of a) the way the levees were (or were not) designed and maintained, and b) the way evacuation of New Orleans was (or was not) carried out.

Airplane crashes can also be ambiguous on this dimension. On the one hand, the making of the plane, its piloting, and the organization of the trip and its route are the result of human activity. On the other hand, planes often crash because of bad weather. Does the latter make it a natural disaster? Does it depend on whether the pilot or the air traffic controllers should have prevented the crash? Fires, shipwrecks, avalanches and the like are yet other examples of events that can bring catastrophic consequences that may be uncertainly labeled as natural or manmade. In the end, it is not clear what is gained by trying to categorize disasters as natural ("acts of God") or not, although those who catalog disasters tend to do so anyway.[5]

C. Types of Losses: Property Destruction or Damage, Death or Serious Personal Injury, Financial Losses, and Other Woes

A large earthquake can easily result in widespread serious injury and death, a huge amount of property damage, and enormous financial losses of other sorts as well. From the perspective of the individual victim of the earthquake, however, the direct consequences are of the same sort as are incurred by victims of individual disasters that are not societal disasters. Put differently, although the Oakland hills firestorm of 1991 was a societal disaster, the deaths that followed yielded losses of the same sort that routinely occur from, say, auto accident fatalities, and the property damage that followed the destruction of 3000 homes was of the same type that flows from ordinary fires (say, from lighted cigarettes or lightning) that burn down single buildings.

In general, the same point may be made about serious personal injuries. These harms bring with them expenses (like medical and rehabilitation expenses), lost income (or at least a diminished ability to earn), and what tort law calls non-economic losses. These latter include the physical pain and consequent suffering that goes along with a physical trauma, the emotional harm that can come from an injury to one's self or a loved one, the disappointment or embarrassment arising from one's changed appearance or altered ability to engage in pleasurable activities and favorite pastimes as a result of an injury, the harm to one's dignity or to one's health from being injured, and so on. Once more, these types of harms are no different if one is badly injured in an earthquake or in an auto accident.

Nevertheless, in some cases the consequences of a similar injury will be greater if it is incurred as part of a societal disaster. For example, in the aftermath of an earthquake or hurricane the local hospital staff may be unable to provide the immediate care it normally provides, thereby leaving victims with more serious permanent harms. Or, the informal family and social support network on which a victim might otherwise rely may itself be severely disrupted and unable to function, thereby leading to larger losses. Or, a victim may be more emotionally scarred from being part of a community-wide trauma rather than an individual one. (On the other hand, a community's heroic response to a disaster might have a positive long term emotional impact of the disaster's victims that would not occur where the injury was an isolated one.)

One tends to think of disasters as involving physical force and physical harm, and indeed those who rank disasters tend to do so in terms of the number of lives lost or the value or physical property destroyed. Yet, a disaster can occur without either of these. For example, to shareholders of Enron, especially those many employees whose retirement savings were largely or exclusively concentrated in the corporation's stock, the company's sudden financial melt-down was very much a disaster.

What seems most special about social disasters, then, is that they are experienced by a wider community (however defined), and indeed, in the case of many major disasters, the lifeblood of the community itself is potentially at risk. Moreover, because of the very widespread nature of some disasters, the recovery effort may be much more burdensome. For example, when one person's home burns down, finding someone else or some group in the community to provide temporary housing while the person relocates (or finding stable interim housing while the person rebuilds), may not be terribly difficult. But if vast numbers are made homeless, both the need for help is much greater and those able to provide help many fewer – as the recent hurricane Katrina experience vividly showed.

Furthermore, certain catastrophic losses may be coherently understood only as societal losses. These include, for example, the extinction of plant or animal species (or other grave environmental harm perhaps not even involving direct harm to private property) or the breakdown of a functioning state or local government.

D. Insured/Insurable Losses (or Not)

The financial consequences of many of the losses that result from catastrophic events may be ameliorated by the advance purchase of private insurance that covers the peril in question. Life insurance, health insurance, disability insurance, and accidental death and dismemberment insurance are all examples of privately sold policies that provide compensation for individuals suffering casualty losses to the person. Property insurance (covering fire and all sorts of other perils) is a private mechanism that provides compensation to those who suffer covered losses to physical property (both real property and personal property); and homeowner's insurance, for example, will often pay, not only for the rebuilding or repair of one's home, but also for temporary living costs.. Business interruption insurance can serve as at least a partial substitute for temporarily lost income or pay for temporarily higher expenses. And while these sorts of insurance policies are primarily used to cover the risk of individual loss in non-disaster settings, they can indeed come into play in the event of a disaster.

Yet, one problem with private insurance solutions is that there is sometimes no private insurance available for certain types of catastrophic risks to which people are subject.[6] Indeed, it is precisely the dramatically large event that leads to widespread disastrous consequences that is frequently specifically excluded from certain standard private insurance policies. For example, the destruction of one's home or other buildings is generally not covered by ordinary property insurance (or homeowners') policies if the harm is caused by things like war, nuclear radiation, floods, and, at least in some places, earthquakes.[7]

Sometimes those catastrophic risks may be specially insured against through privately purchased policies that are narrowly tailored to specific potentially catastrophic events (although sometimes the availability of these private policies requires governmental intervention, as discussed later). But often, no private insurance market exists for these risks.

While this insurance unavailability might be viewed as a market failure, there are usually understandable reasons why insurers won't underwrite certain risks.[8] First of all, they find themselves unable to sensibly price the insurance, both because the precipitating event too infrequently occurs and when it does the amount harm it will cause is not really predictable. Moreover, it is especially worrying to insurers that the catastrophe might occur markedly earlier than expected, so that not enough premiums would yet have been accumulated, thereby putting an insurer at risk of insolvency. Even if the timing and scale of the risk were reasonably predictable, however, insuring against infrequent disasters would require a long accumulation and investment of premium income in a way that is not altogether attractive to insurers (and re-insurers who might be enticed to spread the risk beyond the insurer who initially sold coverage to its customers). Among other things, U.S. tax law rules discourage insurance lines that involve premium collection without payouts, even if funds are set aside for eventual losses. Besides, when the gigantic-loss event finally occurs, insurers could be swamped by the claims-handling process, having to rely on out-of-area and/or inexperienced staff who are likely to be more costly and less efficient. As a result, catastrophic risk coverage might simply be an unattractive product for mainstream insurers to offer.

Two common reasons why underwriters typically don't cover certain risks are also relevant in the disaster setting. One is moral hazard, by which I mean that the insured may do something (or fail to do something) that precipitates the insurable event or the level of its consequences. The other is adverse selection, by which I mean the insurer is not easily able to screen out, or charge more to, those customers with higher than average risks. For example, suppose that a lot of people don't take care of their property in a way to minimize the risk of landslide damage and that insurers cannot monitor this failure to take sufficient precautions. Then, not only are landslide damage claims likely to be larger than predicted, but also insurers may find it infeasible to charge different premiums to those who are more and less at risk, thereby forcing them to set premiums at a rate that discourages purchase by responsible owners. In such a setting, especially given the possibility of enormous landslide claims made by lots of customers in one location, who are all harmed by a single major storm, insurers may prefer simply to exclude this risk. Not all insurance against catastrophic harm is subject to this sort of exclusion, however. For example, "major medical" insurance is designed to cover personally catastrophic risks that would cause the insured to need a great deal of expensive medical care. And this sort of health insurance generally will cover medical costs incurred in connection with any sort of societal disaster. One reason for the availability of this coverage is that, even a major disaster is not likely to cause a large share of any insurer's customer base to file claims.

So, too, large amounts of life insurance are generally available for purchase and proceeds of the policy are normally payable regardless of whether the person died from a societal catastrophe or not. To be sure, in some policies some causes of death are excluded from coverage. These may include suicide for a moderate period of time after the policy is obtained, as well as death from sky diving, bungee jumping, and other specifically listed perils – i.e., what are viewed as extraordinarily dangerous activities that the insured party voluntarily undertakes. But deaths from earthquakes, floods, or terrorism, for example, are generally covered by standard life insurance policies. Again, even a major earthquake is likely to kill only a small share of any one life insurer's clients, and the amount of the insurance payout has been specified (and specifically priced) in advance.

Insurance unavailability is one thing. Yet, even when insurance is available, potential victims may not purchase advance protection against possible losses. This may occur for several reasons. Some people feel they simply cannot afford to buy the insurance (or at least they find it so expensive that they forego it in order have money left to pay for basic essentials of daily living).

Other people, who in important respects clearly could afford to buy private insurance coverage to provide compensation in case of a disaster, do not do so. This might arise from inattention to one's affairs, or a failure to appreciate that one is at risk. Or, if coverage is sold separately for a specific risk, potential victims may psychologically discount nearly to zero that particular danger to them, thereby concluding that insurance is not needed and/or unduly expensive. Moreover, some people may find it psychologically discomforting even to consider he potentially devastating consequences of even very small risks and so, along with repressing their fears, they pay no attention to the possibility of purchasing insurance.

Still others may be very clear-headed about the risk they face, find the quoted premium to be appropriate, and nonetheless choose not to buy as a result of a deliberate decision to take a chance. Indeed, as discussed later, some might elect not to pay for coverage because they believe that, if a societal disaster does occur, government will step in and help out, thereby making it foolish for them to lay out cash in advance.

Regardless of the reasons for insufficient private insurance coverage, the upshot is that a community can find itself dealing with the aftermath of a societal disaster in which large numbers of victims confront devastating uninsured losses. In such settings, the community may be faced with the reality that, if nothing is done to make up for the lack of private insurance, the entire community may suffer wider fallout effects, which would not occur were a single member or a single family of the community devastated or killed by other than a societal disaster.

E. Having a Viable Legal (Tort) Remedy Against the Cause of the Disaster (or Not)

By using the legal system, some victims of certain societal disasters may obtain financial recovery for their losses against those private parties who are responsible for their injuries. But many do not have this remedy.

Perhaps most importantly, losses from wholly natural disasters are not compensable in this way because you cannot sue "Mother Nature" or "God" for "acts of God." (I put aside instances in which the claim is that people should have prevented the harm caused by nature.[9])

Even when victims (or their surviving heirs) technically have a legal remedy, the prospects of successfully recovering compensation from a solvent party vary enormously.

Sometimes, the remedy is worthless because legally liable actors will have little or no money. Other times, the legal remedy is worthless because liable actors cannot be identified, or, even if known, cannot be found. For example, the 9/11 terrorists themselves, besides being dead, are not good targets of legal claims liability, even if they are clearly formally liable for the incredible havoc they caused, because their estates don't have the money to pay the compensation award that would be imposed. Maybe 9/11 victims could win a lawsuit against the presumably wealthy Osama bin Laden, but, at least for now, they cannot get him before the court. More generally, all too often the people who secretly set disastrous fires, set off disastrous explosions, or spread around disastrous poisons remain unknown (recall, for example, the Tylenol scare of some years ago when an unknown person managed to lace bottles of Tylenol with poison).

In still other instances, human actors were in some sense a cause of the disaster, but they were not at fault in doing so. And if the law in those settings requires that fault must be proved as a condition of recovery, then the victims of the disaster have no legal right to compensation from their injurers. To be sure, proof of fault is not always required – say, in the case of a dynamite explosion that unavoidably goes awry and results in a disaster.[10] But for most accidental harms, proof of fault is a condition of legal liability.

Suppose, for example, a drug company carefully tests a drug that appears to be altogether safe and very beneficial to patients. Yet, suppose that, when the drug is used by the population at large, it suddenly becomes clear that the drug is lethal to some people, has already killed hundreds, and should be withdrawn. Assuming that the drug company pulls the drug from the market at the first moment when it could plausibly have known of its dangerousness, then this grim pharmaceutical disaster is probably not its fault. And since the law generally requires victims to prove drug company fault before they can recover in court, on these facts the disaster victims would have no legal remedy.[11]

Finally, in yet other settings, event at-fault, identified, and seemingly solvent actors will escape legal liability. Two very different examples illustrate the point. First, as a disaster unfolds, it is routine that professional rescuers (firefighters, police and the like) will be called to the scene, and it is, alas, predictable that over time some will be injured or killed in the course of doing their jobs. Yet, in nearly all states, even if the danger (say, a fire) has been carelessly caused by an identified and solvent actor, these professional rescuers (or their survivors) will have no legal claim against the wrongdoer because of what is usually termed the "firefighter's" rule.[12] One basis for this rule is that these professionals are already provided reasonably generous compensation for their injuries (and deaths) through advance work-based arrangements. A different justification is that, as professionals who knowingly confront a danger they are paid to confront, they are only entitled to a warning of the peril and have no right to claim that the wrongdoer should have prevented the danger.

Second, the very fact that an event has led to a societal disaster may also prevent victims from recovering in tort. For example, after the huge electricity blackout in New York City in 1977, New York's highest court precluded the claims of victims who were themselves not direct contractual customers of the utility involved (Con Edison), even though it accepted the jury finding that the company was grossly at fault in causing the blackout.[13] At base, the court feared that requiring compensation of all victims could bankrupt the company, disrupt its operations, and quite possibly result in the denial of the public of its basic need for electricity. This is an instance in which, had there merely been a single victim who was not a Con Edison customer (for example, a tenant whose electricity is paid for by the landlord), then (under the same facts) that victim clearly would have been able to recover compensation from the utility. Rather perversely, then, the fact that so many were harmed was what allowed the defendant to escape legal responsibility. (A different justification for this result might be that, when catastrophic results occur, if the defendant has to pay for all of the foreseeable consequences of its misconduct, this would be excessive "punishment." Yet, tort law normally does not require any relationship between the degree of fault and the amount of liability.)

F. Promoting Precautions to Prevent or Minimize Disasters in the Future

Although my general focus here is on victim compensation, a few words may be appropriate on the issue of prevention. If it is not too burdensome to do so, then it will be desirable for people to take action before a disaster occurs that can either reduce the frequency of disasters happening, and/or reduce the severity of the harm that follows when disasters do occur. Government might do several things to promote these outcomes.

1. Stimulating would-be victims to take precautions against disasters

Government might take steps to stimulate potential disaster victims to engage in loss prevention (or reduction) measures. For example, certain sorts of structural enhancements to buildings can sharply limit the harm done by earthquakes of certain magnitudes. And government could provide information to building owners about these measures, provide financial incentives to owners to utilize these measures, require owners to take such precautions now, and/or penalize owners who failed to take such measures and suffer harm in a subsequent quake. Similar actions can be taken by government to encourage precautions for other potentially catastrophic risks like floods or tornadoes.

2. Discouraging manmade disasters

Beyond a focus on would-be victims, government could attend to the causes of disasters and take steps in advance to prevent their happening (or at least reduce their prevalence and/or severity). I have in mind here government actions that stimulate private parties who would later be found responsible for a disaster to take advance precautions. Ordering railways, chemical companies, explosives makers and the like to adopt specific safety measures is one strategy. Threatening such companies with the possibility that their victims (or public prosecutors) could sue them if precautions are not taken and harm occurs is another. Sending in government inspectors to look for conditions that might lead to disasters and then demand risk-reducing actions is yet another strategy. Still another example is requiring private parties to obtain some sort of advance approval from public officials before engaging in activities that could have disastrous consequences – for example, demanding FDA approval prior to the sale of prescription drugs. In some instances, the potential danger from activities is thought to be so great that government might elect to ban it altogether and use a variety of means to enforce such a rule. Certain environmental controls are of this sort.

3. Government itself taking precautionary measures

Sometimes, government itself can directly take measures that are intended to prevent disasters. The Army Corps of Engineers may build dikes or re-direct waterways and the like in an effort to reduce the flood risk to a specific area. Or government may run (and regularly improve) the air traffic control system in hopes of preventing air crash disasters. And so on.

G. Saving People, Fixing Public Property, and Restoring Core Public Functions (Apart from Victim Compensation)

When a disaster occurs, like an earthquake or a hurricane, there can be considerable destruction and disruption of public property and public functions. Clearly, dealing with these consequences is a duty of government. The roads, parks, and beaches may have to be cleared and restored. Public buildings like schools, libraries and civil offices may need to be fixed or rebuilt. The criminal and civil justice systems, regulatory bodies, administrative units and the like may need to get up and running again. If public employees die or are injured in the disaster they have to be replaced. And so on.

Moreover, in the course of a disaster unfolding, public authorities often must send out rescuers in hopes of minimizing harm. For example, fires have to be put out, those cut off by floods need to be retrieved if possible, those already injured need to be taken to places where medical care can be provided, and so on. Moreover, if there is adequate warning, pre-rescue efforts may need to be taken even before the disaster has struck – like facilitating evacuations.

Depending on the extent of the disaster, local government may not be able to bear this effort by itself, and other governments must be called in to help. Local and state governments typically have reciprocal aid pacts in which they pledge to help each other out in cases of such emergencies, and, of course, where the disaster's consequences are wide enough and large enough, the federal government must also step in, say, by providing money and/or federal emergency personnel.

But this sort of governmental effort in dealing with disasters is not my central focus here. Rather, my concern is with the possible roles that government might play with respect to the compensation of individual victims of societal disasters.

II. Roles of Government in Compensating Societal Disaster Victims

Assuming that, despite prevention efforts, major disasters are going to occur anyway, what are roles of government with respect to victim compensation in the aftermath?[14] Note well, that effectively helping victims after a disaster often requires government action beforehand, by putting victim compensation arrangements in place. Note too that, merely because a true societal disaster has occurred, that does not necessarily mean that some special disaster-based scheme must come into play.

A. Facilitating the Receipt of Private Compensation for the Consequences of a Disaster

One basic role of government is to facilitate the availability of private sources of compensation in the event of a disaster. This partly involves the protection of victims' ordinary legal rights. I have two related, but different, jobs in mind here.

1. *Enforcing insurance contracts and ensuring that insurers are solvent*

and pay what they owe

First, by opening up its courts, government can help assure that those who bought insurance before a disaster occurred and later find that their valid claim is rebuffed, are able to sue their insurer and win a judgment against the defendant. In cases of egregious refusals to pay valid claims, government can (and many states do) allow victims to assert and, on proper proof, win substantial additional financial compensation (for pain and suffering, as punitive damages, and so on) as a way to prod insurers to live up to their contractual obligations in the first place.[15]

Beyond that, government may also take steps (as state governments generally do) to assure that insurers will actually have the money to pay valid claims in the event of a disaster.[16] This requires regulators to be certain that insurers are both charging actuarially adequate rates (and not cutting premiums too much in order to obtain more business) and managing the premiums collected in a responsible and secure manner. In addition, to deal with the problem of insurer insolvency, states typically have created guaranty funds though which, in effect, solvent insurers step up and provide at least limited benefits for claimants whose insurers have financially collapsed.

These jobs of helping policy holders collect from their insurers apply, of course, to claims arising out of events that are, and are not, societal disasters. And while assuring insurer solvency may be especially important when it comes to events that occasion multiple, large claims, this is a good example of how more general public action, aimed at a broader problem, comes into play to help societal disaster victims.

It is also worth noting in this context that, although governments often interfere with respect to various terms that are to be included or excluded from insurance contracts in general, they have typically permitted casualty insurers to exclude property damage coverage that is the result of various specified disasters as noted above. Understandably, government must be careful not to require private insurance coverage of the sort that will cause insurers to withdraw from the business entirely.

2. Creating enforceable tort rights against those who cause manmade disasters

I have already briefly discussed the fact that some disaster victims will have valuable tort claims against those who caused their losses, and I simply want to note here that it is another basic role of government both to define the relevant tort rights and then to make the judicial process available to those who make claims that cannot be resolved outside of court.

As mentioned above, however, it is important to appreciate that, in defining the boundaries of tort rights, common law courts have not infrequently curtailed the rights of disaster victims out of a fear that otherwise the financial devastation of the defendant might lead to an even greater harm to the community.

2. *Facilitating charitable/voluntary organizations and efforts to step in and assist victims of disasters*

Finally, I want to emphasize under this heading that, in the aftermath of a disaster, government is hardly the only actor that might step in to help victims. Private actors with no formal legal duty to help might well also "come to the rescue." These can be individuals or local groups of people who spontaneously rise to the occasion, and they can be organizations set up in advance to respond. Indeed, quasi-public groups like the Red Cross (which typically works alongside FEMA) have disaster response as their central mission.[17]

Government can take steps in advance and after a disaster occurs to promote this outpouring of private "charity" (both its quality and quantity). This can be done by encouraging donations to and voluntary service commitments to disaster relief organizations (e.g., by providing tax benefits for donors). It can be done through advance coordination agreements meant to help assure that there is as little duplication of effort as possible once a disaster occurs, that groups are able to take advantage of their expertise, and so on. Government might also simply try to promote a general cultural norm that it is a moral obligation to help one's neighbors, community members, or even fellow countrymen in the event of a disaster (for example, by honoring those who have done do, by promoting this value in schools, and so on).

There is inevitably some tension between the role of private actors and that of government in the provision of disaster relief. Basically, government has to be concerned about discouraging private relief (or indeed, personal advance provision for financial compensation) by promising to take care of everything if a disaster hits (or even simply by being seen to do so once disasters strike, regardless of whether anything specific was promised in advance). Doing so risks causing potential victims and their would-be helpers to ignore the problem and just step aside and leave it to government when a catastrophe happens. Hence, in order to stimulate those private actors, government somehow has to define its role as supplementing and not supplanting that of others. I will discuss this coordination problem further below.

B. Assuring Insurance Availability for Disaster Victims When the Market Fails to Do So

1. *Stepping in when the private insurance market fails to cover property losses from certain disasters*

As noted already, sometimes the private insurance market by itself will not provide insurance coverage for the consequences of certain disasters. In that case, government might act, either by becoming an insurer itself and offering (or even mandating purchase of) the missing coverage or by working with insurers to get (or force) them to provide the coverage.[18]

The latter could involve getting each insurer of similar risks (e.g. property insurers) to take on its "fair share" of the target risk (like earthquakes). Or it could involve creating of a fund paid for by insurers (presumably from extra premiums collected from its customers) that covers the target risk (like earthquakes). Alternatively, government may become the actual insurer of the risk (like earthquakes) although even there government might yet enlist private insurers in the roles of selling the product, collecting the premiums, and perhaps even processing the claims were the covered risk to occur.

The regime supervised by California's current California Earthquake Authority is one example of how government can get involved with creating a market for insurance coverage for a risk that is not covered by nearly all basic property insurance policies sold in California.[19] A somewhat different role is played by the state of Florida under the Florida Hurricane Catastrophe Fund that was created in 1993 in the wake of Hurricane Andrew.[20] The National Flood Insurance Program is an example of how the federal government stepped in to create coverage for a risk that private insurers were generally unwilling to underwrite on their own.[21] Recent governmental interventions designed to assure the availability insurance against the consequences of terrorism (most importantly, a temporary agreement by the federal government to pay for a share of covered losses) is yet another.[22] These schemes are all aimed at physical property damage. Although not now in place, it is imaginable that, with the help of government, the insurance industry could provide property insurance against the full range of natural disasters.[23]

An important issue confronting any such arrangement – either a comprehensive scheme or one aimed at a specific disaster risk -- is the premium structure. Is the government arranged scheme, on average, charging the equivalent of "market" rates, or are taxpayers subsidizing those who buy the insurance? A justification for subsidy might be the otherwise low income status of the victims. A second-best sort of justification might be that, if, after the disaster, political realities would require government to come in with taxpayer money and help out anyway, it might be socially desirable to get at least some contribution in advance from those who are specifically at risk.

Additional critical pricing issues are (1) whether individual or classes of buyers will be charged differently because they run different risks, and (2) to what extent will underwriting investigations be carried out and underwriting conditions be attached so as to promote efficient precautions by those who are at risk. Failure to differentiate among insureds in the way a private market would results in subsidies. To be sure, sometimes these seeming subsidies are justified because price classification is simply too costly to engage in. Other times, failure to discriminate in pricing may reflect a positive choice to favor certain parties who are risk, such as low (or high) income people. In any event, the absence of actuarially sensible risk-related premiums can discourage both insurance companies and certain property owners from participating, and it can cause some people to incur risks they would not run were their insurance costs actuarially fair.

Beyond assuring the availability of certain types of property damage insurance, other federal insurance programs protect against potentially disastrous financial losses. Moreover, unlike, say, the California earthquake program or the National Flood Insurance Program, these financial loss insurance regimes are largely universal (effectively mandatory). They include the programs that insure bank deposits,[24] private pensions,[25] and securities held by stock brokers[26] against the financial collapse of various institutions.

Governments also create social insurance programs that come into play in the event of a disaster, even if these mechanisms are by no means restricted to disaster settings. In this respect they are like efforts to assure insurer solvency, as noted already.

Social insurance is aimed at personal loss, not property loss. For example, in the United States our social security system effectively requires workers to partially insure against loss of income from retirement or death, the Medicare Part A component of social security in effect requires workers to insure against the need for costly hospitalization services when they become elderly (or disabled), and the unemployment compensation system in effect requires workers to partially insure against the loss of wages arising from involuntary unemployment. Their mandatory nature makes them like bank deposit insurance, but unlike flood insurance.

Mandatory social insurance is perhaps best justified on the combined grounds that some workers would otherwise feel themselves unable to afford this sort of insurance and that many would, in any case, simply choose not to purchase coverage that later turns out to be needed. This can be viewed as a kind of collective paternalism that forces people to do what is best for their longer run interests, regardless of their short term preferences. Alternatively, it can be viewed as an effort to force people to contribute in advance their own fair share (or at least something) to a scheme that will help them in times of personal need, rather than having them rely upon taxpayers in general when the time comes.

The key point here is that, when people suffer personally from a societal disaster, general social insurance is already in place, and so certain disaster victims (and their families) can call on this scheme to help compensate for their income loses, medical expenses, and so on. If nothing else, this means that any special disaster victim compensation arrangement needs to consider how to deal with the availability of basic social insurance. And it may well mean that the wider and more generous the underlying social security safety net, the less need there will be for special governmental intervention in case of a disaster.

Furthermore, while not exactly social insurance, it is also vital to appreciate that all sorts of other government "relief" programs that are available to victims of what might be seen as personal disasters are normally intended to be there to help as well when it is a societal disaster that has occurred. This includes income support provided by welfare programs like TANF, housing support programs like public housing units and so-called section 8 housing vouchers, food assistance provided by food stamps and so on. Again, special disaster relief schemes need to take that fact into account.

As an aside, some people will already be receiving benefits from needs-based relief programs and/or social insurance schemes like unemployment compensation when a societal disaster strikes their community. Hence, an a important, and sometimes quite difficult, role for government is simply to assure the continued provision of assistance to those who were already obtaining that support before the event (a problem much exacerbated in the aftermath of hurricane Katrina, for example, because so many claimants were relocated to other states)[27].

C. Providing Victim Compensation Either When Government Should Have Prevented the Disaster or When It Is the Sort of Disaster We Aspire to Have Government Prevent

First, suppose government actors should have prevented a catastrophe from occurring, but failed properly to carry out precautionary obligations, or carried them out in an inadequate or careless manner that facilitates the disaster.

In such settings, the public may believe that, as a result, government has an obligation to compensate the victims. People can have rather different visions of what they mean by "government" in such settings.

One approach is to think of government as some independent body with money, like a corporation or other private enterprise, whose treasury is appropriately tapped when the misfeasance or nonfeasance of its employees or officers brings about a disaster that should have been avoided. Perhaps the more realistic view is that if we collectively (through our elected leaders and our employees) failed to get the job properly done, then perhaps we collectively have an obligation to provide compensation to those who are harmed as a result.

However this is conceived, one way to effectuate this role of government is to allow victims to file tort claims against the government. Yet, in fact, the Federal Tort Claims Act (FTCA)[28] is quite unreceptive to many of the claims that would likely be made with respect to failures by federal officials to prevent disasters. The result is that when the finger of responsibility is pointed at federal government actors, even carelessness, incompetence or both may not suffice to impose financial responsibility via tort law on the deepest of pockets we have – even in cases where, had the wrongdoing actors been private parties, tort recovery would have been allowed (and the actors' employer would be vicariously liable).

This immunity is especially sweeping at the federal level because the FTCA protects government from tort liability for the consequences of discretionary acts (a concept that has been broadly defined). This includes discretionary acts that juries would later have found to be altogether unreasonable. Other federal statutes contain special tort immunity provisions, for example, in legislation governing the flood control and flood insurance program. State tort claims acts often contain weaker governmental tort immunity provisions, although the law in some states is largely parallel to federal law.

This discretionary immunity provision of governmental tort claims acts primarily rests on considerations of separation of powers. The idea here is that the judicial system should not be second guessing the policy (and related) choices made by the executive/administrative branch. The point seems to be that, if the public objects that a wrong decision was made, it is not to register this judgment through juries, but rather through other political processes, such as by pressuring legislators or executive actors to decide differently, by voting those who are misbehaving out of office and so on. Of course, these alternative remedies are of little solace to disaster victims who are now suffering because of incompetent government.

On the other hand, it is important as well to emphasize that immunity under tort claims acts does not necessarily mean that government will, or should, turn its back on its victims. It is simply that their remedy, if any, is not to come through tort law. That, in turn, suggests that a role of government might be to create a specific disaster-compensation scheme (other than tort law) to provide compensation in such instances.

In any event, it is not only for specific instances of public "fault" for which government may be called upon to provide disaster compensation. As a society, we broadly see it as government's job, for example, to provide public security – to protect us against crime, of both the routine sort and the special sort that amount to social catastrophes, like large-scale terrorist attacks. This goal for government is a matter of aspiration, and thoughtful people concede that is simply not feasible for government to prevent all such crimes.

Nonetheless, when such events do occur that are either personal disasters for victims or broader societal disasters, then, as members of society at large, we may conclude that, in effect, we should all chip in and provide compensation to victims.

State "victims of violent crimes" laws[29] are perhaps best viewed as an example of government acting in this way. These schemes (which are neither all that effective nor very generous) are usually meant to provide financial help to those who are made destitute or otherwise devastated by some violent crime to their person. Government aid provided to victims of urban riots might also be viewed in this way.

In hindsight, some might argue that the September 11th Compensation Plan should be seen as a program by which government is taking responsibility for its failures to prevent the terrorist acts of 2001.[30] But, even if one believes that the federal government could not have stopped these terrorist acts (which was the general view at the time the compensation plan was enacted), the 9/11 plan might be justified by the aspirational idea that, since it is government's job to stop terrorism in general, it is government's duty to compensate terrorism victims even if their harms were not reasonably preventable in this instance.

So, too, the scale of the extra-ordinary assistance voted by Congress in the aftermath of hurricane Katrina may be justified either on the basis of specific prevention failings of federal officials (if one believes that) or on the basis of the more general social understanding that flood prevention is a federal responsibility.

D. Providing Victim Compensation as an Alternative to Tort Recovery

Sometimes the prospect that future or existing victims will sue in tort those responsible for a disaster (or potential disaster) is socially daunting. On the one hand, the fear of possible tort liability in the future, were a disastrous accident to occur, may prevent what otherwise is thought to be a socially desirable project from going forward at all. On the other hand, once a disaster has occurred, the potentially crushing burden of tort liability may threaten the very existence of some highly desirable social good or service.

In these settings, one possibility is for government, either ex ante or ex post, simply to bar tort claims (or at least some claims, or at least limit the amount of claims). This is, in effect, what the New York Court of Appeals did in the "blackout" case discussed earlier when, ex post, it cut off the electric company's tort responsibility to those who were not direct customers of Con Edison. This decision followed an earlier New York case (which generally reflects the law across the U.S.) which freed a water company from potentially devastating tort liability for carelessly failing to provide the water it had promised to make available at local hydrants for firefighters to use to contend with burning buildings.[31]

Denying a tort remedy need not necessarily mean that victims simply go uncompensated, however. For fire risks, for example, one explanation for the tort immunity of water companies is that these accidental losses may well be better dealt with via private fire insurance (both because it is both widely available and widely purchased and because that insurance, unlike water rates, is priced to reflect the fire risk attached to the insured building).

But other times, society might conclude that government should provide (or arrange for) a substitute compensation arrangement in lieu of tort law. I next consider three somewhat different settings in which this has occurred.

1. Compensation plans adopted in advance of a (potential) disaster that are designed to facilitate the pursuit of a social good

When the nuclear power industry was getting underway, commercial liability insurers were unwilling to provide broad coverage against the risk of harm from a serious reactor meltdown, presumably on the basis that (1) the likelihood of this happening, although very small, was quite unpredictable, and (2) the amount of harm, while potentially astronomical, was also unpredictable. Faced with altogether inadequate insurance coverage, the nation's electrical utility companies announced that they were unwilling to develop nuclear energy because they were unwilling to risk the company's entire wealth on the even slight chance of serious accident.

Some opponents of nuclear power argued that this was a good reason for never allowing this sort of development in the first place, i.e., an unwillingness of the industry to take responsibility for the social costs it might impose. Yet, politicians concluded that the benefits of nuclear power outweighed the disaster risk, and that society would be harmed were nuclear power to be stalled because of the overhang of tort liability.

Hence, in 1957 Congress adopted the Price-Anderson Act[32] which simultaneously restricted the tort rights of potential victims of a serious nuclear accident and mandated private arrangements to assure at least some compensation to victims were such an accident to happen. This scheme technically did not create a substitution for tort law, but it amounts to much the same thing. Specifically, the Act provided that the power company where the accident occurred would be strictly liable in tort for the consequences (this was probably the law of most states anyway, although there had not then been any cases directly on point). But it limited tort recovery in an inventive way.

First, power companies with nuclear reactors were required to purchase the level of liability insurance that the insurance industry was then willing to sell (and over time as the industry capacity has grown, Congress has amended the Act to insist on higher coverage). Second, since this coverage would be quite inadequate in the event of a grave nuclear accident, the Act further provided that, were there such an accident, then every company in the nation operating a nuclear plant would have to contribute into a fund a specific amount per plant that would be used to pay additional victim compensation in the local area where the disaster occurred. The total contribution that would be available to the fund has increased over time, both as the number of nuclear power plants grew and as the Congressionally-required contribution per plant has been expanded. Through this plan, the government, in effect, forces the entire industry to pool its resources and collectively insure against the risk all of the firms face.

Even this much expanded coverage, however, would presumably not suffice were the U.S. to suffer an accident of the Chernobyl sort. Fortunately, nothing like that has happened in America so far, and so we have no experience with what would happen next. The Act promises vaguely that Congress would then take appropriate action, but does not provide for exactly what that would be or whether it would be other than what the federal government already provides in the event of other disasters, discussed below.

A quite different strategy was employed in 1976 in furtherance of the federal government's effort to get a large share of Americans to take the so-called Swine-flu vaccine.[33] Because they could not get tort liability insurance protection, vaccine makers initially refused to supply the product at a time when federal health officials feared that, without a large nationwide vaccination campaign, a pandemic flu that was predicted for the up-coming flu season could kill a very large number of Americans. In short, the Ford Administration feared a disaster in the making.

To break the log-jam, the federal government relieved the vaccine makers of the tort liability they feared; instead, simply put, Congress agreed that the government itself could be sued as though it were the vaccine provider. Alas, things turned out very different from what was anticipated. The dreaded pandemic did not arrive. The vaccine was taken by a substantial number of people, but, as a bitter irony, it turned out to be highly dangerous in some cases, and many were seriously injured. In the end, the federal government wound up paying substantial victim compensation (through tort law).

2. *Compensation schemes designed to relieve a tort law crisis with respect to a social good*

A somewhat different strategy was embraced with respect to childhood vaccines. In the 1980s, pharmaceutical firms making those vaccines were beginning to be successfully sued by parents on behalf of children who, the parents claimed, were being severely injured by the side effects of vaccines (especially the vaccine aimed at preventing pertussis or whooping cough as it is informally called). Were the claims about side effects correct, the nation had a public health disaster on its hands. While it was very important for children's health to curtail whooping cough, at the same time it would be very bad if many children were being gravely harmed in the process. National public health leaders concluded that, on balance, continued widespread vaccination was the socially more desirable route for the nation to take, especially as there was some doubt in their minds that the vaccines were actually having the claimed side effects. But, faced with potentially enormous tort liability (especially as compared with the amount they could realistically charge for their products), the vaccine makers threatened to cease vaccine production.

Notice, that what is different about this category from that described above, as illustrated by nuclear power and swine flu, is that here injuries have already occurred and tort suits have been filed and some have already been successful. Yet, as with those other examples, the fear of future tort liability was seen to threaten the provision of something vital to the nation.

In response, Congress adopted the Childhood Vaccine Act[34]. This law provides an alternative to the tort remedy. Claims can be filed with the U.S. Court of Claims on behalf of any child who displays certain symptoms within a certain period after receiving the vaccination. The Court then determines a compensation amount that the family is offered. A key element of the compensation package to be offered is that, in no case, will the amount of non- economic loss compensation exceed $250,000 (which is far less than some juries had been awarding for pain and suffering and possibly for punitive damages in certain individual cases).

Families are not required to accept the sum offered by the Court of Claims, but if they reject that sum and decide to sue the vaccine maker anyway, the plaintiffs are then subject to federal rules as to tort liability that make it much harder for them to win, at least in states that had earlier moved in the direction of imposing strict liability on the defendants merely for making a product that a jury might find was the cause of the child's injury.

This plan is not funded by taxpayers generally. Rather, a fee attached to each vaccination, thereby, in a sense, making families as a group insure against the risk that their child might be an unlucky victim (this puts aside issues of whether individual families actually pay this fee or have it waived or paid for by their health insurance).

Later, a scientific consensus developed (although not everyone has accepted it even yet) that the pertussis vaccine was not actually the cause of the harms the claiming children's families were assigning to it – the position of the vaccine makers all along. The initially sharp fall-off in the share of parents getting their children vaccinated has abated. And the number of claims that the whooping cough vaccine is causing severe harm has dropped. Nonetheless the statutory compensation scheme, with its presumption about causation, has continued in effect. And despite paying out benefits to about two thousand claimants, the scheme has faced considerable criticism for its delays and for what are seen as efforts by claims administrators to find creative ways of denying eligibility.

Florida and Virginia have also enacted plans with respect to medical malpractice that are somewhat similarly constructed, although they contain key differences.[35] In those instances, the states were faced with what they feared would become something of a catastrophe in the provision of medical services, especially with respect to the delivery of babies. At the time, large numbers of doctors were said to be refusing to do this work and moving their practices out of state.

The seeming cause of this pending potential disaster in the provision of medical care was a few extremely high medical malpractice awards against a few doctors in so-called "bad baby" cases, where the harms suffered by a severely- damaged newborn were being blamed on malpractice in the delivery process. The doctors asserted that these were unavoidable birth defects or unavoidable consequences of difficult childbirths, and that they were being held strictly liable. Regardless, even for doctors who had never been sued the consequence was that either malpractice liability insurance was no longer available (as some insurers withdrew from the market) or the rates charged obstetricians were skyrocketing, making it financially infeasible for many doctors to do this sort of work in those two states (or so they claimed).

In order to assure the continued provision of obstetrical care, the legislative solution adopted in both Virginia and Florida was intended to take away the right of future "bad baby" claimants to sue in tort, and in its place provide a compensation scheme for these children. As with the federal Childhood Vaccine Act, these state compensation plans, while mandated by legislation, are not funded by taxpayers at large, but instead by various actors who provide medical services (who presumably pass the cost on the public at large through higher fees).

These plans, especially Virginia's, have been criticized from a variety of perspectives and have not been copied elsewhere, although they continue in force. Moreover, creative lawyers have found ways to continue to bring tort claims in certain settings, especially under Florida's plan. Yet, whatever the plans' shortcomings or their contribution to solving the problem they were aimed at, the crisis in the provision of obstetrical services appears to have passed in both states.

3. *Preventing a possible social crisis that tort litigation might create*

As noted at several points already, the terrorist acts of 9/11 lead very quickly to the September 11th Victim Compensation Plan.[36] One justification for the adoption of the plan, as already explained, is that, even if government could not reasonably have prevented these acts (a now much-contested matter), we look to government generally to protect us from terrorism and when it does not, we pitch in as a nation to provide relief to those (or their families) who had the bad luck of being victims.

Yet, because of past practice, it is not altogether easy to explain the 9/11 plan on this basis. For example, even in recent years no such plan was enacted after the terrorist attacks on the ship the USS Cole (although arguably that event, especially since it took place outside the U.S. was not clearly understood to be a national "disaster"), or after the Oklahoma City bombing (although that was carried out by what arguably amounted to a domestic terrorist, perhaps social solidarity to help out victims of terrorists is more clearly felt with respect to foreign terrorists), or after the first World Trade Center bombing (although the harm done actually then was arguably not enough to amount to a disaster).

So, while it is true that the 9/11 terrorist acts were gigantically more harmful than those other examples of terrorism, there was a further feature of this event that I believe played a key role in the adoption of the compensation plan. From the outset it seems that our political leaders wanted to be sure that the national focus would remain centrally on the terrorists as the wrongdoers. In part, this may have been a desire by the Bush Administration to keep attention away from possible security lapses of the federal government, although, as a litigation matter, any such carelessness of that sort was probably immunized from tort liability anyway.

More important for my purposes here was the matter of potential airline tort liability – say, for the failure to secure access to the cockpit, or for failure to better supervise the screening of passengers. Not only might lawsuits against the airlines potentially undermine the foreign affairs line that the terrorists were the only bad guys here, but also, given the enormity of the disaster, tort liability could financially destroy two of our largest domestic carriers (United and American) both of whom were already in deep financial difficulties at the time. After all, earlier on Pan Am had been successfully sued for very large sums in connection with a terrorist destruction of one of its jets over Lockerbie Scotland in 1988.[37]

Hence, somewhat analogous to the Con Edison "blackout" disaster described above, as part of the September 11th Compensation Plan, airline tort liability was restricted by Congress to the maximum of their then in-place insurance policies (amounting to $1.5 billion with respect to each of the four planes that were lost).[38] This put the financial burden of potential tort liability on the insurers, and not the carriers.

But along with limiting airline liability, Congress adopted a compensation scheme that was designed to woo claims with respect to deceased (and injured) victims out of the tort system altogether and into a special benefit plan instead. As with the Childhood Vaccine Act, tort rights were not eliminated, by the 9/11 plan, although some procedural restraints were imposed beyond of the liability cap.

Unlike the Childhood Vaccine Act, claimants under the 9/11 plan were not made a firm offer that they could either adopt or reject and then sue in tort if they wish. Instead, the law provided that merely filing a claim with the plan precluded a tort claim, at least once an award was made by the plan. But not too much should be made of this difference since the 9/11 claims administrator made the claims-award process highly transparent. This meant that nearly all claimants could be quite certain as to approximately how much they would receive were they to make a claim on the plan.

With respect to those who were killed in the 9/11 disaster, the plan was extremely successful in enticing nearly all of those eligible (well more than 95%) to seek recovery from the plan rather than to sue. Perhaps this was because of what many viewed as the generosity of the plan, despite charges that the amounts provided for non-economic loss were too small in the eyes of some and despite complaints about the way the plan dealt with other victim sources of compensation. Perhaps another reason for the success of the plan was that claimants realized that if they sued the airlines they might well not win; for example, it is much easier in hindsight to complain about better searching passengers and better blocking cockpit access. Most of the perhaps 90 or so lawsuits on behalf of deceased victims that remained in play at the time the compensation plan ended continue to be unresolved five years after the disaster, reflecting the generally slow pace of tort cases filed in the aftermath of disasters (although press reports suggest that perhaps 30 of those cases have been settled, the terms of which settlements remain secret).

Note how this category of government action differs from the nuclear power problem because there no harm had yet occurred; and it differs from the childhood vaccine problem because there tort suits had already been brought and won. Moreover, in both of those other categories, the government action was to curtail tort claims arising from future harms, whereas the 9/11 plan was aimed at curtailing claims that technically had already arisen but had not yet been pursued. All three categories, however, share the central feature that future litigation was feared and government acted with the goal of containing that future litigation while at the same time assuring substantial victim compensation (even if not at the level provided to successful tort claimants).

E. Providing Victim Assistance to Overwhelmed Communities for Reasons of Altruism and National Solidarity

I want to turn now to yet a different justification for compensating disaster victims. It draws on notions of altruism combined with an understanding of the role of the larger community in helping out smaller groups in times of need.

As already suggested, if an event is not a societal disaster, then victims who find themselves in need can often look to their friends and neighbors, or perhaps local charities or even the wider (but still local) community, to help out. Indeed, some "disasters" are probably handled in just this way, for example, a mining disaster in which a dozen or so workers are killed.

But when it is a large scale societal disaster, the local community itself may be too undone, too devastated, to carry the burden of relief. In that case, a wider community – even the nation as a whole – may need to step in and help if the community is not to be permanently impaired. Put differently, on such occasions, it may well be that no other institution besides a larger governmental unit (often the federal government) is capable of organizing and delivering the needed help.

One could try to justify the national government providing compensation to victims of, say, erupting volcanoes on the ground that the wider community (here the nation) feels it appropriate for its tax dollars to be used to provide relief because the rest of us feel lucky that we were not victims this time (as we might well have been). That is, perhaps we see this form of aid as a sort of collective insurance.

Yet this way of thinking about the funding and provision of aid to, say, large scale natural disaster victims, is problematic. After all, only a relatively small share of Americans is truly at risk of, say, hurricane damage, and certainly some people are much more at risk than others. So, too, only a relatively small share of Americans is subject to a significant risk of earthquake damage, and so on.

One might argue that when you take into account all of the different societal disaster risks, we are all subject to one or more of them and so we are all happy to chip in to provide a scheme that helps out those of us who are unlucky enough to be victims. Yet, in the end, surely the truth is that people in some localities are much more at risk of societal disasters than are others, and if the compensation plan is paid for by the nation, then thinking this as a kind of collectively desired insurance has some awkwardness to it.

This suggests that insurance may not really be the proper metaphor. I believe it is more a matter of a combination of a widely felt sense of altruism and a sense of national solidarity. Although Americans do contribute aid to disaster victims in other nations (individually, through private charities, and through government aid programs), even greater help is provided to victims of "our own" disasters.

Providing help on those occasions is a way for us to show that we Americans care about each other. We might not routinely make efforts to help out individually devastated people, but when it is a societal disaster, we want to show something of our own humanity – not only perhaps with an individual voluntary gesture, but also by having our government come in with help on our behalf.[39] Moreover, as already noted, when the devastation is broad and deep enough, communities themselves are endangered, or at least temporarily overwhelmed, and so helping out in such circumstances might be an especially effective use of public funds.

Hurricane disaster relief may be best understood in this way. Although the unavailability of private property insurance for flood damage may also be thought to justify such aid as a way of government providing substitute insurance, don't forget that the federal government has already stepped in to this breach by creating the federal flood insurance scheme. Hence, federal aid provided to individual hurricane victims is typically well beyond what the government has seen as its insurance-creator role, and indeed, substantial hurricane assistance goes to those who would not need it, or, more likely, would need less, had they not failed to purchase flood insurance in the first place.

Thinking about disaster victim compensation as a matter of altruism on behalf of the wider community may also help explain why the 9/11 compensation plan was so quickly adopted without any noticeable public objection that this was not a proper use of taxpayer dollars. That is, New York City victims, the passengers on the various planes, as well as Pentagon victims, were understood to have taken a hit for the nation, and we as a nation had an especially strong psychological need to show solidarity with them – even though citizens living in most of the country must have realized, at least afterwards, that Manhattan was a far more likely terrorist target then their community was.

And the strength of that feeling of solidarity may help explain the extent of the compensation provided. Normally, FEMA and its programs are the central ongoing way in which the federal government deals with what might be termed our national disasters. And FEMA played an important role in response to the 9/11 disaster as well. But it is particularly worth emphasizing here that the 9/11 compensation plan was far more generous to the families of those who were killed on 9/11 than FEMA was, for example, to the victims of the Northridge,

California earthquake, especially as FEMA does not provide anything simply on account of a death from a disaster.

Three aspects of disaster relief can make federal aid based on this altruistic instinct somewhat dicey, however. One, noted already, is how to feel about those victims who might have insured but did not and now are suffering devastating losses. That is, how much should these victims be held accountable for their past acts and how much should we be forgiving of what might seem like a prior lapse? In considering the matter, there is also the question of how much should we fear that providing public assistance after disasters occur will send a message that will undermine self-help efforts in the future?

A second concern stems from the reality that some communities are better prepared to deal with local disasters than are others. Sometimes this is a matter of better advance planning and better leadership as the disaster unfolds. When some places need more help because of failings along these lines, the same conflicting instincts come into play as just noted above.

A third concern is that, under the pressure to provide help to large numbers of people amid chaotic circumstances, those managing disaster aid are very much at risk of either burdening desperate people with oppressively bureaucratic requirements or paying out sums to fraudulent claimants. So, too, aid-providers risk either paying too much for rescue, clean-up, and recovery services that in some cases are not needed at all, or else failing promptly to get help where it is very much needed. In short, the good will underlying the public's instinct that a community should be helped to deal with a disaster can easily be undermined by program administration that, alas, is often easily exposed as too tight or too loose.[40]

Notwithstanding these risks, central government help (largely through FEMA) of one sort or another continues to be provided in disaster after disaster. One additional explanation for this may be that, by its past practice, the federal government has created expectations that run throughout the nation that this is one of its important roles, and therefore, to fail to help would threaten a general loss of confidence in government at a critical moment. Put somewhat differently, in the tumultuous times that often follow a societal disaster the public today regularly counts on government to step in to restore order and to get normal social and economic life up and running once more.

In the larger picture, it is also important to appreciate that some communities that suffer from a catastrophic event will (before the event) simply be poorer, and hence structurally less able to help out those of its members who face enormous plights in the aftermath of the disaster. This means that the same physical calamity may call for very different amounts (or types) of help depending on where it occurs. This reality suggests that national disaster assistance may turn out, at least in some cases, to be a re-distributive measure that is disproportionately concentrated on the "have-nots." In one sense we can be comfortable with this result, since helping those with greatest need may be morally laudable.

What may be troubling, however, is that both our willingness to act on this instinct, as well as the level of assistance we seem prepared to provide, appear to be greater in the face of vivid disasters than with respect to, say, the disastrous consequences of every-day grinding poverty. Perhaps this is explicable on the ground that many Americans think that, unlike so many victims of major disasters, all too many routine poverty victims are themselves in some respects to blame for their condition or that routine poverty-assisting schemes (rather than dramatic gestures) are the right way to attack this social problem (which may also explain why many people who think of themselves as generous, and occasionally even impulsive, donors to organized charity do not give to street beggars).

Yet, it may well also be that, given all the need for financial help that exists in our society, we are just unable (or unwilling) to extend ourselves in especially generous ways all the time. We'd like to show ourselves to be generous at least some of the time, however. And from that perspective, helping out when there is a societal disaster is perhaps symbolically most potent, as well as most likely to gain the greatest attention and public recognition, thereby making us feel best about ourselves for providing the aid. This may also explain why those advocates seeking private and public contributions to support their favorite charitable endeavor often claim that the objects of their concern are facing an "emergency" (or some other word or phrase that suggests a temporary but extreme need, like those arising from natural catastrophes).

III. The Nature of the Compensation Provided

Although this is not the occasion to discuss them at length, I want to close by noting a few key issues that arise once we decide that some government assistance to individual disaster victims will be provided. They go to the questions of what sort of aid is to be given and how much.

Disaster victims can be given grants or loans. The federal government provides both, but with respect to efforts to rebuild private property damaged or destroyed in societal disasters, it primarily provides loans via the Small Business Administration ("SBA"), albeit at less than market interest rates, which is an implicit grant. Most other victim compensation is not repayable.

Individual disaster victims can be given cash, or vouchers aimed good for certain purchases, or in-kind aid (like shelter, food, and the like). FEMA provides all of these types of help. The 9/11 compensation plan, by contrast, only provided cash.

The focus of the disaster aid can be on temporary needs or long run needs. In the immediate aftermath of a hurricane, for example, people may need basic temporary shelter; then they may need transitional housing while they are finding a new place to settle or their former homes are cleaned up, fixed, and/or rebuilt; and they may need help with those processes. Between FEMA and the SBA,[41] the federal government offers all of these.

Help can be partial or complete (at least to the extent that money and other sorts of aid can do that). Hence, a key issue in disaster aid is the share of the victim's loss to be replaced. This introduces considerations of deductibles (how much of the initial loss is simply to be borne by the victim?), "co-insurance" (what proportion of the covered loss is to be borne by the victim?), and caps (is there to be a maximum placed on assistance?). The California Earthquake Authority, for example, imposes a relatively high deductible on the policies it sells and puts a cap on the maximum coverage it will offer.

So too, not all losses need be treated the same way. Damage to physical property could be treated differently from personal injury or death on the one hand or loss of intangible property on the other. Even with respect to personal injury and death, non-economic loss could be treated differently from lost income, medical and other expenses and the like. The existing practice is a patchwork quilt. Some of the schemes described earlier provide nothing for personal injury or death; some provide for income replacement, medical care and other expenses, but not for pain and suffering; yet others provide compensation for pain and suffering as well, although in at least some of them the amount is capped.

Finally, as already mentioned, a particularly difficult issue with respect to disaster relief concerns the treatment of multiple possible sources of compensation. Not infrequently, victims find that there is more than one place they can turn for financial help in the face of a catastrophe. The question that all aid providers must answer is how they should deal with those other sources.

There are at least five possible solutions. One is for each source to ignore other sources and thereby risk overcompensation as victims recover for the same loss from more than one compensation provider. A second is to structure the aid providers so that they act in some agreed order, with the first provider paying without attention to the others, and each provider after that taking into account the compensation already provided by those who went before it. A third approach is to cumulate all the aid that all providers might make available to any one victim and then somehow draw a proportionate share of the needed compensation from each. Fourth, victims might be forced to opt to receive aid from one provider only, thereby foregoing compensation that others might have given. Finally, the issue may be sought to be avoided by re-defining the nature of each provider's compensation so that each is aimed at a different sort of need. For example, one provider would attend to temporary needs and the others to longer term needs, and among the latter one would deal with personal losses and the other property losses and so on.

What is clear is that U.S. and state government approaches to disaster compensation have adopted a variety of solutions to this issue as well. In the 9/11 plan, for example, claimants were forced to opt between tort law and plan benefits, and if they selected the latter, they knew that their compensation amount would be reduced by any life insurance proceeds they had, but not by immediate aid they had received from charity groups like the Red Cross. Swine flu vaccine victims, by contrast, were subject to very different rules.

Perhaps this seeming inconsistency along these various benefit parameters reflects genuinely different social understanding of the various programs. But perhaps not. Maybe the diversity in responses is better understood as accidental. Maybe greater awareness of past practice would result in more uniformity.

For now, this takes us to a final, perhaps self-evident, point. When adopted by Congress or state legislatures, the details of any plan providing compensation to victims of societal disasters are fashioned in the crucible of politics, and not infrequently the politics of crisis. In such settings, it might be too much to insist that government always follow certain consistent principles in determining when and how to provide assistance. Yet, at least the key political figures, their advisors, and the interest groups pushing for assistance may benefit from a more thorough understanding of the very different roles that government has played, and might play, in these circumstances. In this essay I have sought to provide such taxonomy.

ENDNOTES

1. http://www.fema.gov/.

2. U.S. General Accounting Office Major Management Challenges and Program Risks: Federal Emergency Management Agency (GAO-03-113 2003).

3. Robert T. Stafford Disaster Relief and Emergency Assistance Act, as amended by Public Law 93-288, June, 2006; http://www.fema.gov/about/stafact.shtm.

4. R. Posner, Catastrophe: Risk and Response (2004).

5. http://www.disastercenter.com/; http://historical.disaster.net/; http://www.disasternews.net/; http://www.redcross.org/services/disaster/ .

6. Paying the Price: The Status and Role of Insurance Against Natural Disasters in the United States (Kunreuther and Roth eds. 1998); Jaffee and Russell, Catastrophic Insurance, Capital Markets, and Uninsurable Risks, 64 J. Risk and Insurance 205 (1997).

7. http://www.ehow.com/how_110961_obtain-disaster-insurance.html.

8. Kunreuther, Has the Time Come for Comprehensive Natural Disaster Insurance? in On Risk and Disaster (Daniels, Kettl, and Kunreuther, eds.) 175 (2006).

9. Schooner and Siuda-Pfeffer, Post-Katrina Reconstruction Liability: Exposing the Interior Risk-bearer, 43 Harv. J. Legis. 287-327 (2006).

10. Restatement of Torts 3rd section 20.

11. Restatement of Torts 3rd Products Liability section 2.

12. Levandoski v. Cone, 841 A.2d 208 (2004).

13. Strauss v. Belle Realty Co., 482 N.E.2d 34 (1985).

14. Trebilcock and Daniels, Rationales and Instruments for Government Intervention in Natural Disasters, in On Risk and Disaster (Daniels, Kettl and Kunreuther eds.) 89 (2006); Rabin (with Bratis), Financial Compensation for Victims of Catastrophes: United States, in Compensation for Victims of Catastrophes: A Comparative Legal Approach (Faure and Hartlief eds.) 303 (2006); Moss, Courting Disaster: The Transformation of Disaster Policy since 1803, in The Financing of Catastrophic risk (Froot ed.) 307 (1999); D. Farber and J. Chen, Disasters and the Law: Katrina and Beyond (2006).

15. Gruenberg v. Aetna Ins. Co., 510 P.2d 1032 (1973).

16. K. Abraham, Insurance Law and Regulation (4th ed.) 108-113 (2005).

17. http://www.redcross.org/index.html.

18. U.S. General Accounting Office, Terrorism Insurance: Alternative Programs for Protecting Insurance Consumers (GAO-02-199T, 2001).

19. http://www.earthquakeauthority.com/.

20. http://www.floir.com/FHCF.htm.

21. http://www.fema.gov/plan/prevent/floodplain/How_the_NFIP_works.shtm

22. http://www.ustreas.gov/offices/domestic-finance/financial-institution/terrorism- insurance/; Levmore and Logue, Insuring Against Terrorism – And Crime, 102 Mich. L. Rev. 268 (2003).

23. Kunreuther, Has the Time Come for Comprehensive Natural Disaster Insurance? in On Risk and Disaster (Daniels, Kettl, and Kunreuther, eds.) 175 (2006); for a recent conference on this broad topic, see Insuring Catastrophic Losses: The Status of TRIA and Proposed Natural Disaster Backstops (University of Connecticut Law School), www.wrf.com/risk2.

24. http://www.fdic.gov/deposit/index.html.

25. http://www.pbgc.gov/.

26. http://www.sipc.org/.

27. Winston, Golden, Finegold, Rueben, Turner, and Zuckerman, Federalism after Hurricane Katrina: How Can Social Programs Respond to a Major Disaster? Urban Institute (2006).

28. http://www.lectlaw.com/def/f071.htm.

29. http://www.nacvcb.org/progdir.html.

30. http://september11fund.org/.

31. H.R. Moch Co. v. Rensselaer Water Co., 159 N.E. 896 (1928).

32. http://www.gao.gov/new.items/d04654.pdf; http://www.nei.org/.

33. http://www.law.duke.edu/journals/lcp/articles/lcp64dAutumn2001p49.htm.

34. http://www.hrsa.gov/vaccinecompensation/.

35. Bovbjerg and Sloan, No-Fault for Medical Injury: Theory and Evidence, 67 University of Cincinnati Law Review, 53 (1998).

36. http://www.usdoj.gov/archive/victimcompensation/; Rabin, The Quest for Fairness in Compensating Victims of September 11, 49 Cleveland State Law Review 573 (2001).

37. In re Air Disaster at Lockerbie Scotland on December 21, 1988, 37 F.3d 804 (1994).

38. http://leahy.senate.gov/press/200109/010921a.html.

39. G. Calabresi and P. Bobbitt, Tragic Choices (1978).

40. For a good example of how a federal aid program sold to Congress as a response to disaster can be converted into something that looks more like "pork barrel" politics, see Gaul, Morgan and Cohen, No Drought Required for Federal Drought Aid, Washington Post, July 18, 2006 A01.

41. http://www.sba.gov/disaster_recov/index.html.

Part IV

Doctrinal Simplification

Much of the 1L Torts course aims to expose students to the current state of tort doctrine, helping them master how tort law got to where it is today. For many students, learning the law of torts is the central objective and learning how to read and analyze common law decisions of judges is a skill that must be acquired along the way – even if instructors might reverse the order of importance of those two matters. The magnitude of the latter is why instructors typically seek to discourage new students from jumping quickly to read outlines, treatises, bar review material and the like. Nonetheless, in due course many students turn to outside reading to supplement their casebook, and unless they opt to read scholarly law journal-type pieces that are referenced in typical torts casebooks, they are likely to turn to modest length books that focus on doctrine.

The chapters in this book so far have been almost entirely about perspectives on tort law other than substantive tort doctrine. This final part is different, but not in the usual way. It is importantly about doctrine. But the chapters are not centrally there to explain current doctrine. Rather they are about proposed changes in doctrine. Most importantly, taken together they are about a dramatic simplification of tort law (at least as applied to personal injury and death).

Chapter 13 calls for the elimination of the doctrine of "assumption of risk" in tort law. It argues that this common law "defense" is unnecessary, confusing, and sometimes leads judges (and students) to the wrong result. Chapter 14 calls for reshaping the "duty" element in the cause of action for negligence. It shows how duty limitations that are now spread throughout tort law can be gathered up into one simple idea, and then it presents in a thematic way the various arguments that justify allowing someone who carelessly injures another to escape liability in tort for that injury. Chapter 15 calls for the elimination of a separate law of land occupier (owner) liability in tort. It argues that recent doctrinal developments mean that what has conventionally been taught as a separate field can and should now be folded into basic negligence law to the betterment of both arenas. Chapter 16 calls for a far more sweeping simplification of tort law (at least as applied to personal injury and death cases), including what are now treated as intentional torts as well as cases of negligence. It points the way towards a future Restatement (Fourth) of Torts. Finally, Chapter 17 presents something of an overview of this entire book in the form of a description and critique of a large project of the American Law Institute, begun in the 1980s and abandoned in the early 1990s. Like this book, that project took a much wider view of the law of torts.

To re-emphasize the point, while readers of this Part will be exposed to the current state of play of tort law in the areas covered, the lesson sought to be taught is different: tort law can be made better and better understood through a radical simplification of much of it.

Chapter 13

Casting Aside "Assumption of Risk"

Suppose you visit one of our great National Parks and you see an advertisement for a ride in a four-seat airplane providing breath-taking views of the area. You go to the ticket office and watch a brief video that provides an indication of what you will be able to see. In the video you are warned that bad weather could limit your views and conceivably cause the plan to crash; you are also told that to reduce the danger to yourself you should always keep your seatbelt fastened while in the air. When you finish watching the video and have decided to take the flight, you see a paper sign that has just been put up in front of the ticket office saying there will be no trips for at least the next three hours because of dangerous weather conditions. You chat up the pilot who says that while the company is always conservative about weather, he thinks it is fine to take a trip now. He remarks that of course the plane could crash; indeed, he jests, it is always possible that he could fly carelessly, though quickly noting that he has been doing this trip for ten years without any problems. You say that you would love to take the trip right now because the views look so beautiful in the video and because your other obligations make it impossible for you to wait around for three hours or more. The pilot says, OK he will take you up now. Before take-off you are asked to sign a standard form that releases the enterprise from any liability for any injury you might suffer during the trip except if its employees are grossly negligent (or worse).

At this point you have assumed several *physical* risks. The plane could crash from bad weather or the pilot's negligence (either in taking the trip at all or in the way he flies the plane); if there is trouble during the flight, you could be injured worse by not wearing a seat belt. If you sign that form, you have also agreed in writing to largely waive your potential right to sue the enterprise in case you are injured (sometimes termed "express assumption of risk").

None of this yet tells us anything about the legal doctrine termed "assumption of risk" or sometimes "implied assumption of risk." "Assumption of risk" is/was a complete defense at common law and where applicable means/meant that the plaintiff is deemed to have assumed the *legal* risk of injury – that is, to bear the loss herself rather than being able to shift it to another through tort law.

This chapter argues that "assumption of risk" is a confusing and unnecessary legal doctrine that can sometimes lead people to the wrong result. Often, the defendant should win the case because she owed the plaintiff no duty or did not breach that duty (i.e., did not act negligently). "Assumption of risk" is unnecessary for such cases. Other times the defendant and the plaintiff were both at fault and the loss should be shared under the modern regime of comparative negligence; in those cases, applying "assumption of risk" leads to the wrong result. Still other times the defendant was at fault and should fully compensate the victim (merely warning of the danger did not fully satisfy the defendant's duty of care); in those cases as well "assumption of risk" leads to the wrong result. This, in simple terms, is the position put forward in this chapter. As will be explained, the hypothetical given here about the planned flight over a National Park, raises all of these problems.

In addition to helping to get the outcomes of cases right, doing away with the doctrine of "assumption of risk" will help eliminate the confusion between assuming physical risks and assuming legal risks. As for "express assumption of risk," that too is an unneeded phrase that is better talked of in terms of an agreement to waive liability for negligence – which agreement may be legally upheld or may be invalidated as against public policy.

This chapter was delivered as the Monsanto Lecture in 1997, an annual invited lecture on tort law hosted by Valparaiso Law School and published as Stephen D. Sugarman, "Assumption of Risk," 31 Valparaiso University Law Review 833 (1997). It is reprinted with the permission of the journal. Since then the American Law Institute's Restatement of Torts (Third) has largely embraced the position set forward here. Some tort decisions are also coming around to the position advanced here, although often in confusing ways.

ASSUMPTION OF RISK

I. INTRODUCTION[1]

There is confusion at the very top. I refer to a famous opinion, known to generations of law students as the case of "the Flopper," authored by that common law giant Justice Benjamin Cardozo.[2] The whole point of the Coney Island amusement park ride was to flop its helpless participants to the floor. That is what made it fun, as every participant clearly realized. If years of experience were any guide, the Flopper was a largely harmless amusement. But on one occasion it yielded an unfortunate accident -- the plaintiff's fractured knee cap. Cardozo's marvelous style foretells the outcome at the outset when he refers to the plaintiff as "a vigorous young man."

The opinion flops, however, when Cardozo reaches for the Latin maxim "volenti non fit injuria." This is usually translated as "he who consents cannot receive an injury." That, of course, is transparently false. The consenting victim in the Flopper case clearly did receive an injury, and a serious one at that. One might quickly retort that the Latin maxim does not mean to refer to the physical injury; rather, it refers to the legal injury. Yet that sweeping pronouncement, too, is clearly incorrect as I will soon demonstrate.

But first I want to underline here a theme to which I will return throughout. All too often it is the victim's apparent consent to the physical injury that has captured the legal mind -- with scant attention given to whether there might properly be a difference between that consent and consent to the legal injury.

Yet there is a difference. Suppose I go to a plastic surgeon to discuss a possible nose job. My doctor says that while I almost surely will look better afterwards, I need to understand that it is always possible that she might carelessly perform the surgery, leaving me with a very distorted face. To which I reply, "Doctor, I trust you. I'll take that chance." Now suppose, as my luck would have it, her hand was not very steady that day, and, as a result of her negligence, I emerge from surgery looking like the after-version of Dorian Gray. Although I clearly chose to run this very risk -- that is, the physical risk -- am I prevented from successfully suing her in malpractice? Of course not. I may not be able to regain my original appearance, but I clearly can win money damages through tort law. In short, volenti non fit injuria simply does not apply.

This illustrates the central problem of the doctrinal muddle I explore here. A so-called principle that may or may not apply is of little help: indeed, it is confusing, unnecessary, and if we are not careful, it will lead us to the wrong outcome.

Of course, if my doctor had me sign a document in which I agreed not to sue her even if she committed malpractice on me, and assuming that in our state such agreements not to sue are legally valid,[3] then I would indeed lose my tort suit against her. But by merely consenting to the physical risk of her carelessly wielded scalpel, I surely did not agree that I would refrain from suing her. In short, I consented to the danger, but I still received a legal injury. I assumed the physical risk, but not the financial risk.

To be quite clear about it, the volenti principle relied upon by Cardozo is just another way of stating the doctrine of "assumption of risk."[4] These are not different ideas; they are the same idea -- the same bad idea. Yes, of course, the plaintiff assumed the risk in the Flopper case, just as I did in my plastic surgery debacle. In the end, he deserves to lose his tort suit, while I deserve to win mine. Assumption of risk, therefore, can have nothing to do with explaining the different outcomes. Rather, I win because my doctor was negligent, and the vigorous young man loses because the amusement park was not.

Cardozo's opinion reads as though assumption of risk is a separate complete defense that the amusement park could offer up even if it were negligent. That, as we will see, is wrongheaded. Worse, Cardozo compounds this confusion with one of his most memorable phrases: "the timorous may stay at home."[5]

Talking this way mis-focuses our attention on the plaintiff, when, in these sorts of situations, we should instead be concentrating on the conduct of the injurer. If my doctor started talking about "timorous" patients, suggesting I should have been content with the looks I originally had, that would get her nowhere.

Two main themes dominate the Sections that follow. The first theme is that when we are tempted to say "assumption of risk" we should instead say something else. Sometimes, we should rely on other tort doctrines that lead to the same result that conventionally has followed from the legal rule of "assumption of risk" -- a defendant's outright victory. These other doctrines are "no breach," "no duty," "no cause," and "no proximate cause," and it is important to appreciate why and where "assumption of risk" is a confusing substitute for each of them. In other situations, the defendant should not win outright, in which case saying "assumption of risk" yields the wrong result. Sometimes, the proper result is a partial plaintiff victory, and those cases should be handled by the partial defense of comparative negligence. Other times, the defendant's conduct merits taking full responsibility for the loss, so that invoking "assumption of risk" would tum the proper result on its head. Again, it is important to understand when and why these two very different outcomes should prevail.

My argument here is something of a mixed positive and normative one. On the one hand, I offer what I believe to be a parsimonious explanation for most of the existing cases, one that rejects "assumption of risk" as both superfluous and unilluminating of the real reason for the result.

On the other hand, by offering a better way of thinking about the cases, my analysis helps correct the mistakes that I believe some courts have made. In those settings "assumption of risk" is dangerously misleading. This mixed descriptive/prescriptive analysis is in the tradition of several prominent so-called "tort theorists" such as George Fletcher,[6] Richard Epstein[7] and Richard Posner.[8]

Re-directing tort doctrine as I propose reveals my second main theme -- the important and too little discussed problem that I call "when is warning enough?" Howard Latin has recently engaged this question in a most insightful way in the product injury field.[9] I offer, however, a more sweeping approach to the question, showing its importance across many types of accidents with which tort law deals. In the process, I explain why the "libertarian" instinct that "warning is always enough" is, and should be, rejected by the legal system, and, in turn, why, in some appropriate settings, the defendant need actually take precautions that reduce the risk of injury in order to avoid liability.

II. Not "Assumption of Risk" but Something Else

A. "Assumption of Risk" as "No Breach"

Many cases in which the courts talk about "assumption of risk" are best understood as ones in which there simply has been no negligence, or more precisely, "no breach" of the duty to exercise due care. Although the Flopper case, which I already discussed, is a prime example, I will focus now on a different, very familiar situation. Suppose you are a spectator at a baseball game and you are struck by a foul ball while seated in an area of the stadium that is not protected from such balls by a screen. Although this sort of injury is often said to be governed by the principle of "assumption of risk," that is a mistake. The reason you lose the case is that the defendant's conduct was reasonable.

Surely it cannot be negligent merely to promote the national pastime. Obviously, we want to attend live baseball games, we don't want baseballs constructed of soft material, and arming each fan with some sort of individual protective shield seems silly as well. Moreover, despite the slight danger, we don't want all the stadium seats fenced, just as we don't want the seats all moved so far back from the game to be out of reach of foul balls. Either of those precautions would deprive the fans of an important pleasure they ought to be able to enjoy -- seeing the game relatively up-close without the annoyance of having to look through a screen. Rather, we only want the seats to be screened where the risk from foul balls is especially great, a precaution that I assume was taken in the stadium where you were injured. That is, I assume you were struck in a location where no case for screening could reasonably be made.

In short, while spectator foul ball injuries are a regrettable by-product of baseball, they are generally not injuries that we should blame on the stadium operators because there was nothing careless about their behavior. Hence "assumption of risk" is beside the point.

Indeed, the "no breach" analysis explains why, for example, even very young children in attendance at the game, who do not really know anything about baseball or the danger of being hit by a foul ball, also properly lose their cases. In the leading California case on the subject, Judge Wood gets into trouble when he writes, "by voluntarily entering into the sport as a spectator he knowingly accepts the reasonable risks and hazards inherent in and incident to the game."[10] Fans struck by foul balls do indeed lose because the risks created are reasonable, but not because they knowingly accepted them. In the case before the court the plaintiff alleged that since she was ignorant of baseball, had never been to a ball park before, and was paying no attention to the game at the time, she "cannot be said to have knowingly assumed the risk."[11] The opinion tries to escape from this seemingly telling point (given the court's analysis) by evading it -- talking about the risks being "common knowledge," and that they are "imputed to her," and that they "should have been observed by her"[12] (piling on yet more confusion by suggesting, quite wrongly I believe, that first-time adult spectators at baseball games are somehow at fault if they choose to spend the afternoon talking with a friend rather than watching the action).

Rather, to repeat, for both the first-time fan and the five-year-old fan, just as for the experienced fan, being hit by a foul ball is just bad luck -- because there is just nothing more that should reasonably have been done to protect the victim from the danger. Obviously, if foul ball injuries were much more common and much more harmful, we might well think differently about the precautions that stadium operators should take.[13]

A parallel point may be made here from the world of intentional torts. When you participate in a properly run boxing match and your opponent injures you with a series of altogether proper punches, you have no cause of action for battery. The traditional explanation for this result is that it cannot be a battery because there was consent -- volenti non fit injuria, assumption of risk.[14] But I think it is quite misleading to think of this as a consent case, when the one thing the plaintiff boxer tried hardest to do was to prevent his opponent from successfully landing a punch. The real reason the plaintiff loses, in my view, is that the defendant did nothing wrong. To be sure the plaintiff's agreement to participate in the boxing match is what legitimates the defendant taking a swing, and to be sure the plaintiff assumes the physical risk of harm. But the reason we want the defendant to win, at the core, is that he acted perfectly reasonably. This approach also better explains those carnival boxing match cases we used to see, where the local yokel gets hoodwinked into fighting the carnival pro (probably to impress his girlfriend) and then has his face smashed in.[15]

Assuming we want the victim to win his lawsuit, it is because we find such matches socially unacceptable and improper for defendants to promote. It is the defendant's wrongdoing, not some legal gambit that allows us to void the plaintiff's consent, that best explains the outcome that holds the defendant responsible.

The examples so far all come from the world of sports and entertainment. But the point applies to many other sorts of cases as well. Suppose, for example, you purchase an automobile with a soft top, a convertible. Now, assume, as bad luck would have it, your car overturns for some reason that is not relevant here, and you sue the manufacturer for the damages you suffered -- claiming simply that the vehicle is defective because it didn't have a metal top that would have saved you from harm. You will lose. Although it is tempting to say "assumption of risk," the best way to understand the case is that the car you bought simply was not defective.

Although this area of law today typically parades under the label of "strict products liability," in fact, the "design defect" claim you would be making here is largely a matter of negligence law.[16] In any event, regardless of the label, the central point is that for you to win we would have to be convinced that, because of the risks involved, the car maker should not have sold you a convertible. But society does not feel that way. Because people like the open air sensation of driving convertibles and, in general, this is not dangerous, we have concluded that it is perfectly all right for car makers to sell, and motorists to buy, vehicles designed like that. As a result, there was "no breach" of the duty to provide a non-defective car.

Consider next a common situation from the medical injury field. Returning to my nose job example, suppose my doctor had told me something rather different. Suppose she said, "I want to warn you that about one percent of the time, people getting nose jobs emerge from surgery looking far worse. This is not because of any carelessness by the doctor, but, apparently, because of something about the bones certain people have. We plastic surgeons have been trying to figure out when this is likely to happen and how to prevent it, but it is all still a big mystery to us." And suppose I respond, "I understand that, doctor. I'll take the chance."

Unfortunately, in my view, this area of the law has come to be headed "informed consent,"[17] and you can bet that today my doctor would have arranged for me to sign a so-called "consent form" acknowledging that I had been informed of and was willing to run that one percent risk. But this situation, too, is best understood as one in which I lose simply because my doctor did not commit malpractice. Of course, she needs my consent to attempt the surgery at all. Otherwise, it would be battery. But when we focus in on the risks of surgery, the better analysis goes like this. Doctors have a duty to make reasonable disclosures of those risks to their patients. My doctor satisfied her duty by telling me what she did. Because I was just one of the unlucky one percent, I cannot fairly blame her for my harm. Since there was "no breach," she does not need the volenti principle as some sort of separate defense.

Next, I want to give an example of my general point from the area of premises liability. You will recall that President Clinton recently badly injured his knee when he fell down some stairs at the home of his good buddy, the golfer, Greg Norman. Imagine that the conversation just before the fall went like this. "Mr. President" (I am assuming here that even friends address the President that way) "Watch out. There are some confusing shadows down at the bottom of this stairway. I would not want you to be injured in my home." "No problem, Greg," replies the President, as I imagine it. And then bang, he falls, and the next thing we know the meeting with Russia's President Yeltsin is delayed for a day. Many of us had previously thought of Gerald Ford as our slip-and-fall President, but no longer. Now suppose Clinton sues Norman. Maybe he would not mind being on the plaintiff side of a case given all of his other legal woes these days. Yet, I trust that the President would lose because (I am assuming at least for the moment) Norman simply was not negligent. We can say to the President "volenti non fit injuria," but assumption of risk is legally beside the point.

Finally, I want to tum to a couple of examples about which some people say "assumption of risk" where that is even more far-fetched. Suppose you are sitting in your living room watching television and suddenly, and amazingly, a car comes crashing in through the window and injures you, the driver having had an unexpected heart attack and blacked out.[18] Or suppose you are out on a walk near a baseball park when suddenly, and to your astonishment, you are struck and injured by a ball hit outside the park for the first time, a feat of such mighty prowess that no one had previously imagined it was possible.[19] In both of these instances, if you sue your injurer, you will lose. And you will lose for the same reason the plaintiff loses in the Flapper case: the defendant simply was not negligent.

Or course, in these cases you never really thought about the risk that eventuated, or had any real reason to do so, and hence in the lay sense it sounds preposterous to say that you agreed to, or assumed, it. Nonetheless, sometimes legal people are heard to say that risks like these are ones that the law "deems" you to have assumed. I admit that this is not an incoherent thing to say, although in that sense, any case in which the plaintiff loses is a "deemed assumption of risk" case. Yet it is especially confusing to bring talk of "assumption of risk" into cases like these when your choice, in effect, was simply to live in a world where freak events occur. This choice, of course, has nothing to do with explaining the legal outcome.

B. Duty v. Breach and the Problem of Saying "No Duty" When What Is Meant Is "No Breach "

In another well-known Cardozo opinion, a young boy was injured when a wire he was swinging, while crossing a bridge, came into contact with the defendant's electric railway wires, thus transmitting a damaging shock to his body.[20] In his lawsuit, the boy was required, among other things, to prove that the defendant was negligent. Establishing that the railroad failed to exercise due care generally necessitates demonstrating not only that the defendant was aware of the dangerousness of its conduct (or should have been), but also that there is some reasonable precaution that the defendant should have taken to avoid the harm. Perhaps the easiest way to justify the railway's victory in this case is on the ground that the danger to the victim was simply unforeseeable.

However, Cardozo goes on to discuss, and dismiss, possible precautions that the defendant might have taken even had it been aware of the danger (or, presumably, that it might take in the future, once it was on notice of this risk). One of those precautions would be to insulate the railroad's wires; another would be to put them underground. But, Cardozo concluded, in neither case was it negligent to fail to take such precautions. On the one hand, the electric railway needed uninsulated wires in order to function, and impliedly it was not negligent to operate an electric rather than, say, a coal-powered system. And on the other hand, demanding that they put the electric wires underground would be asking too much. That is, it would be financially too burdensome and hence unreasonable to ask that of the railway, given the small risk that the overhead wires presented. Therefore, because the boy failed to identify a reasonable precaution that the railway could have taken, the defendant would not have been negligent (and hence not liable to the boy) even if the risk was foreseeable.

This all makes a great deal of sense to me, and is fully consistent with the current understanding of "negligence" as the failure to take reasonable precautions. Put differently, the job of the legal system in such cases (usually the jury, but sometimes the judge) is to decide whether a specifically proposed precaution is appropriate or too burdensome, and it is supposed to do this by weighing the heaviness of the burden against the danger that the precaution would avoid.

The only problem I have with Cardozo's opinion in the case is that, when discussing the possible precautions, he talks about the railroad having no "duty" to underground the wires.[21] This, unfortunately, is a common formulation in judicial opinions. But, to be precise, what Cardozo means is that the defendants did not "breach" their duties to take reasonable care by failing to take the precaution in question. This imprecision would not be a serious problem but for the fact that there is a separate defendant's legal doctrine called "no duty," and this case is not an example of it.

That is to say, sometimes, as I will next illustrate, defendants win cases because they had "no duty" to exercise due care towards plaintiffs in the first place. Hence, the fact that the plaintiff may be able to identify even a simple precaution that the defendant might have taken does the plaintiff no good. For you cannot fail to exercise due care as a legal matter when there is no obligation to do so in the first place.

A classic instance of this concerns the common law principle that you have "no duty" to rescue strangers.[22] Suppose, for example, you are sitting alone at the end of a pier next to a life-saving ring and I come along the pier, accidentally slip into the water, and call out for your help, but you do nothing and I drown. In a lawsuit by my heirs against you, you would prevail even if a jury, if given a chance, would have strongly condemned your inaction as callous -- reflecting the failure to have taken the totally reasonable precaution of having almost effortlessly tossed the life-saving ring out to me. I will discuss the reason(s) why you would win this case shortly.

For the moment the point to be made clear is that you win for a doctrinally quite different reason than the railway wins its case with the boy swinging the wire. You win because the legal system imposes on you no duty to exercise due care towards me. The railway, by contrast, clearly did have a duty to exercise due care to pedestrians and others passing along side of their rail system; it is just that, at least in this situation, the railway in fact exercised due care. Put differently, they win because there was nothing they failed to do that they should have done; by contrast, you win the pier case despite the fact that nearly everyone will say that you failed to do something you had a compelling moral duty to do. The reason, again, is that as a legal matter, you had no duty, whereas the railroad had a duty but did not breach it.

Therefore, because "no duty" is a decidedly different idea, and hence a separate legal concept from "no breach," I find it unnerving and potentially quite deceiving when Cardozo employs the phrase "no duty" when referring to some potential precaution the railway might conceivably have taken, when it would be better to say that the failure to take that precaution was "no breach."

Put more broadly, the difference between the doctrines comes to this. "Breach/No breach" involves the evaluation of a specific defendant. Given what she knew or should have known, is there some way that the community (i.e., the jury, or perhaps the judge) thinks she should have acted otherwise? "No duty," however, is not a matter of making an evaluation of the specific facts of this case. Rather, it is a global determination that, for some overriding policy reason, courts should not entertain causes of action for cases that fall into certain categories.

C. Justifying "No Duty" Rules

Several overriding policy reasons may support "no duty" rules. Three common sorts of justifications I will call: l) trumping values, 2) fears of socially undesirable conduct were a legal duty granted, and 3) judicial manageability. Often more than one such reason may be offered for a specific "no duty" rule.

I will take the space here to discuss at some length these underpinnings of "no duty" rules -- not only to make even more forceful the distinction between "no duty" and "no breach," but also in order to provide the groundwork that will later be needed when I explain why certain cases that may be labeled "assumption of risk" (by others) are better understood as "no duty" cases.

Returning to the "no duty to rescue" strangers rule, this may be justified first by assigning such great weight to the value of "individual liberty." The idea is that the importance of permitting you to do what you want with your time and not have to serve as a "slave" to the needs of others should trump even the slightest social obligation to go to the aid of another. This is a principle that meshes as well with the peculiarly American commitment to the value of "rugged individualism" in which individuals are meant to be self-sufficient and not have the right (or need) to call on others for assistance.

Second, the "no duty to rescue" rule may rest on fears that it would do more harm than good. This could be based on the belief that those who can competently rescue will generally voluntarily do so even without a legal duty, and that imposing a legal duty will only bring out incompetent rescue efforts and officious intermeddlers seeking to provide help where none is needed or wanted. In the same vein, imposing a legal duty might also cause talented rescuers, like physicians, to remove themselves from locations where they might be coerced to rescue, thus undermining their opportunity voluntarily to do so.

Third is the problem of judicial administration. In many rescue settings, such as where people are in distress in public places like on the highways or in auditoriums, there are a large number of potential rescuers, and the courts may well fear that the legal system would not be able either to determine fairly just who should have made the effort, or to handle the caseload if everyone present were permitted to be sued.

I do not mean to argue that each (or any) of these justifications is necessarily persuasive, but only to present them as examples of three types of justifications that may be put forward for a "no duty" rule. Maybe the "no duty to rescue" rule is actually better justified by yet other reasons, for example, by a different trumping value. One possibility is that we need to make room for people to act "heroically" or "charitably" rather than allowing their altruism to be demeaned by being identified as legally compelled.[23] Or perhaps, in the end, the courts are just wrong not to impose a legal duty, at least a duty of easy rescue.[24]

After all, many other common law "no duty" rules of earlier days have since been abandoned or modified. For example, it could once be said in a fairly sweeping way that product makers had "no duty" to exercise reasonable care towards users of their products with whom they had no privity of contract -- which was most users once most manufacturers began selling their products through middlemen.[25] Possible early justifications for this rule were that it was too hard to tell what modifications a user might have made in the product, or that we very strongly valued the idea of "caveat emptor," or that we feared that new and desirable forms of capitalism would otherwise be stymied.

As another example, at an earlier time people in general had no duty to avoid negligently imposing emotional (as contrasted with physical) harm on others.[26] Perhaps early justifications were that allowing such actions would flood the courts with an administratively unmanageable torrent of "hurt feeling" cases, or on a ground that devalued "emotional" injury as beneath public recognition and compensation.

Nowadays, as values have changed, new understandings have emerged about behavioral responses to rules, and new notions of judicial competence have arisen, many of these sweeping no duty rules have been thrown over.

Nevertheless, even beyond the "no duty to rescue" principle, other "no duty" rules remain, and some new ones are regularly being adopted as novel lawsuits are tried out and categorically rejected. For example, when water companies carelessly fail to provide water at hydrants at the time when it is needed to fight a fire,[27] or when power companies carelessly cause massive "blackouts,"[28] victims who had relied on having these "essential" services and were injured by their shortage may well be barred by a "no duty" rule-justified perhaps because of fears that the potential enormity of liability would bankrupt these providers of essential services (thereby possibly depriving the public of the services altogether), or that an avalanche of claims, including faked claims, would overwhelm the judicial system.

Let me complete this illustrative run-through with a contemporary example. Suppose a television program portrays a bizarre and nasty assault by a group of boys on a girl, and the next day, in real life, the conduct displayed on this show is copied by a group of boys who had watched it together.[29] Under ordinary negligence principles, if the girl sued the program's producers (and the network that ran it), she might well win -- if she could convince a jury that it was foreseeable that viewers would be inspired to act out what they watched on that particular program, and that, in view of the danger it presented, it was, on balance, unreasonable to have aired that program at all (at least with the specific attack portrayed in it). But when courts reject such cases, what they are saying is that tort law imposes no legal duty on networks to take reasonable care towards victims who are injured in the way here assumed. That is, plaintiffs are never allowed even to ask a jury to condemn this defendant's specific conduct as negligent because the judiciary has decided in advance to rule out this category of cases.

In this instance, once more, a series of justifications may be offered in support of the "no duty" holding. One is the free speech value of the First Amendment. This does not necessarily mean that the First Amendment itself actually precludes such lawsuits as a matter of constitutional law; the courts usually do not find it necessary to get that far. The point is rather that, as a matter of state common law, such suits should not be allowed because to do so would too much chill the media's exercise of free speech in deciding what programs to run. One way to put this worry is that when a local person has been injured, then local juries will improperly and unwisely devalue the free speech interest in the specific case, condemning a program regardless of its artistic, social or other merit. There is also an administrative worry concerning proof -- that the jury will unfairly find a causal connection between the defendant's conduct and the plaintiff's injury that may well be lacking. In the next case the assault depicted on TV may have been of a generic sort without distinctive features, and in the following case the plaintiff may seek to connect the violence with a program watched weeks ago, or a series watched over a season. The risk then is that mass media operators' fears of open-ended and unpredictable liability for both these reasons would in tum be translated into socially undesirable self-censorship to the overall net detriment of society at large. And to protect against this "chilling effect," a "no duty" rule is adopted. Or put somewhat differently, the courts may conclude that tort law (i.e., decisions by juries) should not be the forum in which we try to resolve the contemporary public debate over the extent to which television violence breeds violence and what sort of censorship, if any, should follow.

Speaking generally, then, we have seen that "no duty" rules are adopted by courts as a way of preventing juries from attempting to award damages to plaintiffs in the individual case -- maybe for fear that the jury will not give the proper weight to the overriding value that the court has identified (like liberty, or free speech), maybe for fear that the jury will make too many mistakes, or maybe for the other sorts of fears already canvassed (e.g., there will be too many cases brought, or bad behavioral consequences will flow from allowing such cases, or excessive liability will fall on and perhaps wipe out this class of defendants).

I want finally to emphasize that a "no duty" rule may also reflect the judgment that the social values the tort system is meant to promote are already being well served through other institutional arrangements so as to make it, in a sense, redundant to provide a tort remedy in the particular setting. This is perhaps best illustrated for the moment with workplace injuries. The idea is that, given the existence of workers' compensation schemes, governmental occupational safety agencies, and union and other bodies to which workers may tum when they discover workplace dangers, it may be concluded that the compensation, safety promotion, punishment, and individual justice objectives of tort law are already sufficiently furthered. And, in fact, the typical American solution has been to create a "no duty" barrier to nearly all lawsuits by workers against their employers-although in this setting, not by judicial adoption, but rather through workers' compensation legislation itself.

D. "Assumption of Risk" as "No Duty"

Now we are prepared to look at that category of cases in which "assumption of risk" is commonly invoked, but which are better understood as "no duty" cases. For example, it was often said that under the early common law a trespasser assumed the risk of any and all dangers he encountered on the defendant's premises.[30] Some years ago considerable attention was given to a California case in which a criminal fell through a high school roof to the gymnasium floor below, sued the school district, and received a substantial financial settlement.[31] The gist of the objection to the case clearly was that if you engage in illegal acts, getting hurt is a risk you take. But in the actual case, talk about "assumption of risk" decidedly puts the emphasis in the wrong place. That trespasser did not knowingly run the physical danger that injured him; rather, he crashed through a painted-over skylight that, in the dark, looked like wood. If you want that trespasser to lose, it is, I suggest, because you support the rule that the defendant simply owes trespassers "no duty" of care. To be sure, the plaintiff's status as an undeserving "outlaw" is one way to understand the reason underlying the traditional "no duty" rule -- something with which the case's critics would no doubt have agreed. But that is quite different from the idea that the trespasser chose to engage any specific peril.

An especially good illustration of my point here is revealed, I believe, by cases in which professional athletes are injured in the course of competition through what they claim is the negligence of others, usually fellow players. On the whole, these plaintiffs lose. For example, in one prominent New York case a jockey, who was hurt through the alleged careless riding of another jockey, sued and was denied recovery.[32]

Notice carefully that we are not talking about inherent risks of the game arising from reasonable conduct by others-such as legitimate tackles in football, appropriate slides in baseball, fair checks in hockey, to say nothing of proper punches in boxing. Nor are we talking about unintended, inevitable accidents of the sport that are not the result of what might properly be considered negligence -- such as the broken baseball bat or the accidental elbow to the body when battling for a basketball rebound. Victims in all of those cases would lose because there was no fault, that is, "no breach." Rather, I am talking here about careless conduct that, the plaintiff alleges, the jury would label as unreasonable if given the opportunity.

Of course, athletes know, in a general way, that they may well be exposed to injury through the careless playing of the sport by others. But, ordinarily, the physical risk they thereby may be said to assume when they elect to play would hardly itself be a ground for denying them recovery. After all, by analogy, passengers know about a parallel danger they face whenever they get on a bus, but assuming that physical risk obviously does not block a lawsuit against a negligent driver.

Still, there may well be good policy reasons generally to prevent lawsuits by professional athletes for injuries suffered as part of the game through the fault of other participants. The broad argument here is one we have seen in the prior Section -- that courts should keep out of the business of resolving disputes within professional athletics because the social objectives that tort law might serve by providing a remedy are already effectively dealt with through parallel institutions.

Specifically, professional sports have their own special rules (and rule- making bodies), their own umpires and referees, and their own penalty structure (both during the game and afterwards when higher-up officials can impose even stronger sanctions). Hence, in most professional sports there already exists, outside the formal legal system, an elaborate structure to deal with goals of deterrence, punishment and justice. Moreover, professional athletes (and their leagues) typically (although not always) have reasonably generous injury insurance schemes that go well beyond what workers' compensation would provide, thereby, arguably, eclipsing tort law's compensatory function. Finally, as an administrative matter, were tort law to try to offer a remedy for ordinary negligence, there might be considerable uncertainty and inconsistency in deciding whether certain conduct was fairly treated as negligence. Examples here include a wild pitch or throw in baseball, or tackling to break up the flow of the game in soccer -- conduct which, on the one hand, may be undesired by the injurer but perhaps not reasonably avoidable in the heat of play, or, on the other hand, conduct which, although "penalized" by the officials, is generally treated by the players as a legitimate "part of the sport."

In sum, it is perhaps well justified to deny recovery in tort to a professional athlete for an injury arising from what would otherwise be viewed by the jury in a specific case as the negligence of another competitor. Nonetheless, as I have shown, the volenti principle is not the persuasive justification, and all the talk by the New York court that the injured-jockey "accepted the risk"[33] once more confuses the assumption of physical risks with the proper legal outcome. Rather, the explanation I have put forward is of the sort classically used to justify a "no duty" rule.

Notice further that, if the sporting behavior in question (or perhaps I should say, the "unsportsmanlike conduct" in question) goes too far beyond the bounds of routine misconduct within the sport, or perhaps if the game's officials are seen by the courts as having lost control of the sport, then the judges may well conclude that tort law has a role to play after all, and they achieve this result by recognizing a legal duty of care.[34] The New York court in the injured-jockey case appreciated this distinction. Yet this line, if and when it is crossed, does not have anything to do with the point at which the risk of physical injury, in any real sense, ceases to be assumed, since athletes voluntarily compete knowing that they are at risk of flagrant infractions as well. Put differently, for the participants, it is not any more "all right" for opponents to carelessly injure them than it is for opponents to recklessly or intentionally injure them. Rather, the courts probably sensibly draw that line on grounds that, once the defendant's conduct has become flagrant, the policy reasons that free an athlete from liability for injuring an opponent no longer apply.

E. "Express Assumption of Risk" as "No Duty"

More than fifty years after the Flopper case, and right around the time of the injured-jockey case, another New York Court of Appeals decision provided further confusing signals in yet another amusement case.[35] A high school senior class arranged for a day of "donkey basketball" as a fund raiser. The defendant company, which provided the donkeys, helmets for participants to wear, and so on, warned everyone that there was a slight chance that the donkeys might buck or put their heads down thereby tossing the riders off. Sure enough, when her donkey put its head down, the plaintiff, a student teacher, fell off and permanently injured her arm.

The issue before the court was whether the plaintiff had expressly assumed the risk. In the torts literature it has long been well understood that "express assumption of risk" is a label applied to what are better termed "express agreements not to sue" -- that is, situations, like that hypothesized earlier involving me and my doctor, where she gets me to sign a waiver of liability by agreeing not to sue her, even if she commits malpractice on me.

However, clearly no such agreement was signed in the donkey basketball case. There was evidence that, in view of the warning, the student teacher expressly assumed the physical risk -- just as I did before undergoing plastic surgery; and just as the vigorous young man riding on the Flopper did. But I trust we have seen by now that this fact by itself is useless in telling us whether the plaintiff should win or lose the case. The donkey riding teacher no more signed away her right to sue than I did in the original version of the plastic surgery fiasco. To hold for the donkey owners on the ground of express assumption of risk, as the New York Court of Appeals did, is altogether the wrong analysis. It fell into this trap by looking no further than the plaintiff's assumption of the physical risk.

Maybe the student teacher should lose her case -- but if so, it is for a different reason. We see that better when, once again, we tum our focus away from the teacher's consent to the physical risk and examine the behavior of the defendant. Maybe, as with the owners of the Flopper, the defendant simply was not negligent. After all, if even normally tame animals very occasionally throw their riders, regardless of what precautions the owners take, then it may well be quite reasonable to provide this sort of amusement, at least when the participants are well warned of the danger. And if the defendants were not negligent, they should win outright.

Unlike the plaintiff in the donkey basketball case, accident victims in recreational activities settings may well have earlier signed an agreement not to sue. For example, suppose before joining a health club you sign a contract providing, in part, that you agree not to sue the club for any injuries you might suffer owing to the club's negligence. Assuming this agreement is valid, its effect is to relieve the club of a legal duty to exercise due care towards you. The club would probably still owe you a duty to avoid grossly or recklessly injuring you, but if, for example, you slipped on the shower floor or strained your back on an exercise machine or hurt your knee in an aerobics class and claimed that their negligence was responsible for your injury, your lawsuit would fail.[36]

Might it make sense for you and the club to make this agreement? Perhaps it does. Both management and club members may realize that it will often be very difficult to determine whether an injury was caused by the fault of the club, or by the carelessness or general health condition of the member, or whether it was just an unavoidable injury. Agreeing that there will not be litigation over such injuries, with the member then on notice to obtain her own first-party insurance elsewhere (if that is what she wants), probably helps keep the dues down. Moreover, since joining a health club is hardly compulsory, and since there are often many health clubs in a community, if people wanted to retain the right to sue, they could probably find a club that offered membership on that basis. Hence, in order to promote individual preferences we generally allow people to sign and then uphold these sorts of agreements not to sue. Although these cases are typically said to involve "express assumption of risk," as I have already noted, the better way to understand the situation is that, by reason of the explicit agreement, there is simply no legal duty to exercise due care.

Not every agreement not to sue is upheld by the courts. For example, the leading California case striking down such a release involved an agreement not to sue hospitals for malpractice connected with medical treatment.[37] If the agreement is voided, the case proceeds as under ordinary tort doctrine and the plaintiff, with the right proof, can win outright. In these settings, public policy precludes the defendant from cutting a deal in advance with the would-be victim which curtails the victim's later ability to sue.[38]

To be sure, some of the reasons for disallowing express agreements not to sue include doubts as to the voluntariness on the plaintiff's side -- such as the plaintiff's critical need for the service from the defendant, or the burying of the disclaimer in the agreement's fine print. On the other hand, Vermont's highest court recently voided a ski resort's efforts to obtain a waiver of liability on the ground (at least in part) that this would undesirably remove the resort's safety incentives.[39] In any event, when an agreement not to sue for negligence is struck down, it is only confusing to say that we are taking away a "defense." Rather, we are saying that the defendant was never properly relieved of his duty of care in the first place.

F. "Assumption of Risk" as "Contributory/Comparative Negligence"

I now tum to another category of cases where "assumption of risk" is not only the wrong way to look at the problem, but also where to do so would reach the wrong result. Suppose you go out dancing at a nightclub. You meet someone who offers to drive you to a second club. Your new friend clearly has been drinking too much, although you have not. But you are in a carefree mood and agree to go along. You see just how unsteady your friend is both while walking to the car and as your friend drives through the parking lot toward the street. Yet you remain in the car and say nothing. Sure enough, about two blocks away your friend smashes the car into a tree, and you are hurt. Assuming your state has neither an automobile guest statute (now a rarity) nor a comprehensive auto no-fault plan (which currently exists in North America only in Quebec), what happens when you sue the car's driver in tort? Volenti non fit injuria -- you clearly assumed the risk. Do you lose? My sense is that the clear majority, if not universal rule, is "no," and properly so.[40]

At common law, simplifying somewhat, if the simultaneously negligent conduct of two parties combined to produce the injury of one of them, that victim would fail in her lawsuit against her injurer. This is because the defense of contributory negligence was a complete bar to recovery. One justification for this rule was that since the plaintiff could have avoided her harm through her own due care, she should have looked to her own precaution for protection and should not now come to the courts for relief. Another justification was simply the common law's abhorrence of anything but all-or-nothing outcomes, and its unwillingness to provide full recovery to someone who was also at fault in causing her own injury.

In recent years, this all-or-nothing thinking about a plaintiffs fault has been overthrown, driven partly by the widespread belief that juries often refused to follow their common law instructions -- finding a careless plaintiff not at all at fault, and then perhaps taking some of that generosity back through a lowered damages award. As well, many commentators sharply objected to a rule that freed from any responsibility a careless (and often insured) defendant whose proper behavior would have avoided the injury, especially when this meant that the careless (and often uninsured) victim would have to bear all of the physical pain of the accident as well all of its financial consequences.

As a result, nearly everywhere today, the plaintiffs fault will serve only as a partial defense, with the plaintiff thereby entitled to recover from the defendant a portion of her loss (assuming, of course, that the defendant is also at fault or otherwise thought legally responsible for the injury).[41] Therefore, through the application of this new regime -- generally called comparative negligence -- the tort law now has an official device for blaming both parties to an accident by making each of them take partial responsibility for paying for its financial consequences.

In other words, the attitude of tort law today towards my example of you riding with your drunk driver friend is "a plague on both of your houses." The driver was clearly negligent in driving while seriously inebriated; you, too, were negligent, however, by accepting a ride in those circumstances. The way we punish you both for your combined foolishness is by making the defendant pay something, but at the same time by denying you full recovery. To be sure, the timorous would have stayed at the first club. But going for the ride is not the same as signing away your right to sue. To be sure, in this instance, even the venturous would have refused the ride. But, as I have just said, your contributory negligence, almost everywhere, is no longer a complete bar; instead, you will obtain a partial recovery, something like, say, three-quarters of your damages.

One more thing. A person might well ask why does tort law consider the drunk driver negligent when the passenger was willing to go along for the ride? The paradigm case for the application of the modern notion of comparative negligence, after all, is one in which both parties are carelessly inattentive -- for example, one motorist is talking to a passenger and not paying attention to his speed or the road ahead while the other motorist pulls away from the curb without checking for traffic from the rear. There is a crash that either driver could have avoided had he been paying proper attention. Under comparative negligence (at least in the pure form), any losses the two then suffer are shared by them in proportion to their fault.[42]

But not all careless conduct is inattentive or oblivious, or the product of misjudgment or poor application of skill. That is to say, sometimes actors may be said to be "knowingly" or perhaps even "deliberately" negligent. That was certainly the case in the drunk-driving example before us. A fundamental policy issue therefore is whether this latter sort of conduct by plaintiffs -- about which it may be said "assumption of risk" -- should be treated in a different way from inattentive negligence. On the whole, the answer has been to treat the two the same.[43]

In order to understand why that is so, the first thing to note is that this is tort law, not contract law. The community sets standards of behavior in tort law, not the parties themselves. Still, one might press, if the parties are willing to run the danger, why does the community demand more of them? Why does it, in effect, paternalize them, telling them to act safer than they apparently felt was necessary? In short, why doesn't it treat the car ride like the Flopper? This actually is a very difficult question about which I will have more to say later. For now, however, let me offer at least three reasons that together seem reasonably compelling in this situation.

First, the drunk driver endangered not just the passenger, but others on the road as well, and since we are eager to discourage and punish drunk driving generally, we are not about to let the driver off completely just because, as it happens, only the passenger was hurt.

Second, the drunk driver was far more dangerous to the passenger than the Flopper was to its participants. And so, even if the passenger and the drunk driver want to get their kicks like this, we, the rest of society, simply do not approve of that in the way we do approve of people running some other risks. After all, if someone is hurt, which is all too likely in this situation, the rest of us are probably going to have to pick up some or all of the tab through public or private insurance arrangements, but we are not eager to do that. This is in contrast to the Flopper situation where we think of the plaintiff as merely a victim of fate, like someone who happens to be hit by lightning and now needs medical care.

Third, even though the passenger willingly got in the car at the time, this is probably the sort of risk that the passenger would candidly acknowledge, in the light of day, that he should not have run. This is unlike the Flopper situation, which presumably continued to draw its patrons, even those in line when the plaintiff in that case was hurt. Indeed, the very victim of the Flopper would probably like to try the ride again, at least if his knee were up to it.

The riding-with-the-drunk example is by no means the only case in this "both at fault" category. Consider two others that come from the defective products area. Suppose you drive your new car home from the showroom, and within a day or two you realize that the brakes are working badly, pulling you sharply to the right whenever you apply them quickly. But rather than immediately taking the car back to be fixed, you are so eager to be behind the wheel that you go ahead and drive the car some more, trying to compensate by braking more slowly. Sure enough, two days later another motorist ahead of you in traffic unavoidably skids on wet pavement, you brake to get out of the way, and your defective brakes pull you into a tree.

You sue your car manufacturer for the personal injuries you suffer. Again, the general rule nowadays is that you will recover some but not all of your damages.[44] In short, both you and the car maker are held responsible for the injury -- the company on the ground that it sold you a defectively manufactured auto and you for your negligence. In other words, comparative fault, or what is sometimes called comparative responsibility, applies not only to pure negligence cases, but also to cases where the defendant is so-called strictly liable.

Even though this may seem like comparing apples and oranges, the jury is nonetheless told to do its best to determine the parties' relative shares of the responsibility for the injury and make its award accordingly.[45] As a result, although, by continuing to drive the defective car after discovering the defect, you clearly assumed the physical risk of just the sort of injury that happened to you, your claim will not be completely barred.

The same rule has been applied to many cases involving the foreseeable misuse of defective products. In those cases, the defendant is held responsible for its inadequate design when it did, or should have, anticipated the likely misuse of its product and had a ready way of preventing the misuse (such as by adding a better guard to a press used in the workplace). When that very misuse occurs (such as when the victim removes the inadequate guard), tort law does not want to let the defendant off. To be sure, the victim, typically, well knew that by misusing the product as he did, he was taking a risk of the very injury that followed. Volenti non fit injuria. Yet, because of the irresponsible behavior on both sides, the typical solution today is to give the plaintiff a partial recovery.[46]

Not all cases will have undisputed outcomes. You come to a skating rink, pay your money, don your rental skates, and just as you start out onto the ice you see that some rowdy teenagers are skating in ways that have made the rink dangerous for everyone. So, you complain to the manager, who assures you that he will immediately deal with the problem. You wait ten minutes, but the rowdies are still at it. Rather than complain again, or ask for your money back and leave, you venture cautiously onto the rink. Sure enough, very soon two of the rowdies bang into you, knocking you down and hurting you. Although you assumed the risk, I have little doubt that the rink owner will nonetheless be held responsible for your injuries (the rowdies, of course, are judgment proof). So, what is clear again is that the volenti principle does not apply to bar your recovery. What is not entirely clear is whether you will only receive a partial recovery on the ground that your own conduct was unreasonable. Although I would consider you partly at fault, perhaps some will disagree.[47]

G. Plaintiff Wins Notwithstanding "Assumption of Risk"

In this Section, I want to address cases in which "assumption of risk" threatens to produce entirely the wrong result, that is, cases in which, rather than losing, plaintiffs should decidedly recover in full. I have already given one example, the first version of my nose job story. But if that sounded somehow fishy to you, consider next this slight variation on another well-known case.[48]

A porter employed by a railroad negligently spills a very slippery substance on a railway platform and does nothing to deal with the danger thereby created. Sure enough, a passenger walking down the platform while awaiting a train slips and falls onto the tracks. This passenger happens to be a two-year-old who then becomes trapped on the rails, both too frightened and too weak to move. The train is now roaring towards the station, and the child's father who had planned to take the helpless infant on a journey with him, faints with terror. But you, our super-hero, seeing that the child will almost surely be killed if nothing is done, jump down onto the tracks, and in a flash pick up the child in your arms and scamper towards safety. Alas, even you could not outrun the oncoming locomotive which rolls over your trailing foot causing you grave injury. The child is safe; you get your picture in the paper and lifelong thanks from the child's family.

Not satisfied with those rewards, you sue the railroad in tort. Its lawyers plead "volenti non fit injuria" -- assumption of risk. But, unlike the victim in the Flopper case, you will win. In yet another of Cardozo's marvelously coined phrases, "danger invites rescue."[49] In these circumstances, harm to a rescuer like you is exactly what the defendant should have expected would happen, and the railroad will be liable to you for the harm resulting from the negligence of its porter. You clearly did assume the risk of physical harm, but not the legal risk; the "timorous" remained on platform, yet you will win your case.

Consider next a similar outcome from an entirely different area of tort law. You buy a power lawn mower. It contains a large caution sign over the hole from which the grass comes out, warning you to keep your hands, feet and the like out of there. Although you know you are supposed to keep away from that hole, suppose that while using the mower you accidentally slip and fall, and sure enough one of your limbs goes part way into the hole and you are badly mangled. At trial your lawyer is able to show that for one dollar more the mower manufacturer could have added a guard to the product that would have prevented your injury. In most jurisdictions today, the so-called "open and obvious danger" rule has been abrogated because of situations just like this.[50] Despite the fact that you clearly realized the risk you were running, courts have concluded that tort law nonetheless should condemn product makers for clear design errors. As a result, the jury is very likely to find the mower to be a defective product and award you full recovery in this example, even though it might be said about you "volenti non fit injuria."

III. When is Warning Enough?

Although I have not especially emphasized it so far, my examples reveal a difficult and too little discussed problem to which I tum next. I will call it: "when is warning enough?"[51] A warning was sufficient in the soft top convertible case, but not in the lawn mower case. A warning was sufficient in the Flopper case, but not in the defective brakes case. A warning was sufficient in the President's slip and fall case, but not in the riding with the drunk case. When I discussed the drunk driver case, I gave some reasons to justify that specific result. In this Section, I want to discuss the issue more generally: when should a clear warning fully discharge the defendant's duty to exercise due care, and when should the defendant be required to take precautions to reduce the danger?

A. No Reasonable Precautions Available

In many situations a warning is sufficient because there are no additional precautions available that the plaintiff can reasonably suggest that the defendant should have taken. I have in mind here cases in which society believes that the product, service or whatever ought to be able to be offered as it was, and to have reduced the danger would have meant a dramatic and unacceptable change in what the defendant provided.

For example, suppose a ski slope operator carefully warns you, through markers, maps and the like, which of its trails are suitable for beginners, which are suitable for intermediate skiers, and which are suitable for advanced skiers. Alas, you, an intermediate skier, break your leg while on an advanced slope where you should not have been. In this instance, the warning will satisfy the operator's duty to exercise due care. So that friends and families can all go to the same mountain, we want ski slope operators to be able to cater to a range of skier abilities. But in order to do that, they need to offer ski runs of increasing difficulty.[52] I am assuming that everyone agrees that it is totally impractical for the resort operator to test skier abilities before every run they take. So, as I have emphasized throughout, if you sue you should lose, although the reason is not "assumption of risk" but rather that there simply was "no breach." The point to be emphasized now, however, is that in this instance an adequate warning was enough.

This category also contains the Flopper case and the convertible case. The amusement park could have turned the Flopper into a very safe moving sidewalk going nowhere, but then who would want to ride on it? And if drivers could only open the windows but not put the top down, the motoring experience just wouldn't be the same.

This analysis applies as well, I believe, to more controversial matters. Take cigarettes, for example. To me the right way to understand the core of the tobacco litigation to date is that society, in the end, has considered cigarettes to be like the Flopper. In short, cigarettes, as a legal matter, have not been treated as a defective product. This is because, despite their great dangers, we have concluded that this product ought to be able to be sold (at least to adults), and so far as we can tell, to take away the risk of cancer, heart disease, and lung disease would also mean to eliminate cigarettes as we now know them. In short, like the Flopper, so long as the dangers are made clear, we have been unwilling to say that they should be taken off the market. Of course, the legal conclusion could change if people start believing otherwise -- either about the viability of a safer cigarette or about the acceptability of selling cigarettes at all.[53]

A nice counter-example makes the point even more sharply. Many years ago I saw a cartoon depicting a customer inside a supermarket looking at two bins of apparently similar products. One has a sign that reads "Mushrooms $2.49 a pound." The other has a sign that says "Mushrooms? 3 cents a pound."

Suppose you actually buy some of the 3 cents a pound product, eat it, and become critically ill because those mushrooms were poisonous. In contrast to cigarettes, I am firmly convinced that we would find it entirely unacceptable for supermarkets to sell such a potentially fatal product, regardless of its low price. Hence, the store would be liable for selling you a defective product, notwithstanding the clearly implied warning that the bin of cheap mushrooms might be deadly to eat.[54] That is, warning was not enough.

In fact, there are actually very few reported cases like the mushrooms example. New Jersey courts started down this route at one point when they concluded that certain backyard, above-ground swimming pools could be deemed defective (and the manufacturers held liable), regardless of any warnings they carried. These pools were viewed as simply too dangerous and thus should not have been sold at all.[55] It has also been suggested that diabolical products like highly dangerous lawn darts are also in this category.[56] But, for understandable reasons, tort law has been very slow to condemn products, services and conditions squarely on the ground that they are so dangerous that their very provision to a seemingly willing plaintiff was socially unacceptable.

B. Available Precautions and Injuries to "Strangers"

So, let me turn then to cases in which the plaintiff can propose a plausible precaution that the defendant might have taken without dramatically transforming the good, service or situation it provides, but where, instead of taking the precaution, the defendant only warned of the danger of addiction, will frequently doom their cases.

In some settings, it seems clear that warning alone will not suffice. Suppose the defendant posts a large sign telling people to be on the lookout for trucks emerging from its building site. You see the sign as you approach the site on foot on the sidewalk and continue on alertly. Just as you are crossing the driveway, you are struck by a truck being carelessly driven out of the site by one of the defendant's employees (say, the driver was going too fast). In that event, the defendant would be liable to you. The warning clearly will not replace the duty of its employees to drive carefully.

Or consider another example. Defendant is a new driver and posts a large "learner" notice on his vehicle. You, an experienced driver, find yourself driving in traffic along side of the defendant and you see and understand the defendant's notice. You don't pull out of the way, but continue to drive as you normally would. The defendant then changes lanes carelessly, crashes into your car, injuring you. Once more the warning alone will not suffice to satisfy the defendant's duty of care.

In other words, in both of these examples the defendant is not permitted to slough off his duty to exercise due care merely by making you aware that he is acting, or might act, carelessly. Even with this knowledge, you are still, as a legal matter, entitled to demand that he actually take the precautionary measure. Perhaps your knowledge entitles us to say of you that by continuing your activity in the face of the warning you assumed the physical risk. But legally saying "assumption of risk" would get us into trouble.

To be sure, there may be some cases in this category in which we would consider it unduly foolhardy for the plaintiff to continue on with her own lawful activity in the face of the defendant's conduct. For example, suppose she saw not just the warning signs, but also the speeding truck heading for the exit, or suppose she saw the novice driver actually weaving out of control. In those situations, her failure to take reasonable precautions to get out of the way (despite minor inconvenience to her) could well be viewed as negligent on her part. But as we have already seen, the consequence of that today, generally speaking, is not a complete bar (as would follow from "assumption of risk") but rather some appropriate reduction of her damage award.

The examples just described involve what we usually would call injuries to "strangers." Although the plaintiff and the defendant may belong to the same community and have been sharing the road or sidewalk or crosswalk, they were not really involved in a transaction together. In such settings, tort law says you may not subject another to unreasonably dangerous risks merely by warning that you are about to do so.

C. Available Precautions and Voluntary Relationships Among Ordinary People

It gets much trickier, however, when there is something of a voluntary relationship between the parties, such as buyer and seller, owner and invitee, employer and employee, doctor and patient, and the like.

Consider first the homeowner with a guest in his house. Let's rerun President Clinton's recent injury with a different script. Now suppose the President hears Greg Norman say, "Watch out when you go down those stairs Mr. President. The handrail broke off last week, and I haven't had time to replace it yet." Or suppose the President simply realizes that, even though the stairs are rather steep, there is no handrail. In that situation, even if the President could convince us that he would not have fallen had there been a hand rail for him to hold onto, he probably will lose.[57] As usual, I would say this is not because he "assumed the risk" but rather because the legal system would conclude that, in this case, a warning is sufficient -- either the personal warning by the defendant or the implicit warning by the open and obvious condition of the stairs themselves.

But why is a warning sufficient here, when it would not be all that difficult for Norman to have replaced the handrail? The right answer, I believe, is that we feel that it is too burdensome to ask ordinary homeowners to make these repairs even if they are not very expensive. In other words, if the homeowner himself is willing to live with this sort of danger (usually not a very large danger), then we conclude that it suffices to satisfy his obligation to exercise "due care" to put the visitor on the same footing.

Historically, this point was broadly captured by the different levels of care said to be owed to invitees and licensees. The paradigm invitee was someone welcomed for business onto commercial premises, whereas the paradigm licensee was a social guest in one's home. Simplifying somewhat, the law allowed the invitee to demand that the owner both reasonably search for dangers and repair those he found, or should have found; whereas the licensee could ask no more than for reasonable warnings of dangers already known to his host.[58]

But now, even in those many jurisdictions where the formal distinction between invitees and licensees is breaking down,[59] the application of the general negligence principle will yield the same result. That is, for social hosts, the exercise of due care will generally be satisfied by warning, so that the victim will generally not succeed if he bases his case on the claim that the danger should have been removed.[60]

Take two seasonally different examples. The weather has brought us snow and ice. I have invited you over for dinner, but I have not cleared my driveway or stairs. You see the danger, but alas you slip and fall and injure yourself. You probably will lose your suit against me for failing to shovel or de-ice.[61]

Alternatively, you come to town to play in a summer tennis tourney and need some place to practice. You ask to use the court I have in my backyard, and I warn you that there is an uneven spot along the baseline that I have not repaired. You decide to practice there anyway and trip at that spot. You will probably lose your case against me.[62]

D. The Inadequacy of the Libertarian Perspective

The outcome of these cases might suggest that the courts have embraced what I will call the "libertarian outlook." But, after explaining what I mean by that, I will then show that this conclusion is a mistake.

From the libertarian perspective, in cases involving "voluntary relationships," an effective warning should always suffice. If the plaintiff did not want to go ahead in the face of the danger, she should not have done so. Because she has chosen to do so, she should not later be able to say that the defendant should have presented the transaction to her on different and safer terms. If the defendant had no obligation to enter into the transaction in the first place, it was sufficient to disclose at the outset the risks involved and leave it to the plaintiff to decide.

Put differently, the libertarian would be opposed in principle to having the legal system step in and allow the jury to conclude that the defendant should have done something different. This would remake the transaction between the parties, and that presumably would over-ride their own (original) preferences and interfere with their private liberty to make the transactions they wish. In short, victims should be stuck with the choices they made relationships, the libertarian outlook cuts the other way. So, as in my learner-driver and truck-pulling-out-of-the-building-site examples, when the plaintiff is out on the road (on foot or in a car) exercising her liberty of movement, the defendant will certainly not satisfy his duty of care by warning, thereby hoping to get away with imposing an unreasonable risk on the plaintiff. This is because doing so would, of course, interfere with the victim's liberty to drive or walk where she has a right to be.

The libertarian perspective puts considerable weight, then, on determining whether a specific relationship is voluntary or not. Even when it is voluntary, it is necessary to determine whether the warning given was truly effective so as to make it fairly said that the plaintiff knowingly made an informed choice to continue in the face of the danger. If these conditions are not met, then the libertarian would also agree that the defendant might be blamed for the injury.

Although the libertarian perspective comfortably explains the Flopper case, the situation with cigarettes (provided we agree that the warning has been adequate}, the tennis court case, the missing handrail case, and so on, it would be wrong to assume that this is the right way to understand today's tort law. This is because it fails to explain a large number of cases, to which I will turn next, in which a clear warning to someone in a voluntary relationship is insufficient. In these cases society, through tort law, insists that the defendant actually take the safety precaution that removes the danger. In other words, the libertarian perspective too much emphasizes contract and consent -- assumption of risk if you will -- without allowing a sufficient role for tort and community standards.

For example, as noted earlier, in most jurisdictions, product makers are very unlikely to escape liability for patent dangers in their products that are readily eliminated by simple redesign strategies. A warning will not suffice. My lawn mower case demonstrates this point. Other illustrations from the product injury field include situations in which the victim uses the product after discovering the defect -- my bad brakes example -- and those in which the product maker realizes that the product will be misused -- my example of the plaintiff using a machine after removing the guard.

But product makers are not the only defendants required to do more than warn. For example, landowners increasingly have duties to take reasonable steps to make safe areas that are open to the public, to protect tenants and patrons from crime and so on. Those defendants are now much less likely to escape liability because the danger is open and obvious or because the defendant had warned of the danger. [63]

A key point to notice here is that these defendants tend to be commercial actors on whom we are willing to impose the burden of taking precautions beyond warnings. This may be seen more clearly in the following example. Suppose you come to my home and I warn you that the chair you propose to sit in has a weak leg. If so, I probably will not be found liable to you when the chair collapses, because I discharged my duty of care to you through warning. I am not obligated to fix these sorts of dangers in my home in order to prevent such injuries to my guests. Hotels, by contrast, would generally not get away with providing their guests with rickety seating even if they did warn of the danger.[64]

E. Why More than a Warning Is Required

But why do we insist on more than a warning from these commercial defendants when the plaintiff himself did not demand more? A generalized response is this: tort law asks more for the same reasons that our society has imposed housing codes on landlords, FDA requirements on food sellers, CPSC regulations on product makers, OSHA restrictions on employers and so on. Simply put, we just do not always trust individual choice and the market to provide the level of safety that society considers desirable.

But, at least in the torts area, what more specifically might be said to lie behind these requirements? Let me offer several arguments. First, we may have generalized doubts as to the voluntariness of the conduct of those in the plaintiff's situation. At the workplace, for example, the libertarian viewpoint simply assumes that when employees accept dangers connected to their jobs they do so truly by choice, by obtaining higher wages in return. But many people today do not generally accept the libertarian's underlying assumption about the free market for labor, reasoning that all too many workers must accept whatever dangers they face on the job for fear that they would otherwise be out of work and out of money. Rather than seeing a worker as someone who prefers to handle a printing press whose guard has been removed, they see that worker as a victim of superior bargaining power-someone who, in effect, has to accept the dangerous machine under duress. Tenants who wind up living in dangerous housing (typically lower income people) are also seen to be other than truly explain why warning is found to be insufficient in cases involving workplace and apartment house accidents.

Note well, that the tort rules applied in these settings that require defendants to do more than merely warn not only reject the generalized libertarian assumption about transactions of these sorts (e.g., in employment and housing), but they also reject its application in an individualized way to the accident in question. This employee will be able to insist that the defendant should have provided a safer machine without having to show that his specific encountering of that machine was effectively coercive rather than voluntary. This tenant will be able to insist that the landlord should have provided better locks and lighting without having to show that she actually had no choice in accepting the apartment in question.

Second, some injuries arise out of situations in which it is widely believed that reasonable people would wish, if they really thought about it, to have been protected against the danger that they faced -- even though, by their conduct, they appear to have willingly confronted that danger. Suppose, for example, you are told about a very small chance of a very serious harm, but because it seems so small you simply disregard it. Now it turns out that there was a way to have paid a bit more to have avoided the risk. The libertarian view is that this is a risk you ran, and you must bear the consequences. But society might nonetheless believe that it well serves people's own best interests -- their true preferences if they really thought about them -- to prevent them from running that risk at all. Tort law tries to do that by telling defendants that it will not be sufficient to warn of the risk, and that to avoid liability it is necessary to take the precaution that eliminates the risk. The problem of momentary inattention and slips-of-the-hand by product users is another example in this same vein. Again, society might well conclude that we, the users, actually want the law to impose a kind of self-paternalism on us, one that keeps us from choosing a product that could hurt us through our momentary carelessness, if it would only cost a bit more to eliminate that risk altogether.

Third, sometimes a warning will suffice for some people, perhaps even most of those who are exposed to the risk. This is because, once forewarned, they are able to deal with the danger in ways so that they will remain uninjured. Yet other people need the defendant to take actual precautions if they are to be protected from harm. Those in the latter group may be especially clumsy, or have bad judgment, or do not properly read, digest, or remember warnings given to them.

Others may be children who are immature or have an exaggerated taste for danger. And so on.[65] The law might well, in the end, treat some of these people as contributorily negligent if it were to come to that, but as we have seen, that defense would only arise as a partial defense to an already liable defendant. And that is the question here. Should some people's need for protection against their own inadequacies, whether or not they are contributorily negligent, create an obligation in the defendant to do more than warn? Assume further, for the moment, that the defendant will have to treat everyone alike, so that the precautions would have to be imposed on some people who do not need them. Even in this setting, however, society may well decide that defendants must do more than warn, and that, on balance, it is better to insist on precautions that may only help some. Mandating air bags, although not quite the right example, illustrates the point. Their primary benefit is to those who should, but for whatever reason do not, use their seat belts. Yet we are now insisting on air bags for everyone. (In fact, air bags also provide some extra safety benefit even for those who are already using seat belts, but even if they did not, the point here is that we might mandate them anyway.)

Fourth, sometimes what seems like a voluntary transaction between two parties also involves risk of harm to third parties. This risk creates what is commonly termed an externality. My earlier example of riding with a drunk driver fits this category. Again, contrary to the libertarian who would hold you responsible for your own choice, tort law today permits you to advance what are, at least in part, the safety concerns of others who were involuntarily endangered by the driver's conduct.

Even more broadly, there may be a desire in cases like this to impose precautions on would-be victims for the benefit of their loved ones who later suffer if the victim is badly injured, and/or for the benefit of society at large which wants neither to lose the productive capacity of needlessly injured workers nor to have to bear the welfare costs of caring for such people. These sentiments might be said to involve a different sort of externality. Nonetheless, they seem directly to reject the libertarian ideology which treats people much more seriously as autonomous individuals.

Economists typically point out that imposing more safety on defendants will result in lower wages, higher rents, more expensive products and the like. If those costs were large, a point to which I return below, we may well be reluctant to impose them. But the general point here is that, in those instances in which the burden of precaution is modest, tort law is a vehicle for promoting the adoption of that precaution when we believe that more than a warning is socially desirable.

Of course, as an institutional matter, tort law imposes these obligations on defendants through juries as guided by judges. People have very different views about how good a mechanism this is to determine community sentiment. Still, since we already depend upon it for the implementation of the negligence standard generally, so long as we have tort law at all, it is the mechanism we have. It might be argued from the libertarian view that at least with stranger injuries we have no choice since somebody has to set the standard, but with relationship cases, the argument goes, we should always defer to the parties themselves. The response of tort law today is this: If those in voluntary relationships do not like tort law imposing on defendants more than the obligation to provide a reasonable warning, they should expressly agree to that, thereby relieving the defendant of any such additional burdens. The law will uphold that agreement -- unless, of course, there appears to be a strong public policy reason not to do so. In short, the default legal rule rests on the assumption that would-be victims want tort law as I have described it to serve as backup-to make reasonable demands on would-be defendants for precautions that they, as consumers, employees and the like, probably should have made themselves.

It is also worth pointing out some more general reasons why we use tort law to insist that commercial defendants (in comparison to individuals) take precautions that victims did not insist upon. First, we are more willing to use enterprises than individuals for social engineering purposes because enterprises are more likely to be responsive to legal signals. That is, because business organizations plan with the "bottom line" in mind, they are more likely to take precautions in order to avoid liability.[66] Second, these defendants are generally in a better position to bear and spread the loss afterwards if the precaution was not taken and the victim is injured. Moreover, we tend to give little moral weight to the liberty interests of what are impersonal entities. Third, through their repeated behavior, commercial actors are more likely to subject more people to risk.

By contrast, as I already noted, when it comes to ordinary individuals in their private settings, things look different. If I have not gotten around to fixing my dining room chair or my stair rail or my tennis court in order to protect myself, then I may well not take these precautions before you come over for a visit as my guest. Besides, unlike the enterprise, I have no product or service into which I can internalize the cost of making my home safer. Furthermore, my liberty to keep my home in the condition I like has substantial social value.

F. The Problem of Options

The analysis so far has pretty much assumed an all-or-nothing resolution of the choice between warning and precautions. But consider those situations in which the victim clearly had options, that is, where there was a choice to confront either a safer or a less safe version. Sometimes, it seems clear that we are pleased that there are options like that, and in such circumstances the informed victim who selects the more dangerous option generally will not recover. We saw that in the example of the intermediate skier who tried the advanced slope. It is also true that Chrysler will not be liable merely for selling you its, say, less safe small and lightweight Neon car just because that model is more dangerous, say, than are Chrysler's Jeep Grand Cherokees. We want people to have these options, if nothing else, because of the great price difference between them.

Indeed, a car maker need not offer both a safe and less safe option to get away with providing only a less safe model. The car market today is filled with many sources of information about autos and their safety. Consumers tend to shop carefully, and models differ along so many dimensions that our society tolerates vehicles with a wide range of passenger safety. Indeed, the government tests many models and reports their relative safety rating based on those crash tests.

For other products, however, it may not suffice for a defendant to rely on the fact that other makers offer safer versions. Consider, for example, safety leg guards for motorcycles. Assume that these are just the sort of thing that will especially benefit inexperienced cyclists, but at the same time are exceedingly annoying and probably of rare help to expert cyclists. In this setting, we probably do not want motorcycle makers to provide the leg guards on every vehicle they sell (although we might think differently if they were not so annoying and we saw that lots of beginners were foolishly going without them). On the other hand, it may not be enough that only some brands offer the guards as an option. That is, perhaps we would term any individual maker's cycles defective if it too did not provide the guards as an option.[67] Otherwise, given the lesser public information about motorcycles as compared with cars, we might fear that buyers who come into their local motorcycle dealer and try out that brand will not be aware that they can obtain this option elsewhere.

There are still other safety features, however, that we probably want to insist upon. In those cases we would hold responsible in tort those defendants who merely provide them as options. One example is the one dollar guard on the power lawn mower, which presumably provides substantial safety benefits without impairing the operation of the machine. In that setting, we would probably consider someone who refuses the model with the guard to be contributorily negligent. Nonetheless, we would still probably want him to recover partially because we find it unacceptable for the defendants to have offered a guard-free version in the first place.

G. Assumption of Risk as "No Cause"

Lurking here is the very difficult issue of how tort law's "cause in fact" requirement should be applied. Suppose the defendant in the guard-less mower case says that even if it had sold its mowers only with the one dollar guard, this buyer, given his actual selection, probably would have removed it. If we allow the argument and believe the assertion, the defendant would get off on the ground that the failure to provide a guard on all of its mowers was not a cause-in-fact of the plaintiff's injury -- that is, the victim would have been hurt anyway.

Courts dealing with this sort of issue have been inconsistent from one area of tort law to the other. In the medical malpractice area, the dominant rule in so-called informed consent cases has the jury decide whether a typical patient would have gone ahead with the operation even had the doctor disclosed the risk that she failed to disclose.[68] If so, then the injured patient loses on cause-in-fact grounds. The usual reason for looking to patients in general, as opposed to the plaintiff, is that, after-the-fact, the plaintiff will always testify that he would not have gone ahead if he had known of the risk. This solution is perhaps overly cautions. After all, there is no reason for the jury automatically to believe what the plaintiff says, and evidence of what other patients typically do could be used to discount such self-serving testimony.

Indeed, in both the product injury area and in the premises liability area, where the claim is that the manufacturer or owner failed to warn of a certain risk, courts do not seem to react the same way. There they ask the jury to decide whether this plaintiff would have acted differently had he known of the danger, perhaps not realizing the inconsistency with the medical malpractice cases.[69]

With this general framework before us, let us return to the situation in which the mower was sold without a guard and the jury thinks that all such mowers should have had a guard. In that setting, it seems clear to me that if we ask whether the typical consumer would have removed the guard, the answer will very likely be "no." Moreover, even if we focus on this buyer, it is rather dubious that, if this mower came with a guard, he would have removed it. Instead, it is far more likely either that he paid no attention to the guard when buying the mower, or else wanted the lowest priced mower. Under those assumptions there is no reason to surmise that he would have removed the guard had it been standard. On this analysis, the defendant will not get off on cause-in-fact grounds regardless of which cause-in-fact test we apply.

But if we now alter the facts a bit, we can create an example in which the cause-in-fact limit would seem to have bite, at least if we direct it toward the actual plaintiff rather than at buyers in general. Consider the sport of hang gliding. Suppose the jury decides that it is negligent for the defendant not to offer a safer version of its product (say, one that contained a safety cage). But suppose we are also convinced that even if that had been done, this particular plaintiff would not have bought the safer version. That might be the case if, say, beginner and intermediate hang gliders would find this extra security very welcome, but some advanced hot shots like the plaintiff found the cage unaesthetic and cumbersome. Although applying the cause-in-fact test to buyers generally might keep the defendant on the hook, if the test is instead applied to this particular plaintiff, then the jury would presumably let the defendant off.[70]

I do not object to that result. The first thing to notice is that the explanation for the victim's loss is not "assumption of risk," but rather "no causation." That conforms to my general thesis. Second, although we are unhappy with the defendant for not offering the optional safety cage, it is probably all right in this setting that the cause-in-fact rule prevents this specific victim, who has a special and understandable taste for danger, from relying on that social objection. After all, this case arises in a context in which the jury was only saying that the defendant should provide an option and not that all hang gliders should come with the safety cage.

H. Harder Cases Where the Precaution Is More Burdensome

Throughout, in the examples I have used, I have made simplifying stipulations in order to demonstrate my general points. But in the real world we confront situations which are far messier. An important category is where the safety feature that the plaintiff says the defendant should have included carries a more substantial cost or significantly interferes with some other feature (productive or aesthetic). In such cases, what is needed to protect the victim is more than what might be termed an "easy rescue," and, therefore, it is more difficult to confidently conclude that the defendants should have done more than warn of the dangers.

A good example is illustrated by injuries incurred in national parks. Assume that the victim is able to identify precautions, such as handrails, that probably would have protected the plaintiff from injury. Yet, a core value at stake in our national park system is allowing people to go out and confront nature without the protective interference of humans -- a value that would be lost were handrails installed. This, of course, does not mean that no safety precautions need be provided in our national parks. Nonetheless, it does show why we are likely to feel conflicted about whether, in a particular situation, the condition that might have been made safer should have been left in its natural state.

It may be agreed that, as a general proposition, where the safety precaution carries a substantial burden, we ought to be much more certain that substantial safety gains will accrue before insisting on the proposed precaution, rather than a clear warning. Even then, we ought to be cautious before imposing the safety feature on everyone. After all, not too far down this line we come to the soft-top convertible and the advanced ski run.

Nonetheless, in clear enough cases, tort law will properly insist on even more than an easy rescue -- as, for example, in the very dangerous above-ground swimming pool and lawn darts examples. Some people may say they want to buy that sort of recreational equipment, and claim they are unhappy having only wading pools or underground pools, or having only bar darts or outdoor nerf darts as their options. Yet, we may conclude that the highly unsafe nature of these products is simply socially unacceptable.

Indeed, there are some cases that are rather like these in which the courts, in my view, have become too caught up in the volenti principle and have refused to condemn unacceptable products outright. One example is a case in which a court tolerated a BB-gun that was much more dangerous than it need be, just because its dangerous design made it look like an old-fashioned rifle.[71]

However we resolve difficult individual controversies like this, let me emphasize once more that "assumption of risk" does not lead us to the answer. "Assumption of risk" would always tell us to conclude that an adequate warning was enough. Rather, as I have explained, we must look to other considerations in order to determine when more than a warning should have been provided.

IV. The Most Difficult Cases: "Assumption of Risk" as "No Proximate Cause"?

Sometimes, a single course of conduct can injure two victims. One is entitled to full recovery, the other none at all. What distinguishes these claimants is that for one type a warning is sufficient to discharge the defendant's duty of care, but for the other it is not. Of course, I resist the notion that the explanation for those cases where plaintiffs lose is "assumption of risk." Rather, it is better, I think, to treat these as cases of "no proximate cause."

This problem is best illuminated by claims brought by professionals whose job is to confront negligently created dangers. Suppose you carelessly allow a fence to fall over and break a power line. You call the power company. Its employee comes over and is accidentally electrocuted while making the repair. Or suppose you carelessly break a water pipe. You call a plumber, who comes to deal with the emergency, but is accidentally injured while trying to stop the flow of water. Or suppose you carelessly knock coals from your fireplace, starting a fire that bums out of control. You call the fire department and a fire fighter who responds is burned while battling the blaze.

Each of these examples fits the same model. You were negligent at what could be called "time 1." A professional, whose job it is to deal with the consequence of your negligence, comes to the scene to confront the danger at "time 2" and is injured. Surely we might say about these events, "Danger invites rescue." Yet, unlike the amateur rescuer who jumps onto the tracks to save the trapped child, the general rule is that these professional rescuers will lose if they sue you.[72] Why?

Some of the claimants in the above examples are denied recovery in many states by the so-called "fireman's rule" -- which generally applies not only to the fire-fighter, but to police officers as well.[73] It should not come as a surprise that I do not like ad hoc, free-standing doctrines like this. We need to know "why" the fireman loses and, in my view, we ought to be able to explain that treatment by reference to more general underlying legal rules. The question, then, is whether we can do that -- and without resorting to "assumption of risk."

One possible explanation for the fireman's rule is that this is an awkward way of saying that the defendant owes the plaintiff no duty of care. This explanation draws on the usual sorts of arguments that justify a no duty result. These include: 1) the fire-fighter's generous disability compensation arrangements make that role for tort law superfluous; 2) because fires tend to burn up the evidence, it is unwise to create a cause of action where the legal system will have difficulty determining fault; and 3) we do not want to give the careless firestarter a perverse incentive not to call the fire department for fear of potential liability. Although merely stating these arguments does not make them convincing, let us assume for the moment that they are.

But even if these explanations disposed of fire-fighter claimants (and perhaps police officer claimants as well), we are still left with the power company worker and the plumber. As to them the "no duty" arguments just made are much less convincing -- except perhaps for the idea that the threat of liability will perversely cause the originally negligent party not to call for help.[74] Yet, tort law generally blocks recovery for plumbers and power company workers as well.[75]

How do we explain this? The general point applicable to all of these claimants is the familiar one discussed earlier: reasonable warning is sufficient. Yet, before, a sufficient warning meant that there was no breach. Here, however, that cannot be said. Clearly, had the fire spread to a neighbor's house, or had the downed power line injured a passing pedestrian, and so on, the defendant would have been liable to those victims. So, if there was a duty and a breach, how do we extricate the defendant from liability other than by saying "assumption of risk"? Clearly the defendant was the cause-in-fact of the injury to what I am calling the professional rescuer, and the victim was not at fault (which, anyway, would only lead to a reduced recovery).

To overcome this difficulty, I suggest that we tum to notions typically employed in connection with the doctrine of proximate cause. Under the Restatement view, you are not the proximate cause of the plaintiffs harm if you were not negligent "toward" the plaintiff, even if you were negligent toward another.[76] Under a somewhat different formulation, you are not the proximate cause of the plaintiffs harm if the plaintiffs harm resulted from a "hazard" that is different from that which would have made you liable to another.[77] And under yet a different formulation, you are not the proximate cause of the plaintiff's harm if your responsibility for the hazard has been superseded by the conduct of another.[78]

We can, I believe, apply each of these formulations in a reasonably convincing way to the professional rescuer setting -- although, I admit, not without some awkwardness. The strongest way to put it, I think, is to say that the arrival of a professional rescuer is superseding, that is, cutting off the defendant's responsibility for the subsequent injury. Consider, for example, the case in which X orders wood from the defendant to build a scaffold, and the defendant negligently sends bad wood. But X discovers that the wood is bad, and yet uses it anyway. X's taking responsibility for the wood, knowing that it is bad, becomes a superseding cause and cuts off the defendant's liability to the plaintiff who is later hurt when the scaffold collapses.[79] The analogy here is that the professional rescuer takes responsibility for the danger once she arrives on the scene. This is a comfortable notion to apply to professionals but not amateurs and thereby helps to explain the different results in the two cases. Yet, I admit that the analogy is not exact, if for no other reason than that the bad wood case involves a third party as the superseding cause, whereas here the victim herself is seen as the superseding cause.

Turning then to the "wrong hazard" notion, we might draw, for example, on the case in which the defendant negligently rented the plaintiff a car with a defective hood latch.[80] As a result, the hood flies open while the plaintiff is on the highway. Had that caused an accident right there, as it might well have, then surely the defendant would have been liable. But suppose instead the plaintiff manages to get the car off the road and into a regular parking place, and while getting out to lower the hood, the plaintiff is struck by a passing motorist. The defendant now wins and the reason is that it seems only coincidental and not legally relevant that the plaintiff happened to be standing outside his car on his way to lower the hood. A driver getting out of his car at a parking space might just as well have been on his way to get an ordinary package out of the trunk. The injury is not a "hazard" for which the defendant is fairly held accountable. Analogously, then, it might be argued that it is not relevant that the fire, downed wire, and broken pipe dangers were negligently created. They might just as easily have been accidentally created because in that instance the plaintiff would equally have been on the scene and equally at risk in the very same way.[81]

Finally, in the famous Palsgraf case[82] it was assumed that the defendant railway workers were negligent towards a passenger they pushed onto the moving train, even though he was not injured. But they were not negligent towards Mrs. Palsgraf. Hence they escaped liability to her when she was injured as a result of scales that fell on her in response to the vibrations caused by the explosion of the fireworks that had been knocked from the arms of that man they pushed onto the train. Analogously, then, it might be argued that although the defendants in these professional rescue cases were negligent toward their neighbors and to passersby, they were not negligent toward the plaintiffs. That is, whereas the former were entitled to precautions, the latter were due only the fair warning they got.

Trickier is to understand why they are entitled only to a warning. Although, in one sense, they depend for their livelihood upon being called out in emergencies, surely in a more immediate way they would rather not put themselves on the line in order to save someone (or someone's property) who should not have created the dangerous predicament in the first place. Nonetheless, thinking back to the cases involving dangers on the property of ordinary homeowners, we saw there, too, that those who come onto the land are typically entitled to no more than a warning. This, however, seems to imply that commercial actors who call out professional rescuers would be held to a higher standard, and yet they do not seem to be.[83]

In sum, I concede that putting the professional rescue cases into the "no proximate cause" category is a little bit awkward. This will lead some to say that what plainly is needed here is "assumption of risk." But let me emphasize again that this is unsatisfactory if for no other reason that it does not explain the different treatment of professional and amateur rescuers. Indeed, in a certain sense the amateur's conduct constitutes a more voluntary encountering of the danger. After all, he can refuse. By contrast, the professionals, certainly the police officer and the fire fighter, have a duty to confront the risk whether they feel like it or not. Of course, those professionals knew about the risk when they took their jobs and, more specifically, when they arrived on the scene. But, as I showed in my discussion of defective products in the workplace, the mere willingness of an employee to accept a dangerous job clearly no longer precludes tort recovery. A manufacturer who readily could have made the work environment safer by providing a different machine, for example, is likely to be held liable notwithstanding the employee's volitional encounter of the machine's danger.

Perhaps these professional rescuer cases are simply wrongly decided. Maybe the courts have been hypnotized by the fact that the victims assumed the physical risk and confuse that with the legal risk. There is indeed some judicial and legislative support for this position.[84] Or maybe the courts are too caught up on the old licensee-invitee distinction with professional rescuers relegated to the less protected category. That aside, and assuming you are still not convinced by the "no duty" argument I made earlier, I then conclude that "no proximate cause" will just have to do to explain the result.

V. Conclusion

Although the Restatement of Torts still provides that assumption of risk is a complete defense to a cause of action in tort, I have tried to show that assumption of risk is a trap-in two senses. First, assumption of risk is both redundant and confusing as a legal doctrine: any result fairly achieved by the application of assumption of risk can also be reached, and is better understood, by the use of one of a number of other familiar doctrines. Second, the mere assumption of the physical tends to be wrongly equated with the legal doctrine, thereby leading to inappropriate bars to legal recovery under the current personal injury law system. The more important and difficult question for courts to ask is when should the defendant's warning suffice, and when that question is thoughtfully answered, often it will be determined that the defendant should have done more.[85]

The ideas I have presented here are perhaps best summed up through one final example. In recent years courts around the country have been presented with a great number of sporting injury lawsuits between participants, but outside the professional sports context. Some cases simply apply ordinary negligence principles, holding careless participants liable for injuries to others, a result that is, of course, consistent with the broad sweep of tort law generally.[86] Most, however, relieve the defendant from liability for ordinary negligence -- at least in so-called "contact" sports settings.[87]

In some of these cases, the courts seem to understand the doctrinal approach I have urged here, and rest their decision on "no duty" grounds.[88]

Typically the emphasis is on, first, judicial manageability (can juries meaningfully distinguish unreasonable from reasonable risk taking in such settings, and will the courts be swamped with cases?) and second, a fear that liability will lead to perverse behavioral incentives (that is, competitors will no longer be willing to go all out to win because of an excessive fear of liability). I concede that these are exactly the sort of arguments that are appropriate to a no duty theory.

Whether they are convincing arguments is another matter, however. If nothing else, I feel confident saying that informal recreational sports settings do not present nearly as many reasons for a "no duty" rule as do professional settings. Specifically, there is no well-structured alternative behavioral control regime and no generous alternative compensation arrangements. In a leading case, for example, some friends decided to play touch football during the halftime of a Super Bowl.[89] The female plaintiff had complained to the male defendant not to be so rough, after he had already run into her, reminding him that it was only touch football after all. He promised to behave better, but on the very next play, according to her complaint and deposition, he negligently knocked her down, seriously injuring her. It is not obvious to me just why courts should be so eager to free defendants, like those portrayed in this complaint, from tort liability for their negligence.

Far worse, however, are those judicial opinions in this area that seem mesmerized by the idea that participants in these activities know that they might get hurt, and so ought not complain about it.[90] Assumption of the physical risk is essentially equated with assumption of the legal risk. It is as though, in the case I just described, the woman having realized that the man was not playing by the rules must have (or at least should have) appreciated that he might do so again (notwithstanding his assurances). If she did not want to take any further chances she should have quit there and then. If there is one single message to take away from this Monsanto Lecture, it is my belief that this is altogether the wrong way to think about tort liability.

ENDNOTES

1. I was truly pleased to give this year's Monsanto Lecture. My many distinguished predecessors have talked primarily about tort reform from the *outside-that* is, through legislation. Even though much of my own torts scholarship is also in that vein, I decided instead to address tort reform from the *inside.* Notwithstanding recent statutory changes, torts remain, of all the law school courses we offer, the queen of the common law subjects. As I will argue here, in at least one important area of tort law, judges should change the way they are looking at and talking about the issues they face. "Assumption of risk" has received considerable attention over the years, yet courts continue to get it wrong. The most important classic writing on the issue is by Fleming James, *Assumption of Risk,* 61 YALE L.J. 141 (1952) and Assumption *of Risk: Unhappy Reincarnation,* 78 YALE L.J. 185 (1968); John Mansfield, *Informed Choice in the law of Tons,* 22 LA. L. Rev. 17 (1961); and Francis Bohlen, *Voluntary Assumption of Risk,* 20 HARV. L. REV. 14 (1906). Recent helpful writing includes Kenneth Simons, *Assumption of Risk and Consent in the LAW of Torts: A Theory of Full Preference,* 67 B.U. L. REv. 213 (1987); Stephanie Wildman& John Barker, *Time To Abolish Implied Assumption of a Reasonable Risk in California,* 25 U.S.F. L. Rev.647 (1991); and John Diamond, Assumption *of Risk after Comparative Negligence: Integrating Contract Theory into Tort Doctrine,* 52 OHIO St. L.J. 717 (1991).

2. Murphy v. Steeplechase Amusement Co., 166 N.E. 173 (N.Y. 1929).

3. On the validity of these sorts of agreements in general, see *Tunkl v. Regents of the University of California,* 383 P.2d 441 (Cal. 1963) and *Dalury v. S-K-1, Lid.,* 670 A.2d 795 (Vt.1995).

4. The Restatement (Second) of Torts sets out "assumption of risk" in Section 496A-G.

5. *Murphy,* 166 N.E. at 174.

6. George P. Fletcher, *Fairness and Utility in Tort Theory,* 85 HARV. L. REV. 537 (1972).

7. Richard A. Epstein, *A Theory of Strict Liability,* 2 J. LEGAL STUD. 151 (1973).

8. Richard A. Posner, *A Theory of Negligence,* 1 J. LEGAL STUD. 29 (1972).

9. Howard Latin, *"Good" Warnings, Bad Products, and Cognitive Limitations,* 41 UCLA L. REV. 1193 (1994).

10. Brown v. San Francisco Ball Club, Inc., 222 P.2d 19, 20 (Cal. Ct. App. 1950).

11. *Id.* at 2L

12. *Id.*

13 One might ask why didn't the stadium operators at least provide a warning to newcomers. I find this suggestion impractical. If an effective warning really were required, then making an announcement over the public address system once people are already in their seats would seem hardly sufficient. It is implausible to expect people already sitting in the open to at that point ask for new seats behind screening or well out of the reach of foul balls.

Hence, a thorough warning would have to come before tickets are purchased. We could imagine that, before buying a ticket at the stadium, every new patron would watch a video which shows people being hit and injured by foul balls and then explains the seating options (with parallel warnings given when people seek to purchase tickets over the phone). But I find it rather preposterous to say that stadium owners are careless for not providing such warnings. Moreover, even if a claimant managed to convince a jury that the defendant was negligent not to have given a warning, it seems to me that the victim would still probably lose on causation grounds. That is, I find it altogether unconvincing that a warned first-time spectator would, as a result, actually choose to sit out of harm's way, which usually means accepting a decidedly worse seat.

14. RESTATEMENT (SECOND) OF TORTS§ 13 (1965); RESTATEMENT (SECOND) OF TORTS§§892-892D (1979).

15. *See* RESTATEMENT (SECOND) OF TORTS § 892C cmt. e, illus. 9 (1979).

16. *See* RESTATEMENT (THIRD) OF TORTS: PRODUCTS LIABILITY§ 2(b) (Tentative Draft No.2, 1995).

17. *See generally* Peter H. Schuck, *Rethinking Informed Consent,* 103 YALE L.J. 899 (1994).

18. This example is based on *Hammnontree v. Jenner,* 97 Cal. Rptr. 739 (Cal. Ct. App. 1971).

19. This example is based on *Bolton v. Stone,* [1951] App. Cas. 850.

20. Adams v. Bullock, 125 N.E. 93 (N.Y. 1919).

21. *Id.* at 94.

22. *See generally* James Barr Ames, *Law and Morals,* 22 HARV. L. REV. 97 (1908).

23. *See* Epstein, *supra* note 7, at 198.

24. *See, e.g.,* Ernest J. Weinrib, *The Case for a Duty to Rescue,* 90 YALE L.J. 247 (1980).

25. *See generally* Winterbottom v. Wright, 10 Meeson & Welsby 109, 152 Eng. Rep 402 (Ex. P. 1842); MacPherson v. Buick Motor Co., 1l N.E. 1050 (N.Y. 1916).

26. *See generally* Falzone v. Busch, 214 A.2d 12 (N.J. 1965).

27. *See, e.g.,* H. R. Moch Co. v. Rensselaer Water Co., 159 N.E. 896 (N.Y. 1928).

28. *See, e.g.,* Strauss v. Belle Realty Co., 482 N.E.2d 34 (N.Y. 1985).

29. This example is based on *Olivia N. v. National Broadcasting Co.,* 178 Cal. Rptr. 888 (Cal Ct. App. 1981).

30. *See generally* Blakely *v.* Camp Ondessonk, 38 F.3d 325 (7th Cir. 1994).

31. For a fuller description of the case and some of the controversy surrounding it, see Stephen D. Sugarman, *Taking Advantage of the Torts Crisis,* 48 OHIO ST. L.J. 329, 337 n.47 (1987).

32. Turcotte *v.* Fell, 502 N.E.2d 964 (N.Y. 1986).

33. *Id.* at 971.

34. *See generally* Hackbart v. Cincinnati Bengals, Inc., 601 F.2d 516 (l0th Cir. 1979).

35. Arbegast v. Board of Educ., 480 N.E.2d 365 (N.Y. 1985).

36. For cases upholding signed releases of liability for negligence in recreational settings, see, e.g., *Barnes v. New Hampshire KaningAss'n,Inc.,* 509 A.2d 151 (N.H. l986) and *Okura v. United States Cycling Federation,* 231 Cal. Rptr. 429 (Cal. Ct. App. 1986).

37. Tunkl v. Regents of the Univ. of Cal., 383 P.2d 441 (Cal. 1963).

38. This follows even if the class of those who signed the agreement not to sue (including the victim) benefitted from the agreement through, say, lower costs of the service or product.

39. Dalury v. S-K-1 Ltd., 670 A.2d 795 (Vt. 1995).

40. *See generally* Gonzalez v. Garcia, 75 Cal. App. 3d 874, 142 Cal. Rptr. 503 (1977) (upon which this example is based); UNIF. COMPARATIVE FAULT Acr § 1(b), 12 U.L.A. 33 (1996).

41. *See generally* Williams v. Delta Int'l Mach. Corp., 619 So. 2d 1330 (Ala. 1993).

42. In the so-called "pure form" of comparative negligence, even the mostly at fault victim may still recover a small share of her damages from her relatively little at fault injurer. Under the "modified" versions, the injurer must be at least either equally or more at fault (depending upon which "modified" form has been adopted) for the victim to be able to recover anything at all. In short, in those latter jurisdictions the domain over which loss sharing operates is more restricted. *See generally* VICTOR E. SCHWARTZ, COMPARATIVE NEGLIGENCE (2d ed. 1986 & Supp. 1993).

43. *See, e.g.* UNIF. COMPARATIVE FAULT ACT § 2 Commentary, 12 U.L.A. (1996).

44. RESTATEMENT (THIRD) OF TORTS: PRODUCTS LIABILITY §§ 2 cmt. I, 12 cmt. b (Tentative Draft No. 2, 1995).

45. *See* Daly v. General Motors Corp., 575 P.2d 1162 (Cal. 1978).

46. RESTATEMENT (THIRD) OF TORTS: PRODUCTS LIABILITY §§ 2 cmts. I, o; 12 cmts. b-e (Tentative Draft No. 2, 1995).

47. This example is based on *Rauch v. Pennsylvania Sports & Enterprises, Inc.,* 81 A.2d 548 (Pa. 1951), a case from the pre-comparative fault era that in my view gets it all wrong, by holding for the defendant on the basis of "assumption of risk."

48. This example is based on *Eckert v. Long Island R.R.,* 43 N.Y. 502 (1871).

49. Wagner v. International Ry. Co., 133 N.E. 437 (N.Y. 1921).

50. This example is based on *Luque v. McLean,* 501 P.2d 1163 (Cal. 1972). *See generally* RESTATEMENT (THIRD) OF TORTS: PRODUCTS LIABILITY § 2 cmts. c, i (Tenative Draft No. 2,1995).

51. For a fine discussion of this problem in the product injury settings, *see* generally Latin, *supra* note 9. For a response to Latin, see Kennelh Weissman, *A "Comment J" Parry to Howard Latin's "Good" Warnings, Bad Products, and Cognitive limitations,* 70 ST.JOHN'S L. REV. 629 (1996). In important respects Weissman seems to be talking past Latin, because, despite all of his criticism, Weissman concedes that plaintiffs should be able to win by showing that the product was defective notwithstanding the provision of a "good" warning. *Id.* at 689. That, however, is also what Latin wants the victim to be able to do. Latin, *supra* note 9, at 1290-92.

52. Obviously, ski slope operators can be at fault on some occasions, either by failing to warn adequately, or by failing to take precautions we do want them to take, such as properly maintaining the chair lifts and closing runs where there are special avalanche dangers. But I am assuming in this example that nothing of that sort is amiss.

53. *See generally* SMOKING POLICY: LAW, POLITICS AND CULTURE (Robert Rabin & Stephen D. Sugarman eds., 1993). To be sure, some smokers today might understandably gripe that the tobacco makers failed to provide them an adequate warning about the risks and addictive nature of the product, especially those people who started smoking as youths. But the United States Supreme Court concluded that Congress has pre-empted those tort claims (at least for those who started smoking after 1965) by deciding that the legally required warnings on cigarette packages are sufficient. *See* Cipollone v. Liggett Group, *505* U.S. 504 (1992). Those who started smoking before the warnings appeared have different legal problems. Some find it hard to prove that the companies themselves knew of the dangers at the time the victim began using the product. Most also confront a cause in fact problem-convincing the jury that they would not have started smoking had they been warned. On this score, their continued smoking in the face of the warnings, notwithstanding claims of addiction, will frequently doom their cases.

54. Perhaps you would be held contributorily negligent for buying the product and have your damages reduced accordingly.

55. O'Brien v. Muskin Corp., 463 A.2d 298 (N.J. 1983). Whether the plaintiff could also be held contributorily negligent is another matter.

56. The New Jersey legislature has restricted *O'Brien* by statute. Now that statute permits a product to be condemned essentially only where the product is "egregiously unsafe," of "little or no usefulness" *and* the ordinary user "cannot reasonably be expected to have knowledge of the product's risks, or the product poses a risk of serious injury to persons other than the user or consumer." N.J. SRAT. ANN. § 2A:58C-3 (West 1996). The proposed Restatement (Third) of Torts: Products Liability, however, does not appear to give such product makers a "warnings" escape hatch. RESTATEMENT (THIRD) OF TORTS: PRODUCFS LIABIUTY § 2 cmt. d (Tenative Draft No. 2, 1995).

57. RESTATEMENT (SECOND) OF TORTS § 342 (1965).

58. *Compare* RESTATEMENT (SECOND) OF TORTS§§ 341, 342 (1965)(regarding licensees) *with* §§ 341A, 343, 343A (regarding invitees).

59. *See, e.g.,* Rowland v. Christian, 443 P.2d 561 (Cal. 1968).

60. In the leading *Rowland* case, for example, there is every reason to believe that the apartment-dweller host would have satisfied her obligation to exercise due care had she warned her guest of the hidden danger in the bathroom. *Id.* at 567.

61. *See, e.g.,* Carter v. Kinney, 896 S.W.2d 926 (Mo. 1995).

62. This example is loosely based on *Heldman v. Uniroyal, Inc.,* 371 N.E.2d 557 (Ohio Ct. App. 1977).

63. A leading case is *Kline v. 1500 Mass. Ave. Apartment Corp.,* 439 F.2d 477 (D.C. Cir.1970). *See also* Woolston v. Wells, 687 P.2d 144 (Or. 1984); Harrison v. Taylor, 768 P.2d. 1321 (Idaho 1989); Ward v. K Mart Corp, 554 N.E.2d 223 (Ill. 1990); Tharp v. Bunge Corp., 641 So.2d 20 (Miss. 1994); Bertrand v. Alan Ford, Inc., 537 N.W.2d 185 (Mich. 1995).

64. *See generally* RESTATEMENT (SECOND) OF TORTS § 343A(I) (1965).

65. *See generally* Latin, *supra* note 9.

66. *See* Howard A. Latin, *Problem-Solving Behavior and Theories of Ton Liability,* 73 CAL.L.REV. 677 (198.5).

67. This discussion is based on *Camacho v. Honda Motor Co.,* 741 P.2d 1240 (Colo. 1987).

68. *See generally* Aaron D. Twerski & Neil B. Cohen, *Informed Decision Making and the Law of Torts: The Myth of Justiciable Causation,* 1988 U. ILL. L. REV. 607.

69. *Id.*

70. I draw this example from Kenneth W. Simons' discussion, *supra* note I; although he sees this as a case of true assumption of risk, I find it better understood as a matter of "no cause."

71. Dias *v.* Daisy-Heddon, 390 N.E.2d 222 (Ind. Ct. App. 1979). For a further discussion, see Latin, *supra* note 9, at 1267-68.

72. See W. PAGE KEETON ET AL., PROSSER AND KEETON ON THE LAW OF TORTS427 (5th ed.1984).

73. *Id.* at 429-30.

74. Prosser considered this argument "rubbish." *Id.* at 431.

75. *See, e.g.,* Cohen v. Mcintyre, 20 Cal. Rptr. 2d 143 (Cal. 1993) (veterinarian injured by dog bite); Hacker v. City of Glendale, 20 Cal. Rptr. 2d 847 (Cal. Ct. App. 1993) (professional tree trimmer electrocuted by power line); Nunez v. R'Bibo, 260 Cal. Rptr. 1 (Cal. Ct. App. 1989) (gardener injured on a ladder); Nelson v. Hall, 211 Cal. Rptr. 668 (Cal. Ct. App. 1985) (veterinary assistant injured by dog bite). *But see* Neighbarger v. Irwin Industries, 882 P.2d 347 (Cal. 1994) (rejecting the application of both the "no duty" rule and the "firefighter's" rule to an oil refiner's safety employees who were injured fighting a fire that the defendant negligently set); Davis v. Cashier, 14 Cal. Rptr. 2d 679 (1992) (dog handler was bit by injured dog).

76. RESTATEMENT (SECOND) OF TORTS§ 281(b) cmt. c (1965).

77. *Id.* § 281(b) cmts. e, f.

78. *Id.* § 440.

79. Stultz v. Benson Lumber Co. 59 P.2d 100 (Cal. 1936).

80. This discussion is based on *Ventricelli v. Kinney System Rent A Car.* 383 N.E.2d 1149 (N.Y. 1978).

81. For a recent decision involving a professional rescuer that follows this general form of analysis, see *Bryant v. Glastetter,* 38 Cal. Rptr. 2d 291 (Cal. Ct. App. 1995).

82. Palsgraf. Long Island R.R. Co., 162 N.E. 99 (N.Y. 1928).

83. *See, e.g,* Giorgi v. Pacific Gas & Elec. Co., 72 Cal. Rptr. 119 (Cal. Ct. App. 1968).

84. *See, e.g.,* the views of Justice Tobriner in *Walters v. Sloan, 511* P.2d 609 (Cal. 1977) (Tobriner, J., dissenting). *See also* N.J. STAT. ANN. § 2A:62A-21 (West Supp. 1996) (discussed in Boyer v. Anchor Disposal, 638 A.2d 135 (N.J. 1994)).

85. I have put aside here the possible role of a defense of assumption of risk" in cases where plaintiffs voluntarily encounter ultrahazardous activities for which the defendant would otherwise be strictly liable. Nor have I considered the role for an entirely new doctrine of assumption of risk in a regime of the sort imagined by Judge Calabresi in which the goal of the system were to identify the "cheapest cost avoider". *See generally* GUIDO CALABRESI, THE *COSTS* OF ACCIDENTS (1970).

86. *See, e.g.,* Lestina v. West Bend Mut. Ins. Co., 501 N.W.2d 28 (Wis. 1993).

87. *See* Hana Miura, Lestina v. West Bend Mutual Insurance Co.: *Widening the Court as a Playing Field for Negligent Participants in Recreational Team Contact Sports,* 1994 WIS. L. REV.1005, at 1008-11; Yancy v. Superior Court, 33 Cal. Rptr. 2d 777 (Cal. Ct. App. 1994) (treating discus-throwing injuries to fellow participants as subject to ordinary negligence principles). Some cases have also distinguished between injuries involving co-participants and those involving students and teachers. *See, e.g.,* Fidopiastis v. Hirtler, 41 Cal. Rptr. 2d 94 (Cal. Ct. App. 1995).

88. *See, e.g.,* Knight v. Jewett, 834 P.2d 696 (Cal. 1992).

89. *Id.*

90. *See, e.g.,* Ross v. Clouser, 637 S.W.2d 11, 14 (Mo. 1982); Kuehner v. Green, 436 So.2d 78, 80 (Fla. 1983); Marchettti v. Kalish, *559* N.E.2d 699, 703-04 (Ohio 1990); Connell v. Payne, 814 S.W.2d 486, 488 (Tex. Ct. App. 1991).

Chapter14

Gathering "Duty" into a Unified Concept

The core principle of negligence law is that if you act unreasonably and cause harm to another, you are liable for the injury. Or put even more broadly, if a reasonably prudent person would have taken precautions you failed to take and those precautions would have avoided harm to the victim, then you are liable for that harm.

But there are limits on this principle, and this chapter focuses on the "no duty" limit. That is, in some settings because you have no legal duty to protect the victim from harm therefore you will not be liable for that harm even though/if your behavior was unreasonable.

When is there "no duty" to exercise due care? Since we generally want people to act in ways that juries would find to be how reasonable people act, there had better be a good reason why it is all right to fail to act in that way and yet escape legal responsibility in tort for the harm you caused. This perspective begins with the presumption that there normally is a duty to act with due care but admits that sometimes for good reason there is no duty to do so. Some scholars and courts begin with the opposite presumption – that there is no duty to another in tort unless there is a reason for having a duty imposed on you. This chapter argues that the former is a better way to think about the problem because, however one starts, the analysis comes down to asking whether in this case, or perhaps better put, in this type of case there is a convincing reason for no duty. After all, the reason for imposing a duty is always straightforwardly the same – you acted (or the victim has alleged that you acted) in an unreasonable manner, and a central goal of tort is supposed to be to encourage reasonable actions and to provide fair compensation to those who are injured when others fail to so act. This chapter provides a substantial expansion of some ideas about "duty" that are introduced in Chapter 13.

Unfortunately, thinking about when there is or is not a duty is often quite confused. The California Supreme Court in the important case of *Rowland v.*

Christian (involving the legal duties of apartment occupiers to their guests) set out what have become known as the "*Rowland* factors" as guides to determining whether or not there is a duty of care in tort: " foreseeability of harm to the plaintiff, the degree of certainty that the plaintiff suffered injury, the closeness of the connection between the defendant's conduct and the injury suffered, the moral blame attached to the defendant's conduct, the policy of preventing future harm, the extent of the burden to the defendant and consequences to the community of imposing a duty to exercise care with resulting liability for breach, and the availability, cost, and prevalence of insurance for the risk involved."

Alas, these factors are largely unhelpful and misleading. First, although many have argued that there can be no duty to another in tort if the risk of harm to that person is unforeseeable, in the end "foreseeability" is a matter of breach, not duty. That is, a reasonable person cannot be expected to take precautions against risks that cannot reasonably be foreseen, and so in such circumstances there has been no failure to act with due care. And therefore, the "no duty" issue does not come into it. The key point here is that if "no duty" is to have any independent meaning, it must be reserved for cases where there has been a breach (or at least the victim has so alleged).

Second, the "certainty" that the victim has suffered an injury may be a helpful consideration in cases involving, say, emotional distress. But for cases of straightforward physical injury the question of certainty is about the plaintiff carrying the burden of proof as to damages and not a matter of duty.

Third, the "closeness of the connection" between the defendant's conduct and the victim's harm seems to be about what used to be called "proximate cause" (which the Restatement (Third) now calls "scope of the risk") and not about "duty."

Fourth, the "moral blame" of the defendant and the "policy of preventing future harm" are factors that would always point to liability in cases where the defendant acted unreasonably (that is, failed to exercise due care) and hence are not helpful factors in deciding when there should be "no duty."

Fifth, the extent of the "burden" of precaution on the defendant goes to whether or not there was a breach, not the question of duty.

Sixth, the availability of insurance is perhaps a consideration as to whether there should or should not be a duty in tort. Yet, one would surely want to know more about why insurance is not generally available before concluding that this suffices to free the particular defendant from liability on grounds of "no duty" – a consideration that is in no way explicated by this *Rowland* factor.

Seventh, and finally, the same goes for the "consequences to the community" of imposing a tort duty on this defendant. Yes, perhaps sometimes those consequences can justify relieving this defendant of a duty, but the way this factor is stated gives no clue as to when that might be or why.

Moreover, not only are these factors – which have been endlessly repeated in case after case in California and elsewhere – worse than unhelpful, they are altogether incomplete. As this chapter argues, there are a series of factors or arguments that can justify a court concluding that the defendant owes the victim no duty of due care and thereby grant the defendant a victory as a matter of law (on the pleadings or on summary judgment). But those factors are very different from the *Rowland* factors. Some of these reasons are instrumental (or pragmatic); others are moral (going to considerations of fairness).

This chapter presents the arguments for these reasons with a wide range of examples. It provides a substantial expansion of some ideas about "duty" that are introduced in Chapter 13. As the examples given here demonstrate, "no duty" arguments are scattered around several places in the law of torts, and this chapter argues that judges, scholars and students would be better served if they were gathered up into a single doctrinal place on which "no duty" considerations could be focused.

Finally, this chapter argues that courts often treat cases as involving "no duty" that are really "no breach" cases because they feel more comfortable ruling for defendants as a matter of law that way. After all, "duty" is widely understood to be an issue for the court, whereas "breach" is ordinarily an issue for the jury. But this is wrong and confusing. Judges should rule that there was no breach as a matter of law when juries could not reasonably decide otherwise. And in instances where judges are convinced of that, they should rule that way. To rule instead that the defendant had "no duty" to prevent the injury when in fact the reason behind that call is, say, that the risk was too small or the burden of precaution too great, is to give the wrong reason (even if, often, the result is correct). This chapter explains that sort of mistake that courts are making through several examples.

This paper was presented at the Seventeenth Annual Clifford Symposium held at DePaul Law School and published as part of a Festschrift honoring Stanford Law School's Professor Robert L. Rabin: Stephen D. Sugarman, "Why No Duty?," 61 DePaul Law Review 669-695 (2012). It is reprinted here with the permission of the journal.

WHY NO DUTY?

SETTING UP THE PROBLEM

Typically, first-year tort students quickly learn that there are several elements in a cause of action sounding in negligence, one of which is the matter of duty. Although it is said that the plaintiff possesses the burden to prove that a legal duty of due care was owed to him, duty is best understood as a defendant's doctrine. Not only is it conventionally the defendant who will contest the issue of duty, but also it is a finding of no duty that allows a defendant to escape responsibility in tort for harming another through behavior that was unreasonable (or could well have been so found).[1]

Why do we allow wrongdoers to avoid tort liability? After all, denying the plaintiff's claim would appear to undermine a wide range of justifications usually given for creating fault-based liability in the first place. Individual justice is sacrificed by not allowing the victim to have the satisfaction of obtaining a determination that the injurer legally wronged him. The role played by tort liability—deterring the sort of unreasonable conduct in which the injurer engaged—is abandoned. No compensation in tort is forthcoming to the plaintiff from the at-fault defendant, with the result that the accident costs of the defendant's misconduct are not thereby internalized into the defendant's activity.

Surely, if we are going to have a common law system of negligence, there must be a very strong reason for allowing someone to get away with causing harm to another by failing to act in a way that a reasonable person would have. I explore those situations and their justifications in this Article.[2]

By way of a bit of ground clearing, I will put aside cases in which the defendant escapes liability because the harm he caused is not fairly part of the careless risk he took. From my perspective, these cases, which we used to call "no proximate cause" cases,[3] raise different issues of individual fairness that are outside my current inquiry. I also put aside consideration of the victim's own ordinary negligence in bringing about his injury. These days, the victim's carelessness results only in a partial reduction of recovery against a negligent defendant under the regime of pure comparative fault.[4] By contrast, a careless defendant with no duty to exercise due care completely escapes liability.[5]

It is also essential to keep the duty issue separate from the question of whether or not there was a "breach" of the duty to take due care— although this is not always easy to do. Someone who owes another a legal duty and harms the other individual through conduct that is judged to be reasonable will not be liable in negligence because there was no breach. For example, if a defendant did not act unreasonably because it was unforeseeable that her conduct would risk harm to another[6] or because the precaution necessary to avoid the harm would have been unreasonably burdensome,[7] there is no breach rather than no duty owed to the harmed individual (at least not on these grounds).

The essence of fault-based liability is that duty and causation are not enough; the defendant's conduct must also have fallen below the level expected of a reasonable person under the circumstances. In other words, when a defendant prevails at trial because there was no breach, this is not a victory on the grounds of no duty (although there are cases, to be sure, in which a defendant is or would be successful on both grounds). Alas, all too often judges and others talking about no-breach cases confusingly use no-duty language.[8] This is unfortunate. This is a theme to which I will return in Part III of this Article.

II. Why Might Unreasonable Defendants Escape Tort Liability on No-Duty Grounds?

In the following sections, I identify six separate reasons that might justify a no-duty determination and provide illustrations. For a number of injuries, one might offer more than one justification for a no-duty result, and so for purposes of explication, some of the examples may illustrate more than one justification.

In discussing some examples, I show that even if the right sort of no-duty argument may be made, it is not necessarily convincing. This is demonstrated in three ways. First, in some cases the law has changed over time as courts have rejected the old no-duty argument. Second, sometimes there is a division among the states, with some embracing the no-duty argument and others declining to do so. Third, for some examples I will offer my own criticism of the no-duty rules. This is all to emphasize that my central goal here is not to reshape the law as to when a tort duty is or is not owed. Rather, my primary objective is to show how no-duty decisions may be gathered up from all corners of tort doctrine and put into six categories. These categories, or types of arguments, seek to justify relieving a tort defendant of liability not because a jury should find his conduct faultless, but rather because of overriding considerations that free from tort liability someone who a jury might have found to have acted in an unreasonably careless way.

I loosely group the no-duty justifications into two bunches. The first bunch appeals to utilitarian considerations, the second to matters of moral value.

A. Tort Is the Wrong Regime to Deal with the Victim's Complaint

One justification for finding that no duty exists is that the victim who turns to tort law is looking in the wrong place for a remedy. There is a place (or are places) to deal with her complaint, but that place is not tort law. A clear example of this is the American law on workplace injuries with regard to claims made by employees against their employers. Employers owe their workers no duty of due care in tort because the workers' compensation system has replaced tort law as the mechanism for providing compensation to victims.[9] In addition, it might be argued that a combination of workers' compensation funding mechanisms and other institutions (like occupational safety agencies and unions) have replaced tort as other ways of assuring workers with reasonably safe workplaces. Of course, this is an instance in which a finding of no duty in tort is brought about by statute, and many of my examples will be common law no-duty cases. But this example illustrates the general point that the claimant who would try to sue in tort would be told that he is in the wrong realm.

The "fireman's rule" provides that property owners who carelessly set fires that require the services of firefighters are not liable in tort to those firefighters who are injured battling the flames.[10] Proponents offer many reasons for the rule, although some criticize the rule and not all states have adopted it.[11] I focus here on the reason that because firefighters already receive generous disability benefits that come with their jobs, they should turn exclusively to that form of compensation rather than to tort law. This is a no-duty way of thinking about the fireman's rule, and it parallels the workers' compensation solution. In effect, the property owner—who pays taxes that are used to hire firefighters and to provide them with disability benefits when injured—is viewed as a temporary employer of the firefighter who was hurt while combating the property owner's blaze.

When initially enacted, the National Vaccine Injury Compensation Program (NVICP)[12] appeared to allow those who said they were victims of the unwanted side effects of vaccinations to recover either from the plan's fund or in tort (subject to the requirement that the victim first go through the fund's claims process).[13] Recently, the U.S. Supreme Court ruled out the tort remedy for design-defect claims against vaccine manufacturers on so-called "preemption" grounds under the National Childhood Vaccine Injury Act.[14] This no-duty result was achieved by Justice Scalia's remarkable grammatical tour de force, in which he interpreted the word "unavoidable" in the statute to mean (or include) "avoidable."[15] I find it utterly baffling that someone like Justice Scalia, who is thought to interpret statutes by the simple reading of the plain text, would reach such a result. His opinion also reflects a misunderstanding of the state of tort law at the time the NVICP was enacted. But all of this carping is for another day. The point is that concerns about whether vaccines were properly designed are now turned over exclusively to the Federal and Drug Administration (FDA), with its expertise, and away from trial judges and juries as a result of the 6–2 decision in Bruesewitz. And if injured victims are to obtain any compensation, it is to come from the NVICP fund and not tort law.

This is but the latest in a line of pro-defendant decisions in which the Supreme Court has interpreted congressional language as preempting the claimant from seeking a tort remedy, thereby freeing the defendant from a tort duty to exercise due care. In these cases, the Court has concluded that tort is no longer a proper place for individuals to try their complaints about, say, the design of medical devices[16] or the warnings contained on cigarette packages and in advertisements.[17] Rather, the FDA or Congress is the final word on whether reasonable precautions were taken, which results in the defendant owing no duty in tort to the claimant.

In the examples so far discussed, the government has created alternatives to tort for airing victim concerns. Consider next the professional athlete who is injured on the field by a carelessly behaving competitor. Generally speaking, for conduct that is merely negligent, there is no tort remedy.[18] One justification for this no-duty solution is that professional sports have privately developed mechanisms for dealing with the social goals said to be advanced by tort law, and they are the method for dealing with careless conduct that injures athletes. More precisely, professional sports have elaborate on-and off-field penalty mechanisms for dealing with misconduct that takes place during the game.[19] These are thought to well serve the punishment, deterrence, and justice goals of tort law. As for compensation, there is a well-developed system outside of tort law as well—the combination of guaranteed contracts (when available) and disability insurance. Those arrangements are ones to which professional athletes have ready access, given that they have agents who know about these opportunities, to say nothing of their typical union membership in a body that is concerned about the future lives of those who are injured while playing, including those injured by the unreasonable behavior of another player.

In a similar vein, most states have concluded that if one's property has burned in a fire because the relevant water company carelessly failed to have water available to fight the fire, the property owner generally has no valid legal claim against the water company because the company owes him no duty to act with due care.[20] This is an example in which the property owner clearly relies on the water being competently supplied, believing that alternative fire-fighting water supplies need not be arranged. Normally one would think that there would be a legal duty owed to the property owner, and a few states reach that result.[21] But where there is no duty in tort, one justification is that, in this setting, the victim should look to the institution of private fire insurance rather than tort law to obtain compensation. Fire insurance is widely available, widely bought, and something that society thinks responsible property owners should obtain. Hence, in reality, the tort claim would generally involve a fight between the fire insurance company and the water company. Viewed that way, many believe that it is better for the loss to fall on the fire insurer because it is in a good position to price its insurance based on each specific piece of property's fire risk; the water company, by contrast, will generally only charge the municipality a bulk rate for the water pressure in the lines that lead to all of the hydrants in the jurisdiction.[22]

For another example, when the media negligently publishes something defamatory about a public figure, that victim may not successfully sue the publisher because, as a matter of federal constitutional law, there is no tort duty of due care owed to the victim.[23] One argument in support of this result is that the Supreme Court has concluded that a wronged public figure should seek a remedy not in tort law, but through a reply in the media—access to which, it is assumed, a public figure will readily have.

The field of financial loss provides yet other instances in which would-be tort claimants are denied recovery on no-duty grounds because courts prefer them to pursue other private remedies instead. Here, the rejection of a tort claim is generally based on the argument that the victim should seek relief in contract law.[24] For example, if someone purchases a defective product and suffers financial losses as a result, then recourse must generally be sought in contract and not tort.[25]

For a different example of this same point, assume that one spouse inflicts emotional distress on the other spouse, who then sues in tort. Some jurisdictions, which generally allow tort actions for emotional distress wrongfully imposed on a clearly foreseeable victim, will deny recovery in such cases on the ground that the offending spouse owes the other spouse no duty of care in tort.[26] One justification for this result is that the wronged spouse should instead seek relief in family law through divorce or separation proceedings.

In sum, what characterizes all of these no-duty arguments is that there is another forum available to the plaintiff to deal with the plaintiff's complaint. To be sure, that other forum may in the end provide no remedy. And even if it does provide a remedy that remedy might not address all of the goals said by some to be served by tort—justice, deterrence, cost internalization, and compensation, for example. Still, if these reasons are to be believed, the point is that the legal system has concluded that it would be better for victims to turn elsewhere, thereby relieving the actor of a legal duty of due care in tort.

B. *The Judicial System Cannot Suitably Administer Claims Like This*

A second justification supporting the absence of a duty in tort is that, in certain types of cases, the judicial process we use to administer tort claims is simply not capable of properly processing the claims that would be brought were there a tort duty of due care.

Consider the rule in states like California, which provides that there is no duty of due care to prevent the negligent infliction of emotional distress upon someone the defendant did not directly physically impact or threaten to impact, unless that person was both present at the scene of the harm and a close relative of the physically injured victim.[27] It is easy to imagine instances in which negligently caused injuries to third parties could also cause emotional harm to dozens, hundreds, or even thousands of individuals who witnessed, read about, or later saw a video of the direct physical injury the defendant caused.[28] Allowing claims in all such cases could produce a flood of claims that has the potential to swamp the judicial system, causing huge delays in the handling of much more serious injuries. This fear of judicial paralysis is frequently offered as a justification for denying a tort duty to those who were in fact negligently so harmed.[29] These victims are generally thought to have suffered smaller injuries, comparatively speaking, and, for the sake of being able to provide justice for other claimants, these victims are denied a tort remedy.

I can also understand the flood-of-claims argument when a court disallows lawsuits by children for both emotional distress and "loss of consortium" every time a parent is seriously injured by a careless defendant.[30] But I am less convinced that a parent who rushes to the scene of an accident where her child lies seriously harmed should be denied recovery because she did not witness the initial crash on the ground that this would open up the courts to too many cases. Yet I concede that the line needs to be drawn somewhere and, on grounds of administrative convenience, those with practical experience in these matters must be trusted to try to draw it sensibly.

A different sort of concern about the inability of the judicial system to administer certain claims is that the courts—especially juries—will regularly make multiple mistakes, or will at least be seen by the public as doing so. This could come in the form of inconsistent decisions about similar facts or outcomes that the public feels confident that it can second-guess and conclude were inconsistent. We cannot expect our system to be perfect or totally free from public criticism. But there could be some types of claims that create an especially acute risk of this result, which could wind up damaging the legitimacy of the judicial system in general and thereby cause far greater social harm. In such cases, it might be thought better simply to deny access to the courts even if that means the actual victims of another's fault would go uncompensated.

Here are two examples that are sometimes justified on this basis. First, in most states, participants in recreational sporting activities owe each other no duty of ordinary due care in tort.[31] One explanation for this is that juries will not be able to sensibly determine whether the victim was harmed by the negligence of the fellow participant or whether the injury was just a risk of the sport. All too often, a finding by the jury of the former would be seen by the public as more properly a case of the latter. Second, products liability claims could historically be brought only against the individual who directly sold the product to the consumer.[32] One explanation given for this result was that, because a product passed from a manufacturer through the hands of another party to the user-victim, juries would never know what the original buyer did to, or with, the product, thereby making it impossible for jurors to properly decide whether it was the initial negligence of the manufacturer or the fault of someone else that caused the injury.

Yet another potential problem area for the judicial system concerns cases in which we worry about collusion between plaintiffs and defendants. Suppose, for example, a husband is driving the family car and is in an accident in which his wife, who is either a passenger or a pedestrian, is injured. If the wife sues the husband, it will probably be to gain access to money provided from the family's liability insurance policy, which would raise a worry that the husband might concede that he was negligently driving when he was not. The old common law family-immunity doctrine would preclude such claims.[33] Although traditionally termed a separate or specialized doctrine, this "immunity" claim is really a no-duty idea, and the fraud concern given in justification of the doctrine is an example of the justification I am exploring here.[34] Most states appear to have abandoned the family-immunity rule,[35] and some states even find that insurance contract terms that exclude coverage when the claim is by another household member contrary to public policy.[36] In those states, insurers are simply left to ferret out any inappropriate collusion on a case-by-case basis. On balance, this might well be the best solution. My only point here is to show how the old doctrine might be justified as applicable to certain intra-family claims on the ground of judicial incompetence to ferret out the truth.

C. Permitting Tort Claims Will Induce Individuals to Respond in Socially Unacceptable (Perverse) Ways

A third category of no-duty cases is somewhat anguishing because it reflects a reluctant acceptance of the idea that in some situations one has to choose the lesser of two evils. I have in mind a setting in which the courts conclude that allowing a tort claim would, alas, result in behavior that is so socially undesirable that, on balance, it is actually better—or less bad—to deny recovery to the wronged and otherwise deserving victim.

One example in this category concerns recreational injuries. As noted above, in a large majority of states, if one skier carelessly knocks down another skier from behind and injures his victim, a tort claim will not lie because the injurer is said to owe no duty of ordinary care to the victim.[37] Another justification for this no-duty rule—the justification I want to focus on here—is the belief that imposing liability would have a highly undesirable social outcome; specifically, fearing the possibility of being sued, individuals would be afraid to engage in sporting activities that carry risks to others and would, in effect, stay at home and get fat. Put differently, some judges believe that imposing liability for negligence among participants will cause recreational activity to come to a halt or, perhaps less dramatically, to be substantially reduced.[38] That outcome, it is said, would be so undesirable that a tort duty will be denied in order to avoid this socially perverse response.[39]

I accept this sort of argument. Yet in this specific setting, I am rather skeptical about whether it is convincing as an empirical matter. Knowing how much individuals enjoy playing sports and how ignorant they are of tort law, I am generally doubtful that skiing and the like would come to a halt, or be sharply reduced, were ordinary negligence law applied. This instinct is reinforced because I have not seen good evidence of the withdrawal from recreational sports in a state like Wisconsin, which applies the regular tort obligation of due care to participants.[40]

The denial of tort recovery to public figures who are merely negligently defamed by the media has also been justified by a perverse-behavioral-response argument—that there will be excessive "self-censorship" by the media so as to chill the exercise of the right to free speech (that society so greatly values).[41] Hence, once more, carelessly harmed victims are denied recovery in tort. Although this justification for a no-duty result rests in the First Amendment to the Constitution, it reflects this category of cases. As the media is hyper-aware of the possibility of defamation actions, I take the concern about excessive self-censorship more seriously here, especially when I think about out-of-state media defendants being sued in local state courts by otherwise popular local state officials.

Most states have concluded that social hosts should not be held liable for carelessly serving drinks to their guests.[42] These cases typically arise when the guest later goes out and, because of her drunken state, carelessly injures the victim, who subsequently sues the host. One justification for this no-duty rule is that the socially valuable enjoyment of alcohol in important social settings (weddings, birthday parties, and the like) will be destroyed as individuals will inevitably overreact in the face of potential liability.[43]

Notice that this is but a specialized illustration of one reason that has historically been used to justify a limited tort duty of social hosts to their guests as a general matter.[44] Fully imposing on hosts the due-care principle, some have argued, would cause individuals to stop (or reduce) hosting others out of an exaggerated fear of liability.[45] More precisely, a fear of this perverse social response has been historically used to justify what at common law was a partial no-duty obligation toward licensees. By now, however, a majority of states have, in general, lumped licensees and invitees together, holding that both are owed the full duty of due care (in the relevant circumstances),[46] which suggests that most courts are no longer concerned about a serious decline in social interaction. But for the minority of states that have retained the old distinction,[47] a fear of perverse behavioral responses still may justify no-duty outcomes. Moreover, even in the majority-rule states, many legislatures have responded to the change in the common law with specialized, so-called "recreational use of land" statutes out of a fear that applying the ordinary tort-duty rules would cause too many individuals who freely allow or tolerate their land being used for recreational activities to fence their land off and deny recreational access to the substantial detriment of individuals seeking to enjoy the outdoors.[48] In effect, legislatures have concluded that it is better to maintain public access than it is to threaten landowners with liability for failing to address dangers they should have known and done something about.

The American rule that strangers owe no tort duty to take reasonable steps to save endangered fellow citizens[49] is justified on many grounds. One justification is the concern that imposing a duty would lead to perverse behavioral responses.[50] One such response might be that some individuals would become officious intermeddlers, rushing in to annoy individuals who do not need help.[51] Another is that some individuals would feel bound to attempt rescues when they are not competent to do so and, in their bumbling, would make things worse.[52] Yet another is that some individuals would be afraid to go out into the world for fear of being held responsible for failing to help others they encounter.[53] In sum, these concerns about perverse behavioral responses have been used to justify no duty in tort. Whether these concerns are empirically justified is another matter. There does not seem to be evidence of these bad outcomes from European nations that impose a tort duty on those who fail to make "easy" rescues.[54] Still, were these fears based in reality, one can appreciate why a no-duty rule would be adopted.[55]

Some have tried to justify the previously discussed fireman's rule on the ground that, without such a rule, individuals who carelessly set fires would refrain from timely calling the fire department and would instead foolishly try to put out the fire themselves, thereby risking not only larger harm to their own property but potentially harm to the property of others.[56] This justification also rests on the ground that such a perverse behavioral response makes it better to deny, rather than allow, recovery to the carelessly injured firefighter. Were this fear truly warranted, I could again appreciate the force of the argument. Yet absent solid empirical evidence, it strikes me as wild speculation that owners would actually risk increased damage to their property because of a vague fear that a firefighter called to the scene might be injured by the flames and then sue the careless owner, especially when the owner's tort liability would normally be covered by his fire insurance policy.

Following the California Supreme Court's decision in Tarasoff v. Regents of the University of California, a majority of states now recognize a duty of mental health professionals to warn a targeted victim when a patient of the professional has seriously threatened to kill or maim that person.[57] Yet, some courts and scholars reject imposing a duty of due care in such settings by raising concerns about perverse behavioral responses. These concerns are threefold: (1) patients will stop seeking therapy or stop being candid with their therapists; (2) therapists will wrongly commit patients to mental institutions so as to assure themselves of not being sued were the patient to attack someone; and (3) by way of overdeterrence, therapists will excessively warn of possible attacks, causing mental harm to third parties. In fact, these concerns seem not to have played out over the years in which a duty has been imposed in such situations, but one can appreciate how courts at the outset might have been apprehensive.[58]

Difficult cases arise when criminals come into places of business and threaten customers with weapons as a way to force employees to turn over their cash. Suppose an employee refuses and the criminal then shoots a customer in anger. Assume the customer or her heirs then sue the business, claiming that a reasonable employee would have turned over the money. Focusing only on the case before it, a jury might well agree and find the defendant liable. Yet, courts might believe that to allow this result would increase the number of now-emboldened robbers, leading not only to more lost cash but, inevitably, more injured bystanders. Once more, I find such a view, which has been used to justify a no-duty rule in this sort of case,[59] to be questionable as an empirical matter. But I concede that it is in the same vein as the position held by many that in the end it is better to stick firmly to the position that "we do not negotiate with terrorists."

In the case of Randi W. v. Muroc Joint Unified School District, the plaintiff-student claimed to have been sexually molested by a school employee who, it appears, had engaged in similar misconduct in the past that his former employer knew about.[60] But when asked for a reference by his potential new employer, his former employer praised him and said nothing about his apparent misbehavior.[61] The plaintiff understandably argued that had the former employer been forthcoming, her district would not have hired the person and she would not have been molested.[62] The California Supreme Court upheld her tort claim against the former employer, at least with respect to allegations of misrepresentation.[63] Defendants argued that allowing such tort claims would undermine the job reference system to such a degree that in the future, former employers would simply acknowledge that X worked for them and would refuse to say anything about X, good or bad. Were this perverse response to occur, it would deprive those on the hiring side from valuable information about prospective employees.[64] For some, this is a good reason to deny the assault victim's claim by deciding that the former employer owed the victim no duty in tort.

Florida's and Virginia's so-called "bad baby" compensation plans might also illustrate this perspective.[65] Those legislatures, some argue, curtailed the tort rights of newborns harmed by the medical malpractice of certain doctors because of their determination that allowing such tort claims would deprive the citizens of the state, more generally, of essential medical services.[66] Doctors, it was thought, would flee—and perhaps were already fleeing—to other states. The NVICP, discussed above,[67] also arguably reflects this justification: Congress curtailed tort rights because of the fear of a socially worse consequence of keeping them in place—the public loss of firms willing to make essential vaccines. Notice that in both these instances, the decision to create an alternative realm for the victims to turn for compensation was driven by the concern that existing duties of care in tort law were creating perverse responses that were socially intolerable.

In contrast, in most of the other examples I have discussed in this category, governments have not created specific alternative compensation plans to which victims can turn. That said, perhaps it is worth mentioning that many states have created "victims of violent crimes" laws, to which some individuals being denied tort claims can apply. Alas, these state compensation plans have functioned poorly and pay very modest benefits, usually only to destitute victims and all too often after extremely long delays.[68]

D. *Trumping Social Values Override the Victim's Claim in Tort*

I put a related fourth category of no-duty cases under the heading of "trumping social values." This brings us to the first of three value-based justifications. In these cases, the courts conclude that a broader and more important social value is at stake, one that would be unacceptably sacrificed if a duty of ordinary care were imposed. Put differently, this value trumps the normal desirability of discouraging and punishing conduct that juries conclude to be unreasonable. In this category, therefore, it does not matter whether imposing a tort duty would result in changed and undesirable behavior. If that were the case, this could shift the example to the "perverse behavioral response" category. As I see it, that prior category concerns an overall appraisal of the net social utility of allowing or disallowing tort claims in such settings, and the empirical reality of how individuals respond to the law matters greatly. By contrast, this "trumping values" category turns on a judicial appraisal of the value of the defendant's behavior.

It is important to see that this no-duty reason is not quite the same as a no-breach reason, although they are quite similar. Take, for example, the already-discussed common law rule that there is no duty in tort to come to the assistance of strangers.[69] Relevant here is a different justification from the belief that perverse and unhelpful behavioral responses would occur if there were such a duty. Rather, I want to focus on the justification that the liberty to remain uninvolved with other individuals' problems trumps the obligation to help them even when, in a specific case, a jury thought or might think it reasonable to do so.

One might argue that the courts in this situation are merely weighing the burden of rescuing against the benefit to the victim and so are making a breach determination for each particular case. But I do not think this is the right way to think about it. Rather, I think that courts are saying that the liberty right to remain uninvolved is of such importance that it trumps the entire idea of holding potential rescuers to a duty of due care toward strangers. It is, in a sense, making a decision at the wholesale level, whereas juries' breach decisions are made one by one at the retail level. Moreover, courts might be concerned that, in considering the burden on liberty in an individual case, juries might not have a wide enough perspective to take the liberty value fully into account. For that reason, courts seize on this category of injuries and decide such cases as a matter of law.

The common law no-duty rule has its special bite in cases in which it was obvious who could have come to the victim's assistance and where a nearly effortless act could have saved the victim from a terrible injury or death. In such cases, juries indeed might find the defendant to have been unreasonable were they permitted to do so. But if courts view the defendant's liberty interest to be important enough, then the no-duty result follows.

For myself, I fail to see why the liberty value is so important to protect in instances in which an obvious defendant could so easily have saved the victim's life, but I acknowledge that others may see this differently. And I concur that our liberty could be compromised if potential victims could begin using tort law to involuntarily enlist us in their aid on the grounds that it would benefit them at what an individual jury might consider to be an acceptable cost.

A similar analysis might apply to cases that exempt from liability movie and television directors who depict an unusual act of violence that is soon thereafter engaged in by copycats who attack the plaintiff-victim.[70] What I am imagining here is a jury that focuses solely on the victim of this attack might well find (with its retail perspective) that the defendant should have known of the risk of a copycat response and was unreasonable in portraying this episode or scene on television or in film. That is, the jury might heavily discount the value of the artistic free expression at stake in a larger sense because it is looking at the burden of eliminating this scene solely in this case. But a court, especially an appellate court, may take a wholesale look at the matter and conclude that artistic freedom is too important and that it would be socially unacceptable in settings like this to burden media presenters with the cost of copycat conduct, even if the jury were to decide that the attack would not have happened but for the showing of the film.

Notice that this justification does not depend upon showing that imposing a tort duty in such settings would have a chilling effect on the director's right of free expression, thereby causing film makers to steer too wide a berth from controversial depictions of violence. That sort of justification falls under the "perverse behavioral response" category discussed above. Rather, the argument here is that the defendant's freedom of expression is especially important to protect from the financial burdens of tort law.

E. The Victims Are Morally Undeserving

A fifth category of no-duty cases concerns victims thought to be so morally undeserving that the courts will not open their doors to such a person even if he has been carelessly injured by another.

I think that this principle initially justified the common law doctrine of contributory negligence. That is, the wrongful nature of the victim's act made the claimant completely undeserving of recovery against someone who carelessly caused him harm. While this common law rule is typically called a "defense," it functioned as a no-duty rule. That is, so far as tort law was concerned, it was alright to carelessly harm such victims because of their unworthiness.

While this rule's complete bar is now generally overturned, there are other examples of tort doctrine that reflect this outlook. First, there is the original and parallel rule that land occupiers owe no tort duty to trespassers.[71] Again, one justification of this rule is that the undeserving nature of trespassers meant that land owners could carelessly cause them harm and escape responsibility for that harm. Of course, over time this rule too was substantially weakened so as to allow certain classes of (less wrongful) trespassers to recover in certain circumstances against merely negligent land owners.[72] And in Rowland v. Christian, the California Supreme Court, in a decision later followed in a small number of other states,[73] completely abandoned this no-duty-to-trespassers rule.[74] And yet in response, the California legislature and the Restatement

(Third) of Torts have concluded as a matter of principle that some especially undeserving trespassers are still owed no duty of ordinary care in tort by land possessors.[75]

Moreover, even in states that seemingly have replaced the complete defense of contributory negligence with pure comparative fault, one can find unusual cases in which recovery is denied to some flagrantly careless victims of other individuals' negligence (outside of the trespasser setting). This might occur, for example, when the victim is engaged in criminal or other highly socially unacceptable conduct, like making a pipe bomb.[76] While, doctrinally, courts might say that comparative fault was not meant to apply in this setting and therefore recovery will be denied in full under the prior contributory negligence principle, a better understanding of this result is that there is no duty of ordinary care owed to such undeserving claimants.

F. Imposing a Duty of Care on This Defendant Would Result in an Unfairly Crushing Liability

I put in this final no-duty category cases in which the defendant has been negligent in the ordinary sense and harm has been done. But the harm is so enormous as compared with the nature of the defendant's wrongdoing that the consequence of the conventional application of tort law would be, in the view of judges, an unfairly disproportionate punishment of the defendant's misconduct. In such instances, we see courts finding ways to limit liability via the invocation of no-duty rules.

Some of these cases concern public utilities (or similar defendants) in which a single lower level employee carelessly acts in a way that causes untold harms to a vast number of individuals. Courts seem quite concerned that, absent a no-duty limit, the defendant would be subject to inappropriately crushing liability. Were the utility to be destroyed by tort law and no other firm would be willing step into the role, then such a case would be best put into the "perverse behavioral response" category. But my sense is that these cases do not depend on the community having to go without this vital public service were tort law to function in its normal way. Rather, it is simply the quantity of liability that sufficiently troubles the courts and causes them to step in and limit the defendant's exposure.

For example, we have seen this sort of justification given by the New York Court of Appeals in support of limiting the recovery of damages to actual customers of Consolidated Edison following the utility's careless causing of the famous New York City blackout.[77]

Similarly, utility-crushing liability is sometimes given as a justification for the no-duty rule with respect to water companies that negligently cause water to be unavailable at fire hydrants when needed to fight fires.[78] For myself, I find these crushing-liability arguments somewhat dubious. Public utilities can generally pass on their tort liability through higher rates to their customers or spread their tort liability among other utilities via liability insurance. There is also something unsavory about allowing one to be let off for carelessly causing a huge amount of harm, as compared with someone who causes only a modest amount of harm. Nonetheless, I do concede the moral argument that the penalty can seem wildly disproportionate in certain cases, and I agree that if one accepts that argument as compelling, then no duty in tort follows.

In a similar vein is Congress's decision to limit, in advance, the potential tort liability of power companies that could possibly arise from the operation of nuclear power plants.[79] Although a statutory solution, rather than one from common law, the congressional vision at the time was that nuclear power was very important for the nation to develop. But the utilities were refusing to provide nuclear power for fear of crushing liability.[80] As a result, victim compensation that might be obtained from the utilities in the event of nuclear accident was restricted (although at the same time at least some compensation was guaranteed).[81]

G. *Summary of No-Duty Grounds*

I believe that these six categories of justifications reflect appropriate arguments in favor of no-duty rules. They are not about the likelihood of harm or the burden of preventing it—the two major inquiries made in determining the reasonableness of the defendant's actions (in other words, whether he breached his duty). To the contrary, they rest on considerations that could lead one to conclude that, overall and on balance, it would be unwise to allow a tort claim by someone who might otherwise be able to recover on the ground that the defendant unreasonably failed to prevent the injury. Perhaps others will put forward different categories of reasons or will decide to regroup the reasons I have advanced in a different way. What is most important for now, I think, is to always keep in mind that the arguments advanced here are in support of freeing a potential defendant from tort liability when a jury found or might reasonably find him to have failed to exercise due care under the circumstances.

III. The Confusion of Breach and Duty

Having now described the sorts of arguments that might justify a no-duty rule, I want to return to a point I raised briefly at the outset: the duty element in tort cases sounding in negligence is much confused and much abused.

It is often said that while breach is a question for the jury (or more generally the trier of fact), duty is a question for the judge—a difference that is perhaps most salient when there is a jury, although even in bench trials it is important to keep the duty and breach issues distinct.[82] Alas, this old saying, about which issue is for which actor, is wrong and contributes to the confusion.

Judges, both at the trial and appellate levels, have roles in the breach question beyond merely stating for the jury the legal principle that breach is a matter of deciding how a reasonable person should act under the circumstances and then gauging the defendant's conduct against that. After all, trial judges may, and indeed do, have an obligation to decide whether the defendant's conduct was reasonable or unreasonable as a matter of law—at least when asked by the appropriate party through a proper motion (for example, a motion for a directed verdict or summary judgment). The test against which these motions are measured is whether a jury could reasonably decide otherwise.[83] If not, then the judge is to step in and assert that there was or was not a breach.

In practice, plaintiffs rarely ask for these rulings because, generally speaking, if the plaintiff's lawyer thinks that the case is strong enough to get a directed verdict, then the lawyer is usually not worried about the jury deciding against her client. And to ask for and have such a motion granted even in a very strong case—when there is any risk that this could be overturned on appeal, thereby causing delay and requiring a new trial—is something that the plaintiff is eager to avoid. Defendants typically feel otherwise. They worry that juries will find them at fault when they were not, and if the judge grants a directed verdict that is later overturned, defendants—who get to keep their money while all of this is going on—are much less bothered by delays. The point, in any event, is that when no jury could reasonably find that the defendant failed to exercise due care and the defendant asks for a directed verdict and gets it, the breach issue has been decided by the trial judge and not the jury.

Moreover, appellate courts sometimes decide the breach issue or make a decision that dictates the outcome of the breach issue. The former happens when the appellate court, in effect, chastises the trial judge for failing to properly grant a directed verdict request by the defendant. For example, even though appellate judges normally defer to the judgment of trial judges, who personally encountered the evidence, including live witnesses, an appellate court will occasionally conclude that, even seen in the best light possible, the plaintiff simply has failed to offer proof that could reasonably demonstrate a lack of due care by the defendant. These cases tend to be of two sorts. On the one hand, the harm that took place may be so unexpected that the appellate court concludes, and explains why, the injury was unforeseeable. And it cannot be unreasonable to fail to avoid harms that you could not plausibly imagine would occur. Hence, because de minimis risk-taking conduct is not something that the reasonable person would avoid, someone taking such a risk may not be found at fault. On the other hand, sometimes the amount of cost or effort that would have been required by the defendant to avoid the harm that took place is so self-evidently overwhelming that it would unquestionably be unreasonable to ask the defendant to bear that burden. In those cases too, appellate courts sometimes decide that there was no breach as a matter of law. For the purposes of this Article, the vital thing to appreciate is that in these cases the judges are deciding the breach issue and not the duty issue.

A good example is Adams v. Bullock, a case in which a boy had swung a wire in the air that caught on overhead trolley wires, sending live electricity into his body and seriously injuring him.[84] For Judge Cardozo, this sort of freak harm was simply unforeseeable; it had never happened before, according to the proof tendered, and the circumstances did not make the live wires appear to Cardozo to be dangerously in harm's way.[85] Moreover, as Cardozo saw it, there was nothing that the trolley company could reasonably do about it anyway.[86] It could not insulate its wires because then the trolley could not function, and having the power train put underground was altogether too much to ask.[87] Hence, looked at from either side of what later has become known as the Hand Formula in deciding the breach issue (is PL greater than B?), both the P (the probability part of the risk consideration) and the B (the burden side of the equation) are overwhelmingly in the defendant's favor.[88] When there can be no other result than a finding of no breach by the defendant, one can understand why Cardozo, speaking for the New York Court of Appeals, reversed the trial judge and the jury verdict for the plaintiff that the trial judge had allowed to stand, and ordered a new trial.[89]

Some qualifications should be offered about this famous opinion. First, it turns out that at that time many children were in fact being injured by coming in contact (usually via other wires) with live train and trolley wires, something that the defendant trolley line probably should have known about—and probably did—although the plaintiff's lawyer oddly failed to offer proof of this past experience.[90] Second, while undergrounding the power might have been too much to ask of the defendant, putting up a shield or guard at the particular point of the injury arguably was not. This was a unique place on the trolley line where individuals were above the wires on a well-used bridge and much closer than normal to the trolley wires, which could be reached (as the plaintiff did) with the help of gravity. So, maybe the outcome of the case is one that is actually best explained by inadequate representation of the plaintiff.

Perhaps more important for my purposes, Cardozo's opinion has a different exasperating feature. As I see it, he is clearly deciding the breach question, and as I have already said, I have no problem with courts doing so when juries could not reasonably decide otherwise. But, he uses the "duty" word.[91] This is wrong and misleading. To be sure, it is a correct usage of the English language to say that the defendant had "no duty" to bury the wires underground. But, as a legal matter, this mixes up duty and breach. There was no issue of "duty" presented to the New York Court of Appeals. Had harms like this been shown to be common and well known to trolley lines and had powerful evidence been presented that this bridge was evidently a specially dangerous locale for such an injury—one that could have been avoided by spending a couple of dollars on a wooden guard over the wire as it emerged from under the bridge—then there seems no doubt that the jury verdict for the plaintiff would have been upheld.

Hence, what Cardozo should more precisely have said was that, under these facts, it was not unreasonable to fail to underground the trolley, that failing to do so did not amount to failing to exercise due care, or that a reasonable trolley line would not have buried the wires—all ways of emphasizing that there was no breach.

In the same vein, consider Harper v. Herman, a case in which a young man dove off a recreational boat and seriously injured himself when it turned out that the water into which he dove was quite shallow.[92] The owner and operator of this small craft knew of the shallow water, where he deliberately anchored for his passengers to go swimming.[93] The court concluded, however, that he had no duty to warn the passenger of the water's depth without adequately explaining why.[94] It seems to me that there is hardly any liberty interest of the boat captain at stake and that a duty of due care should have been imposed. After all, the victim was a welcomed passenger on the defendant's craft. Whether or not there was a breach is another matter, however. It appears that the young man may well have dove in quickly, in a way that the captain did not anticipate, making it not actually unreasonable to have failed to give a warning. But that is not a duty matter.

Frequently the breach question is well understood to be a fresh matter to be decided entirely on the facts of the specific case. Due care, or breach, is a "standard" against which the defendant's conduct is measured by the jury (or fact-finding judge in a bench trial). I have assumed this to be the case in the discussion so far. But in some situations, appellate courts have decided to adopt or announce "rules" that more precisely specify what is or is not due care in a certain type of case.[95]

One advantage of rules is that case results are likely to be more consistent; for example, the same facts will be decided in the same way (either breach or no breach), rather than being left to juries who might find the identical conduct reasonable in some cases and unreasonable in others. A second advantage is that rules make clear to defendants in advance just what is expected of them, which may provide some sense of security to those who want to do things but not run afoul of the law. A third advantage is that cases may well be more quickly settled, or indeed, resolved without formal legal proceedings, when it is reasonably clear to both sides what the legal outcome will be.

Rules have costs, however. They fail to take into account the myriad of little factual variations in cases subject to the rule, and those facts might actually, in close cases, make the defendant's conduct judged to be other than what the rule specifies. The rule that requires motor vehicle drivers to get out of their vehicles at railroad crossings and look down the track if they could not see far enough for safety from the driver's seat is a good example (albeit applicable to plaintiff's, not defendant's fault).[96] It turns out that certain grade crossings have such complex configurations that it would actually be unreasonably foolish to get out to look down the track, but a victim who failed to do so would be deemed negligent under the rule. This problem is nicely illustrated by Justice Holmes's opinion in Goodman, which first set out the rule, and then by Justice Cardozo's later opinion in Pokora, which effectively scuttles the rule.[97]

A different example of a rule would be that it is unforeseeable that a criminal would injure a patron in one's parking lot if this had not happened previously.[98] Hence, the first person harmed on the defendant's property in this way would always lose. In such instances, the failure of the plaintiff to win should be understood as a no-breach determination and not one about there being no duty to take precautions against the harm that happened.

One problem with a rule that exempts first victims from recovery is that sometimes other facts might demonstrate that, in certain areas and with respect to certain property, it was actually not at all unforeseeable that someone might be attacked in the parking lot—say, for example, dozens of these attacks had recently occurred in parking lots right down the block and the defendant was well aware of that. Those considerations favor using the due-care standard over a rule.

When doing so, however, courts sometimes continue to confuse duty and breach. In Posecai v. Wal-Mart Stores, Inc., the victim, who had been shopping at the defendant's store, was attacked in the defendant's parking lot.[99] The court concluded that, given the limited past history of similar attacks, the risk of harm to the plaintiff was slight.[100] (So far, so good.) But it was misleading then to conclude that the defendant owed the victim no duty to protect her from the crime.[101]

Instead it should have said that there was, as a matter of law, no breach of the duty of due care that the defendants clearly did owe to a customer and invitee on their property.

A different cost of a rule is that sometimes the rule reflects an understanding of the available harm-avoiding technology at the time the rule was adopted and yet later on new technology has become available that would make it much easier to avoid the harm in question. Additionally, rules may not reflect the fluid nature of society's understanding of what sort of precautions defendants should reasonably take. For example, society may become more risk averse (or the opposite), or the value of a life saved may be thought to be much more than it previously was. In such situations a defendant could be found not negligent for complying with a rule when a contemporary jury, reflecting today's social judgment, would have found the defendant to be at fault for not preventing the injury.

In my view, these reasons—combined with more talented plaintiff lawyers—have substantially undercut the use of rules and have made negligence law increasingly more a matter of deciding whether there was a breach in the specific circumstances—namely, applying the due-care standard and not applying a due-care rule. Nonetheless, where there is a rule as to what constitutes breach, that rule should be applied by the trial judge both in giving instructions to the jury and, more importantly, in deciding whether the rule was complied with as a matter of law; and if so, deciding for the defendant if the proper motion has been made.

But all of this is about breach. It is all about deciding in one way or another, in one context or another, whether the defendant or plaintiff was at fault. It is not about duty. Hence, if the rule calls for the defendant to do X and the defendant does X but fails to do Y, it is not helpful and only confusing to say that the defendant has no duty to do Y. Rather, the right thing to say is that the defendant did not breach his duty to act with due care by failing to do Y.

IV. Conclusion

In the Restatement of Torts and in the decisions of common law courts throughout the country, the absence of duty in tort arises in what appear to be highly varied contexts. Typically the courts seem to pay little attention to themes that run across doctrinal areas. In this Article, I have attempted to draw together a range of no-duty issues by gathering them under six general headings. These, I hope, show us that there are indeed a number of reasons why we might want to deny potential plaintiffs the right to a tort recovery against someone who carelessly injured another. By seeing that these same themes arise in different settings, we may become more thoughtful about how to decide cases when new no-duty claims arise. We might also be willing to reassess whether or not the reason given for a no-duty result in some specific setting is actually convincing (especially when set alongside other situations in which this same reason has been offered). I also hope that I have succeeded in distinguishing no-duty problems from no-breach problems by demonstrating ways in which courts, while perhaps coming to the right solution, have mislabeled the doctrine under which they are actually justifying the result. That distinction should further help to clear up the point that duty is not about fault.

ENDNOTES

1. The presumption that there is a duty to exercise due care, which in exceptional cases is overridden by "an articulated countervailing principle or policy," is embraced by the Restatement (Third). See RESTATEMENT (THIRD) OF TORTS: LIAB. FOR PHYSICAL & EMOTIONAL HARM §7 (2010).

2. I previously explored this matter in Stephen D. Sugarman, *Rethinking Tort Doctrine: Visions of a Restatement (Fourth) of Torts*, 50 UCLA L. REV. 585, 613–18 (2002), and Stephen D. Sugarman, *A New Approach to Tort Doctrine: Taking the Best from the Civil Law and Common Law of Canada, in* 17 SUPREME COURT LAW REVIEW, 375, 386–90 (2d ser. 2002). For another writing on this general theme, see Robert L. Rabin, *The Duty Concept in Negligence Law: A Comment*, 54 VAND. L. REV. 787 (2001).

3. The *Restatement (Third) of Torts* has embraced a "scope of liability" notion in lieu of the confusing phrase "proximate cause." See RESTATEMENT (THIRD) OF TORTS: LIAB. FOR PHYSICAL & EMOTIONAL HARM ch. 6, at 492 (2010).

4. See RESTATEMENT (THIRD) OF TORTS: APPORTIONMENT OF LIAB. § 7 (2000).

5. I also put aside here the matter of defendants who are more than merely careless; namely, intentional and reckless wrongdoers.

6. E.g., Bolton v. Stone, [1951] A.C. 850 (H.L.) at 858 ("[T]he further result that injury is likely to follow must also be such as a reasonable man would contemplate, before he can be convicted of actionable negligence.").

7. *See, e.g.*, Posecai v. Wal-Mart Stores, Inc., 752 So. 2d 762, 768–69 (La. 1999).

8. *See, e.g.*, Adams v. Bullock, 125 N.E. 93, 94 (N.Y. 1919).

9. It should be noted that the American solution is by no means the only way to deal with such accidents. European nations tend to allow both workers' compensation claims and tort claims (allowing recovery in tort only for damages not already provided by the country's industrial injury scheme), and Israel relies only on tort, not having adopted a specific workplace injury compensation scheme. Hence, unlike employers in the United States, employers in those nations do have a tort duty of due care to their workers.

10. *E.g.*, Levandoski v. Cone, 841 A.2d 208, 209–10 (Conn. 2004).

11. *See, e.g.*, N.Y. GEN. OBLIG. LAW § 11-106 (McKinney 2010) (permitting recovery for "neglect, willful omission, or intentional, willful or culpable conduct"); N.J. STAT. ANN. § 2A:62A-21 (West 2000) (same).

12. 42 U.S.C. §§ 300aa-10 to -34 (2006).

13. *See id.* § 300aa-11(a)(2)(A).

14. Bruesewitz v. Wyeth LLC, 131 S. Ct. 1068, 1082 (2011). Although victims of manufacturing-defect claims continue to be able to sue in tort, those are rarely, if ever, the basis for claims under this program.

15. *See id.* at 1075–76.

16. *See* Riegel v. Medtronic, Inc., 552 U.S. 312, 323–30 (2008). *But see* Wyeth v. Levine, 555 U.S. 555, 581 (2009) (concerning prescription drugs rather than medical devices).

17. *See* Cipollone v. Liggett Grp., Inc., 505 U.S. 504, 524 (1992).

18. *See* Hackbart v. Cincinnati Bengals, Inc., 601 F.2d 516, 520 (10th Cir. 1979).

19. *See, e.g.*, NAT'L FOOTBALL LEAGUE, OFFICIAL PLAYING RULES AND CASEBOOK OF THE NATIONAL FOOTBALL LEAGUE (2011), *available at* http://www.blogandtackle.net/wp-content/uploads/2011/08/2011NFLRuleBook.pdf.

20. *See, e.g.*, H.R. Moch Co. v. Rensselaer Water Co., 159 N.E. 896, 897 (N.Y. 1928).

21. For a discussion of conflicting viewpoints, see Libbey v. Hampton Water Works Co., 389 A.2d 434, 434–35 (N.H. 1978).

22. *See id.* at 435 ("Water companies are in business to supply water, not to extinguish fires. Their rates reflect this assumption; they are uniform, not varying with the greater or lesser inherent danger in given areas.").

23. *See* N.Y. Times Co. v. Sullivan, 376 U.S. 254, 282–83 (1964).

24. *See* RESTATEMENT (THIRD) OF TORTS: ECON. TORTS & RELATED WRONGS § 8 & cmt. e(4) (Council Draft No. 1, 2006) (adopting the "economic loss rule" and discussing when tort is set aside because of the availability of a contract remedy).

25. *See* E. River Steamship Corp. v. Transamerica Delaval Inc., 476 U.S. 858, 872 (1986); Seely v. White Motor Co., 403 P.2d 145, 151 (Cal. 1965).

26. *See* Ira Mark Ellman & Stephen D. Sugarman, *Spousal Emotional Abuse as a Tort?*, 55 MD. L. REV. 1268, 1301–03 & n.24 (1996) (discussing why a jurisdiction should adopt a rule barring interspousal claims for negligent infliction of emotional distress).

27. *E.g.*, Thing v. La Chusa, 771 P.2d 814, 829–30 (Cal. 1989).

28. Think about the driver who carelessly caused the death of Princess Diana or the doctor who negligently caused the death of Michael Jackson.

29. *See, e.g.*, Metro-N. Commuter R.R. v. Buckley, 521 U.S. 424, 433 (1997).

30. *See, e.g.*, Borer v. Am. Airlines, Inc., 563 P.2d 858, 866 (Cal. 1977).

31. *See, e.g.*, Knight v. Jewett, 834 P.2d 696, 711 (Cal. 1992).

32. *See* MacPherson v. Buick Motor Co., 111 N.E. 1050, 1051–52 (N.Y. 1916); Winterbottom v. Wright, (1842) 152 Eng. Rep. 402 (Ex. Div.) 405.

33. *See* Waite v. Waite, 618 So. 2d 1360, 1361 (Fla. 1993) (discussing policy justifications).

34. Other justifications have also been advanced in support of the family-immunity doctrine.

35. *See, e.g.*, Broadbent v. Broadbent, 907 P.2d 43, 50 (Ariz. 1995) (claims by children against parents); *Waite*, 618 So. 2d at 1361 (spousal claims). *But see* Renko v. McLean, 697 A.2d 468, 470 (Md. 1997).

36. *See, e.g.*, Ky. Farmers Bureau Mut. Ins. Co. v. Thompson, 1 S.W.3d 475, 477 (KY. 1999).

37. *See, e.g.*, Knight v. Jewett, 834 P.2d 696, 711 (Cal. 1992).

38. *Id.*

39. *Id.*

40. *See, e.g.*, Lestina v. W. Bend Mut. Ins. Co., 501 N.W.2d 28, 33 (Wis. 1993).

41. N.Y. Times Co. v. Sullivan, 376 U.S. 254, 279 (1964).

42. Nina J. Emerson & Sarah B. Stroebel, *Another Look at Dram Shop Liability*, 73 WIS. LAW., Aug. 2000, at 14, 17.

43. *See* Reynolds v. Hicks, 951 P.2d 761, 764–65 (Wash. 1998).

44. The *Restatement (Second) of Torts* treated a land possessor's obligations to licensees, which include the guests of social hosts, through a variety of provisions. *See* RESTATEMENT (SECOND) OF TORTS §§ 330, 341–342, 343B (1965).

45. *See Reynolds*, 951 P.2d at 764–65.

46. *See* RESTATEMENT (THIRD) OF TORTS: LIAB. FOR PHYSICAL & EMOTIONAL HARM § 51 & cmt. a (Tentative Draft No. 6, 2009).

47. *See, e.g.*, Carter v. Kinney, 896 S.W.2d 926, 930 (Mo. 1995); RESTATEMENT (SECOND) OF TORTS § 330 cmt. h(3) (1965).

48. *See* Bragg v. Genesee Cnty. Agric. Soc'y, 644 N.E.2d 1013, 1017–18 (N.Y. 1994) (discussing recreational use of land statutes).

49. *E.g.*, Farwell v. Keaton, 240 N.W.2d 217, 221–22 & n.3 (Mich. 1976); *see also* RESTATEMENT (THIRD) OF TORTS: LIAB. FOR PHYSICAL & EMOTIONAL HARM § 7(b) (2010) ("In exceptional cases, when an articulated countervailing principle or policy warrants denying or limiting liability in a particular class of cases, a court may decide that the defendant has no duty or that the ordinary duty of reasonable care requires modification.").

50. *See* Saul Levmore, *Waiting for Rescue: An Essay on the Evolution and Incentive Structure of the Law of Affirmative Obligations*, 72 VA. L. REV 879, 882 (1986).

51. *Id.* at 886–87.

52. *Cf. id.* at 905 ("It is also possible that potential finders will actually cause losses and then hide the items that they find from their true owners.").

53. *See id.* at 884.

54. *See* Ernest J. Weinrib, *The Case for a Duty to Rescue*, 90 YALE L.J. 247 (1980).

55. Adding to the empirical argument on this issue, one might claim that even without a legal duty, most competent individuals voluntarily engage in "easy" rescues anyway so that the upside behavioral gain from imposing tort liability in such settings would be minimal at best. But this alone may not overcome the concern on the other side that someone who could easily have

engaged in an easy rescue, but did not, should escape liability. For another possible justification of a no-duty result in such settings, see discussion *infra* Part II.D.

56. W. PAGE KEETON ET AL., PROSSER AND KEETON ON THE LAW OF TORTS 431 (5th ed. 1984).

57. *See* RESTATEMENT (THIRD) OF TORTS: LIAB. FOR PHYSICAL & EMOTIONAL HARM § 42 (Tentative Draft No. 4, 2004); *see also* Tarasoff v. Regents of Univ. of Cal., 551 P.2d 334, 353 (Cal. 1976).

58. *See* Peter H. Schuck & Daniel J. Givelber, Tarasoff v. Regents of the University of California*: The Therapist's Dilemma, in* TORTS STORIES 99, 113–17 (Robert L. Rabin & Stephen D. Sugarman eds., 2003) (discussing the duty imposed by *Tarasoff*).

59. *See, e.g.*, Boyd v. Racine Currency Exch., Inc., 306 N.E.2d 39, 42 (Ill. 1973); *see also* Ky. Fried Chicken of Cal., Inc. v. Superior Court of L.A. Cnty., 927 P.2d 1260, 1266–70 (Cal. 1997) (listing cases).

60. Randi W. v. Muroc Joint Unified Sch. Dist., 929 P.2d 582, 585–86 (Cal. 1997).

61. *Id.* at 585.

62. *See id.* at 586.

63. *Id.* at 595.

64. *See id.* at 590.

65. Florida Birth-Related Neurological Injury Compensation Plan, FLA. STAT. §§ 766.301–316 (2010); Virginia Birth-Related Neurological Injury Compensation Act, VA. CODE ANN. §§ 38.2-5000 to -5021 (1950 & repl. vol. 2007).

66. Peter H. White, Note, *Innovative No-Fault Tort Reform for an Endangered Specialty*, 74 VA. L. REV. 1487, 1496–97 (1988).

67. *See supra* notes 12–15 and accompanying text.

68. For an early analysis and historical background, see Robert E. Scott, Note, *Compensation for Victims of Violent Crimes: An Analysis*, 8 WM. & MARY L. REV. 277 (1967).

69. *See supra* notes 49–55 and accompanying text.

70. *See, e.g.*, Olivia N. v. NBC, 178 Cal. Rptr. 888, 892–94 (Ct. App. 1981).

71. William L. Prosser, *Trespassing Children*, 47 CALIF. L. REV. 427, 427 (1959).

72. *See* RESTATEMENT (SECOND) OF TORTS §§ 334–339 (1965) (allowing recovery under certain circumstances for constant trespassers, known trespassers, and child trespassers).

73. RESTATEMENT (THIRD) OF TORTS: LIAB. FOR PHYSICAL & EMOTIONAL HARM § 52 Reporters' Note cmt. a (Tentative Draft No. 6, 2009).

74. *See* Rowland v. Christian, 443 P.2d 561, 568 (Cal. 1968).

75. *See* CAL. CIV. CODE § 847 (West 2007) (extending immunity from liability to landowners when the injury was sustained during or after the commission of certain felonies); RESTATEMENT (THIRD) OF TORTS: LIAB. FOR PHYSICAL & EMOTIONAL HARM § 52 (Tentative Draft No. 6, 2009)

(lowering the duty owed to flagrant trespassers who are not "helpless" or "unable to protect themselves"). For the background story that led to the adoption of the California statute, see Wendy Lilliedoll, An Unexpected Windfall for California's Tort Reform Movement: *Bodine v. Enterprise High School* 34–44 (2004) (unpublished student paper), *available at* http://www.law.berkeley.edu/sugarman/Wendy_TortStoryFinal_ii.doc.

76. *See, e.g.*, Barker v. Kallash, 468 N.E.2d 39, 40, 44 (N.Y. 1984).

77. *See* Strauss v. Belle Realty Co., 482 N.E.2d 34, 36–38 (N.Y. 1985).

78. *See* H.R. Moch Co. v. Rensselaer Water Co., 159 N.E. 896, 897–98 (N.Y. 1928).

79. *See* Price-Anderson Act, 42 U.S.C. § 2210(e) (2006). Yet because of the seemingly realistic fear that without tort limitation, there would be no nuclear power industry, perhaps this example seems better put in the "perverse behavioral response" category.

80. *See* MARC A. FRANKLIN ET AL., TORT LAW AND ALTERNATIVES 884 (9th ed. 2011).

81. *Id.*

82. *E.g.*, Farwell v. Keaton, 240 N.W.2d 217, 219–20 (Mich. 1976).

83. *See, e.g.*, Andrews v. United Airlines, Inc., 24 F.3d 39, 41–42 (9th Cir. 1994).

84. Adams v. Bullock, 125 N.E. 93, 93 (N.Y. 1919).

85. *Id.*

86. *Id.* at 94.

87. *Id.*

88.. United States v. Carroll Towing Co., 159 F.2d 169, 173 (2d Cir. 1947).

89. *Adams*, 125 N.E. at 94.

90. For the story behind this well-known case, see Elizabeth Smallwood, A First-Year Tort Law Institution: *Adams v. Bullock* (2004) (unpublished student paper), *available at* http://www.law.berkeley.edu/sugarman/adamsfinal-1.doc.

91. *Adams*, 125 N.E. at 94.

92. Harper v. Herman, 499 N.W.2d 472, 474 (Minn. 1993).

93. *Id.* at 473.

94. *See id.* at 475.

95. Akins v. Glens Falls City Sch. Dist., 424 N.E.2d 531, 534–35 (N.Y. 1981).

96. *See* Balt. & Ohio R.R. v. Goodman, 275 U.S. 66, 70 (1927).

97. *See* Pokora v. Wabash Ry., 292 U.S. 98, 102–06 (1934).

98. *See* Posecai v. Wal-Mart Stores, Inc., 752 So. 2d 762, 766–68 (La. 1999) (discussing various rules states have adopted on this issue).

99. *Id.* at 764.

100. *Id.* at 768–69.

101. *Id.* at 769.

Chapter 15

"Land-Possessor" Liability Doesn't Need a Separate Tort Law

When presenting the law of negligence, torts casebooks typically first discuss the concept of "due care" and then later examine special circumstances when there is "no duty" to exercise due care. Within the part on "duty" the law of "landowner" (or "occupier" or "possessor") liability is ordinarily presented.

This organization perhaps made sense in the past when duties to entrants onto land were specially subdivided into three categories depending on the "status" of the entrant – invitee, licensee, or trespasser. But contemporary tort law, at least in a majority of states, has abandoned the idea of three distinct categories, and even where lip service is still given to them there are typically so many so-called "exceptions" that obligations of land occupiers are best seen to fall along a continuum rather than in separate buckets.

The Restatement (Third) of Torts has acknowledged this evolution of tort law by taking the position that the ordinary rule of "due care" (under the circumstances) is the way that land possessors are to be judges with regard to injuries to entrants onto their property – except with respect to what are termed "flagrant trespassers" (toward whom a substantially lesser duty is owed).

Yet the Restatement (Third) of Torts continues to spell out these rules about land possessor liability in a series of independent sections. This chapter argues that we should no longer think of occupier liability as a separate piece of tort law. Rather, it should be folded into the basic structure of negligence law. Landowners, like most actors, normally owe others the basic duty of due care, and, as with some other actors in special situations, there are instances in which the full duty of care is relaxed. For landowners this is with respect flagrant trespassers. This way of looking at things not only helps us think more clearly about just what is due care in the land possessor setting, but also it helps us to see where flagrant trespassers fit in the larger picture of when lesser duties are owed.

Furthermore, judges have an unfortunate habit of deciding cases involving land possessors as a matter of law by treating them as "no duty" cases (since "duty" is an issue for judges) when, on more careful examination, what the judges are actually arguing is that there has been "no breach." While "breach" is ordinarily a question for the jury, judges should themselves decide case outcomes when no jury could reasonably find otherwise. And this chapter argues (as Chapter 14 also argues) that the law would be clearer and more consistent if judges were to decide appropriate land possessor cases in that manner instead of hiding behind the "no duty" cover.

This essay was first presented at a conference held at Wake Forest University to discuss the Restatement's new treatment of land-possessor liability, Wake Forest being the home law school of Professor Michael Green, one of the co-reporters for the ALI's project to update the Restatement of Torts. It was published as Stephen D. Sugarman, "Land-Possessor Liability in the Restatement (Third) of Torts: Too Much and Too Little," 44 Wake Forest Law Review 1079-1092 (2009). It is reprinted with the permission of the Wake Forest Law Review, the copyright holder.

LAND-POSSESSOR LIABILITY IN THE *RESTATEMENT (THIRD) OF TORTS:* TOO MUCH AND TOO LITTLE

INTRODUCTION

In working towards a *Restatement (Third) of Torts,* Michael Green and William Powers, the Reporters for the American Law Institute's ("ALI") project on Liability for Physical and Emotional Harm, have drafted six sections specifically addressing land-possessor liability that are gathered together as chapter 9.[1] This separate treatment is not altogether surprising; the *Restatement (Second) of Torts* also addresses land-possessor liability separately, and these sections are an "add on" effort to the Reporters' initial work. Moreover, in a recent Reporters' Memorandum, they argue not only that the duties of land possessors have historically been treated as a "discrete subject" but also that users of the new *Restatement* "would expect to find consolidated and separate treatment of land-possessors' duties."[2]

I do not object to the substantive conclusions that the Reporters reach about what the law is (or should be) on the liability of land-possessors. My concerns go to their packaging job. I think that it is a mistake to have a separate chapter on land-possessors. Rather, I believe that the ALI and the profession would both be better served by integrating this area of the law into earlier sections of the *Restatement (Third) of Torts* that the ALI has already approved.

Perhaps most importantly, integrating the topic of land-possessors into earlier sections would help us to make progress on two important substantive themes that, I believe, are not very helpfully addressed by the Reporters: (1) What are the reasons that justify any no-duty rule in tort? (2) In deciding what due care requires, when is a fair warning sufficient and when must the defendant eliminate (or at least reduce) the danger by taking additional precautions?

I. THE SHIFT TO A GENERAL DUTY OF DUE CARE OF LAND-POSSESSORS

A. What Section 51 Provides Is Already Covered in Section 7(a)

In section 51 the Reporters make clear that for nearly all of the types of accidents that occur on the land possessor's property, liability is determined by deciding on a case-by-case basis whether there was negligence under the circumstances.[3] I strongly support this position, which moves away from the "rules" that previously dominated this area of the law. But we do not need section 51 to reach this result. Cases involving land-possessor liability for misfeasance can be handled by section 7(a), the new *Restatement's* basic principle about fault-based liability.[4]

People can be injured while on the property of others in many ways. Just to give some examples: (a) they can be harmed by the land-possessor's activities on the premises (e.g., the possessor may be clearing snow and strike the victim with the shovel), (b) they can be harmed by dangers that the possessor has created that lie in wait to injure those who encounter them (e.g., the victim may drown in the possessor's swimming pool), (c) they can be harmed by dangers that have developed with respect to artificial conditions on the premises that the possessor has not fixed (e.g., the victim may fall down a broken stairway), (d) they can be harmed by natural conditions of the premises that become dangerous (e.g., the victim may slip on paths made dangerous by snow and ice, or tree branches may fall on the victim), (e) they can be harmed by third parties on the premises in both criminal and noncriminal ways (e.g., the victim may be attacked in the possessor's parking lot by a third party), (f) they can be harmed by dangers created by prior possessors and left in place (e.g., dangerously piled rocks may fall on victims), and so on.[5]

For all of these settings the Reporters say that the basic common-law rule today is (and/or should be) that the defendant land-possessor may be held liable if he was negligent in failing to take reasonable precautions to prevent the harm that occurred.[6] That is, the basic fault principle is to govern these cases, just as it dominates most of the rest of tort law with respect to physical injury.[7]

By contrast, the traditional common-law approach had been to adopt various rules of law that were tailored to the "status" of the victim-invitee, licensee, or trespasser.[8] Early on, the common-law position appeared to be that if licensees and trespassers were harmed in ways that would otherwise be judged negligent, the land-possessor would not be liable. Only invitees were owed the ordinary duty of due care generally demanded by the fault principle.[9] Over the centuries, it became clear to common-law courts that this regime was often unfairly harsh to non-invitee victims, and over time, in an ad hoc way, both licensees and trespassers were allowed to recover for at least certain acts of negligence towards them. Courts tended to adopt special rules governing specific non-invitees on the land such as child entrants, social guests, and known or discovered trespassers.[10] Simultaneously, even as to invitees, various special rules were adopted by courts, such as those governing "open and obvious" dangers, third-party criminal attacks on people who were on the property of the land possessor, and so on.[11]
These legal rules based on the status of the victim yielded an unduly complicated state of affairs in which judges were deciding issues at the "wholesale" level-that is, as a matter of "law" and frequently labeled as "duty" questions—that negligence law normally reserves for juries to decide at the

"retail" level—that is, whether or not the defendant was at fault in these particular circumstances, which is a question of "breach."

The new section 51 makes clear that, for nearly all of the types of accidents that occur on the possessor's land, both the rules and the categories are out. This was the position taken several decades ago (but after the adoption of the *Restatement (Second))* by the California Supreme Court in *Rowland v. Christian,*[12] since adopted explicitly by about half of the states, and now appropriately embraced by the Reporters.

Although I applaud this embrace of the basic "due-care" standard, we do not need section 51 to reach this result. Cases involving land-possessor liability for misfeasance instead can be handled by-and indeed are already covered by-section 7(a), the basic statement about fault-based liability, which provides: "An actor ordinarily has a duty to exercise reasonable care when the actor's conduct creates a risk of physical harm."[13]

B. *The Limited Duty to Flagrant Trespassers Set Out in Section 52 Is an Application of Section 7(b)*

The Reporters specifically exclude only one set of claimants from the normal operation of the fault principle. These are what section 52 calls "flagrant trespassers."[14] But there is no need for a separate section 52 to deal with flagrant trespassers. Instead, they could be covered in section 7(b), which makes the basic point that sometimes no duty of ordinary care is owed to someone the defendant might reasonably have prevented from being injured.[15]

The approach in section 52 is broadly based on the California statute[16] enacted in response to *Rowland v. Christian* and a subsequent celebrated case of a trespasser who fell through the roof of a public school while in the process of stealing lights and then sued the school district.[17] That statute rather precisely limits the duties of land possessors with respect to those who enter the land to commit and are convicted of certain serious crimes.[18] Section 52 leaves the meaning of flagrant trespasser somewhat vague, allowing room for states to adopt both wider and narrower definitions than did the California

State Legislature. Yet the illustrations in section 52 make clear that serious criminal trespassers are the core actors to be included. [19]

However defined in detail, exempting land-possessors from ordinary due-care obligations to flagrant trespassers is a no-duty conclusion that these claimants are simply undeserving. The notion is that, in these sorts of circumstances, it is simply outrageous to open up our courts to these "bad guys" who deliberately act against the interests of even a negligent land possessor.

Flagrant trespassers who are injured on the premises of others would very often lose anyway, even if there were an ordinary duty of care owed to them, on the ground that there was no breach of that duty. These victims are often unforeseen or the precautions required to protect them from harm are too burdensome to ask the land possessor to take them. But even if the straightforward application of the ordinary negligence principle would have found the land possessor at fault, these undeserving entrants are precluded from recovery. This is a policy determination based upon what I call a "trumping value": the land possessor's ordinary right to control access to the land is too offended if a victim who entered without consent and intent on egregious wrongdoing is allowed to recover in tort from the land possessor. And trumping values are one important reason for concluding that a duty of ordinary care is not owed.

I have no complaints about this result. But the treatment of flagrant trespassers could be offered up as a nice example of the principle provided by section 7(b): "In exceptional cases, when an articulated countervailing principle or policy warrants denying or limiting liability in a particular class of cases, a court may decide that the defendant has no duty or that the ordinary duty of reasonable care requires modification."[20]

Note that section 52 provides that, even as to flagrant trespassers, one has a duty not to inflict willful or wanton injury.[21] I agree that doing so is too much like taking the criminal law into one's own hands and handing out vigilante justice, and hence land-possessors should be liable for harm caused in this way. But once more I would cover this limited obligation to the flagrant trespasser in section 7(b), which already contemplates using no-duty rules only to wipe out the duty of ordinary care (and does not provide immunity for willful and wanton conduct).[22]

The Reporters further provide under section 52 that, in some special situations, flagrant trespassers are owed a duty of ordinary care after all-when they are imperiled and helpless or unable to protect themselves.[23] I support this conclusion as well; it is consistent with other previously adopted positions in the *Restatement (Third)* that impose affirmative rescue obligations on people in certain relationships.[24] Section 37 states the general rule that there is "no duty" to take affirmative steps to help another,[25] but subsequent sections 38 to 44 impose such duties when certain relationships exist.[26]

So the protection for some flagrant trespassers set out in section 52 could be incorporated into an expanded section 40, which currently imposes a duty to take affirmative actions to prevent (or reduce) harm when the parties involved have a relationship of "a business or other possessor of land that holds its premises open to the public with those who are lawfully on the premises."[27] Section 52, in effect, expands section 40 to cover the relationship between a land-possessor and someone not lawfully on the premises, but who is there and is imperiled and helpless.

Beyond that, in my view, even sections 37 to 44 are not needed. I would prefer to collapse them into section 7(a) as well, thereby making 7(a) cover both misfeasance and nonfeasance. The default principle then would be that there is liability when anyone fails to take reasonable steps to help others. There would then be a no-duty exception in section 7(b) to cover cases envisioned by section 37 in which the person in need was essentially a "stranger" to the potential rescuer.

Once placed in section 7(b), the general rule that there is no affirmative duty to help strangers could (like the rule for most flagrant trespassers) be explained by a trumping value: in this case, the liberty interest people have in not becoming involved with the lives of strangers. Notice, then, that a person you do not know whom you pass on the road and who is in obvious need of help would qualify as a "stranger" under this approach. But an imperiled and helpless trespasser whom you discover on your own land would not-on the ground that this is a responsibility that goes along with possessing land. Responsibilities towards such trespassers would then be covered by the basic section 7(a).

II. REDRAFTING PROPOSAL

With respect to the six sections of chapter 9, then, I would first do away with section 50, which defines trespassers in general,[28] because it is only flagrant trespassers to whom special rules apply, and they are covered in section 52. Anything important remaining in the comments to section 50 could be temporarily moved to section 52.

I would also collapse sections 53 and 54 into section 51 because they together provide that the basic negligence principle applies not only to land possessors with respect to those *on* the land (which is covered in section 51, discussed above)[29] but also to land possessors with respect to those *off* the land (section 54), [30]and to a certain type of land possessor—a lessor (section 53).[31] This would leave chapter 9 with but three sections: section 49 on boundaries (which says that chapter 9 is about land possessors), the now more robust section 51 on the general application of fault-based liability to land possessors, and section 52 on the narrow no-duty exception for flagrant trespassers.
Then, as explained above, I would collapse section 52 on flagrant trespassers into section 7 on "no duty" in general. As the Reporters acknowledge in a comment to section 7, land-possessors who are social hosts and who serve alcohol to their guests may well be exempted from liability even if serving alcohol in the specific circumstances would be found to be negligent by a jury.[32] This would be because a court would find that the no-duty principle of section 7(b) applies to such conduct by social hosts.[33] To me, it is not helpful to split up these different no-duty situations involving land-possessors-flagrant trespassers in section 52 and victims of one's alcohol-drinking social guests in section 7(b). Instead, both examples could be provided in section 7(b), along with other special circumstances in which the normal due-care principle is suspended.

As also stated above, I would collapse the now more robust section 51 on the general duty of land possessors to those on the land, plus section 54 on their duty to those off the land and section 53 on the duty of lessors, into section 7(a) on the general obligation to exercise due care. Having done that, there would then be no need for section 49 defining land-possessors, and the entire chapter 9 on Duty of Land-possessors could disappear.

Are there subtleties in the Reporters' analysis that are lost under my proposal? The Reporters skillfully show how the topics covered by a large number of sections in the *Restatement (Second)* are now embedded in the new chapter 9 sections. Consider the following example. The Reporters' comments to section 51 distinguish artificial conditions created by a land possessor from those created by a prior owner.[34] They admit that the due-care duty imposed by section 51 with respect to conditions created by the land-possessor is simply an application of section 7(a) on misfeasance, but they argue that the parallel duty that land possessors have under section 51, with respect to conditions that were acquired, is not. Instead, they argue that the duty to eliminate or ameliorate those acquired risks is analogous to the duty to take affirmative steps under circumstances set out in the sections following section 37 (on nonfeasance).[35]

To me, however, this is just further evidence that sections 37 and following are misplaced and perhaps misconceived. Instead, as already explained, there should be a general duty of due care (the section 7(a) obligation broadened to cover misfeasance and nonfeasance), and then there should be no-duty exceptions to that duty (the section 7(b) exemption) that include circumstances in which one has an insufficient relationship with the risk or the victim.

III. WARNINGS

A. *When Are Warnings Enough?*

I do not believe that the ALI project on Tort Liability for Physical and Emotional Harm pays enough attention to the recurrent issue of when warnings are enough and when the actor must take further precautionary steps to repair or otherwise reduce the danger. In this Part, I suggest that what is involved here may be a matter of the different "social roles" of commercial actors and ordinary people. In my view, these social-role distinctions should be given a prominence that is now lacking in the *Restatement (Third).*[36]

Notice that in the comments to section 51 on the general duty of land possessors to exercise due care with respect to those who come onto the land, the Reporters say, "The rule requires a land-possessor to use reasonable care to investigate and discover dangerous conditions and to use reasonable care to attend to known or reasonably knowable conditions on the property."[37] This is correct. What it does not make clear, however, is when the reasonable care obligation is satisfied by providing the entrant with notice of the danger and when the land possessor must take additional steps to reduce or eliminate the danger. After all, the actor could "attend to" the danger in either way.

Comment *h* to section 51 begins to get at this matter when it discusses the idea that it may well suffice to discharge the duty of due care to social guests by providing warnings as to non-obvious dangers (i.e., it would not be negligent to fail to fix the problems that give rise to those dangers).[38] This is a well-put way of explaining how the *Restatement (Third)* may be read as accommodating the old saw that one's social guests are not entitled to safer conditions than one has chosen to live with, so long as they are reasonably warned of dangers one knows or should know about.

But comment *h* does not then go on to talk directly about whether commercial actors (say, hotels) should also be able to get away merely with warnings in discharging o their duty of due care to their customers. We know that the Reporters think that at least certain commercial actors must do more than warn because in illustration 7 in comment j to section 51, involving trespassers, they make clear, albeit in passing, that a landlord with notice of missing posts in an apartment-house railing will be liable for failing to repair the railing even if the victim (and even a formal, but not flagrant, trespasser) is well aware of the danger.[39] I agree with this position, but the Reporters do not offer a deeper and more thematic explanation for these different treatments of warnings.

Taking up an analogous matter, comment *i* notes that while commercial actors may well be thought to be at fault for failing to inspect their land for hidden dangers, ordinary people (i.e., homeowners) may not be expected so to inspect and therefore are not held in breach for failing to take precautions with respect to dangers they would have discovered through a reasonable inspection.[40] Again, while this distinction between commercial and noncommercial actors may reflect traditional common-law distinctions between duties owed (usually by commercial actors) to invitees and those owed to licensees, nothing more than a broad generalization is offered in its defense.

Turning next to the issue of "open and obvious" dangers in comment *k,* the Reporters make clear that if all that is required in such settings is a warning, then additional warnings are generally superfluous, as the conditions themselves generally warn as effectively as a written or oral warning would.[41] But they also rightly make clear that in some settings a warning may not suffice, and it will be a breach of the duty of due care to fail to take steps to repair or otherwise fix the dangerous condition.[42] Yet again they do not even attempt to explain why and when some actors should have to do more than warn, remembering that they earlier said in comment *h* that a warning from a host to a social guest may well suffice.

In sum, one comes away from reading the Reporters' comments with the sense that, when it comes to taking due care, ordinary homeowners need neither inspect their property for dangers nor fix those they know about. Rather, they are to be held liable basically for failing to warn of known risks. But why? For the Reporters, in the end, whether the land-possessor should have inspected or not, as well as whether the possessor should have done more than warn about a danger the land possessor knew (or should have known) about seems simply to be a jury question on the issue of breach.

B. *Social Roles*

To me, something more seems to be involved here. I see it as a matter of what I call "social roles." Commercial actors are expected in our society to play different social roles than noncommercial actors; they are expected to be more attentive to risks, better able to plan actions to reduce risks, better able to train their employees to act in more careful ways, better able to spread the cost of repairs (through the pricing of their goods and services), and better able to spread the loss if held liable. For these reasons, it seems more appropriate for society to use the law to call on commercial actors to take risk-reducing precautions as part of their business practices.

Put differently, in many situations we do not want commercial actors to shift the risk to their customers (and others) merely by warning of dangers. Rather, we want them to repair the problem or otherwise make changes to reduce or eliminate the danger. Think about supermarket, hotel, or apartment-complex owners. We do not want them simply to point out dangers on their premises like broken stairs, missing handrails, slippery floors, unshoveled snow, and the like. We want them to take reasonable steps to get rid of these risks. That is their social role. It is a condition we, in effect, impose on them as part of the price of doing business and making profits. We seem to do this because we have confidence that commercial actors can sensibly respond to the law in ways that make life in our society safer in ways that we as a society want. We do not want slightly cheaper markets, hotels, and apartment buildings that contain these dangers. We are content to pay slightly more for greater safety.

Ordinary folks, by contrast, do not function in the same way and do not have commercial activities into which they can internalize either the costs of precautions or the burden of losses if held liable. Society does not expect ordinary folks to be experts in risk reduction in the same way it expects commercial actors to be. Hence, ordinary folks play a different social role and, as among themselves, it is often sufficient to provide an adequate warning. This, I think, better explains why the tort system would decide that ordinary homeowners have not committed a breach of their duty of ordinary care when they have warned guests of dangers that they as hosts know about, while commercial land possessors would be said to have breached their duty of ordinary care if they fail to take further precautions to fix those same dangers.

In other words, under the circumstances, a commercial actor would have breached its duty by merely warning because the benefit of the extra precaution is worth its cost, whereas this is not true for a noncommercial actor. After all, when the former fixes a dangerous condition, it is likely to prevent more harms than when a noncommercial actor does so. But I think there is more to it than that. This argument is not meant to be a plea to recreate the invitee and licensee categories. If nothing else, my argument is that shopping malls can be held liable for merely warning and failing to fix dangers when the victims are only licensees and that homeowners can be freed from liability to business visitors to their homes (invitees) merely by warning of dangers and not fixing them. Moreover, I do not want to return the regime of land-possessor liability to one of "duty" rules, but I do want to argue that our understanding of what is and is not a breach is importantly influenced by what I am calling "social roles."

Furthermore, in my view, this difference in the obligations that go along with different social roles is not restricted to the land- possessor setting. It applies too, for example, with respect to transportation. We have different expectations of measures that airline companies, bus companies, railroads, and even taxi companies should take to protect passengers as compared with what precautions ordinary folks should take with respect to their passengers. The safety condition of the vehicle is one example in which a warning to passengers (say, about a lack of air bags) may suffice for ordinary folks but would not suffice for commercial vehicle operators.

As a different example, in my view, physicians (and other professionals) are expected to play a different social role than other business actors because we view the former more like trustees or fiduciaries. This helps explain why, when we apply the concept of the duty to warn to physicians, we expect certain doctors to tell us both about other treatment options and about the risks of not having treatment at all. By contrast, we generally do not look to regular businesses to tell us about differences between their products and those of their competitors. Rather, we rely on the market (and consumer shopping and independent rating sources like *Consumer Reports)* to bring out those differences. By contrast, when we go to the doctor, we are looking to him or her to provide independent advice about options that we cannot count on sensibly obtaining in other ways.

In sum, these social-role distinctions should be given a prominence that is now lacking in the *Restatement (Third),* a prominence that would be much more readily and coherently provided were all of the duties to exercise due care collected under section 7(a). Operationally perhaps, giving prominence to social roles might be translated into jury instructions that call upon juries to take different social roles into account in deciding whether there was a breach. But I leave this procedural detail for another occasion.

IV. GROUNDS FOR "NO DUTY"

In this last Part, I will suggest that, were the various categories of no-duty rules gathered together in section 7(b) instead of being distributed throughout the *Restatement (Third),* we might be better able to appreciate the common justifications for them.[43]

I have already set out one reason for relaxing the normal duty to exercise due care in certain circumstances: the existence of *trumping values* that would be put seriously at risk were juries allowed to decide the breach issue on a case-by-case basis.[44] I pointed out that both the individual's liberty interest in not having to aid strangers and the land-possessor's interest in being free from the intrusion of flagrant trespassers can be understood as trumping values that bar the imposition of liability, even if a jury might find that there was a breach on the ground that there were simple precautions that the defendants might have taken to prevent harm to these victims.[45]

A second reason for a no-duty rule is what I call the *perverse behavioral response* concern. Here the idea is that, even though this defendant might have been negligent, if we allow victims to sue and win such cases, people will change their behavior in ways that will have even worse social consequences-with the result that it is, regrettably, less bad to allow some careless defendants to escape liability than it would be to impose tort sanctions on them. Indeed, this sort of reason might, for some, justify the rule that there is no duty to come to the aid of strangers. That is, some might believe that imposing such a duty with respect to strangers would not in practice promote additional careful rescue efforts but instead would generate clumsy efforts by officious intermeddlers.

This same sort of reasoning has been used by some courts that allow ordinary citizens engaged in recreational activities to escape liability for negligently harming fellow participants-i.e., to impose liability would have such a chilling effect as to cause many people to shrink from engaging in such activities to the substantial detriment of society as a whole. Whether one should believe these empirical predictions is another matter. But accepting them for these purposes, they might be seen to justify no-duty rules on perverse behavioral response grounds.

Yet a third reason for a no-duty rule is what I call the *administrative* concern. Indeed, this reason might also be advanced in support of the rule that there is no duty to come to the aid of strangers. The argument would be that it is very often too difficult to decide just who should have aided the stranger. Other sorts of administrative concerns might justify other no-duty rules. For example, sometimes we fear that if we allowed people to sue for certain harms, small-value claims would flood the system, thereby creating costly delays in the handling of more serious cases (a reason that may justify limiting duties regarding emotional distress damages, for example).

A fourth reason for a no-duty rule is that the matter is better, or at least adequately, handled though some *alternative mechanism(s)* to tort law. This is a reason that may, for example, justify exempting from the tort system most injuries incurred by professional athletes in the course of play. Leagues and other bodies already have elaborate penalty systems in place to serve the deterrence and punishment goals of tort law, and players, especially in unionized team sports, have ready access to generous disability- insurance arrangements to deal with the compensation goal.

The current discussion in section 7(b) does not richly explore these four sorts of no-duty justifications. One reason for that, in my view, is that the no-duty positions with respect to land possessors are put in chapter 9,[46] the no-duty positions with respect to what the Reporters call "affirmative actions" are put in section 37,[47] the no- duty provisions with respect to emotional harm are put in the separate sections dealing with that sort of loss,[48] and so on. Were all of the no-duty rules instead gathered together in section 7(b), we might be better able to appreciate the common themes among them.

Here is an illustration of my point. Comment *m* to section 51 takes up the so-called "firefighter's rule" that, where embraced, exempts from liability a land possessor who, for example, carelessly starts a fire that then burns a firefighter who tries to put it out.[49] The Reporters make clear that under section 51 (as would be true under section 7(a)), the firefighter may no longer be denied recovery because of his or her status as something other than an invitee because the status distinctions are now abandoned.[50] Moreover, the firefighter is clearly not a flagrant trespasser. The Reporters rightly say that firefighter recovery could well be denied under a no-duty rule adopted pursuant to section 7(b), although they do not take a position on this matter.[51]

I think that section 7(b) is indeed the right place to deal with the question of whether there should be no duty to firefighters. There, we would naturally focus on whether this is properly a matter of, say, perverse behavioral responses. Although Dean Prosser finds it quite unconvincing as an empirical matter (and I agree), some have sought to explain the firefighter's rule on the ground that if land possessors owed firefighters a duty of ordinary care, then those who carelessly set fires might be too frightened to call the fire department for help, thereby risking harm not only to the land possessor's property but to neighbors as well.[52] Some courts have justified the firefighter's rule on the basis of "alternative mechanisms"—firefighters are already well compensated for this risk through special workers' compensation schemes, and land-possessors are already adequately enticed to take reasonable care via the pricing of their fire insurance. Or maybe, in the end, the firefighter's rule is justified by "social role" considerations noted earlier—i.e., when it is your professional job (your "social role") to rescue people and their property even from their own folly, you are entitled from them only to a warning as to the danger (which the fire itself of course provides), and you should not be able to complain about the earlier carelessness that created the fire. In this respect the firefighter may be like a doctor who cannot complain that he or she caught a contagious disease or an infection from a presenting patient who carelessly caught the disease or incurred the infection in the first place.[53] To see this possible analogy, once more it would be helpful for all of these examples to be gathered together in section 7(b), rather than having the firefighter's rule separately set out in a comment to a section on land-possessors.

CONCLUSION

In sum, chapter 9 on land-possessor liability is both too much and too little-too much because everything it provides is already, in effect, covered by other sections, and too little because by spreading this and other topics around the new *Restatement,* the Reporters miss an opportunity to identify and analyze both the common themes that run through the whole range of no-duty rules and the function that social roles play in determining what sort of warnings are expected and whether warnings are enough.

ENDNOTES

1. RESTATEMENT (THIRD) OF TORTS: LIAB. FOR PHYSICAL & EMOTIONAL HARM §§ 49-54 (Tentative Draft No.6, 2009).

2. *Id.* reporters' memorandum at xx.

3. *Id.* § 51 cmt. i ("Thus, the facts relating to the entrance onto the land, not status, bear on whether reasonable care was exercised.").

4. *See* RESTATEMENT (THIRD) OF TORTS: LIAB. FOR PHYSICAL HARM § 7(a) (Proposed Final Draft No. 1, 2005).

5. *See, e.g.,* RESTATEMENT (Third) OF TORTS: LIAB. FOR PHYSICAL & EMOTIONAL HARM § 51 cmt. b, illus. 1, cmt. h, illus. 2-4, cmt. i, illus 5, cmt. j,illus. 6-7, cmt. u, illus. 8-13 No.6, (Tentative Draft 2009).

6. *Id.* §51.

7. I can think of two important exceptions to this claim about the fault principle. First, as the Reporters well appreciate, if the land-possessor engages in abnormally dangerous activities (e.g., dynamiting in urban areas), then the possessor may be strictly liable for the ensuing harm. This narrow set of circumstances is already covered by section 20. *See* RESTATEMENT (THIRD) OF TORTS: LIAB. FOR PHYSICAL HARM § 20 (Proposed Final Draft No. 1, 2005). Second, so too is it possible for a land possessor to cause harm with respect to the use of defective products on the possessor's land in ways that would give rise to strict products liability. The Reporters realize this as well and note that if a land possessor is using a defective chainsaw and injures someone on the land with the saw, products liability law will apply. *See* RESTATEMENT (THIRD) OF TORTS: LIAB. FOR PHYSICAL & EMOTIONAL HARM ch. 9 scope note at 5 (Tentative Draft No.6, 2009). I put these matters aside.

8. KENNETH S. ABRAHAM, THE FORMS AND FUNCTIONS OF TORT LAW 239 (3d ed. 2007).

9. *Id.*

10. *See* G. EDWARD WHITE, TORT LAW IN AMERICA: AN INTELLECTUAL STUDY 190 (2003); *see also* RESTATEMENT (SECOND) OF TORTS § 342 (1965) (setting out special liability of land-possessors to licensees).

11. *See, e.g.,* RESTATEMENT (SECOND) OF TORTS § 343 (1965) (setting out special liability of land possessors to invitees); *id.* § 343A (describing open and obvious dangers).

12. 443 P.2d 561 (Cal. 1968).

13. RESTATEMENT (THIRD) OF TORTS: LIAB. FOR PHYSICAL HARM § 7(a) (Proposed Final Draft No. 1, 2005).

14. RESTATEMENT (THIRD) OF TORTS: LIAB. FOR PHYSICAL & EMOTIONAL HARM § 52 (Tentative Draft No. 6, 2009).

15. *See* RESTATEMENT (THIRD) OF TORTS: LIAB. FOR PHYSICAL HARM § 7(a) (Proposed Final Draft No. 1, 2005).

16. CAL. CIV. CODE§ 847 (Deering 2005).

17. *See generally* Wendy Lilliedoll, An Unexpected Windfall for California's Tort Reform Movement: *Bodine v. Enterprise High School* (2004) (unpublished comment), http://www.law.berkeley.edu/ faculty/sugarmans/#Torts.

18. CAL. CIV. CODEMM § 847.

19. RESTATEMENT (THIRD) OF TORTS: LIAB. FOR PHYSICAL & EMOTIONAL HARM § 52 cmt. i, illus. 2-4, cmt. m, illus. 9 (Tentative Draft No. 6, 2009).

20. RESTATEMENT (THIRD) OF TORTS: LIAB. FOR PHYSICAL HARM § 7(b) (Proposed Final Draft No. 1, 2005).

21. RESTATEMENT (THIRD) OF TORTS: LIAB. FOR PHYSICAL & EMOTIONAL HARM § 52(a) (Tentative Draft No. 6, 2009).

22. RESTATEMENT (THIRD) OF TORTS: LIAB. FOR PHYSICAL HARM § 7 cmt. A (Proposed Final Draft No. 1, 2005).

23. RESTATEMENT (THIRD) OF TORTS: LIAB. FOR PHYSICAL & EMOTIONAL HARM § 52(b) (Tentative Draft No. 6, 2009).

24. *See* RESTATEMENT (THIRD) OF TORTS: LIAB. FOR PHYSICAL HARM §§ 38-44 (Proposed Final Draft No. 1, 2005).

25. *Id.* § 37.

26. *See id.* §§ 38-44.

27. *Id.* § 40.

28. RESTATEMENT (THIRD) OF TORTS: LIAB. FOR PHYSICAL & EMOTIONAL HARM § 50 (Tentative Draft No. 6, 2009).

29. *Id.§* 51.

30. *Id.§* 54.

31. *Id.§* 53.

32. *See* RESTATEMENT (THIRD) OF TORTS: LIAB. FOR PHYSICAL HARM § 7 cmt. c (Proposed Final Draft No. 1, 2005).

33. *See id.*

34. RESTATEMENT (THIRD) OF TORTS: LIAB. FOR PHYSICAL & EMOTIONAL HARM § 51cmt. e (Tentative Draft No. 6, 2009).

35. *Id.*

36. For further discussion of the need to spell out due-care obligations in more detail, see Stephen D. Sugarman, *Rethinking Tort Doctrine: Visions of a Restatement (Fourth) of Torts,* 50 UCLA L. REV. 585, 597 -601 (2002).

37. RESTATEMENT (THIRD) OF TORTS: LIAB. FOR PHYSICAL & EMOTIONAL HARM §51 cmt. a (Tentative Draft No.6, 2009).

38. *Id.* § 51cmt. h.

39. *Id.* § 51 cmt. j, illus. 7.

40. *Id.* § 51 cmt. i.

41. *Id.* §51 cmt. k.

42. *Id.*

43. For further discussion of "no duty" policy arguments, see Stephen D. Sugarman, *A New Approach to Tort Doctrine: Taking the Best from the Civil Law and Common Law of Canada,* 17 SUP. CT. L. REV. 375, 388-89 (2002); Sugarman, *supra* note 36, at 613-18.

44. *See supra* Part I.B.

45. *See supra* Part I.B.

46. *See, e.g.,* RESTATEMENT (THIRD) OF TORTS: LIAB. FOR PHYSICAL & EMOTIONAL HARM §§ 52(a), 54(c) (Tentative Draft No. 6, 2009).

47. RESTATEMENT (THIRD) OF TORTS: LIAB. FOR PHYSICAL HARM § 37 (Proposed Final Draft No. 1, 2005).

48. *See, e.g.,* RESTATEMENT (THIRD) OF TORTS: LIAB. FOR PHYSICAL & EMOTIONAL HARM §§ 46-47 (Tentative Draft No.5, 2007).

49. RESTATEMENT (THIRD) OF TORTS: LIAB. FOR PHYSICAL & EMOTIONAL HARM § 51 cmt. m (Tentative Draft No. 6, 2009).

50. *See id.*

51. *See id.*

52. *See* W. PAGE KEETON ET AL., PROSSER AND KEETON ON THE LAW OF TORTS 431 (5th ed. 1984) (calling this argument "preposterous rubbish").

53. *See, e.g.,* Fritts v. McKinne, 934 P.2d 371 (Okla. Civ. App. 1996} (noting that a doctor cannot assert a contributory negligence defense when being sued for a botched-and ultimately fatal-surgery on a drunk driver).

Chapter 16

The Restatement of Torts (Third) is a Nice Jumping off Point for a Better Restatement (Fourth)

Law professors are apt to say that the central teaching mission of the 1L year is to get students to "think like a lawyer." More precisely, students are repeatedly engaged by their instructors in the close reading and careful analysis of judicial opinions. This is especially true in Torts where the material under examination is little distracted by the need to consider legislative or regulatory enactments. That is, Torts is very much a common law subject and hence "judicial reasoning" is again and again the core topic day after day. In order to provide variety, the Torts class moves through tort doctrine, and so in the process students (it is hoped) not only learn the key skill of thoughtful case reading and analysis but also master tort "law."

Indeed, there is a great deal of tort doctrine to learn. But does it really need to be so complex? Can't tort law be dramatically simplified? This chapter argues that it can. A new simplified structure of tort law is presented, a structure that, beyond making the law easier to understand, could bring with it two substantial additional advantages. First, by bringing together under a few headings legal rules that are currently spread out all over the place, we might more clearly recognize inconsistencies within tort law that are now largely ignored and would instead be forced to contend with them. Second, with a simpler structure that draws now diffuse doctrine under one heading, we would have a richer set of materials to bring to bear on new problems to which tort law must give answers.

As a brief preview, this chapter presents this architecture for a future Restatement (Fourth) of Torts at a time that the American Law Institute is still in the process of adopting the Restatement (Third). And while the current project contains a number of simplifications over the Restatement (Second), it is but a step in the direction proposed here.

Imagine the law of torts being organized like this.

> Division One: One who unreasonably harms another is (generally) liable to compensate the victim for his or her loss.
>
> Division Two: Occasionally one is strictly liable for harms to another (i.e. notwithstanding the reasonableness of the injurer's conduct).
>
> Division Three: There are three defenses: 1) the victim conduct was unreasonable (this is a partial defense); 2) the injury to the victim is outside of the scope of the risk taken by the injurer; and 3) over-riding considerations sometimes exempt an unreasonable injurer from having to compensate the victim.
>
> Division Four: Victim compensation is (generally) in the form of money and awarded in amounts as provided here.

To highlight here just a few points, Division One covers what are often termed the "breach" and "cause" issues in negligence law, but also would include liability for most intentional torts; Division Two covers all the instances of strict liability including liability for abnormally dangerous activities, vicarious liability of employers and others, and liability for products with manufacturing defects; Division Three covers comparative fault, what used to be called "proximate cause," and matters of "no duty"; Division Four covers remedies – the law of compensatory and punitive damages.

A theme emphasized throughout is that of "social role." In Division One, for example, in deciding whether one has acted unreasonably or not, it is generally necessary for the victim to point to how the injurer should have acted and that generally requires showing that the injurer should have either said something or done something different from how the injured actually behaved. But whether one should have "warned" of a danger or "fixed" the danger (as well as what effort should have been made to be aware of the danger in advance) will often turn on our collective understanding of the social role played by the defendant. For example, we may well expect a physician both to know more about and tell us more about possible treatment options than we expect a social host to tell us about household dangers or than we expect a product seller to tell us about competitor products.

While Chapter 13 argues for simplifying the law of torts by casting aside the "assumption of risk" concept, and Chapter 15 argues for simplifying the law of torts by folding "land possessor liability" into ordinary negligence law, this chapter takes the simplification project many steps further. It also provides a preview of the material covered in Chapter 14 in which "no duty" justifications are gathered together in one place.

This chapter was first presented at a conference held at UCLA Law School in honor of Professor Gary Schwartz, who had recently died while serving as the chief Reporter for the Restatement (Third) of Torts. It was published as Stephen D. Sugarman, "Rethinking Tort Doctrine: Visions of a Restatement (Fourth) of Torts," 50 UCLA Law Review 585-619 (2002), and is reprinted with permission of the journal.

RETHINKING TORT DOCTRINE: VISIONS OF A RESTATEMENT (FOURTH) OF TORTS

INTROUCTION

The American Law Institute (ALI) is currently at work on the *Restatement (Third) of Torts,* portions of which have already been adopted. Some important changes from the *Restatement (Second)* [1] have been approved, and more are in the works. In many respects the *Restatement (Third),* on which UCLA Professor Gary T. Schwartz was working at the time of his death, represents a step forward. Yet, I believe that we in the torts field would be better served if the entire way we structure, discuss, and analyze tort doctrine were altered. Although I do not have this restructuring completely worked out yet, the main features are reasonably clear in my mind. For now, I call it Visions of a Restatement (Fourth) of Torts. Were the Restatement (Fourth) of Torts to evolve in the direction I elaborate here, it would, in my view, be a suitable extension of the work Professor Schwartz began for the *Restatement (Third)* and provide a fine tribute to our lasting memory of him.

I. BACKGROUND ON THE *RESTATEMENT OF TORTS*

The original *Restatement of Torts 2* and its subsequent revisions have been monumental undertakings. University of Pennsylvania Professor Francis H. Bohlen was appointed by the ALI as the original Reporter in 1923, and he served until he became ill in 1937. Most of the original *Restatement of Torts* was the product of his efforts (aided by a distinguished group of advisers). It was adopted by the ALI at meetings held over the course of the years 1934-1939.

Berkeley's then Dean William L. Prosser was appointed as the Reporter to revise the *Restatement of Torts* in 1954, and he presented a preliminary draft to his advisers in 1955. It was not until meetings in May of 1963 and 1964, however, that the first two volumes of what have become the *Restatement (Second) of Torts* were adopted by the ALI. Prosser continued to serve until 1970 (and died in 1972). He was replaced as Reporter by Vanderbilt Professor John Wade, who saw the remaining volumes three and four of the *Restatement (Second)* through to their approval in 1977.

Because the first *Restatement of Torts* project took sixteen years and the *Restatement (Second)* took more than two decades, it was perhaps understandable that in 1986 the ALI adopted a different strategy. Rather than then launching a *Restatement (Third)* project, it instead commissioned a major, nondoctrinal policy review of the way that U.S. society handles, and should handle, the problem of personal injuries caused by enterprises. Moreover, rather than turning directly to scholarly giants from within "torts" (like Bohlen and Prosser), the ALI instead recruited to lead the project very distinguished scholars whose fame lay in adjacent fields. New York University Professor Richard Stewart (then of Harvard) was the first Chief Reporter of this project, and in 1989, when Stewart was called to serve in Washington, the mantle was passed to his Harvard colleague, Professor Paul C. Weiler. Weiler had been serving as one of the Associate Reporters, most of whom like Stewart and Weiler, were at that time best known for research other than doctrinal work in torts. The Reporters' Study titled *Enterprise Responsibility for Personal Injury3* (in two volumes) was presented for discussion by the ALI in 1991. Although this ambitious project importantly advanced our understanding of where torts fit in the wider context of other compensatory and regulatory systems, and although it offered several novel and insightful suggestions for tort reform, it received a hostile reception at the ALI meetings and the effort was essentially abandoned.[4]

Thereafter, the ALI promptly reverted to its old ways. But concluding that a comprehensive revision of the *Restatement (Second)* was too large an effort for a single project with a single Reporter, it decided instead to break up the next round into several parts. The ALI first appointed frequent coauthors Professors James A. Henderson, Jr. and Aaron D. Twerski, of Cornell and Brooklyn Law Schools, respectively, as co-Reporters to deal with the topic of products liability. Although their efforts were sharply criticized by some as pro-defendant,[5] this first segment of the *Restatement (Third) of Torts* [6] was adopted by the ALI in 1997. Alongside this project on product injuries, the ALI commissioned now Dean William C. Powers, Jr. of the University of Texas School of Law and Wake Forest School of Law's Professor Michael D. Green (then at the University of Iowa College of Law) as co-Reporters for a segment of the *Restatement (Third)* covering apportionment of liability.[7] This effort was adopted by the ALI in 1999.

While these two other efforts were underway, the ALI appointed Professor Schwartz as Reporter for a project intended to set forth general principles concerning tort liability for accidental physical harm to people and property. It remains unclear precisely how much and which sections of the *Restatement (Second)* are intended to be supplanted by this effort. However, it is clear that, even when the general principles project is combined with the completed projects on products liability and apportionment, a great deal of material covered in the *Restatement (Second)* remains to be addressed.

Professor Schwartz produced a partial discussion draft in 1999 and a longer and revised Tentative Draft Number I[8] for discussion by the ALI in May 2001. Alas, by the time of that meeting Professor Schwartz had become ill. He eventually died in the summer of 2001.

Professor Schwartz's effort was the subject of the John W. Wade Conference on the Third Restatement of Torts, held in September 2000 at Vanderbilt University Law School, and the papers presented there now appear in the April 2001 issue of the *Vanderbilt Law Review*[9] Moreover, all three ALI projects concerning the *Restatement (Third)* were the subject of an academic conference held at the University of Kansas School of Law, and overviews of those presentations appear in the fall 2000 issue of the *Kansas Journal of Law and Public Policy.*[10]

Even before Professor Schwartz's illness, Professor Green had been appointed as a co-Reporter to work primarily on certain forthcoming sections of the project concerning causation; after Professor Schwartz's death, Professor Green was joined as co-Reporter by Dean Powers, his collaborator on the apportionment project. In response to discussions at the ALI meeting in May 2001 and in the academic literature, Green and Powers have produced both revisions to some of Professor Schwartz's principles and new sections (primarily on topics conventionally termed "cause in fact" and "proximate cause"). This Tentative Draft Number 2[11] was discussed by the ALI in May 2002, when most of it won tentative approval.

A simple explanation for the ALI's products liability project is readily apparent. When Dean Prosser convinced the ALI in 1964 to adopt section 402A[12] concerning product liability, it appeared that a regime of strict liability in tort might be in the process of taking over an entire area of the law previously dominated by a combination of negligence in tort and the intricacies of warranty on the contract side. As it turned out, this has not occurred. Although defendants are now generally strictly liable in tort for so-called "manufacturing defects," in most jurisdictions the negligence principle, in effect, applies to all other product injuries. One important purpose of this portion of the *Restatement (Third)* is to reinforce that idea—although, oddly enough, Henderson and Twerski (who openly champion the negligence principle over the strict liability principle in their own scholarship) have actually clouded the point, by having the *Restatement (Third)* declare defendants liable for product "defects"[13] and then by defining so-called "warning" and "design" defects in ways that require proof of fault.[14] Products liability was also seen by the ALI as ripe for attention both because, as a practical matter, product injury lawsuits had become extremely important since 1964, and because new doctrine had developed to deal with many important peripheral issues not contemplated by Dean Prosser's language (or by his Reporter's comments to section 402A). Add to this the fact that many torts casebooks, scholars, litigators, and judges seem to treat product injuries as a reasonably self-contained area of the law, and the appeal to the ALI of updating the law on this specific topic becomes self-evident.

Yet, it remains to be seen whether commissioning this project was actually a good idea. As I will explain below, the Restatement (Fourth) of Torts that I envision contains no separate portion on products liability.

It is also readily understandable why the ALI would create a project on apportionment of liability, even though it combines the two very different matters of (1) the sharing of damages between plaintiffs and defendants and (2) the sharing of damages among defendants. Nonetheless, the law in both areas has changed sharply since 1964. First, the principle of contributory negligence as a complete bar to the plaintiffs recovery, which is the clear "black-letter law" in the *Restatement (Second),*[15] has by now been abrogated in nearly all U.S. jurisdictions. Second, the issue of how multiple defendants do and should share liability has gained a great deal of judicial, legislative, and scholarly attention of late, with the law becoming far more detailed than it had been. Moreover, the law in this latter area seems to be increasingly different from state to state (a problem that caused the Reporters for the apportionment of liability project to include several different "tracks" rather than a single dominant or preferred position).[16]

Professor Schwartz's project is something rather different, however. The idea seemed to be to let one of America's most distinguished torts scholars loose over a vast terrain of tort doctrine to see if he could come up with fewer and better-presented basic principles that could come to replace a great number of the sections scattered throughout the four volumes of the *Restatement (Second).* Yet, even Professor Schwartz recognized that there had to be limits on the scope of his undertaking, so he largely restricted himself to thinking about general principles that would cover accidental physical injuries to people and property. This meant, for example, excluding other injuries such as emotional harm, dignitary harm, and pure economic loss.

Interestingly enough, Professor Schwartz actually gives brief attention to nonaccidental physical injuries, offering up a basic principle that calls for the imposition of tort liability on one who intentionally causes physical harm [17] (and in section 1 of his draft he goes to great lengths to define and discuss the meaning of "intent"[18]). However, as for any further details concerning liability for such intentional harms (including both defenses and other qualifications),

Professor Schwartz simply refers the reader to the existing and elaborate provisions of the *Restatement (Second).*

The upshot is that this project, now renamed Liability for Physical Harm (Basic Principles), as augmented by Green and Powers, primarily addresses (1) the law of negligently caused physical injury and property damage and (2) some special areas of the law where strict liability is imposed on those who cause physical injury or property damage. Yet, because this effort does not call for the abandonment of the Henderson and Twerski project, product injuries apparently are not to be absorbed into these basic principles, [19] even though there are some references to product injury examples in Professor Schwartz's discussions.[20]

Professor Schwartz's project decidedly represents a step in the right direction. But, in my view, it does not go far enough. Hence, my vision is that however these basic principles become incorporated into a *Restatement (Third),* this piecemeal effort will eventually be replaced by a more comprehensive Restatement (Fourth) of Torts rooted in the broad thinking that underlies Professor Schwartz's effort.

II. Architecture For A Restatement (Fourth) Of Torts

I envision four major divisions in my Restatement (Fourth) of Torts. First would come the fault liability division, and the core principle of my Restatement (Fourth) is that, in general, someone suffering an injury because of another person's failure to act reasonably is entitled to compensation for the injury in the form of monetary damages. In terms of conventional doctrinal categories, this division would cover "breach of duty" and "cause in fact."

Next would come the strict liability division, which carves out an exception to the core principle. Covered here would be a few special instances in which there is a strongly felt social understanding that injurers should be held responsible for the consequences of their conduct, even if it has not been unreasonable.

The third division would contain a series of defenses that either reduce or eliminate the liability that the prior principles would otherwise impose. The three main subparts of this division would cover topics that currently are addressed under the doctrinal headings of "plaintiffs fault," "proximate cause," and "no duty."

The fourth and final division would concern remedies. This division would focus primarily on the nature of the monetary (or other) damages that victorious plaintiffs may recover and from whom they may be recovered amongst possible defendants (thereby borrowing heavily from the second half of the apportionment of liability project). But it would also include provisions on enhanced fault-encompassing those special situations in which an injurer's unreasonable conduct amounts to reckless disregard for the interests of the victim (or worse). In such instances, the victim additionally is entitled to punitive damages.

III. Some Problems With Existing Tort Doctrine

Before discussing these four divisions in more detail, I want to address what I see as the main problems with tort doctrine today. This should help to explain why my vision for a Restatement (Fourth) of Torts would be very different from both the *Restatement (Second)* and what is emerging as the *Restatement (Third)* and why I favor the particular approach that I have just briefly introduced.

First, in my view, there are simply too many separate "torts." Rather than starting from the civil law notion that there is one basic principle of "delict" (or liability for what might be termed fault), the common law approached and developed the field now known as torts in a piecemeal fashion. This is especially vivid in Volume 1 of the *Restatement* (Second), which contains a laundry list of some of the classic intentional torts, such as battery,[21] assault,[22] and false imprisonment.[23] Further torts, such as misrepresentation,[24] defamation,[25] invasion of privacy,[26] unjustifiable litigation,[27] and interference in domestic relations,[28] appear in Volume 3 and still others such as nuisance,[29] interference with contractual relations,[30] interference with water use,[31] and interference with dead bodies,[32] appear in Volume 4. Partly, this proliferation of separate torts was the product of the writ system.[33] Partly it was a result of the very nature of the common law, in which judges create new law by recognizing new torts as they address new problems.

One undesirable consequence of this "many torts" approach, however, is that several of the different torts have their own special language, even though the doctrinal words seem to be trying to convey the same essential ideas expressed in other torts through other language. the principle of "consent" used for intentional torts, for example, seems to be intended to convey much the same idea as that of "assumption of risk," which is sometimes used in negligence cases; yet, both actually tum out to mean one of several other things, such as "no duty" or "no breach."[34]

A second undesirable consequence (as I will illustrate below) is that seemingly similar problems appear to be resolved differently, perhaps with judges not even being aware of the inconsistency, as they approach the terrain covered by each of the separate torts with blinders on as to tort law generally. Third, when addressing new problems, judges tend to draw from analogies and experience in prior cases in the same narrow doctrinal area, when a fuller understanding of the matter might be gained by looking to how other parts of tort law have addressed this matter.

Hence, my vision of the Restatement (Fourth) of Torts would include but two principles of liability. Plaintiffs could only hope to win if either (1) they demonstrate the fault of the defendant, or (2) they show that their injury was one of those special cases that should attract liability in the absence of defendant fault. Professor Schwartz moves somewhat in this direction by adopting three categories of liability for physical harm: intentional physical harms in section 5,[35] negligent physical harms in section 6,[36] and strict liability in chapter 4.[37] But as already noted, a great deal of tort law is excluded from his project. Moreover, it is important to emphasize that my vision contains no separate category of intentional harm.

Furthermore, I believe that current tort doctrine is not sufficiently detailed regarding those types of things that at-fault defendants should have done differently, or those types of precautions that re required of different sorts of defendants. Hence, my vision of the Restatement (Fourth) of Torts would spell out due care obligations in more detail. Professor Schwartz addresses this topic a bit in his comments and notes to section 3,[38] which defines negligence, and to section 18,[39] which explores the notion of the negligent failure to warn.

Additionally, I believe that, in addressing whether or not a defendant exercised due care, courts often undesirably interchange the words "breach" and "duty" -- concepts that I believe should be carefully separated. I would break up these ideas in a Restatement (Fourth) of Torts. Besides, current doctrine, in my judgment, is much too thin in setting out the types of reasons why one should have, or not have, a duty to exercise due care towards another. Hence, my vision of the Restatement (Fourth) of Torts would more thoroughly articulate and defend the "no-duty" categories. Professor Schwartz and his successors have begun to elaborate upon this topic in section 7.[40]

Finally, as I see it, tort law today confusingly uses the word "cause" to encompass the very different ideas of historical causation and what is now often termed "proximate cause." Moreover, some problems are dealt with under the "duty" label (or elsewhere) that should be handled with a renamed "proximate cause" analysis (a misstep largely resulting from the way that Judge Benjamin Cardozo handled the famous *Palsgraf v. Long Island Railroad* Co.[41] case). Hence, my vision of a Restatement (Fourth) of Torts would address these matters quite differently. Powers and Green have helpfully separated the two "causation" ideas, by covering what they term "factual cause" in their Chapter 5,[42] and by putting the proximate cause topic in their Chapter 6,[43] where it has been re-titled "scope of liability."

I now elaborate on my vision of a Restatement (Fourth) of Torts, describing each of my four "divisions" in some detail, and explaining, among other things, how I would attempt to deal with the problems of existing tort doctrine that I have just described.

IV. The Core Principle: Fault-Based Liability

Division 1 is where, in practice, most of tort law fits. That is, liability is usually imposed on those who engage in unreasonably dangerous conduct that causes harm. Hence this division would express the core principle that one is (provisionally) liable if one unreasonably fails to act in a way that would have prevented the injury suffered by the victim.

Therefore, this division would apply to most carelessly caused medical injuries, transportation injuries, injuries on the premises of another, product injuries, most nuisances, and all of the other injuries that now lead to claims sounding in negligence (including not only physical injuries, but also harms to other interests of the victim, such as emotional distress, economic loss, and more). This means that product injury claims based on fault with respect to warning or design, now appearing in the separate provisions of the *Restatement (Third) on Products Liability,* would be folded into my Division 1 under the core fault principle.

A. Including Intentional Torts

In addition to ordinary negligence cases, most of the cases that might today be brought as so-called intentional torts would also be covered in my Division 1 on fault-based liability. Professor Schwartz, as noted above, would continue the separate treatment of intentional torts.[44]

Consider, battery, for example. I reject the idea that we benefit from having a separate tort for unconsented-to, offensive, physical touching. Rather, I believe we should ask whether the touching of one by another was reasonable or not. If it was reasonable, then generally there should be no liability, and certainly not fault-based liability. On the other hand, if the conduct was unreasonable, then the defendant should normally be liable. Thus, for example, when two prizefighters box, it is unwise in my view to claim that each consents to blows inflicted by the other, as the law now appears to do. After all, they are in fact trying their best to prevent such blows. Instead, the real reason they cannot sue for harms received by punches to the nose is that, under the circumstances, it is reasonable to deliver such punches.

So, too, if one brushes against another while moving down the aisle of a. crowded bus, or if one gently taps a stranger on the shoulder to ask the time, and we think these defendants should not be liable for their conduct, then the reason is that such behavior—unlike spitting on another's shoe in contempt, for example—is reasonable. This is exactly what the *Restatement (Second)* is saying when it deems such conduct not "offensive."[45] Similarly, when battery doctrine now allows a defense of self-defense,[46] it is basically saying that when self-defense is properly exercised, the actor, who has inflicted harm, has acted reasonably. My vision of the Restatement (Fourth) of Torts would express this directly, without requiring the complexities of a prima facie case plus a defense.

Consider next a reasonable effort made in self-defense that causes harm to an innocent victim. Imagine bank guards who reasonably exchange bullets with bank robbers and, without fault, shoot an innocent bystander. It is somewhat awkward to arrive at a defense victory under the conventional doctrine governing battery. Nonetheless, the *Restatement (Second)* appears to reach that result by introducing considerations of the reasonableness of the guards' conduct.[47] But, when this problem is addressed under my fault-based liability division, the guards win in a straightforward way. This is because we judge their conduct not to be wrongful.

In the same vein, consider the reasonable but mistaken detention of suspected shoplifters. I have in mind here a defendant who engages in self-help to protect his own property and makes a reasonable mistake, briefly detaining someone who is quickly determined to be an innocent party after all. The basic provisions of the *Restatement (Second)* would normally impose strict liability on such a defendant, on the ground that his actions constitute false imprisonment[48] and/or a false arrest.[49] And, there is reason to believe that this was indeed the traditional common law result.[50] However, some courts have created a special exception for such situations[51] that (very much like special statutes enacted in many states) permits businesses that reasonably believe someone is a shoplifter to detain the person on the premises for a reasonable time. Once more, if there is to be no liability in this setting, then under my Division 1, this result would be straightforwardly achieved on the ground that the defendant acted reasonably.

Although I will not elaborate on the details here, it should be evident that other separate intentional torts also readily would be folded into my Division 1. One good example is defamation, which now, as a matter of constitutional law, requires proof of fault as a pre-condition of liability. The requirement of proof of even graver fault in defamation cases brought by public figures would be handled in my Division 3, as discussed below. Another example is the intentional infliction of emotional distress, which, along with the negligent infliction of emotional distress, would simply illustrate fault-based liability under my Division 1. The extra exemplary damages for which one is eligible when the conduct causing his emotional distress is "outrageous," along with the availability of such additional damages for many of what are now termed intentional torts would be covered in my Division 4 in the section on punitive damages. The unavailability of recovery for certain instances of wrongful infliction of emotional distress would be covered in my Division 3, as discussed below.

B. Characteristics and Circumstances of Individual Defendants

Torts casebooks and Professor Schwartz's Tentative Draft Number 1 deal thoroughly with the question of the extent to which tort law should formally take into account features of the individual defendant in deciding whether he or she acted unreasonably. The main topics usually addressed include emergencies, child defendants, defendants with physical or mental disabilities, and special knowledge or talents that the defendant may possess or lack.[52] .

I do not object to including this topic in my Division 1, and I would generally be content to embrace what Professor Schwartz has said on the topic in his draft. Moreover, as will become clear shortly, I especially approve of the way that tort law doctrine, when considering children, now generally takes into account the "social role" that the child was playing at the time—that is, distinguishing between children acting in adult roles, such as driving a car, and those acting in children's roles, such as playing hopscotch on the sidewalk.

But while they appropriately pay attention to these individual characteristics, tort doctrine and the *Restatement (Second)* do not, as I stated earlier, pay sufficient attention to the ways in which one might, as a general matter, have acted to avoid harm to another or to which of those ways are required of people in various social roles. In my view, *Restatement (Second)* sections 300 and 301, which vaguely address this issue as a general matter, are woefully inadequate. Instead, if these matters are dealt with at all by tort doctrine, this tends to be done on an ad hoc basis in separate doctrinal areas, without an effort to synthesize what is common among or different among those areas. Hence, while the *Restatement (Second)* has special rules for possessors of land,[53] doctors,[54] and product sellers,[55] my vision is to approach these complexities from the opposite end.

C. Types of Unreasonable Conduct

It is ordinarily up to the plaintiff to specify how the defendant should have acted, and to convince us that a reasonable person in the defendant's position would have acted this way and that, had the defendant so acted, the victim would not have been injured. As I see it, in specifying how the defendant should have acted, the plaintiff basically has two general ways of characterizing the defendant's conduct as wrongful:

First is the failure to have said the right thing—either because the defendant said nothing, or because the defendant did not say enough, or because the defendant said the wrong thing. Simply put, the plaintiff in these instances is complaining about the failure of the defendant to have properly disclosed dangers about which the defendant knew or reasonably should have known.

Second is the unreasonable failure to have acted differently. Either the defendant failed to make safer his or her activity, product, service, property, or the like, or the defendant carried out its conduct in the wrong place, or the defendant should not have engaged in its activity at all.

An important feature of my vision for a Restatement (Fourth) of Torts is that, in determining what disclosures should reasonably have been made, or whether precautions beyond disclosure should have been undertaken, it would be clear that it is not only proper, but crucial, to take the injurer's *social role* into account.

1. Disclosure: How Much?

Consider first the obligation to disclose. My broad point is that it is unwise to treat quite separately, as we generally do today, the obligation of doctors to obtain the informed consent of their patients, the responsibility of product sellers to warn of product dangers, and the necessity of land occupiers to notify those who come on to the land of the hazards lurking there. For me, these obligations are all part of the obligation to disclose risks and should initially be gathered under that single broad heading. But, and here is the next key point, the precise contours of the disclosure obligation further depend, in my view, upon the social role the defendant plays with respect to the victim.[56]

I believe, for example, that doctors are understood in today's society to be fiduciaries and that, as such, they should disclose to their patients not only the risks of the treatment they propose, but also the risks of nontreatment, as well as a range of benefits and risks associated with reasonably plausible alternative treatments that might be tried, if there are any. This is because a fiduciary is someone we turn to in order to obtain the full range of information that is needed to make a sound decision. If we understand doctors in that way, then this will help us think through the range of disclosure obligations of others who we might conclude are also serving in a fiduciary capacity.

By contrast, I believe that most commercial actors—like product makers and land occupiers—are not viewed by society as fiduciaries. Hence, their disclosure obligations are appropriately more limited. It seems rather that our social expectation for ordinary enterprises is that they should let us know about dangers associated with their products, or their land, or their commercial activity—including both nonobvious dangers they are aware of, and dangers they could have been aware of if they had made reasonable efforts to discover them (for example, through inspection). Hence, we should think about a range of similarly situated enterprises when we address the disclosure obligations of supermarkets with respect to debris on their floors, machinery sellers as to the dangers of their products, and spectator sports promoters as to the risks of watching from the stands.

However, there are perhaps yet different social expectations for noncommercial actors with whom we have a relationship of the guest/host sort. In such relationships, it is perhaps quite appropriate for this social role to carry with it the obligation to disclose only those nonobvious dangers actually known to the host (that is, inspecting for dangers is not viewed as a reasonable requirement).

In any event, the more general point is that it is appropriate to focus on whether there is something about the social relationship of the parties that makes it acceptable for this defendant not to have provided the sort of warning that we would have expected from a normal commercial provider. Professor Schwartz less explicitly acknowledges the importance of social role in his discussion of warnings in section 18 of his Tentative Draft Number 1. There, he explores the question of the extent of the effort that a defendant must take to acquire information about risks and states that some of the relevant criteria are "the status of the defendant, the relationship between the parties, and the expectations which that relationship occasions."[57]

Notice that, in emphasizing the importance of social role, I do not mean, for example, to embrace the classifications of invitee, licensee, and trespasser that used to dominate the law of occupier liability (and which still reign in many jurisdictions).[58] Yet, I do want to acknowledge that, at least in some respects, the different obligations said to be owed to these different classes of persons injured on the premises of another reflect the different sorts of social expectations that I have in mind. The problem with these traditional categories is that they soon became misaligned with social expectations in many important cases, thereby forcing the development by the courts of numerous so-called "exceptions."

2. Is Disclosure Enough, or Must the Actor Also Take Precautions?

A related key area for me concerns the question of when merely disclosing (or warning) of dangers suffices, and when someone additionally is required to take precautionary actions to reduce or eliminate the risk. This, too, is a problem that runs through all sorts of factual settings that tend to be treated quite distinctly today. These separate doctrinal areas would also be gathered together under my vision of a Restatement (Fourth) of Torts.

But again, for me one's social role is central. Consider first commercial actors such as supermarkets, hotels, landlords, and the like. They should not be able to get away with merely warning their customers, tenants, and so on about reasonably avoidable dangers on their premises. That is, it just will not do for a Safeway store to put up a sign saying that it is not bothering to clear up broken glass in its aisles, or for landlords to ignore staircases with broken treads and hand railings even after all the tenants in the building know of the danger. Rather, parties occupying those social roles are expected to take reasonable steps to prevent dangers in the first place and to eliminate dangers once they have developed.

By contrast, however, ordinary homeowners might well be viewed as appropriately satisfying their full obligation to act reasonably when they warn their guests of similar hazards in their homes. That is, because of the different social relationship, we might find it appropriate for the host fully to shift the responsibility to the guest for safely negotiating his or her way down a staircase once the danger has been clearly pointed out, whereas we no longer tolerate commercial providers completely escaping responsibility for dangers merely because these hazards are open and obvious (that is, well warned about but not fixed). Professor Schwartz also recognizes that sometimes warnings are sufficient,[59] but he does not link the question of when a warning may suffice to one's social role.

This, of course, does not mean that commercial actors must always take every feasible step to eliminate all dangers associated with their activity or product. Plainly, some risk reduction will deprive those served by the activity or product of important benefits that society does not want people to have to forego. For example, with respect to recreational activities in particular (whether the victim is a participant or spectator), warnings of modest dangers generally will suffice, and additional precautions generally will not be *required.* This explains why baseball stadium owners need not screen all of the seats or why it is was permissible for an amusement park to operate something called "the Flopper."[60] A similar point applies to various products used for recreational purposes.

Were similar levels of risk to arise in the work context, however, it might well be deemed unacceptable merely to warn employees, even if investment in precaution implied a minor reduction in wages. That trade-off, in the end, is no different from the one made when tort law imposes obligations to "fix" obvious dangers on hotels and supermarkets—tort law insists on safety even though that might imply a minor increase in price. In the case of these workplace or commercial property dangers, this insistence on safety precautions is a reflection of a societal determination that there are risks that we simply do not want potential victims to run. This determination is based on a judgment that, in fact, most potential victims indeed would prefer to pay for the risk reduction and/or a decision to paternalize them and avoid the danger in the name of the greater social good. By contrast, in the recreational activities examples noted above, society has decided not to paternalize consumers once it is determined that the socially approved benefit that comes with the danger is one the potential victim class is eager to enjoy.

Another example of where the nature of the social relationship between the parties apparently leads judges to decide that a warning suffices is the case of professional rescuers, such as firefighters who arrive to put out fires negligently set by landowners or electricians who come to fix careless wiring jobs started by do-it-yourself homeowners. Indeed, the overriding point of all the examples given here is that the social relationship between injurer and victim is critical in determining the question of whether a warning is sufficient.

D. Disputes over Wrongdoing

In easy cases, there is no dispute over either what happened or what should have happened. We know what the defendant did or what the defendant said, and it is clear whether that is how a reasonable defendant should have behaved. Cases become difficult when the parties are in conflict over one or more of these matters. I envision that Division 1 would attend systematically to the different types of disputes.

1. Disputes over What Happened

First are disputes over what happened. The victim may claim that the defendant was speeding or drove his/her car across the center line, but the defendant may deny the allegation (and perhaps claim some specific alternative behavior). The same goes for a victim's claim that he/she was never warned, when the defendant argues, "But I told you...." These factual disputes are classically matters for juries in the United States, with ordinary rules of procedure and evidence determining whether either side would be entitled to a directed finding (if requested) on the matter at issue.

There is nothing terribly special about torts cases in this respect, although it is perhaps worth emphasizing that judges through the years have been especially attentive to the ability of personal injury victims to prove their cases by circumstantial evidence, in view of the requirement that they may win merely with a preponderance of the evidence and need not prove what happened beyond a reasonable doubt, as in criminal cases.

The doctrine of res ipsa loquitur has been drawn into this question but, probably having done more harm than good, it would be better if it were retired. Instead, two very different situations should be distinguished. In one, common sense and/or common experience tells us that the defendant acted in a wrongful manner, even if we cannot know precisely how the defendant acted and therefore the precise nature of the defendant's misconduct. The famous case of the flour barrel falling out of a warehouse window and onto a passerby that ushered in the res ipsa expression is a good example.[61] We do not know whether the defendant and his/her employees carelessly pushed the barrel out of the window, they carelessly tied it down and it somehow rolled away, they carelessly knocked against it, or what. But we are reasonably confident that the explanation for the falling barrel was some wrongful behavior of that sort, and not alternatives that we can imagine. Even when added together, we understand those alternatives, such as a criminal seeking to harm the plaintiff sneaking into the building and throwing the barrel at the victim, or an earthquake shaking the barrel down, to be rather unlikely.

Very different are those cases in which common sense and common experience will not carry the day for the victim, but there is something special about access to the evidence as to what did happen. In such circumstances, judges sometimes conclude that it would be unjust to impose the ordinary burden of proof on the victim. In such cases, the courts should openly state that (and justify why) the burden is being placed on the defendant(s). Res ipsa is altogether the wrong expression for these situations, because, unlike in the flour barrel case, the facts by no means speak for themselves. Examples of this second sort of case might include those in which young children come home from day care settings with unexplained injuries, those of exploding soda bottles that the victim thinks occurred because of carelessness at the bottling plant, and the famous *Ybarra v. Spangard*[62] case, in which the plaintiff awoke from surgery with an injury that was almost surely caused by one of the independent contractors involved in the surgery but in which the patient had no way of knowing which medical professional was responsible.[63] Some believe that modem rules of discovery make it no longer necessary for courts to shift the burden in such circumstances. This appears to be Professor Schwartz's viewpoint; however, he still retains the phrase of "res ipsa" in his heading.[64]

2. Disputes over Foreseeability

A quite different type of dispute between the litigants concerns whether the defendant knew or should have known that his/her behavior had endangered the victim. This raises the general issue of foreseeability. It is widely agreed that one cannot really be blamed for harming someone when, at the time one acted, one did not anticipate and could not reasonably have anticipated, that acting in the way one did risked harm to another. This is because, in such circumstances, it seems unfair to say the defendant should have acted differently. Disputes about foreseeability also broadly concern facts—what the defendant knew and, by reference generally to what others knew, what the defendant should have known. Again, this is normally a matter for the jury, and the main concern here is preventing juries from being too heavily influenced by hindsight. Just because it turns out that the defendant injured the victim that does not prove that the defendant should have realized the dangerousness of his conduct at the time he acted. Yet, it is all too easy to project knowledge of what has happened backwards and perhaps draw an improper conclusion as to what should have been known at the time. This concern, I believe, must simply be handled by the proper admonishing of the jury by the trial judge and by the advocacy skills of the defense lawyer.

3. Disputes over Wrongfulness

Still different, and much more difficult, are disputes over whether the defendant's conduct was wrongful or not. The victim's initial and perhaps simple-minded position could usually be stated in a straightforward way: You knew (or should have known) that your conduct endangered me, and you should not have done that. Or perhaps somewhat more subtly, the victim's position could initially be put: You knew (or should have known) that I was at risk of harm and that by your doing or saying something different I would not have been hurt; thus, you should have acted differently.

The problem is that there are all sorts of circumstances in which the social judgment dictates that it was all right for the defendant to subject the victim to that risk of harm after all (for example, striking back in self-defense) and, therefore, that it was all right for the defendant to have acted as he/she did and not in the way the plaintiff says he/she should have acted. Determining those circumstances is not a matter of fact finding. The jury can find as a matter of fact what the defendant alternatively might have done that would have prevented harm to the victim -- although this is more of a finding of hypothetical fact, rather than a finding of fact as to what actually happened.

Yet it is not really a question of fact whether the defendant was wrong in failing to act in an alternative way. Rather, I believe, answering that question requires making a social judgment. This perhaps explains why some term the issue of breach (that is, whether or not the defendant's behavior was wrongful) something of a mixed question of law and fact. It may also explain why judges often find themselves intruding into aspects of the breach question in various ways, thereby managing to take back for themselves this question of what would have been reasonable conduct under the circumstances.

Unfortunately, judges sometimes do this by seemingly terming the matter a question of duty, and I find that confusing. For example, in a famous case in which a boy was injured when a wire he was swinging struck the electric power line of a trolley company, Judge Cardozo held that the trolley company had no duty to place the wires underground.[65] It would have been better had he made clear that it was not a breach to have failed to put them underground. The "duty" term, in my view, should be left for matters that I take up below in my Division 3. I do not object to courts declaring that, as a matter of law, there was a breach of the duty to behave reasonably, or that there was no breach of that duty. Indeed, I believe that judges have an obligation to make such a finding (when asked by the relevant party) if, in a particular case, no jury reasonably could find otherwise.

Perhaps more important than the question of allocating functions to judge and jury is consideration of the reasons why it might indeed be all right for a defendant to have endangered a victim. Much attention has been given in the past thirty years to the so-called "Hand formula" set out in *United States v. Carroll* Towing.[66] Judge Hand presents a kind of cost-benefit algebraic formula, in which he says that determining whether or not the defendant acted reasonably is a matter of balancing the risk to the victim (comprised of the probability of harm or "P," multiplied by the likely loss that the victim will suffer if the risk comes to pass or "L") against what he terms the "burden of adequate precautions" on the defendant (or "B").[67] As Judge Hand saw it, if the burden on the defendant of avoiding the risk is too great in comparison to the risk to the victim, it is acceptable for the defendant to proceed and run the risk and not pay for the consequent harm when it occurs.[68]

I want to emphasize, however, that whether or not the burden on the defendant of avoiding the harm to the victim is too great is very much a social judgment, albeit one that a jury is probably reasonably well-suited to make. In short, we look to the legal system to tell us whether the defendant's injury-causing behavior was socially acceptable or not. And society's view of the burden may be markedly different than the defendant's view. In turn, this means that when the jury finds that the burden of avoidance is something the defendant should have born, but the defendant attaches much higher value to doing what he/she did, we should appreciate that, while tort law may punish the defendant, threatening such liability may well not prevent this sort of injury from occurring in the future.

It is also important to appreciate that, while the burden on the defendant might be money or something readily converted into a dollar value, frequently it is not (for example, driving more carefully). Perhaps even more significantly, one should not understand this "burden" always to be a matter of the defendant advancing his/her exclusively selfish interests against those of the victim. To be sure, sometimes the defendant succeeds in convincing us that the financial cost of the precaution the victim proposes that the defendant should have taken is so great as compared with the small nature of the risk run that the jury will conclude that it was all right for the defendant not to have spent his/her money on that precaution. But often the burden of avoiding the injury will be deemed by society to be too great (and hence the defendant's conduct in causing the injury to be not wrongful) because of the social benefit the defendant's conduct brings about. As a simple example, it is reasonable for companies to offer airplane passenger service even if they know that there are going to be some unavoidable crashes (for example, from totally unexpected changes in weather). Of course, allowing this commercial venture permits airline companies to make profits. But, the real point is that the burden on our society would be too much if we had to give up air travel. Just because the passengers are aware of the risks and choose to take them hardly ends the inquiry. There are also involuntary victims on the ground. Moreover, it can often be unreasonable from society's viewpoint for the defendant to have acted in a certain manner, even if the victim earlier had been happy for the defendant to have done so. Consider, for example, a friend who goes out for a joy ride in a car with an intoxicated buddy and who is injured when the buddy crashes the car into a tree. Professor Schwartz deals with several of these matters, including the roles played by statute and custom in helping the tort system to decide whether or not conduct was wrongful.[69]

E. Cause in Fact

Although my Division 1 would include provisions on what has been called "cause in fact" and what Green and Powers call "factual causation,"[70] I will address this topic only briefly here. Generally, I support the Green and Powers approach of including under the heading of "factual causation" both cases in which the defendant can be shown to be the "but-for" cause of the plaintiff's loss[71] and certain other very special cases in which that cannot be demonstrated and yet the defendant is nonetheless held liable.[72]

This latter category is comprised of what Green and Powers call "multiple sufficient causal sets"[73] or what many others call the problem of over-determined causation. I certainly agree that when there are two independently negligent actors and each of their acts, absent the act of the other, would have sufficed to injure the plaintiff, it is morally unacceptable to allow each to point the finger at the other and thereby allow both to escape liability because neither is technically the "but-for" cause of the harm. To be sure, each may show that the plaintiff would have been no better off had he (and he only) not been negligent. But, just as clearly, had there been no negligence at all, the victim would not have been injured at all. And so, in my view, just as surely the victim should not lose completely because of the coincidence of two simultaneous negligent acts. Of course, it is a policy choice to reject the "but-for" test in such settings, but it is widely considered the correct choice, as Powers and Green make clear.[74]

A much more difficult case involves the combination of the negligence of a defendant and some concurrent act of nature/fate/God, either of which would have sufficed to injure the victim. In such a setting, in the absence of negligence, the victim still would have been injured. Therefore, to hold the negligent party liable for the loss would mean putting the victim back in a better position than he/she would have been in absent the defendant's negligence. Cutting the other way, of course, are (1) the misconduct of the defendant toward the victim and (2) the actual harm to the victim. Yet, these factors alone are normally insufficient to impose tort liability. Indeed, the central purpose of also requiring the plaintiff to show "but-for" causation is to further the conventional "corrective justice" understanding of tort law as a mechanism for righting individual wrongs. In their Tentative Draft Number 2, however, Powers and Green conclude that the weight of current authority favors the imposition of liability in at least some simultaneous cause settings, even when one cause is nontortious—although they present arguments on both sides of this issue.[75] I will not explore this matter further in this Article.

Earlier, I mentioned a role for courts in shifting the burden in special cases in which proof of breach is difficult because of the victim's inability to muster all of the relevant evidence. This problem exists with respect to the issue of proving historical causation as well, and Division 1 would address those situations in which, for a number of policy reasons, it has been thought appropriate to shift the onus of negating the evidentiary connection to the defendant.[76]

V. The Exception: Strict Liability

A. The Major Existing Exceptions

I next turn to my Division 2, governing cases of liability without fault. So far, I see this division as clearly including three important categories: (1) dangerous activities that are not commonly carried out in the place where they were performed, (2) the production or sale of commercial products containing manufacturing defects, and (3) the vicarious liability of employers for the torts of employees. In each of these situations, the defendant is held liable without requiring the victim to show that the defendant in any way acted unreasonably (although admittedly in the last category, the victim must demonstrate that the employee acted unreasonably).

Coverage of these three matters is now strewn around the *Restatement (Second) of Torts* as well as the *Restatement (Second) of Agency.* [77] Moreover, each of them is taken up by a separate one of the three projects that so far comprise the *Restatement (Third).* Strict liability for what are called "abnormally dangerous activities" is dealt with by Professor Schwartz's basic principles;[78] strict liability for manufacturing defects is in the products liability portion;[79] and strict vicarious liability is treated briefly in the apportionment of liability portion.[80]

This divided treatment suggests that these three matters are quite unrelated and does little to help us to understand why there are important sets of cases on both sides of the fault/no-fault gulch or to decide whether newly identified problems should go on one side or another. As Chicago Professor Harry Kalven noted long ago, although the twentieth century saw a dramatic simplification of negligence law and the elimination of all sorts of difficult-to-justify inconsistencies, it also made more vivid the stark contrast between requiring proof of unreasonable conduct as a prerequisite for recovery in some situations and not in others.[81] I prefer to put these three major categories of strict liability cases together in the hopes that we can thereby better discern their similarities and better decide whether, in the future, additional matters should be resolved on a strict liability, rather than on a fault liability, basis.

Moreover, I believe there is a common theme connecting these three main examples of strict liability in tort. Namely, in each of these instances, commercial actors are viewed by society, because of the social role they play, as having special responsibilities to pay for harms they caused, even if their conduct was not blameworthy. But I admit this is something of a conclusory theme. It points to the combination of commercial activity and special obligations arising from the particular commercial role being played. Yet it hardly explains what precisely creates different social expectations in these settings as contrasted with other commercial settings. To dig further into that requires a closer look at each of these three problems.

The basic criteria for the "abnormally dangerous activities" category are that the activity is both quite dangerous and uncommon. This simplified and improved characterization of the doctrine, as compared with the confusing multiple criteria set out in the *Restatement (Second),* is well-captured by Professor Schwartz in his Tentative Draft Number 1, section 20. More precisely, in these situations a commercial actor has come to the type of location where this sort of dangerous thing is not normally done. And, although we are not saying he should not have done what he did, his violation of the expectations of substantial dangers that are ordinarily run in that sort of location is seen to thrust on him the obligation to compensate his faultless victims. Professor Schwartz, by contrast, appears to emphasize administrative reasons over the alteration of social expectations as the explanation for strict liability for abnormally dangerous activities.[82] In my view, these administrative reasons would at best justify shifting the burden of proof to the defendant to show that its dangerous and uncommon activity nonetheless was reasonably carried out in the location where it took place.

For the second category—products with manufacturing defects—expectations are also key in my view. Our social understanding of today's packaged and highly advertised products is that they will be safe. Unlike humans, who of course sometimes cause unavoidable injuries in the delivery of services, our society somehow has infused commercial products (i.e., objects) with a different meaning. And when our expectations about those products are violated, then strict liability is imposed. Again, the society is not saying that the defendant was at fault in selling such a product (or in making the product), but rather that, in view of consumers' expectations, the defendant is obliged to compensate the victim. The *Restatement (Third)* portion on products liability instead emphasizes administrative, economic, and deterrence objectives in justifying strict liability for manufacturing defects.[83] In my view, these arguments would apply equally to the provision of many sorts of commercial services, such as airline transportation, and hence do not really justify tort law's special treatment of products.

Finally, for the third category—vicarious liability for the torts of one's employee (and in some cases, one's independent contractor)—social expectations once more are critical. Simply put, our social understanding is that when someone acting on behalf of, and for the benefit of, an enterprise carelessly harms us, the enterprise will take responsibility for that actor. Otherwise, it would be viewed as quite unacceptable for enterprises to hire judgment-proof employees, to set them to work in ways that predictably will cause them on occasion to harm others negligently, and then to wash their hands of any responsibility for the resulting injury.

In short, I suggest that the existence of special social expectations is the common justification for imposing strict liability in each of these three important areas, in which the law contains exceptions to the normal rule that one may be held liable only on the basis of one's own fault.

B Additional Categories?

Beyond these three categories of cases, there are additional candidates for inclusion in my Division 2 covering strict liability. Let us, for example, reconsider both the case of the reasonable but mistaken shooting of a bystander by bank guards and the case of the reasonable but mistaken detention of a suspected shoplifter by store security guards. An important issue, in my view, is whether the enterprise defendants in these instances should be strictly liable for the harm caused by their employees to innocent victims. These problems, and the issue they raise, might be characterized even more generally: Should an individual who acts reasonably in self-defense for his own benefit be liable in a situation like this? I am not certain what the right answer to this question should be. I am confident, however, that trying to answer this question by applying the complex rules of battery and false arrest law is not helpful.

I would prefer instead to address the question by exploring the social expectations theme I advanced to explain strict liability in the categories of abnormally dangerous activities, manufacturing defects, and vicarious liability. In the same vein, perhaps it could be argued that victims of the conduct of the bank guards and the security guards cannot really imagine they might be accidentally singled out for the injury they suffer. So, when such mistakes occur, our violated social expectations demand victim compensation. On the other hand, we might decide instead that these experiences are no more than bad luck to which no special expectations attach. If so, they are rightly understood simply as instances of the much wider default category of not-reasonably-avoidable accidents, the financial consequences of which fall on victims, not injurers.

Were we to decide to keep these bank guard and security guard cases in Division 1, requiring proof of fault before the victims may recover, this might force us to reexamine the common law rule concerning private necessity, now set out in the *Restatement (Second)* in section 197[84] and section 263.[85] According to the *Restatement (Second),* unlike bank guards acting in self-defense or security guards acting to detain suspected shoplifters, reasonable conduct by a defendant in the private necessity setting does not suffice to avoid liability for harm reasonably imposed. This rule rests on the classic case of *Vincent v. Lake Erie Transportation* Co.,[86] which Professor Bohlen explicitly drew upon to set out the Restatement position on private necessity. There, because the defendant had a self-protection privilege to tie its ship to the plaintiffs dock in order to avoid its ship being damaged badly by a tremendous storm, it was not liable for trespass.[87] Nevertheless, the Minnesota Supreme Court held the defendant strictly liable to the dock owner for the damage the boat did to the dock when pounded by a storm.[88] Just why the innocent dock owner can recover, but the innocent yet suspected shoplifter and the innocent victim of the bank guard's bullets cannot, is something of a mystery to me. Clearly, in each of these cases, the defendants acted reasonably in self-defense of person or property, and each of the defendants, in furtherance of his own interests, imposed a loss on an innocent party. And it is even more troubling to me that the successful plaintiff in *Vincent* is a commercial actor, whereas the losing plaintiffs in the examples are ordinary citizens. Perhaps there are different social expectations that attach to the private necessity situation. At least my approach should force a more consistent evaluation of these problems, rather than leave them scattered about the Restatement as though they were altogether different matters.

As for other possible inclusions in my Division 2, I leave for another occasion any consideration of Professor Schwartz's remaining and somewhat exotic categories of wandering livestock,[89] wild animals,[90] and abnormally dangerous animals.[91] Also, there are other examples of what, in effect, is the imposition of strict liability in the intentional tort area (beyond the private necessity example already discussed). These matters also would be covered in my Division 2 and thereby clearly would be separated from most intentional torts, which rest upon wrongful conduct and would be covered under my Division 1.

VI. Defenses

As noted earlier, there are three main defenses in my Division 3. I will set out their general terms, and then I will discuss each in tum. As a preliminary matter, however, I want to emphasize what I mean by a defense. My main point is that a defendant who has otherwise been shown (or alleged) to have either wrongfully injured the victim or injured the victim through conduct to which strict liability attached needs to offer a convincing reason why he/she should not be held fully liable for the loss. I do not mean for now to attend to the niceties of pleading or the order in which the various issues in a case should be addressed.

First, in general, if the victim also could have avoided or reduced his or her injury by acting reasonably, then the damages that the victim might otherwise have been awarded are appropriately reduced based upon an appraisal of the victim's share of the responsibility for his or her own loss.

Second, if the victim's injury is not fairly understood to be part of the risk taken by the injurer's conduct, then the injurer is not liable at all for the victim's loss.

Finally, injurers are not liable in tort for certain consequences of their conduct, when the judiciary concludes that the overall social benefits of exempting a particular injurer and similar injurers from liability clearly outweigh the social benefits of holding that injurer responsible for the consequences of his or her unreasonable (or otherwise strict liability-attaching) conduct.

A. Victim Fault

As for victim fault, I am merely including in my Division 3 the general principle of comparative fault. This has been set out in Topic 1 of the apportionment of liability project for the *Restatement (Third)* .[92] And, I am generally in accord with what is presented there. Of course, in their details, the rules of comparative fault vary considerably from state to state, and I have my own personal preferences as to which regime is the most just (largely in line with the choices made in the Uniform Comparative Fault Act93). But this is not the occasion to address those differences.

Rather, for now I will address only one issue. Consider, for example, the situation in which you wrongfully attack me with your fists and I respond in self-defense but use unreasonably excessive force, injuring you. You then sue me. Under my approach, your lawsuit would be covered under Division1, which deals with my wrongful behavior, that is, my unreasonable use of force that causes you injury. But the following question would then vividly arise: Why should I not be able, under the defenses provided by Division 3, to reduce your damages because of your fault in attacking me in the first place?

The very separate structure of the law of intentional torts in the United States long seems to have stood in the way of assimilating the comparative fault regime into such lawsuits. Clearly, the *Restatement (Second)* rejects considering the fault of the initial aggressor in his/her lawsuit against the person who was attacked but responded with excessive force.[94] But under my reformulation, we could readily do that. Powers and Green in their apportionment of liability project are thoughtfully alert to this issue.[95] Moreover, they helpfully point out several situations in which courts are now beginning to apply comparative fault principles in cases brought as intentional torts.[96]

B. Harms Outside the Scope of the Risk Taken (No "Proximate Cause")

In the second defense in my Division 3, rather than speaking in terms of legal cause or proximate cause or superceding cause or other phrases that use the word "cause," I adopt a different approach. Instead, I provide a defense for an injurer who can persuade the court that the injury that occurred is not fairly understood to be part of the risk he took.

In a variety of circumstances the defendant may be able to convince the court that the victim's injury is most fairly attributable to something other than the defendant—perhaps another party, or fate, or nature, or the like. Examples of these circumstances are spelled out in the elaboration of this defense. They include the defendant persuading us that (1) this injury was not the result of the hazard that the defendant created, (2) this was not the victim that the defendant endangered, (3) the defendant did not enhance the victim's risk of being injured as he was, or (4) some other party unexpectedly came between the defendant and the victim and his act eclipsed the defendant's responsibility. The thrust of the argument in each of these circumstances is captured in the master principle of this part of my Division 3—namely, that the defendant has demonstrated that what happened is not fairly part of the risk he took.

Although I have used somewhat different language here, my views are largely in accord with those of Powers and Green.[97] They want to get away from both the word "cause" and an obsession others have to use special language to express the moral sentiment applicable to these cases. Their proposal is that a defendant is not liable for "harm different from the harms whose risk made the actor's conduct tortious,"[98] leaving it for the comments and notes to try to spell out what constitutes a "different harm."[99]

I want to emphasize further that casting this defense in terms of the "scope of the risk taken" (or as a "different harm," as Powers and Green would) might also help courts to better articulate than the *Restatement (Second)* just why it is that defendants are liable in certain cases and not others. For example, liability is avoided in "unexpected hazard,"[100] "unexpected plaintiff,"[101] or "superceding cause"[102] cases, and yet defendants are usually fully liable in so-called "unexpected extent,"[103] "unexpected manner,"[104] and mere "intervening cause"[105] cases. Powers and Green maintain these distinctions.[106] It is less clear whether they have yet offered a convincing reason why it should be that some defendants are not liable for certain "unforeseen" harms, because they are characterized as "different harms," whereas other defendants are liable for other "unforeseen" harms, which somehow are not viewed as "different harms." I leave this very thorny topic for another occasion.

C. Policy Arguments Trumping Liability ("No Duty")

Turning finally to what are typically called the "no-duty" rules, I cover in my Division 3 those situations in which the defendant is not held liable because, even if he were at fault, there is some overriding policy reason for his escaping liability after all. My goal is to capture and articulate, in one place, the range of policy arguments that may be used to let individual defendants escape having to pay for harm they impose on individual victims. These are situations that, if narrowly judged in terms of this one injury, might well seem to be ripe for the imposition of liability, but that, when viewed in the wider context, are instances in which judges are convinced that broader social values preclude tort liability.

Below, I set out five important policy arguments. For each type, I will give a general statement of the reason why tort liability should be denied and then an example that arguably illustrates the reason. I want to make clear at the outset, however, that for some of my specific examples the denial of liability might actually be justified by more than one of the policy arguments I will set out, a point I will subsequently expand with further examples.

> (1) A well-functioning alternative justice system, itself providing deterrence, punishment, and compensation, is available. This system makes providing tort remedies not only superfluous but also unwise, as it would interfere with the alternative and its socially effective governance structure. This is a good reason for judges to decide that tort law will not provide a remedy for a victim of unreasonable conduct. This reason may explain, for

example, why professional athletes in the United States (who have generous disability insurance coverage and are subject to penalties by both on-the-field and league officials) are generally not permitted to sue each other for ordinary negligence that occurs during the course of their sporting event.

(2) Were liability imposed, then administrative burdens (that is, a "flood of cases") would be imposed on the judiciary that would be so large as to preclude the courts from providing prompt justice in other, more compelling cases. If this fear is well-grounded, then it, I believe, provides another good reason for judges to deny recovery to victims of wrongful conduct. This reason might justify precluding lawsuits for the negligent infliction of emotional distress upon strangers, which courts apparently think would unleash a potentially huge number of small injury claims.

(3) Imposing liability will generate perverse behavioral responses that will be even more undesirable than denying recovery. Again, if this fear is truly well-grounded, it is perhaps just for judges to keep tort law from doing more harm than good, even at the expense of an otherwise deserving victim. This appears to be the justification in many states for denying recovery to those who suffer recreational injuries at the hands of careless fellow participants.[107] That is, the courts that reject plaintiffs in these cases seem convinced that imposing liability would dramatically discourage participation in such activities. I must confess, however, that I have substantial doubts about the correctness of the predicted behavioral response to imposing liability on carelessly dangerous recreational activity. In short, I doubt whether the fear expressed by the courts is truly well grounded.

(4) If the victim is allowed to win here, then crushing liability might well follow that genuinely risks depriving the public of essential goods and services. Again, if this fear is truly well-grounded, it is probably just for judges to keep tort law from causing more harm than good in this particular way, even at the

expense of individual victims. This reason perhaps explains why New York's highest court, in the well-known Consolidated Edison case, limited the public utility's liability in connection with New York City's famous "blackout."[108] However, I must again confess that I find highly dubious the underlying empirical argument, here concerning the risk to the provision of essential services. I find it unlikely that allowing suits like the plaintiffs truly jeopardized the provision of electrical services. (This policy reason might help to explain limits that many states impose on the responsibilities of lawyers, accountants, and other financial actors for economic losses that their careless conduct imposes on people who are not their own clients.)

(5) There are important and trumping social values at stake that otherwise might be trampled were the decision in an individual case made with a focus precisely on the events of the case instead of on the wider systemic consequences of liability. This may be the most difficult reason to justify the denial of recovery because it means that judges are making a social judgment about what values are of paramount importance. However, in the U.S. system, which relies upon juries to determine the reasonableness of one's conduct in individual cases, judges may well be justified in precluding what they appropriately fear might be the narrow focus of individual juries. Moreover, if the identification by the courts of certain trumping values is viewed as inappropriate, then, at least in the ordinary case, it can be overturned by the legislature, which perhaps is a more legitimate body for identifying such values. This reason may explain why courts would deny recovery to a child who is suing his or her mother for injuries suffered because of alleged misconduct by the mother during pregnancy. [109] Courts might wisely conclude that the strong social value favoring the mother's autonomy with respect to her own body trumps all other considerations and that juries should not be asked to weigh that value in general against the specific risk to the plaintiff in the individual case. This reason also may explain why

in the United States the media is not liable for merely negligently defaming public figures.[110] Simply put, the First Amendment free speech value is thought to trump consideration by the jury of the alleged careless reporting in the individual case. (Of course, in this setting, because the U.S. Supreme Court has rested the media's rights on the U.S. Constitution, no legislative overruling is available.)

This list of five reasons is meant to be only illustrative, not comprehensive. Other reasons that might be added to the list include, for example:

(6) Allowing a tort action for the conduct in question would unwisely interfere with the handling of the dispute between the parties in a different judicial forum.

(7) The facts to be uncovered and/or matters to be resolved are of a sort such that the judiciary is as likely to decide the case wrongly as rightly, so that to allow lawsuits of this sort to proceed will probably bring about widespread disrespect for the judiciary with accompanying detriment to the society in general.

(8) Allowing lawsuits like these will unleash collusion between plaintiffs and defendants that will so unfairly involve the courts in injustice as to make it socially more desirable to disallow such claims altogether.

(9) Permitting recovery would run afoul of separation-of-powers concerns, leading to the judgment that complaints, for example, about policy judgments made by executive and administrative actors should be brought, not as torts to be resolved in court, but rather through legislative, rule making, or other political processes instead.[111]

Before completing this discussion of what are usually termed "no-duty" rules, let me briefly address three more examples. One concerns the question of whether therapists should be obligated to take reasonable steps to protect third-party potential victims from threats to their lives made by the therapists' clients. This matter was addressed by the California Supreme Court in *Tarasoff v. Regents of the University of California,*[112] where a duty to act was imposed. But suppose a court were to rule that the therapist had no obligation to act even in a situation in which a jury would have concluded that the threat was so clear, and the readily available warning to the police so easy to give, that it was decidedly unreasonable for the therapist to have remained silent—a result reached in jurisdictions that reject *Tarasoff.*[113] Several of the many reasons set out above might justify such a result. One would be the trumping value of therapist/client privacy. A second would be the risk of perverse behavioral responses. For instance, dangerous clients may no longer seek counseling or no longer make disclosures in counseling that would promote helpful therapy. Or, therapists may involuntarily commit too many patients to mental hospitals. It might even be believed by some courts that therapist liability in these sorts of cases would drive all too many high-quality therapists from the profession—although common experience in California after *Tarasoff* strongly suggests the opposite.

Consider next possible claims by one divorcing spouse against the other (or both against each other) for the infliction of emotional distress. Although liability for this sort of wrongful conduct is allowed by some jurisdictions, it is rejected in others.[114] Again, more than one of the policy reasons earlier presented in support of "no-duty" rules might explain why courts would follow the latter route. One might be that allowing lawsuits risks upsetting the state's no-fault divorce regime by turning most divorces into fault-based tort contests. Another might be that the private understandings between spouses as to what is legitimate conduct in their marriage are so impenetrable that allowing such lawsuits threatens either a high proportion of erroneous decisions or the imposition of external standards that unwisely trump the autonomy of the parties to have the marital arrangement they created for themselves.

Finally, I tum to the still solid U.S. rule that there is no duty to go to the aid of "strangers." This rule means that affirmative assistance owed to another must rest upon a relationship that the courts view as more than a stranger relationship—a relationship that appropriately calls upon one to act for the benefit of another. The justification for the basic rule, however, is by no means self-evident, and it arguably rests upon one or more of the "no-duty" policy reasons set out above. Perhaps the broad liberty value not to get involved with others trumps a specific determination in this case that a trivial and evident effort was reasonably available to the defendant. Or perhaps this rule is based on the reason that imposing liability would lead to perverse behavioral responses—by unleashing unwanted and officious inter-meddlers, or by causing clumsy rescuers who now hold back to join in and do more harm than good, or by causing people undesirably to withdraw from social interaction with others. Or perhaps there are overriding concerns in the administration of justice that it will often be unclear toward whom the finger of responsibility to help the victim actually has been pointed. This would thereby lead to lawsuits either against an army of defendants or against one who is arbitrarily and unfairly singled out. I note that when a duty to aid another is imposed, it is because of the social relationship that the defendant has to the victim, a third party, or some property or the like of the defendant's. Hence, it might be argued that this consideration of social role should go with my discussion of social role under my Division 1. However, because the lack of any recognized social role grounds the denial of liability as a policy matter, I am content for that to be an issue for the defendant to assert and convince us about for one or more of the reasons that count under my Division 3.

VII. Remedies

I will say little here about my vision of Division 4, concerning remedies. I want only to emphasize that this would cover punitive damages. Traditionally, one of the main benefits of alleging and proving an intentional tort is that there is a good chance that punitive damages will be awarded (although clearly not for all such torts). Today, punitive damages are increasingly available for highly wrongful conduct that is not intentional in the traditional sense. Hence, my preference is to have initial liability based upon fault of whatever degree and to cover that liability, as noted already, in Division 1. Then for Division 1 cases of grave wrongdoing, the possibility of additional punitive damages would be addressed by the standards set out in Division 4.

Conclusion: A Restatement (Fourth) Of Torts And The Teaching Of Torts

In closing, I want to point out that were my approach adopted, it might alter considerably the way law professors would teach torts. I can envision a time when professors would first talk about cases in which victims claim that injurers should have said something different and then about cases in which victims claim that injurers should have done something different. Under both headings, a variety of injury contexts would be addressed, not limited only to physical harm to person or property. Next we would examine cases in which victims seek recovery without claiming that injurers should have acted differently at all. The two main heads of liability having been addressed, we would then examine cases in which defendants seek to reduce or eliminate their legal obligations for the sorts of defense reasons I discussed earlier. Last would come cases concerning the nature of the recovery that winning plaintiffs could obtain. With this much simplified structure, tort law, in my view, would be much easier to teach and to learn.

Experienced instructors will have noticed already that my approach eliminates several concepts, doctrines, and categories that are today commonly part of tort law. These include such matters as "immunity," the right to "informed consent," "assumption of risk," "the firefighter's rule," "occupier liability," and the like.

This simplification of tort doctrine would also give those who teach torts more time to focus on other topics, including alternatives to tort. Those topics are now all too often placed, if at all, in the back part of the casebooks and treatises. Often, they are not addressed in the first-year class, or only lightly covered. With more time, not only could we teach about alternative compensation mechanisms (both focused and general compensation schemes), but we could also give at least some attention to alternative means of serving the other goals of tort law (like promoting safety and punishing wrongdoing) through social interventions, including regulatory regimes, criminal law, and more.

ENDNOTES

1. RESTATEMENT (SECOND) OF TORTS: (1965).

2. RESTATEMENT OF TORTS: (1934).

3. AMERICAN LAW INSTITUTE, REPORTERS' STUDY, ENTERPRISE RESPONSIBILITY FOR PERSONAL INJURY (1991).

4. For my extensive review of the Reporters' Study, see Stephen D. Sugarman, A *Restatement of Torts,* 44 STAN. L. REV. 1163 (1992).

5. *See, e.g.,* Howard A. Latin, *The Preliminary Draft of a Proposed Restatement (Third) of Torts: Products Liability,* 15 J. PRODS. & TOXICS LIAB. 169, 177, 182 (1993).

6. RESTATEMENT (THIRD) OF TORTS: PRODUCTS LIABILITY (1998).

7. RESTATEMENT (THIRD) OF TORTS: APPORTIONMENT OF LIABILITY (2000).

8. *See* RESTATEMENT (THIRD) OF TORTS: LIABILITY FOR PHYSICAL HARM (BASIC PRINCIPLES) (Tentative Draft No. 1, 2001) [hereinafter Draft No. 1].

9. Symposium, *The John W. Wade Conference on the Third Restatement of Torts,* 54 VAND L. REV. 639 (2001).

10. Symposium, *The Restatement (Third) of Torts: and the Future of Tort Law,* 10 KAN J.L. & PUB. POL'Y 1 (2000).

11. RESTATEMENT (THIRD) OF TORTS: LIABILITY FOR PHYSICAL HARM (BASIC PRINCIPLES) (Tentative Draft No. 2, 2002) [hereinafter Draft No. 2].

12. RESTATEMENT (SECOND) OF TORTS: § 402A (1965).

13. *See* RESTATEMENT (THIRD) OF TORTS: PRODUCTS LIABILITY § 1 (1998).

14. *See* id. § 2(b)-(c).

15. *See* RESTATEMENT (SECOND) OF TORTS: PRODUCTS LIABILITY § 467 (1965).

16. *See* RESTATEMENT (THIRD) OF TORTS: APPORTIONMENT OF LIABILITY §§ A18-E21, at 160-271 (1999).

17. *See* Draft No. 1, *supra* note 8, § 5.

18. *See* id. § 1 & cmts.

19. *See* id. ch. 4 scope note, at 291-92.

20. *See, e.g.,* id. § 18 reporters' note.

21. RESTATEMENT (SECOND) OF TORTS §§ 13-20 (1965).

22. *Id.* § 21.

23. *Id.* § 35.

24. *Id.* § 525-557 A.

25. *Id.* § 558-581A.

26. *Id.* § 652A-6521.

27. *Id.* § 653-682.

28. *Id.* § 683-707A.

29. *Id.* § 821A-821F.

30. *Id.* § 762-774A.

31. *Id.* §841-864.

32. *Id.* § 868.

33. Gary T. Schwartz, *The Character of Early American Tort Law,* 36 UCLA L. REV. 641, 648-53 (1989).

34. *See generally* Stephen D. Sugarman, *Assumption of Risk,* 31 VAL U. L. REV. 833 (1997).

35. Draft No. I, *supra* note 8, § 5.

36. *Id.* § 6.

37. *Id.* §§ 20-25.

38. *Id.* § 3 cmts. & reporters' note.

39. *Id.* § 18 cmts. & reporters' note.

40. *Id.*§ 7; Draft No.2, *supra* note 11, § 7.

41. 162 N.E. 99 (N.Y. 1928)

42. Draft No. 2, *supra* note 11, § 26-28.

43. *Id.* §§ 29-34.

44. See Draft No. 1, *supra* note 8, § 5 & cmt. c.

45. *See* RESTATEMENT (SECOND) OF TORTS § 19 (1965).

46. *See* id. § 63.

47. *See* id. §§ 18, 63, 75.

48. *See* id. § 35.

49. *See* id. § 129.

50. For a thorough discussion, see DAN B. DOBBS, THE LAW OF TORTS 196-98 (2000).

51. *See* RESTATEMENT (SECOND) OF TORTS § 120A (1965).

52. *See,* e.g., Draft No. 1, *supra* note 8, §§ 9-12.

53. *See* RESTATEMENT (SECOND) OF TORTS §§ 328E-387 (1965).

54. *See* id. § 299A.

55. *See* id. §§ 388-4028.

56. For a more general appraisal of the role of social expectations in determining common law rights, see MELVIN A. EISENBERG, THE NATURE OF COMMON LAW 14-19 (1988).

57. Draft No. 1, *supra* note 8, § 18 cmt. g, at 263.

58. *See* RESTATEMENT (SECOND) OF TORTS §§ 329-32 (1965).

59. *See* Draft No. 1, *supra* note 8, § 18(b).

60. These injuries to recreational participants and spectators, illustrated by cases such as *Murphy v. Steeplechase Amusement* Co., 166 N.E. 173 (N.Y. 1929), which involved a ride called "The Flopper," and *Davidoff v. Metropolitan Baseball Club,* 463 N.E.2d 1219 (N.Y. 1984), are sometimes unhelpfully characterized as involving "assumption of risk." Better understood, they are simply examples of no breach, i.e., the defendant exercised due care. More precisely, they are examples of situations in which the defendant acted reasonably merely by warning, rather than by reducing or eliminating the risk.

61. *See* Byrne v. Boadle, 159 Eng. Rep. 299 (Ex. Ch. 1863).

62. 154 P.2d 687 (1944).

63. *Id.* at 688.

64. *See* Draft No. 1, *supra* note 8, § 17.

65. Adams v. Bullock, 125 N.E. 93, 94 (N.Y. 1919).

66. 159 F.2d 169 (2d Cir. 1947).

67. *Id.* at 173.

68. *See* id.

69. Draft No. 1, *supra* note 8, §§ 3, 13-16.

70. Draft No. 2, *supra* note 11, §§ 26-28.

71. *Id.* § 26.

72. *Id.* § 27.

73. *Id.*

74. *See id.* § 27 reporters' note (discussing cmt. a).

75. *See* RESTATEMENT (THIRD) OF TORTS: APPORTIONMENT OF LIABILITY § 4 (2000); Draft No.2, *supra* note 11, § 27 cmts.

76. *See, e.g.,* Summers v. Tice, 199 P.2d 1 (Cal. 1948).

77. RESTATEMENT OF AGENCY (1958).

78. *See* Draft No. 1, *supra* note 8, § 20.

79. *See* RESTATEMENT (THIRD) OF TORTS: PRODUCTS LIABILITY § 2(a) (1998).

80. *See* RESTATEMENT (THIRD) OF TORTS: APPORTIONMENT OF LIABILITY § 13 (2000).

81. *See* Harry Kalven, Jr., *Tort Watch,* 34 J. AM. TRIAL LAW. ASS'N 1, 2 (1972).

82. *See* Draft No. 1, *supra* note 8, § 20 cmt. b.

83. *See* RESTATEMENT (THIRD) OF TORTS: PRODUCTS LIABILITY § 2 cmt. a (1998).

84. RESTATEMENT (SECOND) OF TORTS § 197 (1965) deals with entry into land.

85. *Id.* § 263 (dealing with the conversion of chattels).

86. 124 N.W. 221 (Minn. 1910).

87. *Id.* at 221; *accord* Ploof v. Putnam, 71 A. 188, 189 (Vt. 1908).

88. 124 N.W. at 221-22.

89. Draft No. 1, *supra* note 8, § 21.

90. *Id.* § 22.

91. *Id.* § 23.

92. *See* RESTATEMENT (THIRD) OF TORTS: APPORTIONMENT OF LIABILITY §§ 1-9 (2000).

93. UNIF. COMPARATIVE FAULT ACT, 12 U.L.A. 123 (1996 & Supp. 2002).

94. *See* RESTATEMENT (SECOND) OF TORTS §§ 63, 70 (1965).

95. *See* RESTATEMENT (THIRD) OF TORTS: APPORTIONMENT OF LIABILITY § 1 cmt. c (2000).

96. *See id.* § 1 reporters' note.

97. *See* Draft No. 2, *supra* note 11, §§ 29-34.

98. *Id.* § 29.

99. *See* id. § 29 cmts. & notes.

100. Overseas Tankship (U.K.) Ltd. v. Morts Dock & Eng'g Co., (Wagon Mound I) [1961]1 A.C. 388 (P.C.) (appeal taken from Austl.).

101. Palsgraf v. Long Island R.R. Co., 162 N.E. 99 (N.Y. 1928).

102. Stultz v. Benson Lumber Co., 59 P.2d 100 (Cal. 1936).

103. Benn v. Thomas, 512 N.W.2d 537 (Iowa 1994).

104. McLaughlin v. Mine Safety Appliances Co., 181 N.E.2d 430 (N.Y. 1962).

105. Hines v. Garrett, 108 S.E. 690 (Va. 1921).

106. *See* Draft No. 2, *supra* note 11, § 30 (dealing with "unexpected extent" or the "eggshell skull"); id. § 33 (dealing with "intervening/superceding" causes).

107. *See, e.g.,* Knight v. Jewett, 834 P.2d 696,710-12 (Cal. 1992) (finding no duty for injury suffered during a touch football game).

108. *See* Strauss v. Belle Realty Co., 482 N.E.2d 34, 38 (N.Y. 1985).

109. See, for example, the Supreme Court of Canada's decision in *ex rel. Dobson v. Dobson* [1999] D.L.R. 148, in which no duty was found. *But see* Bonte v. Bonte, 616 A.2d 464, 466 (N.H.1992) (finding a duty).

110. N.Y. Times Co. v. Sullivan, 376 U.S. 254 *passim* (1964).

111. For an even longer list of possible reasons for denying a victim the right to recover in tort, see Jane Stapleton, *Duty of Care Factors: A Selection from the judicial Menus, in* THE LAW OF OBLIGATIONS: ESSAYS IN CELEBRATION OF JOHN FLEMING 59,92-95 (Peter Cane &Jane Stapleton eds., 1998).

112. 551 P.2d 334 (Cal. 1976).

113. *See,* e.g., Nasser v. Parker, 455 S.E.2d 502 *passim* (Va. 1995).

114. *See generally* Ira Mark Ellman & Stephen D. Sugarman, *Spousal Emotional Abuse as a Tort,* 55 MD. L. REV. 1268 (1996).

Chapter 17

The American Law Institute's "Enterprise Liability" Project was Abandoned too Soon

In 1986, the American Law Institute ("ALI") launched a project charged with taking a wider view of U.S. tort law, and in 1991 the ALI published "Enterprise Responsibility for Personal Injury." This chapter provides a substantial review and evaluation of this project. Volume I of the Reporters' Study provides a wealth of information about the wider field of compensation of those suffering personal injuries, as well as a somewhat wider look at safety promotion outside of tort law. Volume II explores a range of possible legislative reforms of tort law. In a sense this project can be seen as something of a launching pad for this book of essays.

This ALI project came at a time when "tort reform" was decidedly on the political front burner. But the legislative agenda realistically under consideration was a series of one-way cutbacks in victim rights that was being promoted by defense-side interests. The Reporters' Study provides a far more balanced set of recommendations.

Nonetheless, as described in this chapter, the ALI membership did not know how to deal sensibly with the project's output. Plaintiff personal injury lawyers, as described in Chapter 2 of this book, had become the effective voice for victims, and their political goal was to maintain the status quo so far as the legislative process was concerned. Clients of defense lawyers probably thought they were doing better and could ultimately achieve more by keeping to their agenda rather than what was proposed in the ALI report.

ALI members are supposed to put their own and their own clients' financial interests aside as they carry out ALI business – never an easy role for a number of the members. This seemed especially so when a report came before the membership that envisioned legislative action in the realm of personal injury law – a far cry from the traditional "Restatement" work of the ALI. In the end the ALI dropped this project and took up instead a multi-decade process of turning out the Restatement (Third) of Torts – a process that is still going on.

While that change in direction was perhaps inevitable, the "enterprise liability" project was abandoned too soon. This chapter revives that effort. Readers will see early signs of the various "ideological" outlooks on accidents that are more fully discussed in Chapter 1 of this book. There are also discussions of damages reform that are further explored in this book in Chapters 7 and 8 from a comparative law perspective, as well as potential changes in how we deal with medical injuries as described in more detail in Chapter 10 of this book. With tort reform currently much less of a hot-button political issue, perhaps it is time to return to a consideration of the wider findings and recommendation of the Reporters' Study.

This review of the Reporters' Study was published as Stephen D. Sugarman, "A Restatement of Torts," 44 Stanford Law Review 1163-1208 (1992) and is reprinted with permission of the journal.

A Restatement of Torts

I. INTRODUCTION AND THE WIDER CONTEXT

In 1986 the American Law Institute (ALI), which is most well known for its "Restatement of the Law" efforts, launched an ambitious project to evaluate contemporary personal injury law. Five years later, the ALI published and put before the membership of the Institute the results of that project in a massive two volume Reporters' Study.[1]

In May 1991, at the Institute's meetings devoted to discussion of the Study, which I attended, several members complained that this project was, unfortunately, unlike the ALI's previous endeavors. They argued that the study was inappropriately political or policy-oriented, in contrast to what a Restatement (Third) of Torts might have been.

These complaints are ironic. First, most of the important recommendations of the Study can readily be described as modifications of the ALI's Restatement (Second) of Torts. At the same time, it is naive to suggest that key changes made in the first Restatement of Torts by the second were not also driven by policy or politics. The most obvious and important example is section 402A concerning manufacturers' strict liability for product defects.[2] Section 402A did not "restate" the dominant common law rule in America circa 1964; rather it reflected the judgment of the ALI as to what the law should be.[3] With the ALI's imprimatur, the new doctrine soon swept the nation.

If important policy-driven changes in tort law were comfortably ushered in by the Second Restatement, why did this ALI report generate so much criticism? Why was Dean William Prosser, the ALI's Chief Reporter for the Second Restatement able to obtain consensus in the 1960s, but in 1991 no real consensus could be reached within the ALI with respect to any of the important recommendations made by the Study?[4]

Tort law is much more politicized today than it was in the early 1960s, when personal injury attorneys mainly handled auto accidents. Today a sophisticated and specialized bar exists in the fields of products liability, medical malpractice, and environmental torts. Similarly, tort law then was neither a major concern of, nor a threat to, most large enterprises. All this, of course, has changed.[5]

One symptom of this change is that, while the project was underway, several subgroups within the ALI were fiercely battling each other over tort reform in numerous legislative and other arenas. Predictably, these factions were unwilling, even in a more august forum, to cast aside positions they have long and vigorously argued, tum their backs on the interests of their clients and constituents, and compromise.[6] The reform proposal that the Study offers is itself a compromise. Whether it is the right compromise is another matter, one to be addressed in due course. But discussion at the ALI meetings might have been more fruitful and less harsh, cynical, and adversarial had the members on both sides of the battle line regarded the recommendations as a package rather than as a series of individual ideas to attack.

Another thing that contributed to the Study being attacked is the fundamental change in the academic study of tort law that has occurred since the last ALI report was undertaken. When Prosser was the reporter for the Restatement (Second) of Torts, he was already the author of his famed horn-book.[7] As such, he was immersed in "doctrine"; his approach was shaped by his own distillation of countless decisions by countless courts over countless years. He, and the other leaders of the time, like Yale's Fleming James, were interested in "policy" and the social functions of tort law. However, he promoted change in traditionally familiar language suited to common law evolution.

Today, the study of tort doctrine is not so fashionable. Case law analysis has been supplanted in academia by an onslaught of theoretical and empirical analyses from various schools of thought, including "law and economics," "moral philosophy," "critical legal studies;' and "law and society." Moreover, arguments for detailed changes in tort law are as likely to be directed at the legislative as the judicial process.

In fact, the tide was already turning at the time of the ALI's endorsement of Section 402A. Alfred Conard and his colleagues were just reporting on their monumental study of the auto accident compensation system;[8] Jeffrey O'Connell and (now) Judge Robert Keeton's blueprint for auto no-fault was in the making;[9] and Dean Guido Calabresi's path breaking work that lead to the publication in 1970 of his *The Costs of Accidents* [10] was underway.

To be sure, doctrinal development did not die with the adoption of Section 402A. To the contrary, when I began teaching torts in 1972, an enormous number of the rules I had learned during my first year at Northwestern Law School in 1964-65 had already been overturned. By the time I published my first substantial article in the field in 1985,[11] the subject had been transformed. Nevertheless, it is my strong belief that as my generation of torts professors have more new "law" to keep up with, we also write less about "law" in Prosser's way. Indeed, judging by the Study, one of the last places to find lucid thinking about the desirable direction of tort law is in the published opinions of state and federal judges.

Evidencing this shift away from doctrinal concerns was the appointment by Professor Geoffrey Hazard, the ALI director, of Richard Stewart as the original Chief Reporter for the new ALI torts study in 1986. Stewart is a brilliant scholar, best known for his work in administrative law and environmental law, but he is not generally considered a "torts man." Similarly, when Stewart left the project part way through to go to the Department of Justice, his replacement, Paul Weiler, was known primarily for his splendid work in the labor field, not tort law. Indeed, several of the very talented Associate Reporters and lead Contributors for the project are more noted for their work in other, albeit sometimes adjacent, fields. For example, while Robert Rabin is plainly one of the torts "stars," Kenneth Abraham and Alan Schwartz are more closely associated with insurance and contract law, respectively.

Selecting a team of reporters not primarily steeped in tort doctrine would have seemed odd in 1960, but given the changes in the field, it was an astute choice in the late 1980s. Hazard and Stewart are to be commended for their insight. Yet the predictable upshot of these changes in context between the Restatement (Second) of Torts and this study, indicative of the times and the talent, was that the Study reads very differently from the reports that Prosser and his colleagues produced.

Not surprisingly, then, the loudest cries of protest against the un-abashedly policy-driven report came from judges and lawyers whose first allegiance is to the more doctrinal approach of Prosser. Another consideration seems to have been that some ALI members still see the function of the Institute as one of sorting through and making sense of the case law, and then taking a leadership role in the guiding of future common law decision- making. But this is a process that is very difficult to undertake for tort law today when, for several years now, so much of the action has been in the legislative arena.

I do not mean to suggest that no law professors launched attacks on the report. Some did, and, in a few cases, they attacked passionately. These critics generally shared the view that the common law of torts is both good and important because it compensates individual victims who have been wronged and that, on balance, the Study is pro-defendant and therefore needs to be discredited. Ironically, compared to legislative reforms in some jurisdictions, adopting the recommendations of the Study in full arguably would produce substantial gains for plaintiffs.

Some professors complained that the study disregarded important intellectual perspectives on tort law. This is a delicate problem. A report that takes a reasonably coherent stance on the future direction of tort law could not possibly embrace the enormous diversity of opinion currently present in academia.[12] The Reporters had little choice but to emphasize their preferred perspective -- which is best described as Calabresian.

In *The Costs of Accidents,* Calabresi argued that society's policy towards accidents should be to minimize the sum of primary, secondary, and tertiary accident costs. Reducing primary costs concerns promoting safety (while not discouraging, if possible, socially desirable innovation). Reducing secondary costs concerns spreading the costs of compensation paid to accident victims. Tertiary costs are the transactions costs; these costs include the costs of lawyers' fees, insurance administration, the parties' time, and court costs.

While the Study pays lip service to other aims of tort law, in the end it evaluates the existing regime and its potential alternatives primarily in terms of their role in primary and secondary cost reduction: (1) how well they channel human behavior in socially desirable ways, and (2) how well they provide accident victims appropriate compensation.

To its credit, the Study employs the Calabresian framework in an expansive way. Whereas Calabresi has given some attention to auto no-fault as an institutional alternative to tort law, he has not focused a great deal of attention on other institutional alternatives.[13] By contrast, the Study does so. Launching a serious inquiry into a wide range of institutional alternatives is Stewart's most important contribution.[14]

Although I believe that there is widespread support within the academy for Calabresi's framework, there plainly are other points of view. Not everyone sees tort law and its alternatives in such an instrumental way. For example, many commentators, including the academics who complained at the ALI meeting, emphasize individual justice. These commentators believe that people who are wronged deserve to have a mechanism through which they can right those wrongs, and it is an obligation of our democratic society to provide such a mechanism no matter the cost.

In my writing I have largely devalued this corrective justice goal because I am convinced both that we have no coherent and agreed theory of corrective justice and that, in practice, tort law ill serves any defensible theory of justice. [15] The Study likewise dismisses the idea of a quest for justice.[16] Following Calabresi, it adopts the position that the principles of justice essentially serve as a constraint on the way that accident cost minimization is implemented.

Having studied the alternatives, the Study concludes that there still is an important role for personal injury law, albeit a reformed law. The reporters believe that enterprise liability for personal injury has important, socially desirable behavioral consequences for primary cost reduction that should not be abandoned. Furthermore, they believe these results cannot be achieved as well through other institutional arrangements. Also, the Study finds that at least some needy people are well compensated by tort law, and is skeptical about the political viability, or (in some cases) the desirability, of alternatives. Notwithstanding these strengths, the Study recognizes that the current tort system is expensive to administer and proposes some cost reduction techniques.

Were I to flatter myself, I would say that the Study is a long response to my odyssey through Calabresi's framework, one which led me[17] to quite a different conclusion. I too canvassed the institutional alternatives, but found them far more promising, at least in principle. In addition, I found the primary cost reduction effects of tort law unpersuasive compared with available alternatives. Ironically, I stand together with the advocates of tort law as a provider of individual justice on this: We are skeptical that so much of the Study's defense of tort law can be sustained on appeals to its positive behavioral consequences. As a result, I find the tertiary costs of operating the current system more damning than does the Study.

Although we part company on the broader analysis, when it comes to the details of how tort law should be reformed now, the Study and I are close on many important items, especially those in which the Study turns away from the imperatives of behavioral channeling and to the requirements of sensible compensation.

II. THE INSTITUTIONAL ALTERNATIVES

Before turning in detail to the Study's recommendations, contained in volume II, I will describe and discuss volume I, "The Institutional Framework." Although it bears the hallmarks of separate authorship, volume I is a skillfully knit and bountiful primer on a wide array of important topics. What's more, in certain places it is quite insightful. Volume I is especially helpful background reading both for torts people who are unaware of the wide range of institutional alternatives discussed in recent scholarship and for the ALI's general membership, whose main work lies outside tort law. I too found many chapters quite informative.

Volume I tells the same story four times. First comes Weiler's overview of the Volume. The following seven chapters discuss the various institutional settings considered by the Study. These include the tort law/liability insurance (chapter 2) and its many complementary and/or competing schemes, such as first-party insurance, regulation, markets, and focused compensation plans (chapters 3-8). Chapters 9 through 12 examine similar issues organized in terms of the injury setting. In particular, the Study examines workplace, product, medical, and environmental injuries. Chapter 13 offers a second overview, comparing the competing arrangements' ability to modify behavior, provide compensation, and other desirable social functions as revealed by empirical data. In my view, to be told something four times by different, thoughtful people with different points of view is not a bad thing.

A. *Five Models*

Tort law and its alternatives may be categorized in many ways. In this section, I offer five competing institutional arrangements for handling accidents. My models are not water-tight, but I offer them for heuristic purposes; moreover, I have given them labels drawn from political philosophy, broadly, right to left, that are meant to be suggestive, more than definitive.

1. *The Libertarian model*

The first model is the Libertarian alternative. Under this approach, members of society rely primarily upon the market to determine standards of conduct and provide compensation for accidental injuries. Government protects property from theft and intentional destruction, enforces contracts and, I suppose, punishes fraud. Voluntary market transactions, however, determine the degree of risk people will accept in the goods and services they consume. The market also provides insurance of all kinds. The dominant value is liberty; the social picture is a result of millions of decentralized decisions about risk.

2. *The Conservative model*

The historic tort law/liability insurance option I call the Conservative model, both because it reflects the status quo for many types of accidents and because many of the values it embodies are conservative. In this model, government establishes legal rights and wrongs with respect to risk-taking beyond those created by contract. But those rights are enforced only when they are asserted by individuals. Fault is the fundamental criterion by which both wrongdoing and the right to compensation are identified. Behavior is meant to be controlled through private threats to assert these rights via lawsuits claiming money damages. (Hence, the judiciary, not the executive, is the public agency of social control.) Compensation, when provided, is intended to be full, with two further conservative consequences. First, by providing more compensation to the disabled high earner than to the disabled laborer, the law reinforces pre-existing inequalities in income and wealth that were upset by the injury-triggering event; second, by compensating for intangible loss ("pain and suffering"), the law caters to individual feelings of indignity and outrage)[18]

3. *The Liberal model*

Focused compensation plans, of which workers' compensation is the most prominent example, characterize what I call the Liberal model. This alternative is more interventionist than traditional tort law in several ways. Like other liberal ideas, little weight is put on individual fault. Instead, larger institutional forces are thought to be responsible for causing the majority of injuries, and institutions are obligated to compensate their victims. Compensation, although comprehensively wide (perhaps excluding intentional self-injurers), is not meant to be full. The aim is to assure that the basic material needs of the ordinary citizen are met. The focused compensation plan, like the traditional tort system, can be seen as a single societal instrument used both to control conduct and provide compensation. Because the funding mechanisms of these plans internalize the costs of accidents to specifically responsible institutions, they are meant to discourage dangerous activities and promote their safe performance.

4. *The Collective model.*

What I call the Collective model is more interventionist than the Liberal model in two critical ways. First, accident victims are not singled out based upon the specific type of accident they suffer, e.g., auto, medical, or product. In fact, accident victims are not treated separately or differently from the disabled generally; accident victims, like those suffering from disease, birth defects, and so on need medical care and income protection. Indeed, accident victims may be treated as part of a much broader class of citizens, including the unemployed and the retired, for whom collective protection against loss is assured. Social insurance is the mechanism used to compensate the protected class and, as with focused compensation plans, its goal is to meet the basic material needs of its beneficiaries. Social insurance funding may be unrelated to behavior-channeling goals, relying instead on effective revenue-generating devices such as payroll and income taxes. This gives rise to the second contrast with focused compensation schemes. Under the Collective model, behavior control must be accomplished independent of compensation, through government regulation.

5. *The Socialist model*

Finally, there is what I call the Socialist alternative.[19] Its compensation side is not sharply differentiated from the Collective option. However, this alternative precludes the range of wealth and income inequalities permitted or encouraged by the other alternatives. It protects accident victims and others by nationalizing health care and providing a minimum guaranteed income for all. Under the Socialist model, behavior control is accomplished by a collective commitment to risk-sharing that is far greater than under other models. There is less freedom for individual risk-taking and risk-creating, and hence less diversity in the risk levels to which people are exposed. This greater equality with respect to the exposure to risk comes about not only through reductions in the levels of risk created in the society but also through collective ownership of, and worker control, over large enterprises that create risk.

Our actual experience in the United States, of course, neither runs the gamut of these five models, nor always fits neatly into just one of the boxes. But the models represent ideologically distinctive approaches to the control of risk and the personal injury consequences of risk. As we move through the models, managing risk and providing compensation shift from individual matters to matters of increasingly wider social responsibility. Thus, the focus of compensation shifts away from the individual and the particular to the group and the general, and the process for determining which risks are socially acceptable shifts from the decentralized to the increasingly centralized.

Obviously, as tort law shifts towards mass victim claims proceedings, ignores defendant fault, reduces its insistence on clear defendant-plaintiff causal-connections, and pays out damage amounts that are much less finely tuned to individual circumstances, it ceases to be traditional tort law. It thereby loses many of its conservative characteristics and begins to take on those of the focused compensation plan of the Liberal Model, albeit a compensation plan organized and operated under the supervision of the judiciary.

Combined models, which reject ideological purity in favor of pragmatic considerations, offer additional possibilities. Viewing the models as complementary rather than mutually exclusive, society could employ both cascading compensation arrangements (tort plus compensation plans and/or social insurance) and cascading control mechanisms (tort plus focused plan funding plus government regulation). Society, too, at least in certain respects, can decide to apply one model to some accidents and another model to others.

Before 1900, the United States largely combined reliance on the Conservative and Libertarian models. Today, no modem industrialized society relies exclusively, or even predominantly, on the Libertarian model. At present our nation's policy towards those suffering personal injuries and the prevention of accidents is decidedly mixed, combining elements of the Conservative, Liberal, and Collective models. This is contrasted, for example, with New Zealand where the Collective model predominates.

B. *Markets, First Party Insurance, and The Libertarian Model*

The Study gives little support to the Libertarian model even though it is keen on the idea that social welfare is maximized when individual consumers decide how much risk they are willing to assume and how much they will pay for safety.[20] The Study nonetheless recognizes that unregulated markets are unlikely to achieve the socially optimal level of risk.

One shortcoming of the Libertarian model, although the Study gives it precious little attention, is that many accidents involve parties with no market relationship to each other. Environmental spills, ultrahazardous activities such as dynamite blasting or other conduct covered by section 520 of the Restatement (Second), and fires that spread from one land owner to another are likely to involve injury to parties previously unknown to each other. Extreme libertarians might imagine these problems being solved through private land use schemes -- voluntary covenants, entered into in advance, that would control conduct and provide remedies if breached. But this solution would entail enormous transaction costs to make the necessary arrangements. Therefore, most people find this solution implausible, believing that collective standard setting, through either tort law or government intervention, is required to regulate these externalities.

Even in circumstances where the parties are in a market relationship, there are market failure problems. One of the central problems the Study identifies is that the market alone may not provide sufficient information for consumers to make reasoned choices about risk, and that, even if well informed, consumers may mistakenly make choices that are not in their best interest.[21] Government intervention beyond that contemplated by the Libertarian model is then necessary to deal with these market failures.

The authors emphasize that much could be gained if social intervention assured that people were adequately warned.[22] Without doubting that in the slightest, adequate warning alone fails to contend with other problems already identified, namely, unforeseen third parties, harm to others, and people's failure to act in their own best interest. Moreover, it is, of course, one thing to favor effective warnings and another to believe that tort law actually promotes them (a matter to be taken up below).

One empirical finding on risk perception that the authors stress is that although people devalue risks of which they are unaware, they tend to overreact to small risks of which they are somewhat aware: They might, for example, refuse to purchase a product when it would really be in their best interest to do so.[23] This shows that social intervention to make people realistic about risk in both directions has its place. On the other hand, being told once about a small risk by no means assures that when later confronted by it a person is still meaningfully informed; those settings may prompt under reaction, rather than over reaction.[24] The authors acknowledge this point by emphasizing the concept of the salience of a risk.[25]

This would have been a splendid occasion to provide a synthetic analysis of a range of problems concerning the inadequate awareness of, and inappropriate response to, risk. Examples include the issue of informed consent to medical treatment, the sorts of warnings landowners are required to give different classes of occupiers, and the related question of when warnings are inadequate, requiring instead that the danger be removed, as well as the role of warnings in product liability cases. The current tort law responses to these issues are strewn throughout the Restatement. Unfortunately, the Study misses this opportunity and focuses only on product dangers.

Private disability and life insurance, which in the Libertarian model provide financial protection for losses arising from accidental injury or death, are discussed in chapter 5. The Study explains that private disability insurance today plainly fails to cover all those disabled by accidents. For example, it notes that "loss insurance does not come close to paying the full economic losses of those who bring tort actions" and emphasizes that the gaps are "most severe for the seriously injured victim."[26] From the Libertarian perspective this might simply mean that many individuals have elected not to insure against the risk of their own disability. But, as the Study points out, incomplete coverage of disability insurance is an inevitable result of the first party insurance market.[27]

Like insurers generally, those selling individual disability insurance policies must worry about adverse selection and moral hazard. Adverse selection concerns the problem of purchasers who are at greater risk than the insurer realizes. This is a particularly acute problem for disability insurers because buyers may be aware of their own physical and mental condition in ways unfathomable to the insurer. Moral hazard concerns the problem that the existence of the insurance itself has a tendency to increase what otherwise would be the incidence of disability. The insured may act in ways which increase his chances of becoming disabled, or he might feign disability. Insurers respond to adverse selection through underwriting practices. They scrutinize potential buyers and set premiums in accordance with risk classifications. They try to combat moral hazard, among other things, by providing only partial replacement of the loss of current income and by requiring participation in rehabilitation.

In practice, this means that useful disability insurance is not widely marketed to individual blue collar workers or to those more concerned about protecting their anticipated future earnings than their current income, such as children, students, temporary homemakers and the unemployed. Even among white collar workers and professionals, those who are evidently most at risk may well be uninsurable. Furthermore, many of those who might purchase disability insurance fail to appreciate the nature of the risk they face and gamble against becoming disabled contrary to their own best interest. Others make this gamble because they overestimate how well they are protected by other forms of disability insurance such as job-based group disability insurance and social security. Group disability insurance that is provided to an enterprise's entire workforce eliminates some of the coverage problems; but it, of course, is only available where employers choose to provide it (even if they make the employees pay for it)—and today many don't.

The Study gives brief attention to the idea of mandatory disability insurance.[28] This, of course, would not be a solution for the Libertarian model, nor the Conservative or Liberal models. Mandatory disability insurance, rather, is one way to implement the Collective model. Therefore, it may be misleading to say it would be dramatic overkill (and very expensive) to deal with the compensation goals of tort law through mandatory disability insurance, as the authors do.[29] After all, on this basis the existing, and effectively mandatory, life and disability insurance provisions of the social security system are already overly broad when it comes to compensating accident victims, let alone victims of another's fault, because social security also protects victims of disease and of congenital disabilities, as well as those who carelessly injure themselves. But it hardly seems sensible to criticize this over breadth. It simply reflects the fact that the Collective model identifies those to be compensated differently than do other models.

From the viewpoint of the Collective model, the real question is whether social security's existing disability insurance scheme should be expanded. It might, for example, provide more generous benefit levels, cover some partial disabilities, and apply to people who do not have substantial recent attachment to the labor force. In the alternative, similar results could be sought through insurance schemes organized at the state level or through required employment-based disability insurance.

Chapter 5 seeks to distance tort reform from reform that guarantees disability protection, suggesting only that the latter "does warrant careful evaluation on its own terms."[30] This is somewhat unsatisfying, both because the Study does not go on to make that evaluation and because, were disability (and health) insurance to be provided to everyone, the compensatory role for tort law would be dramatically decreased and possibly eliminated.

C. *Workers' Compensation and the Liberal Model*

The Study, in chapter 3, paints a reasonably positive picture of the workers' compensation system. Adopted in America in the 1910s and sharply strengthened since 1970, workers' compensation exemplifies the Liberal alternative to tort law. It provides reasonable medical, income replacement, and rehabilitation benefits to workers injured on the job, promptly and without much attention to fault. Because the job setting is broadly under the control of employers, they are required to pay regardless of whether there is anything they might have done to avoid the accident.

The Study identifies several problems with this system, particularly regarding victim compensation.[31] First, the system's coverage of occupational disease is poor. Second, periodic payments to those suffering long term disabilities have not been subject to regular cost of living adjustments. Because these benefits may seriously erode in value, they fail to provide the compensation intended by the Liberal model. Third, because the future work prospects of those suffering from partial permanent disabilities are so unpredictable, compensation is problematic. The traditional system, which awards a worker a specific sum on the ground that she has been X percent disabled or has suffered type Y impairment, over compensates some and under compensates others. Finally, administrative costs for seriously injured workers are high, especially when compared to social security. Nevertheless, workers' compensation remains an administrative bargain compared to tort law.

As a technical matter, the inflation problem can readily be solved; it is a matter of political will. As for the prediction problem confronting those with partial permanent disabilities, the Study points out that important strides already appear to have been made in some jurisdictions. Benefits in these jurisdictions more carefully track actual individual wage loss over time and separately award compensation for the impairment itself.

The occupational disease problem, however, is more difficult. Employees change jobs. Many of these diseases are the result of cumulative exposure, including non-job exposure. Causal links between individual workers and job exposure are often hard to prove. Hence, solving this problem may require moving away from the Liberal model to the Collective model, in which connecting the disease to a specific institutional source is not relevant. As the Study suggests in chapter 3, this shift should also reduce administrative costs. To the extent the Collective model is already in place in America through the social security system, we are again faced with the policy issue described in the previous section. Social security already covers occupational diseases with serious consequences. Thus, the question is whether social security should be improved generally, which in turn would benefit those disabled from occupational diseases.

On the other hand, it is clear that the Study authors worry that abandoning the focused funding obligation of workers' compensation could lead to an increase in the injury rate. On the behavioral impact side, the Study reports that the more generous the workers' compensation benefits are, the higher the level of claims filed. This is especially true for "'softer,' less visible muscle or back injuries."[32] At the same time, recent work has found that because the funding obligation of worker's compensation is focused on employers and, for medium and large employers, varies with their claims experience, it has had a powerful impact on reducing the injury rate. Presumably, employers have increased their efforts to provide a safe work-place in order to save compensation costs.[33]

I am skeptical that the workers' compensation system is truly as powerful in promoting safety as the Study suggests. Apart from workers' compensation premiums, government regulation, and tort suits, employers already have strong incentives to make the workplace safe. On-the-job injuries cause disruption, loss of morale, and productivity losses. A replacement must be hired and trained. Without the workers' compensation obligation, the employer might well be concerned about the medical costs the worker would impose on the employer's health plan.

More generally, the Study's examination of focused compensation plans is both somewhat narrow and fragmented. For example, it fails to deal with the overlap in coverage between workers' compensation and the typical employer's health insurance plan. It never discusses focused compensation plans, existing and proposed, as a package. Chapter 13 of volume I discusses some of these ideas briefly.[34] Further discussions of compensation plans are also contained in chapters 14 and 15 of volume 11.[35]

D. *Health Insurance, Social Insurance, Regulation, and the Collective Model*

I was delighted to see the Study devote chapters to institutional arrangements that are essential to evaluating the alternative I have called the Collective model. Tort law professors and practitioners are often accused of knowing little about health insurance and social insurance. Chapters 4 and 6 of the Study provide some good basic information.[36]

Chapter 4 traces the history of health insurance in the United States to its current, unsatisfactory, hodgepodge of arrangements.[37] Group plans sponsored by employers form the core of our system. Medicare and Medicaid provide important governmental support for the elderly, the disabled, and the poor. Unfortunately, our nation's health care costs are out of control, there are many holes in the system, and those without regular health insurance arrangements receive fewer and lower quality health services than do other Americans.

As the Study notes, "It would be rash, therefore, to dismiss out of hand the role that tort damage awards play in providing a form of health insurance for the victims of enterprise injuries."[38] But this conclusion is less a form of praise for the Conservative model than a commentary on our failure to embrace the Collective health care model. The Conservative model, after all, provides health care only to certain accident victims, and at enormous cost. Many other industrialized societies have long had health care systems that are reasonably comprehensive. Were we to adopt, say, the Canadian system that has been much discussed of late—or even some sort of mandatory employer-provided health insurance combined with broadened coverage by Medicare and Medicaid—the role for tort law could be sharply curtailed. Whether broad health care reform of that sort is soon forthcoming is difficult to predict, even though nearly all those who have studied our health care system agree that it demands prompt attention.

The Study could have said more about the extent to which seriously injured tort victims eventually gain access to Medicare and Medicaid. Also, a discussion of the ways in which tort law's definition of medical damages relates to typical health insurance coverage would be useful. But, apparently, little hard data is currently available on these questions.

The Study's remarks in chapter 6 on social insurance also reveal that the United States has not embraced the Collective model with regard to income replacement the way competitor nations have.[39] Our social security system does provide moderate, wage-related benefits to totally disabled people, their young children, and dependent spouses when the disabled person has had substantial recent attachment to the labor force. Also when former workers die (including death from accidents that might be covered by tort law or workers' compensation), social security provides moderate wage-related pensions to surviving children and to the decedent's elderly dependent spouse or parents. But there is no national scheme for the partially permanently disabled or the temporarily disabled.

State workers' compensation plans fill part of the income replacement gap but also overlap partially with social security. For non-occupational disabilities, however, there is no comprehensive state-level scheme. A few states provide temporary disability insurance programs for workers. Otherwise, most people must rely upon their own savings and whatever sick leave and temporary disability insurance their employers might provide.

Once more, tort law can fill some gaps in the compensation system. It remains, however, an expensive and incomplete system for filling those gaps. Our nation could more fully implement the Collective model with respect to income replacement; many creative options exist. For example, even without action by the federal government, states could require workers' compensation benefits to cover employees and their dependents around the clock. Alternatively, they could focus the workers' compensation income replacement function on serious injuries, make reasonable sick leave plans mandatory, and adopt employee-paid, temporary income replacement plans covering disabilities of all sorts.

On the compensation side, a true Socialist model would imply even more dramatic changes both in the health care system[40] and in the income transfer system. But the Study does not really begin to address this alternative.

The Study examines regulation in chapter 8.[41] Recognizing the need for effective behavior control mechanisms and acknowledging the shortcomings of the market, the Study characterizes the policy choice in terms of the Collective model (government regulation) and the Conservative model (tort law). The Socialist approach to risk control is ignored, and, more surprisingly, no comparison is made to the Liberal model's focused obligations to fund compensation plans, despite the Study's support for workers' compensation.

The Study also confines itself to federal regulation. While national regulation is uniform, more well-known, and has been the subject of careful empirical studies, ignoring state and local regulation is a significant omission. In any event, the Study offers fair criticisms of existing regulatory schemes, noting for example, their inadequate enforcement and their incomplete coverage of risks.[42] It recognizes, however, both that these problems might be alleviated and that tort law, as a system of behavior control, has serious shortcomings.[43]

E. *Tort Law, Liability Insurance, and the Conservative Model*

In the introductory chapter to volume I, the Study states, "Anyone conducting a fair-minded review of trends and analyses over the last several decades would have to concede the flaws in tort law's performance."[44] But the Study's general chapter on tort law and liability insurance does not address those "flaws" as the reader might expect. Rather, after providing basic information on the tort system's financial scale, its increasing cost over time, and the growing number of large verdicts,[45] the Study in chapter 2 turns its attention to the liability insurance crisis of the mid-1980s.

The Study attempts to make sense of the many competing explanations for the skyrocketing liability insurance rates (especially for product liability, medical malpractice, and municipal liability insurance) and the occasional complete unavailability of insurance associated with the tort crisis.[46] It asserts that "the evolution of the underwriting cycle, the growth of tort law, the tendency of this body of law in some instances to promote adverse selection, market conditions, and increased uncertainty regarding the scope and magnitude of modern tort law" all played a part.[47] As for the relative importance of these factors, the

Study concludes "we are persuaded that a significant share of the responsibility for what occurred in the liability insurance markets during the decade of the 1980's was caused by developments within the civil liability system."[48] At the same time, the Study is skeptical that the reforms so far enacted in response to the crisis have had, or are likely to have, much of an impact on tort costs and insurability. The main exception noted is the imposition of a tight cap on recoveries for pain and suffering; that solution, however, is one which the Study opposes for reasons explained in volume II. Further discussion of the Conservative model is provided in the context of specific accident settings referred to by the Study as the "upper tiers of high-stakes and very-high-stakes litigation."[49]

The Study's chapter on product injuries draws two significant conclusions. Regarding compensation, the Study says: "It is generally more efficient to insure once and for all against the entire set of risks a person faces rather than purchase insurance on a product by product basis, as occurs, in effect, through product liability."[50] This conclusion takes no stance on the comparative desirability of either the Libertarian solution, in which individuals elect whether to purchase insurance, or the Collective solution, in which insurance is assured. With respect to safety promotion, the Study concludes: "[A] general endorsement of the efficiency of the tort system is unwarranted. [T]he amounts of compensation provided are generally insufficient to promote efficient levels of deterrence."[51]

It has been strongly asserted that tort law discourages desirable product innovation.[52] On that issue, the Study concludes that the evidence to date is mixed.[53] On the other hand, it expresses concern about negative impacts on product development from another direction. In contrast to the tenor of its chapter on regulation generally, government control of product safety, the Study asserts in chapter 9, is often too stringent, rather than incomplete or unenforced.[54] By demanding more safety than is socially desirable, government regulation keeps some products from the public and makes others more expensive than they need be.[55]

The Study finds fault with tort law's response to medical malpractice as well. Tort law, the study concludes, vastly under compensates most malpractice victims, if it compensates them at all.[56] The tort system also falls short as a deterrent. The Study notes, for example, that "it is questionable whether [more] suits would reduce the amount of malpractice."[57] The "apparently ...limited effect" tort law has in producing safer medical care is attributed to the fact that it is directed towards individual physicians, most of whose errors "consist in inadvertent mistakes and slipups caused by momentary inattention-the kind of behavior that the tort system is least likely to influence effectively."[58] The Study also attributes medical malpractice insurance's fiscal crisis, marked by unpredictable rate increases and fabulously high premiums in some specialties, to the fact that this insurance is directed at, and generally paid for by, individual physicians.[59]

The Study is also not much impressed with the record to date of the Collective model's regulatory approach to physician control.[60] However, the Study does suggest that recently required hospital risk-management programs might have some positive effect.[61]

F. *Conclusion: Volume I*

Perhaps the dominant theme of volume I of the Study is best captured in the phrase "nothing is perfect." For example, many accidents that would be prevented under other systems would occur under the Libertarian model. Moreover, many accident victims would not be compensated under the Libertarian model, including both those whose best interests should have, but didn't, cause them to be insured, and those whom the rest of us want to be insured regardless of their own preferences. Yet the social intervention models attempting to correct the shortcomings of the Libertarian model are also flawed. The Conservative model, for example, is an ineffective behavioral channeling mechanism, compensates a limited share of victims (even of tort victims), provides uneven and unpredictable compensation, and costs a great deal to administer. Unable to rely on the moral power that attaches to injurer fault, the Liberal model runs into political objections by those forced to pay the bill. As a result, there is a risk that plan benefits will be inadequate, forcing victims to look as well to Conservative and Libertarian model remedies (lawsuits and their own insurance) for sufficient compensation. This undermines some of the efficiency gains that, in principle, attach to the Liberal model. It is also by no means clear that we can sensibly design focused compensation plans for the wide range of accidents covered by the Conservative model. Product injury compensation plans? Transportation injury compensation plans? Premises injury compensation plans? Medical injury compensation plans? Some of these might work, others not. Finally, despite some encouraging evidence, it remains unclear how effective the Liberal model can be in shaping behavior through the use of financial incentives created by plan funding arrangements.

The Collective model can effectively assure victim compensation at low administrative costs. But its embrace requires a feeling of collective and mutual responsibility that may be absent in a nation such as ours with a strong ideological commitment to individual responsibility and individual desert. Moreover, the compensation paid would likely be of a common denominator sort, less carefully tailored to individual circumstances than in other models. This reflects the model's common citizen orientation. Having separated behavior control from the compensation mechanism, the Collective model must resort to government regulation. Yet, American experience with current governmental efforts to promote safety is mixed at best.

The Study failed to address the Socialist model. Had it done so, it surely would have predicted inefficiency of government ownership of basic industries, including the health care system. Also, it would have doubted the feasibility and desirability of equalizing exposure to risk. This, the Study would have reasoned, would sharply reduce individual welfare by preventing people from voluntarily accepting risk in exchange for other benefits they want. Undoubtedly, the authors would also have concluded that a policy of assuring greater equality of income in America is politically implausible in the near future, quite apart from concerns about potentially undesirable social consequences resulting from dampened individual initiative.

If there is no ideal solution, then one must judge which is the most promising despite its flaws. At the least, one can select the elements of each model that appear most able to deal with various personal injuries. This is the subject of volume II.

III. APPROACHES TO LEGAL AND INSTITUTIONAL CHANGE

Volume II of the Study contains the project's recommendations. Consistent with its broad appraisal of the institutional alternatives in volume I, the Study insists that "it is essential to avoid a 'tort-centric' approach to personal injury policy."[62] Yet, it concedes that its policy proposals "are largely devoted to tort law alone."[63] It offers two justifications for that focus: first, it concludes that "tort plays a valuable role in the broader personal injury picture"; and second, it asserts that "as a group of tort scholars, that is where our comparative advantage lies."[64]

To illustrate the latter point, the Study says, "the more we learned about the problems as well as the virtues of disability insurance, for example, the more we realized how presumptuous it would be for us to judge whether social security disability insurance might be expanded to cover partial as well as total disability."[65] I find this expression of modesty rather disingenuous. The project leaders planned the expansive nature of their inquiry, so why did they not shape its personnel to be competent to make broad judgments beyond tort law? In addition, at least two of the core participants in the project, Kenneth Abraham and Lance Liebman, do know a great deal about disability insurance and social security, and wrote about those topics for volume I. If more diverse expertise was needed, other prominent legal scholars specializing in social security's disability insurance role could have been added. Jerry Mashaw is one name that comes to mind. Besides, the project did include social and private insurance experts who were not law professors, such as Kip Viscusi, a very talented economist, who made important contributions to the products liability, markets, and regulation chapters. Other non-lawyers could have been added to the team as well.

In any event, the heart of volume II addresses recommendations for reforming the Conservative model. Volume II does not completely ignore other institutional arrangements; the Libertarian, Liberal, and Collective models are briefly revisited near the end of the volume. Nevertheless, those who would prefer a wholesale replacement of personal injury lawsuits with, for example, a comprehensive accident compensation scheme similar to New Zealand, will find the Study regrettably timid.

The Study has not shied away from proposing "serious tort law reform."[66] Still, most of Volume II, however thoughtfully argued, re-plows very familiar ground and offers few surprises. Indeed, most of the tort reform recommendations could have been cast as proposed revisions of existing sections of the Restatement (Second) of Torts.

A. *Tort Damages*

In chapters 5-10 of volume II, the Study proposes substantial changes in the rules for determining the amount of damages payable to tort victims.[67] Chapter 47 of the Restatement (Second) of Torts is devoted to principles of damages, and several its sections would have to be altered to accommodate the Study's recommendations.

1. *Collateral sources.*

Section 920A(2) of the Restatement (Second) states the common law collateral source rule. Simply put, tort law ignores the fact that the victim is eligible for compensation for his medical expenses, wage losses, and other accident related costs from sources such as health insurance, disability insurance, sick leave, and social security.[68] Payment from these sources either results in double recovery to the victim, or is returned to the payors via their contractual or equitable subrogation rights. This rule reflects the Conservative model value that tortfeasors should internalize the full costs they impose.

In chapter 6, the Study authors "recommend virtually complete reversal of the collateral source rule."[69] Damage awards would be reduced by sums received from collateral sources, and those payors would lose reimbursement rights against the plaintiff's award. (The Study authors also emphasize elsewhere that the same principle would apply in cases where employees receiving workers' compensation sued third parties.)[70]

This is hardly the first time that reversing the collateral source rule has been advocated. In recent years, the U.S. Attorney General's Task Force appointed by the Reagan Administration urged reversal,[71] as did my own proposal for "serious tort law reform."[72] Moreover, several jurisdictions have already adopted various formulations of the collateral source rule similar to the one recommended by the Study. Indeed, section 920A of the Restatement (Second) of Torts already acknowledges the possibility of statutory change in the rule.[73] An important effect of combining the collateral source rule reversal with the adoption of compensation schemes of the Liberal and Collective models is that tort law's compensation role is eroded from within; the more those plans pay, the less tort law does.

2. *Pain and suffering.*

Section 924(a) of the Restatement (Second), which in turn refers to section 912 (concerning certainty), and section 905 (generally discussing compensatory damages for nonpecuniary harm), sets out the common law right of personal injury victims to an open-ended monetary award, determined by the trier of fact, to compensate for past and prospective pain and suffering.[74]

The Study proposes restricting pain and suffering awards in various ways. First, no damages for pain and suffering would be awarded unless the victim has suffered "significant injuries."[75] The Study cites the verbal threshold in Michigan's motor vehicle accident law as an example. That statute requires "proof of serious impairment of bodily function or permanent and serious disfigurement as a precondition to recovery of damages for pain and suffering."[76] The Study authors, however, favor a slightly more generous rule that would award pain and suffering damages to "more serious, albeit temporary, injuries inflicted by tortious behavior,"[77] at least absent a new scheme that assures pecuniary compensation to such temporarily disabled victims.

A second reform recommended by the Study is an inflation-adjusted ceiling on allowable pain and suffering damages in serious injury cases. As the Study goes to great lengths to explain, this ceiling is not simply a cap on general damages applied by the judge to truncate the jury's open-ended award. Rather, the ceiling is the top of a scale (or set of guidelines) that would be developed for serious injuries generally, with injuries of differing degrees of seriousness located along the scale. The jury's job is to place the injury in question at a suitable point along the scale and award the designated sum. The Study does not establish a specific dollar value for the ceiling although it does insist that "substantial monetary awards [be] paid to the permanently disabled who can use the additional funds to adjust to and better enjoy life in their future disabled state."[78] The authors defer to the political process to establish the precise number.[79]

As with the collateral source rule, other commentators have also recommended both thresholds for awarding pain and suffering damages, and ceilings on those awards. My own proposal is along the same lines, though without the Study's more sophisticated "scale." Instead I proposed allowing the common law to develop reasonable awards in reference to the ceiling as it has done in England.[80] Indeed, the Australians have also recently put such a scheme in place through statutory reform.[81] On the principle that compensation for the seriously injured should be fair but not excessive, I proposed a ceiling that would generate income in the admittedly arbitrary amount of about $1,000 a month in the late 1980s, to be increased with inflation. Hence my proposed ceiling would be close to $200,000 today. The Australian ceiling is $180,000 Australian.

The Reagan Administration advocated a simple cap, first in the amount of $100,000,[82] later $200,000.[83] Several American jurisdictions have capped pain and suffering awards, although the amount of the cap has varied considerably. However, many of these caps have been invalidated on state constitutional grounds.[84]

3. *Punitive damages.*

Sections 908 and 909 of the Restatement (Second) cover punitive damages. Section 908(2) requires a finding of the "defendant's evil motive or his reckless indifference to the rights of another" and permits taking "the wealth of the defendant" into account in awarding punitive damages.[85] In effect, this requires finding serious fault at the managerial level of the corporation before the enterprise can be held liable for punitive damages based upon its employee's conduct.[86] Again, the Restatement (Second) already recognizes that many states have adopted statutes governing liability for punitive damages.[87]

The Study calls for raising the Restatement (Second)'s standard by adding "clear and convincing evidence" to the required showing of "reckless disregard for the safety of others in the decision made by management officials or other senior personnel" before punitive damages can be awarded. In contrast to the Restatement, it urges that evidence of the defendant's wealth be excluded, although it would allow evidence of the "profits earned from the specific tortious activity"[88]

In calculating the amount to award, the Study favors a scheme in which punitive damages are calculated as a ratio of compensatory damages. The Study fails to endorse any specific ratio (e.g., 1/1 or 3/1). Alternatively, the Study urges that judges should be able to bifurcate trials, trying the punitive damages part of the claim separately to the same jury. If the amount of the award is not set by the ratio formula, it urges "serious consideration" of having judges fix the amount after juries decide punitive damages are warranted. Finally, it proposes in mass tort cases, that the punitive damage issue be tried in a single, national mandatory class action, to avoid cascading awards in individual litigation over the same course of conduct.[89]

My proposal regarding punitive damages calls for judges to decide whether and how much to award.[90] The Reagan Administration first proposed applying the $100,000 pain and suffering cap to punitive damages as well, but later separated the two and called for a variety of restrictions on the punitive damages award.[91] In recent years, states have adopted a wide range punitive damage reforms and some have even eliminated them altogether.[92]

4. *Joint and several liability.*

Chapter 44 of the Restatement (Second) covers contributing tortfeasors, recognizing that much of the law in this area is governed by statute. Section 875 states the general joint and several liability principle if two or more tortfeasors are liable for a single harm, each is liable for the full damage claim.[93] The plaintiff can obtain a full judgment against any or all of them, although she can only collect her full judgment once.[94]

Restatement (Second) section 886A sets out the general rule that defendants who are jointly and severally liable have contribution rights against each other.[95] The Restatement (Second) recognizes that the traditional rule of pro-rata contribution, whereby three solvent defendants are each liable for a third of the judgment, has been giving way to a rule of contribution based upon the relative fault among the defendants.[96]

Two situations that frequently give rise to practical difficulties are those in which one of the jointly and severally liable defendants is insolvent (or absent), or has settled with the plaintiff for less than what otherwise would be his share under the contribution rules. In the former case, the Restatement (Second)'s rules place the risk of insolvency on the defendant from which the plaintiff has collected;[97] his right to contribution is worthless.

Section 467 of the Restatement contains the common law rule that the plaintiff's contributory negligence is a complete bar to recovery, while the special note to section 467 recognizes that several states have adopted a comparative negligence regime in which an at-fault plaintiff's recovery may be reduced in proportion to her fault. Since this section was issued, comparative negligence has swept the country. This, in turn, has highlighted the need to decide whether an at-fault plaintiff should share, proportionately along with solvent defendant(s), in the insolvency of other defendant(s). For example, in a 2-auto collision in which the victim driver is 20 percent at fault, the injurer driver is 40 percent at fault (but is insolvent), and the local municipality is 40 percent at fault for failing to maintain the highway properly, should the plaintiff share the burden of the other driver's insolvency with the municipality? This is the solution recommended by the Uniform Law Commissioners in the Uniform Comparative Fault Act of 1977, although states are divided on the issue.[98]

On the risk of under-settling, the Restatement (Second) makes no endorsement, but acknowledges three alternative outcomes.[99] First, the settling defendant is still liable in contribution to the non-settling defendant(s). This, however, tends to discourage settlement. Second, the settling defendant is released from further liability and the shortfall is born by the other defendant(s). This encourages low settlements with D1 where Dl agrees to be a witness against D2. That, in turn, prompts legal requirements that the settlement with D1 be in "good faith" and requires that the standards be policed. Lastly, the risk of under-settling is borne by the plaintiff. The settling party's liability is discharged in full, thereby reducing the liability of the other defendant(s), even though that share was not fully paid. This solution discourages settlements with defendants of limited solvency, such as drivers with limited auto insurance coverage, provided that the insolvent-defendant rule is more favorable to the plaintiff. This point suggests yet another alternative, which is that the risk of under-settling is borne by the parties, including the plaintiff, on the basis of fault. As the Restatement (Second) points out, the Uniform Comparative Fault Act of 1977 opts for the third solution.[100]

The Reagan Administration urged the elimination of joint and several liability altogether. Instead, multiple tortfeasors would each be liable only in proportion to their fault.[101] This solution was considered especially fair in cases in which a "deep pocket" defendant is minimally at fault, perhaps even less so than the plaintiff, but nonetheless would be liable for a large percentage of the damages under the rule of joint and several liability when the other defendant doesn't pay the appropriate share. It has never been clear to me whether advocates of abolishing joint and several liability truly favor this solution in cases when, for example, a landlord whose negligent failure to provide adequate security leads to the rape of a tenant. Is the landlord really only to be liable for a small share of the victim's damages (on the assumption that the rapist, who is typically either judgment proof or simply not apprehended, was primarily at fault)? That certainly seems to be the consequence of holding a defendant liable only for her share of the fault in causing an injury. In any event, in recent years, several states have modified their rules on joint and several liability in a variety of ways, including a few that have abolished the rule.[102]

Chapter *5* of the Study rejects abolishing joint and several liability. When the defendants have contracted among themselves, such as the parties in the chain of distribution of a product, or doctors and hospitals, the Study favors retaining joint and several liability. The risk of insolvency is borne by the defendants, to be allocated by them contractually in advance. When the defendants are not in a position to contract in advance, the Study adopts the Uniform Law Commissioners' approach, in which the risk of insolvency is shared by plaintiffs and defendants in proportion to their share of the fault. Like the Uniform Comparative Fault Act, the Study also favors the position that the risk of under-settling should fall on the plaintiff. [103]

Altering the rule of joint and several liability was not part of my proposal, so to that extent I join the Study in opposition to the Reagan Administration proposal. However, in contrast to the Study, under my plan in multiple defendant cases the risks of insolvency and under-settling would fall fully on the defendant(s). This is flows from another part of my proposal that is considerably more dramatic: The plaintiff's fault would not reduce her recovery at all. [104] Not content to stop at comparative fault, I would move all the way to the principle articulated in compensation plans under the Liberal and Collective models, in which the victim's negligence is simply disregarded. This has long been the case in workers' compensation, for example. Exceptions would arise in cases of intentional self-injury, and perhaps when the plaintiff is more than 50 percent at fault. The Study does not address this proposal.

5. *Attorneys' fees.*

Under the common law, as reflected in section 914 of the Restatement (Second), a tort victim's damages do not ordinarily include attorneys' fees or other expenses of litigation such as expert witnesses and deposition fees.[105] The Study, in chapter 10, proposes the opposite solution. Reasonable attorneys' fees and other litigation costs should be part of the plaintiff's damage.[106] This portion of the Study's package of recommendations is critical. The collateral source rule and the unconstrained award of pain and suffering damages are both now often justified, albeit awkwardly because of the poor match, as serving the practical function of providing money to pay for the victim's legal expenses. The Study favors changing both of those rules contingent upon allowing attorneys' fees and costs to be awarded as damages.

The Study's proposal is not the same as the so-called English rule in which the loser is generally liable for the legal expenses of the winner. Rather, when combined with the American practice of contingent fees, if the plaintiff wins or settles, the defendant pays the legal expenses of both sides. If the plaintiff loses, the defendant would still pay its own expenses and the plaintiff's lawyer would go unpaid. This is also what I proposed.[107]

The Study does not make a firm proposal for the method of calculating the fee, but suggests that defendants pay approximately what the "market" has traditionally generated.[108] Thus, liability for attorneys' fees would probably be in the range of an additional one-third of the plaintiff's recovery for compensatory damages. This would likely be reduced somewhat for settled cases and increased somewhat for appealed cases. The Study rejects both basing the award on hours worked) and scaling the percentage awarded to the amount of the recovery.

My proposal and that of the Study diverge on the latter score. I proposed, for most cases, that a decreasing proportion of the award be added for lawyers' fees as the award increases. The sliding scale contingent fee rule applicable to medical malpractice cases in California, although it governs how much of the plaintiff's award his own attorney can take as a fee, serves as an example.[109]

The Reagan Administration, by contrast, did not advocate making the plaintiff's legal expenses part of their tort damage award. Rather, it proposed simply restricting the amount that the plaintiff's lawyer could charge, as in the California rule for medical malpractice cases just noted. Some states have adopted this kind of solution.[110]

6. *Conclusion: Tort damages.*

Taken as a whole, the changes recommended by the Study would make tort compensation more closely reflect the principles of the Liberal model a move that I favor. The Liberal model values meeting actual need over punishing wrongdoing. Awards are less individualized in the interest of greater uniformity and more simplified administration. If lawyers continue to be necessary to help people press their claims, the cost of litigation is not taken out of awards that are intended for other purposes.

As I have shown, this does not mean that victims' awards are simply to be reduced. On the contrary, as a result of the proposal concerning attorneys' fees, a balance of interests is struck between plaintiffs and defendants that is fair even when compared to the common law rules. Moreover, as compared with the law in states that have already adopted one or more of the Reagan Administration proposals, the Study's recommendations are less threatening to, and even supportive of, plaintiff interests. For example, in California medical malpractice cases, attorneys' fees are already restricted, pain and suffering damages are capped at $250,000, the collateral source rule is essentially reversed, tighter controls have been imposed on punitive damages, and relatively few people sue who haven't suffered serious injuries.[111] There, the most important consequence of the Study's proposals on damages would probably be the shifting of the burden of paying the plaintiff's legal expenses to the defendant. This would be a substantial pro-plaintiff change.

My own proposal differs from the Study's recommendations on several important points. First, depending upon local politics, the awards for pain and suffering favored by the Study might be more generous than I have recommended. On the other hand, a substantial proportion of claimants would benefit more under my proposal because victim fault would be largely ignored in awarding damages. In addition, as I will explain in more detail below, my proposal for reforming tort damages rules would also assure first-party compensation for tort victims outside the tort system.

B. *Tort Substance and Procedure*

Chapters 2, 3, 4, and 12 of the Study examine substantive standards for tort liability in product injury cases, the effect regulatory compliance should have in tort cases, the substantive liability for medical malpractice, and the substantive law governing environmental injury. The next section discusses these issues.

1. *Product defects and warnings.*

Section 402A of the Restatement (Second) appears to have played an important role in generating widespread support among courts and commentators for its core principle, namely that manufacturers are liable for injuries caused by manufacturing defects in their products without proof of negligence in the manufacturing process.[112] Section 402A effectively supersedes section 395 which states the rule of *MacPherson v. Buick Motor Co.*[113] holding manufacturers liable for injuries caused by products that become dangerous because they are negligently manufactured.[114] Illustrations of manufacturing defects plainly covered by section 402A include the exploding soft drink bottle, the automobile whose steering mechanism goes awry, and the loaf of bread with a pin in it. The manufacturer will concede that this particular product did not conform to ordinary manufacturing standards and hence is "defective"[115]

For manufacturing defects, the courts have had to decide additional issues such as whether, for example, the manufacturer is strictly liable to a pedestrian run over by a car with a defective tire; whether retailers should be held strictly liable; whether component part manufacturers should also be strictly liable when the defect is in the part they provided. Although the ALI left these three issues unresolved in 1964 when it adopted section 402A, the law governing them has since matured and a revised Restatement would take these developments into account. So, too, a revised section 402A would address the liability of others who, though not manufacturers, may nonetheless be strictly liable. The courts have addressed this issue in cases involving lessors, financiers, franchisors, rebuilders, repairers, and sellers of used goods. Unfortunately, the Study does not address these matters.

Instead, the Study focuses its attention on warning and design defects. Prior to the adoption of section 402A, the Restatement (Second) provided for liability in cases both of negligent product design and negligent failure to warn.[116] After the adoption of section 402A, however, plaintiffs sought to convince courts that strict liability should attach for both defective design and failure to warn. The main issue here concerns knowledge and technology that change over time. A product that appeared reasonably safe and was reasonably designed according to the state of the art available at the time of manufacture may appear defective if judged as of the time of trial. When that happens, should an innocent manufacturer nonetheless be liable for a product that it would be negligent to sell in the same condition today? The Restatement (Second) takes no clear position on the question; courts, legislatures and commentators have split.[117] Although the Study does not seriously engage this issue, the authors apparently favor judging the product as of the time of sale.[118]

Another thorny issue is whether a product may be deemed defective in design simply because it contains an unavoidable risk of injury that is well understood by both the manufacturer and user. A good example is a valuable medicine that nonetheless contains the risk of harmful side effects; another is good whiskey. The Restatement (Second) rejects strict liability for "unavoidably unsafe products."[119] Again, courts and commentators are split on this issue. Some believe that manufacturers should be forced to bear the costs imposed by products, which in tum encourages efforts to eliminate hazardous products. Others, on the other hand, fear that imposing strict liability would cause manufacturers to remove desirable products from the marketplace. The Study rejects imposing tort liability on such products and, more generally, rejects the "insurance" or "compensation" argument for imposing strict products liability.[120]

A different issue is whether a jury ought to be able to condemn what the Study calls a "generic category of product," (such as lawn darts, all-terrain vehicles (ATVs), cigarettes, soft-top convertible cars, or above-ground swimming pools) on the ground that the product's dangers so outweigh its benefits that it is "defective" to market it at all (or, I would say, negligent to market it at all). This issue is different from the question of "unavoidably unsafe products" because there the question is whether the danger alone might be the basis for strict liability. Here the dangers are weighed against the benefits. Thus, while no one would argue that a life-saving drug should not be marketed at all, risky side effects notwithstanding, some might argue that the risks associated with lawn darts, or ATVs, for example, outweigh their benefits. Although there are exceptions, courts have not been inclined to permit generic categories of products to be deemed defective on the basis of a jury's cost/benefit (or risk/utility) analysis, and the Study strongly agrees. The authors argue that, so long as the consumer is reasonably well informed of the risks, the market, not the jury, should determine whether the benefits are worth the risks. [121] It is noteworthy that the concern raised in volume I, that informed people might nonetheless foolishly make decisions not in their own best interests, has seemingly been forgotten in volume II.

A closely related issue concerns products for which an alternate safer design is available, but the manufacturer nonetheless markets a more dangerous version, together with a warning about the danger. Although some have argued that in this case, the market should determine which risks are socially acceptable, the Study rejects this result on the ground that, in practice, because of imperfections in the market for information, consumers may not actually make informed choices. Notwithstanding its somewhat self-contradictory presentation, the bottom line for the Study is that the jury ought to be able to find a product "defective" where a feasible alternative design exists that would have avoided the harm, and where implementing the alternative is cost-justified in terms of the injuries avoided. [122]

While I don't disagree with its proposals on these last two issues, it is important to appreciate that the boundary between the two categories that the Study creates is ambiguous. Is the generic product category ATVs or all "Jeep-like" vehicles? Is the generic product category limited to lawn darts with sharp metal points, or does it include lawn darts using foam and velcro, or even all lawn target games? Is the generic product category above-ground swimming pools, or all swimming pools? The more broadly one describes the generic product category, the more likely it is that feasible alternative designs exist with which the jury would be permitted to make cost/benefit comparisons; the narrower, the less likely. Unfortunately, the Study doesn't really give us criteria for defining the generic product category.

Another important issue addressed by the Study is how to decide whether a warning is adequate. The fact that the Study has rejected the view that lawsuits should always be disallowed against products where the complaint is made against a patent danger, including a danger made patent through warning, does not mean that warning defects no longer merit discussion. Dangerous products without feasible, cost-justified alternative designs, and generic categories of dangerous products must carry adequate warnings. One might rely upon the market to provide proper warnings, as in the Libertarian model, but the Study again expresses its distrust for the market. Instead, it concludes that tort law must police the market: Manufacturers are to escape liability only where a legally adequate warning has been given.[123] To determine what should constitute an adequate warning, the Study (harkening back to some the points made in Volume I) wisely calls for the following improvements: wider use of experts in evaluating warnings; the development of what it calls a "uniform national vocabulary" to be used to communicate risk levels; and, where appropriate, deference by the tort system to warning requirements established by governmental agencies.[124]

Finally, candidly displaying its "law and economics" outlook,[125] the Study urges that where an adequate warning has not been given, the courts should presume that the consumer would have read the warning and heeded it.[126] This eliminates the traditional requirement that the plaintiff prove that if the defendant had acted differently, it would have made a difference in this case. Were the Study's position on causation adopted, it would require a further change in sections 402A and 388 of the Restatement (Second).[127] I do not claim that this provocative position is not persuasively argued, but it is unfortunate that the Study does not address its more sweeping implications. For example, would the authors of the Study also eliminate the requirement that patients who assert that their doctor failed to obtain "informed consent" before administering treatment prove that they (or a reasonable patient in their position) would have refused the treatment had they been fully informed?

It is also disappointing that the Study did not address the question of whether there are analogies to manufacturing defects in mass-production enterprises other than manufacturing. For example, when an airplane crashes, why does the crash not constitute a defective service so far as the passengers on board are concerned? Or, if the roof falls in or a shelf falls over in a Wal-Mart store, would it not be as appropriate to invoke a concept of "defective premises" in this context as it is to invoke strict liability against General Motors for one of its defective Buicks? I don't mean to argue that the analogies are necessarily apt rather I present these questions merely to illustrate my view that the authors of this sweeping review of "enterprise liability for personal injury" focused their attention too narrowly.

2. *Regulatory compliance.*

Section 288C of the Restatement (Second) provides that while compliance with an administrative regulation is evidence of due care, the legal standard of care is set by the trier of fact in the torts case.[128] The Restatement (Second) is concerned about regulations that may establish only minimum standards when the "reasonable man" would have taken more precautions. Its position also reflects a fear of agency capture by industry.

The Study's primary concern regarding regulatory standards is that imposing liability on enterprises even though they have complied with relevant regulatory requirements may deter socially desirable conduct by those enterprises. It is also concerned about the competence of juries to second guess the regulators. As a result, chapter 3 of the Study proposes a stronger role for what it calls a "regulatory compliance defense."[129] As noted by the authors, several states have already attempted to fashion regulatory compliance defenses.[130] Under the Study's proposal, if a specialized agency has focused on the risk at issue and adopted standards specifying the level of permissible risk, and if the defendant has fully complied with the agency's requirements, then it should presumed to have exercised due care, provided that one further test is met: The defendant must have disclosed to the agency all material information it possesses about the risks it has taken.[131] The Study recognizes that "such a defense would probably not have a very extensive application."[132]

Adopting a regulatory compliance defense might have two desirable side effects. First, realizing their regulations set a presumptive liability threshold, agencies might strengthen their requirements. Second, hoping to take advantage of the rule, enterprises might disclose known risks that they now keep secret. This last point suggests a potentially productive interaction between strategies of the Conservative and Collective models. Currently, many agencies, such as the Consumer Products Safety Commission (CPSC), already have rules that require enterprises to come forward with information about risks. This command so far has not worked well, as all too many of the hazardous products the CPSC has learned about came through disclosure other than by the manufacturer.133 The

Study's tactic is to provide an incentive in the tort system to improve compliance.

Elsewhere, I have suggested that bounties be paid to private citizens who point out hazardous products to the CPSC before the manufacturer discloses them. The bounties would be financed with fines imposed on such nondisclosing manufacturers.[134] My idea is meant both to direct the energy of the public, consumer groups, and plaintiff tort lawyers to the discovery of dangerous products and to stimulate greater self-disclosure of dangers by manufacturers.

3. *Medical malpractice.*

One of the project's most innovative and stimulating proposals concerns liability for medical malpractice. The Study pays scant attention to the criteria for imposing tort liability for medical injuries. Rather it argues for "organizational liability," a very sharp change in the current regime.

Under the common law, as reflected in section 409 of the Restatement (Second), employers of independent contractors are not ordinarily vicariously liable for the torts of those contractors.[135] Today, the large majority of physicians who commit malpractice in hospital settings are not employees of the hospital; they are independent contractors with "privileges" to treat their patients in the hospital. Hence, absent negligence of the hospital itself, the patient plaintiff must sue the doctor and not the hospital. (In exceptional cases, hospitals have been found negligent for granting continued privileges to physicians they know to be incompetent. These decisions follow Restatement (Second) sections 410-415 which state when those who employ independent contractors may themselves be found negligent with respect to that employment.[136])

The Study's proposed reform in this area has a wider sweep. Its first, and most important, feature is that hospitals would be liable for the malpractice of a physician that occurs in the hospital even if the doctor is an independent contractor and even if the hospital itself was not negligent. Sections 416-429 of the Restatement already constitute a kind of grab-bag list of exceptions to the general rule of Section 409-situations in which the employer of an independent contractor is vicariously liable for the torts of that contractor even though the employer itself is not negligent. The Study's proposal would, in effect, add a new situation to the existing list of common law exceptions. In addition, under the proposal, the doctor could not be sued individually. This would be quite a radical change, although it is not clear how important it would be in practice.

The Study's goals here are two-fold, based upon findings reported in volume I discussed above. The first aim is to eliminate the current practice in which malpractice insurance for torts committed by doctors in hospitals is financed and carried by individual doctors. In the current system, doctors have difficulty incorporating unpredictable increases in medical malpractice insurance rates into their fees. The authors of the Study believe that this problem would be sharply reduced if the insurance were carried by hospitals instead of doctors. Second, believing that medical malpractice law now fails to promote safer medical practice in the way the Conservative model envisions (and has negative social consequences too), the authors conclude that the prospects for improved medical care would be enhanced by imposing the financial burden on the relevant larger enterprise, namely, the hospital.

Although the Study articulates this proposal effectively, and defends it against likely objections from within the tort system,[137] the authors realize, and I agree that it is not clear the strategy of organizational liability is best pursued through the Conservative model. Rather, organizational liability is an attractive possibility for a medical accident compensation scheme adopted pursuant to the Liberal model.

4. *Environmental injuries.*

The Study reports, in chapter 12, that "there has been comparatively little litigation alleging environmental hazardous substance-produced personal injury" even though there are at least "10,000 environmentally related cancer deaths per year."[138] The Study authors believe that this gap between the high number of injuries related to environmental hazards and the low number of lawsuits in this area is primarily the result of the difficulty of proving causation. At the same time, the authors believe that many of those who do win these sorts of cases do so on scientifically dubious evidence. This, in tum, has caused some judges to demand an even higher evidentiary standard for causation before allowing cases to proceed.

To improve the tort system's treatment of such cases, the Study recommends changes in the use of class actions and science panels, advocates early monetary awards to pay for medical monitoring of future harm, and seeks liberalization of the statute of limitations.[139] Some of these points tie into the Study's discussion in a separate chapter which proposes, in more detail, the creation of a Federal Science Board to assist the judiciary in the handling of tort litigation about hazardous substances. The Board's role would include identifying experts, convening "science panels" in certain cases, and generally assisting courts to cope with the uncertainty that often plagues hazardous substances litigation.[140] These are plausible improvements in the system, upon which I will not elaborate here. Two other issues that bear further consideration, however, are the standard of liability and the award of proportionate compensation.

Under the common law, persons engaged in "abnormally dangerous activities" may be held strictly liable for the consequences of their actions, and the Restatement (Second) lists six factors for determining if an activity is ultrahazardous[141]. Essentially, the Restatement (Second) allows strict liability to be imposed on activities that create a substantial risk of harm and are uncommon for the place in which they are carried out, even though the activities are not nuisances and are not conducted negligently.[142]

Chapter 12 asserts that environmental risk cases should be judged, generally speaking, by the law of "abnormally dangerous activities." But this is neither persuasive nor sufficiently analytical. First of all, if the victims of environmental risk can demonstrate liability on the basis of negligence or nuisance principles, they should prevail on those grounds. The strict liability principles applicable to abnormally dangerous activities should be better understood as potentially available for those cases where wrongdoing through the creation of environmental risks cannot be demonstrated by the victim. Second, the Study concedes that not all the externalities of enterprise activity that could be labelled "pollution" should qualify for strict liability. I agree that "ordinary manufacturing activities involving the emission of smoke or fumes,"[143] provided that they are not carried out negligently or in an inappropriate place, presumably would be seen as common activities and hence not abnormally dangerous. The key issue then becomes which non-negligent environmental risks are sufficiently uncommon to be appropriate targets for strict liability. Unfortunately, the Study does not discuss this question.

Instead, the Study addresses an issue raised above in the discussion of product injuries: Is it relevant that, at the time the pollution was created, the defendant either could not reasonably know of the risk or had no feasible way to prevent it without ceasing the activity altogether? Acknowledging that it may be taking a different approach from that proposed for product injuries, the Study argues that while unknowable risks should be exculpating, unavailable means of prevention should not. This inconsistency should not be the cause of great alarm, however, because the proposal for environmental risk fits the basic structure of strict liability for abnormally dangerous activity. If the enterprise could not have known at the time that its conduct was dangerous, it can hardly be said to have chosen to engage in a dangerous activity, and understandably escapes strict liability. By contrast, if the conduct is known to be dangerous and uncommon, the whole point of the abnormally dangerous activity doctrine is to impose strict liability even though no reasonable precautions could have been taken to avoid the harm. (Products differ, according to the Restatement (Second) approach, because, when buyers are made aware of the unavoidable danger, they accept the risk, thereby making the product not defective.)

Finally, the Study endorses a limited use of what has become known as probabilistic causation to award proportionate damages. Where toxic substances are emitted into the environment, the typical facts are is that a class has been exposed to a risk, sometime in the future plaintiffs complain of physical injury (such as cancer), but there is a good chance, perhaps a better than 50 percent chance, that the harm was actually caused by something other than the risk created by the defendant. Traditional tort law would require proof of "more likely than not" causation in each case. This is often enough to defeat the claims of all the victims in the exposed class, even though we might be confident that, for example, 40 percent of those in the class were actually harmed by the defendant's risk. On the other hand, when there is a 66 percent chance that anyone in the class was in fact injured by the defendant's risk, tort law's all-or-nothing approach might allow everyone in the class to recover in full. In place of tort law's sharp cutoff rule, the Study proposes a proportionate compensation substitute. When the chances are between 20 percent and 80 percent that the defendant's risk caused the victim's harm, recovery would be proportionate to the chance. Those with less than a 20 percent chance would get nothing. Those with an 80 percent or more chance would be compensated 100 percent.

The adoption of this proposal would seemingly require modification of Restatement (Second) section 433B which states the traditional tort causation standard of preponderance of the evidence.[144]

While there is a certain attractiveness to the Study's proposal for proportionate compensation, especially from the viewpoint of those who can show that the chances that the defendant's activity injured them was between 20 percent and 50 percent, it also has drawbacks. The Study admits that much of the behavior control function for these risks must be taken up through mechanisms other than tort law. The long latency quality of these problems makes it especially unlikely that individuals within an enterprise will alter their present conduct because they may expose the firm to liability long in the future. Proportionate liability is also an unsatisfactory compensation mechanism because victims only partially compensated through tort law will have to tum to other broader sources anyway; and if those other sources were themselves adequate, then proportionate liability would be unnecessary. Indeed, under the Study's proposal on the collateral source rule, the availability of the other sources would actually relieve the environmental risk-creating defendant from having to pay. Hence the Study's recommendation, in the end, seems most appealing as a symbolic commitment to group justice or what some have called "good social cost accounting."

5. *Conclusion: Torts substance and procedure.*

As was true of the Study's recommendations concerning the reform of tort damages law, its proposals pertaining to substantive and procedural changes are balanced. Changes advanced for environmental torts are certainly intended to open up the courts to more plaintiffs. While the adoption of organizational liability for medical injuries may not formally benefit claimants much, in practice plaintiffs might find significant advantages in proceeding against an enterprise instead of an individual doctor. The Study also seeks to help defendants by creating the regulatory compliance defense and by narrowing some of the grounds for holding manufacturers liable for product injuries.[145]

Thematically, the recommendations canvassed by the Study authors seek generally to improve tort law's ability to signal potential defendants as to what conduct is acceptable so that they will know what actions to take to avoid liability. A lesser, and somewhat contradictory theme of the authors is to concentrate liability on certain defendants in order to encourage them to intensify their own search for injury reduction efforts.

Like the reversal of the collateral sources rule, the Study's recommendations for tort reform acknowledge and interface with features of the institutional alternatives. Unfortunately, the Study does not really compare the package of proposed reforms with potential improvements in the institutional alternatives, such as government regulation. In other words, although the project addresses possible synergies between tort law and the CPSC or the FDA, it does not even follow up on its own observations in volume I about improving government regulation to determine whether those sorts of changes might make tort law's behavior modification role largely redundant. Consider two examples: First, applying its talent to enhancing regulation, the Study team might well have devised new ways of prompting hospitals to be more effective in policing their practicing doctors without imposing organizational tort liability on them; second, if regulatory agencies are to create a new national vocabulary for warnings as recommended, the authors might well have identified ways of assuring the widespread use of this new vocabulary without involving tort law. My modest efforts in this direction, for example, centered on increasing citizen participation in the regulatory process, hoping in part to harness and redirect some of the energy that now goes into bringing tort suits.[146]

More effective regulation alone, of course, does not take care of a person's need for compensation when accidents do happen, which brings me to the final set of chapters in the Study.

C. *Beyond Tort*

1. *Contract alternatives: Revisiting the Libertarian model.*

Should potential personal injury victims be permitted to waive their tort rights in advance, and thus on a one-by-one basis, revert from the Conservative model to the Libertarian model? The Restatement (Second) supports only a limited right to assume the risk of harm (i.e. to waive liability) by express agreement.[147] The Restatement recognizes that such agreements are often invalid because they are against public policy.

The Study rejects the idea of generally allowing outright disclaimers of liability. On the other hand, the Study authors support the proposal that people should be able to purchase products and services that include no-fault insurance coverage in lieu of the right to sue the manufacturer. The Study also gives some consideration (not especially favorably) to a proposal permitting those who already have adequate first party protection to accept contract disclaimers of tort liability.[148] By contrast, the Study authors are intrigued with the idea of allowing sellers to set two prices for their goods and services -- one with tort rights and the other without. Yet the authors reject this option for the time being, fearing that existing market failures would make it unworkable in practice.[149]

Allowing individuals to use contract to arrive at solutions they judge better for themselves reflects the core principle of the Libertarian model. The Study favors allowing parties to contract around tort liability only where other compensation arrangements would be available. The proposals the Study considers differ formally on the basis of whether people accepting disclaimers are to rely primarily on private individual protection, no-fault protection provided by the injurer, or broad-based collective protection provided by employers and/or society at large for compensation in the event of injury.

But there is a broader issue here as well. If disclaimers are to be permitted only when the victim is otherwise protected, is the role of contract law here really to promote variety and individual choice as in the Libertarian model? Or, alternatively, should contract law be viewed as a device aimed at facilitating the eventual adoption of compensation plans under either the Liberal or Collective models? This point is made even more vividly in the next discussion.

2. *Revisiting the Liberal model I: Medical no-fault plans.*

The Study, in chapter 15, proposes taking even further the "organizational liability" notion advanced with respect to medical malpractice liability: Hospitals would become liable on a no-fault basis for all medical accidents that occur on their premises, provided that the accident resulted in serious injury.[150] This scheme would replace medical malpractice tort suits. Benefits would cover expenses and lost income (up to moderate limits) not covered by other sources, plus modest, scheduled payments to compensate for the impairments themselves.

In the past, many commentators have assumed that a broad no-fault medical accident scheme would be prohibitively expensive, especially considering that there are perhaps four times as many victims of medical accidents as there are medical malpractice suits, and only one in thirty victims now recovers in tort.[151] Nevertheless, the Study authors assert that their proposal would cost no more than the current regime because recovery would be restricted to the most seriously injured victims, payments would not be duplicated by collateral sources, and administrative costs would be far less than they are under the existing system.

Scholars have also previously assumed that determining what constitutes a "medical accident" would be terribly difficult and expensive, thus under-cutting the theoretical advantages of a no-fault plan.[152] The Study down-plays that concern, however, based upon a recent Harvard Medical Practice Study, which found that in most instances, this determination is not difficult to make.[153] Moreover, as noted earlier, the Study argues that no-fault hospital liability would promote safer medical practice than does the current malpractice regime.[154]

The Study authors do, however, acknowledge some potential problems with the proposal, such as the handling of medical injuries occurring outside of hospitals and the real-world administration of the eligibility requirements, especially were lawyers to become heavily involved.[155] Consequently, they advocate implementing it on an elective basis, along lines previously proposed by Professor O'Connell.[156]

I will not say much more about this rather exciting proposal here because I have written more extensively about it elsewhere.[157] I do, however, want to register my concern about treating differently, as this proposal would, those who are injured in medical accidents while in the hospital and those who are injured in other ways. Why have a special plan for those who lose the use of a leg due to a surgical accident, but not for those who are born with only one functioning leg, who contract a disease that disables the use of one leg, or who lose the use of one leg in an industrial or recreational accident? This, of course, is a general argument favoring the wider compensation scheme of the Collective model over the focused compensation plan of the Liberal model.

3. *Revisiting the Liberal model II: An administrative compensation scheme for toxic harm*

Early in chapter 14 the Study states, "there is no substantial reason for looking beyond the toxic harm area in assessing the case for mass injury no-fault putting aside consideration of a universal, New Zealand-type compensation plan."[158] I find this unpersuasive.

For example, the Study concludes that current tort law responds to non-toxic mass tort cases, such as those arising from commercial airline crashes sufficiently well, so that changing over to the focused compensation scheme envisioned by the Liberal model is not needed. But I have not been convinced by either the Study's conclusions or those of the RAND report on aviation accidents [159] on which the Study relies.[160] The Study concedes that, on top of the benefits paid to claimants, an additional 33 percent, or more, is expended in claims administration. Furthermore, the Study acknowledges that those with minor losses are over compensated while those with major losses are under compensated. It is also true that the payment of claims from commercial airline crashes is sometimes long delayed.[161]

Compare this state of affairs with two hypothetical alternatives.[162] Under the first, all airline tickets would come with an insurance policy with predetermined death (say, $250,000) and disability benefits, and tort liability would be eliminated. In the event of an accident, claims would be promptly paid with minimum administrative cost. Most passengers would be well aware of their entitlement, and could make an informed decision about whether or not to carry additional insurance. In addition, this scheme would be more equitable since the claimants, unlike plaintiffs in wrongful death actions today, would not receive radically differing awards despite paying the same amount for their tickets.

Under the second hypothetical plan, commercial air crashes would automatically lead to the payment of no-fault benefits to the passengers' heirs based upon the projections of what would have been the future earnings of the deceased, as well as the payment of medical expenses and lost wages for those who survived but suffered injuries. This sum would be reduced by any social security payments or workers' compensation payments to which the heirs are entitled. If politically desirable, it could also be augmented by a legislatively determined lump sum designed to compensate for the death itself (as a substitute for tort damages now allowed under some state's wrongful death statutes for what is, in effect, loss of consortium). Again, I believe that this solution would pay faster and more fairly, and would incur considerably lower administrative costs than the tort system.

Unfortunately, the Study neglects to engage the question of the comparative advantages or disadvantages of these sorts of Liberal model alternatives to the current system, not only in air crash cases, but also in other mass harm situations where they might plausibly apply, such as commercial building collapses from forces like fire and earthquakes.

Although the Study ignores focused compensation plans of the sort just mentioned, at least chapter 14 seriously addresses the issue of whether there should be an administrative compensation scheme for victims of toxic harm broadly defined.[163] The Study authors consider this solution after concluding that the tort system has not handled well cases involving claims of wide-spread injury following mass exposure to toxic substances. The Agent Orange, asbestos, DES, and Dalkon Shield litigations are all examples of this kind of claim.· Earlier, the Study proposes procedural reforms to improve the ability of tort law to deal with such problems, including mandatory class actions in federal courts, the mandatory creation of a fund for future victims of past exposure and the payment of scheduled, as opposed to, individualized damages.[164] But in chapter 14, the authors admit that they are doubtful those changes will truly suffice and proceed to explore an explicit administrative compensation scheme.[165]

If there is to be a no-fault compensation system for toxic harm, there must be some way to identify the "designated compensable event."[166] Of course, private parties could be given the right to petition the administering agency to create a list of toxic substances and their known hazards in advance, adding to the list as scientific knowledge expands. Injuries from substances on the list would come within the compensation plan. But past experience with asbestos and the Dalkon Shield, for example, teaches that people may not be aware of the dangers associated with a particular substance until after they have been exposed to the harm or actually injured. To deal with the problem, chapter 14 considers what it calls a "switching mechanism" by which these cases are somehow diverted from the tort scheme to the compensation scheme once they become known and before enormous litigation expenses are incurred. The authors admit, however, that there are likely to be many bugs in this switching mechanism which they have not yet worked out (including just what proof would be necessary to trigger it).[167]

Turning to the level of benefits such a scheme might provide, the Study argues for payments equivalent to those of a generous workers' compensation plan.[168] Again, the Study is confronted with the uncertain-causation/ probabilistic-compensation issue discussed in Section III.B.4. above in relation to environmental injuries. [169] Here the Study argues that for an administrative compensation scheme, partial compensation on probabilistic grounds is inapt. Rather, full benefits are to be paid, but, to control costs, higher proof thresholds are to be required if it appears that "too many" claimants will otherwise recover. This too has its shortcomings; we will be reasonably confident that the injurer's toxic chemical injured or killed some people, but the claimants will go without compensation from the administrative compensation scheme for toxic injuries, and instead will have to pursue other compensation sources.

Another question raised by the Study is whether tort law should be retained as a supplemental or alternative remedy to the toxic harm administrative compensation scheme. It concludes that tort should certainly not provide a supplementary remedy. [170] On the other hand, as a way of both trying to assure that the compensation scheme functions well and saves administrative costs, the Study suggests that claimants might be required to make an early binding election to pursue one remedy or the other.

Finally, on the matter of funding the scheme, the Study suggests several alternatives, including a flat tax on the gross revenue of the listed substances, more precisely calibrated charges on the listed substances as payout experience is gained, and subrogation rights against enterprises that generate obligations of the fund. It recognizes, however, that the last alternative could be costly to operate, but that without it serious fairness claims would arise, especially when a substance is "switched" onto the list only after it has caused harm, but before its manufacturers have contributed anything to the fund to provide for those injuries.[171]

Taking all the pluses and minuses into account, chapter 14 first concludes that "if there were a clear prospect of a significant number of discrete mass tort cases occurring in the future on the scale of asbestos or the Dalkon Shield ...the case for resorting to a broad-based no-fault scheme would be very strong."[172] But in view of the uncertainty of such mass injury events occurring, and in light of the potential for great problems with the compensation plan it has outlined, the Study ultimately suggests that perhaps the better approach is "a wait-and-see attitude for now."[173]

Many of the problems of an administrative compensation scheme for toxic substances that the Study identifies simply disappear under the Collective model. Therefore, I found extremely disappointing the Study's initial dismissal of Collective model alternatives in a footnote in chapter 14: "comprehensive no-fault along the lines of New Zealand is almost certainly not politically feasible in the United States at this time ..." [174] Although this short run political appraisal is probably true, it is an insufficient reason to avoid evaluating the longer-run, social desirability of Collective model alter- natives, especially in light of the Study's self-appointed task to avoid being "tort-centric."

At the end of chapter 14, the Study returns to the Collective model, concluding, as I would, that "it may well be that a really satisfying [solution to the toxic substances problem] ...may be found only in the continuing development of the social insurance mechanisms and regulatory approaches discussed in other sections of this Report."[175]

4. *Expanding social insurance: Revisiting the Collective model*

One thousand pages after it began, the Study reaches its final chapter, entitled "Filling Compensation Gaps with Social Insurance."[176] Stating that the ALI "did not charge this Project with the task of recommending a new and coherent social welfare system," chapter 18 nonetheless goes on to "outline the implications for this Project's recommendations of changes in the American social welfare system that have received serious scholarly if not political consideration."[177] After all, were such social welfare changes forthcoming, they might alter the role of tort law.[178]

For example, if there were a comprehensive health care and income loss protection system for those suffering from illness or injury, there would arguably be little need for tort law to compensate accident victims.[179] Recognizing this, in order to impose financial pressures on those who cause accidents, the Study authors suddenly seem to back-pedal a bit on their proposed reversal of the collateral source rule.[180] In addition, they seem to favor keeping tort law alive so that richer people, whose earnings are not likely to be fully covered by the comprehensive compensation plan, can be more completely compensated.[181] I find both of these perspectives highly unattractive. In the latter instance, wealthier people are subsidized by consumers as a group, who must pay a premium on goods and services to insure producers against tort suits brought by the well-to-do. Since they are concerned about behavioral incentives, the Study would have been far more helpful here if the authors instead explored the possibility of funding comprehensive health care and income loss protection schemes, at least in part, through charges targeted to those who cause harm.

Various proposals have been made for improving the income replacement for those who are temporarily out of work. Some of these proposals focus on those temporarily disabled in an accident while others include those not working for any of many socially acceptable reasons.[182] The Study authors express mixed feelings about these proposals. The authors are again concerned that a needed deterrent would be lost if tort is replaced, however they also recognize that benefits would accrue by removing from the tort system what would otherwise be lots of little injury claims. [183] Unfortunately, the discussion of these proposals is too thin to come to grips with their competing behavioral channeling incentives. For example, the authors mention my proposal for Short Term Paid Leave in which employees would earn one day of paid leave for a certain number of days worked.[184] These earned days off would substitute for unemployment compensation, temporary disability insurance, paid public holidays, paid vacations, paid sick leave, and the income replacement part of workers' compensation for temporary disabilities, and would relieve tort law from covering the first six months of lost earnings. Although this plan would remove certain existing financial pressures on employers to avoid injury and unemployment, it would create new ones that might be more effective. For example, employees would have more of an incentive not to call in sick when they are well, not to become disabled, to return to work more quickly after a temporary disability, and to accept more promptly a new job after a layoff.

Suppose social security's disability insurance system were substantially expanded (or some equivalent state-level scheme were adopted)? The Study considers the possibility and expresses concern yet again about the loss of financial incentives given its earlier proposal concerning the collateral sources rule.[185] It suggests keeping tort and/or no-fault schemes in place, largely at the inter-insurance company level, for the purpose of reallocating costs to the sources of injury.[186] My impression is that this closely resembles the schemes in places like Germany which have generous and well developed social insurance networks. Regrettably, the Study fails to engage the alternative solutions of improved regulation and/or direct funding of the social insurance mechanism by the sources of injury. Based on the New Zealand experience, the Study authors might have been convinced that the administrative costs of targeting costs are not worth the positive behavioral consequences to be attained.

Finally, the Study thoughtfully highlights several acute problems facing broad compensation plans, including the workers' compensation system, aimed at those with partial permanent disabilities. [187] I concede that the problems of prediction and proof can be extremely difficult in these cases. Ultimately, however, there is no reason to believe that the tort system is any good at dealing with partial permanent disabilities either; the same problems are simply buried through the use of general jury verdicts and settlement agreements. Worse, the outcomes turn more, I fear, on the quality of one's lawyer and not one's real loss.

5. *Conclusion: Beyond tort.*

In sum, apart from continually harping on the potential work-disincentive effects of income support plans to an extent that would probably make former President Reagan and other welfare-bashers proud, the Study concerns itself more with the implications for tort law than with the desirability of a serious institutional change, such as to a fuller American embrace of the Collective model. Maybe such an evaluation should not have been expected from those who tell us they know mainly about tort law. A retreat to this limited point of view, however, misses a potentially important opportunity.

At the beginning of volume I, the Study refers to the approximate $100 billion direct annual cost of the tort law. [188] Enterprises and individuals might well be convinced to support any number of expansions in our social welfare system if, as part of the package, they could be relieved of most or all of the cost of personal injury law.[189] The potential for such a change is perhaps not well appreciated by non-tort scholars. While those who wrote the Study did not give as much explicit attention to this proposal as I would have liked, those who read it ought to be well positioned to begin to make such an appraisal for themselves.

IV. POSTSCRIPT

The Study ends with a postscript and so will I. The ALI study is an important contribution to torts scholarship. An unbelievably dazzling range of issues is surveyed and intelligently commented upon in a well organized way. Although most of the project's main recommendations can be considered as revisions to the rules currently stated in various sections of the Restatement (Second) of Torts, I believe it was ultimately proper that the Study did not explicitly cast its proposals in that way. Tort law reform is now the property of a far wider audience than the ALI membership and other leading players in common law development, including attorneys, judges, and torts professors. The ALI in a certain sense is wedded to what I have called the Conservative model because that is what a traditional restatement of torts necessarily implies. But by casting the Study in this wider form, rooted as it is in the approaches and techniques of contemporary legal scholarship, and presented in ways that appeal to a broader audience as well, the authors at least open up the possibility of envisioning a restatement of torts in which social insurance plans and regulatory devices of the Collective model play the featured roles.

ENDNOTES

1. Thousands of additional pages of output from the project are available, or soon will be, in the form of preliminary reports to the ALI and separately published articles and books by the key participants in the effort. For my review of an important book by the chief reporter of the ALI Report, see Stephen D. Sugarman, *Doctor No,* 58 U. CHI. L. REV. 1499 (1991) (reviewing PAUL C. WEILER, MEDICAL MALPRACTICE ON TRIAL (1991)).

2. RESTATEMENT (SECOND) OF TORTS § 402A (1965).

3. George L. Priest, *The Invention of Enterprise Liability: A Critical History of the Intellectual Foundations of Modern Tort Law,* 14 J. LEGAL STUD. 461 (1985).

4. Indeed, it ought to have been clear in 1986, when the Reporters' Study was launched, that it was exceedingly unlikely that a consensus could be reached by the ALI (or the project's advisers, the project's consultative group, or the ALI's Inner Council) about any important recommendations that such a report might make. Just what the ALI originally thought it was getting into with this project is not clear; however, because in 1986 the country was in the middle of what was widely being called a torts "crisis," it would not be surprising if the ALI, as did other groups, simply concluded that it ought to examine the "crisis" and attempt to solve it, Stephen D. Sugarman, *Taking Advantage of the Torts Crisis,* 48 OHIO ST. L.J. 329 (1987). In his Forward to the Study, the ALI's director, Geoffrey Hazard, explains that the ALI Inner Council, divided on the Study's recommendations, authorized its publication as a report "to" the Institute, rather than a report "of" the Institute. Vol. I, p. xi.

5. The Study states that the direct liability insurance (and self- insurance) costs of the tort system are roughly $100 billion a year, about half of which are for auto accidents. Vol. I, pp. 57-58.

6. They certainly did not at other "high level" conferences I have attended, such as the American Bar Association's conference in Kentucky in 1985 or the American Assembly on Tort Law in New York in 1990.

7. WILLIAM L. PROSSER, PROSSER ON TORTS (2d ed. 1955).

8. ALFRED F. CONARD, JAMES N. MORGAN, ROBERT W. PRATT, JR., CHARLES E. VOLTZ & ROBERT E. BOMBAUGH, AUTOMOBILE ACCIDENT COSTS AND PAYMENTS: STUDIES IN THE ECONOMICS OF INJURY REPARATION (1964); Alfred F. Conard, *The Economic Treatment of Automobile Injuries,* 63 MICH. L. REV. 279 (1964).

9. ROBERT E. KEETON & JEFFREY O'CONNELL, BASIC PROTECTION FOR THE TRAFFIC VICTIM (1965).

10. GUIDO CALABRESI, THE COSTS OF ACCIDENTS: A LEGAL AND ECONOMIC ANALYSIS (1970).

11. Stephen D. Sugarman, *Doing Away with Tort Law,* 73 CAL. L. REV. 558 (1985).

12. Given my radical position that would combine "doing away" with personal injury law and strong public law substitutes, I sometimes think of myself as being at one end of the range of academic opinion. STEPHEN D. SUGARMAN, DOING AWAY WITH PERSONAL INJURY LAW (1989). But, because such diverse work is now being done in the field, it is by no means clear whether I am better seen as at the end of a line or, say, at one outer point of a star; nor do my critics seem to agree whether, on the political spectrum, I should be put at the far left or the far right.

A few years ago two Berkeley colleagues, Robert Cooter and Daniel Rubinfeld, and I taught a 2-year seminar on "tort theory and policy." We tried to put academic opinion into different "schools." Among these were the law and economics school, starting with Calabresi and Judge Richard Posner and later followed by "real" economists and other fellow travelers; the moral philosophy school, as exemplified by Jules Coleman, Richard Epstein, and Ernest Weinrib; the no-fault compensation school, epitomized by O'Connell; and the critical legal studies school, with a small list of contributions, mostly by Richard Abel and Allen Hutchinson. This methodology, however, was not altogether satisfactory. Members of the various schools often did not even share common starting points, and there was enormous disagreement within the schools. Also, this type of categorizing left out many important contributors to contemporary torts scholarship, including John Fleming and Gary Schwartz. In many respects, the "schools" that Cooter, Rubinfeld, and I identified all have something fundamentally critical to say about existing tort law how it is conceived, how it functions, and so on. Other scholars, however, largely delight in the way tort law has been (or had been) developing, especially its incorporation of more grounds on which more victims could recover. Marshall Shapo falls into this category. Shapo was the Reporter for an earlier American Bar Association study of tort law, which found everything pretty much hunky-dory. REPORT TO THE AMERICAN BAR ASSOCIATION, TOWARDS A JURISPRUDENCE OF INJURY: THE CONTINUING CREATION OF A SYSTEM OF SUBSTANTIVE JUSTICE IN AMERICAN TORT LAW (1984). The work of still others is more descriptive and analytical than normative, and therefore has never been included as a "school." Peter Schuck's fascinating account of the Agent Orange saga fits in this category. PETER SCHUCK, AGENT ORANGE ON TRIAL: MASS TOXIC DISASTERS IN THE COURTS (enlarged ed. 1987). Our response in the seminar was to include the work of many of these authors on an ad hoc basis.

The ALI project might have set its task as one of organizing torts scholarship. Perhaps it could have produced a well worked out map of the different intellectual approaches of contemporary tort law scholars. Recent intellectual history, however well rendered, hardly translates directly into an understanding of the torts crisis or a program for whatever reform, if any, is needed. And, reform—especially practical and politically plausible reform—is what the project's chief reporters and their colleagues seem to have had their eyes on from the start. *See* vol. I, p. 10.

13. Guido Calabresi, *The New York Plan: A Free Choice Modification, 11* COLUM. L. REV. 267 (1971). In my judgment, in terms of practical application, Calabresi's writings about accident costs primarily provide insights into how the tort law might decide whether to impose liability on persons or institutions, thereby internalizing the accident's costs. For Calabresi, the answer lay in the elusive "cheapest cost avoider," the party who could best appraise how to reduce the sum of accident costs and act on that appraisal. How are we to decide who that party is? In my opinion, the main problem is that Calabresi never provided convincing criteria for deciding at which level of generality to answer the question. For example, are we supposed to ask who is the cheapest cost avoider while thinking about the provision and use of a power lawn mower without certain guards but containing certain warnings; about the sale and use of power mowers generally; about the sale and use of lawn mowers of all sorts; about the decision to have lawns and arrangements for their upkeep generally? As the target of the inquiry changes, the ultimate cheapest cost avoiders change.

In what appears to be an attempt to tame the uncertainty in Calabresi's analysis, Howard Latin bas proposed that the Calabresi-type inquiry be turned into a scrutiny of whether either of the parties involved in the class of accidents at issue is a "problem solver." *See* Howard A. Latin, *Problem-Solving Behavior and Theories of Tort Liability,* 73 CAL. L. REV. 677 (1985). If so, there may be good reason to impose accident costs on him, her, or it. Problem solvers are those actors who rationally respond to legal threats to impose accident costs. Of course, Latin's structure, too, is fraught with uncertainty in defining the relevant class of accidents. Should it be car accidents involving drinking, in which case the alcoholic beverage makers are a potential candidate for liability? Or is it auto accidents generally, as Latin seems to prefer, in order to impose liability on the auto makers to stimulate them to make safer cars? Or is it all roadway accidents, in which case highway designers become an equally promising target under Latin's criteria? At least Latin's framework recognizes that while tort law might be appropriate for some settings, focused compensation schemes and social insurance plans might be more appropriate for others.

14. For his own first cut, see Richard B. Stewart, *Crisis in Tort Law? The Institutional Perspective,* 54 U. CHI. L. REV. 184 (1987).

15. S. SUGARMAN, *supra* note 12, at 55-63.

16. Vol. I, pp. 24-25.

17. S. SUGARMAN, *supra* note 12.

18. Admittedly, some self-styled "liberals" are strong supporters of the tort/insurance model and might resent my "conservative" label. Indeed, they might well believe that American tort law better serves their values than would the other models. They revel in examples of the "little guy" and his or her lawyer taking on and defeating powerful enterprises by convincing that very democratic institution, the jury, of corporate wrongdoing. Because they tend to associate the label "conservative" with the power of business, a model that facilitates David taking on Goliath hardly seems conservative to them. Furthermore, lawyers and academics, with the cooperation and urging of judges and the support of juries, have helped make American tort law far more pro-plaintiff than it was before the 1960s. Tort liberals, in this sense of the word, do not want to give up these gains, nor, in many cases, do they wish to trade them for the compensation and behavior control mechanisms of the more centralized models. They are skeptical that other mechanisms for controlling corporations will work as well as the present system, and fear that the compensation delivered by other models will be less than promised. In other words, as a pragmatic matter, these liberals are fearful of the fate of the Liberal model when their opponents exercise their political clout in the legislature.

As Mies Van der Rohe said, "God is in the details." And friends of the tort law/insurance model in the abstract-including both plaintiff and defense attorneys, many "conservative" economists, liability insurers, and certain consumer activists like Ralph Nader—fiercely disagree as to its details. As substantial tort reform has been undertaken in recent years in legislatures throughout the country, these strange bedfellows, rather than fending off devotees of other models, have been at each other's throats. For my purposes, however, so long as tort law at its core stands for a private law remedy through which individuals seek redress from their injurers, it is "conservative" in the ways I have already explained.

19. For this model I draw on the writings of Richard Abel. *See generally* Richard L. Abel, *A Critique of Torts,* 37 UCLA L. REV. 785 (1990).

20. Vol. I, pp. 203-07.

21. Vol. I, pp. 207..08.

22. Vol. I, p. 232.

23. Vol. I, pp. 223-26.

24. Professor Howard Latin has pointed this out to me in private conversation.

25. Vol. I, p. 226.

26. Vol. I, pp. 165-66.

27. Vol. I, pp. 168-75.

28. Vol. I, pp. 178-80.

29. Vol. I, p. 178.

30. Vol. I, p. 180.

31. Vol. I, pp. 113-21.

32. Vol. I, p. 124.

33. Vol. I, p. 125. The study describes and analyzes other evidence about workplace injuries and the workers' compensation system at vol. I, pp. 335-47, 427-41.

34. Vol. I, pp. 391-97 (medical injuries), 411-12 (product injuries).

35. See vol. I, pp. 441-516.

36. *See* vol. I, pp. 129-56, 181-202.

37. Vol. I, pp. 129-54.

38. Vol. I, p. 156.

39. Vol. I, pp. 181-202.

40. This would probably call for some variation on the traditional British health service in which health care professionals are employees of the state.

41. Vol. I, pp. 233-51.

42. Vol. I, pp. 249-51.

43. Vol. I, pp. 249-51.

44. Vol. I, pp. 33-34.

45. Vol. I, pp. 56-66.

46. Vol. I, pp. 66-97.

47. Vol. I, p. 97.

48. Vol. I, p. 102.

49. Vol. I, p. 10.

50. Vol. I, p. 262.

51. Vol. I,. p. 264. For an appraisal of the largely indeterminate empirical evidence on the impact of tort liability in the product area, see vol. I, pp. 398-402.

52. *See generally* PETER W. HUBER, LIABILITY: THE LEGAL REVOLUTION AND ITS CONSEQUENCES (1988).

53. Vol. I, p. 277. For some more recent evidence, see THE LIABILITY MAZE: THE IMPACT OF LIABILITY LAW ON SAFETY AND INNOVATION (Peter W. Huber & Robert E. Litan eds., 1991).

54. Vol. I, pp. 279-83.

55. Vol. I, pp. 279-83. The Study's review of governmental safety regulation in the product area finds a mixed outcome, suggesting that agencies might do best by making more use of required warning labels and safe use information. *See* vol. I, pp. 404-11.

56. This is further confirmed in chapter 13. *See* vol. I, pp. 381-85.

57. Vol. I, p. 297.

58. Vol. I, p. 298. The more thorough presentation of the empirical evidence in chapter 13 finds the impact "inconclusive." Vol. I, p. 379.

59. *See* vol. I, pp. 285-92.

60. Vol. I, p. 294.

61. Vol. I, pp. 385-91.

62. Vol. II, p. 6.

63. Vol. II, p. 7.

64. Vol. II, p. 7.

65. Vol. II, p. 7.

66. A great number of the positions it takes parallel those I made in an article with that very title. Stephen D. Sugarman, *Serious Tort Law Reform,* 24 SAN DIEGO L. REV. 795 (1987). My proposals draw on earlier ideas of Professor O'Connell's.

67. Although the Study's focus, as noted, is on certain types of high stakes cases, there is no reason to suppose that the authors wish their rules regarding damages reform to be limited to such cases.

68. *See* RESTATEMENT (SECOND) OF TORTS § 920A(2) (1979).

69. Vol. II, p. 182.

70. Vol. II, p. 197.

71 U.S. ATTORNEY GENERAL TORT POLICY WORKING GROUP , REPORT ON THE CAUSES, EXTENT, AND IMPLICATIONS OF THE CURRENT CRISIS IN INSURANCE AVAILABILITY AND AFFORDABILITY (1989) [hereinafter WORKING GROUP].

72. Sugarman, *supra* note 66, at 819-23.

73. RESTATEMENT (SECOND) OF TORTS § 920A cmt. d (1979).

74. *Id.* § 924(a) cmt. b (1965).

75. Vol. II, p. 230.

76. Vol. II, p. 220 n.23; *see also* MICH. COMP. LAWS Ann.§ 500.3125(1) (West 1990).

77. Vol. II, p. 221 n.3.

78. Vol. II, p. 230.

79. Vol. II, p. 229.

80. Sugarman, *supra* note 66, at 823-30.

81. For a recent discussion of the application of the New South Wales statute, see Southgate v. Waterford, 21 N.S.W.L.R. 427 (c.a. 1990).

82. WORKING GROUP, *supra* note 71, at 66-69.

83. U.S. ATTORNEY GENERAL TORT POLICY WORKING GROUP, AN UPDATE ON THE LIABILITY CRISIS, 78-81 (1987) [HEREINAFTER UPDATE).

84. Vol. II, p. 203.

85. RESTATEMENT (SECOND) OF TORTS§ 908(2) (1965).

86. *Id.* § 908 cmt. b.

87. *Id.* § 908 cmt. f.

88. Vol. II, p. 264.

89. Vol. II, p. 265.

90. Sugarman, *supra* note 66, at 830-34

91. WORKING GROUP, *supra* note 71, at 66-68; UPDATE *supra* note 83, at 78-83.

92. Vol. II, pp. 243-52; *see, e.g.,* CAL. CIV. CODE§ 3294 (West Supp. 1987); COLO. REV. STAT. § 13-31-102(4) (Supp. 1986); IOWA CODE ANN. § 668A.l (West Supp. 1987); N.H. Prod. Liab. Rep. (CCH) ¶ 93.025.

93. RESTATEMENT (SECOND) OF TORTS§ 775 (1965).

94. *Id.* § 885(3).

95. *Id.* § 886A.

96. *Id.* § 886A cmt. h.

97. *Id.* § 886A cmt. f.

98. Vol. II, p. 156.

99. RESTATEMENT (SECOND) OF TORTS § 886A cmt. m (1965).

100. *Id.*

101. WORKING GROUP, *supra* note 71, at 64-65.

102. Vol. II, pp. 136-40.

103. Vol. II, pp. 156-57.

104. Sugarman, *supra* note 66, at 838-40.

105. RESTATEMENT (SECOND) OF TORTS § 914 (1965).

106. Vol. II, p. 315.

107. Sugarman, *supra* note 66, at 834-38. The Study goes on to propose some sophisticated "offer of settlement" rules. Simply put, if the plaintiff rejects another and in the subsequent trial fares worse, his right to attorney fees is reduced. *See* vol. II, pp. 283-90. The Study also addresses prejudgment interest, groundless litigation, and other matters beyond the scope of this discussion.

108. Vol. II, pp. 297-395.

109. CAL BUS. & PROF. CODE § 6146 (West 1990); *see* Sugarman, *supra* note 66, at 835. The Study and I also disagree about whether the plaintiff should be allowed to contract with his lawyer for an additional fee beyond that to be paid by the defendant. The Study would permit such agreements. Vol. II, p. 305. On both counts our disagreement stems from the Study authors' confidence in the market for lawyers and from my belief that the market for lawyers is quite imperfect. Most tort victims do not "shop" and, in any case, lawyers rarely compete on price. My view is based on my belief that victims are very risk averse in selecting lawyers, and cannot accurately judge how good a lawyer someone is. In this context an attorney who offers to work for less risks signaling low quality that will frighten the plaintiff off.

110. WORKING GROUP, *supra* note 71, at 72-74.

111. CAL BUS. & PROF. CODE § 6146 (West 1990) (restricting attorney fees); CAL. CIV. CODE. § 3333.2 (West 1990) (capping damages); CAL. CIV. CODE § 3333.1 (West 1990) (collateral source rule).

112. RESTATEMENT (SECOND) OF TORTS § 402A {1965).

113. 217 N.Y. 382, 111 N.E. 1050 (1916).

114. RESTATEMENT (SECOND) OF TORTS § 395 (1965).

115. The Reagan Administration expressed concern about the whole concept of strict liability. WORKING GROUP, *supra* note 71, at 61-63. In recent years, several states have adopted a wide variety of statutory changes that modify the way their courts have treated product liability issues. *See* vol. II, pp. 35-40.

116. RESTATEMENT (SECOND) OF TORTS §§ 388, 398 (1965).

117. *See, e.g.,* Gary T. Schwartz, *Foreword: Understanding Products Liability,* 67 CAL. L. REV.435 (1979).

118. I say this because the Study calls for abolishing the so-called consumer expectations test, which some courts have used to hold defendants strictly liable when a product has surprised both the manufacturer and the victim by its dangerousness. *See* vol. II, pp. 44-47. Some courts have, mistakenly in my view, thought that comment k to section 402A of the Restatement (Second) sheds light on the solution to the problem of changing knowledge over time. *See, e.g.,* Brown v. Superior Ct., 44 Cal. 3d 1049, 751 P.2d 470, 245 Cal. Rptr. 412 (1988).

119. RESTATEMENT (SECOND) OF TORTS § 402A, cmts. h, k (1965).

120. Vol. II, pp. 47-51.

121. Vol. II, pp. 54-57.

122. Vol. II, p. 57. The issues discussed in these last two paragraphs plainly could be seen as inquiries into the legal meaning of design negligence under RESTATEMENT (SECOND) OF TORTS § 398 (1965).

123. Vol. II, pp. 70-72.

124. Vol. II, pp. 72-75.

125. This is to be contrasted with the "corrective justice" outlook in which proof of causation is generally thought essential.

126. Vol. II, pp. 77-80.

127. Perhaps changes would also be needed in section 430 and other sections of the Restatement (Second) dealing with "causation" generally.

128. RESTATEMENT (SECOND) OF TORTS § 288C (1965).

129. Vol. II, p. 95. This is a broader version of chapter 2's position, noted above, that regulatory standards should play a stronger role in determining what is an adequate warning.

130. Vol. II, pp. 90-94.

131. Vol. II, pp. 95-97.

132. Vol. II, p. 101.

133. Robert S. Adler, *New CPSC Act: A Disappointment,* TRIAL, Nov. 1991, at 19; Robert S. Adler, *Manufacturers Blind CPSC to Product Hazards,* TRIAL, Oct. 1990, at 20.

134. S. SUGARMAN, *supra* note 12, at 156-60.

135. RESTATEMENT (SECOND) OF TORTS § 409 (1965).

136. *Id.* §§ 410-415.

137. Perhaps relieving the doctor from personal liability is required to assure the financial shift and to create the desired incentive structure, but this is not obvious. After all, it has not been necessary to relieve airline pilots of personal liability to have the litigation concerning commercial air crashes directed at the airline itself. Hence, it may suffice for the Study's goals simply to create vicarious liability for hospitals. For further discussion of the proposal, *see* Sugarman, *supra* note 1, at 1514-15.

138. Vol. II, p. 355.

139. Vol. II, pp. 358-64, 375-81.

140. Vol. II, ch. 11.

141. RESTATEMENT (SECOND) OF TORTS §§ 519, 520 (1965).

142. Comparing dynamite blasting, the paradigmatic abnormally dangerous activity, with driving an automobile illustrates this point. Blasting can cause substantial injury even when carried out with extreme care in a suitable location. The same can be said of driving. The difference between these two activities is that blasting is uncommon, while driving is an ordinary occurrence.

Unfortunately, the Restatement's explanation of ultrahazardous activities does not include a definition of "uncommon" if "uncommon" implies an activity that takes place infrequently, attaching strict liability can be justified on the ground that potential victims are unlikely to create similar risks, nor are they likely to be attuned to, and prepared for, the risks entailed. If, on the other hand, uncommon implies that few people engage in the activity, strict liability can be seen as the price exacted by society for allowing persons to exploit their particular expertise. Apparently, the Restatement (Second) favors the former meaning because it has specially set out section 520A which calls for strict liability for ground damage from aircraft. It appeared necessary to set out a special section because, although only a few carry out the activity, it is common. *But cf.* Langan v. Valicopters, Inc.,88 Wash. 2d 855, 567 P.2d 218 (1977) (imposing strict liability on crop dusting, which the court found to be frequent but carried out by relatively few persons).

143. Vol. II, p. 367.

144. RESTATEMENT (SECOND) OF TORTS § 433B (1965).

145. Especially because defendants have already won beneficial changes in many state legislatures, the Study's recommended product liability regime would, on balance, benefit plaintiffs, at least in some jurisdictions.

146. S. SUGARMAN, *supra* note 12, at 156-60.

147. RESTATEMENT (SECOND) OF TORTS § 496B (1965).

148. Robert Cooter and I imagined that the quid pro quo for the disclaimer would usually be better employee benefits and that the transaction would be handled for people by their employers. Robert Cooter

& Stephen D. Sugarman, *A Regulated Market in Unmatured Tort Claims: Tort Reform by Contract, in* New Directions In Liability Law 174 (Walter Olson ed., 1988).

149. Vol. II, pp. 521-36. These ideas are to be distinguished from a quite different contractual alternative to tort that the Study cautiously supports: With some consumer protection provisions in place, the Study favors the right of tort victims to sell their claims to others who would pursue them against the injurer. *See* vol. II, pp. 517-21.

150. Vol. II, pp. 487-512. For example, a disability of more than six months could become the standard.

151. *E.g.,* Sugarman, *supra* note 1, at 1500-02.

152. *E.g.,* Clark C. Havighurst & Laurence R. Tancredi, *"Medical Adversity Insurance"—A No-Fault Approach to Medical Malpractice and Quality Assurance,* 51 Milbank Mem. Fund Q. 125 (1973).

153. Harvard Medical Practice Study Group, Patients, Doctors, And Lawyers: Medical Injury, Malpractice Litigation, And Patient Compensation In New York (1990).

154. *See* text accompanying notes 136-137 *supra.*

155. Vol. II, pp. 512-15.

156. Jeffrey O'Connell, *Expanding No-Fault Beyond Auto Insurance: Some Proposals,* 59 Va. L. Rev. 749 (1973).

157. Sugarman, *supra* note 1.

158. Vol. II, p. 445.

159. Institute For Civil Justice, Executive Summaries Of The Aviation Accident Study (1988).

160. Vol. II, pp. 444-45.

161. Elizabeth M. King & James P. Smith, Institute For Civil Justice, Dispute Resolution Following Airplane Crashes 16-18 (1983).

162. These are discussed in greater detail in Stephen D. Sugarman, *Right and Wrong Ways of Doing Away With Commercial Air Crash Litigation: Professor Chalk's "Market Insurance Plan" and Other No-Fault Follies,* 52 J. Air L. & Com. 681 (1987). After imagining and exploring various air crash no-fault plans, I express my preference for broad social insurance mechanisms that would treat air crash victims as part of a broader category of persons whose injuries and deaths are to be compensated as part of a collective plan. *See id.* at 703-07.

163. Vol. II, pp. 441-83.

164. Vol. II, pp. 412-29. Notice that these procedural mechanisms, if taken to their extreme, effectively create an administrative compensation scheme run by the judiciary.

165. Vol. II, p. 476.

166. Vol. II, pp. 457-66.

167. Vol. II, pp. 463-65.

168. Vol. II, pp. 466-70.

169. *See* text accompanying notes 138-143 *supra.*

170. Vol. II, pp. 470-73.

171. Vol. II, pp. 473-75.

172. Vol. II, p. 480.

173. Vol. II, p. 482.

174. Vol. II, p. 445.

175. Vol. II, pp. 482-83.

176. Vol. II, p. *555.*

177. Vol. II, p. 559.

178. Vol. II, p. 559.

179. The authors express their doubts about whether these changes are politically likely. *See* vol. II, pp. 559-61.

180. Vol. II, p. 561.

181. Vol. II, p. 561.

182. For example, I propose the adoption of a substantially expanded version of California's temporary disability income plan, together with the mandatory imposition on employers or a paid sick leave plan. *See* Sugarman, *supra* note 66, at 808-15.

183. Vol. II, pp. 561-65.

184. Vol. II, p. 562 n.16 (citing Sugarman, *supra* note 66). This proposal is set out in far more detail in Stephen D. Sugarman, *Short Term Paid Leave: A New Approach to Social Insurance and Employee Benefits, 15* CAL. L. REV.465 {1987).

185. Vol. II, pp. 565-68.

186. Vol. II, p. 568.

187. Vol. II, pp. 568-72

188. Vol. I, p. 57.

189. For example, I have recently proposed replacing tort liability for auto accidents with what I call the Auto Accident Compensation Corporation (AACC), which would pay generous no-fault benefits to all those injured in motor vehicle accidents. The AACC would be funded by new gasoline taxes, charges on drivers (based on their driving record and years of experience), and charges on vehicles (based on their safety features and record). In return for paying these new costs, motorists generally would be relieved of even larger auto insurance premiums. *See* Stephen D. Sugarman, *Nader's Failures?,* SO CAL. L. REV. 289 (1992); Stephen D. Sugarman, *California's Insurance Regulation Revolution: The First Two Years of Proposition 103,* 27 SAN DIEGO L. REV. 683, 711-14 (1990); Stephen D. Sugarman, *Foreword: Choosing Among Systems of Auto Insurance for Personal Injury,* 26 SAN DIEGO L. REV. 977, 988-92 (1989).

www.ingramcontent.com/pod-product-compliance
Lightning Source LLC
LaVergne TN
LVHW082011200926
848481LV00010B/2836